EFFORTLESS ENGLISH

LEARN TO SPEAK ENGLISH LIKE A NATIVE

A.J. HOGE

Effortless English

Effortless English is published by Effortless English LLC
1702 A. Street, Ste. C
Sparks, NV 89431

Inquiries: events@effortlessenglishclub.com
Website: www.effortlessenglishclub.com

ISBN: 978-1-942250-00-5
LCCN: pending
Library of Congress Cataloging-In-Publication Data Has Been Applied For

Cover design and typesetting: Enterline Design Services LLC

EFFORTLESS
ENGLISH

LEARN TO SPEAK ENGLISH LIKE A NATIVE

Effortless
English

Contents

CHAPTER 1

A Better Way to Learn English

If you've picked up this book, chances are you've wanted to speak English for a while. Maybe you've even taken classes. You probably need English to improve your career. Maybe you want to travel internationally or study abroad. You know that English is the key to international business and international travel. So let me ask you something.

Do you feel nervous or shy when you try to speak English? Do you still struggle to understand what someone is saying to you despite years of study? Are you embarrassed about your pronunciation or worried you speak too slowly? Are you frustrated that despite all the time you've invested in learning English you still can't speak it? Despite your goals, is it difficult for you to actually use English in your job, travels, or studies? Do you sometimes feel that you'll never master spoken English?

If you answered yes to any of these questions, you're not alone. In fact, you're fairly typical. Most English students feel this way. Most adult English learners are stressed and frustrated about their speaking ability. Some feel completely hopeless and feel they'll never be able to speak English powerfully. Not because they're bad at languages, but because, like you, they've been taught using the wrong methods.

The good thing is that it doesn't have to be like this. There is nothing wrong with you. You can learn to speak English naturally and with ease. You can use English effectively in your job, travels, and studies. You can feel relaxed and confident every time you speak English. In fact, as a long-time English teacher, I've helped thousands of students all over the world become fluent and powerful English speakers.

How did I do it? I did it using a teaching method I developed called Effortless English™. Effortless English™ enables you to learn English naturally and automatically – the way children learn before they enter school. Too often, English classes get so focused on tests, textbooks, grades and "levels," students forget why they're there in the first place. They forget about the real world goals of a more successful career and exciting international travel. With Effortless English™ you never lose sight of the fact that the ultimate goal of learning a language is communication. Instead, you learn to speak English both quickly and with more precision.

Effortless?

I understand if you're skeptical – particularly if you've been trying to learn English the traditional way. You've put in the hours: memorizing vocabulary lists, doing grammar drills, reading boring textbooks. "How?" you're thinking, "can speaking English possibly be effortless?"

Believe me, I feel your pain.

Back when I started teaching 15 years ago, my students were all excited to begin conversing in English. And I was excited to help them. At that time, I taught in the usual way. I used textbooks and I focused on teaching grammar. I thought this was the best way to teach, and none of my students complained.

I still remember one particularly intelligent student of mine from Venezuela named Gladys. Gladys was determined to speak English well. Talk about effort! Gladys attended every one of my classes. She always sat in the center of the front row. I can still picture her eager and smiling face. She took detailed notes. She listened to every word I said. She also studied at home. Every day Gladys studied her English textbooks for four hours or more. She also tried to learn 50 new vocabulary words by memorizing word lists. Gladys was my star student and I, too, was sure she would succeed.

Six months later, however, she still could barely speak English. Her speech was hesitant and unnatural. She constantly made grammar mistakes with even the simplest sentences. Her pronunciation was difficult to understand. She still thought in Spanish and tried to translate to and from English when she spoke. Worst of all, Gladys felt nervous every time she tried to speak English. Speaking English was a painful experience for her.

Gladys was extremely frustrated. After so much effort, she had barely improved. As her teacher, I too was frustrated. I was sure Gladys would improve quickly and couldn't understand why she had not. I followed all of the traditional teaching methods. I used the standard textbooks and the standard classroom activities. Gladys was intelligent, disciplined and consistent, and yet her English speaking barely improved.

Sadly, I realized that Gladys wasn't the only one who had not improved. Her classmates also had barely improved. It was frustrating, and I felt like a complete failure as a teacher. But when I asked my colleagues for help, it turned out they had the same problem – very few of their students were improving either! At that point, I realized something was wrong – something *is* wrong with standard methods for teaching English. The worst part for me was that everyone accepted this situation as "normal." The other teachers didn't seem to be concerned about their students' lack of progress. All the teachers were using the same methods and getting the same poor results.

In most parts of the world, students study English in school for years. Yet, the vast majority of them never learn to speak English well. After years of study, they still have trouble with real English conversations. They still feel nervous and shy about speaking.

A few years after my experience with Gladys, I got a job as an English teaching assistant in Japan. I was excited and eager to help these young students learn my language. I still remember my first day. I was sitting at the front of the class next to the main teacher, who was Japanese. As the students came into the room, they saw me and giggled nervously. They sat down and continued to shyly glance up at me. They were sweet and curious.

Then the class started. The main teacher wrote an English sentence on the board. I don't remember the exact sentence, but it was something like, "The little girl goes to school." The teacher pointed to the sentence and began to talk in Japanese. The students all grabbed their notebooks and began writing. Everyone was very serious.

Next, the teacher circled the word "goes." She pointed at the word and continued speaking in Japanese. She talked and talked and talked, in Japanese. The students wrote quickly, filling their notebooks with information. Finally, the teacher drew a line from the word "goes" to the word "girl." And then she talked more, on and on and on, in Japanese.

This continued for the entire class. The teacher drew lines, circles, and squares. She used different colored chalk. And she continued speaking Japanese.

I was totally confused. I am a native speaker of English, and I was sitting in a beginning English class. Yet I could not understand anything in the class (except for that one sentence). I was thinking to myself, "What could this teacher possibly be talking about so much? It's just one sentence." Yet the teacher spent an entire hour analyzing, explaining, and dissecting that one simple sentence. Finally, at the end of the class, the teacher asked me to read the sentence aloud "for pronunciation." I read the sentence a couple of times, and that was the only real English input the students got that day.

Sadly, this same pattern repeated every day. Day by day, I watched the students' enthusiasm and curiosity disappear. They became bored. They became stressed and confused. Every day they wrote pages of notes, mostly in Japanese. Every day the teacher talked and talked and talked, mostly in Japanese. I couldn't understand why an English class was being taught mostly in Japanese. During the average class, the students were listening to Japanese 90% of the time or more. They heard very little English. No wonder they never learned to speak! No wonder they were frustrated and confused.

Honestly, it broke my heart to watch as the school crushed these students' natural love of learning. It was terrible to watch them grow bored, frustrated, and stressed. And six months later, none of the students could speak to me at all, not even the simplest conversation.

This kind of situation is repeated in English classes all over the world.

My experiences with Gladys and in Japan convinced me that traditional English language education is broken. I knew there had to be a better way to help my students speak English than what we were doing. So I began the search for a better way. I devoured books about English teaching. I constantly tried out new methods in my classes. I read research studies. I traveled and taught English in other parts of the world.

What surprised me was how little the actual research supported traditional teaching methods. As eminent University of Southern California linguist Stephen Krashen noted: "We acquire language when we understand what people tell us and what we read….there is no need for deliberate memorization." If most of us knew, intuitively, that the best way to learn English was naturally, I wondered, why were so many teachers and students still choosing to use unnatural, ineffective and old methods of teaching?

Eventually, I went back to school and got a master's degree in (TESOL) Teaching English to Speakers of Other Languages. Along the way, I did more research and discovered the incredible new methods that would become the basis for the Effortless English™ program.

I also did my own informal research. I searched for excellent English speakers who had learned the language as an adult. Whenever I found such a person, I interviewed them. Over time, I noticed patterns. Most of these successful speakers were independent students who mastered spoken English outside of school. Most of them used similar methods, the very same methods supported by my master's research. Most avoided the traditional methods used in most schools.

I changed my teaching, and when I used these new strategies in classes, my students improved quickly. I couldn't believe it! They learned to speak easily and powerfully. And even better – they were enjoying themselves! After years of searching and experimentation, I had finally found methods that worked.

Effortless English Today

Over the years, I've continued to test and adapt these methods and developed the Effortless English™ system. I've organized the program to include seven essential rules for learning English, which have led countless students to fluency. To build on the success of my classes, I created audio courses and began offering them online to English students around the world. My audio lessons are currently bestsellers in 25 countries.

In addition, I founded the Effortless English Club™ to create an international English learning community where students can communicate with other members. I wanted to create an environment that encouraged confidence and success with English, because so many learners struggle with nervousness, shyness, frustration and fear when speaking. In fact, for many people these negative emotions are the worst part of speaking English.

In our Effortless English Club™ students are able to interact on our forums and speak with each other online. It is an extremely positive and encouraging community, where everyone is free to "play with English," make mistakes, and communicate without fear. In my opinion, we have the best members in the world. Every one of our members is focused not only on their own success, but also on helping other members achieve success too. The result is a supportive "family" of learners and international leaders.

This book is another resource for students looking to speak English powerfully and fluently. It is designed to guide you on the road to fluency, to speed your journey to confident, powerful, effortless speaking. In this book, you will learn how to re-program your negative emotions about English, develop confidence when speaking, and follow a powerful and effective road to fluency. You'll also learn how to use English to improve your career and achieve the success you want.

Over the next several chapters, I will describe the Effortless English™ system in detail, explain the philosophy behind it, and tell you why both psychology and method are important for language learning. I'll also tell you exactly how to use the system to reach your goals.

Join me and enjoy the journey. You really have nothing to fear by leaving the old education system behind. So let go of the pressure, the stress, the fear and the boredom. I promise you this natural learning system is fun, friendly, and energetic – the opposite of most school classrooms. There is no pressure – just friendly encouragement and support.

Trust me. I have helped students everywhere in the world... and now I am eager to help you. I promise I will always do my best to help you speak excellent English.

NOT "LAZY" ENGLISH

So what is Effortless English™? By "effortless" I certainly don't mean lazy English. On the contrary, "effortless English" is going to be the result of the work you put in every day. By following my system, you will make progress and achieve the result of speaking naturally and "effortlessly" (unforced, without stress, hesitation or nervousness).

In other words, "effortless" is the result, not the beginning. Your goal is to speak English effortlessly. You want the words to flow out without thinking, without translating, without worry or hesitation. You want to speak English just as you speak your own native language. Effortless speaking is the final result, and sometimes it takes a lot of effort to become effortless!

It is possible, however, to thoroughly enjoy that effort. The example I like to use is that of an athlete or artist "in the zone." "In the zone" means performing excellently and effortlessly. When an athlete is "in the zone" at one level, they are working very hard – expending a lot of energy, pushing, totally focused. However, when they are enjoying themselves and completely focused, the activity FEELS effortless to them. There is no feeling of forcing, straining, etc.

In fact, the name Effortless English™ was inspired by the Taoist idea of "wu wei" or effortless effort. It's a description of that flow state where you can be expending a lot of effort and yet it feels totally effortless and natural, not forced.

So the point is that Effortless English™ is not about laziness, quick fixes, or impossible scams... but rather about finding that state of "effortless effort" or "wu wei." Effortless English means you speak English fluently. You don't struggle as you speak. You don't feel nervous or stressed. You don't think about grammar rules or translations.

When you speak English effortlessly, you communicate your ideas clearly. You express your feelings powerfully. You focus on connecting with other people, not on conjugating verbs. You thoroughly enjoy the process of speaking English as you work, travel and learn.

CHAPTER 2

The Problem with Schools

My teaching experiences in different parts of the world convinced me that something is wrong with English education. Everywhere I went, it was the same situation. The students were bored, frustrated, stressed, and nervous. Most students, even after years of studying English, failed to speak the language fluently. You are not alone, because it's a global problem.

One of my students, Seiko from Japan, described this combination of failure and stress as "English trauma." Seiko said that she hated English. She felt that learning English was boring and stressful and speaking English was even worse. In fact, the thought of speaking to a native speaker immediately made Seiko feel extremely nervous and shy. Seiko felt she had developed a psychological problem with English and had named it "English trauma." A "trauma" is a deep wound or injury. "How sad," I thought to myself, "that so many people now think of English as a kind of injury or mental disease."

Throughout my teaching career I've met many students who had similar feelings about English. I discovered that Seiko was not alone. Rather, "English trauma" is a global epidemic. Though most people feel they must learn to speak English, very few seem to enjoy it. Most who learn the language struggle with the same feelings of nervousness and frustration that Seiko had.

As I encountered this problem more and more, I began to look for the root causes. I realized that before I found a solution, I needed to understand the problem. Just as a doctor must first diagnose a disease before treating it. Think about it. What is the cause of all this misery and failure? Why do so many people fail to speak English effortlessly despite years of study? What is wrong with English education?

The first and most obvious problem I found with schools was the way in which they teach English. Most schools, everywhere in the world, use the grammar translation method. As the name implies, the focus of this method is on grammar analysis and the memorization of translated vocabulary. This method breaks English into an endless series of grammar formulas to memorize. Of course, each grammar formula has exceptions and these must be memorized too.

Schools like the grammar translation method because it appears to be serious, academic and complex. The grammar translation method fits the way schools teach most subjects — with textbooks, lectures, notes, memorization, and tests. The only problem, as you know, is that it doesn't work. In real conversations, there simply is no time to think about grammar formulas and their exceptions. The failure rate for this method, therefore, is absolutely horrible. Despite the failure of most students to speak English fluently, schools continue to use this method. This is an epic failure of our education system.

Recently, because students find the grammar translation method so boring, some schools have added "communication activities" to their curriculum. Occasionally, the teacher puts the students into pairs or groups. The students then read or repeat dialogues from a textbook. Sometimes they might answer a few questions from a worksheet. Of course, these activities are unnatural, nothing like real English conversation. Consequently, the failure rate of "communication activities" is just as bad as grammar translation.

Obviously the English teaching methods used in schools do not work. That was easy to see. I knew it. The students knew it. And many teachers know it too, though few will admit it.

However, as I continued to investigate the problem with schools, I found even deeper problems in the education system. These problems are less obvious, but in many ways far more damaging to the students. I call these problems "the hidden curriculum" because they are the hidden lessons taught by schools.

The Hidden Curriculum

Most schools, everywhere in the world, share a similar hidden curriculum. One element of this curriculum is student passivity. In schools, students are trained to be passive, not active. They sit in chairs, in rows. When they are young, they are told to be quiet and obey the teacher. As the teacher lectures, the students take notes. Later, they are told to memorize these notes in preparation for a test. The message is clear — learning is a passive activity. You listen to the teacher, you take notes, you memorize the notes.

The problem is that speaking English is not a passive activity. You must connect with other people. You must constantly ask and answer questions. You must communicate ideas, emotions, and descriptions. You must be ready for the unexpected. You must be spontaneous. You must actively interact. English is not something you passively study, it's something you do.

Related to the problem of passivity is the issue of energy. Sitting for a long time is a low-energy activity. The longer you sit, the more your energy drops. And as your energy drops, so does your concentration. What's worse, we know that some learners need physical movement in order to learn effectively. These people are called "kinesthetic learners." The truth is we are all "kinesthetic learners" to some degree, because we all benefit from physical movement. Schools stick us in chairs and drain our energy. Eventually, an inactive body leads to an inactive mind.

The One Right Answer Mentality

One of the greatest flaws of school education is the idea of "one right answer." One right answer is a powerful part of the hidden curriculum. It is a result of using textbooks and tests.

In school, you are frequently taught that there is one, and only one, correct answer to a question or problem. For example, you may be asked to choose the correct verb tense on a test, or you may be taught "proper" English greetings. The hidden message is that the teacher's way is always right.

Real life, and real English, is not this way. For example, sometimes I will tell a story using the present tense, even though the events happened in the past. This is a technique commonly used by native speakers. However, when English learners hear these stories, many are confused and upset. They are convinced that the past tense is the "right answer" and the only correct way to tell the story. Some get quite upset and even argue with me about it. These students are so convinced that there is only "one right answer" that they will argue with native speakers!

These students have been trained to believe that there is only one correct way to say things in English. The truth is there are always many ways to say the same thing. We can change verb tenses in order to change the feeling of the story. We can use different vocabulary and different phrases. And we even break grammar rules all the time! 'One right answer' thinking limits and confuses English learners. Effective communication requires flexibility while the "one right answer" mentality trains students to be rigid and unimaginative.

Connected to this problem is another dangerous part of the hidden curriculum — fear of mistakes. This is one of the most negative and traumatizing messages taught in schools. How is the fear of mistakes taught? Through tests and corrections. In nearly every school all over the world, teachers regularly give quizzes and tests. The teacher asks questions and the students must provide the one right answer. Of course, the one right answer is always the teacher's answer.

What happens if the student provides a different answer? They are punished with a lower score. Students are smart, and they quickly understand that in school, mistakes are bad and must be avoided. They also understand that truth is unimportant and the best way to succeed is to simply give the answer that the teacher wants. Even worse is when a student, already feeling nervous, tries to speak English with the whole class listening. They are just learning, so of course they will make mistakes. When the teacher corrects these mistakes, the student is embarrassed and becomes even more nervous. Eventually, most students try to avoid speaking English because the situation is so painful.

By punishing and correcting mistakes, schools punish risk taking. Little by little, they train students to avoid risk and avoid doing anything they can't do perfectly. Yet there is no perfection with English speaking. Even native speakers make mistakes. We make grammar mistakes. We mispronounce words. We forget vocabulary words. It doesn't matter, because we are focused on communicating, not on tests and grades.

Of course, the fear of mistakes goes far beyond English class. After years of school, most people learn to avoid risk in most parts of their life. School trains them to be passive, rigid, timid, and obedient. This not only hurts your English speaking, it also harms your career and limits your success in all areas of life. Fortune favors the bold. Those who are active, flexible, and passionate are the ones who achieve the greatest success in life. The passive and obedient rarely live their dreams.

You will make many mistakes as you improve your English speaking. There is no need to be upset by this. The truth is, most native speakers don't care. They don't care if you make grammar mistakes. They just want to communicate with you. They want to share thoughts, ideas and feelings. They want to communicate with you as a human being, not as an "English student." To communicate effectively, you must forget the idea of perfection and learn to be flexible.

The Dirty Secret of English Teaching

If the hidden curriculum is so bad, why do schools and teachers continue to follow it? The truth about our education system is that the curriculum exists to benefit the schools, not the students. Teachers use these methods because they are easier for the teacher, not because they are good for the student. The hidden curriculum creates passive students. It creates obedient students. Passive and obedient students are easier to control, making life easier for teachers and school administrators.

Textbooks, for example, make the teacher's job much easier. By using a textbook, the teacher doesn't have to plan new lessons for every class. Planning lessons is hard work, and a textbook makes it much easier. The teacher can simply follow the textbook with minimum effort. Many teachers are little more than textbook readers. Every day they read the textbook to their students, slavishly following the lessons. In my opinion, they can barely be called "teachers" at all. Perhaps we should call them "textbook readers" instead.

Another benefit of textbooks, for the schools, is that they standardize learning. By using a textbook, the school ensures that every English class is learning exactly the same thing. School officials like this because it makes testing and ranking students easier. Schools are like factories, the bosses want everything to be the same.

The same is true for tests and grades. These provide little to no benefit to English learners. In fact, as we have discussed, tests and grades increase stress and create a fear of making mistakes. Tests and grades are a primary cause of "English trauma." On the other hand, tests and grades are a powerful tool of control for teachers. When students fear bad grades, they obey the teacher more. They learn that the teacher is always right, because if they don't agree with the teacher's answer they are punished with lower scores.

Grades are a means of ranking students. Most teachers and administrators are focused on ranking students rather than helping all succeed. In many schools, the official policy is that a certain percentage of students in every class must get poor grades, a certain percentage must get "medium level" grades, and only a small percentage can be given excellent grades. In other words, the system is designed to create failure for a large number of students.

While working at a university in Thailand, I was told directly by my boss that too many of my students had high scores. My boss insisted that I fail more students in my class. I was shocked and angry. I quit the job rather than purposely fail dedicated students. Sadly, this mentality of "designing for failure" is present in most school everywhere in the world. Schools benefit from ranking and controlling students.

The grammar translation method also benefits the teacher but not the student. By teaching grammar rules, the teacher can simply lecture from the textbook. Because linguistics is a complicated subject, the teacher appears knowledgeable and thus establishes a position of superiority over the students. Even if the teacher is a non-native speaker with terrible English ability, he or she can pretend to be an expert by teaching complex grammar from a book. The shocking truth is that many non-native English teachers, in fact, speak English very poorly. By focusing on grammar they disguise their inability to speak well.

What about communication activities? Surely they are designed to help students. Actually, they are not. These activities, as we discussed previously, are unnatural. They are nothing like a real conversation, and thus do not prepare students to have real conversations. However, communication activities are great for teachers. The teacher puts the students into pairs or groups and asks them to follow a textbook activity. Often, the students simply read a written dialogue from the book or answer pre-written questions from the book. The advantage for the teacher is that once such an activity is started, the teacher can rest and do nothing. While the students go through the textbook activity, the teacher relaxes. It's a secret among English teachers that communication activities are a great way to waste time and avoid work.

One particularly horrible version of communication activities is the use of movies. Used correctly, movies can be a powerful English learning tool. Most teachers, however, simply use movies as a way to waste time. They put in a movie, turn out the lights, and push play. For the remainder of the class, the teacher happily does nothing. The students are usually happy, too, because watching a movie is far more interesting than grammar, even if they can't understand most of the film.

Passive Low Energy Benefits the Teacher

Finally, let's look at the low energy situation in most schools. From childhood, students are forced to sit for hours, motionless in chairs. They are told to be quiet and obedient. By adulthood, most people are thoroughly trained. They accept passive lectures and low energy as a normal part of learning.

Why would schools and teachers want low energy? Again, because low energy students are easier to manage. A teacher must work much harder with curious, energetic students. Sadly, most teachers prefer the easy way. It's much easier for them to lecture quietly to passive students.

The truth is that many teachers are tired and stressed. Because of this, they constantly look for ways to make their own job easier. Their first concern is not the students. They are not obsessively focused on getting better results for the learners. Rather, they just want to get through their workday as easily as possible. There are many reasons for this situation, but the end result for the student is boredom, frustration, and poor results.

This is the ugly truth of education. This is the reason you cannot speak English well, despite years of study. This is the reason you find English to be stressful, difficult, and boring. This is the cause of English trauma. This is the source of the problem.

Happily, there is a solution. The Internet has made independent learning easy for all. No matter where you live or what you do, it is possible to master spoken English without schools. All you need is an Internet connection!

In the next chapter, I will introduce the solution to English trauma. You will learn how to heal and how to finally get the results you want with English speaking.

CHAPTER 3

Psychology Is More Important Than Grammar and Vocabulary

Most people have suffered with English for so long they worry there is no solution. Trained by schools to be passive, fear mistakes, and search for just one right answer, most English learners are stressed and frustrated. Some feel nearly hopeless. They have spent years in English classrooms. They have spent years memorizing grammar rules and vocabulary lists. They have spent years studying for exams such as the TOEFL, IELTS, or TOEIC.

Despite all this work and effort, most English learners are frustrated. Many struggle with even simple conversations. Many feel nervous any time they must speak English. They have memorized countless grammar rules, yet even simple conversations feel difficult. Likewise, despite years of study, most learners still cannot understand American TV or movies.

After so many years of traditional learning, students are confused. When they try to speak, they constantly think about grammar and translations. First they think of a sentence in their own language, then they translate it to English, then they think about the grammar, and finally they speak.

When they listen, they go through a similar process. They hear the English, translate it into their own language, think of a response in their own language, translate their response into English, and then think about the grammar to be sure their response is correct. No wonder their speech is so slow and unnatural! No wonder English feels so stressful and difficult! Real conversations are fast, and it's nearly impossible to do all of this thinking fast enough, especially when talking to a native speaker.

If you think about translations and grammar during a real conversation, you will quickly become lost. Instead of listening carefully to the other person, you'll be translating your own responses and trying to remember grammar. Your speech will be hesitant. Often, the other person will become frustrated by your lack of understanding. Of course, if you see the other person is losing patience, you will usually become even more nervous. It's a terrible downward spiral that most English learners know too well.

There is a solution. There is a way to escape the hidden curriculum. There is a road to English fluency and you can travel on it. You can speak English powerfully. You can speak English clearly, naturally, and effortlessly. This solution, however, will require you to completely change your beliefs about education and completely change the way you learn English.

I call the solution the Effortless English™ system and it has two parts: the psychology and the method. Most schools, most teachers, and most learners focus only on method. In other words, they are solely focused on the pieces of the English language — vocabulary and grammar. As we learned in the last chapter, schools primarily use the "grammar translation" method, with some "communication activities" added.

While schools are focused just on method, they completely ignore the first part of the Effortless English™ system — the psychology. Yet, psychology is probably the most important element for success with English speaking. When you think of your own English speaking, you'll realize that your nervousness, lack of confidence, and frustration are major problems. How do you change these?

Without an effective psychological system, you will struggle to find success with even the best language teaching method. Let's use a story to understand these two important parts of the Effortless English™ system. Imagine that you are on a road. You are driving on the road to English fluency.

What kind of car would you want? Let's say all you have to drive is an old slow car that often breaks down. In addition, you fill this old car with cheap gasoline. What kind of trip will you have? How fast will you go on this road to fluency? Most likely, your trip will be slow and frustrating, with frequent breakdowns. In fact, you probably will not reach your destination.

Now, you could put some high quality gas in that old car, but even then it will likely take you a long time to reach your destination. Better gas will help a little, but the trip is still likely to be slow and frustrating.

Now imagine instead that you'll be driving a Formula 1 racing car on this road to fluency. This car is made for speed and performance. Clearly, it will go faster than the old, slow car. But what if you fill it up with cheap, low quality fuel? There will likely be problems. Racing cars need racing fuel or they will not perform well.

Obviously, the best situation would be to put high quality racing fuel into your Formula 1 racing car! With this car and this fuel, your trip on the road to fluency will be fast and exciting.

This is how learning English works. If you've been studying for a while, you know by now that there are all sorts of systems. Traditional classes at universities. Private lessons from language schools. Online or packaged software courses. Immersion programs that put you in the country where they speak the language you're studying. In other words, you've got a lot of different cars to choose from. Some may be better than others, some may be faster. But even the greatest of these methods, the Ferrari of language teaching, if you will, needs fuel to make it work.

A method, after all, is only an engine. And if you don't give an engine the proper fuel, even a great one won't work the way you'd like it to. To succeed, you need both quality fuel and a powerful engine.

The right engine + the right fuel = success

Obviously, I believe the right engine would be the Effortless English™ system.

What is the fuel? The fuel is your psychology. It is the beliefs, emotions, and goals that power your learning. Your fuel is your motivation, your confidence, your energy, your enthusiasm.

Your Fuel: Success Psychology

If your psychology is weak, even the best method will fail. In other words, if you have connected stress, fear, nervousness, and doubt to the process of speaking English you will have a lot of problems. Unfortunately, this is exactly what happens in most schools. The tests, the error corrections, and the boring and ineffective methods used in schools combine to create powerful negative emotions in most students.

Even if you're using my Effortless English™ method, you must have strong psychology. Unless you bring the proper emotional energy to the language-learning process, it won't be enough.

The Effortless English™ system is based upon a success psychology system known as Neuro-Linguistic Programming, or NLP. Developed by Richard Bandler and John Grinder, NLP is focused on the psychology of success, high-performance, and motivation. Rather than study mentally ill people, Bandler and Grinder researched the psychology of the most successful people in the world. They then created a psychological system designed to help individuals achieve the highest levels of success and happiness in their lives.

What Bandler and Grinder found was that happy, motivated and energetic people actually learn better. They perform better. They achieve more success in all aspects of their lives. The opposite is also true: If you're feeling bored, stressed, sad, frustrated or even tired, your brain actually functions more slowly and has a harder time remembering information.

Clearly, it is important to connect positive, rather than negative, emotions to the process of learning and speaking English. The process of connecting emotions to an experience or process is called anchoring. Anchoring can be positive or negative. For example, imagine that you listen to a specific song when you are feeling extremely happy. If the emotion is strong enough, a connection will be formed between the song and the emotion. And if you are feeling very happy when you hear the song again, that connection will become stronger.

Eventually, you will create a very strong connection between the song and the feeling of happiness. At that point, anytime you hear the song you will automatically find yourself feeling happy. That's what happens with your favorite songs and that's great!

However, this process also works with negative emotions. Imagine that you have a stressful experience in English class. Maybe the teacher corrects one of your errors when you are speaking and you feel embarrassed. Now imagine that you continue to have a series of negative emotional experiences in English classes. You frequently feel bored, nervous and stressed while learning and using English.

Eventually, a strong connection forms between English and the negative emotions. This is a negative anchor. Once this is formed, whenever you try to use English you will automatically begin to feel more nervous and stressed. This is why many "advanced" English learners still have so much trouble when trying to speak.

Sadly, most learners now have powerful negative anchors connected to their English speaking. The good news is that negative anchors can be broken and reprogrammed. This, in fact, is your first step towards speaking English powerfully.

Instead of feeling nervous, imagine if you suddenly and automatically felt powerful every time you spoke English? What if you automatically felt more excited every time you learned English? This change alone would improve your speaking.

Through the power of anchoring, you can indeed connect these powerful emotions to English. The secret to breaking a negative anchor and creating a new positive one is intensity. The more powerful an emotion is felt (while using English), the faster and deeper the connection.

So, to create a strong positive anchor for English requires a few steps.

First, you must create a very intense positive emotion. Most people believe that emotions are something that happen to them, but in fact, we create our emotions. It is possible to choose your emotions and to create them consciously.

For example, if you wished to feel tired and sad right now, what would you do? Let's start with your body. How would you use your body to create a tired and sad feeling? Would you pull your shoulders back, or hunch them forward? Would you look up or down? Would you smile or frown? In fact, by simply changing your body you would change your feelings.

To make yourself feel even worse, you would think about sad and negative things. Perhaps you would think about a big problem you have, or about a big regret. And what about your voice? You could moan, cry, or whine, and that would make you feel even worse.

After doing all of the above for a few minutes, you would genuinely begin to feel sadder and more tired. This is how you consciously can create a negative emotion.

Of course, this process works for positive emotions too, and that is good news! How would you make yourself feel more excited right now? Again, start with the body. Pull your shoulders back and push your chest up and out. Bring your head up and look straight ahead. Put a big smile on your face and hold it.

Next, change your thoughts. Think about something great in your life. Think about the biggest success you have ever had. Think about your future success speaking English powerfully. Smile bigger. First you are just pretending, but eventually you will feel stronger and happier. That's because your emotions change when your body changes. It's a simple technique.

Of course, you can feel even better by using your body even more. Instead of just standing and smiling, raise your arms over your head. Then jump in the air like you are celebrating a big victory. And use your voice. Shout and cheer loudly as you jump and smile and think of wonderful things. Go crazy! This is called a "peak emotional state," an intensely powerful positive emotion.

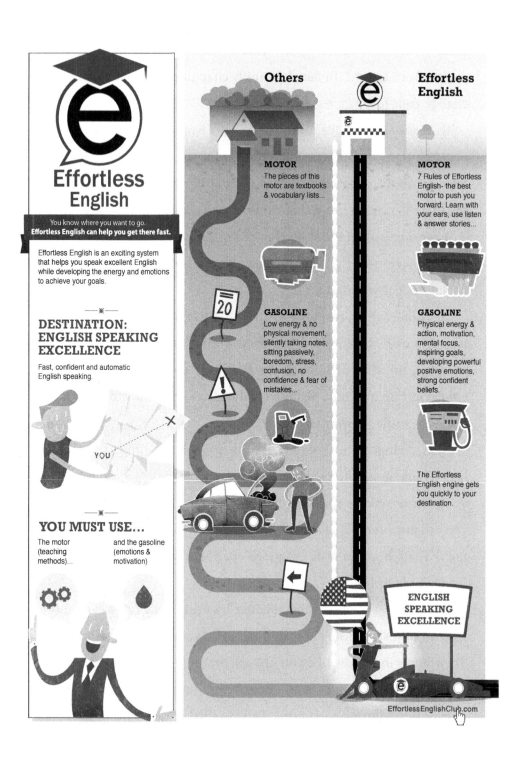

Effortless English

You know where you want to go.
Effortless English can help you get there fast.

Effortless English is an exciting system that helps you speak excellent English while developing the energy and emotions to achieve your goals.

DESTINATION: ENGLISH SPEAKING EXCELLENCE

Fast, confident and automatic English speaking.

YOU

YOU MUST USE...

The motor (teaching methods)...

and the gasoline (emotions & motivation)

Others

Effortless English

MOTOR
The pieces of this motor are textbooks & vocabulary lists...

MOTOR
7 Rules of Effortless English- the best motor to push you forward. Learn with your ears, use listen & answer stories...

GASOLINE
Low energy & no physical movement, silently taking notes, sitting passively, boredom, stress, confusion, no confidence & fear of mistakes...

GASOLINE
Physical energy & action, motivation, mental focus, inspiring goals, developing powerful positive emotions, strong confident beliefs.

The Effortless English engine gets you quickly to your destination.

ENGLISH SPEAKING EXCELLENCE

EffortlessEnglishClub.com

The final step, of course, is to connect this great feeling to English. So, still feeling great, immediately start listening to an easy English audio. As you are listening, continue to smile and move your body in a strong, positive way.

Each day, just before you begin learning English, you will create this peak emotion. As you repeat this process every day, these strong, positive feelings will become connected to English. Eventually, every time you hear or use English you will automatically feel energized, positive and excited. You have broken the old negative anchor and replaced it with a new positive one.

And there is more good news. Research has shown that people who are excited and energized while learning actually learn more quickly. They remember more and they remember longer. They perform better. In fact, you will speak English better right now simply by being in a peak emotional state. Creating this positive anchor to English, therefore, is your first step to faster travel on the road to fluency.

Why Happy Students Learn More

Dr. Stephen Krashen, a linguist at the University of Southern California and one of the top researchers on second language learning, believes negative emotions act as a filter, reducing the amount of new language input you're able to learn. As a result, students who feel bad, anxious or worried remember less vocabulary and don't speak as well. Essentially, they learn more slowly.

The best way to counter this, Krashen says, is by keeping students interested, reducing stress in classrooms and boosting learners' self-confidence.

In one study, researchers found that when they compared the performance of students who were energized and enjoying themselves in class with the performance of students who were just being drilled in material, the energized students did better. The same was true when they tested these students again at three months and later at six months.

I see the same thing in our Effortless English Club™ community. When you look at our most successful members, you'll find a common factor. They are all extremely enthusiastic. They have a lot of energy. They're very, very positive. They have very strong positive emotions. When you use peak emotions you can speak better – right now.

Therefore, each and every time you study English, create a peak emotional state. Change your body and your mental focus in order to create excitement and positive energy. Build a strong anchor, a strong connection, between English and your most positive emotions. Heal your English trauma.

CHAPTER 4

Your Beliefs Determine
Your English Success

In the last chapter, you learned the importance of fuel, or psychology, for English speaking success. You also learned how to anchor (connect) strong positive emotions to English.

In addition to peak emotions, there is another important element of psychology that you must master in order to speak English powerfully: belief. Beliefs are our most powerful "brain programs." They guide our decisions, our feelings, and our thoughts. They tell us what is possible and what is not. They open us to success or limit us to failure.

We can put beliefs into two general categories: limiting beliefs and empowering beliefs. A limiting belief is typically a negative "program" that limits your potential and performance. In other words, limiting beliefs limit your success.

The hidden curriculum is the source of most negative beliefs about English. Over time, schools consistently program limiting beliefs into the minds of their students. After years in school, most students share some or all of these limiting beliefs:

- English is complicated and difficult.
- It takes many years to speak English well.
- English is stressful.
- Grammar study is the key to English speaking.
- I'm not good at English.
- There is one right answer. There is one right way to say it.

- Something is wrong with me because I still can't speak English well.
- My test scores are low, therefore I can't speak English well.
- The best way to learn English is to sit in a class, take notes, and read a textbook.
- Only a few special people can learn to speak English powerfully.
- English learning is boring and frustrating.

The problem with these negative beliefs is that they lead to negative emotions (about English). The negative beliefs and emotions then lead to bad decisions, and the bad decisions lead to disappointing results.

For example, someone who believes that English is stressful, complicated, and difficult is unlikely to be motivated to work hard every day. Rather, they will constantly be struggling to force themselves to learn English.

Someone who feels only a few special people can master English will likely become frustrated very quickly. They will assume that something is wrong with them, that they are "not good at English." Again, their progress will be slow.

Finally, those who believe that classes, textbooks and grammar study are the key may spend years using these ineffective methods, driving their old slow car on the road to fluency and never achieving success.

This is why beliefs are so important. They are the central programs in our brain that create feelings, decisions and actions. Beliefs are what make the difference between ultimate success or a lifetime of frustration with English.

Beliefs tell you what an experience means. Whenever you have an English language experience, your brain must decide the meaning of what happened. In other words, your brain generalizes the experience. Your brain decides what the event means to your life as a whole. And with each negative experience, the belief can grow stronger and stronger. Eventually you become completely certain about the belief.

For example, maybe you were repeatedly corrected by an English teacher. After each of these embarrassing experiences, your brain had to decide the meaning of what happened. Based on these events, maybe you decided that you were bad at English. Maybe you decided that English was painful and stressful. Each negative experience made the belief stronger.

The problem is that these beliefs then affected all of your English experiences that followed. So whenever you had another encounter with English, it was always with these negative limiting beliefs. Because of this, you automatically viewed every new experience with English more negatively. If your beliefs are strongly negative and you don't change them, you can completely destroy your ability to succeed as an English speaker. Many English learners completely lose hope and simply quit, never to succeed.

You must, therefore, replace your limiting beliefs with strong empowering ones. "Empowering" means "giving power." So an empowering belief is one that gives you power!

What kind of empowering beliefs do you need for English speaking success?

Here is a sample list:

- English is easy, fun and exciting.
- I can speak English fluently in about six months.
- Mistakes are normal and necessary. Even native speakers make mistakes.

- Communication, not a test score, is the purpose of English speaking.
- Grammar study kills English speaking.
- Anyone can learn to speak English powerfully.
- There's nothing wrong with me, I've just been using a bad method and I can change that.

I'm sure you can see how much stronger these beliefs are. You can see that these beliefs are more likely to create success than the limiting ones. You can probably imagine the greater feelings of confidence and excitement that these beliefs create. But how do you create these beliefs? Clearly the empowering beliefs are more desirable, but how do you truly re-program your mind?

One powerful method for changing beliefs is called modeling. Modeling simply means to find a successful person and study them carefully. If you want to speak English powerfully, for example, you find another person who has learned to do it. You learn about them. You learn what they did and how they did it. If possible, you talk to them and learn about their psychology and their methods. Finally, of course, you do your best to do exactly what they did.

The more you model successful people, the more your beliefs will change automatically. By focusing on success instead of failure, you gradually re-program your brain. This is why I created the Effortless English Club™. In our community, the most successful members guide and advise newer members. While I hope this book will help to change your beliefs, there is nothing more powerful than hearing from another person, just like you, who achieved success.

Your job now is to find successful English speakers and model them. You might find them in your town. You will certainly find them online.

When you do find them, ask them about their beliefs and methods. Study their psychology and their success. This is exactly what I did when I developed the Effortless English™ system. I studied the most successful English learners. I interviewed them. I studied their emotions, their beliefs, their goals, and their learning methods. That is how I created a system based on success, not failure.

Remember, beliefs are created by the meaning we attach to experiences. The more you focus on and think about negative experiences, the stronger the limiting beliefs become. You can make empowering beliefs stronger in the same way. In other words, you can use "selective memory" to create and strengthen your positive beliefs.

How do you do this? Simply by reviewing all of your past experiences with English. As you remember all of your past experiences, search your memory for any that were positive. Maybe you remember a fun activity. Maybe you enjoyed reading a short story in English. When you remember these positive experiences, write them down. Create a list of all the positive experiences you have ever had with English.

Most people can identify at least a few such experiences. The next step is to focus your attention on these memories every day. Each day, review your list of positive English memories. Remember each experience. See each one in your mind and feel those positive feelings again.

Then write down a new empowering belief about English. You might write "English is easy and fun." You might write "I enjoy learning English and I'm good at it." Write this belief at the top of your list and also review it each day.

And of course, every time you have a new positive experience with English, add it to your list. Your list will grow longer and longer. And as it grows, your empowering beliefs will get stronger and stronger.

We all know the computer programming term "garbage in, garbage out." Beliefs are our brain programs. Garbage (negative limiting) beliefs create negative emotions, bad decisions, and low motivation. These, in turn, create "garbage out" – terrible results. Those bad results then create new and stronger negative beliefs, and the whole cycle starts again, even worse. This is called a "downward spiral."

Positive beliefs, on the other hand, create an upward spiral. Empowering beliefs create more positive emotions, better decisions, and better motivation. These, in turn, create better results. Better results then create even stronger empowering beliefs. The whole cycle repeats again and again, getting stronger each time. This upward spiral is the key to rapid success with English.

CHAPTER 5

English Is A Physical Sport

One of the greatest errors of the hidden curriculum is that schools teach English as an academic subject. In school you study English. You learn about English. You analyze the parts of the language (grammar, vocabulary, etc.). You take tests about this knowledge.

The problem is, English is not a subject to be studied. English is a skill to be performed or "played." Speaking is something you do, not something you analyze and think about. Perhaps you can see the problem.

Real English conversations are very fast and they are unpredictable. The other person speaks quickly and you never know exactly what they will say. You must be able to listen, understand, and respond almost instantly. There simply is no time to think about grammar, translations, or anything else you learned in English class.

English conversation is more like playing soccer (football). A soccer player must act and react almost instantly. The player must play the game intuitively. Soccer players do not study physics formulas in order to play well. They learn by doing. They "play" soccer, they don't "study" it.

Studying grammar rules to speak English is much like a soccer player studying physics to play soccer. It might be interesting (or not!), but it certainly won't help performance. Your job, therefore, is to stop "studying" English and start "playing" it!

Remember that your fuel is an important part, perhaps the most important part, of your Effortless English™ engine. Learning to play English, rather than study it, is a powerful way to develop strong psychology and go much faster on the road to fluency.

When we first discussed fuel, we learned how to use our bodies to change our emotions. It turns out the body is, in fact, a very important (and neglected) key to learning English. By using physical actions while learning, it is possible to learn faster, remember more, remember longer and speak better.

Dr. James Asher, a psychologist and professor emeritus at San José State University, found that using physical actions in language class actually helps students learn vocabulary better. Dr. Asher became curious about the link between language and movement after watching how young children learned to speak. He noticed that when parents said something, their children typically would respond with a word and some sort of action. He also noticed that parents frequently used actions and gestures while speaking to their babies.

Based on his research and observations, Asher developed the Total Physical Response system of language teaching in which students respond to teacher commands in the new language with whole body actions. These actions strengthen the meaning of the phrase and make it easier to remember. Dr. Asher believes that students can learn 12 to 36 words in an hour using this method. I've had similar success using a version of it in my lessons and seminars.

Of course, this is the complete opposite of what happens in most English classes. In school, you are told to sit still in your chair. You sit for an hour or more. Naturally, the longer you sit, the more your energy drops. As your energy drops, your concentration drops, too. And as your concentration drops, you learn less and forget more. Of course, this lower energy frequently leads to feelings of boredom. Less movement, less energy, lower concentration, and boredom naturally produce worse results, no matter what the method is, and so we have another downward spiral.

While everyone benefits from physical learning, some people absolutely need it. These people are called "kinesthetic learners." They learn best when they connect learning to physical movement. This kind of learner tends to struggle in traditional classrooms, where they are required to sit motionless for hours. Schools and teachers often label these people as being "learning disabled" or as having "attention deficit disorder."

The problem, however, is not that "kinesthetic learners" are disabled. Rather, the problem is a teaching disability — the failure of schools to teach active learners in an effective way.

My Effortless English™ seminars and classes are quite different. Many have described them as "English rock concerts." In an Effortless English™ seminar, we frequently jump, dance, shout, laugh, and move. In fact, it is rare for learners to sit for more than 15 minutes in one of my seminars. I want them moving. I want them energized. Because I know that active and energized people learn faster, learn more, remember longer and perform better!

Remember, English is a performance skill, not a subject you study. The more you use your body while learning, the more success you will achieve. One way to use movement while learning English is to use the Action Vocabulary method. In this method, you connect a unique physical movement to a new vocabulary word. You shout the word (or phrase) and perform the movement. The movement should remind you of the meaning of the word.

By doing this repeatedly, you connect the word, its meaning, and the unique physical action. This combination creates a stronger and deeper memory, resulting in faster and deeper vocabulary learning. This is far more effective than simply trying to memorize long lists of words.

Another simple way to use your body is to walk while learning English. With a smart phone you can make your learning mobile! Instead of sitting on your butt, slowly losing energy, put on your headphones and go for a walk while listening to English. As you walk, your heart will pump and your brain will get more blood. You'll feel more energy and thus you will concentrate better. You'll probably enjoy learning more, too.

There is no reason to be limited by the old school methods. You do not need to sit motionless in a chair while you learn. You do not need to remain silent. You do not need to be bored and tired. As an independent learner, you are free to learn in the way that is most effective and most enjoyable for you. You are the master of your own learning. Enjoy it!

Remember the peak emotion exercise you learned? This is another excellent way to use your body while learning English. Take a short "energy break." Play your favorite energetic music. Jump, shout, smile, cheer and dance for a couple of minutes. Fully energize your body and create peak emotions. Then continue learning English. Take these energy breaks every 20-30 minutes every time you learn English. I guarantee you will get better results.

Watch children when they are playing. They are happy, energetic and active. Children learn best while playing. They bring an attitude of play to everything they do. Small children don't need much effort or discipline. They are energized by curiosity. They learn actively. They learn by playing and play while learning.

It is time for you to rediscover these natural qualities. As an adult, you still learn best in this way. You, too, benefit from being active and energized while learning. You, too, benefit from physical movement and an attitude of play. As you use the techniques and methods in this book, always do so with a fun and playful attitude!

There are two major parts to the Effortless English™ system: the psychology and the method. You know that psychology is the fuel that makes the engine go. You must develop that fuel to create higher and higher energy for learning. You have learned how to use peak emotion anchoring, beliefs, and physical movement to create that fuel. You have learned the importance of an active, playful attitude.

In the next chapter, you will learn another psychological technique for creating the most powerful fuel possible for English learning.

(See below)

ACTION VOCABULARY

So many students waste time trying to memorize English vocabulary. They study long lists of words. They repeat the lists many times, trying to memorize the English words and their translated meanings. Unfortunately, research shows that 80% of vocabulary learned in this way is forgotten in less than a year. That's a lot of wasted time and effort.

There's another problem with this vocabulary learning method — it's boring, and it kills long-term motivation. As a student, you must be very careful— killing your motivation is the worst thing you can do. Learning English is a marathon, it's a long run. It requires high levels of motivation that are sustained for many years.

Using boring vocabulary learning methods, therefore, is doubly bad: it is inefficient and it weakens motivation.

There is a better way, as participants in my breakthrough seminars have found out. It is possible to learn new vocabulary in a way that is far more powerful AND is a lot of fun. When you learn in this way, studies show that you can remember 80% one year later! That's powerful.

The key to deep, powerful, long term vocabulary learning is movement. When you combine strong physical movements with understandable new vocabulary, you create deep connections in your brain and body. These connections are long term. They last! The key is to use a movement that reminds you of the meaning of the vocabulary.

For example, imagine you want to learn the phrase "to proclaim." First you would find the meaning of the word, which is "to say or announce publicly, often in a loud way." After you know the meaning, you create an action that reminds you of it. You might put your hands to your mouth and pretend you are yelling loudly ("to say publicly and loudly"). Finally, you would shout the phrase "to proclaim" as you did the gesture at the same time.

The more loudly you shout and the more energetically you do the gesture, the stronger the connection you make in your brain. By simply shouting the phrase and doing the movement vigorously several times, you will create a stronger and deeper memory of the meaning.

In a recent seminar I did in Vietnam, I taught a number of new words using this action vocabulary method. The students shouted the new words with me, while simultaneously using the strong actions I showed them. Each action was connected to the meaning of the new word or phrase. By the end of the lesson, they knew those words completely, never to forget them.

But that's not all. Since Effortless English™ is a deep learning system, I repeated those new words again — this time in a story lesson. Each time I used one of the new words in the story, I asked the students to use the same strong gesture we had practiced. Through the Mini-Story lesson, the students got even more repetition of the vocabulary, with emotion and strong actions.

Finally, I gave the students homework: download the audio of the same Mini-Story lesson, and listen to that audio every day for one week. If students do this, they will learn these new vocabulary words very deeply, and will remember them forever. That is the power of the Effortless English™ system, and that is the power of using physical movement while learning!

EIGHT SIMPLE STEPS TO CHANGING YOUR EMOTIONS

1. Find some exciting, energetic music that you LOVE.

2. Before you start listening to your English lesson, play the music.

3. As this exciting music plays, raise your head. Look up. Change your body.

Pull your shoulders back. Stand tall. Then smile… smile a big smile.

Take deep breaths.

4. Next, move your body. Dance with the music. Keep looking up. Keep smiling. Jump and dance. Lift your arms over your head as you jump and dance and smile. Feel the happiness and energy from the music.

5. Stop and say loudly, "Yes!" Say it again, "Yes!" One more time, "Yes!"

6. Now play your English lesson. As you listen, keep your shoulders back. Keep your eyes up. Keep smiling. In fact, stand up and keep moving. Walk and breathe deeply as you listen to the lesson.

7. When you listen to my Mini-Story lessons, answer each question loudly. Don't be shy. Shout your answer! Keep your head and eyes up. Keep a big smile on your face as you answer with a loud voice.

8. If you begin to feel tired or bored at any time, pause the lesson. Play your favorite music again and repeat all of these steps. Add more energy to your body and your emotions. Then play the lesson again.

By managing your emotions in this way, you will study longer, you will re-member more, and you will learn 2-4 times faster. You'll also teach yourself to be strong and confident when you speak English.

CHAPTER 6

Use Big Real World Goals To Motivate Yourself For Success

Why, exactly, are you learning English? Why do you want to speak English powerfully? Surprisingly, many people have only a vague idea. They know that English is the "international language" and they feel they should learn it. In school, they are told that English is important. Some people are focused on tests scores. They are studying English in order to get a high score on the TOEFL, TOEIC, IELTS or other exam.

Where do these goals come from? Typically, they come from the school system. In other words, they are external goals that are promoted by other people. Students are told these goals are important and thus spend years focusing on test scores. The problem is that external goals (goals provided by outside people) feel like work. These goals feel like an obligation.

These goals are weak and uninspiring, and that's a problem because goals are our brain's targeting system. Goals tell our brains what we want, when we want it, and why we want it. A powerful goal energizes, inspires and motivates us to do more and be more. A great goal can totally change your life. Weak goals, on the other hand, produce weak results.

Another step in developing your Effortless English™ fuel is, therefore, to develop stronger goals. But what makes a strong goal? A strong goal is one that creates a positive obsession in your mind. A strong goal is emotional. A strong goal not only motivates you, it seems to pull you towards action and success.

A great goal is like a positive addiction. The goal keeps you focused on what is important in your life. You can't forget about it. In fact, with a truly powerful goal, you will find it difficult to stop thinking about it. This goal guides you and motivates you even through difficult times.

To be powerful, a goal must be intensely emotional in a positive way. This is why test score goals are so weak. Who gets excited and inspired by tests? In fact, for most people, tests are negative experiences that produce feelings of nervousness, fear and stress. That's not very energizing or inspiring. No wonder so many people feel bad about English.

So how do you find and create truly powerful goals? Begin by asking yourself power questions. These are questions that help you find your deeper reason for speaking English. As you go deeper, you will find more inspiring goals. And the best power question of all is simply, "why?"

Repeatedly asking why is an easy way to find your deeper purpose for English. For example, you might first ask yourself, "Why am I learning English?" Maybe your first answer is, "To get a high TOEFL score." That's a weak external goal. So you ask yourself again, "Why do I want a high TOEFL score?" Maybe you answer, "To get a better job." Again you ask, "Why do I want a better job?" Now you are going deeper, finding your true purpose. Maybe you answer, "To make more money for my family." And then you ask, "Why do I want to make more money for my family?" And you might answer, "Because I love them and want to provide an abundant and wonderful life for them." You have found your big internal goal.

Your big goal is not to get a high TOEFL score, your true goal is to create a wonderful life for your family. English is a tool to help you with that goal. Isn't that more powerful and emotional? Doesn't that excite and inspire you more? Doesn't that create much more fuel for your engine?

Of course, everyone is different. Maybe your big goal is to travel the world and live a life of adventure – and you know that English is the international language. Maybe you dream of being a rich and success-ful international businessperson, and English will help you achieve that dream. Maybe you dream of studying abroad at an American university. Maybe you want to make international friends from many countries around the world. Maybe you have more than one big goal for English.

The point is that English is a tool for communication. Just knowing a lot of words and grammar is useless. You must use the language to unleash its power. So the key to finding your big goal is to figure out how you want to use English in the real world.

With English, you must focus on your real world reasons for speak-ing the language.

Goals must excite you. You should feel enthusiastic and energized just thinking about your goals.

Even though I'm writing on this topic, I too have sometimes been guilty of having weak goals. For example, I recently did a series of seminars and presentations in Thailand. My initial goals were:

- To teach people about the Effortless English™ system.
- To connect with more people.

Now these were certainly positive goals – but they had no power. They didn't excite me. They didn't create passion. So I thought more deeply. I asked myself, "Why do I want to teach people about the Effortless English™ system? Why do I want to connect with more people? What do I want to contribute? What do I want to accomplish?"

Better goals instantly came to my mind, including:

- I want to inspire people and change their lives!
- I want to awaken people's passion and love of learning.
- I want to awaken their imaginations!
- I want to heal their English trauma!
- I want to totally change the way people learn English.
- I want to help people achieve their dreams using English as a tool!
- I want to build an international family of super enthusiastic learners!
- I want to give people incredibly positive & powerful emotional experiences!
- I want to give them happiness, laughter, passion, and powerful confidence.
- I want to free people from doubt, from insecurity, from boredom, from hesitancy.
- I want to help them achieve their dreams!

Now these were exciting goals! These goals immediately gave me energy and power. They made me want to jump out of bed and get to work! They made me want to do a fantastic job as a teacher. They inspired me to learn and grow better and better. They made me want to create an amazing demonstration – not just some boring lecture.

Such is the power of big and meaningful goals. Why do you want to learn English? What is the most exciting outcome you can imagine speaking English will bring you? What truly inspires you about learning English? Think bigger. Dream bigger!

Do yourself a favor: Choose big, audacious, powerful goals for learning English. Ignite your passion!

CHAPTER 7

Program Your Brain For English Success

While teaching English at a university in Thailand, I had a student named Ploy. On the first day of class, Ploy sat in the back row. During that class, she did her best to hide from me. She hunched her shoulders and tried to disappear behind the student who sat in front of her. Ploy remained silent during the entire class.

After class I asked her to stay a minute. I could see that something was wrong and wanted to find out how I could help her. I told her, "I noticed you were hiding during class, is everything okay?" She said, "I'm not good in English." Ploy then described her longtime frustrations with English, including bad grades, bad test scores, and embarrassment. Because of this history, she was convinced that she had a flaw and was "bad at English."

After talking with Ploy, I thought about her problem and her beliefs. I realized that other students in the class probably had similar feelings. Before I taught them English, I knew I had to find a way to help them reprogram their beliefs. That week I researched more psychology techniques and discovered the method of "mental movie programming."

The following week, I taught the technique to the class and continued to use it throughout the semester. In just a few weeks, I noticed a dramatic difference. Ploy grew more confident and outgoing. First, she sat in the front row instead of the back row. Then, she began to participate in class. Her classmates likewise grew more confident week by week.

This experience showed me the power of psychology and why it is so important to program yourself for success.

This chapter is the final step to reprogramming your psychology for English success. You'll learn exactly how to program the beliefs, goals and peak emotions you need to develop race-car fuel for your Effortless English™ engine.

The problem for learners is not a lack of intelligence, nor a lack of will power. You are not "bad at English." What most people lack is control over their mind and emotions. In fact, you have all the talent, intelligence and power you need to master spoken English at the highest possible level. You simply need to learn how to control your power and use it to change your emotions, beliefs, and actions in an instant, exactly as you want.

Like many English learners, perhaps you too suffer from "English trauma." Perhaps you hold limiting beliefs, and feel frustrated, nervous or stressful when trying to speak. You want to feel confident and powerful when speaking, and to do so, you must learn to control your internal movies.

Your internal movies are the programs you use to create feelings, beliefs and goals. You create these movies with your five senses: sight, hearing, touch, taste and smell. Your memories and your dreams are recorded in your mind as a combination of these senses. These are the ingredients you use to write and direct your own internal movies. These movies then create your emotions, thoughts and actions.

When you want to change the results you get with learning English, you want to change two things: how you feel when speaking English and how well you actually speak. In other words, you want to feel confident while speaking and you want to speak skillfully. This chapter is about how to change your internal movies so they program you for both powerful feelings and skillful performance while speaking.

As you think about the movies you make in your mind, realize that there are two things you can choose: What is in your movies and how that movie is made. If you frequently think about memories of embarrassment with English, that will change the way you feel. How that memory is structured is also important. For example, perhaps you remember a time when you were corrected by a teacher in class, and that memory creates nervousness about English. That memory is a movie in your mind. Internally, you see the event happening, you hear the teacher correcting you, and you feel the embarrassment (sight, hearing and physical sensations are the most common and powerful ingredients used in internal movies).

For most people, if you make that negative movie larger in your mind, the bad feelings will get stronger. Likewise, if you make the teacher's voice louder, the bad feelings are likely to get worse. And you could focus on the sensations or feelings of embarrassment and move them faster in your body, again making them stronger. By changing how the movie is played in your mind, you change its power.

These movie qualities are called "sub-modalities." They are the specific qualities of each sense used in your internal movies. Each of the senses has several sub-modalities that can be controlled and changed.

Visually, for example, you can change the colors of a movie, or remove color completely to make it black and white. You can change the size of the images in your mind, making them larger or smaller. If you imagine the movie showing on a screen inside your mind, you can change the distance to the screen, bringing it closer or pushing it away. You can change the brightness of a movie. You control the movement of your internal movies and can make them fast, normal, or slow motion. You can change the "camera angle" of your movie, changing the view of any scene.

Internal movies have soundtracks, and these too can be controlled and changed. You control the loudness of the sounds in your movie. You control the rhythm. You can change the tone and pitch, making sounds higher or lower.

And you also control the feelings or physical sensations in your movies. You control the temperature (colder, hotter), the pressure (more, less), and the location of sensations. You also control the intensity of emotions and can make them vibrate faster or slower in your body.

Essentially, you are the movie director of your own mind. The question is, will you control these movies and consciously direct them, or will you let them control you? A good director controls the images, camera angles, sounds, etc. in a movie to create exactly the thoughts and feelings he or she wants the audience to experience. As director of your own mind, you can do the same.

You can, for example, change your memory recordings. Memories are simply internal movies you have created about an experience you had in the past. For most people, these movies were created without conscious choice. The good news is you can re-direct these movies in order to make them weaker or stronger, and change the effect they have on your life.

Let's do it now. Think of a very happy memory. It can be anything, any memory that makes you smile. Close your eyes, smile, and think of that memory now. As you remember, notice the image or movie in your mind. What do you see? Then notice what you hear: does your movie have sound? And what about the feelings: how do you feel in this movie? Where are the feelings in your body? Do you feel vibrations in your body, or feelings of tension or relaxation? Just notice the details of this happy internal movie.

Now become the director of this memory. If you only see a still photograph, make it into a movie by adding movement. Then make the image bigger in your mind, bring it closer to you. As you make it bigger, notice how your feelings change. For most people, making the movie bigger increases the power of the emotions (negative or positive). With a happy memory, you can make it even happier by making the movie bigger!

Of course, you can also change the sound and the feelings. Try making the sounds a bit louder, especially the pleasant sounds. When you notice the good feelings, locate where they are in your body and how they are moving. Feelings are physical and are usually experienced as a vibration or energy in the body. Make that happy vibration faster, and have it move through your body more. For most, this will also increase the feeling of happiness.

Congratulations, you just directed your first internal movie. You learned how to increase feelings of happiness by becoming a better director. You can use this same skill with negative memories, thoughts and beliefs. Let's try it.

Remember a negative experience with English. Perhaps it's a bad experience from school, or a time when you felt nervous, frustrated, bored or foolish trying to speak English. As you remember this bad experience, again notice the details of your internal movie. See the memory in your mind. Notice if this movie has sound, and notice how you feel in the movie.

First, bring this negative movie screen closer to you, making it bigger. Make the sounds louder and vibrate the feelings faster. Most people will feel worse by doing this. That's not what you want. So now do the opposite. Push the movie screen farther away, making the movie smaller. Then make the movie darker and harder to see in your mind. Imagine this movie screen has a button that controls volume. Grab that button and turn it down, making the sounds quieter. In fact, turn off the sound completely. Finally, take a deep breath and calm your feelings.

By doing all of these things, you'll notice that the negative feelings are much weaker, or gone completely. You have taken an unhappy memory and made it powerless by consciously directing your mind. Most people believe that memories are unchangeable, but you have just proven that you are, in fact, in control of your memories. The same is true of your thoughts.

You have a choice. You can be the conscious director of your mind or you can let your brain run wild. Most people do the latter and they feel powerless. They are controlled by negative thoughts and memories and bad experiences. This is not necessary. You can choose to run your brain, directing it to produce the thoughts, feelings and actions you desire.

You can make the negative powerless and you can also increase the strength of positive memories, thoughts, beliefs and goals. You can control your brain instead of being controlled by it. This process not only works for memories, it also works for goals you want to achieve in the future. Think of a big goal for English, one of those large and inspiring goals that will change your life.

Close your eyes as you think of this goal. Now consciously make a movie for that goal. You are the director! See yourself speaking

English powerfully to other people. Choose a situation that inspires you. As you look at this movie, notice the faces of the other people as they listen to you. See them smiling as they understand and enjoy your English! Grab that movie screen in your mind and bring it closer, so the movie is much bigger. Then make the colors more beautiful. Make the image a little brighter.

As you continue watching this great movie, notice the soundtrack. Hear one of the listeners say, "Wow, your English is great! How did you learn to speak so well?" Turn up the sound so you can hear this loud and clear! Notice how you feel when you hear this compliment. You'll feel the pride and happiness in your body somewhere. Where is it? Wherever it is, make that happy vibration faster and stronger and then move it around all of your body. Feels great!

You have just created your English power movie, and you are the movie star. You are confident and skillful. You are happy. You are amazing, speaking English effortlessly! Feels great!

With this directing power, you start to program your brain for the exact beliefs, emotions and outcomes that you want. You focus on this power movie every day, and each time you create the movie it becomes stronger. Anytime a negative movie arises in your mind, you use your directing skill to make it smaller and weaker. Day by day, by consciously mastering your mind, you completely change your life.

Of course this requires daily practice. Those old movies were created over many years, so you need to consciously create your power movies every day. By doing so, step by step you will re-program yourself for English success.

One particularly powerful way to reprogram your movies is by using a method called "the swish." The swish is a classic technique of success psychology and NLP. A swish is a way to instantly and automatically change a negative internal movie into a power movie that makes you feel great. For example, if you frequently feel nervous when speaking English, you can program your mind to automatically change to feeling powerful and confident every time you speak.

You must practice and train this "swish" technique daily, but once it is programmed deeply, you will not need to think about it. Whenever you need to speak English, you will effortlessly feel strong and confident.

Here are the steps for using the swish technique:

1. Identify the feeling or action you want to change. Maybe it's a feeling of nervousness when speaking English. First, make a movie of that negative situation. See, hear and feel what's happening in this negative movie.

2. Next you will create a power movie that represents your goal, what you want to feel and do instead. You could, for example, use the power movie in the previous example... a movie of yourself speaking powerfully and feeling great.

3. Use the "swish" to connect the two movies and create an automatic change from the negative to the power movie. Essentially, you are anchoring the power movie to the old negative situation.

This is how you do the swish specifically:

Close your eyes and start by making a big picture of the negative situation you want to change. See it clearly. Then imagine there is a small dark square in the corner of that picture. That small square is your power movie. So you have the big negative movie on the screen in front of you, and in the corner of that screen is a small square which contains the power movie.

Next, say "Wooosh!" and imagine that the small square explodes and becomes a huge movie screen. As it explodes, it completely destroys the negative movie and replaces it. Now you see your power movie in front of you. It is big, bright, and colorful. It has a great soundtrack and it feels great. Notice the movie and let those happy feelings grow stronger.

Be sure to say the word "Woosh!" loudly and powerfully, with a lot of excitement. Remember peak emotion and use a strong body gesture, too, in order to increase the positive feelings. You are creating a connection, an anchor, between the word, the gesture, and the power movie.

Next, open your eyes for a moment to reset. Then close your eyes and repeat the entire swish process. Each time, make the explosion happen faster. The power movie explodes and destroys that old image. Shout "Woosh!" loudly and make the peak emotions of your power movie even stronger.

Then open your eyes for a moment, reset, close your eyes, and do it again. Keep repeating the process, again and again. Each day, practice doing this ten times or more. Do it daily. It may take thirty or more days to program an automatic response. Once programmed, you will notice an amazing result. When you are in an English speaking situation, you may feel a brief moment of nervousness. Then suddenly, you'll feel better — more powerful, more relaxed and more confident. It will happen automatically and effortlessly. This is the result of the swish programming.

Make this a daily habit. You can do this swish process every morning when you wake up and it will only take a few minutes. During these few minutes, you program your unconscious mind for success.

You change the old negative movies. You develop more powerful beliefs and feelings about English. You take control and become a skilled director of your own mind.

You now have all the tools you need to develop powerful success psychology. You know how to create peak emotions and connect them to English. You know the importance of beliefs and how to change them through modeling. You know how to use physical movement to create emotions and enhance memory. You know the motivational power of big goals and how to find your deeper reasons for learning English. And you know how to consciously direct your mind to success by using internal movies.

On the road to English fluency, you need two things: powerful fuel and a powerful car: strong psychology and a great method. You now know how to create the premium fuel you need.

In the next section, you will learn what to do with that fuel — the specific English learning methods you must use in order to speak English powerfully. It is time to learn the Effortless English™ engine.

CHAPTER 8

Babies Learn Best — The Effortless English™ Engine

You have now learned the first part of the Effortless English™ system: the fuel or psychology. You know how to create high-quality emotional fuel to power your journey on the road to English fluency. Now it's time to focus on the engine that will use that fuel. This is what I like to call the Ferrari of language learning – the Effortless English™ method.

As I noted earlier, Effortless English™ is a system I developed over a period of several years of teaching and research. Through trial and error, I've been able to improve and adapt this method to suit the needs of learners all over the world. As long as you bring the proper psychology and emotional fuel to the method, I guarantee you'll arrive quickly at English fluency.

For purposes of clarity, I have broken the Effortless English™ method into seven steps. I refer to these steps as the "seven rules." In this chapter, I'll introduce these rules and briefly explain how they work. I'll also describe how this section will be organized, so that you can get the maximum benefits from studying English each time you sit down.

Each of the seven rules is a piece of "profound knowledge" that will completely change the results you get with English. Professor Edwards Deming described profound knowledge as a new idea, strategy or distinction that powerfully changes the quality of results. Profound knowledge is often a simple change that creates a big improvement.

Each of the seven rules is simple, but when used each will produce large improvements in your English speaking. Used together with strong psychology, the seven rules speed your travel along the road to fluency.

I should warn you that this method is completely different from the hidden curriculum you have used in the past. Remember, Effortless English™ doesn't depend on traditional methods. Instead, it is designed to follow the natural order of language learning seen with small children.

Babies Know Best

In fact, babies and small children are the best English learners in the world! They easily learn to speak as a native speaker, with excellent grammar, vocabulary, fluency and pronunciation. Instead of studying textbooks, perhaps we should look at babies and how they learn English.

When a baby first starts to learn English, or any language, it mostly just listens. In fact, for many months, the baby or child will only listen without any real speaking. This period of listening is called the "silent period" by linguists. During the silent period, the baby is learning to understand the language. Of course, when a baby is silently learning the parents do not get worried. They don't teach the baby grammar. They don't get angry if the baby doesn't speak.

What do the parents do? They simply talk to the baby using very simple English. They use actions while they talk. For example, they point to Mom and say, "mama, mama," over and over again every day. Eventually the baby realizes that "mama" is the word for his or her mother.

Eventually, the baby will begin to speak. Perhaps one day they finally say "mama." What happens? Do the parents correct the baby's pronunciation? Do they try to teach the baby grammar? Of course not. Rather, everyone goes crazy with happiness because the baby said one correct word (usually with bad pronunciation). Everyone is smiling and laughing. Speaking English is a very happy time for the baby!

During the next few years, the baby will continue focusing on listening. Its speech will gradually become better. The baby will use more words. Its grammar will improve, even though it never studies grammar rules! The baby's pronunciation will improve. And yet, for many years, its listening will still be better than its speaking. The baby will understand more than it can say.

This is the natural way of learning English. As you can see, it is very different than the way you learned in school. In school you focused on reading textbooks from the beginning. Perhaps you were forced to speak very soon, even though you were not ready. You focused on studying grammar rules. When you made a mistake, the teacher corrected you.

Unlike the baby, you did not improve quickly. You didn't improve your grammar naturally and effortlessly. Your pronunciation never seemed to get much better. And your speaking always seemed too slow. For you, English probably was not a joyful experience. English was not a playful and natural experience that you loved.

Clearly there is something wrong with the traditional way of teaching English in school. Clearly we need a better method, a method that closely follows the natural way that humans are designed to learn a language.

The truth is, your brain is an incredible language-learning machine. When you have strong psychology and an effective method, you learn

English quickly. Even better, when you follow a natural approach, you enjoy the process of learning because you are no longer fighting against nature and your own brain.

You have learned Effortless English™ psychology. Now it is time to learn the engine, the method, of Effortless English™. Each of the seven rules is an important part of this method. Each rule is a new way to "play English." As you learn and use the seven rules, be sure to maintain a playful attitude. Be flexible. Have fun. Enjoy this new process of learning.

The seven rules are interconnected and work synergistically. "Synergistic" means the rules are more powerful when used together than they are individually. Each rule makes the other rules stronger. Together they form a powerful method for achieving fluency and skill with English.

How to use this section

The purpose of this section is to help you learn to speak English confidently and fluently. Now that I've explained the psychology of Effortless English™, my goal is to make the material in these pages as practical and useful as possible. In the next several chapters, I'll be explaining each of the seven rules of Effortless English™ in detail. I'll also be including more motivational tips, teaching examples and sample practice exercises to assist you on your road to fluency.

As you learn each rule, you'll get another piece of the Effortless English™ method. Together they form a complete learning system. At the end of this section I will teach you how to put these rules together to create your own daily individual learning plan. You'll learn exactly what to do, each day, to achieve spoken English mastery.

Enjoy the ride.

CHAPTER 9

The First Rule – Learn Phrases Not Words

If you've taken English classes, chances are you've had plenty of experience memorizing lists of vocabulary words.

With Effortless English™ you are not going to do that anymore. Why? Because vocabulary lists are a waste of time. Yes, you heard me right. Trying to memorize a bunch of random individual words is not an effective way to learn. Instead, you're going to use the first rule of the Effortless English™ method and learn phrases not words.

What do I mean by "phrases?" Phrases are groups of words that are related, and focus on an idea. Another way to describe phrases is as "natural chunks of language." In any language, certain words naturally go together in a certain way. For example, in English we say "I am on an island." We don't say, "I am at an island." Why? There is no logical reason. One is simply a common and acceptable phrase and the other is not.

Here's another example. Let's say that *hate* is one of the new words you want to learn. In a traditional class, you'd write down the word *hate* and then go look it up in the dictionary to find its meaning. You'd see that it means to have a strong and intense dislike for something; to loathe or detest. Then you'd memorize it – *hate, hate, hate, hate, hate.*

That's the old way – kind of the textbook way, right? In school, you probably used this strategy to remember a lot of individual words. You had those big vocabulary lists, and you tried to memorize all of them for the test. For verbs, you also tried to memorize conjugation charts.

Even worse, you probably learned these words by memorizing translations in your own language. Because of this, you often find yourself translating in your head when trying to speak English. First you think of the word in your own language, then you try to remember the translation in English. This extra step slows both your speaking and your listening ability.

Trust me. It's much better if you learn a phrase – a group of words. It's easy. You listen to someone speaking real English, and when you hear a new word, you write it down. Or when you read a story and you see a new word, you write it down. Only you don't want to just write down that one word. You want to write down the whole phrase or sentence that it's in.

In other words, you learn the language in chunks. So, instead of just writing down the word *hate*, you would write down *John hates ice cream*. You would write down the whole phrase and its meaning.

It's easy to look up words in an English language dictionary, which most students own. Phrases can present more of a challenge, since they can't always be translated literally. That's why I recommend all my students get a good idiomatic dictionary, or dictionary of English idioms. Idioms are common phrases or sayings in a language. If you just search online for "dictionary of English idioms" you'll find a ready selection of these books to choose from.

Why do we do this? What's the power of phrases? Well, for one thing, phrases give you a lot more information. They give you much more information than you would get from a single word. As a result, phrases are easier to remember, because they have deeper meaning. They present you with a kind of picture or story, especially when you get them from something you are listening to or reading. When you hear, *John hates ice cream,* you remember the whole little story. You remember who John is. You remember that he had ice cream, and then you remember he hated it. He didn't like it, right? So you have all these extra pieces of information. This extra information puts the word in context. It helps you remember the meaning of the phrase as well as the meaning of that word! This might not seem like much, but in fact this is a huge improvement for memory. By learning phrases, you will learn more vocabulary, you'll learn it faster and you'll remember it longer.

There's also another bonus. When you learn phrases, you are not just learning the individual word, you're learning grammar, too. You're learning how to use that word correctly with other words. You don't need to think about the grammar. You don't need to know the rules or worry about word order or verb tenses. It's automatic. You'll use the word correctly in a phrase because that's how you remembered it.

In the Effortless English™ system, this is one way that you learn grammar intuitively and unconsciously, without thinking about grammar rules. Phrases teach you natural spoken English grammar. By learning phrases, you are automatically learning both grammar and vocabulary at the same time. Two for one!

Learning the Natural Way

This is actually how native speakers first learn English grammar. It's how you learned your own language. When we're children, we learn in phrases. We learn in groups of words. *Give it to me. Walk across the street. He fell down.* (Note: in some cases the phrases I'll refer to could be full sentences, since they contain both a subject and a verb like the previous example: *He fell down.* In other cases, a phrase could be just a few words within a sentence. In this book I am using the word *phrase* to describe any natural word group).

The point is: we learn groups of words, not just one word. Word by word is slow and it doesn't help with grammar. But when you learn a whole phrase, you are getting extra information. Maybe you don't know it, but you are.

Let's return to our example: *John hates ice cream.* Remember, our initial word was *hate.* But now you see there's an "s" at the end – *hates,* right? *John hates.* You know from grammar study that you're making the subject and verb agree, but you don't need to think about that. You learn the grammar from just that word in the phrase, that "s" on the end, *hates.* And in the future, whenever you say John hates ice cream or he hates ice cream, you will automatically add the "s" because that's how you learned it. You won't have to spend time trying to remember the conjugations of the verb "hate" because you learned it correctly from a phrase and now it's automatic.

Of course, you don't actually have to think about all of this consciously. Just by learning the phrase, you will automatically learn the correct verb conjugation. You eliminate the extra step of labeling and analyzing grammar terms. That's why learning phrases leads to faster speech and faster understanding.

On the other hand, if you learn all of this from a textbook, you'll often just learn the root of the word "to hate" and you'll focus on this form: hate, hate, hate. So you study it and you memorize it. That's when you start making mistakes, because you memorized it mostly in this way, without other words. Later, you try to remember all of the conjugations of the verb. But because you didn't learn this with other words, sometimes you might say "he hate ice cream." You'll forget the "s" because you never learned it correctly in a sentence, in a phrase. And in a real conversation there is no time to think about verb conjugations.

Learning phrases will also help your pronunciation. One of the biggest problems I see with English learners is they speak with strange rhythm and intonation. Rhythm and intonation are the "music" of English. While many students worry about the pronunciation of individual sounds such as v, b, r, and l, their biggest problem is unnatural rhythm.

The rhythm of English is created by the natural pattern of pauses. Native speakers naturally pause between phrases. They speak the language in phrases, in short chunks of English. Because they learned English mostly from phrases, their pronunciation is clear and easy to understand. On the other hand, many students learn English by memorizing individual words, and when they speak, they speak word by word, one at a time. As a result, they often pause in strange places. They create unnatural word groupings. This creates a very strange and unnatural rhythm that many native speakers struggle to understand. This is very frustrating for the speaker and for the listener.

One of the easiest ways to improve speaking, therefore, is to learn phrases and to speak in phrases rather than word by word. This simple change will make your English speaking much clearer and much easier to understand. You'll sound more natural. The words will flow out more easily. You'll improve both pronunciation and fluency. You'll even learn grammar.

Where to Find Phrases

So where does a student get these phrases? How do you know which ones to learn? The good news is that you can find them everywhere. Any natural English content contains a wealth of phrases. In a future chapter, I will tell you specifically where to get useful English phrases. But for now, focus on getting phrases from whatever English you are listening to or reading.

To do this you need to start keeping a "phrase" notebook. Every time you see or hear a new word or phrase, write that phrase in your notebook. When you find new English vocabulary in a lesson, in something you are listening to, in a book, or in an article, write down the phrase. Not just one word, write down the entire phrase, and then review that phrase again and again each day. By doing this, you will create a notebook full of phrases and sentences you can use, not just individual words. You'll be programming yourself to speak in phrases instead of word by word.

If you're watching a movie about a bank robbery, for example, you might hear a character say, *"They're getting away!"* You know *get* means "to obtain" something, and you're pretty sure *away* refers to "being at a distance" – like far away. But it's confusing. So you write it down, *"They are getting away."* Then when you look it up in an idiomatic dictionary, you learn that one meaning of "to get away" is to escape. You might also discover that sometimes when people are going on vacation, they say they are *"getting away."* Even if you had previously memorized the words *get* and *away* on some vocabulary list, you still might not understand what the character in the movie is saying. But since you wrote down the phrase, you now know a new expression you can use in many different situations.

Here's another example. Let's say someone describes their former pet by saying, "*He was a bad dog.*" It's a fairly simple phrase, but you write it down in your notebook. Every time you review, you study that complete phrase. By doing that, you are getting free grammar – *he was*. You know this is something that was true in the past, not *he is*, which would mean the dog still was around. You're also getting some free tips about word usage. We don't usually say he was a *horrendous* dog, for example, even though the meaning is correct. In normal spoken English, we don't usually use that word to describe a dog. This is not what you would learn from studying the definition of horrendous. You learn it by studying a phrase.

When you write down a phrase, write where it came from. If you saw this in a newspaper article about the economy, put that down because that is going to trigger your memory. It will remind you of how the word was used and in what context. You'll start to learn when certain phrases and words are used and when they are not. This way, you'll begin to get a feeling about what is correct and how to put sentences together.

IMPROVING YOUR PRONUNCIATION

Pronunciation is a big worry for many English learners. Learning phrases will help, but there is another exercise you can do to improve even more. One of the greatest challenges with pronunciation is the problem of feeling strange when trying to use a native accent.

For example, many learners feel unnatural when trying to use an American accent. They feel they are not being normal, or not being themselves.

Their voice sounds strange to them. This is normal because speaking a different language naturally forces you to create different sounds.

So how can you develop more natural English pronunciation? One strategy I suggest is to play a little game with movies. In this game you try to become your favorite English speaking actor or actress. This is a variation of the movie technique, which I will describe in more detail in a later chapter. When you speak, pretend you are that actor. Instead of worrying about your English, concentrate on speaking exactly the way the actor would.

In fact, it's important to think of this as a game and to even exaggerate the actor's pronunciation, movements and facial expressions.

Sometimes in my own classes I imitate the famous actor John Wayne, who played the hero in many old Westerns and was seen as the typical American. I'll walk around my classes like I'm wearing cowboy boots and ready to go after some bad guys. Maybe you'll feel more comfortable playing Tom Cruise, Julia Roberts or another movie star . . . the idea is to exaggerate their pronunciation and push yourself to speak just like them. Have fun, and you'll be surprised how much this will help your pronunciation.

The first rule of the Effortless English™ method is very simple. Yet this very small change to the way you learn vocabulary affects your grammar, your pronunciation and your memory of new words. Rule one is a piece of profound knowledge that works synergistically with the other rules.

In the next chapter you'll learn, perhaps, the most surprising rule of the Effortless English™ system. Rule Two frees you from the grammar translation method used in school and removes much of the boredom and pain of English learning.

CHAPTER 10

The Second Rule: Grammar Study Kills Your English Speaking

The second rule of the method is the most shocking for most learners. After years of studying English in schools, most people believe that grammar study is the key to English speaking. In fact, many learners simply cannot imagine learning English without studying grammar rules. They have strong beliefs deeply programmed by the hidden curriculum.

That is why the second rule is such a huge change. The second rule of the Effortless English™ method is: Do NOT study grammar! Now I know this might be a tough idea for you to accept. Let's face it: for as long as you've been studying English, you have been told that you must learn grammar rules – in middle school, in high school, in university, in language schools, everywhere in the world it's grammar, grammar, grammar, grammar.

So my first question is: How did this strategy work for you? Was it successful? If you are reading this book, you've likely studied English for years and you focused a lot on grammar rules. But can you speak English easily, quickly and automatically right now? Did all of this grammar study produce the result you want?

If the answer is no, you are normal. Because despite what you learned in school, the truth is that grammar study actually hurts your English speaking. The problem with studying grammar is that instead of speaking English you focus on *analyzing* it. You become like the soccer player who is studying physics in order to improve. You learn a lot of information but your skill never seems to get much better.

In other words, you *think* about English instead of doing it. You think about the past tense, the present tense, the future, the present perfect, the past perfect. Now for writing English, that's not as bad. When you write English, you have time. You can think about things slowly and take your time. You can erase your mistakes. It's less of a problem. You don't need to write fast.

But when it comes to speaking, there's no time. You don't have time to think about the rules for the present perfect tense in English when you are talking to people. If someone asks you a question, you have to answer it immediately. You don't have time to think about prepositions. You don't have time to think about verb tenses, possessives, phrasal verbs – all the other linguistic terms you've learned. There's no time.

A student of mine in Barcelona named Oscar once struggled with this very issue. He wanted to improve his conversational skills, however, all he could think of was grammar. *Should I be using present perfect or another tense?* That kind of thing. He said he felt like he was chained up and the words just wouldn't come. So he stopped studying grammar. Over the next few months, his speaking dramatically improved. "It just started flowing out instead of me consciously thinking about it."

Research supports this, which is why linguists like Stephen Krashen recommend a more natural approach. Learning a language, Krashen notes, "doesn't require extensive use of conscious grammatical rules and does not require tedious drill."

In a meta-analysis of grammar instruction, researchers found that studies over the last century have failed to find a significant effect for the teaching of grammar directly. The research is clear: Learning grammar rules does not improve your spoken grammar. You have seen this with your own speaking. How many times have you made a grammar mistake when speaking, even though you "knew" the correct rule?

For example, many students who do well on grammar tests have terrible spoken grammar. They can tell you that the past tense version of "teach" is "taught." Yet, when speaking, they will say "last year he teach me." They know the rule intellectually, but this does not help their speaking.

Another common problem is slow and hesitant speech. While speaking, a student will constantly be thinking of verb conjugations. All this analyzing slows their speech, making it painful and unnatural for the listener. Even when they manage to speak correctly, they kill natural communication by being so slow and hesitant.

What Real English Sounds Like

Real English conversation is tricky. Real conversation isn't like what you learned in school. In fact, it often feels totally different.

One key difference is the fact that real speech very rarely uses full or "grammatically correct" sentences. Of course, in school, those are the only kinds of sentences you learned. You learned about Subject-Verb-Object. You learned to avoid sentence fragments.

Then you hear a real English conversation with real native speakers and you discover that they MOSTLY use sentence fragments!

This is something I immediately noticed when I read the transcripts for some of our Effortless English™ lessons. I knew that most of us tend to use a lot of fragments in normal speech, but even I was surprised at just how often we do this.

In fact, we constantly speak in partial sentences. We constantly use "run on" sentences. We constantly interrupt our own sentences and change our thoughts in the middle of speaking. A transcript of a real conversation – that is, a totally spontaneous and natural conversation – is completely different than anything you will find in a textbook.

And that is only one difference – there are many other major differences between real English conversations and textbook conversations or so-called "dialogues."

This helps to explain why even "advanced" English students have such trouble when they come to the United States. While these students may have good individual vocabulary (usually formal), they have absolutely no exposure to real spoken English. In school they learned how people "should" speak English – but what they really needed to learn is how people actually DO speak English.

THE TRUTH ABOUT GRAMMAR

Sometimes people will ask me, "A.J., why are you against grammar?" I think it's important to clarify that I most definitely am NOT against grammar. I just think people need to learn it intuitively. As a teacher, I need to teach it indirectly.

What does "intuitive grammar" mean, exactly? Intuitive mastery of spoken grammar is based on a "feeling for correctness." This is the method that native speakers use to learn and master English grammar. By avoiding grammar study, learning phrases, and using other natural methods, the native speaker learns to identify what "sounds right."

You do the same with your own language. As you speak, you do not think about verb tenses or other grammar. If you hear another person make a mistake, you know it's a mistake because it "sounds wrong."

Intuitive grammar mastery is the only kind of grammar learning that works for fast English conversations. Your intuition is fast, your conscious analytical mind is not. You must learn to trust the natural process and let your grammar improve automatically.

My students usually fall into two categories: those who are excited about rule two and those who are skeptical. I usually tell this second group to take a leap of faith. Be a scientist. You've spent many years trying to learn English the traditional way and look at the result.

So try a little experiment. For the next six months, dedicate yourself completely to the Effortless English™ method. Use the psychology system. Use all of the seven rules. Give all of your effort for just six months.

Then check the result. Did your English speaking improve? Compare the results you got from six months of Effortless English™ to the results you got with the old school methods. If the Effortless English™ results are better, and for most people they are, then continue using Effortless English™. If you still feel that grammar translation is better for you, you can always return to the method.

The Hidden Curriculum Can Be Hard to Break

When I was teaching English in San Francisco, I had two Korean students named Jinny and Jacky (their American nicknames). Each of these students was struggling with her speaking and each wanted to attend an American university. In order to be accepted into a university, the students had to pass the new TOEFL test, which included listening and speaking sections.

Jinny and Jacky had spent years studying English grammar in Korea. As a result, their speech was slow, unnatural, and hesitant. They felt nervous when speaking, constantly worried about making a mistake.

As students in my class, I taught each of them Rule Two. I told them to stop studying grammar. I told them to get rid of their grammar books and their TOEFL books. I told them to do their best to stop even thinking about grammar.

At first, both students were skeptical because this advice went against everything they had ever learned in school. Jinny eventually decided to accept my advice, while Jacky did not. Over the next several months, Jinny completely avoided grammar study. Jacky, unfortunately, continued. I would often see Jacky studying grammar and TOEFL books in a cafe after class.

Gradually, Jinny began to feel more relaxed about English. Her speaking became more natural and fluent. She was thrilled with the improvement! Jacky did not improve. She came to me and again asked for advice. She had once again failed to achieve the required TOEFL score.

Again I gave Jacky the same advice, stop studying grammar. Yet, despite her continued failure, she just couldn't believe me. The beliefs of the hidden curriculum were so strong in her that she simply couldn't accept another way. So she continued to focus on grammar books and TOEFL books.

When I left that job, Jinny had moved on to an American university. Jacky, however, was still stuck in the language school. She was still studying grammar and still failing to achieve success.

Jinny and Jacky's story is powerful because it shows us how strong the hidden curriculum can be. Despite years of frustration and failure, some people just can't seem to break free from grammar study. They will continue using the same failed method for years, never learning to speak English powerfully.

To me, that is the worst tragedy of the hidden curriculum. These limiting beliefs imprison many people into a downward spiral of failure. It saddens me to see this cycle of frustration and stress.

For some, it may be difficult to accept Rule Two, but this rule is essential for your speaking success. As Jinny and countless Effortless English™ members have proven, spoken grammar can be mastered without studying grammar rules.

What I want you to remember is very simple: Do not study grammar rules. If you focus on grammar rules, it will hurt your speaking. You will speak more slowly. You will understand more slowly. To put it strongly, grammar kills your English speaking.

So if you have grammar books, throw them away. Say goodbye to grammar books forever. If you want, you can even burn them, set them on fire. Have a little celebration. Because grammar translation is worse than useless, it is actually harmful to your speaking ability.

For Practice

Exercise: Take a grammar holiday. For the next six months, just decide you are not going to study grammar. In fact, do your best to completely forget about grammar rules. Unlearn this information by avoiding grammar books. Whenever you catch yourself thinking about grammar, immediately change your focus. During this time, instead of worrying about mistakes, accept them. Accept that mistakes are normal and necessary.

Focus on communicating. The truth is that native speakers will still understand you even if you make grammar mistakes. While schools hate mistakes, normal people really don't care. They simply want to hear your ideas, your feelings, your thoughts. In fact, native speakers make grammar mistakes, too, and they don't get upset about them.

CHAPTER 11

The Third Rule: Learn With Your Ears, Not With Your Eyes

My third rule for learning to speak English is simple, yet powerful. In fact, I usually say this is the most important rule because this is how we all learn language as children. It's such an easy thing to do that you have to wonder why most English classes don't emphasize it more.

Here it is: *Learn with your ears, not with your eyes.* That's right. If you want to speak excellent English, you have to listen. Listening, listening and more listening is the key to speaking excellent English. If you listen a lot, you are going to learn vocabulary. You will learn grammar. You will get faster at speaking and you will understand what people are saying to you. You will do all of this in a more natural and enjoyable manner. You will imitate the process that babies and small children use to learn a language.

Academic research on language learning has consistently found listening to be the biggest factor in overall language ability – particularly in the early stages. In fact, this is true even if you don't understand most of what you're hearing. That's because our ability to learn new words is directly related to how often we have heard combinations of the sounds that make up those words, says Dr. Paul Sulzberger, a researcher at Victoria University in New Zealand who conducted a 2009 study on the subject. "'Neural tissue required to learn and understand a new language will develop automatically from simple exposure to the language," Dr. Sulzberger said. "This is how babies learn their first language."

Remember the process used by babies and children? Babies learn through listening. They don't study grammar rules. They don't use textbooks. They don't take tests. Yet small children master spoken English, including grammar. In fact, experts say, 80 percent of your time studying English should be spent listening, even after you're no longer a beginner. Unfortunately, most traditional language classes don't emphasize listening. So if you studied English in school, you probably learned mostly with your eyes. I have observed many English classes in many different countries, and they're all the same. Most English teachers – whether in middle school, high school, university or private school – focus on textbooks in the classroom. There may be short "communication exercises," but the entire class is defined and driven by a textbook.

Now, if your goal is to get a degree in English from a university, this is a great way to study. But if you want to speak real English, these kinds of traditional methods won't get you there. Why? Because even if you study for many years, you've basically learned English analytically. You learned to think about English, talk about English and translate English. You also may know a lot about grammar rules. In fact, you know more about grammar rules than most Americans, most Canadians, most British people because native speakers don't study that stuff very much.

English conversation is different.

Native speakers learned to speak English with their ears by listening, listening, listening, and that's what you must do if you want to speak English quickly, automatically and naturally just like a native speaker.

The most important factor for learning English is what Dr. Stephen Krashen calls "comprehensible input." In other words, understandable input. Input refers to what is coming into your brain. You get English input in two ways: through listening and through reading. Certain kinds of reading are very useful and beneficial. However, the most powerful kind of input for learning to speak is listening.

Comprehensible (understandable) input methods have been shown to be more effective than traditional methods (grammar study, drills, exercises, speaking practice). The research shows that speech happens as a result of listening.

Think of babies and children again. Listening is always the first step. No child starts talking before they understand through listening. They always listen for a long time, until they understand a lot of the language. Then, and only then, do they begin to speak. This listening "silent period" is vitally important to the process of natural language learning.

Another property of natural language learning is that speech emerges naturally from listening. Speech is not a skill that is consciously practiced or taught. Rather, after enough understandable listening, a child will just suddenly begin to speak. Its seems to happen by magic. The speaking ability grows out of the listening ability.

Researcher James Crawford has found that speaking English is the result of listening and that English fluency frequently occurs from listening alone. He states that English learning is an unconscious process, and while it's happening we are often not aware that it is happening.

You can think of this like a seed in the ground. The seed, the potential for speaking, is always there. However, the seed needs water in order to grow and emerge from the ground. Likewise, our brains need a lot of understandable listening for effortless speech to emerge.

As you might imagine, because children spend so much time listening before they speak, their listening ability is always higher than their speaking ability. In other words, children always understand more English than they can actually use in speech. As you use the Effortless English™ system you will experience the same thing. Your listening ability will naturally grow faster than your speaking ability. Some learners worry about this but it is the natural and correct process.

Another way to think of this is that listening leads speaking and pulls it along. Listening is like a balloon with a string tied to speaking. As the listening level rises, it pulls the speaking ability up with it. They go up together, but the listening ability will always be higher.

 "BUT I CAN UNDERSTAND WRITTEN ENGLISH PERFECTLY."

I hear this a lot from students who don't understand why they have great comprehension of written English, but can't speak it well. One reason is because English conversation is quite different from English reading. Conversation uses a different type of English, including different vocabulary.

English conversational vocabulary is much more casual. In English, this means we use more words of Saxon or Old English origin during conversation. We also use more phrasal verbs (two- or three-word phrases with either a verb and an adverb or a verb and a proposition, such as *get away, calm down* or *cheer someone up).*

The difference between conversation and more formal English is one reason that even "advanced" students have difficulty with everyday conversations. The problem is that students learn more formal English in school. Formal English tends to use more words of French and Latin origin. This kind of English is, in fact, much easier for students who speak Romance languages such as Spanish,

Italian, Portuguese, or French. These students often do quite well when reading English, but have a lot of trouble understanding normal speech.

So, if you want to communicate with native speakers, it's very important to learn from English conversation and audios – not just textbooks and reading.

Learn English Conversation

This is why listening is so important. Listening provides the foundation for speaking. As your listening ability improves, it will pull your speaking ability up, too. Too many learners are focused solely on speaking and they neglect listening. However, what use is speaking if you can't understand the other person?

Another reason listening is important is because the dynamics of spoken English are completely different from those of the written language. For starters, the grammar is different since we rarely speak in complete sentences. The vocabulary is also different with a lot more idioms and slang being used in speech. (See box.)

And most importantly, the speed is different. Speech is fast. Super fast. So fast that you have no time to think about translations, or grammar rules, or textbook lessons or pronunciation. There is no time. Your conscious brain simply cannot analyze, translate, and organize real speech. This is the reason your speech is so slow. This is the reason you can't understand two native speakers talking to each other.

In fact, in order to perform at real speaking speeds, you must turn off your conscious brain and let your subconscious do its job. To do that, you must use methods which awaken your subconscious. You must learn holistically, intuitively, and naturally.

Primarily, this means listening to lots of understandable English speech... and doing it repeatedly. As you listen, you quiet your conscious mind and just allow your brain to understand the whole meaning of the words. You don't try to pick out individual words. You don't worry about the few words you don't understand. You relax and you let the meaning wash over you. Your mind is open and quiet. And then, when you speak, you just let the words come out. You don't struggle. You don't analyze. You don't think about rules. You don't worry about mistakes. You don't think about translations. You just let the words pour out of your mouth effortlessly. This is what my students have learned to do. It takes time, but as you focus on listening and learning English effortlessly, your fluency, confidence and correctness will grow.

Less Stress

There's another benefit to spending a lot of time listening to English – it reduces the anxiety people often feel when speaking a new language. Many English classes push new students to speak right away, but this is an unnatural approach.

In fact, being required to speak too soon can slow down language learning. Your brain hasn't had enough time to process the new words and store them in your memory. So while you may be able to repeat familiar phrases in English, you still won't understand what people are saying to you. This is an unnatural and stressful situation.

In one study of beginning-level English students, researchers found that those who weren't forced to speak but were trained in listening comprehension did better than students taught using conventional methods. In addition, delaying speech also had a positive effect on students' overall attitudes about English, and kept the classroom free of anxiety.

Dr. J. Marvin Brown took this idea even further. The director of a Thai language program for foreigners, Dr. Brown created a program that mimics the silent period of babies and small children. In his AUA Thai program, students listen to understandable Thai every day but they do not speak for six months or more. The students focus completely on learning with their ears.

For many foreigners, Thai is a difficult language to pronounce. Dr. Brown found that the silent period had a strong positive affect on learners' pronunciation, eventually producing superior pronunciation much closer to that of a Thai native speaker.

The same principle works with English. Though a silent period is not necessary for most intermediate learners, you still might try it. Why not focus completely on English listening for a few months, and then return to English speaking? You'll likely find that your speaking has improved even though you never practiced it.

What Should You Listen To?

The most important thing to keep in mind is that you must listen to easy English. It has to be easy for you. That means you should understand 95% or more of what is being said. That's without stopping the audio and without a dictionary. So it should be quite easy. I say this because the natural desire of most students is to pick something harder, thinking it will help them. It sounds more impressive to say I'm listening to CNN rather than a children's program. If you choose something too difficult, you can get frustrated. With something easy, you get confidence.

Remember Dr. Krashen's idea of understandable input. If you don't understand, you are not learning. No understanding means no improvement. Easier listening is almost always better than difficult. Eventually, you will be ready for more difficult material, but take your time and listen to plenty of easy English.

If you're just starting out, try listening to children's programs since the English tends to be simpler. You can buy audio books online as a download, and get the audio book immediately so you can get started.

If you find yourself listening to something more difficult, you can still use it, but you usually need the text. You can get an audio article or a speech, and use the text so you can read and listen at the same time. For more advanced learners, another great source of casual English conversation is film. Listen to American and English movies and read the subtitles. This will also help you. Just remember, listening is the most important thing. To get the most from films, use the movie technique below.

If you don't have an audio player or smart phone, get one. It will enable you to listen to English conveniently whenever you can. Listen in the morning when you get up. Listen when you go to work, or when you are at home. Listen when you are at lunch. Listen when you are coming home from work. Listen in the evening – lots and lots and lots of English listening, lots of easy listening. I even have a free Effortless English™ podcast on iTunes and you can listen to that. Listen, Listen, Listen.

Rule Three is the reason that all of my courses are based on audio. Effortless English™ is a listening system where most learning is done through the ears. It's okay to use text to help understanding, but focus most of your time and efforts on learning with audios.

No matter how you choose to do it, it's important to listen to English as much as you can. Some of my students have been reluctant at first. But most of them say that getting to choose what they listen to starts to make it enjoyable. Instead of suffering through yet another boring textbook drill, you can relax and listen to something that is interesting to you.

MORE LISTENING PRACTICE

Looking for another great way to practice listening to English? Perhaps you might want to follow my weekly Effortless English™ Show. I do a talk show about mastering spoken English. This show is a great way to get easy English listening. As most Effortless English™ members know, easy and relaxed English listening is an important key to speaking English fluently.

To speak English fluently, you must listen to a lot of English – preferably easy and understandable English. My show is one way to get plenty of English audio. These are a great supplement to other English lessons or materials.

It's very easy to get my show! Just "Follow" me on Twitter. Go to Twitter.com/ajhoge. If you don't have an account, create one. Then go to my page and click "Follow." That's all! It's super easy.

Each week, check my Twitter page for "tweets" about the next Effortless English™ Show. Click on the link in each tweet to watch the video and download the audio.

If you prefer, you can search for the "Effortless English™ Podcast" on iTunes, where I put all of the audio recordings of the show.

The video recordings of past shows are also available on my You-

Tube channel, which is another source of learning suggestions and English audio.

Subscribe to my YouTube channel at: <u>Youtube.com/ajhoge</u>

Listening Practice

To help students improve their listening, I often suggest an exercise known as the "Movie Technique." To do this, you need to pick an English-language movie that you enjoy. Again, pick a fairly easy one, where you will understand most of the words used.

Begin by watching the first scene. This should take about 3 to 5 minutes. Turn on the English subtitles. As you go through it, pause if there is a something you don't understand. Look up the meaning of the word or phrase in an idiomatic dictionary. Watch the scene until you know all the words of it and understand.

The next day, watch the same scene again, several times. Once you understand the vocabulary, turn off the subtitles. Then watch the scene again, listening without the subtitles. Do this every day for the next five days or so. You might spend four or five days on one scene, but that's okay. Each repetition improves your English listening ability.

Now watch the scene again, but try pausing after each sentence or phrase. Repeat the sentence out loud. In fact, don't just repeat the sentence, act out the scene. Copy the speech of the actors. Copy their movements, facial expressions, and emotions. Pretend you are the characters in the scene. Remember the movie pronunciation exercise? This is another version of it.

This entire movie technique might take you a whole week for just one scene. When you feel you have mastered the scene, you can start the entire process again with the next scene. It might take several months to get through one movie, to really learn it, but that's the point. The movie technique is a way to thoroughly learn and master all of the English used in a film. This method will improve your listening, your fluency, and your pronunciation. If you just watch a movie once, without using this process, you get little to no benefit from it.

 WILL LISTENING TO MUSIC IMPROVE MY ENGLISH?

I get this question a lot. Personally, I don't suggest learning English through music. I get students coming to me with lyrics, and I can't understand half the words the singer is saying. Music is an art form with lots of imagery in the language. Even native speakers often don't know what the singer is trying to say. Likewise, the pronunciation used in songs is not normal. Singers frequently change the natural pronunciation in order to fit the words into the melody of the music. In terms of learning English, it's much more efficient to use television or movies. The meaning of what people are saying is usually clearer, and you also have video to provide visual cues that help you understand. So yes, please listen to English language music if you like how it sounds, but don't expect it to help your own communication in English.

CHAPTER 12

The Fourth Rule – Repetition Is The Key To Spoken Mastery

You want to learn English and you want to speak it well RIGHT NOW. The problem is most language classes move too quickly for students to master material before moving onto something new. In this chapter, we'll focus on the fourth rule of Effortless English™ which advises you to take your time and *learn deeply*.

What does it mean to learn deeply? To learn deeply means to learn English to the point where speaking and understanding are automatic. Often people know a lot of English grammar and vocabulary, but they don't know it deeply. When it comes time to speak, they're translating vocabulary and analyzing tenses in their heads or struggling to understand the meaning of what someone is saying to them. Effortless English™ emphasizes training for mastery.

Deep learning means repeating what you have learned, again and again. This might feel very different from the way you learned in school. Most schools have a lot of pressure to move fast. They're always pushing the students to learn more grammar or a certain number of new words every week. The teachers rely primarily on textbooks, and try to finish them on schedule. The problem for students is that you learn a lot of stuff but then you forget it. Or you remember the basic idea, but you can't use it.

Take the past tense, for example. If you've studied English before, chances are you learned the past tense. Chances are also good that you studied it in a textbook and then *BOOM* very fast, you moved on. You went on to learn more grammar, possessives, the future tense or the present perfect tense.

Now, if someone asks you if you know the past tense, you'd say, "of course." But the truth is you haven't mastered the past tense. You moved through the material so quickly that you never learned it deeply, like a native speaker. That's why you still make mistakes with the past tense. Even though you may have studied English for many years, you still make mistakes because it's not automatic. You haven't learned it deeply.

Master the Fundamentals

To better understand deep learning, once again let's look at the world of sports. Imagine, for example, a professional golfer. How does a professional golfer master the game and continue to improve?

The most important skill for a golfer to master is their swing. A professional will practice their swing five hundred times a day or more, every day. A good golfer never says, "OK, I already know how to swing, so now I need to do something else."

Golfers understand that the best way to master the game is to master a few fundamental skills. They practice these same few skills hundreds of times a day, for years and years — possibly for their entire lives.

Unfortunately, many English learners fail to understand the importance of deep learning. In my English classes, I frequently spent a long time repeating and reviewing the most common and most useful language. Sometimes a student would complain. They would say, for example, "I want to learn advanced grammar. I already know the past tense."

Yet, in a casual conversation, this same student frequently made mistakes with the past tense. He said "go" when he should have said "went." He didn't understand the difference between knowledge and skill.

Remember, knowledge is something you analyze and think about. Skill is something you do. Knowing the past tense is useless. You must be able to use the past tense instantly and automatically in real conversations. You need English skill, not English knowledge.

How To Learn Deeply

If this sounds familiar, don't despair. You can move much closer to your goal of speaking excellent English simply by adjusting the way you learn. You just need to slow down and repeat everything you learn again and again. For example, I tell members of my courses to repeat each lesson daily for at least seven days. This is the case even if they think they know it well after listening to it twice. If it's still difficult, I advise them to listen to the lesson daily for two, three or even four weeks. Remember, it's not a race. The point is not to memorize, or recite the phrases back like a bird, but to truly deeply understand the phrases you are learning.

Often I get a question like this from a student: "A.J., can I learn two lessons in a week?" That's a good question. People want to go faster. They want to do more. I understand that. But if you ask any of my advanced students, they will all give you the same answer: No.

Why? Because deep learning is important. You need to repeat each audio every day for seven days. More is fine. Yes, 14 days is better, 30 days is even better than that. Less than seven won't get the job done. You won't be doing enough repetitions to have the material sink in deeply. It's challenging to pace yourself, because I know many people think that faster is better. But it doesn't work that way. You need to repeat each audio at least once a day for seven days. You're doing this because you want your knowledge to go deeper and deeper. You are learning for mastery.

Julia, a student from Italy, at first had a hard time accepting this idea. She thought she would get bored and that it might be a waste of time. But she wanted to improve her English, so she was willing to try it. Over time, she says, she realized she had spent years learning English but not in a deep way. "When I studied the second lesson," she says, "I had already forgotten the first. "

These days, Julia sometimes listens to an audio for an entire month before she moves on. "It's not hard work anymore," she says. "I've developed a way to listen and learn deeply and it has really helped my English."

So if you have an audio article or podcast, something you listen to and like, don't just listen to it once. One time is not enough. Five times is not enough. You should listen to that article, speech, whatever it is 30 times. Or perhaps 50 times, 100 times or even more.

After you've learned the vocabulary, keep listening. Because knowing the vocabulary means that you can take the test and say the meaning, but when you hear it do you instantly understand it? Can you use it quickly, easily and automatically? If the answer is no, you need to study it again, you need to listen to that same audio again. Many, many times. This is one of the secrets to speaking faster and to really learning grammar and using it correctly.

You are like the professional golfer who practices his swing hundreds of times per day. The golfer is always looking for ways to improve that same fundamental skill. The golfer realizes that mastery of the fundamentals is more important than a lot of advanced knowledge.

For example, you might listen to a story in the past tense over and over for two weeks. After that, you'll listen to another story for two weeks, and maybe another story in the past tense for the same length of time. You never stop. I am a native speaker and all my life I have been learning the past tense. I still listen to the past tense now, and I will as long as I live. I've heard the same common vocabulary words every day thousands and thousands of times and will continue to hear them. That has enabled me to use them quickly and automatically.

That's the secret. You never stop. You just need more repetition. Focus on the most common words, most common verbs, most common phrases through listening and then repeat, repeat, repeat. When you do that, you develop that "feeling for correctness" and will use English more naturally and automatically.

Perhaps you are thinking to yourself, "But won't I get bored listening to the same thing again and again?" Of course this is possible. The best way to avoid boredom is to choose material that is compelling to you. Compelling means "extremely interesting."

How do you find compelling content? One way is to learn about something you love, in English. For example, if you love romance novels in your own language, get them in English! Find easy romance audiobooks and listen to them every day. Find the text versions of the books, too, and read while you listen. If you love business, then learn about business in English. Use English as a means of learning other knowledge and other skills. The more you focus on this compelling content, the easier it will be to repeat it often. You'll enjoy hearing it again and again.

Deep Learning Practice

Exercise 1:   Pick an audio that's ten minutes long. This is going to be your main audio for the week. Listen to it a few times. Repeat this process every day for the next week. Really commit yourself to mastering it. The idea is you're not trying to memorize it, but rather to thoroughly know it. Imagine that each time you listen to and understand the audio, it is going deeper into your brain. It's like a seed you are planting in your mind. Plant it deep and water it with many repeated listenings.

After you have mastered the first audio, pick two additional audios. They should each be 5-20 minutes long. Listen to these in the same way as you did the first.

You will notice yourself going through different learning stages as you do this. Try to be conscious of these stages. The first will be, "Oh no, I don't understand." You may need to use a text for total understanding. You'll know you've hit the second stage when you can listen to the words and phrases without reviewing any of them. The third stage will be when you're hearing and easily understanding without the text. How long does it take you to get to the third stage? How does listening to longer audios affect your understanding?

How quickly will you progress and how many repetitions are required? Much of this will depend on your state of mind during repetition. Are you relaxed? Energized? When I teach action vocabulary in seminars, students can often master new words and phrases in just a few minutes because they are moving and excited. Repetition with half-concentration and low energy is not as good as repetition with engaged emotional energy. So as you are repeating the audios, stand up, move around, and even shout the phrases to yourself. If you're feeling self-conscious, close your door and do this in your room until you get more comfortable with it.

Exercise 2: Select an audio for listening practice. A common complaint I hear from students about deep learning is that they get bored listening to the same thing day after day. So in this exercise, every few days you're going to change your focus. On the first day, concentrate on just learning the vocabulary. On the next day, play a game where you're just trying to understand the audio completely without the text. A day later, play a sentence, pause the tape and shout the sentence. Copy the speaker's rhythm, tone, and emotion. Work on your pronunciation. Next, try a game where you play two sentences and then repeat them loudly, with emotion. The next day, return to just listening and understanding. Basically, each day you shift your focus on the same material so that you learn from many different angles. The important thing is that each repetition you do has a purpose.

CHAPTER 13

The Fifth Rule: Learn Grammar Intuitively And Unconsciously

I've promised that you can learn to speak English well, without studying grammar rules. I've even told you to throw your grammar books away because you don't need them. Now I'm going to show you what to do instead.

It's actually a very simple technique – one that I believe is the best way to learn grammar – not only to learn English grammar, but grammar for any language. The fifth rule of Effortless English™ is: Use Point-of-View Stories. These are small, short stories in which we change the point of view. In other words, we change the time frame and we change the grammar to create multiple versions of the same story.

By reading and listening to these story variations, you can learn grammar intuitively without thinking of tenses, conjugations, etc. Point-of-view stories are easy and fun. Best of all, they allow you to absorb the grammar naturally by understanding the context of stories. That is the key point. Rather than studying abstract grammar rules, you acquire spoken grammar skill from meaningful and memorable English.

Point-of-view stories were first developed by Blaine Ray, the creator of the TPRS learning system. In the 1990s, Ray was a high school Spanish teacher in California who was looking for ways to engage his students beyond the traditional drill and memorization methods used in language classes. TPRS stands for Total Physical Response

Storytelling (also described as Teaching Proficiency) through Reading and Storytelling (see box). It was Ray's belief that students could learn to speak Spanish more naturally by listening to certain kinds of simple stories.

I immediately recognized the power of these stories, and decided to modify them for my own teaching system. Point-of-view stories are now a very important part of the Effortless English™ system.

How do point-of-view stories work? In the simplest version, you start by listening to a main story – usually told from the past point of view. In other words, the story is mostly about events that happened in the past.

Next, you listen to another version of the story, with a different point of view. So, for example, you might hear the same story told again in the present. Then you listen to yet another version, told as if it will happen in the future. Or even another version that talks about past events that have continued to the present.

Each point of view story is basically the same, but the change in time creates changes in the language used… especially the verbs. By listening repeatedly to these stories, you easily and naturally absorb the most common and most useful English grammar tenses. Because you learn them subconsciously and intuitively, you will actually USE them correctly when you speak – and you won't have to think about it!

An important focus of point-of-view stories is that they should focus on the most commonly used grammar structures. Some students become obsessed with extremely rare forms of grammar while neglecting the forms that native speakers constantly use on a daily basis. For example, "He slept for six hours" is far more commonly used than "He will have been sleeping for six hours." It's far more important to master the first form of the sentence (the simple past) as it is far more useful for communication. Thus, the point-of-view stories you use will be limited to only the most common forms.

The great thing is, you only need to listen to these stories a few times every day. You don't need to analyze the grammar changes... and you certainly don't need to identify the linguistic grammar rules. There is no need to identify which version is the "simple past," or which is the "past perfect." These terms may be useful to linguists, but they are distracting to those who wish to speak quickly, easily and automatically.

You must trust your intuition and simply listen to each version of the story without analyzing it. Try to quiet your analytic mind. Relax and focus on the events of the story. With time, you will absorb the grammar intuitively, and use it correctly without effort.

 PUTTING THE PHYSICAL INTO STORYTELLING

Dr. James Asher, a psychologist at San José State University, was one of the earliest researchers to identify the importance of physical movement in learning. Asher developed the "total physical response" method (TPR) after discovering that students learned language more effectively if they associated words and phrases with meaningful movement. He taught language without translation, solely through the use of actions. For example, he would say to a class, "Sit down," and then he would demonstrate the action of sitting. Then he would say, "Stand up," and he would demonstrate standing. After repeating this series a few times, students quickly understood the meaning of the phrases "Sit down" and "Stand up."

In the next phase of the lesson, Asher indicated to the class to join him. So when he said "Stand up," the whole class stood up together with him. And when he said "Sit down," the class demonstrated their understanding by sitting.

In the final phase, Asher gave the commands but did not demonstrate them. Rather, he watched to be sure the class understood. This eliminated the need for translation, as the students connected the phrases to the actions.

With time, students in Dr. Asher's class were able to learn and demonstrate very complex commands such as, "Stand up, turn around five times, then walk backwards to the door and close it." Dr. Asher built core fluency entirely through the use of commands and actions. Later, Dr. Asher and other researchers modified TPR, adding gestures to represent more abstract terms like "think" or "hope."

TPR was a predecessor of Blaine Ray's TPRS (Total Physical Response Storytelling). Ray realized that if the actions and gestures were combined to create a story, students would learn even more quickly. TPRS is a method for getting students to physically and verbally interact as part of storytelling. This technique was the starting point for much of the Effortless English™ system.

A Sample Point-Of-View Story

Let me give you a very simple example of a point-of-view story: *There is a boy. His name is Bill. Bill goes to the store. He buys a bottle of water. He pays two dollars for the water.*

Ok, that's it. That's our little story right now. It's not very interesting, but you understand it easily. It's in the present tense, and all you need to do is just understand it. If this was an audio story, you would listen to it every day for a week or more. Remember, we're striving for deep learning, so you're going to repeat it a lot of times.

Next, I tell you the same story again, but now it's in the past: *There was a boy named Bill. Yesterday, he went to the store. He bought a bottle of water. He paid two dollars for the water.*

Ok, that's all. Very simple. Of course, in my lessons my point-of-view stories are longer. They're more difficult and they are more interesting. But this is a simple example to help you understand the concept.

So now you've read or heard Bill's story in the present and the past. Ideally, you have audio versions and you listen to that story in the past many times. When you listen, don't think about the grammar rules. You don't need to analyze, "Oh, this is the past tense" or "Oh, 'paid' is an irregular verb." No, no, no – no need to think about that. Just listen to each story version and understand the meaning. That's all you need to do. Listen to the first story – understand the meaning. Listen to the second story – understand the meaning. That's all. It's easy, effortless grammar learning.

After that, you would listen to the future version of the story: *Imagine there will be a boy. His name will be Bill. He'll go to the store, and buy a bottle of water. He's going to pay two dollars for the water.* That's the end of our short example in the future.

Again, all you do is just listen to this little easy story. You listen to the present version. You listen to the past version. You listen to the future version. Every day for seven days or more, you listen to each one.

We can even add more versions. We can practice any kind of grammar with this. For example, I might say: *There was boy. Since last year, he has gone to the store every day. He has bought a bottle of water every day. He has paid two dollars for the water.* You don't need to know the name of the grammar or the verb tense that I'm using. It's called the present perfect, but you don't need to know that. I don't want you to think about that. All you need to do, again, is listen to this version of the story.

Of course, I'm using extra phrases to help you understand the meaning. I said, "Since last year," so now you understand that these verbs change because something happened in the past and it has continued for a while, but you don't need to think about that. That's why these stories are so easy and powerful. You just listen. You listen to story number one. You listen to story number two, and you listen to story number three and to story number four, and you learn the grammar like a native speaker. Like a child.

When you learn grammar like this, using these kinds of stories, you are training like an athlete and you are freeing yourself from the hidden curriculum. This is the difference between learning grammar as abstract knowledge and acquiring the skill of using grammar in real speech. You want the skill. You want to use correct grammar without thinking about it.

HOW TO LISTEN TO POINT-OF-VIEW STORIES

To get the most out of a point-of-view story, do your best to focus on the story and imagine it in your mind as you're listening to it. Turn off that part of your brain that labels the tenses or thinks about grammar. Instead, think of a line going through your body. Behind you is the past. In front of you is the future. Imagine now that the story you're hearing is inside a box or radio. As you hear the past version, try to imagine that box sitting behind you, back in the past. When you listen to a future version, picture the box in front of you, up in the future. Imagining where you would put this box or radio on the line gives the story a visual component, which will help you to more intuitively understand the grammar.

While it's easy to understand this idea by reading sample point-of-view stories, it is essential that you use audio versions. Remember Rule Three: listening is the key to speaking. You not only want to learn grammar intuitively, you also want to learn *spoken* grammar. That means, just like vocabulary, you need to learn grammar with your ears.

Learning grammar with audio point-of-view stories develops your "feeling for correctness," the same skill used by native speakers. Each repetition and each variation develops this feeling. Eventually, you will instantly know correct grammar because it will sound right to you. No need to think about linguistic terms. That's when you know the point-of-view stories are working.

Remember that true grammar skill must happen instantly. In a real conversation, you must produce the correct grammar without hesitation. There is no time to think about rules. This instantaneous grammar skill can only be developed subconsciously and point-of-view stories are one of the best ways to do this. By using these stories, you skip the unnecessary step of thinking about abstract rules. You produce correct English grammar intuitively, without conscious thought. In this way, you use grammar like a native speaker. It takes time and repetition, but point-of-view stories give you the most effective training for spoken grammar mastery.

The Psychological Benefits

We have discussed the benefits of point-of-view stories to your English. These are significant. However, the psychological benefits of these stories are perhaps even more powerful.

For most learners, abstract grammar study is one of the most painful aspects of studying English. Most people find grammar study to be boring, confusing and frustrating. Many dread the idea of trying to memorize yet another grammar rule. Most English learners have bad memories of grammar lessons and grammar tests.

Grammar study has a way of making intelligent people feel stupid. They study and memorize countless conjugations. They analyze the use of English articles, prepositions, countable and uncountable nouns. Yet, when it's time to actually speak, they find themselves constantly making mistakes. Even though they "know" the grammar, they struggle to use it. "What's wrong with me?" they ask themselves. "I know this."

They are not stupid. They have simply confused knowledge with skill. Leave grammar knowledge to the professional linguists. Your job is to acquire grammar skill intuitively, and point-of-view stories are the best way to do that.

Practice Exercise

Here's a fun way to create your own point-of-view stories. Find a simple story about something that interests you. The story might contain a few words or phrases that you don't understand and have to look up in a dictionary. However, it should be easy. Five new words is the maximum that should appear in the story.

Now, show this story to your English teacher, or an English-speaking friend. Ask them to rewrite the story from different points of view. They will write different versions for at least the past, the present and the future. After they write each version, ask them to read each one and record it. Then, for the next week or two, listen to all versions of the story every day.

Once you have mastered those stories, repeat the process again with a completely new story. Simply by listening each day, you will develop your spoken grammar ability. Just like an athlete, you'll train yourself in the skill of using correct grammar automatically.

CHAPTER 14

The Sixth Rule: Learn Real English And Trash Your Textbooks

You've been studying English for years. But when you hear someone speak it doesn't sound like the English you learned. You find it hard to understand, and when you speak, people look confused.

Sadly, this experience is fairly common. It's what happens when you've been taught English the traditional way where your teacher relies heavily on textbooks and classroom drills.

That's why we don't use textbooks in Effortless English™. In fact, you have my permission to throw your textbooks away. Go ahead. Pitch them in the trash. As I've said before, textbooks aren't the way to learn a language. With Effortless English™, you learn real English, and that is Rule Six.

Textbooks have a number of problems. First, they are grammar-focused. We have already discussed the reasons you should avoid grammar study. Another huge problem is that textbooks mostly teach the formal form of English. This is the form of English you commonly find in writing. Textbooks rely heavily on written dialogues that are completely unnatural.

Perhaps you recognize this one:

"Hello"

"Hello. How are you?"

"I'm fine, and you?"

The textbook may be accompanied by an audio, in which actors read this dialogue using strange rhythm and completely unnatural pronunciation.

So what happens in real life? You study this textbook dialogue, and you think you know English. Then you travel to an English speaking country such as the United States. You meet a person at the bus stop and they say, "Hey, what's up?" Of course, they are just greeting you and asking, "How are you?" but they are using the real casual English that is much more common among native speakers.

In fact, as a teacher in San Francisco, I heard this common complaint most often from students. They traveled from many countries to study in America. Many new students thought of themselves as advanced English learners. Many had great test scores.

However, when they tried to communicate with real people, they had tremendous problems. I remember one student named Humberto saying to me, "I can't understand what anyone is saying. I don't understand people at the bus stop. I don't understand the waitresses in restaurants. I thought I was advanced, but I can't understand anyone." Like most students, Humberto had studied formal textbook English but had never learned real conversational English. He did well on tests but could not function in the real world.

Real pronunciation is also much different than what you'll find in textbooks and their audios. This is another source of difficulty for those who learn using traditional methods. Schools typically teach the formal dictionary pronunciation of English words. While the textbook will teach you "How are you?" a real American speaker is likely to say something like, "Howya doin'?" "Howzit goin'?" "Hey, whassup?" or "Nice-ta meetcha."

To really communicate in English, you absolutely must understand this real English. And these are only the simplest examples of greetings. The entire language is full of such examples. No wonder even "advanced" textbook English learners struggle to communicate with real people.

Idioms are another common problem for textbook learners. Spoken American English is full of idioms, yet you'll learn few of them from textbooks. Recently, I recorded a conversation with my Dad on the topic of business. Later, as I reviewed the recording, I was shocked by just how many idioms we used in that short conversation.

Idioms are phrases that have a meaning different from the individual words in it. They are often based on metaphors or cultural topics and can be quite hard to understand logically. For example, in a business meeting, a colleague might say, "We scored a touchdown on that project." This idiom comes from the sport of American football, and it means to have a big success or victory. You're unlikely to learn this phrase in a textbook, yet it is very commonly used by Americans.

Clearly, textbooks are ineffective learning tools. What tools will you use then? You'll learn the same way native speakers do: by using real authentic materials. *Use only real English materials*: the sixth rule. What do I mean by real? Well, I'm talking about English materials that are for native speakers or that are very similar to those used by native speakers. They can be books, articles, audio books, podcasts, videos, etc.

You can find plenty of real English listening material on the Internet. Podcasts are perfect. I have a Podcast. You can go to effortlessenglish. libsyn.com and listen to me talking about English, talking about learning, talking about my ideas. It's free. It's easy. You can just listen, listen, and listen – there are a lot of real materials. I'm just talking normally and I'm a real native speaker. I'm not acting and I'm not reading.

And there are a lot of other podcasts out there. You can pick English learning podcasts, or better yet, a podcast on any topic you like. If you like sports, find English podcasts that talk about sports. If you like cars, find ones that talk about cars. If you like exercise or health, find podcasts about that.

Audio books are another great way to practice your listening. An audio book is just a book that someone's reading and they record it. So instead of reading the book, you listen to the book. The key is to choose audiobooks that were created for native speakers. Also, choose audio books that are easy for you. You may need to start with children's storybooks. That's okay. I can guarantee that listening to a children's storybook is more interesting and more useful than some boring textbook.

One of my favorite examples of good authentic materials is a children's book with an audio version. These are useful because you can listen and read along at the same time. You can also easily look up unknown vocabulary in a dictionary. I often have to tell my adult students not to be too proud to get a book for kids. You'll probably find a book by Dr. Seuss is more interesting than a textbook, because it is a real story written for native English speakers.

As you get better, when your English level is higher, you can listen to audio books for young adults or for older children. Just keep listening to real English. When something gets too easy, choose something a little more difficult until that gets easy. Eventually, when you are advanced, you can listen to CNN or the BBC, or American movies, British movies, Australian movies, etc. But again, that's at an advanced level. Start with easy stuff.

By focusing on real English materials, you are immersing yourself in the language used by native speakers. You are not learning a strange special language taught only to students. By listening to real English, you guarantee that you are learning useful language that is used in the real world. At the same time, because the material you use is authentic, you also learn idioms and culture – which are vital to understanding spoken English.

I have created an audiobook version of this book so you can use this book for English practice. See the back of the book for more details.

Real English materials will even help you improve faster on exams such as the TOEFL. Research by Dr. Ashley Hastings found that students who learned with authentic materials (books, movies, TV shows) improved 35% more than students who studied in a TOEFL preparation course using sample tests.

What about reading? While listening will be your main focus, reading authentic materials is also powerful. With reading, you follow the same principles as you did with authentic listening materials. You read easy English story books or easy English novels. You choose books that are pleasurable. Pick something you enjoy, something that's interesting – maybe a romance or maybe an adventure story or any topic or category that fascinates you.

Dr. Krashen calls this "free voluntary reading" and it is the most powerful way to increase your English vocabulary. Reading authentic materials has been shown to increase vocabulary much faster than studying lists of words. As you'll see in a future chapter, this kind of reading is also the best possible activity you can do in order to improve your English writing ability. Research finds that reading and listening for pleasure leads to superior TOEFL performance. I always recommend my students start with children's novels, usually something for elementary or middle school age. For beginners, graded readers can be useful. I also like series of books such as *Goosebumps*, *The Hardy Boys* and *Nancy Drew*. These include a lot of books, more than 30 in some cases. They are easy reading and they will help your writing ability, reading speed, and vocabulary.

As you improve, you'll naturally seek out more difficult books and audios. One strategy is to find an author you like and read every one of his or her books. For example, if you enjoy scary stories you could read every book written by Stephen King. If you enjoy romance, why not read all of Danielle Steele's books? If you can find audiobook versions for these, even better. By the time you finish an entire series of books, you will have improved your real English skills dramatically.

In my Effortless English™ courses, I often focus on topics such as self-improvement and success. I want members to focus on the topics and real English in my lessons, not on the parts of the language. The more you connect emotionally to a topic in the real world, the easier you will learn the English.

In fact, the perfect situation is when you are so interested in the topic that you completely forget you are listening to or reading English. When this happens, language learning happens without any effort at all.

 TOO EASY? TOO DIFFICULT? OR JUST RIGHT?

How should you decide what to listen to or read? Often, my students worry that they'll pick something too easy. My recommendation: it's best to pick something you can understand without too much difficulty, but that stretches you a little. Linguists call this "comprehensible input plus one" which they describe as material that is just one level above where you are currently. They believe students learn a second language best when they are in a low stress situation and are interested in the topic being discussed.

An easy test of difficulty is whether or not you need a dictionary. You should be able to read and listen quickly, with only a few unknown words per page. Because you understand most of the material, you can guess the meaning of those unknown words without interrupting yourself. Just keep going, because you will eventually encounter those same new words again. When you do, you'll make another, even better guess about the meaning. Eventually, you'll learn this new vocabulary simply by enjoying real English without using a dictionary.

When you listen to real English materials, you get the real English that is actually used by Americans, Canadians, Australians, the British, etc. That's how we really speak. By replacing textbooks with these materials, you will be prepared for real world communication. When someone greets you on the street, you'll understand them. When someone uses a common idiom, you'll understand them. Eventually, you'll completely understand TV shows and movies too.

Rule Six is the key: learn real English.

LEARNING CASUAL CONVERSATION

In San Francisco where I used to live, I met many students with high English test scores, and great grades in their English classes. Yet, when they sat in a café, they couldn't understand what people were saying around them. They had absolutely no idea what normal Americans were saying.

They had been trained in formal, academic English – with a focus on grammar rules. I think this is totally backwards.

Common, casual conversation should be the first thing you learn. The first need, after all, is to communicate with other people. You want to chat with people in a café. You want to make friends and understand what they are saying. You want to talk to your co-workers. You want to understand TV shows and movies.

Common English should be what you learn first… then, and only if you need it, focus on academic English.

To help you, we have a new collection of recorded, real, spontaneous conversations. These are real conversations with friends, family, and business partners. We aren't reading scripts. We aren't actors. You'll learn the real English that we use every day with each other – including slang, idioms, swear words, jokes, cultural references, etc.

You'll hear filler words, too (such as "ah," "um," "you know," "like"), which are a common element of English that is missing from textbooks. You'll hear the natural rhythm of English – the way we go back and forth, the way we use phrases, the ways we interrupt each other.

We have all the conversations transcribed, and include short notes to explain the slang, idioms, etc. that you can't find in a dictionary. We did this because there's a huge need. In fact, it's probably the biggest need our members have.

My friends and I created a course from these conversations, with text and explanations. You can find them at www.learnrealenglish.com

CHAPTER 15

The Seventh Rule:
Learn English With Compelling Stories

The primary purpose of Effortless English™ is to teach you to speak and understand English quickly, correctly and automatically. That "automatic" part is what separates this method from so many others, and automatic comes from thinking in English.

When you think in English, you no longer translate. You no longer think about grammar or pronunciation. The language has become a deep part of you, just like your own native language.

At this stage, you have achieved effortless English. You understand instantly, with no stress. Because you think in English, words flow out of your mouth quickly and easily. You use correct grammar, yet never consider grammar rules. If someone asks how you do it, you probably say, "I don't know. I just know what sounds right."

Speed is the most obvious change at this stage. You are able to instantly understand and instantly respond. The hesitation is gone. The strain, the stress, the doubt, the confusion – all gone. You are like the professional soccer player, performing with power and grace.

At this point on the road to fluency, you have learned most of the Effortless English™ system. You have just one more rule to learn and I have saved the best for last.

Rule Seven is the method that trains speed. So what is it? Listen-and-answer stories. That's the seventh and final rule of Effortless English™. *Learn to think in English with listen-and-answer stories.*

What are listen-and-answer stories, or, as I sometimes call them, mini-stories? Well, remember in the past when you went to English school? You probably were taught with a lot of listen and repeat drills. You know, when the teacher would say, "Repeat after me. Hi, how are you?" And everyone in the class would say in unison, "Hi, how are you?" Then the teacher would continue, "I'm fine, and you?" Then all of the class together said, "I'm fine, and you?" This is listen and repeat. It's an old way to learn English. But, it's not powerful.

Why? When you listen and repeat, you don't need to think in English. You don't need to think at all. You just repeat what the teacher said. You don't even need to understand what you are saying, but still you repeat. It's a mindless exercise with little benefit.

Now sometimes, after you've gotten used to listening and repeating in one of these traditional classes, the teacher will start asking you questions so you can answer with some of the responses you've learned. For example, instead of having you repeat, she'll ask: "How are you?" You'll say, "I'm fine, and you?" This is a bit better, since you're at least answering questions and not just repeating phrases you may or may not understand.

The problem is, these are scripted answers. When the teacher asks, "How are you?" you always say, "I'm fine, and you?" You already know what the teacher is going to say and you already know what you are going to say. Yet, real conversations are unpredictable. You never know what is coming next. You have to be ready for anything. Listen-and-answer stories are much more powerful.

Perhaps the first question we should ask is, "Why stories?" In Rule Five, I taught you about point-of-view stories. In Rule Six, I encouraged you to read and listen to authentic materials, especially stories.

Now I'm telling you the key to automatic English is listen-and-answer stories.

Stories are incredibly powerful, because they are an ideal way to deliver information to the brain. Human beings have used stories to teach and learn for thousands of years, since well before the invention of writing. What makes them powerful?

Stories are emotional. We love the heroes and hate the villains, and that's important because emotions create stronger memories. This is why religions have used stories for thousands of years to teach their principles. They could just teach the principles directly, but they know that stories create a stronger and deeper impression.

And when a story is designed to be strange, funny, or highly emotional, it is even easier to remember. This is why listen-and-answer stories use strange characters and exaggerated events. Which is easier to remember: a normal person with brown hair, or a person who is only one meter tall with green hair? If you meet both briefly at a party, which are you most likely to remember a year later? Usually it's the one that is not "normal."

In addition to being strange, funny, or exaggerated, listen-and-answer stories use a very specific technique called "asking a story." Please note, I did not say *telling* a story. I said *asking* a story. This is a technique developed by Blaine Ray. The teacher creates the story by asking a lot of very simple and easy questions. Why?

Because the questions train you to understand and respond more quickly. A listen-and-answer story is not a passive activity. You must constantly understand a barrage of endless questions, and you must instantly respond to them. The teacher slowly builds the story by adding more details.

An important aspect of these stories is that the questions are always easy and your answers are always short. Most of the time, you will answer with only a couple of words. The focus of these stories is speed, not length. Remember, to achieve the highest levels of English speaking, you must be fast. You must understand and respond instantly.

As you listen, sometimes the teacher will ask a question and you won't know the answer. When this happens, you are encouraged to immediately shout out a guess.

So the process is a non-stop series of questions and answers. Through this process, you overwhelm your slow analytic brain. Because there are so many questions and you must answer so quickly, there simply isn't time to think about grammar, vocabulary, or anything else. This is how listen-and-answer stories train you for speed.

When you use these listen-and-answer stories, you teach yourself to understand quickly and to respond quickly. You have to speak quickly and automatically, without thinking, "What does that word mean?" That's why these stories are so powerful. You learn to think in English, and you learn to speak quickly without translating.

How Mini-Stories Work

Let me give you a very easy and simple sample of a question-and-answer mini-story, just a couple of sentences. Now, imagine you have a short little story about a monkey. In listen-and-answer stories, it would work this way. As a teacher, I would say: "Class, there was a monkey. Was there a monkey?" You would shout: "Yes!" You could also shout, "Yes, there was a monkey!" but a one word answer is sufficient.

Then I would say, "Was there a monkey or was there a girl? You would immediately shout: "A monkey – a monkey."

And I would say, "Ah, so there was a monkey?" Again, you would shout, "Yes, a monkey."

I would say, "Ah, I see there was a monkey. What was his name?" Here you don't know, so you guess quickly – John or Jim – anything – you would shout an answer as fast as possible.

"Actually," I would say, "his name was Reggie. Was Reggie a monkey or was Reggie a girl?" And you would shout again, "A monkey!"

This continues for twenty minutes or more, slowly building the story. I continue to ask more questions, and because you are constantly answering questions, you learn to think in English. You learn to respond, to answer faster and faster in English. Now of course, this example is very simple. My real mini-story lessons are longer and much more interesting, and there are a lot more questions. (You can download a free sample Effortless English™ lesson, including a listen-and-answer story, at: http://EffortlessEnglishClub.com/point-of-view-grammar.) And when you use these lessons, you will gradually train yourself to think in English.

Listen-and-answer stories are a form of active brain exercise. Because they are stories, you can visualize what's happening. You learn the phrases, grammar and vocabulary in a meaningful context. Because the stories are strange and funny, you remember the English used in them much longer. Because you constantly answer questions, you learn to think and respond in English faster and faster.

In fact, a good listen-and-answer story skillfully combines all elements of the Effortless English™ system into one powerful learning tool. I know of no better tool for rapid improvement in spoken English.

HOW KNOWING THE CULTURE HELPS YOU SPEAK MORE FLUENTLY

When I put together mini-stories, I try to make them funny or strange so that they're easy to remember. I also try to reflect American culture, as you'll see in the practice example at the end of this chapter.

Why do I do this? Well, research has shown that you will learn a language more quickly if you can begin to identify with the culture. For example, according to Dr. Stephen Krashen and contrary to popular belief, even people who learn English as an adult can develop a perfect accent. What holds them back is not some inability to make new sounds, but rather their connection to their home country and its culture. When a child comes to the U.S. and learns English, they really want to fit in, so they will do everything they can to be like other Americans. Adults, on the other hand, have more established identities and tend to stay more rooted to their native culture.

But there are ways to get around this. The best thing you can do if you're trying to learn English is find some part of American culture that you really love (or British or Australian culture, if you're studying English there), and can immerse yourself in. It can be anything – music, movies, food, martial arts, whatever – as long as you find it interesting. It's especially useful if you can find something that is unique to the culture, like American football, for example. Most important, you must connect to and share your interest with native English speakers who love the same thing.

Try it and see. This will not only help you speak more fluently, but it will also help your pronunciation as well.

Movement and Mini-Stories

I mentioned the importance of movement in earlier chapters. Dr. James Asher's total physical response (TPR) system emphasizes the link between movement and learning. Blaine Ray's TPRS method (Total Physical Response using Storytelling) links movement to stories. Effortless English™ uses both systems.

When I do a live event, one of the first things I tell my students is that they need to make listening to a mini-story a whole body activity. Much of the power of (listen-and-answer) mini-stories comes from how powerful your responses are.

In any (listen-and-answer) mini story, you will hear only three types of sentences. You must respond to each type of sentence in a particular way. The first type of sentence is a statement. A statement is not a question, but you should still respond by saying "ahhhhhhhhh." Remember, stronger movements and emotions are more powerful, so don't just say "ahhhh," shout it and move your body at the same time. Pretend the statement is the most interesting information you have ever heard! Nod your head and smile as you respond.

The second type of sentence is a question you know the answer to. When you hear this kind of sentence, you want to shout an answer as loud as you can, using a full body gesture that shows you're really excited about it. Exaggerate. Throw your arms up as you shout, "Yes!"

The third and final type of sentence you will hear in a mini story is a question where you don't know the answer. As I mentioned previously, in this case your job is to shout a guess as quickly as possible. As with the other sentence types, shout your guess loudly and use exaggerated gestures as you do so.

The combination of speed, shouting, and movement locks in the memory of the sentence. Instead of just sound, you're getting sound and movement and emotions. You'll need fewer repetitions to remember it. You'll also start to connect speaking English to that excited enthusiastic feeling because, at the same time, you are creating a positive anchor.

There's no stress with mini-stories because anyone can say yes or no. That's why the questions are designed to be super easy. It is not a memory exercise, it's a response exercise. You bypass the whole analysis part and go straight into fast responses.

Another exercise we do at live events is story retelling. Once students have listened to a story and they know it well, they retell it to a friend. They stand up and use their whole body with big, strong gestures and tell the story in a loud, enthusiastic voice. The idea is to tell the story as quickly as possible, focusing on speed, not accuracy.

You will do this as well. After you have mastered the questions and answers, turn off the audio mini story. In a peak emotional state, retell the story out loud as fast as you can. Shout the story and use big gestures as you speak. Make it a game and aim for speed. It's okay to make a mistake and it's even okay to change the details of the story. Just practice speaking as fast as you possibly can.

The point is that the best learning happens when you are in a peak state, involved and active. My live lessons are like "English rock concerts" and everyone has tremendous energy. To recreate this at home, put on your favorite music. Close the door so no one can see you. Now jump around just before you do the mini-story. Feeling energized, begin listening to the mini-story. As you're doing the mini-story, get excited. Get crazy. Really shout out the answers. Finish with a fast retelling of the story. Remember, the more powerful your responses are and the more energy you use, the deeper your learning will go.

Practice Exercise

Here is a more advanced mini-story, without the questions. Note: the bolded words are the vocabulary I would teach my students in advance at a seminar. I've included part of the transcript to give you an idea.

For a full audio version of this lesson, including the questions, go to: http://effortlessenglishclub.com/point-of-view-grammar

Listen and Answer Mini Story: The Race

It's five o'clock and Allen is riding his motorcycle in San Francisco. He is riding down Van Ness Street and comes to a stop light.

A red Ferrari pulls up next to him. The driver's wearing dark sun glasses. He looks over at Allen.

Allen looks at him and realizes that the driver is Tom!

Tom sneers at Allen. He says, "When the light turns green, let's race."

Allen says, "All right, you're on!"

Tom says, "I'm gonna smoke you!"

Allen says, "You wish. I'm gonna beat you and your sorry-ass car."

Allen and Tom wait at the light. They rev their engines.

Suddenly, the light turns green. Allen and Tom take off! They zoom down Van Ness at top speed.

Tom is winning.

But suddenly, blue and red lights appear behind Tom – it's the police. They pull him over.

Allen zooms past Tom, laughing. He yells, "Better luck next time!"

Allen is the winner!

Download the audio version of this story, including the questions.

Listen and respond to the story every day for seven days or more (and remember, more is better because of deep learning). Each time you finish listening and responding, turn off the audio and retell the story as fast as possible. Notice as your speaking gets faster each day.

CHAPTER 16

Your Daily English Learning Plan

So are you ready to speak English effortlessly? Are you ready to feel relaxed and confident every time you speak? Are you ready to let go of grammar study, textbooks, vocabulary lists, worksheets and drills? Are you ready to rediscover the joy of learning? Are you ready to focus on goals that inspire you? Are you ready to focus on communication with real people? Are you ready to "play English" instead of studying it?

You now know the core Effortless English™ system. I have laid out a plan to help you learn to speak English naturally, fluently and with ease. Using the latest research and my own experience from more than two decades of teaching English language classes to thousands of students all over the world, I've shown why traditional language teaching methods don't work. If you've been struggling with English for a while, I've also tried to give you hope. It's not that you're bad at English. Trust me. You just haven't been taught the right way, the natural way.

When you learn English naturally – the Effortless English™ way – you finally escape from the hidden curriculum. You don't rely on textbooks or repetition drills. Instead you use the simple methods of the Effortless English™ system:

- Anchor positive peak emotions to English
- Change limiting beliefs into empowering beliefs
- Energize and move while learning
- Direct and control your internal movies

- Focus on learning phrases not words
- Don't study grammar
- Learn with your ears, not your eyes; devoting 80 percent of your studying time to listening
- Learn deeply; be willing to put in the time and the numerous repetitions necessary to truly master spoken English
- Use point-of-view stories to master grammar
- Learn real English by focusing on authentic English materials that native speakers use
- Learn to think in English with listen-and-answer stories, which train you to respond automatically without translation

The seven rules are the key to the Effortless English™ method. This method is the motor that will drive you to English fluency. But like any good engine, the Effortless English™ method is only as effective as the fuel you put into it. The fuel you need to learn English, or anything, really, is the emotional energy and motivation you bring to your studies. That's why I've focused so much on the psychological aspects of learning. I've shown you how to generate the necessary emotional fuel for learning English by setting big goals. I've discussed how moving and using your body can help you learn more quickly. I've also demonstrated ways to channel your fears into the energy necessary to speak powerful and relaxed English.

All you need to do now is get out there and do the work. After all, it's not enough to just know these steps, you have to take action. "Work", however, is the wrong word to use because the Effortless English™ system is most effective when combined with a playful mindset. You no longer need to fear mistakes. You no longer need to find the "one right answer." You no longer need to stress over exams or grades.

In fact, you will no longer "study English," you will "play English." You will enjoy your natural curiosity. You'll use fun, interesting, compelling, real materials. You'll feel energized and excited. You'll move your body. You'll smile and laugh while learning.

Fortunately, there's never been a better time to learn English. There have never been more resources available. Thanks to the Internet, there are few things you can't access online – whether it's a website on English learning, or articles, books, audio and video that can all be used to practice. You can even hire a teacher or get a language partner to work with you online.

You are no longer dependent on schools. You don't need to follow the hidden curriculum any longer. You are now the master of your own education. English mastery is within your reach.

A Day in the Life of Effortless English™

I've done my best to explain the Effortless English™ system. At this point, maybe you've decided you like the sound of learning English the natural way. You want to speak English effortlessly. The question is: How do you get started? How can you take all of what I've told you and put it into a typical day of learning English? What would that day look like?

It is vitally important that you establish daily English learning rituals. What is a ritual? A ritual is a habit that is emotional, even sacred, for you. Your progress depends on consistency. By continually making tiny improvements each week, you will accelerate on the road to fluency. Each improvement builds on the ones that came before, creating momentum.

Week by week, your listening improves. For a while, nothing seems to happen with your speaking. You understand more but speaking seems to be no different. Then, suddenly, after a few months, something amazing happens. English phrases begin to come out more quickly and easily. It happens a little at first, then more and more each week. By the time you reach six months, you notice significant improvement in your speaking.

This improvement is built through consistent daily rituals. When I teach seminars, I encourage students to create Effortless English™ rituals for the morning, the day, and the evening. For example:

In the morning, immediately upon waking, play your favorite energizing music. As you listen to this music, take out your list of positive English experiences and empowering beliefs. Read each item on the list, and remember the emotion of the positive experience. Next, think about your biggest goals for English – how you will use the language to create a better life for yourself and your family. Finally, use the "swish" technique ten or more times to direct and program your power movies.

At this point you are feeling great, so you've worked yourself into a peak emotional state. With the music still playing, jump, smile and shout until you feel fantastic! Now you are ready to listen to English. Play an easy English audio. Ideally, you will play a listen-and-answer mini story, followed by several point-of-view stories. As you listen, shout your answers to the questions and use big movements and gestures. If, at any point, you notice your energy dropping, play the music again and create a peak emotional state. Then start listening to English again.

This whole morning ritual might take only thirty minutes. You start your day feeling great, improving your English. At that point, it's probably time to go to work, or school. Use your travel time to listen to more English. Since you'll probably be around other people, this is a good time to listen quietly to an audiobook.

At lunch you'll have more free time, so spend another thirty minutes or more listening to a mini-story or point-of-view story. If you have privacy, shout your answers just as you did at home.

Travel home is another opportunity for more easy English listening. Perhaps you repeat that same audiobook chapter from the morning. If you stay at home with your kids, find moments of listening time when your kids are playing or napping. If you walk somewhere, or stand in line, listen to English. Use every available free moment to listen.

When you are home in the evening, do more English listening. Ideally, choose the same time every night and once again listen to the same mini story and point-of-view stories in a peak state. This might take you another thirty minutes. Go into your room if necessary to shout out the answers and really put your full energy and emotion into it.

Then you might use the movie technique, studying and practicing a movie scene. And even when you are doing other tasks, such as cooking dinner, always have an English audio playing in the background. Surround yourself with the sounds of English all day long.

By building these daily habits, and dividing your study time into four or more chunks throughout the day, you create intensity. The next day, you repeat the same rituals. Because you want to learn deeply, you repeat the same audios again. Listen to the same mini-story and point-of-view stories. Listen to the same audiobook. Watch the same movie scene. Do this for seven days or more to really master each of those audios. Next week, start over.

The great thing about audio story lessons is that they can be done anywhere. You can read and listen at the same time. Or you can take a walk and listen, which is even better. Do whatever works for you. Just do it, and soon you'll be speaking English fluently and with ease.

For best results, dedicate yourself to an intense schedule for six months. During that time, listen to English every free moment you have, however short. Always carry English audios on your phone or audio player. Always have it with you. Use private time for mini stories, point-of-view stories, and the movie technique. When in public, listen quietly to audiobooks or other English audios. Fill every moment of your life with English.

This consistent habit is the secret to your success. By focusing intensely for six months, you will make dramatic improvements in your English speaking ability. You will develop confidence and power. No, you will not speak perfectly, but no one is perfect, not even native speakers.

You have used the old methods for years and are not happy with the results. Give Effortless English™ at least six months. During this time, be fully committed to the system. At the end of six months, notice the improvement and compare it to the old methods. You will be pleasantly surprised.

You will, finally, develop the ability to speak effortless English. The words will come out automatically. The grammar will improve automatically. The feelings of confidence will appear automatically.

Welcome to Effortless English™.

In the final section of this book I will discuss advanced topics and common questions. However, you should not focus on these advanced methods until you have spent at least six months using the core Effortless English™ system as described. Most learners will only need this core system.

LEARNING ENGLISH ONLINE

As I noted earlier, the web now has everything you need to learn English online. You can buy English lessons, find a private teacher, use a translation dictionary, save and review new words, improve your English grammar, and chat with other English students. All of this, you can do online. This has been great for language learners. Even students who find it difficult to get regular access to native English speakers can now hear and speak English every day by simply logging onto the Internet. Here are some of my recommendations on getting the best from the web:

- **Download MP3 English Lessons From The Internet** Your first step is to find natural English courses online. You want lessons that use real English, not grammar or reading lessons. You also want audio lessons, not textbooks.

  Audio lessons have several advantages. One advantage is that you download them immediately. Another advantage is that they are portable – simply put the lessons on your phone or audio player and you can learn English anywhere, anytime. As you know, audio lessons in general are much more effective than written textbooks.

- **Find An Online English Community** There's no need to pay for an expensive tutor or English school. You can find English conversation partners online, often at very reasonable prices.

Most conversation partners use voice chat programs which make it easy to talk to anyone in the world for free. Thus, you can easily find a native speaker or an advanced English learner – no matter where you live. Some people use video chat – even better!

A community also gives you support and encouragement. You'll get great ideas from other learners. You'll also make new friends from all over the world. Members of Effortless English™ courses automatically join our international online community and can use our forums and social site.

- **Online English Dictionary and Word Saver** As you use your English lessons, you'll sometimes want to look up new words in a dictionary or find a translation in your language. Online dictionaries are simply great – much faster than text.

  You will need two types of dictionaries. The first is a standard dictionary. This can be a translation dictionary for your own language or you can use an English-only version. The other type of dictionary you need is an idiomatic dictionary. As you might guess, this type of dictionary contains the common English idioms (phrases) you won't find in a standard dictionary.

- **Audio and Video** The Internet is a buffet of authentic audio and video material. As I noted in a previous chapter, you can find podcasts and audio books on virtually any topic with a simple Internet search. You can watch American and British movies and television on a variety of websites as well.

  More advanced students can listen to copies of actual conversations. These are best for learners who need to understand casual speech.

CHAPTER 17

The Power of Pleasure Reading

You are using the Effortless English™ system every day. You focus most of your time on listening to compelling stories. You listen to point-of-view stories to learn grammar naturally. You learn deeply. As a result, your English speaking is improving. Each month you speak more easily and effortlessly. Your confidence is growing. You are mastering the core, high-frequency English used most commonly by native speakers.

As you continue improving, eventually you will want to advance to a higher level of English. Perhaps you want to study abroad in America or Canada. Perhaps you want to work for an international company that requires English. Perhaps you need to pass an exam such as the TOEFL, TOEIC, or IELTS.

When you reach this point, what is the best way to improve your English reading? How can you learn to read faster? How can you use reading to learn more words faster? How can you improve your reading comprehension? What's the best way to combine reading and listening?

Most schools teach reading using an academic skill-building approach. Typically, students read difficult articles and then answer questions about them to test their comprehension. Students are taught how to identify the main idea of the article, how to answer multiple choice questions about the article, and how to guess the meaning of unknown words. They are then graded on their performance.

During my teaching career, I have found that most students are bored by this approach. Worse, a tremendous amount of research shows that this method is inferior to one that is much more enjoyable and natural. Students who use this natural method write better, have better vocabularies, have better grammar comprehension and perform better on the TOEFL test than those who use the traditional methods found in schools and textbooks.

Just what is this powerful natural method? The research is clear that simply reading for pleasure is the most effective reading method of all. In other words, all you need to do is read interesting and fairly easy books in English. No exercises are necessary. No tests are necessary. No complex reading strategies are necessary. No lessons are necessary. No required books are necessary.

Easy High Volume Pleasure Reading

There is no big secret to reading in English. In fact, the answer couldn't be simpler. You need to read books (in English) that are interesting and fairly easy to you. You need to read them every day and you need to read a lot of them.

It turns out that volume is the key to improvements with reading. In other words, the key to better English reading is to read more pages every day, and more books every month. Choosing extremely difficult books is counter-productive. Some learners think they'll improve faster by reading difficult material but the opposite is true. The best reading materials are ones you can read without the use of a dictionary.

Compelling content is also vital. You must choose books that are extremely interesting to you. Of course, this will be different for everyone. If you love science, then you should read easy books about science and science fiction. If you love romance, then you should read easy romance books. If you love comic books, then read your favorite comic books in English!

In the beginning, you may need to read books that are designed for young adults. Read as many as you can every week. The more you read compelling material, the faster your reading will become and the faster it will improve. Soon you'll be reading novels and non-fiction books that are designed for adults.

Kill Two Birds With One Stone

The very best approach to pleasure reading is to combine it with listening. When you listen and read at the same time, you "kill two birds with one stone." In other words, you accomplish two goals at the same time: you improve your listening (and thus your speaking) and you improve your reading ability.

Whenever possible, get the audiobook version of the book you are reading. Be sure to get the "unabridged" audiobook. The unabridged version will have every word of the book — in audio form. You'll then be able to listen to each chapter as you read along at the same time. By doing this, you'll automatically learn the correct pronunciation of new words you encounter. You'll also learn to read a bit faster as you must follow along with a native speaker who is reading the book aloud for you.

Combined listening and reading will build both your written and your spoken vocabulary. You will continue learning new English phrases from real natural materials at a more advanced level. As your English ability becomes more advanced, novels, nonfiction books and audiobooks will become increasingly important. At the advanced level, you'll spend most of your time reading and listening to books that are compelling to you.

It's as simple as that! Read what you love and read a lot. Listen to the audiobook version whenever possible. This is the fastest and most enjoyable way to improve your English reading. As we'll see in the next chapter, it's also an excellent way to improve your writing.

For Practice

Go online and buy an English language novel for young adults. I recommend starting with a series of books such as "The Hardy Boys" or "Nancy Drew."

Read one chapter in the book each day. On a calendar, track the number of pages you read.

After one week, increase average daily page count. Read a little more. Your goal every week is to read more pages than you read in the previous week.

When you finish the first book, read another in the series. Continue reading books in the series until you have completed all of them. You will then be ready for somewhat more difficult material.

Of course, get the audio versions of your books whenever possible.

CHAPTER 18

The Secret To Good English Writing

Years ago, I was teaching an advanced writing class in San Francisco. My students were foreign learners who hoped to enter an American university. They had just finished writing an essay about why they wanted to study in the USA.

Each student handed me their paper and then walked out of class. I sat down, grabbed the first one, and began to read. I read the first paragraph and was completely confused. The introduction was a mess. The sentences were extremely long and complex and were written in the passive voice. The vocabulary was complex and was used incorrectly.

As I continued to read, I was horrified. The student's essay was unintelligible. I couldn't even understand his main idea. Frustrated, I put the paper aside and grabbed another. I began to read the second essay and encountered the exact same problems. Once again there were long complex sentences that were impossible to follow or understand. Once again the student used complex vocabulary that was inappropriate and used incorrectly. Once again I had no idea what she was trying to say.

Bewildered, I went through every essay and found the same problems in each of them: convoluted sentences, overly complex vocabulary, overuse of the passive voice, and no clear message or point. The essays were unreadable.

"What a mess," I said to myself as I put down the last paper.

The Problem of Academic Writing

Why were these essays so bad, and why were they bad in such similar ways? The answer lies, again, with the hidden curriculum of schools. Each of my students had learned English writing in school. In their classes, they had been taught an academic style of writing that emphasized complex sentences, complex vocabulary, and the passive voice.

Both teachers and students use this style of writing in an attempt to sound intellectual. The truth is, however, that most academic writing is terrible. Academic journals, for example, are filled with convoluted sentences that seem designed to be as confusing as possible. Students, influenced by their professors, attempt to model this kind of writing. As my San Francisco class showed, the results are typically disastrous.

Write Like Hemingway

In contrast to academics, Nobel prize-winning writer Ernest Hemingway was famous for his simple, direct style of writing. Hemingway typically used short sentences, simple phrases, and common vocabulary to create beautiful and powerful stories.

Though you are unlikely to write as well as Hemingway, his general style of writing is the best one to use. Most English learners write badly because they make their writing overly complex. They are trying to sound "intellectual" but instead end up sounding unintelligible. The solution is to write more conversationally. In other words, write like you speak.

Conversational writing is similar to (though not exactly the same) as speaking. When you speak English, you likely use clear, simple, direct sentences. You express your ideas as simply as possible.

Short, direct sentences are best. Break long sentences into a series of short, simple sentences. In most cases, use the active voice rather than the passive. Model your writing on journalists and Hemingway rather than on professors, journal articles, or other academic material.

Good writing is a process of cutting and simplifying. Your goal, therefore, is to communicate your ideas using as few words as possible. The simpler you make your writing, the more clear and powerful it will be.

How To Develop Your English Writing

So how do you develop a simple, conversational, and direct writing style? It turns out you already know the answer! In the last chapter we discussed the importance of pleasure reading. The research shows that this kind of reading is not only a great way to improve your reading speed, reading comprehension, and vocabulary — it's also the best way to improve your writing.

Just as listening is the key to speaking, reading is the key to writing. The same principle applies: Understandable, compelling input is the foundation for effective output. In other words, listening is the foundation for speaking and reading is the foundation for writing.

Just as you focused on fairly easy listening to improve your speaking, you'll focus on fairly easy reading to improve your writing. Just as you focused on listening to real stories and authentic audios to master English speaking, you'll read stories and authentic books to master English writing. You needed a lot of listening to speak effortlessly and you'll now need a lot of reading in order to write effortlessly.

This is why your number one activity for writing is reading. Nothing beats high-volume pleasure reading for improving written grammar, written vocabulary, sentence structure, spelling, and clarity. The more you read for pleasure, the more you intuitively absorb English sentence structures. In other words, you learn to write best by modeling your writing after good writers. The best way to imitate good writers is to read their books.

Remember, when it comes to pleasure reading, the amount is what is most important. Your goal is to constantly increase the number of pages you read in English every week. Read novels that you love. Read non-fiction books that fascinate you. Read comic books. Read simple articles. It's the amount you read that is most important, not how difficult it is. In fact, easier material is usually best, especially for the purpose of improving your writing.

Daily Writing Practice: Speed Writing

Too many English learners focus themselves on writing academic essays. As noted previously, these kinds of essays are often overly complex. Even when well written, academic writing is challenging and is one of the most advanced levels of writing.

This is why most learners benefit by first focusing on simpler forms of writing. One of the best ways to do this is to write a daily journal. Daily journal writing helps you to improve sentence structure, write faster and write more clearly.

The key to journal writing is to keep it short and simple. Each day, choose one clear topic to write about. You might write about something you did the day before. You might write about one of your goals. You could write about something you recently read, communicating your thoughts or feelings about it.

The next step is to set a timer, with an alarm, for ten minutes. When you are ready to begin, press "start" on the timer and write as quickly as possible. The most important point is to never take a break. You must write during the entire ten minutes without pausing. Do not pause to think of what to write next. Do not pause to correct mistakes. Do not pause to think of a better phrase. Do not let your hand stop moving — continue writing anything that comes into your head for the entire ten minutes.

This technique is called "timed writing" and is commonly used by professional authors. By writing quickly, without pausing, you bypass your critical brain and learn to let the words flow out. When you first try this you will probably feel frustrated. You'll struggle to think of what to write. Your writing will be disorganized. You'll make a lot of mistakes. Don't worry.

As you continue doing timed writings each day, you will improve. Your writing speed and fluency will get faster. You'll find yourself naturally using phrases that you read in a book or article. Because you are writing fast, you'll be forced to write more simply. You won't have time to think about grammar rules.

Week by week, your sentence structure will improve. Perhaps more importantly, your confidence with English writing will improve. If you feel confident enough, you could post your journal publicly online by writing it as a blog. Each day, publish a new post of your timed writing.

Rewriting Is The Secret To Good Writing

Reading for pleasure and daily timed writing are the foundation of your English writing practice. However, you will not become a great writer by only using these two methods. In fact, your timed writings will probably never be great. They'll always have mistakes and problems, and that's fine.

In fact, your imperfect journal writing will be in good company. This is a secret that few writers discuss, but all know: almost all first drafts are bad! In other words, even professional native speakers, who get paid hundreds of thousands of dollars for their books, can write badly. All writers make grammar mistakes. All writers make spelling mistakes.

Great writers know that the secret to good writing is rewriting. You see, with writing we have a great advantage compared to speaking. We have time. You have time to read what you wrote. You have time to identify your mistakes. You have time to correct those mistakes. You have time to completely rewrite everything. You even have time to show your writing to other people and get their help!

For casual writing, such as a blog post or email, it's not usually necessary to rewrite. However, for important communication such as business proposals, school essays, important emails, professional articles, etc., rewriting is absolutely essential.

The good news is that you don't need to write perfectly. It is acceptable to make mistakes in your first draft. We all do. It's even acceptable for your first draft to be terrible. With writing, only the final draft is essential and it must be mistake free.

You create your great final draft through the editing process. First, use timed writing to quickly write your first draft. Get your ideas on paper. Make mistakes. Just write quickly.

Once you have the first draft, you have something to work with. Think of yourself as a sculptor and the first draft is your clay. Read the draft, imagining yourself as the final reader (your audience). Are the ideas clear? Is everything stated as directly as possible? What's confusing? Are the ideas well organized?

Undoubtedly, you will find many problems. That's when you rewrite. Correct the problems. Cut the mistakes. Rewrite whole sections, or the whole thing, if necessary. Your focus is to make the second draft simpler, clearer and more direct.

When you finish your second draft, save it and put it aside. If possible, wait a day and then reread it. Again imagine you are the final reader. Look for overly complex sentences. Look for unclear ideas. Fix the problems again and rewrite for the second time.

For many kinds of writing, two rewrites will be enough. However, if the writing is particularly important, you'll need to do more. For this kind of writing, it's best to get outside help from an editor. Your editor might be a friend, or a tutor, or even a paid professional. This person will read your third draft and offer advice. Ask them to quickly rewrite any sections that are problematic.

Working with an editor will help you create the best writing possible. It's not always necessary, but do it whenever you can, and carefully notice their rewrite suggestions.

After a few rewrites with your editor, you'll be ready to publish what you have written. Before you do so, be sure to use spell check to catch spelling mistakes you may have missed.

For Practice

Do a ten minute timed writing exercise every day. During this time, write as quickly as possible without stopping.

The next day, reread the previous day's journal entry. Quickly identify problems and mistakes. Rewrite your journal entry to make it clearer. Cut out anything that is unnecessary.

On day three, you'll go back to step one and do another timed writing. Continue following this pattern, alternating timed writing with rewrites.

CHAPTER 19

Why You Should Not Practice Speaking

During my first English teaching job in Korea, I worked with a staff member named Seo. Seo worked in the sales office of the school. His job was to convince parents to enroll their children. Seo was an energetic and friendly guy. He was also determined to improve his English, which wasn't great.

Since Seo worked at an English school which employed over twenty native speakers, his strategy was to "practice" his English with us at every opportunity. Each day Seo would look for one of the teachers. When he'd find one, he'd corner them and talk as much as he could using broken English. He was especially interested in idioms and made a great effort to use them during these chats.

During my year in Korea, I was cornered by Seo many times. Though he was a likable person, I quickly began to dread my encounters with him. The other teachers felt the same. Whenever we saw Seo, we walked the other way. No one wanted to talk to him!

What was happening? Were we being mean? The truth is, we avoided Seo because he was trying to use us as free English tutors. Rather than communicate with us as friends, he "practiced" English on us. He asked us to correct his mistakes. He asked us to confirm that he was using idioms correctly. He asked for pronunciation advice. Chats with Seo soon felt like teaching an English class rather than communicating with a friend.

By seeing us merely as practice opportunities, Seo killed the possibility for a true friendship. We felt he was trying to use us. Conversations with him were unnatural and annoying because his focus was solely on the English language rather than on true communication.

Because of this approach, Seo never made friends with any of the teachers. Ironically, had he just talked to us as people, without focusing on English, he would have easily made a number of English-speaking friends. He would have had the opportunity for many more real conversations.

Unfortunately, Seo is not unique. Many learners are obsessed with "practicing" their English. Because their focus is on practice, these learners search desperately for "conversation partners." Yet, by insisting that others correct their mistakes or offer English advice, these learners usually drive away native speakers who would otherwise be happy to chat with them.

This is why you must not try to "practice" English with native speakers. Instead of practicing, simply focus on being a true friend. Communicate, without focusing on the English language. Talk about your shared interests. Ask questions and listen to their answers. Show your appreciation and understanding. In other words, treat them just as you would a friend who speaks your own language.

One of the best ways to do this is to meet people who share a common passion. For example, if you love movies, join online forums dedicated to movie lovers. Join international fan clubs dedicated to your favorite movies or musicians. Connect with others who share a hobby with you.

When you communicate with these people, talk about your shared passion. Never ask them to correct your English. Don't apologize for your English. Don't ask for any English advice at all. They are not your English teachers, they are your friends. You'll learn far more by just chatting with them than by trying to make them your personal tutor.

Error Correction Is Useless Anyway

A meta research study at the University of Southern California found that error correction has no impact at all on spoken English. In other words, students whose verbal errors were corrected showed no improvement, and were similar to students who were not corrected. The conclusion: verbal error correction is useless.

In fact, it's worse than useless. Error correction harms you by forcing you to constantly think about grammar. Instead of focusing on communicating your ideas, you increasingly focus on just the language itself. Doing so usually leads to more anxiety, which we know slows your learning and harms your performance. This is why you must never ask a teacher or friend to correct your spoken English. It is a waste of their time and yours. Error correction will also poison your relationship with English speakers and drive them away, just as Seo annoyed the teachers at the school in Korea.

This truth is a difficult one for many learners. Yet the research is clear. You will get no benefit from having your spoken errors corrected (note that writing is different because it is a slow process that can be done consciously and methodically). So rather than ask for error correction, ask others to avoid correcting your errors. If you pay a conversation partner, ask them to avoid correcting your mistakes. If they notice an error, ask them to simply restate the idea using correct English. By hearing your idea restated correctly, you'll intuitively learn to improve without thinking consciously about English.

Listen During Most Of Your Speaking Time

When thinking of conversations, most learners focus on speech. They worry about speaking correctly. They worry about remembering vocabulary words. They fear making mistakes. In my experience, most English learners focus 90% of their energy on speaking.

Yet, the true power of real life conversations comes from listening, not speaking. Think about it. When you talk to a native speaker you have a tremendous opportunity. Because they are a native speaker, they are automatically the best possible source for authentic spoken English. They will naturally use high-frequency phrases, idioms, slang and grammar.

If, during a conversation with a native speaker, you spend most of the time speaking — you have missed a great opportunity. When you speak to a native speaker, how exactly are you learning? You might get a little practice, but you will not learn anything new.

On the other hand, as you listen to a native speaker you get a wealth of learning. You'll hear true native pronunciation. You'll learn natural phrases. You'll learn new words. You'll learn idioms and slang. In fact, most of the benefit of having English conversations happens when you are listening.

This is good news, because most people love to talk. You don't need to feel stressed about talking with a native speaker because it's very easy. All you have to do is ask them a lot of questions. Ask them about their life. Ask about their job or school. Ask about their family. Ask about their hobbies and interests. Ask about their past experiences.

Then listen. Listen carefully. As they speak, look at their eyes and the rest of their face. Seek to understand as well as possible. If you don't understand something, ask more questions for clarification.

When your goal is to listen rather than talk, you'll learn more English and you will also be a better friend. Everybody loves a good listener! The added benefit to you is that you can relax. You don't need to feel pressured to speak. With a few simple questions you will have all the conversations you want.

Mini Story Retells

We have discussed natural conversation situations and how to approach them. In this last section, I'll teach you how to practice speaking and improve your pronunciation. Though you'll always spend the vast majority of your time listening, advanced learners can also benefit from a little bit of speaking practice daily.

Speaking practice is only recommended for advanced learners who are already speaking effortlessly. At that point, you are ready to work on your pronunciation and speed.

One of the easiest ways to practice speaking is to do mini story retells. As the name suggests, you will use the same mini stories described in Rule Seven: listen and answer mini stories. You will continue listening to the stories daily. You'll continue shouting your answers to the questions.

Then you will add this next step. After you finish listening to the story, turn off the audio. Stand in front of a mirror. Get yourself into a peak emotional state — jump, shout, smile. Get energized!

When feeling great, retell the mini story you just heard. Do not try to tell the story exactly, word for word. Do not try to memorize it word for word. Rather, as quickly as possible, retell the story using your own words. You can even change the story if you want.

The most important point is to do this quickly. Strive for speed! In a loud and energetic voice, tell the story to yourself in the mirror. This will only take you a few minutes. When you finish, take a short break and then repeat the process again. Try to retell the story even faster the next time.

The purpose of fast retells is to bypass your logical (and slow) left brain. By speaking quickly, you are forced to speak more naturally and more intuitively. As you do this daily, your fluency will increase. You'll speak faster without effort. English will flow out of you more and more easily. At this point, you are ready for the final step: pronunciation.

Pronunciation Retells

Earlier in the book, I described the movie technique and taught you a method for using it to improve pronunciation. You can use a similar technique with mini story retells.

First, repeat the steps in the previous section. Do a few fast retells of the story. When you can do that easily, it's time to work on pronunciation.

Play one sentence from the mini story and then pause the audio. As you play this sentence, listen very closely. Focus especially on the rhythm and intonation. Notice when the speaker pauses. Notice when the speaker's voice goes up and when it goes down. Notice when it gets louder and when it gets softer.

Then say the same sentence and copy the speaker's voice exactly. Again, imagine you are an actor trying to exactly imitate this speaker. Use their voice. Use their emotion. Even use your face and body as you imagine the speaker would. Try to become this person as you speak.

Then play the next sentence and pause, repeating the process. In this way, go through the entire mini story. Be sure to mimic both the questions and the answers.

Of course, it's best to choose a speaker that you like!

Using the methods in this chapter, you will take your speaking to an advanced, near-native level.

English Is The Language Of International Business

A few years ago I was reviewing business proposals. Our company needed new graphics for our website, so I had posted a job on an international freelancer forum. We got over twenty responses to our job posting. Each posting contained a bid for our project.

As I reviewed the bids, I noticed the nationalities of the graphic artists. There was a company from Argentina. There was an artist from Hungary. There was a Japanese bidder. There was a German and a Malaysian. There were several from the United States and Canada.

As I looked them over, I was struck by this clear example of globalization. These people were all participating in an online international marketplace. Then I realized the obvious: they were all using English to do so. Every bid was written in English. Therefore, each of these artists was competing not only based on their artistic ability, but also on their ability to communicate their strengths in English.

Clearly, English is the international language of business. It is for this reason that schools, everywhere in the world, offer English classes. English language ability is a competitive advantage to any and all who have it. English opens the world, to companies and freelance artists alike. Lack of English closes opportunities and puts you at a disadvantage in our global economy.

These are simply the facts, be they pleasant to you or not. The simple truth is that English is growing increasingly important to the global economy. More and more jobs, in more and more countries, are requiring spoken English proficiency. Some companies, such as the Japanese company Rakuten, are making English their official language.

Rakuten's founder and CEO Hiroshi Mikitani created an English-only policy for the web commerce company. Mr. Mikitani said "one of the things holding back Japanese firms from competing globally is a language barrier that prevents them from fully grasping overseas competition." He also said that lack of English proficiency limits Japanese companies from pursuing global talent and retaining non-Japanese staff.

With the new policy, all employees are required to use English for company communications, including meetings, presentations, emails, proposals, and other documents. The company expects employees to be proactive about learning English independently.

While this is a developing trend for Japan, many international companies are increasing their requirements for English. Many, like Rakuten, are instituting English-only policies. As this trend grows, the demand for business English grows with it.

Increasingly, in the business world there is simply no escape from English.

It's Still English

Business English opens economic opportunities. Because of this, a large variety of business English classes, schools, textbooks and lessons have arrived to fill the need. Not surprisingly, most of these use the same old methods to teach business English as they used to teach general English.

Business English, however, is not a separate type of English. The happy truth is that most of the English used in business situations is the same English used commonly in other situations. In business, you'll find the same common vocabulary, the same common idioms, and the same grammar.

The main addition to business English is simply vocabulary related to specific business topics. This vocabulary falls into two categories: general business terms and specialized jargon.

General business terms are those used throughout the business world. These are common phrases often used in meetings, proposals, and presentations. These are quite easy to learn, using the same Effortless English™ methods you are already using.

The Easy Way To Learn Business English

Learning business English is simply a matter of selecting real materials that are related to business topics. In other words, you use the exact same Effortless English™ method.

First you focus on fuel, your psychology. You change your limiting beliefs. You put yourself into a peak emotional state. Then you use the seven Rules. You spend most of your time listening. You learn deeply. You avoid grammar books and textbooks. You listen to mini stories and point of view stories — choosing stories about business topics that use business English vocabulary.

For extra listening, listen to real business English materials such as business podcasts, business newscasts, and business audiobooks. When possible, get both the text and audio versions. Read and listen simultaneously.

Just as you did with general English, choose materials that are interesting to you. If you are a salesperson, choose materials related to sales. If your area is finance, then focus on audios and text related to finance.

You have nothing special to do. Just follow the same Effortless English™ system, using business materials.

Learn Specialized Jargon Last

Some fields of business have a large number of specialized words. This specialized vocabulary is called "jargon." For example, accountants have a large number of accounting terms which are used extensively in their jobs. This specialized vocabulary is vital for accountants.

While necessary, jargon is the final type of business English you will learn. Before learning jargon you should first focus on general business English. Master the most common business phrases by listening to and reading real business content. Only after you have done this should you concern yourself with jargon.

Of course, you'll learn your field's jargon in exactly the same way as you learned general business English. When you are ready, simply change the material you are listening to and reading. Gather real materials that are specifically related to your field.

Choose material that is useful. Rather than focusing on the English, focus on learning more about your field from English sources. Develop your knowledge and skills using these sources and you'll automatically improve your business English at the same time.

How To Give Powerful English Presentations

I was standing at the side of a stage, waiting to give my first public speech to a group of thirty people. My heart was beating quickly. My breathing was tight and shallow. My entire body felt jittery. I looked down at my hands and they were shaking. I tried to control the shaking, but failed. I thought to myself, "What if I forget everything and freeze?"

Suddenly, I heard my name as I was introduced to the audience. I walked onto the stage. The audience applauded but I couldn't hear them. I glanced up and viewed them through tunnel vision. My sight was narrowed and my peripheral vision had turned black.

As I started to speak, I felt my throat tighten. My voice sounded strange — high pitched and weak. I fixed my gaze on the wall at the back of the room and rapidly gave my presentation. My only goal was to finish as fast as possible and get off that stage. Though the speech was only three minutes long, it felt like hours.

When I finished, I rushed quickly off the stage and sat down. My hands were still shaking uncontrollably.

Few activities are as terrifying as public speaking. Speeches are continually ranked as one of the most feared and stressful life experiences — dreaded by nearly all people. This nerve-wracking experience is made even more difficult when English is not your native language.

When you feel fear, you have both a mental and a physical reaction. It is the physical reactions that are particularly difficult to handle. When terrified, your body produces an adrenaline response. The adrenal glands release adrenaline into your blood, preparing you for "fight or flight."

The physical responses to adrenaline are fairly consistent and predictable and include sweating, increased heartbeat, shallow rapid breathing, muscle tension, shaking, upset stomach, tunnel vision, and loss of fine muscle control.

Adrenaline produces mental changes as well. Your sense of time changes. Most people experience a "slowing down" of time while some experience "time speeding up." Worst of all for speakers, adrenaline causes your higher brain activities to slow. Brain activity shifts to the more primitive and emotional sections of the brain. This is why you can speak perfectly well to one person but struggle terribly when speaking in front of a group. Your brain is not working as well.

Clearly the great challenge with public speaking is overcoming these fear reactions.

Psychology Is Eighty Percent Of Success

I could hear the crowd of three thousand in the room next door. Loud rock music echoed through the venue. A buzz of energy grew as the event organizer began my introduction.

Backstage, my excitement built. I jumped, shouted and smiled. I yelled to myself, "I am here to contribute! I will give all my energy and ability to help this audience today! I'm ready to rock! Yes! Yes! Yes!"

I walked to the door and peeked through it to view the audience. They were standing on their feet, applauding. And then they began to chant my name. "A.J. Hoge! A.J. Hoge! A.J. Hoge!" A surge of energy went through my body. I jumped and then ran onto the stage. The audience continued to shout my name.

As I stood facing that audience of three thousand people, I felt no fear. My breathing was deep, my body relaxed. In place of fear, I felt tremendous enthusiasm. In place of nervousness, I felt eagerness instead.

My experience of public speaking has totally transformed. Before a big speech, I now feel powerful — an incredible mix of confidence, excitement, and enthusiasm.

How did I make such a dramatic change? I did it using a few simple techniques, practiced hundreds of times.

The good news is that you can do what I have done. No matter how much fear you have for English presentations, by practicing a simple technique you can train yourself to feel strong and confident every time you give a public speech.

Feeling strong and confident is eighty percent or more of public speaking success. You already know how to speak. Once you overcome the fear of public speaking, you won't have any problem making great English presentations.

Confidence Must Be Trained

Confidence does not just happen accidentally. To overcome the fear of public speaking, you must develop emotional mastery at a very high level. Doing that requires practice and training. Great speakers train constantly.

You will use a very basic technique to achieve the emotional mastery necessary for public speaking. This technique is designed to overcome the natural fear response and replace it with feelings of confidence.

For this technique to be successful, you must practice it many times before giving a speech. Ideally, you will repeat this technique hundreds of times before taking the stage. You'll do this before each and every speech you ever make.

You Can't Suppress Fear, You Can Only Transform It

The adrenaline response is powerful. Once it is triggered, it is almost impossible to suppress. You can't fight it. In fact, any attempt to suppress the fear will make it worse.

For example, if your hands begin to shake before giving a speech, it is nearly impossible to stop them. The same is true for a rapid heartbeat, shallow breathing, muscle tension, etc. Once these reactions have started, they can't be fought. The adrenaline is already in your blood and your body will respond. If you try to fight against the reactions, you'll grow frustrated by your inability to change them. Your fear will multiply as you realize you are not in control, and the symptoms will worsen.

Once the adrenaline response is triggered, you have only one choice — channel the energy into something positive. Remember the purpose of adrenaline — it prepares you for flight or fight. This means you can use the same fear/flight reactions to create courage and fighting spirit instead. This is how I transformed my own fear of public speaking.

By using the energy instead of resisting it, you make yourself into a dynamic and confident speaker. The physical responses of fear and excitement are nearly identical. When you are excited your heartbeat increases, your breathing gets faster, and your muscles tension increases. When extremely excited, you may sweat and your hands may shake. In other words, your body reacts the same. So what makes the difference between extreme fear and extreme excitement?

It is the thoughts and feelings you attach to the physical reactions that determine whether you experience fear or excitement. By connecting positive experiences to the physical sensations, you will train yourself to feel excited and powerful rather than afraid.

How To Convert Fear Into Power

We will once again return to the technique of anchoring to program your brain for public-speaking confidence.

The first step is to recreate, as best you can, the physical sensations of fear. You want to get your heart beating faster. You want to increase your breathing. You want to tighten your muscles. The easiest way to do this is to use the peak state exercise you learned in the beginning of this book.

Put on your favorite loud, high-energy music. As you listen to this music, begin to jump and move your body. Little by little, jump higher and jump faster. Put a huge smile on your face. Make strong powerful gestures with your arms. Shout aloud, "Yes! Yes! Yes!" Keep going until your heart is beating fast and you are breathing heavily.

Turn off the music and, while still breathing heavily, begin to talk about your topic. Talk about the main ideas. If you have already planned the speech, do the whole thing. As you talk, move your body. Walk from one point of the room to another. Use strong gestures to make your point. Continue to smile.

At first this will likely be difficult, as you'll be out of breath. Your heart will be beating fast and it may be difficult to think of your speech. It's okay. Continue smiling and do the best you can. When you finish, turn on the music again and repeat the entire process.

Repeat this exercise at least four times a day. Each day, try to get your heart beating even faster before you practice your speech.

This exercise accomplishes several things. First, you create a positive anchor. By playing music you love and jumping and having fun, you generate strong positive emotions. Feeling great, you then begin your speech. With repetition, these great feelings become connected to the act of giving a speech. Eventually, just thinking about doing a presentation will make you feel excited automatically.

This exercise also trains you to deal with the major symptoms of nervousness: fast heartbeat, fast breathing, sweating, etc. Most people practice a speech when they are feeling calm. Because they always practice in a calm emotional state, they are unready for the flood of emotions that come just before the real speech. By practicing with an elevated heart and breathing rate, you are training your mind to expect these reactions and handle them. On the day of the speech, you won't get scared by these symptoms because they'll be normal and familiar to you. Instead, you'll be used to channeling this physical energy into positive emotions and strong actions.

This is the difference between training and practicing. Those who practice simply review their speech. Those who train do their best to recreate the emotional and physical conditions that will occur during the real speech. By training, you prepare yourself fully and will be ready for anything.

Practice Emotional Mastery Techniques Daily

Peak state training takes time. It's not enough to do this just a few times. Ideally, you will do this training hundreds of times prior to every speech you ever give. Preparation and training are what make you a great speaker.

You simply must practice daily in order to improve and master the fear of public speaking. It's not easy, but it is highly rewarding. Public speaking mastery will open many opportunities. When you speak to an audience, you are able to reach tens, hundreds, or even thousands of people at a time. Your influence grows. As your influence grows, so too will your career.

CHAPTER 22

English Connects You With The World

Think about why you are studying English. Chances are it has something to do with communicating or connecting with other people. English conversation is about connection. That is the purpose of English conversation – to connect with people around the world. We want to connect personally and emotionally. We want to connect with business partners, clients, and customers. We want to connect with professional peers. We want to connect with new friends.

In short, you need a community to use English. As a learner, it's especially useful to join a community of other English learners in order to practice and improve. The kind of community you join, however, is very important.

Your peer group has a strong effect upon your ultimate success. A "peer group" is simply a group of people who are interconnected with each other. Your friends are a peer group. Your family is another peer group. If you join an English class in a school, your classmates become your peer group. When you join an online community of English learners, they become your peer group.

Peer groups influence their members because, as a group, they share and promote certain values and behaviors. The group as a whole has certain standards and every member of the group is pulled towards those standards. This group effect can produce powerful positive or negative results.

A negative peer group is one with generally low standards. These groups are typically characterized by frequent criticism, focus on errors, complaints, and even insults among members. Such a group tends to pull down its members, discouraging and distracting them from success. Sadly, such groups are especially common in schools and online – the two most common English learning environments.

You want a peer group to pull you up. You want to join a group that encourages you, that feeds you positive thoughts, that interests and entertains you. You want a group that will boost you when you are struggling, and celebrate when you are successful.

Peer groups create spirals, either upward or downward. Through their shared interactions, standards and values, peer group communities exert ever-increasing influence upon you. Participation in a toxic peer group will eventually erode your confidence, no matter how strong you are. On the positive side, an inspiring peer group will empower you to improve, grow, and achieve tremendous success, even if you now feel hopeless.

Choose carefully. When considering a class or online English community, research it thoroughly. Notice how the members interact with each other. When a member is successful, are they celebrated, or do other members gossip jealously? When a community member struggles, do other members jump in to encourage and help them or are they ignored?

While it seems obvious, many students forget the ultimate reason they are learning. In traditional English conversation classes it's easy to get too focused on tests, textbooks, grades, and "levels." After a while, you as a student are so worried about these artificial measurements that you forget your ultimate purpose for study.

At the deepest level, English conversation is about international community-building and sustaining meaningful connections between people. What kind of people do you want in your English speaking community?

One of my ongoing goals is to use our seminars and courses and online groups as a way to create strong international communities. I want to help people connect and communicate in positive and meaningful ways – and help them stay connected. One way you can do this is through our member forums and conversation clubs. They're designed to allow you to interact and ask questions of other students who are learning English just like you.

I also want you to always keep in mind why you are studying English in the first place. Forget grades, tests and worrying about mistakes or how you might sound to others. Just focus on communicating and trying to connect with positive people. Surround yourself with enthusiastic people who love speaking English.

The more you connect with people who are excited about English, the more excited you will become. Enthusiasm is contagious! So is negativity. Choose your peer group wisely.

COMMUNITY IS IMPORTANT

When learning anything, especially when learning English, it's important to have a community – a club of other enthusiastic learners. This is why people continue to go to schools, even though they know the schools' methods are terrible. People want a community. They want to join with other people. They want the increased motivation, support, and inspiration that a good community can provide.

This is why our website is called the Effortless English Club™ (Effort-lessEnglishClub.com). Effortless English™ is more than great courses – it's also a community of very positive and enthusiastic learners. In fact, we are very careful about membership in our community. We only accept the most motivated – English learners who are very positive and enthusiastic.

We monitor our club quite closely, and we have zero tolerance for the negative, insulting, or childish behavior usually seen in internet communities. On most internet forums, for example, you find a massive amount of insults and arguing. We don't allow that. Such members are quickly and decisively eliminated from the club, and are never allowed to re-join.

Yes, this is a tough policy. But it is necessary. It can be difficult to create a great international learning club online. And I admit – I am not interested in accepting and tolerating everyone. My goal is to create an international English learning club of only the most positive learners. I want the most enthusiastic, the most supportive, the friendliest, the most energetic members in the world... and that, in fact, is exactly what we have.

The members of the Effortless English Club™ are absolutely amazing. The level of enthusiasm and friendliness is tremendous. New members are always very happy to discover such a fun and supportive learning club. We have many super members who will answer your questions, give you learning advice, encourage you when you feel discouraged, and inspire you with their success.

We made that community even stronger when we launched our new VIP Program. For us, VIP stands for Vision, Inspiration, Persistence... a monthly membership site where the most dedicated members meet... and get new lessons from me every month. All lessons have video, audio and text, so you can understand everything... but more importantly, the lessons focus on three powerful topics: Advanced Learning Strategies, The Psychology of Success, and Positive Leadership.

The VIP Member Program focuses not only on English, but also on Learning and Success in general. This is a place where our most motivated students (the top 1 percent) meet and learn together – a powerful club and community of the Best of the Best. They are the best not because of their starting English ability, but because of their positive attitudes, persistence, and devotion to learning.

CHAPTER 23

The Effortless English Code and Mission

The Effortless English™ community is held together by our purpose, code, mission and values. Obviously, our main purpose is to help you speak English powerfully and correctly. We share, however, a deeper code, mission and values.

It is the code, mission and values that have created our positive and enthusiastic community, with members from every continent of all ages, genders, and types of people. The code of Effortless English™ is our simple, three part code of conduct. All members of our community, upon joining, agree to follow the code.

The Code of the Effortless English Club™ is:

1. We Do The Best We Can

2. We Do The Right Thing

3. We Show Each Other We Care

We do the best we can means that we try hard to improve but we know that perfection is impossible. We don't worry about perfection. We don't get upset about mistakes. Our focus is always on improvement, not "the one right answer."

We do the right thing means we do not lie, gossip, or insult other members. We treat each other as good friends and family members. We follow "the Golden Rule" by being kind and polite within our community.

We show each other we care means we go beyond just avoiding negative behavior. Rather, we actively encourage and support other members. When another member is feeling bad, we encourage them. When another member succeeds, we cheer them, congratulate them, and compliment them sincerely. We are always looking for ways to help each other.

In addition to mastering spoken English, our community shares a deeper mission. Our mission is:

To explore new opportunities for growth,

To bring confidence, vitality and happiness to people all over the world,

To boldly go where we have never gone before.

To explore new opportunities for growth means we are always looking for new ways to learn and improve. We are dedicated to lifelong learning. As we improve, we share our success with other people. We help others to feel stronger, more energetic and happier. We do this within the Effortless English Club™. We do this within our families. We do this anywhere we can. Finally, we strive to live boldly with open minds. We are eager to try new things, consider new ideas, and travel to new places. We have an adventurous attitude toward life.

The mission is connected to our community values. We have seven values:

1. Devotion to the Mission

As members of the Effortless English™ community we all share the mission. The mission is something we do together, as a team, as an international family.

2. Enthusiasm

Enthusiasm is vital for success in any area of life. Enthusiasm generates peak emotion and fuels our learning engine. We consciously choose to develop our enthusiasm for learning and life.

3. Constant and Never-Ending Improvement

As our mission suggests, we are dedicated to constant and never-ending improvement. We know that big success is the result of small but consistent improvements. We know that learning makes life more interesting and enjoyable and we continue learning as long as we are alive.

4. Contribution

Personal success is important and so is sharing that success. As we improve, we focus on helping others do the same. We are delighted by the success of others in our community. We do our best to help others in whatever way we can.

5. Self-Reliance

Members of the Effortless English Club™ are independent learners. We do not wait for teachers, schools or experts to tell us what to do. We don't wait for others to solve our problems. We take responsibility for our own lives and our own problems. We are proactive learners.

6. Persistence

Success is impossible without persistence. When something is important to us, we do not quit. Despite hardships, despite challenges, despite temporary failures, we keep going. We continue to move forward until we achieve our goals.

7. Positive Leadership

Every member of the Effortless English Club™ is a leader because each of us can encourage and inspire others. In our community, we lead by example. We don't tell others what to do. Rather, we strive to be good role models. We work hard to show the way. As leaders, we want to make others stronger, more successful, and more confident.

It is my belief that all schools should operate with such a code, mission and values. Many of the problems in education would be solved if teachers, administrators, and students were guided by the above principles.

One of the great problems in schools is that teachers have failed to recognize they must do more than lecture to and discipline their students. Truly great teachers are more than just lecturers, they are leaders and coaches who inspire their students to greatness.

Think of your favorite sports coach – someone who helped his or her team achieve greatness. These people do not simply teach the skills of the game. Great coaches lead and inspire. They are experts in practical psychology. They know how to energize and motivate their players. They make their teams stronger, more confident, and more successful.

This is why I typically call myself an English "coach" rather than a teacher. The word "coach" reminds me to be more. It reminds me to focus on energizing, leading and inspiring my team members. As a coach, I must do more than simply teach English, I must help you believe in yourself. I must convince you that you can succeed with English, that, in fact, you will succeed.

I hope this book has done exactly that. I hope you feel more confident. I hope you are convinced that you can and you will finally succeed with English speaking. The past does not equal the future. Whatever struggles you have had with English are gone. Let them go. Today is a new day and you now have a completely new system.

Today is your day. You are now on your way to Effortless English™ speaking.

Enjoy the journey!

GET THE
AUDIOBOOK

As a service to English learners, I have recorded an audio version of this book. Get the audio version on this book's website: **EffortlessEnglish.com**

Use the audio and text version of the book chapter by chapter. Learn deeply by first reading and listening to a chapter at the same time. Do this for a few days. Then put aside the text and just listen to the audio chapter for a few days. Once you have mastered the chapter, begin the process again with the next chapter.

A.J. HOGE
THE WORLD'S #1 ENGLISH TEACHER

A proven method with guaranteed results!

EFFORTLESS
ENGLISH

LEARN TO SPEAK ENGLISH LIKE A NATIVE

Effortless English

EFFORTLESS ENGLISH™
COURSES

Accelerate your English improvement and results by training with A.J. in one of the Effortless English™ courses. Train to be a skillful and confident English speaker.

Every course is designed using the methods described in this book. When you join an Effortless English™ course you'll improve your spoken English using audio and video lessons taught by AJ himself.

This is the easiest way to use the Effortless English™ system for the fastest possible success.

Join one of AJ's courses today at: **EffortlessEnglishClub.com**

AJ HOGE
SPEAKING &
TRAINING

AJ prepares people to thrive in the global economy using English fluency as a stepping stone. AJ consults to international companies on 4 continents, speaks at corporate seminars and public venues in the U.S., Asia, Europe, and South America.

AJ speaks on topics related to English, teaching and training, public speaking, career development, and online marketing. He will customize his presentation to meet your organization's needs.

Effortless
English

LEARN REAL ENGLISH COURSES

Learn real English, including idioms, slang and casual English, with the Learn Real English team: A.J., Kristin Dodds, and Joe Weiss.

These courses use natural conversations, teaching you the everyday language used by native speakers.

Get more information about Learn Real English courses at:

http://LearnRealEnglish.com

About The Author

 A.J. Hoge is the founder and director of Effortless English LLC, and co-founder of Learn Real English and Business English Conversations. He has been described as "the world's #1 English teacher" and is famous as the host of The Effortless English Show, with over 41,000,000 downloads worldwide. He has a master's degree in TESOL and has been teaching English since 1996. A.J. teaches seminars around the world on the topics of English, public speaking, effective training methods, career development, and online marketing.

Connect With AJ:

AJHoge.com

twitter.com/ajhoge

youtube.com/ajhoge

plus.google.com/+effortlessenglishclub

facebook.com/effortlessenglish

Effortless English Audiobook

EffortlessEnglish.com

Speaking, Seminar, and Live Event Booking

events@EffortlessEnglishClub.com

Media Inquiries

events@EffortlessEnglishClub.com

CPSIA information can be obtained
at www.ICGtesting.com
Printed in the USA
LVOW01s1528121115
462272LV00019B/881/P

D*TE DU*

tina
598-9230

99391

ry

> > > > > >

PROBLEMS >
>
>
AND >
>
>
SOLUTIONS >
>

Physical Chemistry

Leonard C. Labowitz
Stern College for Women, Yeshiva University

John S. Arents
The City College of the City University of New York

ACADEMIC PRESS
New York   London

ACADEMIC PRESS, INC.
111 Fifth Avenue, New York, New York 10003

United Kingdom Edition published by
ACADEMIC PRESS, INC. (LONDON) LTD.
24/28 Oval Road, London NW1

LIBRARY OF CONGRESS CATALOG CARD NUMBER: 68-8430

Third Printing, 1972

PRINTED IN THE UNITED STATES OF AMERICA

To *Michael*
and *Gabriele*

>

>

>

>

>

Preface

The purpose of this book is to provide a study aid and a supplementary source of problems for advanced undergraduate and beginning graduate students in physical chemistry.

The material in each chapter has been subdivided into three different categories, according to relative difficulty. The exception is Chapter 15, where many of the problems are sequential in nature. The "I" problems are relatively easy, the "II" problems intermediate, and the "III" problems difficult. It is hoped that the "III" problems will stimulate the students' interest in physical chemistry. Generally speaking, the problems on this level require an unusual understanding and "feeling" for physical chemistry... and some imagination. The "II" problems require sufficient understanding of the subject matter to handle situations that are a little difficult or that require a little "twist" making the viewpoint slightly different from what one has met with in class. The "II" problems require some understanding of the material beyond the mere "plug-the-number-into-the-formula" level. The "I" problems are mainly of the classical variety. All three types of problems are required for a well integrated course in physical chemistry.

We have used barred letters ($\overline{V}$, etc.) for both molar and partial molar quantities; other notations are standard or explained as they appear. We have followed the common practice of writing equilibrium constants as dimensionless numbers, with the understanding that pressures are in atmospheres and concentrations in moles per liter.

The authors are grateful to Professors Edgar F. Westrum, Jr., Robert G. Parr, and Ernest M. Loebl for their interest and encouragement and many helpful suggestions, to our families for their patience and fortitude, and especially to Michael Labowitz, who spilled milk on the manuscript.

New York

LEONARD C. LABOWITZ
JOHN S. ARENTS

Contents

PROBLEMS
AND
SOLUTIONS

>
>
>
>
>
>

Physical
Chemistry

>

>

>

>

>

Problem >
statements

CHAPTER 1

Gases

SECTION 1-1

1-I-1. A bubble with a diameter of 1 cm at the bottom of the Okeefenokee Swamp, where the temperature is 5°C and the pressure is 3 atm, rises to the surface, where the temperature is 25°C and the pressure is 1 atm. What will be the diameter of the bubble when it reaches the surface? (Ignore the presence of water vapor in the bubble.)

1-I-2. The molecular weight of ozone was determined by the Regnault method by Karrer and Wulf [*J. Am. Chem. Soc.*, **44**, 2391 (1922)], and the following data were obtained:

Temperature = 28.2°C
Weight of bulb filled with ozone = 6.7624 g
Weight of evacuated bulb = 6.5998 g
Pressure of ozone in bulb = 274.4 torr
Volume of bulb = 235.67 cm³

Calculate the molecular weight of ozone from these data.

1-I-3. MacInnes and Kreiling [*J. Am. Chem. Soc.*, **39**, 2350 (1917)] determined the molecular weight of diethyl ether by the Victor Meyer method and obtained the following data:

Weight of ether = 0.1023 g
Volume of air displaced = 35.33 cm³
Temperature = 32.5°C
Atmospheric pressure = 743.95 torr

Calculate the molecular weight of the ether.

1-I-4. A certain gas has the following densities at 300.0°K:

Pressure, atm	0.4000	0.8000	1.0000
Density, g liter^{-1}	1.512	3.088	3.900

Find the molecular weight of the gas as accurately as you can with the given data.

1-I-5. The density of gaseous methylamine as a function of pressure at 0°C was investigated by Arthur and Felsing [*J. Am. Chem. Soc.*, **68**, 1883 (1946)]. The following data were obtained:

Pressure, atm	0.200	0.500	0.800
Density, g liter^{-1}	0.2796	0.7080	1.1476

Determine the molecular weight of this compound.

1-I-6. Using Maxwell's law of distribution of molecular energies, $dn = K \sqrt{\epsilon}\, e^{-\epsilon/kT}\, d\epsilon$, write an expression for the fraction of all molecules in an ideal gas that have translational kinetic energies greater than a certain value ϵ_0.

1-I-7. Perrin [*Ann. Chim. Phys.*, **18**, 1 (1909)] determined the value of Avogadro's number by investigating microscopically the distribution of colloidal gamboge particles suspended in water as a function of height. In one set of measurements he obtained the following data at 15°C:

h, height, μm	5	35
n, relative number of particles at height h, averaged over a period of time	100	47

The density of the particles was 1.206 g cm^{-3}. The density of the water was 0.999 g cm^{-3}. The radius of the particles was 0.212 μm. 1μm $= 10^{-4}$ cm. On the basis of this information calculate Avogadro's number.

1-I-8. Plot the probability density function $f(v)$ versus molecular speed v for hydrogen at 0°C.

1-I-9. Calculate the mean free path of argon molecules at 25°C and 1 torr. The molecular diameter of argon is 2.86 Å.

1-I-10. Calculate the collision frequency of nitrogen molecules per cubic centimeter per second at 1 torr and 25°C. The molecular diameter of N_2 is 3.16 Å.

1-I-11. A mixture consisting of 90 mole percent hydrogen and 10 mole percent deuterium at 25°C and a total pressure of 1 atm is permitted to effuse through a small orifice of area 0.30 mm². Calculate the composition of the initial gas that passes through.

1-I-12. Calculate the pressure in atmospheres exerted by 2.00 moles of chlorobenzene vapor confined to 10.0 liters at 25°C (a) using the ideal gas law, and (b) using the van der Waals equation. $a = 25.43$ liter² atm mole⁻², $b = 0.1453$ liter mole⁻¹.

1-I-13. The compressibility factor $Z = PV/nRT$ for CO_2 at 0°C and 100 atm pressure is 0.2007. Calculate the volume occupied by 0.1 mole of the gas at 100 atm and 0°C (a) by the ideal gas law, and (b) by making use of the compressibility factor.

1-I-14. The compressibility factor $Z = PV/nRT$ for N_2 at −50°C and 800 atm pressure is 1.95; at 100°C and 200 atm it is 1.10. A certain mass of nitrogen occupied a volume of 1.00 liter at −50°C and 800 atm. Calculate the volume occupied by the same quantity of nitrogen at 100°C and 200 atm.

1-I-15. For a van der Waals gas $\bar{V}_c = 3b$, $P_c = a/27b^2$, and $T_c = 8a/27bR$. Evaluate numerically the compressibility factor of a van der Waals gas at the critical point.

1-I-16. The boiling point of n-hexane at 760 torr is 68.9°C. Make a rough estimate of the critical temperature of this substance.

SECTION 1-II

1-II-1. The coefficient of thermal expansion of helium as a function of pressure is given below [Henning and Heuse, Z. Physik, **5**, 285 (1921)]. Calculate the temperature in degrees Celsius corresponding to absolute zero.

P, torr	504.8	520.5	760.1	1102.9	1116.5
$\alpha \times 10^6$	3658.9	3660.3	3659.1	3658.2	3658.1

1-II-2.   The density ρ (in g liter^{-1}) of a certain gas at 300.00°K is given by the equation $\rho = 2.000\ P + 0.0200\ P^2$, where P is the pressure in atmospheres. Calculate the molecular weight of this gas to four significant figures.

1-II-3.   Gray and Burt [*J. Chem. Soc.*, **95**, 1633 (1909)] determined the atomic weight of chlorine by the method of limiting densities applied to gaseous hydrogen chloride. In one set of of measurements they found that a glass bulb with a volume of 465.856 cm^3 contained the following weights of hydrogen chloride at the indicated pressures and 0°C:

Weight of HCl, g	0.76097	0.75731	0.75481	0.75968
Barometric pressure, mm Hg	756.76	753.38	750.83	755.79

In another set of experiments they obtained the following data on the PV product of hydrogen chloride as a function of pressure at 0°C:

P, mm Hg	829.50	604.71	384.13
V, cm^3	66.012	90.815	143.259
PV	54757	54917	55030
P	243.40	157.57	
V	226.401	349.978	
PV	55106	55146	

They also found that the limiting density-pressure ratio of oxygen at 0°C was $\lim_{P \to 0} (\rho/P) = 1.42762$ g liter^{-1} atm^{-1}. The measurements were made in London, where the force of gravity is 1.000588 times that at 45° latitude. All of the data have been corrected for the adsorption of gas on the walls of the container. Determine the limiting density of hydrogen chloride and the atomic weight of chlorine.

1-II-4.   The thermal coefficient of cubic expansion of mercury is given by the expression

$$\alpha = \frac{1}{V_0}\left(\frac{\partial V}{\partial T}\right)_P = 1.817 \times 10^{-4} + 5.90 \times 10^{-9}t + 3.45 \times 10^{-10}t^2$$

where t is the Celsius temperature and V_0 is V at $t = 0$. If an ideal gas thermometer and a mercury thermometer are set to agree at 0°C and 100°C, what apparent temperature on the mercury scale would correspond to 50°C on the ideal gas thermometer?

1-II-5. Each of the following definitions of absolute temperature (T) is possible and workable. Describe briefly how each definition differs from the official definition (adopted in 1954 by the International Committee on Weights and Measures), and give one or more reasons why you think each of these definitions is not commonly used. The official definition is

$$T = \frac{1}{nR} \lim_{P \to 0} (PV)$$

where n is the number of moles of gas, V is its volume, P is its pressure, and R is a constant chosen so that $T = 273.16°$ (exactly) at the triple point of water.

(a) $T = 100 \left(\dfrac{l - l_f}{l_b - l_f} \right) + 273.15$

where l is the length of a mercury column of constant cross section at the temperature T, and (l_b, l_f) is the length of the same column at the (boiling, freezing) point of air-saturated water under a pressure of one standard atm (1.01325×10^6 dyne cm^{-2}).

(b) $T = PV/nR$, where V is the volume at one atm pressure of n moles of pure oxygen of the isotopic composition found in the earth's atmosphere. One mole is defined as that quantity of oxygen (approximately 31.9988 g) which contains the same number of molecules as there are atoms in exactly 12 g of the pure nuclide ^{12}C. R is a constant so chosen that $T = 273.16$ at the triple point of water.

1-II-6. A certain mixture of helium and argon weighing 5.00 g occupies a volume of 10.0 liters at 25°C and 1.00 atm. What is the composition of the mixture in weight percent?

1-II-7. Calculate the density in g liter^{-1} of air saturated with water vapor at 25°C. The vapor pressure of water at this temperature is 23.7 torr. The composition of dry, CO_2–free air is 78.1 percent N_2, 21.0 percent O_2, and 0.9 percent Ar by volume.

1-II-8. The pressure of a gas as function of height is given by the formula

$$\ln \left(\frac{P_0}{P} \right) = \frac{Mg(h - h_0)}{RT}$$

where P_0 represents the pressure of the gas at height h_0, and P represents the pressure of the gas at height h, $h > h_0$; M is the molecular weight of the gas, g is the gravitational acceleration constant $= 980.6$ cm sec^{-2}, and R is the gas constant $= 8.314 \times 10^7$ ergs °K^{-1} mole^{-1}. (a) Calculate the atmospheric pressure at the top of the Empire State Building (height 1248 ft) if the pressure at ground level is 1.00 atm and the temperature is 25°C, assuming no complications such as turbulence or temperature gradients. (b) Explain how you could construct a straight-line graph relating altitude to air pressure. The apparent molecular weight of air is 29.

1-II-9. Derive the barometric formula

$$P = P_0\, e^{-Mgz/RT}$$

by solving a differential equation obtained as follows: The pressure difference $(-dP)$ between height z and height $z + dz$ is equal to the weight (not mass) per unit area of a layer of gas of thickness dz. Then equate these two, express everything (by means of the ideal gas law) in terms of the two variables P and z, and separate these variables.

1-II-10. The acceleration of gravity, g, varies in magnitude with distance r from the center of the earth, in accordance with the formula $g = Gm_E/r^2$, where G is a proportionality constant called the gravitational constant and m_E is the mass of the earth. Derive a modified form of the barometric equation that takes this variation of g with altitude z above the earth's surface into account.

1-II-11. In the lower part of the atmosphere the temperature of the air is not uniform but decreases linearly with altitude in accordance with the equation $T = T_0 - az$, where a is a proportionality constant, z is the altitude, T_0 is the temperature at ground level, and T is the temperature at altitude z. Derive a modified form of the barometric equation that takes this temperature dependence into account.

1-II-12. Your answers to this question should be expressed in terms of the given quantities and universal constants. They may contain integrals that you have not evaluated. (a) In an ideal gas at the temperature T in which each molecule has mass m find the fraction of the molecules that have speeds greater than v_0. (b) Find this fraction in a two-dimensional ideal "gas" with the molecules confined to a plane.

1-II-13. The external surface area of an average human being is estimated to be about 2.0 m². Calculate the number of collisions per second of air molecules (20 mole percent O_2, 80 mole percent N_2) with the total surface of an average person at 25°C and 1 atm.

1-II-14. The vapor pressure of scandium was determined by the Knudsen effusion technique [Krikorian, *J. Phys. Chem.*, **67**, 1586 (1963)]. In this method the weight of gas effusing through a small opening in a known interval of time is measured. The following data were obtained:

temperature, 1555.4°K
time, 110.5 min
weight loss, 9.57 mg
diameter of orifice, 0.2965 cm

Calculate the vapor pressure of scandium at this temperature in atmospheres. 1 dyne cm^{-2} = 9.87 × 10^{-7} atm.

1-II-15. Two ideal gases, A and B, are in separate containers at temperatures T_A and T_B, with concentrations c_A and c_B in moles per liter, respectively. Their molecular weights are M_A and M_B; the molecular diameters are σ_A and σ_B. We assume that the molecules are hard spheres. For each of the following quantities find the ratio of its value for gas A to its value for gas B: (a) average kinetic energy per molecule, (b) average speed of a molecule, (c) mean free path, and (d) number of intermolecular collisions suffered by a single molecule per unit time.

1-II-16. According to the kinetic theory of gases the viscosity of a gas is proportional to $T^{1/2}\sigma^{-2}$, where σ is the molecular diameter. Explain why the viscosity (a) increases with increasing temperature, (b) depends on the diameter of the molecules, and (c) is independent of pressure at constant temperature. Why does this independence fail at very low pressures?

1-II-17. It has been proposed that intergalactic space contains hydrogen atoms at a temperature of $7.8 \times 10^{5\circ}$K, with about 1 atom per 100 liters. Assume that the collision diameter of a hydrogen atom is 2.0 Å. (a) Calculate the mean free path of an atom in intergalactic space in light-years. (b) What is the approximate average time, in years, between collisions of a given atom ?

1-II-18. The Boyle temperature of a gas is the temperature at which $[\partial(PV)/\partial P]_T = 0$ when $P = 0$. For each of the following equations of state evaluate T_B, the Boyle temperature, in terms of the known constants A, b, R, P_c, T_c, etc.:

(a) $P\bar{V} = RT + \left(b - \dfrac{A}{RT^{3/2}}\right) P$

(b) $P\bar{V} = RT \left\{1 + \dfrac{9}{128} \left(\dfrac{P}{P_c}\right)\left(\dfrac{T_c}{T}\right)\left[1 - 6\left(\dfrac{T_c}{T}\right)^2\right]\right\}$

1-II-19. Evaluate the Boyle temperature of a van der Waals gas in terms of the constants a, b, and R. The final expression for T_B should contain only a, b, and R. Suggestion: Since the van der Waals equation is difficult to rearrange into the virial form, which would permit T_B to be evaluated by inspection, set up the van der Waals equation in the form

$$P = \frac{nRT}{V - nb} - \frac{n^2 a}{V^2}$$

multiply through by V, and set

$$\left(\frac{\partial[PV]}{\partial P}\right)_T = 0$$

at $P = 0$. Remember that when $P = 0$, $V = \infty$.

1-II-20. Show that at low densities the van der Waals equation

$$\left(P + \frac{a}{\bar{V}^2}\right)(\bar{V} - b) = RT$$

and the Dieterici equation

$$P = \frac{RT}{(\bar{V} - b)} e^{-a/RT\bar{V}}$$

give essentially the same result for P. Hint: Expand the Dieterici equation in terms of the infinite series $e^x = 1 + x + x^2/2! + x^3/3! + x^4/4! + \cdots$.

1-II-21. A certain gas has the equation of state

$$P = \frac{RT}{\overline{V} - bT} - \frac{a}{\overline{V}^3}$$

where $\overline{V}$ represents molar volume, and a, b are constants characteristic of the gas. Show that

$$a = \frac{4RT_c\overline{V}_c{}^2}{3} \quad \text{and} \quad b = \frac{\overline{V}_c}{2T_c}$$

where $\overline{V}_c$ and T_c are the critical constants.

1-II-22. A certain nonideal gas has the equation of state $P\overline{V} = RT + APT - BP$, where $\overline{V}$ is the molar volume and A and B are constants characteristic of the gas. For this gas (a) find the Boyle temperature, and (b) ascertain whether this gas has a critical point. If so, find the critical constants; if not, explain why not.

1-II-23. A hypothetical gas the equation of state

$$P = \frac{RT}{\overline{V} - b} - \frac{a}{\overline{V}}$$

where a and b are constants distinct from zero. Ascertain whether this gas a critical point. If it has, express the critical constants in terms of a and b. If it has not, explain how you arrive at this conclusion.

1-II-24. For a Dieterici gas, $P(\overline{V} - b)\, e^{a/RT\overline{V}} = RT$; $\overline{V}_c = 2b$, $T_c = a/4Rb$, and $P_c = a/4e^2b^2$. Rewrite the Dieterici equation in reduced form—that is, in terms of reduced temperature, $\theta = T/T_c$, reduced pressure, $\pi = P/P_c$, and reduced volume, $\phi = \overline{V}/V_c$. In the final equation π, ϕ, and θ should be the only variables and the constants a, b, and R should not appear at all.

SECTION 1-III

1-III-1. In filling a barometer tube some air was trapped at the top of the column, as was evident from the fact that the instrument read 3.0 mm low when the true pressure was 720 torr (mm Hg) and the room temperature was 20°C. The total length of the barometer tube measured from the lower index was 780 mm. Work out a formula from which the true pressures could be determined with this instrument under all room conditions. Solve for the correction to be applied to the reading.

1-III-2. A glass cylinder 100 cm long, closed at one end, and filled with dry air at 1.00 atm and 25°C is inverted in a pool of mercury until the closed end is flush with the surface of the pool (see the figure). The barometric pressure is 1.00 atm. (a) What will be the height of the mercury column inside the cylinder? (b) What will be the final pressure of the trapped air?

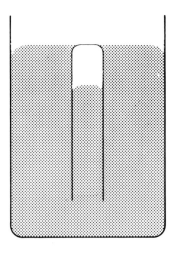

1-III-3. The J-shaped tube shown in the figure is filled initially with air at 1.00 atm and 25°C; then liquid mercury is poured into the open end. The barometric pressure is 1.00 atm. (a) What will be the height of the mercury column in the long arm when mercury is just starting to spill over the top of the short arm? (b) What will be the pressure of the trapped air at this point?

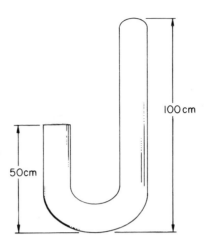

1-III-4. Two hollow, spherical vessels with a capacity of 22.4 liters each are each filled with 1.00 mole of nitrogen at 25°C and 1.00 atm pressure and connected by a thin, hollow tube of negligible volume. Then one sphere is placed in a thermostat at 100°C, and the other sphere is placed in a thermostat at 0°C. What will be the final pressure in the system and what will be the final number of moles of nitrogen in each sphere?

1-III-5. In an attempt to derive the formula $PV = KT$, where K is a constant, by combining the laws of Boyle and Charles (or Gay-Lussac) the following incorrect argument was proposed:

$$PV = k_1 \quad (1) \qquad\qquad V = k_2 T \tag{4}$$

$$\frac{V}{T} = k_2 \quad (2) \qquad\qquad \frac{k_1}{P} = k_2 T \tag{5}$$

$$V = \frac{k_1}{P} \quad (3) \qquad \frac{k_1}{k_2} = k_3 = PT, \quad \text{or} \quad PT = K \tag{6}$$

Equation 6 is obviously incorrect. What is the error? At what step was it introduced? Give a correct derivation.

1-III-6. A chemical engineer wishes to construct a simple, straight-line graph by means of which he could read the composition of a mixture of helium and oxygen in mole percent off one axis by looking up the density, in grams per liter, at 25°C and 1 atm total pressure on the other axis, assuming ideal gas behavior. (a) Explain the basis on which such a graph can be constructed. (b) Draw the graph and use it to determine the composition of a helium-oxygen mixture that has a density of 0.820 g liter^{-1} under the specified conditions.

1-III-7. The three components of the velocity of a gas molecule are v_x, v_y, and v_z. The speed is $v = (v_x{}^2 + v_y{}^2 + v_z{}^2)^{1/2}$.
(a) Write an expression for $\overline{v_x{}^4}$, the fourth power of v_x averaged over all molecules. (This and later answers may be left in the form of unevaluated integrals. However, they should contain only the mass m of each molecule, the temperature T, universal constants, and the variable(s) of integration.)
(b) Write a similar expression for $\overline{v^4}$.
(c) If there is a difference between your two expressions, other than the substitution of v for v_x, explain how it arises.

1-III-8. Sketch a representative isotherm for 1 mole of a gas that obeys the equation of state $P(\bar{V} - b) = RT$, where $b > 0$. Interpret the physical significance of the slope and the $P\bar{V}$ intercept and discuss the validity of this equation of state for real gases at low pressures.

1-III-9. For a certain hypothetical gas the thermal coefficient of expansion is given by

$$\alpha = \frac{1}{V}\left(\frac{\partial V}{\partial T}\right)_P = k_1\left(\frac{C_P}{C_V}\right) T^{(C_P/C_V)-1}$$

and the coefficient of isothermal compressibility by

$$\beta = -\frac{1}{V}\left(\frac{\partial V}{\partial P}\right)_T = \frac{k_2}{P}$$

What is the equation of state of this gas? Assume that C_P, C_V, k_1, and k_2 are constants.

1-III-10. For a van der Waals gas show that $T_c = 8a/27bR$, $V_c = 3nb$, and $P_c = a/27b^2$, where T_c is the critical temperature, V_c is the critical volume, and P_c is the critical pressure. Van der Waals' equation is

$$\left(P + \frac{n^2a}{V^2}\right)(V - nb) = nRT$$

1-III-11. A gas has the equation of state $(P + aP^2)(V - b) = RT$, where a and b are constants. Ascertain whether this gas has a critical point. If it has, write the equation of state in reduced form.

1-III-12. For a gas described by the Berthelot equation,

$$P = RT/(\bar{V} - b) - a/T\bar{V}^2,$$

express a, b, and R in terms of the critical constants and write the equation of state in terms of reduced variables.

1-III-13. Show that the critical constants T_c, $\bar{V}_c$, and P_c for a gas with the equation of state

$$P = \frac{RT}{V - b} \cdot e^{-A/RT^{3/2}\bar{V}}$$

are given by

$$T_c = \left(\frac{A}{4bR}\right)^{2/3}, \quad \bar{V}_c = 2b, \quad \text{and} \quad P_c = \frac{R}{b}\left(\frac{A}{4bR}\right)^{2/3} e^{-2}.$$

1-III-14. The following equation of state for a nonideal gas is proposed:

$$P = \frac{RT}{\bar{V} - B} - A\bar{V}^m$$

where $\bar{V}$ is the molar volume, and A, B, and m are constants characteristic of the gas. If this equation is to be applicable to a real gas, it must predict (i) the approach to ideal behavior at zero pressure or infinite volume—that is, $P\bar{V}/RT \to 1$ as $\bar{V} \to \infty$; (ii) the existence of a critical point, with $\bar{V}_c$, T_c, and P_c all positive. We wish to ascertain what conditions must be imposed on the constants A, B, and m in order that the equation will make these two predictions. (a) Express $P\bar{V}/RT$ in terms of A, B, m, R, T, and $\bar{V}$. (b) If A and $B \neq 0$, what requirement(s) must be imposed in order that $P\bar{V}/RT \to 1$ as $\bar{V} \to \infty$? (c) Express $(\partial P/\partial\bar{V})_T$ and $(\partial^2 P/\partial\bar{V}^2)_T$ in terms of A, B, m, R, T, and $\bar{V}$. (d) Express the critical volume $\bar{V}_c$ in terms of A, B, m, and R. (e) What requirement(s) must be imposed on A, B, or m in order that $\bar{V}_c$ be positive ? (f) Express the critical temperature T_c in terms of A, B, m, and R. (g) What further condition(s) must be imposed on A, B, or m in order that T_c be positive? (h) Discuss the physical significance of the conditions which A, B, and m must satisfy.

CHAPTER 2

The first law

of thermodynamics
and thermochemistry

Table 2.1

*Standard Enthalpies of Formation
and Heat Capacities[a]*

$\Delta H^{\circ}_{f,298}$, kcal mole^{-1} and $\bar{C}_P = a + bT + cT^2 + dT^3 + fT^{-2}$ cal$^{\circ}$K^{-1} mole^{-1}

Substance	$\Delta H^{\circ}_{f,298}$	a	$b \times 10^3$	$c \times 10^7$	$d \times 10^9$	$f \times 10^{-5}$	Range, $^{\circ}$K
C (graphite)	0	4.03	1.14	0	0	−2.04	298–2000
CO(g)	−26.4157	6.79	0.98	0	0	−0.11	298–2000
CO$_2$(g)	−94.0518	10.57	2.10	0	0	−2.06	298–2000
H$_2$O(g)	−57.7979	7.219	2.374	2.67	0	0	298–1500
H$_2$O(liq)	−68.3174						
H$_2$S(g)	−4.815	6.955	3.675	7.40	0	0	298–1500
NH$_3$(g)	−11.04						
O$_2$(g)	0	6.148	3.102	−9.23	0	0	298–1500
SO$_2$(g)	−70.96	6.796	11.588	−3.015	2.057	0	298–1500

[a] These data are to be used as needed for the problems in this chapter.

SECTION 2-I

2-I-1. Show that for the process of heating an ideal gas

$$\Delta E + (P_2 V_2 - P_1 V_1) = n\bar{C}_P(T_2 - T_1)$$

2-I-2. From the equation $(\partial E/\partial V)_T = T(\partial P/\partial T)_V - P$ show that $(\partial E/\partial V)_T = 0$ for a gas that has the equation of state $P\bar{V} = RT$.

2-I-3. Derive a mathematical expression, involving only constants and readily measurable physical properties, for the work done on the surroundings when a gas that has the equation of state $PV = nRT - n^2a/V$ expands reversibly from V_i to V_f at constant temperature.

2-I-4. Find the work done when 1 mole of a gas that has the equation of state $P\bar{V} = RT + APT - BP$ expands in an isothermal, reversible process from volume $\bar{V}_1$ to volume $\bar{V}_2$. $\bar{V}$ is the molar volume and A and B are constants characteristic of the gas.

2-I-5. The valve on a cylinder containing initially 10 liters of an ideal gas at 25 atm and 25°C is opened to the atmosphere, where the pressure is 760 torr and the temperature is 25°C. Assuming that the process is isothermal, how much work in liter atmospheres is done on the atmosphere by the action of expanding gas?

2-I-6. One mole of a monatomic ideal gas is put through the reversible cycle shown in the figure. Fill in the blank spaces in the tables below.

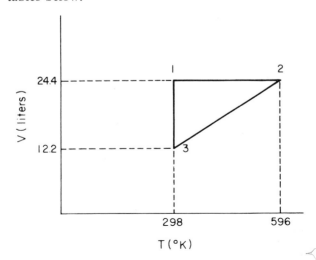

Stage	P, atm	V, liters	T, °K
1	1	24.4	298
2	—	24.4	596
3	—	12.2	298

Step	Nature of Process	q, cal	w, cal	ΔE, cal	ΔH, cal
1 → 2	isochoric	———	———	———	———
2 → 3	isobaric	———	———	———	———
3 → 1	isothermal	———	———	———	———
Total cycle		———	———	———	———

2-I-7. One mole of a monatomic ideal gas is put through the reversible cycle shown in the figure. Fill in the blank spaces in the tables given below.

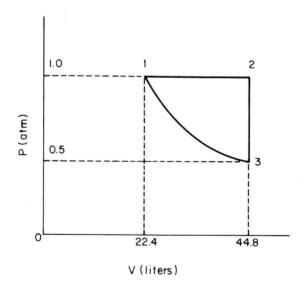

Stage	P, atm	V, liters	T, °K
1	1	24.4	300
2	1	48.8	—
3	0.5	48.8	—

Step	Nature of Process	q, cal	w, cal	ΔE, cal	ΔH, cal
1 → 2	isobaric	————	————	————	————
2 → 3	isochoric	————	————	————	————
3 → 1	isothermal	————	————	————	————
Total cycle		————	————	————	————

2-I-8. One mole of a monatomic ideal gas is put through the reversible cycle shown in the figure. Fill in the blank spaces in the table given below.

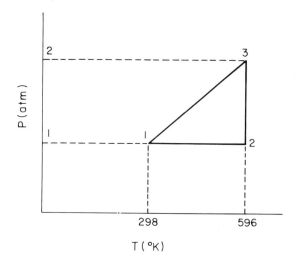

Stage	P, atm	V, liters	T, °K
1	1	————	298
2	1	————	596
3	2	————	596

Step	Nature of Process	q, cal	w, cal	ΔE, cal	ΔH, cal
1 → 2	isobaric	————	————	————	————
2 → 3	isothermal	————	————	————	————
3 → 1	isochoric	————	————	————	————
Total cycle		————	————	————	————

2-I-9.   Calculate the final temperature for the adiabatic reversible expansion of 100 g of argon, initially at 25°C, from 10 liters to 50 liters.

2-I-10.   Calculate the maximum work obtainable by (a) the isothermal expansion, and (b) the adiabatic expansion of 2 moles of nitrogen, assumed ideal, initially at 25°C, from 10 liters to 20 liters. Assume $\bar{C}_V = (5/2)R$.

2-I-11.   Starting with $\mu_{JT} = (-1/C_P)(\partial H/\partial P)_T$, derive the formula

$$\mu_{JT} = -\frac{1}{C_P}\left[\left(\frac{\partial E}{\partial V}\right)_T \left(\frac{\partial V}{\partial P}\right)_T + \left(\frac{\partial (PV)}{\partial P}\right)_T\right]$$

2-I-12.   The Joule-Thomson coefficient of oxygen is $+0.366$°C atm^{-1}. Assuming the coefficient to be independent of temperature under the conditions of this problem, calculate the final temperature of the gas if 10 moles of oxygen initially at 20.0 atm and 0°C is allowed to expand adiabatically through a porous plug, as in a Joule-Thomson experiment, until the final pressure is 1.0 atm.

2-I-13.   In a determination of the enthalpy of combustion of naphthalene ($C_{10}H_8$) by oxygen bomb calorimetry, Richards and Davis [*J. Am. Chem. Soc.*, **42**, 1599 (1920)] found that the temperature of the calorimeter system rose 4.0630°C on the combustion of a 1.1226 g sample of naphthalene. The mean temperature of the run was 18°C. The temperature rise given here is corrected for the enthalpy of combustion of the cotton fuse and the formation of soot, carbon monoxide, and nitric acid. The heat capacity of the calorimeter system is 2660.0 cal and the formula weight of naphthalene is 128.11 g mole^{-1}. Calculate the enthalpy of combustion per mole of naphthalene at 18°C.

2-I-14.   The calorific value of food (actually the enthalpy of combustion of the food per unit mass) may be determined by measuring the heat produced by burning a weighed sample of food under constant-volume conditions in a bomb calorimeter. The heat released by the total combustion of a 1.00 g (3.00×10^{-3} mole) sample of chicken fat under these conditions (constant volume) was found to be 10,000 cal at

37°C. Calculate the calorific value of the chicken fat in cal g^{-1} at 37°C under constant pressure; that is, calculate the standard enthalpy of combustion of the chicken fat at 37°C. The reaction may be represented by the equation,

$$C_{20}H_{32}O_2(s) + 27O_2(g) \rightarrow 20CO_2(g) + 16H_2O(l)$$

2-I-15. On the basis of the following data calculate the enthalpy of fusion of ice in cal mole^{-1} at $-10°C$:

$\bar{C}_P H_2O(s) = 9.0$ cal mole^{-1} °K^{-1}
$\bar{C}_P H_2O(l) = 18.0$ cal mole^{-1} °K^{-1}

$\Delta \bar{H}$ for the fusion of ice at 0°C is 1435 cal mole^{-1}.

2-I-16. According to Torgeson and Shomate [*J. Am. Chem. Soc.*, **69**, 2103 (1947)], the enthalpies of solution in 1.000 N HCl of certain compounds of the type $nCaO \cdot mB_2O_3$ at 298.16°K are as follows:

Compound	Enthalpy of Solution in 1.000 N HCl, cal mole^{-1}
$3CaO \cdot B_2O_3$	$\Delta H_1 = -82{,}423$
$2CaO \cdot B_2O_3$	$\Delta H_2 = -50{,}287$
$CaO \cdot B_2O_3$	$\Delta H_3 = -20{,}259$
$CaO \cdot 2B_2O_3$	$\Delta H_4 = -10{,}080$
CaO	$\Delta H_5 = -46{,}380$
B_2O_3	$\Delta H_6 = -3286$

Calculate ΔH for the reaction $3CaO + B_2O_3 = 3CaO \cdot B_2O_3$.

2-I-17. For the reaction $2A_2(s) + 5B_2(g) = 2A_2B_5(g)$, $\Delta E_{298} = 15.000$ kcal. Calculate ΔH_{298} for this reaction.

2-I-18. The standard enthalpy of combustion of solid naphthalene $(C_{10}H_8)$ is $\Delta H^{\circ}_{298} = -1231.6$ kcal mole^{-1}. The products are CO_2 and liquid H_2O. Find the standard enthalpy of formation of naphthalene at 25°C.

2-I-19. (a) The standard enthalpy of combustion (ΔH_c°) of crystalline benzoic acid, C_6H_5COOH, to $CO_2(g)$ and $H_2O(l)$ is -771.72 kcal mole^{-1} at 25°C. Find ΔH° and ΔE° of formation of benzoic acid from its elements at 25°C. (b) Find $\Delta H°$ of formation of crystalline benzoic acid at 100°C. Assume that the following heat capacities are constant over the temperature range involved:

	$C_6H_5COOH(c)$	C (graphite)	$H_2(g)$	$O_2(g)$
$\bar{C}_P°$, cal °K⁻¹ mole⁻¹	35.1	2.0	4.9	5.0

2-I-20. On the basis of the following enthalpy changes evaluate $\Delta \bar{H}°$ for the ionization of aqueous m-chlorophenol (m-CP) [O'Hara and Hepler, *J. Phys. Chem.*, **65**, 2107 (1961)].

$$m\text{-CP}(l) \to m\text{-CP}(aq) \qquad \Delta H_1° = 674 \text{ cal mole}^{-1}$$
$$m\text{-CP}(l) + OH^-(aq) \to m\text{-CP}^-(aq)$$
$$+ H_2O(l) \qquad \Delta H_2° = -7540 \text{ cal mole}^{-1}$$
$$H_2O(l) \to H^+(aq) + OH^-(aq) \qquad \Delta H_3° = 13,500 \text{ cal mole}^{-1}$$

2-I-21. At 298.16°K the standard enthalpy of combustion of *cis*-hexahydroindan (C_9H_{16}) is -1351.60 kcal mole⁻¹[Browne and Rossini, *J. Phys. Chem.*, **64**, 927 (1960)]. The combustion process may be represented by the equation

$$cis\text{-}C_9H_{16}(l) + 13O_2(g) \to 9CO_2(g) + 8H_2O(l)$$

(a) Calculate the standard enthalpy of formation of 1 mole of *cis*-hexahydroindan from the elements at 298.16°K. (b) How would the answer be changed if diamond instead of graphite were chosen as the standard state of C?

$$C(\text{diamond}) \to C(\text{graphite}), \quad \Delta H_{298}° = -0.45 \text{ kcal.}$$

2-I-22. On the basis of the following data [Huff, Squitieri, and Snyder, *J. Am. Chem. Soc.*, **70**, 3380 (1948)], evaluate the standard enthalpy of formation of tungsten carbide, $WC(s)$.

$$C(\text{graphite}) + O_2(g) \to CO_2(g) \qquad \Delta H_{298}° = -94.052 \text{ kcal}$$
$$WC(s) + \tfrac{5}{2}O_2(g) \to WO_3(s) + CO_2(g) \qquad -285.80$$
$$W(s) + \tfrac{3}{2}O_2(g) \to WO_3(s) \qquad -200.16$$

2-I-23. Kistiakowsky and co-workers [Kistiakowsky, Ruhoff, Smith, and Vaughan, *J. Am. Chem. Soc.*, **57**, 876 (1935); **58**, 137, 146

(1936)] measured the standard enthalpies of hydrogenation of cyclohexene and benzene and obtained the following results:

Reaction	$\Delta H°$ of hydrogenation, kcal mole^{-1}

(a)

$+ H_2 \rightarrow$

−28.59

(b)

$+ 3H_2 \rightarrow$

−49.80

On the basis of (a) estimate the standard enthalpy of hydrogenation of benzene and explain why the answer thus obtained is quite different from the measured value of 49.80 kcal mole^{-1}.

2-I-24. The standard enthalpy of combustion of aluminum borohydride, $Al(BH_4)_3(l)$, was found to be −989.1 kcal mole^{-1} at 298.2°K [Rulon and Mason, *J. Am. Chem. Soc.*, **73**, 5491 (1951)], the reaction being:

$$Al(BH_4)_3(l) + 6O_2(g) \rightarrow \tfrac{1}{2}Al_2O_3 \text{ (crystal, corundum)}$$
$$+ \tfrac{3}{2}B_2O_3 \text{ (crystal)} + 6H_2O(l)$$

Calculate the standard enthalpy of formation of $Al(BH_4)_3(g)$. The enthalpy of vaporization of $Al(BH_4)_3(l)$ is 7.2 kcal mole^{-1}, and the standard enthalpies of formation of some other compounds necessary for the calculation are as follows:

$$Al_2O_3\text{(crystal, corundum)} = -399.09;$$
$$B_2O_3\text{(crystal)} = -303 \text{ kcal mole}^{-1}$$

2-I-25. At 298.2°C the standard enthalpy of formation of $Mg(NO_3)_2$ is −188,770 cal mole^{-1}, and the standard enthalpy of solution is −21,530 cal mole^{-1}; the standard enthalpy of formation of of the NO_3^- ion is −49,320 cal (g ion)$^{-1}$. Calculate the standard enthalpy of formation of the Mg^{2+} ion at this temperature. [Stephenson, *J. Am. Chem. Soc.* **68**, 721 (1946)].

2-I-26. The standard enthalpy of combustion of pyridine (*l*) at 298.15°K is −664.95 kcal mole^{-1} [Hubbard, Frow, and

Waddington, *J. Phys. Chem.*, **65**, 1326 (1961)]. Calculate the standard enthalpy of formation of pyridine at 298.15°K.

2-I-27. Find (a) $\Delta H°$ and $\Delta E°$ at 25°C for the reaction $4NH_3(g) + 3O_2(g) \rightarrow 2N_2(g) + 6H_2O(l)$.

(b) $\Delta H°$ for the reaction of (a) at 50°C, assuming the following heat capacities at constant pressure:

Substance	$\bar{C}_P°$, cal °K^{-1} mole^{-1}
NH_3	8.89
O_2	6.97
N_2	6.94
$H_2O(l)$	18.02

2-I-28.

	$\Delta H_{300}°$ of formation, kcal mole^{-1}	$\bar{C}_P°$, cal °K^{-1} mole^{-1}
A	0	5.00 + 0.0020 T
B	−50.00	7.00
AB$_2$	−80.00	8.00

(a) Obtain an expression for $\Delta H°$ for the reaction

$$A + 2B \rightarrow AB_2$$

as a function of temperature. Your expression must contain only T and actual numbers.

(b) Evaluate $\Delta H°$ for this reaction at 1000°K.

2-I-29. Given the following data:

		$\Delta H°$, kcal (at 18°C)
(a)	$Fe(s) + 2HCl(aq) \rightarrow FeCl_2(aq) + H_2(g)$	−21.0
(b)	$FeCl_2(s) + aq \rightarrow FeCl_2(aq)$	−19.5
(c)	$HCl(g) + aq \rightarrow HCl(aq)$	−17.5
(d)	$H_2(g) + Cl_2(g) \rightarrow 2HCl(g)$	−44.0

	$Fe(s)$	$Cl_2(g)$	$FeCl_2(s)$
$\bar{C}_P°$, cal mole^{-1} °K^{-1}	6.0	8.2	18.5

For solid $FeCl_2$, find (a) $\Delta H°$ of formation at 18°C, (b) $\Delta E°$ of formation at 18°C, and (c) $\Delta H°$ of formation at 118°C.

2-I-30.   Using bond enthalpies from the following table evaluate ΔH for the isomerization of ethyl alcohol to dimethyl ether:

$$CH_3CH_2OH(g) \rightarrow CH_3OCH_3(g)$$

Empirical bond enthalpies at 25°C	
Bond	ΔH, kcal mole^{-1}
H$-$H	104
O$-$O	33
O$-$H	111
C$-$H	99
C$-$O	84
C$-$C	83

2-I-31. $dU = xy^2\,dx + x^2y\,dy$ $dW = (\sin y)\,dx + (\sin x)\,dy$

(a) Ascertain whether dU and dW are exact (perfect) or inexact differentials.

(b) For each differential that is exact find the function (U or W) of which it is the differential by integrating over a suitable path. Show in a diagram the path that you choose.

SECTION 2-II

2-II-1.   Since $C_V = (\partial E/\partial T)_V$ by definition, one often writes, without any restrictions understood, "$dE = C_V\,dT$." It is not generally true, however, that $dE = C_V\,dT$; $dE = C_V\,dT$ only under special circumstances. What are the circumstances?

2-II-2.   Show that the work involved in the reversible adiabatic expansion of 1 mole of an ideal gas is given by the formula

$$w = \bar{C}_V T_1 \left[1 - \left(\frac{P_2}{P_1} \right)^{R/\bar{C}_P} \right]$$

if $\bar{C}_V$ and $\bar{C}_P$ are independent of temperature.

2-II-3. In an infinitesimal compression of a liquid or solid under a pressure P the changes in energy E, volume V, and temperature T are approximately related by the expression $d\bar{E} = \bar{C}_V\, dT + (kT - P)\, d\bar{V}$, where k is a constant characteristic of the substance. Obtain an equation relating the initial and final volumes to the initial and final temperatures in a reversible, adiabatic compression of a liquid or solid with constant heat capacity $\bar{C}_V$.

2-II-4. An imaginary gas has the equation of state $PV^2 = n^2KT$ (where K is a constant), and its heat capacity C_V is independent of temperature and pressure. For this gas $\bar{E}$ depends only on T, as for an ideal gas.
(a) Obtain an equation that relates the initial and final pressures to the initial and final temperatures in a reversible adiabatic expansion of this gas.
(b) Find $\bar{C}_P - \bar{C}_V$ for this gas in terms of P, T, and K.

2-II-5. For a gas described by van der Waals' equation, $(\partial \bar{E}/\partial \bar{V})_T = a/\bar{V}_2$. Obtain an equation that relates the initial and final temperatures to the initial and final volumes in a reversible adiabatic expansion of a van der Waals gas for which $\bar{C}_V = A + BT$ with A and B constant.

2-II-6. Derive the general formula

$$\mu_{\mathrm{JT}} = -\frac{1}{C_P}\left(\frac{\partial H}{\partial P}\right)_T$$

2-II-7. Evaluate the Joule-Thomson coefficient

$$\mu_{\mathrm{JT}} = \frac{1}{C_P}\left[T\left(\frac{\partial V}{\partial T}\right)_P - V\right] = \left(\frac{\partial T}{\partial P}\right)_H$$

in terms of a, R, T, and C_P for a gas that has the equation of state $V = nRT/P - na/R^2T^2$. Would the gas have an inversion temperature? Explain.

2-II-8. The Joule-Thomson coefficient of a van der Waals gas is given by the equation

$$\mu_{\mathrm{JT}} = \frac{1}{C_P}\left(\frac{2a}{RT} - b - \frac{3abP}{R^2T^2}\right).$$

Derive an expression for the inversion temperature as a function of pressure.

2-II-9.   Show that

$$\left(\frac{\partial C_P}{\partial P}\right)_T = -\mu_{JT}\left(\frac{\partial C_P}{\partial T}\right)_P - C_P\left(\frac{\partial \mu_{JT}}{\partial T}\right)_P$$

2-II-10.   Prove that for any substance

$$C_P - C_V = \left[P + \left(\frac{\partial E}{\partial V}\right)_T\right]\left(\frac{\partial V}{\partial T}\right)_P$$

2-II-11.   Show that each of the formulas listed below simplifies to $\bar{C}_P - \bar{C}_V = R$ for the special case of an ideal gas.

(a) $\bar{C}_P - \bar{C}_V = \left[P + \left(\frac{\partial E}{\partial V}\right)_T\right]\left(\frac{\partial \bar{V}}{\partial T}\right)_P$

(b) $\bar{C}_P - \bar{C}_V = -T\left(\frac{\partial \bar{V}}{\partial T}\right)_P^2 \Big/ \left(\frac{\partial \bar{V}}{\partial P}\right)_T$

(c) $\bar{C}_P - \bar{C}_V = T\bar{V}\alpha^2/\beta$

where

$$\alpha = \frac{1}{V}\left(\frac{\partial V}{\partial T}\right)_P \qquad \text{and} \qquad \beta = -\frac{1}{V}\left(\frac{\partial V}{\partial P}\right)_T$$

2-II-12.   (a) In an experiment to determine the enthalpy of neutralization of HCl with NaOH, Hale, Izatt, and Christensen [*J. Phys. Chem.*, **67**, 2605 (1963)] mixed HCl and NaOH solutions in a precision calorimeter and the temperature of the contents of the calorimeter rose $0.2064°C$. The amount of water produced by the reaction was 3.407_5 millimoles. Furthermore it was determined electrically that the heat capacity of the calorimeter and its contents was 223.9 cal $°C^{-1}$. Calculate the enthalpy of neutralization per mole HCl. It is necessary to add algebraically a correction of $+155$ cal per mole H_2O produced to the final result to adjust for the enthalpy of mixing HCl and NaOH solutions before the reaction takes place.

(b) In another experiment the same workers found that the enthalpy of neutralization of $HClO_4$ is, within experimental error, the same as that of HCl. On the other hand the enthalpy of neutralization of acetic acid with NaOH is -13.300 kcal mole^{-1}. How do you account for the fact that the enthalpies of neutralization of HCl and $HClO_4$ are identical but different from that of acetic acid?

2-II-13. For the reaction C (graphite) $+ CO_2(g) \rightarrow 2CO(g)$, express $\Delta H°$ as a function of temperature. Your result should contain only T and actual numbers. State the range of temperature in which your expression is valid.

2-II-14. For the reaction $H_2S(g) + \frac{3}{2}O_2(g) \rightarrow H_2O(g) + SO_2(g)$, (a) Find $\Delta H°$ and $\Delta E°$ at 25°C; (b) find $\Delta H°$ at 1000°K. (c) Do you have enough information to find $\Delta H°$ at 2000°K? Explain.

2-II-15. For the reaction $3A_2(g, 1 \text{ atm}) = 2A_3(g, 1 \text{ atm})$, $\Delta H°_{300} = -35,000$ cal. Making use of this fact and also the information given in the table below, derive a general expression of the form $\Delta H° = A + BT + CT^2 + D/T$ valid over the temperature range 300 to 500°K for the standard enthalpy of reaction as a function of temperature. Evaluate all constants numerically.

$$\bar{C}_p° \text{ (cal mole}^{-1} \text{ °K}^{-1}) = a + bT + c/T^2$$

	a	$b \times 10^3$	$c \times 10^{-5}$	Range of Validity
$A_2(g)$	2.00	2.00	4.00	300–500°K
$A_3(g)$	6.00	5.50	8.00	300–500°K

2-II-16. Find $\Delta H°$ at 1000°K for the reaction $O_2(g) \rightarrow 2O(g)$. $\Delta H°_{298} = 117.04$ kcal. $\bar{C}_p(O) = \frac{5}{2}R$.

2-II-17. Derive an equation for $\Delta H°$ of the following reaction as a function of temperature. The final equation must contain only T and numbers.

$$A(s) + 2B_2(g) \rightleftharpoons AB_4(g), \qquad \Delta H°_{300} = 500,000 \text{ cal}$$

$\bar{C}_p(A, s) = 5.00 + 3.00 \times 10^{-3}T$ cal mole^{-1} °K^{-1}
$\bar{C}_p(B_2, g) = 6.00 + 4.00 \times 10^{-3}T$ cal mole^{-1} °K^{-1}
$\bar{C}_p(AB_4, g) = 7.00 + 5.00 \times 10^{-3}T$ cal mole^{-1} °K^{-1}

2-II-18. For the hypothetical reaction $2A(g) \rightarrow A_2(g)$, $\Delta C_p = 1.00 + 2.00 \times 10^{-3}T$ cal °K^{-1} and $\Delta H°_{298} = -5.000$ kcal. Estimate the temperature at which $\Delta H° = 0$ for this reaction at constant pressure.

2-II-19. Calculate the maximum possible temperature produced by a flame consisting initially of 1 part by volume of $H_2(g)$ and 5 parts by volume of air (20 volume percent $O_2(g)$, 80 volume percent $N_2(g)$), if the ignition temperature is 25°C. What are you assuming about the given heat capacity expressions?

$$\bar{C}_P = a + bT \text{ cal mole}^{-1} \text{ °K}^{-1}$$

	a	$b \times 10^{-3}$
$H_2(g)$	6.947	−0.200
$O_2(g)$	6.095	3.253
$N_2(g)$	6.449	1.413
$H_2O(g)$	7.219	2.374

2-II-20. On the basis of the following thermodynamic information [Parris, Raybin, and Labowitz, *J. Chem. and Eng. Data*, **9**, 221 (1964)], estimate the enthalpy of combustion of the compound triethylenediamine (*s*). The products are $CO_2(g)$, $H_2O(l)$, and $N_2(g)$. Formula:

Property	Value, kcal mole^{-1}
(a) C−C bond energy	83.1
(b) H−H bond energy	104.2
(c) C−H bond energy	98.8
(d) ΔH_f° $CO_2(g)$	−94.0518
(e) ΔH_f° $H_2O(l)$	−68.3174
(f) ΔH_f° $CH_3CH_3(g)$	−20.236
(g) $\Delta H_{combustion}^\circ$ $(CH_3)_3N(g)$	−583.7
(h) $\Delta H_{sublimation}^\circ$ $N(CH_2CH_2)_3N$	14.8

2-II-21. Ascertain whether $dz = xy\, dx + \frac{1}{2}x^2\, dy$ is an exact (perfect) differential. If it is, discover the function z of which it is a differential. If it is not, exhibit two different values for $\int dz$ obtained from two different paths of integration between the same points.

2-II-22. Let $dz = xy(dx + dy)$

(a) Ascertain whether dz is an exact or inexact differential.
(b) Evaluate $\int_{(0,0)}^{(1,2)} dz$ along any two different paths joining the origin to the point $x = 1, y = 2$.

SECTION 2-III

2-III-1. (a) For a van der Waals gas, $(\partial \bar{E}/\partial \bar{V})_T = a/\bar{V}^2$. Find $(\partial T/\partial \bar{V})_{\bar{E}}$ for a van der Waals gas for which $\bar{C}_V = \frac{3}{2}R$, in terms of a, R, and $\bar{V}$. (b) The gas described in (a) is xenon. One mole of xenon is allowed to expand adiabatically into a vacuum from an initial volume of 1.00 liter to a final volume of 2.00 liters. For xenon, $a = 4.19$ liter^2 atm mole^{-2}. Calculate the temperature change of the gas in this expansion.

2-III-2. A student made the following erroneous statement in a laboratory report on bomb calorimetry: "$\Delta H = \Delta E + P \Delta V$. Since the bomb calorimetry process is a constant volume one, $\Delta V = 0$, and $\Delta E = \Delta H$." Explain why this argument is incorrect.

2-III-3. The heat capacity, $C = dq/dT$, is usually measured at constant pressure or constant volume; however, other variables may be held constant instead of P or V. Express C_H (at constant enthalpy) in terms of any or all of the quantities T, P, V, C_P, $(\partial V/\partial T)_P$, and $(\partial V/\partial P)_T$. Assume that the system is closed, homogeneous, and has only two degrees of freedom (T and H in this case), and that no work other than $P - V$ work is done.

2-III-4. Prove that if $(\partial E/\partial V)_T = 0$, then it follows that $(\partial E/\partial P)_T = 0$.

2-III-5. Prove that it does not necessarily follow that if $(\partial E/\partial V)_T = 0$, then $(\partial H/\partial V)_T = 0$.

2-III-6. From the formula

$$\mu_{JT} = \frac{1}{C_P}\left[T\left(\frac{\partial V}{\partial T}\right)_P - V\right]$$

it can be seen that the mathematical condition for the inversion temperature T_i is that $T_i(\partial V/\partial T)_P - V = 0$. We can rewrite this condition in terms of the reduced variables $\pi = P/P_c$, $\phi = V/V_c$, and $\theta = T/T_c$, in which case the condition becomes $\theta_i(\partial\phi/\partial\theta)_\pi - \phi = 0$. Apply this last expression to the reduced form of the van der Waals equation

$$(\pi + 3/\phi^2)(3\phi - 1) = 8\theta$$

and show that

$$\theta_i = \frac{3(3\phi - 1)^2}{4\phi^2} \quad \text{and} \quad \pi_i = \frac{9(2\phi - 1)}{\phi^2}$$

2-III-7. For a gas that has the equation of state $P(\bar{V} - nb) = nRT$, $(\partial E/\partial V)_T = 0$. For this gas derive an expression involving only constants (such as b and R) and readily measurable physical properties (such as P or $\bar{V}$, and n, T, $\bar{C}_P$, and $\bar{C}_V$) for:

(a) The coefficient of thermal expansion, α, where

$$\alpha = (1/V)(\partial V/\partial T)_P$$

(b) The work done upon the surroundings by the gas during its isothermal reversible expansion from $\bar{V}_i$ to $\bar{V}_f$.

(c) The function of T and $\bar{V}$ for the reversible adiabatic expansion analogous to the ideal gas formula $(T_1/T_2) = (\bar{V}_2/\bar{V}_1)^{\gamma-1}$, where $\gamma = \bar{C}_P/\bar{C}_V$. Assume that $\bar{C}_P$ and $\bar{C}_V$ are constant.

(d) The Joule-Thomson coefficient,

$$\mu_{JT} = \left(\frac{\partial T}{\partial P}\right)_H = \frac{1}{C_P}\left[T\left(\frac{\partial V}{\partial T}\right)_P - V\right]$$

CHAPTER 3

The second law

of thermodynamics

SECTION 3-1

3-I-1. $\Delta S = \Delta H/T$ for which one of the following cases:

(a) A process for which $\Delta n_{gas} = 0$?
(b) A process for which $\Delta C_P = 0$?
(c) A process at constant pressure?
(d) An adiabatic process?
(e) An isothermal, reversible phase transition?

3-I-2. The molar heat capacity of a certain metal at 20°K is b cal deg^{-1} mole^{-1}. The absolute entropy of this metal at 20°K is best given by which of the following expressions:

(a) $\int_0^T \frac{C_P \, dT}{T} = b \ln \frac{20}{0}$?

(b) $\int_0^T \frac{bT^3}{T} \, dT = \int_0^T bT^2 \, dT = \frac{b}{3} T^3 = \frac{b}{3} (20)^3$?

(c) The graphical integration of $\bar{C}_P/T$ vs. T?

(d) $(20)^{-3} \int_0^T bT^2 \, dT = \frac{b}{3}$?

(e) $b(20 - 0)$?

(f) $\frac{1}{b} (20 - 0)$?

3-I-3. Calculate ΔS for the isobaric heating of 1 mole of N_2 from 300°K to 1000°K.

$$\bar{C}_P = 6.4492 + 1.4125 \times 10^{-3}T - 0.807 \times 10^{-7}T^2.$$

3-I-4. 200 g of tin [heat capacity 6.1 cal (g atom)$^{-1}$] initially at 100.0°C and 100 g of water (heat capacity 18.0 cal mole^{-1}) initially at 25.0°C are mixed together in a calorimeter. Assuming that the heat capacities are constant and that no heat is lost or gained by the surroundings or by the calorimeter itself, what is (a) the final temperature of the system, and (b) the entropy change for (i) the tin, (ii) the water, and (iii) the universe?

3-I-5. Calculate the maximum theoretical efficiency of a reversible heat engine operating between 25°C and 100°C.

3-I-6. The efficiency of a refrigerator cycle is defined in terms of its coefficient of performance,

$$\omega = \frac{q_1}{-w} \leqslant \frac{T_1}{T_2 - T_1}$$

where T_1 and T_2 are the temperatures of the cold box and of the surroundings, q_1 is the amount of heat withdrawn from the cold box, and $-w$ is the work required.

(a) Calculate the maximum ω for a refrigerator that operates between 25°C and -5°C.

(b) Calculate the minimum amount of work that must be done by the motor to withdraw 1 calorie of heat from the cold box at -5°C and release it to the room at 25°C.

3-I-7. A heat pump is essentially a refrigerator operated in reverse; that is, it is used to heat the system at a higher temperature T_2 by cooling (pumping heat from) the surroundings at a lower temperature. Thus a heat pump could be used to warm a house by pumping heat from the cold outdoors and delivering it to the warm interior of the house. The advantage of this method over conventional methods of heating is that the maximum efficiency of a refrigerator is so much greater than that of other methods of heating. Consider, for example, a heat pump with a coefficient of performance

$$\omega = \frac{-q_1}{w} = \frac{T_1}{T_2 - T_1} = 7.0$$

where q_1 is the amount of heat absorbed at the lower temperature. Calculate q_2/w, the ratio of the heat liberated at the higher temperature to the work done.

3-I-8.   Two moles of an ideal monatomic gas initially at 1 atm and 300°K are put through the following cycle, all stages of which are reversible: (I) isothermal compression to 2 atm, (II) isobaric temperature increase to 400°K, (III) return to the initial state by the path $P = a + bT$, where a and b are constants. Sketch the cycle on a P-T plot and evaluate numerically ΔE and ΔS for the working substance for each stage of the cycle.

3-I-9.   Calculate $\Delta \bar{S}$ for the mixing of 1 mole of nitrogen with 3 moles of oxygen at 25°C and a final total pressure of 1.00 atm. The initial pressure of each gas is 1.00 atm.

3-I-10.   For an ideal gas (or a real gas at 0 pressure), which of the following is (are) true? (a) $f = P$, (b) $\gamma = 1$, (c) $f/P = 0$, (d) $f/P = f/0 = \infty$, (e) $\gamma = 0$. f is fugacity, P is pressure, and γ is the fugacity coefficient.

3-I-11.   Evaluate $\ln \gamma$ for a gas that has the equation of state $P(\bar{V} - b) = RT$.

3-I-12.   The normal boiling point of benzene is 80.1°C. Estimate the molar heat of vaporization of benzene at this temperature.

SECTION 3-II

3-II-1.   The process $2H_2(g, 1 \text{ atm}, 25°C) + O_2(g, 1 \text{ atm}, 25°C) \rightarrow 2H_2O$ (liq, 1 atm, 25°C) is usually regarded as "spontaneous" (that is, thermodynamically possible). Is it possible to carry out the process under conditions of (a) isolation, (b) constant temperature and pressure, (c) constant temperature and volume? Explain.

3-II-2.   Let us define a new thermodynamic function ψ by the equation

$$\psi = A + RT$$

where A, R, and T have their usual meanings. Prove that $\Delta\psi_{T,V}$ can be used as the basis for a criterion for equilibrium. That is, show that $\Delta\psi_{T,V} = 0$ for a reversible process and $\Delta\psi_{T,V} < 0$ for a spontaneous process.

3-II-3.   Write a mathematical expression for the entropy change taking place in the working substance under each of the following circumstances:

(a) Free expansion of 1 mole of an ideal gas from V_1 to V_2;
(b) Reversible, isothermal phase transition;
(c) Reversible, adiabatic expansion of 1 mole of an ideal gas from V_1 to V_2;
(d) Reversible, isothermal expansion of 1 mole of an ideal gas from V_1 to V_2.

3-II-4.   For a certain gas, the following is true:

$$\bar{C}_V = a + bT + cT^2$$

and

$$P(\bar{V} - B) = RT$$

Derive an expression for the entropy change of 1 mole of this gas that accompanies a change in its state from T_i, $\bar{V}_i$ to T_f, $\bar{V}_f$.

3-II-5.   Calculate (a) ΔS, (b) ΔH, (c) ΔE for the process

1 mole H_2O (*liq*, 20°C, 1 atm) → 1 mole H_2O (*g*, 250°C, 1 atm)

given the following data:

$\bar{C}_P$ (*liq*) $= 18.0$ cal deg^{-1} mole^{-1}
$\bar{C}_P$ (*g*) $= 8.6$ cal deg^{-1} mole^{-1}
$\Delta\bar{H}$ for vaporization of H_2O at 100°C and 1 atm $= 9720$ cal mole^{-1}

3-II-6.   (a) Find $\Delta H°$ at $1000°K$ for the reaction

$NaCl(s) \rightarrow Na(g) + \frac{1}{2}Cl_2(g)$

For this reaction

$\Delta H°_{298} = 124.1$ kcal

and

$\Delta C_P° = -1.585 - 3.82 \times 10^{-3}T - 0.34 \times 10^5 T^{-2}$

(b) Is it true that $\Delta S° = \Delta H°/T$ for (i) the reaction in (a) at $25°C$; (ii) the reaction $NaCl(s) \rightarrow NaCl(g)$ at $25°C$; (iii) the reaction $NaCl(liq) \rightarrow NaCl(g)$ at $1413°C$, the boiling point of NaCl? Explain in each case. Assume that the gases are ideal.

3-II-7. $\Delta \bar{H}$ of fusion of H_2O at $0°C = 1436$ cal mole^{-1}. The values of $\bar{C}_P$ for the solid and liquid are 8.9 and 18.0 cal deg^{-1} mole^{-1}, respectively. Calculate (a) $\Delta \bar{H}$, (b) $\Delta \bar{S}$, and (c) $\Delta \bar{G}$ for the process,

$H_2O\ (s,\ -10°C) \rightarrow H_2O\ (liq,\ -10°C)$

at constant pressure, 1 atm.

3-II-8.   For a certain process

$\Delta G°_{298} = B$ cal mole^{-1}

$\Delta H° = D + aT + bT^2 + cT^3$

Derive an expression for $\Delta G°$ for this process as a function of temperature.

3-II-9.   Make a rough sketch of the following cycle on a T-S diagram:

Step A. Isothermal expansion (at T_1) from P_1 to P_2.
Step B. Isochoric heating from P_2, T_1 to P_3, T_3.
Step C. Isobaric cooling from P_3, T_3 to P_1, T_1.

3-II-10.   The four stages of the Otto cycle are (see figure) I: isentropic compression, II: isochoric heat addition, III: isentropic expansion, IV: isochoric heat rejection. Show that the efficiency of a reversible Otto cycle with 1 mole of an ideal gas as the working substance is given by

$\eta = 1 - r^{(1-\gamma)}$

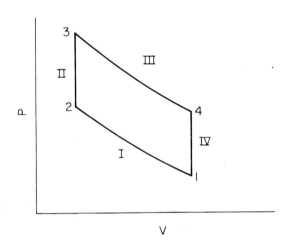

where $\gamma = C_P/C_V$ and r is the compression ratio (the ratio of the initial volume to the final volume for the compression process). What effect would an increase in the compression ratio have on the efficiency of the cycle?

3-II-11. Process A: One mole of an ideal monatomic gas expands isothermally at 300°K into a vacuum from an initial volume of 10 liters to a final volume of 20 liters.

Process B: One mole of the same gas expands isothermally and reversibly at 300°K from 10 to 20 liters.

(a) For each of the two processes, calculate q, w, ΔE, ΔH, ΔA, and ΔG.

(b) Describe a process by which the gas could be restored to its initial state after each of the processes A and B. Show how the surroundings could also be restored to their initial state after one process, and how the surroundings could not be restored to their initial state after the other process.

3-II-12. One mole of an ideal monatomic gas $(\bar{C}_V = \frac{3}{2}R)$ passes through the following reversible cyclic process (process A): (i) The gas is compressed adiabatically from pressure P_1 and temperature T_1 to pressure P_2 and temperature T_2 ; (ii) The gas is expanded isothermally from P_2 and T_2 to the initial pressure P_1 ; (iii) The gas is cooled isobarically (constant P) to the initial temperature T_1 .

(a) Express P_2 in terms of P_1 , T_1 , T_2 , and (if necessary) R.

(b) Find q, w, ΔE, and ΔS for the gas in each of the three steps (i), (ii), and (iii), and in the entire process in terms of any or all of the quantities P_1, T_1, T_2, and R.

(c) In process B steps (i) and (iii) are the same as the corresponding steps in process A, but step (ii) is carried out irreversibly by allowing the gas to expand into a vacuum to attain the same final conditions P_1 and T_2. Find q, w, ΔE, and ΔS for the gas in step (ii) of process B and in the entire process.

3-II-13. One gram of liquid water at $100°C$ is initially at 1.00 atm pressure and is confined to a volume in which no vapor is present. A valve is then opened and the water evaporates into an evacuated space of such volume that the final pressure is 0.10 atm. The entire apparatus is in a heat reservoir at $100°C$. ΔH for the vaporization of H_2O is 540 cal g^{-1} at $100°C$. Assume that the vapor is an ideal gas and that the volume of the liquid is negligible as compared to the volume of the vapor. Find q and ΔS for (a) the water, (b) the reservoir, and (c) the universe. (d) Describe a reversible process by which the water could be brought to the same final state. Show in what way the final state of the universe after this reversible process would differ from its state after the actual process.

3-II-14. (a) Show that $(\partial V/\partial S)_P = (\partial T/\partial P)_S$.

(b) Find $(\partial V/\partial S)_P$ for an ideal gas in terms of P, T, $\bar{C}_P$, and universal constants.

3-II-15. The thermodynamic equation of state,

$$(\partial E/\partial V)_T = T(\partial P/\partial T)_V - P,$$

applies to all substances. Derive it starting only with the first and second laws of thermodynamics and any necessary definitions and mathematical principles.

3-II-16. Starting only with definitions and mathematical principles, derive the formula $(\partial H/\partial P)_T = V - T(\partial V/\partial T)_P$.

3-II-17. Evaluate ΔS for the isothermal, reversible expansion at temperature T from volume V_1 to V_2 of 1 mole of a gas that has the equation of state $P\bar{V} = RT + A$. You may assume that $\Delta E = 0$ for this process.

3-II-18. Show that

$$\left(\frac{\partial S}{\partial P}\right)_T = \frac{nRV^2}{2n^2a - PV^2}$$

for a gas that has the equation of state

$$PV = nRT - \frac{n^2a}{V^2}$$

3-II-19. Evaluate ΔG and ΔA for the isothermal reversible expansion of 1 mole of a gas with the equation of state $P\bar{V} = RT(1 + B/\bar{V})$ from volume $\bar{V}_1$ to volume $\bar{V}_2$ at temperature T.

3-II-20. Show that for a van der Waals gas

$$\left(\frac{\partial T}{\partial \bar{V}}\right)_E = -\frac{a}{\bar{C}_V \bar{V}^2}$$

3-II-21. (a) Show that for a van der Waals gas

$$\left(\frac{\partial \bar{V}}{\partial T}\right)_S = \frac{-\bar{C}_V(\bar{V} - b)}{RT}$$

(b) Obtain an equation relating the initial and final temperatures to the initial and final volumes in a reversible adiabatic expansion of a van der Waals gas, preferably by using the result of (a). Assume that $\bar{C}_V$ is independent of T and $\bar{V}$.

3-II-22. The Dieterici equation of state is

$$P = \frac{RT}{\bar{V} - b} e^{-a/RT\bar{V}}$$

Show that for a Dieterici gas

$$\left(\frac{\partial E}{\partial V}\right)_T = \frac{ae^{-a/RT\bar{V}}}{(\bar{V} - b)\,\bar{V}}$$

3-II-23. Evaluate ΔG for the isothermal, reversible compression from P_1 to P_2 of 1 mole of a gas that has the equation of state

$$P\bar{V} = RT\left\{1 + \frac{9}{128}\left(\frac{P}{P_c}\right)\left(\frac{T_c}{T}\right)\left[1 - 6\left(\frac{T_c}{T}\right)^2\right]\right\}$$

where P_c and T_c are the critical constants.

3-II-24. The Berthelot equation of state is

$$P = \frac{RT}{\bar{V} - b} - \frac{a}{T\bar{V}^2}$$

where a and b are constants characteristic of the gas. For a gas that is described by this equation, show that

(a) $\left(\frac{\partial S}{\partial V}\right)_T = \frac{R}{\bar{V} - b} + \frac{a}{T^2\bar{V}^2}$

(b) $\left(\frac{\partial E}{\partial V}\right)_T = \frac{2a}{T\bar{V}^2}$

(c) $\left(\frac{\partial C_V}{\partial V}\right)_T = -\frac{2a}{T^2\bar{V}^2}$

(d) $\left(\frac{\partial \bar{V}}{\partial T}\right)_S = -\frac{\bar{C}_V}{T}\left(\frac{R}{\bar{V} - b} + \frac{a}{T^2\bar{V}^2}\right)^{-1}$

(e) $\left(\frac{\partial \bar{V}}{\partial T}\right)_P = \frac{[-R/(\bar{V} - b)] - [a/(T^2\bar{V}^2)]}{[-RT/(\bar{V} - b)^2] + (2a/T\bar{V}^3)}$

(f) $\bar{C}_P - \bar{C}_V = \frac{-T\{[R/(\bar{V} - b)] + [a/(T^2\bar{V}^2)]\}^2}{[-RT/(\bar{V} - b)^2] + (2a/T\bar{V}^3)}$

(g) For the special case in which $a = 0$ and $\bar{C}_V$ is independent of temperature obtain an equation that relates the initial and final volumes to the initial and final temperatures in a reversible adiabatic expansion of a Berthelot gas. Show how the result follows from one or more of the equations given in (a)–(f) above.

3-II-25. For N_2O at 0°C the fugacity (activity) coefficient $\gamma = f/P$ is 0.9847 at 3 atm and 0.6961 at 60 atm [Hirth and Kobe, *J. Chem. and Eng. Data*, **2**, 229 (1961)]. Evaluate ΔG in calories for the isothermal, reversible compression of 1 mole of this substance from 3 to 60 atm at 0°C, (a) assuming ideal gas behavior, (b) using the fugacity data given above.

3-II-26. A certain gas has the equation of state

$$P\bar{V} = RT + aP^{1/2} + bP + cP^{3/2}$$

Derive an equation relating the fugacity coefficient (γ) of this gas to the pressure P at constant temperature T.

3-II-27. A certain gas has the equation of state

$$\bar{V} = \frac{RT}{P}(1 + AP + BP^2)$$

where A and B are functions of temperature only. Find the fugacity coefficient $\gamma(=f/P)$ for this gas in terms of any or all of the quantities P, A, B, and universal constants.

3-II-28. At 10.3084 atm and $-15°C$, the molar volume of N_2O is 1.8566 liters [Hirth and Kobe, *J. Chem. and Eng. Data*, **2**, 229 (1961)]. Estimate the fugacity coefficient $\gamma = f/P$ for N_2O under these conditions.

3-II-29. Let a mixture of two gases, X and Y, have the equation of state

$$\frac{PV}{RT} = (n_x + n_y)(1 + \beta P) + \alpha(n_x n_y)^{1/2} P$$

where α and β may depend on T, but not on P, n_x, or n_y.
(a) Find the partial molal volume $\overline{V}_x$ in terms of P, T, α, β, n_x, n_y, and R.
(b) Find

$$\Delta \overline{G}_x = \int_{P_1}^{P_2} \overline{V}_x \, dP$$

for an isothermal expansion of the gas mixture from P_1 to P_2.

3-II-30. The volume V of liquid water at $t°C$ and 1 atm is related to the volume V_0 at $0°C$ and 1 atm by

$$V = V_0(1 - 6.427 \times 10^{-5} t + 8.5053 \times 10^{-6} t^2 - 6.7900 \times 10^{-8} t^3);$$

this expression is valid from 0 to $33°C$. The compressibility of water near $0°C$ and 1 atm is 5.25×10^{-5} atm^{-1}. Find the internal pressure $(\partial E/\partial V)_T$ of liquid water at $1.00°C$ and 1.00 atm. Indicate and explain any noteworthy difference between this result and the internal pressures of most liquids.

SECTION 3-III

3-III-1. Is the oribtal motion of the earth around the sun a case of perpetual motion and hence a violation of the laws of thermodynamics? Explain.

3-III-2. Is the ceaseless, chaotic motion of molecules in a gas a case of perpetual motion and hence a violation of the laws of thermodynamics? Explain.

3-III-3. (a) Is the Joule-Thomson experiment reversible? Explain by describing how one could, or could not, restore the gas to its initial state by the same path.

(b) Is the entropy of the gas constant in the Joule-Thomson experiment? If not, express $(\partial S/\partial P)_H$ in terms of any or all of the variables P, V, T, C_P, and C_V.

3-III-4. Two bodies at different temperatures are connected by a wire with infinitesimal thermal conductance so that heat flows infinitely slowly from the hot body to the cold body until they are at the same temperature. Is this process reversible? Explain briefly.

3-III-5. A person who has a superficial acquaintance with thermodynamics consults you about the following difficulty: "For the reaction $2H_2 + O_2 \rightarrow 2H_2O$, ΔS is negative as we can see in the tables of third-law entropies. Entropy has to increase in every process. Should we conclude that this reaction is impossible?" Explain what the incorrect assumption is, what the corresponding correct statement is, and the special conditions, if any, under which the original assumption and conclusion would become correct.

3-III-6. A person who has a superficial acquaintance with thermodynamics consults you about the following difficulty: "I thought that every spontaneous process is accompanied by an increase of entropy, but on calculating the entropy change for the freezing of 1 mole of supercooled water at $-5°C$, which I know intuitively to be a spontaneous process, I obtain an entropy change of -5.04 cal $°K^{-1}$ mole^{-1} for the H_2O. Since this is a spontaneous process, why isn't the entropy change positive?" Explain what the incorrect assumption is, what the corresponding correct statement is, and the special conditions, if any, under which the original assumption and conclusion would become correct.

3-III-7. Each of the following statements is true in some cases and not in others. Describe the conditions under which each is true, and show how it should be modified or replaced in order to obtain a statement that would be more generally true.

(a) $dG = -S\,dT + V\,dP$.

(b) For a process in which a liquid freezes to a solid, $\Delta S = \Delta H/T$.

(c) When two phases (α and β) are in equilibrium, $a_{i\alpha} = a_{i\beta}$, where a_i is the activity of component i.

3-III-8. For an adiabatic process $q = 0$ (by definition) and therefore $q/T = 0/T = 0$. Why, then, is there an entropy increase ($\Delta S > 0$) in an adiabatic expansion into a vacuum?

3-III-9. A solid at its melting point T_m is melted to liquid at T_m by transferring irreversibly to it a quantity of heat q. It is true that for this process $\Delta S = q/T_m$? If it is true, why and under what assumptions are we justified in ignoring the fact that the process is irreversible? If it is false, how can a correct expression for ΔS be obtained?

3-III-10. Why in the use of entropy as a criterion for spontaneity do we have to consider $\Delta S_{\text{universe}} = \Delta S_{\text{system}} - \Delta S_{\text{surroundings}}$, but in the case of the Gibbs free energy we have to consider only ΔG_{system} (not $\Delta G_{\text{universe}} = \Delta G_{\text{system}} - \Delta G_{\text{surroundings}}$)?

3-III-11. The functions A and G are useful as criteria for spontaneity because

$$dA_{V,T} = dq - T\,dS$$

and

$$dG_{P,T} = dq - T\,dS$$

that is, they both reduce under the indicated restrictions to $dq - T\,dS$. Why not, then, define a new function, X, such that $dX = dq - T\,dS$ directly with no restrictions on P, V, or T?

3-III-12. (a) The following argument, intended to apply to any isothermal process, contains several fallacies. Point them out and describe the special circumstances (if any) under which each statement would become correct.

$$\Delta S = \frac{q}{T} \tag{1}$$

$$\Delta H = q \tag{2}$$

$$\Delta G = \Delta H - T \Delta S \tag{3}$$

$$= q - T \left(\frac{q}{T} \right) = 0 \tag{4}$$

(b) By suitable revisions of the argument in (a) obtain the result

$$\Delta G = q' - q''$$

where q' and q'' are the quantities of heat absorbed when the system goes from the initial state to the final state by two different paths. Describe each of these paths.

3-III-13. Using the equations $dE = T\,dS - P\,dV$ and $H = E + PV$, prove that

$$\left(\frac{\partial E}{\partial S} \right)_P = T - P \left(\frac{\partial T}{\partial P} \right)_S$$

3-III-14. Prove that

$$\left(\frac{\partial S}{\partial E} \right)_H = \frac{-C_P}{T[C_P(P\beta - 1) + PV\alpha(1 - T\alpha)]}$$

where

$$\alpha = \frac{1}{V} \left(\frac{\partial V}{\partial T} \right)_P \quad \text{and} \quad \beta = -\frac{1}{V} \left(\frac{\partial V}{\partial P} \right)_T$$

3-III-15. Prove that

(a) $\left(\dfrac{\partial S}{\partial P} \right)_H = -\dfrac{V}{T}$

(b) $\left(\dfrac{\partial S}{\partial V} \right)_P = \dfrac{C_V}{TV\alpha} + \dfrac{\alpha}{\beta}$

3-III-16. Prove each of the following relationships:

(a) $\left(\dfrac{\partial V}{\partial S} \right)_P = \dfrac{T}{C_P} \left(\dfrac{\partial V}{\partial T} \right)_P$

(b) $\left(\dfrac{\partial T}{\partial P} \right)_H = T \left(\dfrac{\partial V}{\partial H} \right)_P - V \left(\dfrac{\partial T}{\partial H} \right)_P$

3-III-17. For a gas that has the equation of state

$$P\bar{V} = RT - BP + APT,$$

where $\bar{V}$ is the molar volume and A and B are constants characteristic of the gas, show that

$$\bar{C}_P - \bar{C}_V = R\left(1 + \frac{AP}{R}\right)^2$$

3-III-18. Two samples (1 and 2), 1 mole each, of the same ideal gas occupy equal volumes V and are initially at temperatures T_1 and T_2 with $T_2 > T_1$. The molar heat capacity $\bar{C}_V$ is independent of temperature. The two containers are placed in contact through a heat-conducting but gas-impervious wall and the gases are allowed to come to the same temperature T_3, their volumes remaining constant. There is no leakage of heat except between the two gases. The containers have negligible heat capacities. Call this process A.

(a) Find T_3 in terms of the given quantities.

(b) Devise a reversible process (process B) by which the gases can be transferred from the initial state to the same final state. (There are at least two simple ways in which the temperature of a gas can be changed reversibly.)

(c) Find ΔS for each gas sample, for the surroundings, and for the universe in each step of process B and in the entire process.

(d) Find ΔS for each gas sample, for the surroundings, and for the universe in process A.

3-III-19. Consider a gas that has the equation of state

$$\frac{PV}{nRT} = 1 - \frac{n\beta}{VT}$$

(a) For this gas, show that (for $n = 1$ mole)

$$\left(\frac{\partial S}{\partial V}\right)_T = \frac{R}{V}$$
$$\left(\frac{\partial E}{\partial V}\right)_T = \frac{\beta R}{V^2}$$
$$\left(\frac{\partial H}{\partial V}\right)_T = \frac{2\beta R}{V^2}$$

Two identical flasks, each of volume V, are connected through a tube controlled by a stopcock. The flasks are immersed in a thermostat consisting of an equilibrium solid-liquid mixture, such as ice water. The thermostat is enclosed in a perfect thermal insulator. Initially one flask contains 1 mole of this gas; the other is empty. The stopcock is then opened and time is allowed for the restoration of equilibrium. Call this process A.

(b) Devise a reversible process (using different apparatus if you wish) by which the gas can be transferred from the same initial state to the same final state. Call this process B.

(c) For each of the processes A and B, find q, w, ΔE, and ΔS for (i) the gas; (ii) the surroundings, including the flasks, the thermostat, and any other apparatus that you introduced in process B; (iii) the universe.

3-III-20. A gas has the equation of state $(P + aP^2)(\bar{V} - b) = RT$, where a, b, and R are constants. Express $\bar{G} - \bar{G}°$, $\bar{S} - \bar{S}°$, and $\bar{H} - \bar{H}°$ for this gas in terms of P, T, a, b, and R. $\bar{G}°$ is defined as $\lim_{P \to 0}(\bar{G} - RT \ln P)$.

3-III-21. For a van der Waals gas,

(a) Show that

$$\left(\frac{\partial S}{\partial V}\right)_T = \frac{nR}{V - nb}$$

$$\left(\frac{\partial S}{\partial P}\right)_T = \frac{V - nb}{(2na/RV^3)(V - nb)^2 - T}$$

$$\left(\frac{\partial E}{\partial V}\right)_T = \frac{n^2a}{V^2}$$

$$\left(\frac{\partial H}{\partial P}\right)_T = \frac{V - nb}{(2na/RTV^3)(V - nb)^2 - 1} + V$$

$$\left(\frac{\partial E}{\partial P}\right)_T = \frac{(V - nb)^2}{(2/V)(V - nb)^2 - (V^2RT/na)}$$

(b) Evaluate ΔE, ΔH, ΔA, ΔG, and ΔS for an isothermal expansion.

(c) Obtain expressions for $\bar{G}$, f (fugacity), and $\gamma = f/P$ as functions of either P or V at constant T.

3-III-22. Two identical flasks, each of volume V, are connected through a tube controlled by a stopcock. The material of which this apparatus is constructed is a perfect thermal insulator.

Initially, n moles of a monatomic van der Waals gas are confined to one flask at a temperature T_0 and the other flask is empty; the stopcock is then opened and time is allowed for restoration of equilibrium. Assume that the gas has the same heat capacity ($\bar{C}_V = \frac{3}{2}R$) as if it were ideal. Find q, w, ΔE, ΔT, and ΔS for the gas in this process in terms of n, V, T_0, the van der Waals constants a and b, and universal constants.

3-III-23. For a van der Waals gas express the following in terms of T, $\bar{V}$, R, a, b, and $\bar{C}_V$:

(a) $(\partial \bar{C}_V / \partial \bar{V})_T$

(b) $(\partial T / \partial \bar{V})_E$

(c) $(\partial T / \partial \bar{V})_S$

These results may be of use in the remainder of the problem. One mole of a monatomic van der Waals gas at the initial temperature T_1 is confined to a volume V_1. It is then allowed to expand adiabatically

(d) Into an evacuated space

(e) Reversibly

so that its final volume in each case is V_2. Express its final temperature T_2 in terms of T_1, V_1, V_2, R, a, and b, for each of the processes (d) and (e).

(f) Evaluate T_2 numerically for each of the processes in (d) and (e), with $T_1 = 300°K$, $V_1 = 1.00$ liter, $V_2 = 100$ liters, $a = 10$ liter^2 atm mole^{-2}, and $b = 0$.

3-III-24. For a certain substance, $(\partial H / dP)_T = 0$ and $(\partial E / dV)_T = 0$.

(a) Show that this substance is an ideal gas (that is, has the equation of state $PV = kT$, where k is a constant).

(b) Ascertain whether either of these equations taken alone suffices to imply that the substance is an ideal gas.

3-III-25. A certain fictitious gas has at low pressure the approximate equation of state $\bar{V} = rT/P^2$, where $\bar{V}$ is the molar volume.

(a) Express the molar free energy $\bar{G}$ as a function of P, at fixed T, for this gas at low pressure.

(b) Define for this gas a standard molar free energy $\bar{G}°$, a fugacity f, and a fugacity coefficient $\gamma = f/P$ (such that

$\lim_{P \to 0} \gamma = 1$), in ways analogous to those used for real gases. Obtain a formula by which γ can be calculated when the exact equation of state is known.

3-III-26. The molar magnetization of a certain imaginary substance is given by $\bar{I} = (\bar{C}_1 \mathcal{H} / T^2)$, where $\bar{C}_1$ is a constant and $\mathcal{H}$ is the magnetic field. Show that for this substance

$$\left(\frac{\partial T}{\partial \mathcal{H}} \right)_S = \frac{2\bar{C}_1 \mathcal{H}}{T^2(\bar{C}_0 + (3\bar{C}_1 \mathcal{H}^2 / T^3))}$$

where $\bar{C}_0$ is the molar heat capacity at constant pressure and zero magnetic field.

3-III-27. A strip of rubber may be regarded as thermodynamically analogous to a confined gas. Stretching the rubber corresponds to compressing the gas. The work done on the rubber is $-dw = f\, dl$, where f is the contractile force exerted by the rubber and l its length.

(a) Define analogues of the Helmholtz and Gibbs free energies (A and G) for a strip of rubber.

(b) Show that for a process at constant T, $-dw \geqslant dA$, and that for a process at constant T and f, $-dw_{\text{useful}} \geqslant dG$. Formulate your own definition of w_{useful}. State the general thermodynamic principles from which your proofs begin.

(c) Obtain an equation for $(\partial E/\partial l)_T$ in terms of any or all of the quantities T, f, l, and their derivatives with respect to each other.

(d) An ideal rubber is one for which $(\partial E/\partial l)_T = 0$. Show what implications can be drawn about the equation of state (f-l-T relation) for an ideal rubber.

CHAPTER 4

The third law

of thermodynamics

SECTION 4-I

4-I-1. The heat capacity of uranium metal is 0.727 cal deg^{-1} mole^{-1} at 20°K [Flotow and Lohr, *J. Phys. Chem.*, **64**, 904 (1960)]. Calculate the standard absolute entropy of this substance in cal°K^{-1} mole at 20°K.

4-I-2. Estimate the zero-point entropy of NO.

SECTION 4-II

4-II-1. Explain the following statements in statistical terms:

(a) The entropy change in a chemical reaction usually approaches zero as the temperature approaches 0°K.

(b) The reaction $2C(graphite) + O_2(crystal) \rightarrow 2CO(crystal)$ is an exception to this rule.

4-II-2. A certain substance has a molar heat capacity $\bar{C}_P$ given (in cal mole^{-1} °K^{-1}) by the following equations:

$$\bar{C}_P(s) = 4.0 \times 10^{-5}T^3, 0 < T < 50°K$$
$$\bar{C}_P(s) = 5.00, 50 \leqslant T < 150°K$$
$$\bar{C}_P(liq) = 6.00, 50 < T < 400°K$$

At the melting point, 150°K, $\Delta \bar{H}$ of fusion = 300 cal mole⁻¹.

(a) Calculate the third-law molar entropy of this substance in the liquid state at 300°K.

(b) Calculate the molar enthalpy of fusion, entropy of fusion, and Gibbs free energy of fusion at 100°K. Is the sign of $\Delta \bar{G}$ reasonable?

4-II-3. On the basis of the following data [Giauque and Gordon, *J. Am. Chem. Soc.*, **71**, 2176 (1949)] calculate the molar entropy of ethylene oxide gas at the boiling point. Graphical integrations are required. Use the Debye T^3 law below 15°K.

T, °K	$\bar{C}_P$, cal mole⁻¹ °K⁻¹	T, °K	$\bar{C}_P$, cal mole⁻¹ °K⁻¹
15	0.60	160.65	19.80
20	1.43	170	19.66
25	2.34	180	19.55
30	3.30	190	19.49
35	4.26	200	19.47
40	5.21	210	19.50
45	6.02	220	19.56
50	6.77	230	19.67
60	8.16	240	19.82
70	9.22	250	20.00
80	10.06	260	20.21
90	10.76	270	20.46
100	11.43	280	20.67
110	12.06	285	20.77
120	12.77		
130	13.58		
140	14.47		
150	15.39		
160	16.30		
160.65	16.35		

Melting point = 160.65°K

Boiling point = 283.66°K

Enthalpy of fusion = 1236.4 cal mole⁻¹

Enthalpy of vaporization = 6101 cal mole⁻¹ at 1 atm

4-II-4. Calculate the standard molar entropy of gaseous platinum at 1000°K. Use only the following data, together with the

assumption that Pt is an ideal monatomic gas with negligible
electronic excitation below $1000°K$.

T, °K	$\dfrac{\bar{G}° - \bar{H}°_{298}}{T}$, cal mole^{-1} °K^{-1}
298.15	−45.96
1000	−49.17

4-II-5. By measurement of the equilibrium constant for the reaction
$H_2O(liq) + CO(g) \leftrightharpoons HCOOH(liq)$, Branch [*J. Am. Chem.
Soc.*, **37**, 2316 (1915)] found that the standard free energy of
formation of formic acid from the elements is −85,200 cal
mole^{-1} at 298°K. Gibson, Latimer, and Parks [*J. Am. Chem.
Soc.*, **42**, 1533 (1920)] found the standard free energy of
formation of formic acid from the elements at 298°K to be
−85,370 cal mole^{-1} by heat capacity measurements. The
two results may be considered to be identical within limits
experimental error. How does the agreement between the two
results offer experimental evidence for the validity of the third
law of thermodynamics?

CHAPTER 5

Liquids
and the liquefaction of gases

SECTION 5-1

5-I-1. The vapor pressure of a certain liquid is 2 torr at 300°K and 100 torr at 400°K. What is the vapor pressure at 500°K?

5-I-2. Make a rough estimate of the molar enthalpy of vaporization of *n*-pentane. The normal boiling point is 36°C.

5-I-3. Calculate the vapor pressure of the pure liquid of molecular weight 100 that loses 1.0000 g in weight when 0.5000 mole of N_2 at 1.00 atm is bubbled through it at 20.0°C. Assume that the N_2 is completely saturated with the vapor.

5-I-4. The viscosity of $OF_2(liq)$ was determined [Anderson, Schnizlein, Toole, and O'Brien, *J. Phys. Chem.*, **56**, 473 (1952)] using the Ostwald method. The viscosimeter was calibrated with water at 20°C and it was found that 363.4 sec were required for the flow of the water between the marks. The viscosity of water at 20°C is 1.005 centipoise; the density is 0.9982 g cm^{-3}. The time required for the flow of $OF_2(liq)$ between the marks at −145.8°C was 67.6 sec. The density of the $OF_2(liq)$ at this temperature was 1.523 g cm^{-3}. Calculate the absolute viscosity of the $OF_2(liq)$ at −145.8°C.

5-I-5. A steel ball with a radius of 1.00 mm and a density of 7.87 g cm^{-3} falls through a liquid of density 1.26 g cm^{-3} at a constant rate of 10.0 cm sec^{-1}. Calculate the viscosity in centipoise. The gravitational acceleration is 980.7 cm sec^{-2}. Stokes' law is

$$v = 2gr^2(\rho_s - \rho_{liq})/9\eta$$

5-I-6. How much effect would doubling the cross-sectional area of a capillary tube have on the height to which a liquid would rise in the capillary?

5-I-7. In an experiment to determine the surface tension of ethyl acetate by the capillary rise method, a student calibrated his capillary tube with benzene and observed that at 20.5°C benzene of density 0.878 g cm^{-3} and surface tension 28.8 dynes cm^{-1} rose 2.71 cm. He then found that ethyl acetate of density 0.900 g cm^{-3} rose 1.96 cm at the same temperature. Calculate (a) the radius of the capillary, and (b) the surface tension of the ethyl acetate at that temperature. What assumptions are made about the contact angles in (a) and (b)?

5-I-8. From the following data for acetic acid (molecular weight 60.1) determine the constant k in the Ramsay-Shields equation and the critical temperature of the liquid.

t, °C	20.0	75.0
γ, dynes cm^{-1}	27.4	22.3
ρ_{liq}, g cm^{-3}	1.049	0.9892

The Ramsay-Shields equation is

$$\gamma \left(\frac{M}{\rho}\right)^{2/3} = k(t_c - t - 6)$$

5-I-9. Orthobaric density data for the compound ethyl mercaptan are given below. ρ_v refers to the saturated vapor. The critical temperature is 225°C. Using a graph determine the critical density of this substance.

t, °C	100.0	200.0
ρ_{liq}, g cm^{-3}	0.74	0.53
ρ_v, g cm^{-3}	0.01	0.10

5-I-10. For a certain compound (molecular weight, 100) the following data are known. ρ_v is the density of the saturated vapor.

t, °C	0.0	20.0	40.0	60.0
ρ_v , g cm^{-3}	0.01	0.01	0.01	0.04
ρ_{liq} , g cm^{-3}	1.35	1.29	1.23	1.14
t	80.0	100.0	105.0	
ρ_v	0.10	0.26	0.34	
ρ_{liq}	1.02	0.80	0.70	

Determine (a) the critical temperature, (b) the critical density, and (c) the critical molar volume.

SECTION 5-II

5-II-1. The rate of change of vapor pressure with temperature is given by the Clapeyron equation,

$$\frac{dP}{dT} = \frac{\Delta \bar{H}_v}{T(\bar{V}_v - \bar{V}_{liq})} \tag{1}$$

where $\Delta \bar{H}_v$ is the molar enthalpy of vaporization and $\bar{V}_v$ and $\bar{V}_{liq}$ are the molar volumes of the vapor and liquid, respectively. One often sees a modified form known as the Clapeyron-Clausius equation,

$$\frac{1}{P}\frac{dP}{dT} = \frac{\Delta \bar{H}_v}{RT^2} \tag{2}$$

(a) Show how (2) can be derived from (1), pointing out any approximations that must be introduced.

(b) Let P_1 and P_2 be the vapor pressures of a liquid at the temperatures T_1 and T_2 , respectively. Using (2), find P_2 in terms of P_1 , T_1 , T_2 , $\Delta \bar{H}_v$, and R. Point out any further approximations that must be introduced.

5-II-2. Derive an equation for the temperature dependence of the vapor pressure of a liquid (analogous to the integrated form of the Clapeyron-Clausius equation) assuming that the vapor has the equation of state $P\bar{V} = RT + K$, where K is a constant. (Hint: Integrate by the method of partial fractions.)

5-II-3. Show that the variation of vapor pressure with temperature can expressed by the approximate formula,

$$P = k\left[1 - \left(\frac{\Delta\bar{H}_v}{RT}\right) + \frac{1}{2}\left(\frac{\Delta\bar{H}_v}{RT}\right)^2 - \frac{1}{6}\left(\frac{\Delta\bar{H}_v}{RT}\right)^3 + \cdots\right]$$

if $\Delta\bar{H}_v$ is independent of temperature.

5-II-4. According to a certain handbook the normal boiling point of ethylene glycol (formula weight 62.1) is 197°C and the enthalpy of vaporization is 191 cal g^{-1}. Estimate the temperature at which this substance would vacuum-distill in a system maintained at 30 torr.

5-II-5. Explain why the viscosity of a liquid decreases rapidly with increasing temperature.

5-II-6. In the double-capillary method for determining surface tension the difference Δh between the heights that a given liquid will rise in two capillaries of different radii is measured.

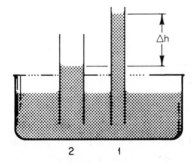

The apparatus is shown in the figure. Show that the surface tension of the liquid will then be given by the formula

$$\gamma = \frac{1}{2}\Delta h\left(\frac{r_1 r_2}{r_2 - r_1}\right)\rho g$$

where the subscripts refer to tubes 1 and 2, respectively, and $\Delta h = h_1 - h_2$.

5-II-7. The following data for the surface tension of benzene as a function of temperature were obtained by Sugden [*J. Chem. Soc.*, (London) 1167 (1924)]:

t, °C	20.0	32.5	41.5	54.8
γ, dynes cm^{-1}	28.88	27.30	26.08	24.28

The critical temperature of benzene is 561.6°C. Show that the data fit the Block equation, $\gamma = k(t_c - t)^n$, and evaluate the constants k and n.

5-II-8. The following data on the density and surface tension of liquid sulfur dioxide as a function of temperature were selected from those obtained by Stowe [*J. Am. Chem. Soc.*, **51**, 410 (1929)]:

t, °C	−20.3	−10	0.2	9.9
γ, dynes cm^{-1}	30.74	28.29	26.30	24.45
ρ, g cm^{-3}	1.4846	1.4601	1.4350	1.4095
t	20	30	40	50
γ	22.75	20.54	18.75	16.73
ρ	1.3831	1.3556	1.3264	1.2957

Show that these data fit the Ramsay-Shields equation, $\gamma(M/\rho)^{2/3} = k(t_c - 6 - t)$. Evaluate k and t_c.

5-II-9.

	ϵ	ν	n	ϵ/n^2
o-dichlorobenzene	7.47	10^6	1.5518	3.10
m-dichlorobenzene			1.54570	
p-dichlorobenzene	2.86	10^4	1.52104	1.24

ϵ is the dielectric constant; ν is the frequency in cycles per second at which ϵ was measured; n is the index of refraction for sodium light, which has a frequency of 5.10×10^{14} cps.

(a) The electromagnetic theory of light predicts that $n^2 = \epsilon$. Explain the conflict between this prediction and the data shown above.

(b) How would you expect ϵ/n^2 for *m*-dichlorobenzene to compare with the corresponding quantities for the *ortho* and *para* compounds? Explain.

5-II-10. Carbon disulfide, SCS, has linear molecules like those of carbon dioxide. It melts at $-109°C$ and boils at $46.3°C$. Its dielectric constant at $20°C$ for the frequency $9 \times 10^5 \text{ sec}^{-1}$ is 2.647. Estimate its index of refraction at $20°C$ for visible or infrared radiation. Explain.

5-II-11. In a substance composed of polar molecules the molar polarization (a) depends on the temperature and (b) is very different from the molar refraction. Explain.

CHAPTER 6

Solids

SECTION 6-I

6-I-1. For the cubic unit cell shown in the figure, how many ○ atoms and how many ● atoms are there per unit cell?

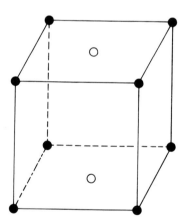

6-I-2. The Weiss indices of a certain crystal face are $\frac{1}{2}$, $\frac{2}{3}$, ∞. What are the corresponding Miller indices?

6-I-3. For the crystal face shown in the figure, what are the Weiss indices and what are the Miller indices?

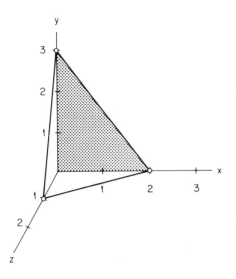

6-I-4. X-ray studies [Ring and Ritter, *J. Phys. Chem.*, **65**, 182 (1961)] indicate that potassium silyl, $KSiH_3$, formula weight 70.18, has a cubic structure of the NaCl type, with potassium at positions at 000, $\frac{1}{2}\frac{1}{2}0$, $0\frac{1}{2}\frac{1}{2}$, $\frac{1}{2}0\frac{1}{2}$ and silicon positions at $00\frac{1}{2}$, $\frac{1}{2}00$, $0\frac{1}{2}0$, $\frac{1}{2}\frac{1}{2}\frac{1}{2}$. The edge of the unit cell is 7.15 Å in length. No effort was made to locate the hydrogen atoms, all of which are held in the form of the silyl anion, SiH_3^-.

(a) Sketch a representative unit cell showing the relative positions of the potassium and silicon atoms.

(b) Calculate the distance in Ångstrom units between nearest potassium-silicon neighbors.

(c) Calculate the density of the crystal.

6-I-5. According to Soldate [(*J. Am. Chem. Soc.*, **69**, 987 (1947)], sodium borohydride, $NaBH_4$, has a face-centered cubic structure with four sodium atoms at 000, $0\frac{1}{2}\frac{1}{2}$, $\frac{1}{2}0\frac{1}{2}$, $\frac{1}{2}\frac{1}{2}0$, and four boron atoms at $\frac{1}{2}\frac{1}{2}\frac{1}{2}$, $\frac{1}{2}00$, $0\frac{1}{2}0$, $00\frac{1}{2}$. a_0 (unit cell edge length) = 6.15 Å.

(a) Sketch the unit cell, indicating the relative positions of the sodium and boron atoms.

(b) Calculate the density of the crystal.

6-I-6. Cesium bromide crystallizes in the cubic system. Its unit cell has a Cs^+ ion at the body center and a Br^- ion at each corner. Its density is 4.44 g cm^{-3}. Determine (a) the length of the unit cell edge, and (b) the d_{200} distance.

6-I-7.   CsI has the same structure as CsCl (two interpenetrating simple cubic lattices). The radii of the Cs^+ and I^- ions are 1.69 and 2.16 Å, respectively. Find (a) the volume of a unit cell in CsI, and (b) the density of CsI in g cm^{-3}.

6-I-8.   KCN has a density of 1.52 g cm^{-3} and crystallizes in the NaCl-type structure [Bozorth, *J. Am. Chem. Soc.*, **44**, 317 (1922)]. Calculate d_{100} for the unit cell.

6-I-9.   Calculate the density of silver. The metal is known to crystallize in the face-centered cubic form and the distance between nearest neighbor atoms is 2.87 Å.

6-I-10. The silver perchlorate-benzene complex, $AgClO_4 \cdot C_6H_6$, is orthorhombic with unit cell dimensions $a_0 = 7.96$, $b_0 = 8.34$, and $c_0 = 11.7$ Å. The formula weight is 285 and there are four molecules per unit cell [Rundle and Goring, *J. Am. Chem. Soc.*, **72**, 5337 (1950)]. Calculate the density of the crystal.

6-I-11. Lithium borohydride, $LiBH_4$, has an orthorhombic structure with four molecules per unit cell and unit cell dimensions of $a_0 = 6.81$, $b_0 = 4.43$, and $c_0 = 7.17$ Å [Harris and Meibohm, *J. Am. Chem. Soc.*, **69**, 1231 (1947)]. Calculate the density of this crystal.

6-I-12. A certain organic compound crystallizes in the orthorhombic system. The unit cell has edges of 12.05, 15.05, and 2.69 Å. There are two molecules per unit cell. The density of the crystal is 1.419 g cm^{-3}. Find the molecular weight of the compound.

SECTION 6-II

6-II-1.   What is the physical significance of the n (the "order" of the x-rays) in the Bragg equation, $n\lambda = 2d \sin \theta$?

6-II-2.   The crystal structure of potassium cyanide was studied by Bozorth [*J. Am. Chem. Soc.*, **44**, 317 (1922)], who found the following angles of reflection from the 100 planes:

Angle of reflection	5°23′	10°51′	4°47′	4°40′
Order of reflection	2	4	2	2
Wavelength, Å	0.614	0.614	0.545	0.534

The structure is cubic. Index the lines and indicate the type of cubic lattice. The following table will be helpful:

hkl	100	110	111	200	210	211	220	221, 300
$h^2 + k^2 + l^2$	1	2	3	4	5	6	8	9

hkl	310	311	222	320	321	400
$h^2 + k^2 + l^2$	10	11	12	13	14	16

6-II-3.   LiBr, NaBr, KBr, and RbBr all have the same crystal structure. X-ray diffraction, however, indicates that RbBr has a simple cubic lattice, and that the other three have face-centered lattices. Explain.

6-II-4.   Explain why a crystal cannot have an axis of greater than sixfold symmetry.

6-II-5.   List the symmetry elements of the solid shown in the figure. *bcd* is an equilateral triangle; the other three faces are congruent isosceles triangles.

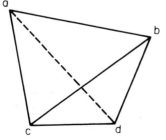

6-II-6. List the symmetry elements of the crystal shown in the figure.

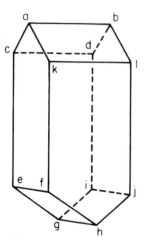

6-II-7. How many twofold axes of symmetry are possessed by the crystal shown in the figure? Sketch them in. The crystal is a perfect cube except for the beveled corners.

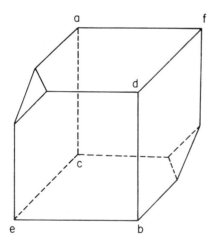

6-II-8. Show that a twofold axis of rotary inversion ($\bar{2}$) is equivalent to a mirror plane.

6-II-9. (a) Sketch a two-dimensional lattice of closest-packed identical circles, indicating a suitable unit cell.

(b) Find the fractional void area in this lattice. (For a triangle with sides a, b, c, the area is $[s(s - a)(s - b)(s - c)]^{1/2}$, where $s = \frac{1}{2}(a + b + c)$.)

6-II-10. Three uni-univalent ionic crystals, AX, AY, and AZ, are composed of ions having the following radii (in arbitrary units):

A^+	X^-	Y^-	Z^-
1.00	1.00	2.00	3.00

Assume that the ions are hard spheres.

(a) Predict whether each crystal will have the sodium chloride or the cesium chloride structure. Explain.

(b) Assuming that your predictions are correct, find the volume of the unit cell in each of the three crystals.

SECTION 6-III

6-III-1. Using the following ionic radii, find the fractional void volume in (a) CsCl, (b) NaCl, (c) LiCl. Assume that the ions are hard spheres in contact.

Ion	Radius, Å
Li^+	0.60
Na^+	0.95
Cs^+	1.69
Cl^-	1.81

In CsCl the positive ions and the negative ions each comprise a simple cubic lattice. Each ion has eight oppositely charged ions as nearest neighbors. In NaCl and LiCl the ions of each sign comprise a face-centered cubic lattice. Each ion has six oppositely charged ions as nearest neighbors.

CHAPTER 7

Solutions

SECTION 7-I

7-I-1. Explain why, even in a nonideal solution, the vapor pressure of the solvent is given by Raoult's law when the solution is sufficiently dilute.

7-I-2. The freezing-point depression constant for camphor is $40.27°C$ (kg camphor) (mole solute)$^{-1}$. In a certain experiment 0.0113 g of phenanthrene lowered the freezing point of 0.0961 g of camphor by $27.0°C$ [Rozenberg and Ushakova, *Zh. Obshch. Khim.*, **30**, 3531 (1960)]. What is the molecular weight of phenanthrene in camphor?

7-I-3. The cryoscopic constant for benzene is $5.085°C$ (kg benzene) (mole solute)$^{-1}$. A 0.07734 molal solution of tetraisoamylammonium thiocyanate in benzene had a freezing point $0.01573°C$ lower than that of pure benzene [Copenhafer and Kraus, *J. Am. Chem. Soc.*, **73**, 4557 (1951)]. Calculate the association number of the quaternary ammonium salt (that is, the ratio of the apparent molecular weight to the formula weight) in benzene.

7-I-4. Beckmann [*Z. Physik. Chem.*, **6**, 437 (1890)] found that a solution consisting of 86.52 g of carbon disulfide and 1.4020 g of anthracene had a boiling point $0.220°C$ higher than that of pure carbon disulfide at 740.5 torr pressure. The addition of 1 mole of solute per 100 g CS_2 elevates the boiling point of this solvent 23.7°C. Assuming an ideal solution, calculate the molecular weight of the anthracene.

7-I-5. The law of osmotic pressure is $\pi \overline{V}_1 = X_2 RT$, where $\overline{V}_1$ is the partial molar volume of the solvent and X_2 is the mole fraction of the solute. 10 g of a solute B were dissolved in 100 g of a solvent A. The molecular weight of A is 100; its density is 1.00 g ml^{-1}. The observed osmotic pressure at 300°K was 0.50 atm. Find the molecular weight of B. Point out any approximations that you are obliged to introduce other than those used in deriving the given equation.

7-I-6. Calculate the activity coefficient of bromine in a bromine-carbon tetrachloride solution above which the partial pressure of bromine is 10.27 torr. The composition of the solution in terms of mole fraction is $0.0250 \, Br_2$, $0.9750 \, CCl_4$. The vapor pressure of pure bromine at the same temperature is 213 torr. Take pure liquid bromine as the standard state for bromine.

7-I-7. The Bunsen absorption coefficient of oxygen in water at 19.94°C is 0.03097 atm^{-1} [Douglas, *J. Phys. Chem.*, **68**, 169 (1964)]. How many moles of oxygen from air (21 percent by volume O_2, 79 percent by volume N_2) at a total pressure of 1 atm could be dissolved in 1 liter of water at that temperature?

7-I-8. At 30°C, 244.0 ml of water dissolved 2.265 ml of helium (measured at 30°C and 1 atm) [Cady, Elsey, and Berger, *J. Am. Chem. Soc.* **44**, 1456 (1922)]. Evaluate α, the Bunsen absorption coefficient, for helium at this temperature.

7-I-9. The Bunsen absorption coefficients of oxygen in water at 0°C and 10°C are, respectively, 0.04889 and 0.03802 atm^{-1}. Calculate the enthalpy of solution of oxygen in water.

7-I-10. When 1.046 g of cadmium is dissolved in 25.23 g of mercury, the vapor pressure of the resulting amalgam at 32.2°C is 0.920 times that of pure mercury. What are (a) the activity, and (b) the activity coefficient (on the mole fraction scale) of of mercury in the amalgam? [Hildebrand, Foster, and Beebe, *J. Am. Chem. Soc.*, **42**, 545 (1920)].

SECTION 7-II

7-II-1. A and B form an ideal solution. The vapor pressure of pure A at 25°C is 100.00 torr. The vapor pressure of pure B is zero. The vapor pressure at 25°C of a solution consisting of 1.00 g B and 10.00 g A is 95.00 torr. Find the ratio of the molecular weight of B to the molecular weight of A.

7-II-2. In order to find out whether the formula of the sodium-tellurium complex in liquid ammonia is $NaTe_x$ or Na_2Te_x, Kraus and Fuchs [*J. Am. Chem. Soc.*, **44**, 2714 (1922)] measured the vapor pressures of a series of solutions prepared by dissolving sodium metal in liquid ammonia in the presence of an excess of solid tellurium. The results of one such series of measurements are given below. The vapor pressure of pure liquid NH_3 at 20°C is 6428 torr.

Weight Na = 0.1398 g, $t = 20°C$

Weight $NH_3(liq)$, g	Mole fraction Na $\times 10^4$ $= \dfrac{n_{Na}}{n_{Na} + n_{NH_3}} \times 10^4$	Vapor pressure depression, ΔP, torr
38.909	26.5	8.2
28.767	35.9	12.0
20.904	49.3	17.0
15.272	67.3	22.8
11.362	90.6	32.0

On the basis of these data, which of the two formulas for the sodium-tellurium complex is the correct one? Explain.

7-II-3. In the derivation of the formula for the relationship between concentration of solute and freezing point of the corresponding solution, it is usually assumed that the enthalpy of fusion of the solvent does not vary with temperature. In the case of water, however, this is not a good assumption inasmuch as the enthalpy of fusion of ice changes at the rate of approximately 1.6 percent per degree in the vicinity of 0°C. Derive a formula for the mole fraction of solute in the solution, X_2, as a function of freezing point, making use of the empirical equation

$$\Delta H_{\text{fusion}}(ice) = -6997 + 63.68\ T - 0.1586\ T^2 \text{ cal mole}^{-1}$$

which takes this temperature dependency of ΔH_{fusion} into account.

7-II-4. For the solute (2) in dilute solutions in a certain solvent the partial molal volume is given by $\overline{V}_2 = a + bm$, where m is the molality of the solute and a, b are constants. Express the partial molal volume $\overline{V}_1$ in terms of a, b, m, and quantities characteristic of the solvent.

7-II-5. The vapor pressures of C_2H_5OH and H_2O over solutions of these two at 20°C are as follows:

Weight percent C_2H_5OH	$P_{C_2H_5OH}$, torr	P_{H_2O}, torr
0	0	17.5
20.0	12.6	15.9
40.0	20.7	14.7
60.0	25.6	14.1
80.0	31.2	11.3
100	43.6	0

Find the activity and the activity coefficient of each component in a solution 40 percent C_2H_5OH by weight. Take the pure substance as the standard state for each component.

7-II-6. A saturated aqueous solution, A, of isobutyl alcohol (74.12 g mole^{-1}) contains 8.2 percent alcohol by weight at 25°C. The second phase, B, in equilibrium with this solution contains 83.2 percent alcohol by weight. Find the activity of the alcohol in solution A, referred to pure alcohol as the standard state. Make whatever reasonable (though, perhaps, rough) approximations are necessary and point out what these approximations are.

7-II-7. The compositions of certain liquid solutions are specified by giving the weight fractions, y_A and y_B, of the components A and B. The molecular weights are M_A and M_B. Give answers in terms of any of the quantities y_A, y_B, M_A, and M_B.

(a) Find the relation between $\mu_A{}^\circ$, the standard chemical potential of A on the weight fraction scale with pure A as the reference state, and $\mu_A{}^*$, the molar free energy of pure A.

(b) Find the relation between the activity, b_A, of A on the weight fraction scale and the activity, a_A, of A on the mole fraction scale, both referred to the pure substance as the standard state.

(c) Find the relation between the activity coefficients for the two activity scales.

(d) Assume that the solutions are ideal. Find the activity coefficients of A on the weight fraction scale when the weight fractions are $y_A = y_B = 0.50$.

7-II-8. Let y_1 and y_2 be the weight fractions of solvent and solute, respectively, and let b_1 and b_2 be activities so defined that $\lim_{y_1 \to 1} b_i/y_i = 1$. Similarly let x_1 and x_2 be the mole fractions and a_1 and a_2 be activities so defined that $\lim_{x_1 \to 1} a_i/x_i = 1$. Find the ratio b_2/a_2 in terms of quantities characteristic of solvent and solute. Prove that your result follows from the definition of activity in terms of chemical potential.

7-II-9. Derive the following equation relating the activity coefficient γ_2 on the molarity (concentration) scale to the activity coefficient γ_2' on the molality scale in terms of the density ρ of the solution, the density ρ_0 of the pure solvent, the molality m_2, and the molecular weight.

$$\frac{\gamma_2}{\gamma_2'} = \frac{\rho_0}{\rho}\left(1 + \frac{m_2 M_2}{1000}\right)$$

7-II-10. The activity coefficient γ_2 (on the mole fraction scale) of the solute in a certain dilute solution is given by $\gamma_2 = e^{AX_2{}^2}$, where A is a constant at constant temperature. Obtain an expression in terms of A and X_2 for the activity coefficient γ_1 (on the mole fraction scale) of the solvent in this solution.

7-II-11. A certain diver has 5 liters of blood, and he is breathing a mixture of 20 mole percent O_2 and 80 mole percent He. Calculate the total volume of gas that would be liberated from his blood stream if he rose suddenly from a depth of 100 ft, where the water temperature was 25°C, to the surface, where atmospheric pressure is 1 atm and the ambient temperature is also 25°C. The density of water is 62.5 lb ft⁻³. Assume that the Bunsen absorption coefficients of He and O_2 are the same in blood plasma as they are in water, namely: He, 0.00861; O_2, 0.02831 atm⁻¹.

7-II-12. The Bunsen absorption coefficients α for CO_2 at various temperatures are given below.

t, °C	30	40	50
α, atm⁻¹	0.665	0.530	0.436

(a) By a suitable graphical method estimate the value of α for CO_2 at 100°C.

(b) Using your answer for (a) calculate the number of moles of CO_2 remaining in 1.00 liter of distilled water initially saturated with air (0.03 percent CO_2 by volume) at room conditions but subsequently boiled at 100°C to remove CO_2.

7-II-13. The graph gives the integral heat of solution of H_2SO_4 in water at 18°C. Determine the differential heat of solution of

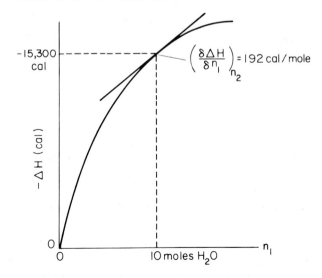

solute, $\overline{\Delta H_2}$, for a solution containing 1 mole of H_2SO_4 in 10 moles of H_2O.

7-II-14. At 25°C the integral heat of solution of a certain acid in water is given by the formula

$$\Delta H \text{ (cal)} = 2.00\, n_1^{1/2} + 3.00\, n_1^{3/2} + 4.00\, n_1^{5/2}$$

where n_1 is the number of moles of H_2O per mole of acid. Evaluate $\overline{\Delta H_2}$ (that is, $(\partial \Delta H/\partial n_2)_{P,T,n_1}$) for a solution that is 10 mole percent acid.

7-II-15. The following data on the integral heats of solution of NaCl in water at 2°C were selected from the work of Mischenko and Yakovlev [*Zh. Obshch. Khim.*, **29**, 1761 (1959)].

m, moles NaCl per kg H_2O	$\overline{\Delta H}$, cal mole^{-1}
0.0624	1846
0.2001	1780
0.4003	1650
0.7504	1531
1.0058	1439
1.9457	1187
3.1064	946
4.0012	767
4.9966	619
6.0004	454

How much heat would be absorbed upon adding 126 g of H_2O to 100 g of a solution, initially 10.0 weight percent NaCl, at this temperature ?

7-II-16. Using data from the table below (compound $1 = H_2O$, compound $2 = H_2SO_4$) calculate the following:

(a) The total amount of heat released when 4 moles of H_2O are added to a solution consisting initially of 6 moles of H_2O and 1 mole of H_2SO_4 .

(b) The total amount of heat released when 3 moles of H_2O are mixed with 6 moles of H_2SO_4 .

Integral and Differential Heats of Solution
for 1 Mole H_2SO_4 in Water at 25°C

Moles H_2O (n_1)	ΔH (cal)	$\overline{\Delta H_1}$ (cal mole^{-1})	$\overline{\Delta H_2}$ (cal mole^{-1})
0	0	−6,750	0
0.50	−3,810	−6,740	−438
1	−6,820	−4,730	−2,090
2	−9,960	−2,320	−5,320
3	−11,890	−1,480	−7,450
4	−13,120	−1,040	−8,960
6	−14,740	−570	−11,320
10	−16,240	−233	−13,910

7-II-17. The solubility of nickel dimethylglyoxime in water was observed at a series of temperatures [Fleischer and Freiser, *J. Phys. Chem.*, **66**, 389 (1962)] and the following results were obtained:

t, °C	Solubility, moles liter^{-1} × 10^5
25.0	0.105 ± 9 %
30.0	0.139 ± 4 %
35.0	0.184 ± 2 %
40.0	0.240 ± 2 %
45.0	0.307 ± 2 %

(a) Evaluate $\Delta H°$, the enthalpy of solution of nickel dimethylglyoxime in water, in kcal mole^{-1}.

(b) What is the meaning of the ° in the expression $\Delta H°$?

7-II-18. If you were conducting an experiment to determine the enthalpy of solution of neptunium metal in 1.00 M HCl, what correction would you make per mole of Np (s) for the heat involved in the vaporization of water as water vapor mixed with the escaping H_2 [Argue, Mercer, and Cobble, *J. Phys. Chem.*, **65**, 2041 (1961)]? The vapor pressure of pure water at 25°C is 23.756 torr, the enthalpy of vaporization of pure water at 25°C is 582.2 cal g^{-1}, and the reactions taking place are:

$$Np(s) + 3H^+ \rightarrow Np(III) + \tfrac{3}{2}H_2$$
$$H^+ + Np(III) + \tfrac{1}{4}O_2 \rightarrow Np(IV) + \tfrac{1}{2}H_2O$$

The temperature and pressure are constant at 25°C and 1.00 atm.

SECTION 7-III

7-III-1. A and B are liquids. At the temperature T their vapor pressures are P_A° and P_B°, respectively; their molar heats of vaporization are $\overline{\Delta H_A}$ and $\overline{\Delta H_B}$. The vapors are ideal gases. When A and B are mixed, the solution is ideal. Let P_A and P_B be the partial pressures of A and B vapors above a solution containing n_A moles of A and n_B moles of B.

(a) Express P_A and P_B in terms of n_A, n_B, P_A°, and P_B°.

(b) The following process is carried out reversibly at the constant temperature T. For each step and for the entire process find ΔH and ΔG for the system consisting of n_A moles of A and n_B moles of B. (There is no heat effect in the formation of an ideal solution).

(i) The pure liquids are evaporated separately.

(ii) The vapors are expanded separately to the pressures P_A and P_B.

(iii) The vapors are mixed so that their partial pressures in the mixtures are P_A and P_B.

(iv) The vapor is condensed to a liquid solution.

(c) Find ΔS for the process of mixing the two liquids, in terms of n_A and n_B.

(d) If the vapors were not ideal but the liquids still formed an ideal solution, how would your answer to (c) be affected? Explain.

7-III-2. The apparent *specific* volume (ml g^{-1}) of component 2 in a solution is defined as

$$\phi_2 = \frac{V - w_1 v_1^\circ}{w_2}$$

where V is the volume of the solution, v_1° is the specific volume of pure component 1, and w_1, w_2 are the weights (in grams) of the two components. We shall take w_1 to be 1 g, so that w_2 is the weight ratio of component 2 to component 1.

(a) Obtain an equation for $\partial\phi_2/\partial w_2$ in terms of the densities ρ of the solution and ρ_1° of pure component 1, w_2, and $\partial\rho/\partial w_2$.

(b) Use your equation to evaluate the partial specific volume

$\bar{v}_2$ of glycerol in a 50 percent (by weight) aqueous solution given the following densities:

Weight percent glycerol	0	49	50
Density of solution (g ml^{-1})	0.9982	1.1236	1.1263

7-III-3. (a) A solution contains n_1 moles of component 1 and n_2 moles of component 2. Their molecular weights are M_1 and M_2, respectively. Obtain an expression for the partial molar volume $\bar{V}_2$ of component 2 in terms of n_1, n_2, the density ρ of the solution, the derivative(s) of ρ with respect to n_2 at constant n_1, and the molecular weights.

(b) Let X_1 and X_2 be the mole fractions of 1 and 2 in the solution. Show that

$$\bar{V}_2 = \frac{M_2}{\rho} - (M_1 X_1 + M_2 X_2) \frac{X_1}{\rho^2} \frac{d\rho}{dX_2}$$

(c) The density in g ml^{-1} of a water-methanol (CH_3OH) solution at 25°C is given by the equation

$$\rho = 0.9971 - 0.28930\, X_2 + 0.29907\, X_2^2 \\ - 0.60876\, X_2^3 + 0.59438\, X_2^4 - 0.20581\, X_2^5$$

where X_2 is the mole fraction of methanol [Mikhail and Kimel, *J. Chem. and Eng. Data*, **6**, 533 (1961)]. Calculate $\bar{V}_2$ in a water-methanol solution at 25°C with $X_2 = 0.100$.

7-III-4. Given the following vapor pressures of chloroform (C), $CHCl_3$, and acetone (A), $(CH_3)_2CO$, over a solution of these components, at 35.17°C:

Mole fraction, X_C	P_C, torr	P_A, torr
0	0	344.5
0.0588	9.2	323.2
0.1232	20.4	299.3
0.1853	31.9	275.4
0.2970	55.4	230.3
0.5143	117.8	135.0
0.7997	224.4	37.5
0.9175	267.1	13.0
1.0000	293.1	0

(a) Find the activity coefficients (γ) of C and of A on the mole fraction scale, referred to the pure substances as the standard states, in a solution 51.43 mole percent C.

(b) Find the Henry's law constant k (where $P = kx$) for each of the components in the other as nearly as you can without elaborate analysis of the data.

(c) Find the activity coefficient (γ_C') of C on the mole fraction scale, referred to the infinitely dilute solution of C in A, in a solution 51.43 mole percent C. $(\gamma_C' \to 1$ as $X_C \to 0)$.

(d) Calculate the ratio γ'/γ for each of the components. Is the result dependent on the mole fraction?

(e) Find ΔG for the process of mixing 0.5143 mole C and 0.4857 mole A at 35.17°C.

7-III-5. A nonideal solution contains n_A moles of A and n_B moles of B. The total free energy of this solution is given approximately by the equation

$$G = n_A \mu_A^\circ + n_B \mu_B^\circ + RT(n_A \ln X_A + n_B \ln X_B) + \frac{C n_A n_B}{n_A + n_B}$$

where X_A, X_B are mole fractions, and C is a constant characteristic of the A-B pair.

(a) Obtain an expression for the chemical potential of A in this solution $(\mu_A$ or $\bar{G}_A)$ in terms of the quantities appearing on the right side of the equation above. Some useful formulas are

$$\left(\frac{\partial \ln X_A}{\partial n_A}\right)_{n_B} = \frac{1}{n_A} - \frac{1}{n_A + n_B} ; \qquad \left(\frac{\partial \ln X_B}{\partial n_A}\right)_{n_B} = -\frac{1}{n_A + n_B}$$

(b) Obtain a similar expression for the activity coefficient (γ_A) of A. Under what conditions does $\gamma_A = 1$?

7-III-6. In a certain solution the activity coefficient γ_2 of the solute is given by $\ln \gamma_2 = -km^{3/2}$, where m is the molality of the solute and k is a constant.

(a) Express $\ln \gamma_1$ in terms of k, m, and the molecular weight M_1 of the solvent.

(b) Ascertain the power n for which

$$\lim_{m \to 0} \left(\frac{\ln \gamma_1}{m^n}\right)$$

is neither zero nor infinite.

Some useful information is contained in the following formulas:

$$\int \frac{x}{a + x}\, dx = x - a \ln(a + x) + \text{constant}$$

$$\ln(1 + x) = x - \tfrac{1}{2}x^2 + \tfrac{1}{3}x^3 - \cdots$$

7-III-7. The activity coefficient of Zn (2) in dilute solutions in Hg (1) is given approximately by $\gamma_2 = 1 - 3.92\,X_2$ at 25°C.

(a) Find a general expression in terms of X_2 for the activity coefficient γ_1 of Hg in such a solution at 25°C.

(b) Show that $1 - \gamma_1$ becomes approximately proportional to X_2^2 at very small X_2 (that is, show that

$$\lim_{X_2 \to 0} \left(\frac{1 - \gamma_1}{X_2^2} \right)$$

is finite and distinct from zero).

7-III-8. In a certain solution the activity coefficient γ_2 of the solute, on the molality scale, is given by $\ln \gamma_2 = A m^p$, where m is the molality of 2, and A and p are constants.

(a) Obtain an expression for the activity coefficient γ_1 of the solvent on the mole fraction scale in terms of m, A, p, and n_1, where n_1 is the number of moles of solvent per kilogram of solvent.

(b) What restriction must be imposed on the possible values of p in order for the result of this problem to be meaningful?

7-III-9. A and B form an ideal solution. We decide, for some reason, to specify the composition by giving X_B^2 instead of X_B. Try to define a scale of activities a_B, with the corresponding μ_B and γ_B, based on X_B^2, in the sense that $\lim(a_B / X_B^2) = 1$ as (a) $X_B \to 1$; (b) $X_B \to 0$. Show the relation of each μ_B° to μ_B^*, the chemical potential of pure B, and give an expression for each γ_B. Discuss any difficulties that you encounter.

CHAPTER 8

Free Energy
and Chemical Equilibrium

SECTION 8-1

8-I-1. Starting with the equation $\Delta G° = -RT \ln K$, derive the equation

$$\ln K = \frac{-\Delta H°}{RT} + C$$

where C is an integration constant.

8-I-2. List of all the conditions under which the following formula is valid:

$$\ln \left(\frac{P_2}{P_1}\right) = \frac{-\Delta H_v}{R} \left(\frac{1}{T_2} - \frac{1}{T_1}\right)$$

8-I-3. Ethylene (C_2H_4) can be purchased in cylinders or tank cars or by pipepline. For the reaction

$C_2H_4(g) \rightarrow 2C(\text{graphite}) + 2H_2(g)$ at 25°C, $\Delta G° = -16$ kcal.

(a) Is the decomposition of C_2H_4 spontaneous?
(b) Does C_2H_4 decompose at room temperature?
(c) Explain any apparent discrepancy between your answers to (a) and to (b).

8-I-4.   The following data for the equilibrium composition of sodium vapor at 10.0 atm total pressure and 1482.53°K have been selected from an extensive series of such measurements made by Makansi, Selke, and Bonilla (reported in *J. Chem. and Eng. Data*, **5**, 441 (1960)).

71.30 weight percent sodium monomer (Na, g)
28.70 weight percent sodium dimer (Na$_2$, g)

Calculate K_p for the reaction $2Na(g) \leftrightharpoons Na_2(g)$ under these conditions.

8-I-5.   In a publication on the reaction

$$\tfrac{2}{3}Bi(liq) + \tfrac{1}{3}BiI_3(g) \rightleftharpoons BiI(g)$$

[Cubicciotti, *J. Phys. Chem.*, **65**, 521-523 (1961)] data are given for several different combinations of equilibrium partial pressures of $BiI_3(g)$ and $BiI(g)$ *at the same temperature.* The logarithms of these partial pressures were plotted with log P_{BiI} as abscissa and with log P_{BiI_3} as ordinate.

(a) Give a theoretical reason why you would expect the graph to be a straight line.

(b) What is the numerical value and the physical significance of the slope dy/dx?

8-I-6.   At 298.2°C the standard free energy of solution of $MgCl_2 \cdot 6H_2O$ is -6180 cal mole^{-1} and the standard free energies of formation of $MgCl_2 \cdot 6H_2O$, H_2O, and $Cl^-(aq)$, are $-505,410$ cal mole^{-1}, $-56,693$ cal mole^{-1}, and $-31,340$ cal (g atom)$^{-1}$, respectively. Calculate the standard free energy of formation of the aqueous magnesium ion at this temperature. [Stephenson, *J. Am. Chem. Soc.*, **68**, 721 (1946)].

8-I-7.   Using data from the table below calculate the value of the equilibrium constant for the reaction

$$3HC{\equiv}CH(g) \rightleftharpoons C_6H_6(g)$$
acetylene   benzene

at 25°C assuming ideal gas behavior. Would you recommend this process as a practical method for making benzene? Explain.

	ΔG_f° , cal mole^{-1}
$HC{\equiv}CH$	50,000
C_6H_6	29,760

8-I-8.   At $300°K$, the equilibrium constant K_p for the reaction

$N_2O_4(g) \rightleftharpoons 2NO_2(g)$

is 0.174 [Hisatsune, *J. Phys. Chem.*, **65**, 2249 (1961)]. What would be the apparent molecular weight of an equilibrium mixture of N_2O_4 and NO_2 formed by the dissociation of pure N_2O_4 at a total pressure of 1 atm at this temperature?

8-I-9.   According to Eastman [*J. Am. Chem. Soc.*, **44**, 975 (1922)] the equilibrium constant for the reaction

$Fe_3O_4(s) + CO \rightleftharpoons 3FeO(s) + CO_2$

at $600°C$ is 1.15. If a mixture consisting initially of 1 mole of Fe_3O_4, 2 moles of CO, 0.5 moles of FeO, and 0.3 moles of CO_2 were heated to $600°C$ at a constant total pressure of 5.00 atm, what would be the amount of each substance at equilibrium?

8-I-10.   For the reaction

$3Fe_2O_3(s) \rightleftharpoons 2Fe_3O_4(s) + \frac{1}{2}O_2(g)$

$\Delta H^{\circ}_{298} = 55.5$ kcal and $\Delta G^{\circ}_{298} = 46.5$ kcal.
(a) Calculate the equilibrium constant K_p at $25°C$ for this reaction.
(b) Calculate the equilibrium constant for this reaction at $125°C$.
(c) Point out any approximations that you make in the calculation of (b).

8-I-11.   For the reaction

$CO(g) + SO_3(g) \rightleftharpoons CO_2(g) + SO_2(g),$

$\Delta H^{\circ}_{298} = -44.14$ kcal and $\Delta G^{\circ}_{298} = -44.72$ kcal.
Calculate (a) ΔG°_{398}; (b) $K_{p,398}$. Assume that $\Delta C^{\circ}_P = 0$ between 298 and $398°K$.

8-I-12.   According to the observations of Adler and Stewart [*J. Phys. Chem.*, **65**, 172 (1961)], K_p is 1.46 at $100.0°C$ and 0.54 at $140.0°C$ for the reaction

$2B_5H_{11}(g) + 2H_2(g) \rightleftharpoons 2B_4H_{10}(g) + B_2H_6(g).$

Estimate ΔH° for this reaction in kilocalories.

8-I-13. On the basis of the following data for the vapor pressure of solid palladium metal as a function of temperature [Hampson and Walker, *J. Res. Natl. Bur. Std.*, **66***A*, 177 (1961)], evaluate ΔH_S°, the mean enthalpy of sublimation of palladium, in kcal mole^{-1}.

T, °K	P(torr) $\times$ 10^6
1294	2.17
1308	3.19
1322	5.23
1333	6.01
1350	8.22
1396	24.5
1406	29.0
1426	47.8
1459	88.6
1488	168

8-I-14. For a certain compound Y, the vapor pressure of the solid and the vapor pressure of the liquid are given as follows:

Vapor Pressure of Solid Y		Vapor Pressure of Liquid Y	
200°K	25 torr	300°K	150 torr
250°K	75 torr	400°K	300 torr

Calculate (a) the enthalpy of sublimation, (b) the enthalpy of vaporization, (c) the enthalpy of fusion. All calculations are to be in cal mole^{-1}.

8-I-15. The vapor pressure of methyl bromide is 13.0 torr at -70.0°C and 117 torr at -36.7°C. Evaluate (a) the molar enthalpy of vaporization of methyl bromide, (b) the vapor pressure of methyl bromide at -50.0°C.

8-I-16. Calculate the equilibrium constant at 25°C of the reaction
$$4HCl(g) + O_2(g) \rightleftharpoons 2Cl_2(g) + 2H_2O(g),$$
using the following data:

	$(\bar{G}^\circ - \bar{H}_0^\circ)/T$ at 298.15°K, cal °K^{-1} mole	$\bar{H}_0^\circ$, kcal mole^{-1}
$O_2(g)$	-42.06	0
$Cl_2(g)$	-45.93	0
$H_2O(g)$	-37.17	-57.107
$HCl(g)$	-37.72	-22.019

8-I-17. Find the equilibrium constant K_p at 1000°K for the reaction

$$C_2H_4(g) + H_2(g) \rightleftharpoons C_2H_6(g)$$

using the following data:

	$(\bar{G}° - \bar{H}_0°)/T$ at 1000°K, cal °K^{-1} mole^{-1}	$\bar{H}_0°$, kcal mole^{-1}
C_2H_6	-61.11	-16.52
C_2H_4	-57.29	$+14.52$
H_2	-32.74	0

8-I-18. Making use of data given in the table below, calculate the equilibrium constant for the reaction $A(g) \rightleftharpoons 2B(g)$ at 600°K.

	$-(\bar{G}° - \bar{H}_0°)/T$, cal °K^{-1} mole^{-1}, at 600°K	$\bar{H}_0°$, kcal mole^{-1}
$A(g)$	48.0	-94.000
$B(g)$	27.0	-27.000

SECTION 8-II

8-II-1. Derive the formula

$$\left[\frac{\partial}{\partial T}\left(-\frac{\Delta A}{T}\right)\right]_P = \frac{\Delta E}{T^2}$$

8-II-2. Estimate the pressure required to melt ice at $-1.0°C$. The specific heat of fusion of ice is 80 cal g^{-1}. The density of the liquid is 1.00 g cm^{-3}; that of the solid is 0.92 g cm^{-3}.

8-II-3. At 298.15°K and 1.00 atm, ΔG for the conversion of rhombic sulfur to monoclinic sulfur is 18 cal mole^{-1}. Which of the two phases is stable under these conditions? The density of rhombic sulfur is 1.96 g cm^{-3}; that of monoclinic sulfur, 2.07 g cm^{-3}. Estimate the minimum pressure at which the other phase would be stable at 298.15°K.

8-II-4.   The following data for the reactions

$$FeO(s) + CO(g) \rightleftharpoons Fe(s) + CO_2(g) \qquad K_1 = P_{CO_2}/P_{CO}$$
$$Fe_3O_4(s) + CO(g) \rightleftharpoons 3\,FeO(s) + CO_2(g) \quad K_2 = P_{CO_2}/P_{CO}$$

were obtained by Eastman [*J. Am. Chem. Soc.*, **44**, 975 (1922)]:

t, °C	K_1	K_2
600	0.871	1.15
700	0.678	1.77
800	0.552	2.54
900	0.466	3.43
1000	0.403	4.42

Calculate the temperature at which Fe, FeO, Fe_3O_4, CO, and CO_2 could all coexist in equilibrium.

8-II-5.   Explain why it is permissible to omit the concentrations of pure solids and liquids in calculating K_c for a heterogeneous reaction.

8-II-6.   Zinc oxide was left in contact with carbon monoxide, initially pure, at 1300°K and a total pressure of 1.00 atm until the reaction

$$ZnO(s) + CO(g) \rightleftharpoons Zn(g) + CO_2(g)$$

had reached equilibrium. The density of the gas mixture was then 0.344 g liter^{-1}. Find (a) the average (apparent) molecular weight of the gas, (b) the fraction of the CO that had reacted with the ZnO, and (c) the equilibrium constant K_p for the reaction given.

8-II-7.   In the reaction $XY_2 \rightleftharpoons X + 2Y$ all three substances are ideal gases. A 10.0 liter flask contains, initially, 0.40 mole of XY_2. A catalyst for dissociation is then introduced. When equilibrium is attained, the pressure of the mixture is 1.20 atm. The temperature is 300°K. Find the equilibrium constant K_p for the given reaction.

8-II-8.   This problem refers to the reaction

$$2SO_2 + O_2 \rightleftharpoons 2SO_3$$

0.100 mole each of SO_2 and SO_3 are mixed in a 2.00 liter flask at 27°C. After equilibrium is attained, the pressure is 2.78 atm. Calculate (a) the mole fraction of O_2 at equilibrium,

(b) K_p , and (c) the percent dissociation of SO_3 if initially the flask had contained 0.100 mole of SO_3 and no O_2 or SO_2 .

8-II-9. In the vapor state acetic acid is known to exist as an equilibrium mixture of monomer, HOAc, and dimer, $(HOAc)_2$, in accordance with the equation $(HOAc)_2(g) \rightleftharpoons 2HOAc(g)$. At 51.2°C the pressure of a certain mass of acetic acid vapor was found to be 25.98 torr in a container with a volume of 359.8 ml. At the end of the pressure measurements the vapor was condensed and titrated with standard $Ba(OH)_2$. 13.80 ml of 0.0568 N $Ba(OH)_2$ was required. Calculate (a) α, the degree of dissociation of the dimer under these conditions, and (b) K, the equilibrium constant for the dissociation of the dimer. [Taylor, *J. Am. Chem. Soc.*, **73**, 315 (1951)].

8-II-10. Caffeine (K) and benzoic acid (HBz) form a water-soluble 1 : 1 complex (K · HBz) in accordance with the equation K(*in solution*) + HBz(*in solution*) $\rightleftharpoons$ K · HBz(*in solution*). In order to determine the dissociation constant of this complex in water, $K_c = [HBz][K]/[K \cdot HBz]$, Higuchi and Zuck [*J. Am. Pharm. Assn., Sci. Ed.*, **41**, 10 (1952)] performed a series of experiments such as the following. 1.000 g of benzoic acid and an accurately weighed portion of caffeine were placed in a glass-stoppered bottle, and 50 ml of water and 50 ml of "Skellysolve-C" (a commercial solvent that is completely immiscible with water) were added. The bottle containing these chemicals was then shaken continuously in a constant temperature bath for 2 hours at 0°C. Aliquots were then removed from each layer and titrated with alcoholic potassium hydroxide solution using α-naphtholbenzein as the indicator. The concentration of benzoic acid (both free as HBz and combined as K · HBz) in the aqueous layer, corrected for the dissociation of HBz, was found to be 20.40×10^{-3} moles liter^{-1}. The total concentration of benzoic acid (as HBz) in the Skellysolve-C layer was found to be 28.43×10^{-3} moles liter^{-1}. The partition coefficient K_d for the distribution of benzoic acid between water and Skellysolve-C, determined in a separate experiment, is given by

$(HBz)_2$ (*in Skellysolve-C*) $\rightleftharpoons$ 2HBz (*in water*)

$$K_d = \frac{[HBz]^2 \ (in \ water)}{[(HBz)_2] \ (in \ Skellysolve\text{-}C)}$$
$$= 5.02 \times 10^{-3}$$

Note that the benzoic acid exists as a monomer in aqueous solution and as a dimer in Skellysolve-C solution. The total concentration of caffeine in the aqueous layer (both free and complexed) was 2.691×10^{-2} moles liter^{-1}. Both the caffeine and the $K \cdot HBz$ complex are completely insoluble in Skellysolve-C. Evaluate K_c.

8-II-11. Given the following standard free energies of formation at 25°C:

$CO(g)$	$CO_2(g)$	$H_2O(g)$	$H_2O(liq)$
-32.807	-94.260	-54.635	-56.69 kcal mole^{-1}

(a) Find $\Delta G°$ and the equilibrium constant K_p for the reaction $CO(g) + H_2O(g) \rightleftharpoons CO_2(g) + H_2(g)$ at 25°C.

(b) Find the vapor pressure of H_2O at 25°C.

(c) If CO, CO_2, and H_2 are mixed so that the partial pressure of each is 1.00 atm and the mixture is brought into contact with excess liquid H_2O, what will be the partial pressure of each gas when equilibrium is attained at 25°C? The volume available to the gases is constant.

8-II-12. In the reaction $A(g) + 2B(g) \rightleftharpoons C(s) + 2D(g)$, A, B, and D are ideal gases; C has a very small vapor pressure and a negligible volume. The following processes take place at one temperature:

(a) A and B are introduced into a container until their partial pressures, before any C or D has been formed, are each 1.00 atm. When the reaction has come to equilibrium under a constant total pressure of 2.00 atm, 75.0 percent of the A originally present remains unreacted. Find the partial pressure of D at equilibrium and the equilibrium constant K_p for the given reaction.

(b) A and B are introduced into a container of fixed volume until their partial pressures, before any C or D has been formed, are each 1.00 atm. Write an equation in which the only unknown is the partial pressure of D at equilibrium.

(c) Predict whether the equilibrium pressure of D will be greater in (b) or in (a). Explain your prediction.

(d) Calculate, to two significant figures, the partial pressure of D for part (b).

8-II-13. (a) Pure iodine monobromide was introduced into a vessel of fixed volume at 25°C until its pressure, before any reaction had occurred, was 0.50 atm. When the reaction

$$2IBr(g) \rightleftharpoons I_2(s) + Br_2(g)$$

had come to equilibrium at 25°C, the partial pressure of bromine was 0.17 atm. Find the equilibrium constant K_p for the reaction given.

(b) Iodine monobromide was kept at 25°C and a constant total pressure of 0.50 atm until its dissociation had come to equilibrium. In the presence of solid iodine the partial pressure of iodine vapor is constant at 4.0×10^{-4} atm. Find the partial pressure of bromine in the equilibrium mixture assuming that no bromine condensed to a liquid.

8-II-14. For the reaction $Br_2(liq) + Cl_2(g) \rightleftharpoons 2BrCl(g)$, $K_p = 2.032$ at 25°C. The vapor pressure of $Br_2(liq)$ at 25°C is 0.281 atm. Pure $BrCl(g)$ was introduced into a closed container of adjustable volume. The total pressure was kept constant at 1.000 atm and the temperature at 25°C. $Br_2(liq)$ was present at equilibrium. Find the fraction of the BrCl originally present that has been converted to Br_2 and Cl_2 at equilibrium. Assume that the gases are ideal.

8-II-15.

$$PuF_4(s) + F_2(g) \rightleftharpoons PuF_6(g)$$
$$K_p = 26.6 \times 10^{-4} \quad \text{at} \quad 300°C$$

Fluorine gas at 1 atm is passed into a tube containing $^{239}PuF_4(s)$ at 300°C. Assuming that equilibrium is attained (a) what is the composition (in mole percent) of the exhaust gas leaving the tube? (b) How many moles of pure $F_2(g)$ would need to be introduced into the tube in order to produce 1.00 g of $PuF_6(g)$ under these conditions?

8-II-16. K_p for the reaction

$$HD(g) + H_2O(g) \rightleftharpoons H_2(g) + HDO(g)$$

is 2.6 at 100°C. The concentration of HD in natural hydrogen is about 0.0298 mole percent.

(a) Calculate the fraction of the initial HD that would remain in a stream of natural hydrogen after equilibrium had been attained at this temperature in a mixture consisting of 0.50 atm natural hydrogen plus 0.50 atm $H_2O(g)$.

(b) If the natural hydrogen treated in this manner were recovered and recycled under the same conditions, what fraction of the original 0.0298 mole percent $HD(g)$ would now remain?

8-II-17. (a) Find the equilibrium constant K_p for the reaction $C_2H_4(g) \rightleftharpoons H_2(g) + C_2H_2(g)$ at $1000°K$ using the data below.
(b) C_2H_4 was kept at $1000°K$ and a total pressure of 10.0 atm until the reaction of (a) had come to equilibrium. Find the partial pressure of H_2 at equilibrium.

	$-(G° - H_0°)/T$ cal $°K^{-1}$ mole^{-1}, $1000°K$	$H_0°$ kcal mole^{-1}
$H_2(g)$	32.74	0
$C_2H_4(g)$	57.29	14.52
$C_2H_2(g)$	52.01	54.33

8-II-18. A, B, and C are ideal gases; D is a solid of negligible volume and negligible vapor pressure. For the reaction

$$A + 2B \rightleftharpoons C + D(s)$$

the equilibrium constant is $K_p = 1.0 \times 10^{-3}$ with pressures in atmospheres. A and B are introduced into a container until the partial pressure of each, before any reaction takes place, is 1.00 atm. Find the partial pressure of C at equilibrium:

(a) When the volume of the container is held constant.

(b) When the total pressure is held constant at 2.00 atm. The temperature is constant in both cases. In each case show the equations which, when solved, will yield P_C exactly; then solve with the aid of suitable approximations.

(c) Your results for P_C may not be sufficiently accurate to show any difference between (a) and (b). Predict in which case the fraction of the reactants converted into products at equilibrium would be greater. Explain your conclusion in both physical and mathematical terms.

8-II-19. For the reaction

$$2H_2S(g) + 3O_2(g) \rightarrow 2SO_2(g) + 2H_2O(liq)$$

$\Delta H^\circ_{298} = -1130.5$ kilojoules, $\Delta S^\circ_{298} = -388.3$ joules $^\circ K^{-1}$, and $\Delta C^\circ_P = 74.0$ joules $^\circ K^{-1}$. Express ΔH°, ΔE°, ΔG°, and ΔS° for this reaction as functions of temperature, containing only T and actual numbers. Make, and point out, any reasonable and necessary approximations.

8-II-20.

	CO(g)	CO$_2$(g)	Pb(s)	PbO(s)
ΔH°_{298} of formation, kcal mole^{-1}	−26.42	−94.05	0	−52.40
ΔG°_{298} of formation, kcal mole^{-1}	−32.81	−94.26	0	−45.25
$\bar{C}^\circ_P$, cal $^\circ K^{-1}$ mole^{-1}	6.95	8.76	6.34	11.07

Assume that the heat capacities are constant between 25 and 127°C.

(a) Find ΔH°, ΔG°, and K_p at 25°C for the reaction

$$PbO(s) + CO(g) \rightleftharpoons Pb(s) + CO_2(g)$$

(b) Express ΔH° as a function of temperature, valid for all temperatures between 25° and 127°C.

(c) Find K_p at 127°C.

8-II-21. Derive a general mathematical expression for ΔG° as a function of temperature at constant pressure for the reaction $Y_2(g) \rightleftharpoons 2Y(g)$. Evaluate all constants. The expression should contain ΔG° and T as the only variables.

	$\bar{H}^\circ_{300}$ kcal mole^{-1}	$\bar{S}^\circ_{300}$ cal $^\circ K^{-1}$ mole^{-1}	$\bar{C}_P$ cal $^\circ K^{-1}$ mole^{-1}
Y(g)	−150.000	10.00	$3.00 + 2.00 \times 10^{-2}$ T
Y$_2$(g)	−250.000	30.00	$4.00 + 5.00 \times 10^{-2}$ T

8-II-22. (a) For the reaction

$$2Ag(s) + 2HCl(g) \rightleftharpoons 2AgCl(s) + H_2(g)$$

find ΔH°, ΔG°, and K_p at 25°C. Use the following data:

	HCl(g)	AgCl(s)
$\Delta \bar{H}^\circ_{298}$ of formation	−22.06	−30.36
$\Delta \bar{G}^\circ_{298}$ of formation	−22.77	−26.22

(b) Silver and silver chloride are placed in an evacuated flask. Hydrogen chloride is introduced at 25°C until the pressure is 0.50 atm. The contents of the flask are then allowed to come to equilibrium, the total pressure being maintained at 0.50 atm and the temperature at 25°C. Some of each solid is still present and in contact with the gas at equilibrium. Find the partial pressures of HCl and of H_2 in the equilibrium mixture. Consider the gases ideal. (Hint: Adopt as your unknown a quantity that you expect to be small.)

(c) Assume that the following molar heat capacities are constant between 0 and 50°C:

	Ag	AgCl	H_2	HCl
$\bar{C}_P$, cal °K^{-1} mole^{-1}	6.01	12.61	6.80	7.09

Express $\Delta H°$ as a function of temperature, valid between 0 and 50°C.

(d) Express log K_p as a function of temperature in the same interval.

(e) Find K_p at 50°C.

8-II-23. For the reaction $I_2(s) + Br_2(g) \rightleftharpoons 2IBr(g)$, $K_p = 0.164$ at 25°C. The following table gives standard enthalpies of formation at 25°C and molar heat capacities (at constant pressure) for temperatures between 0 and 125°C:

	$I_2(s)$	$Br_2(g)$	$IBr(g)$
$\Delta H_f°$	0	7.34	9.75 kcal mole^{-1}
$\bar{C}_P°$	13.3	8.8	8.7 cal °K^{-1} mole^{-1}

(a) $Br_2(g)$ is introduced into a container in which excess $I_2(s)$ is present. The pressure and temperature are kept constant at 0.164 atm and 25°C. Find the partial pressure of IBr at equilibrium. Assume that the vapor pressure of $I_2(s)$ is much less than 0.164 atm.

(b) Find K_p for the given reaction at 125°C.

(c) Explain why the enthalpy of formation of $Br_2(g)$ in the table above is not zero even though Br_2 is an element.

8-II-24.

At 300°K	$\Delta H°$, kcal	$\Delta G°$, kcal
$2(CH_2OH)_2(liq) + 5O_2(g) \rightarrow$ $4CO_2(g) + 6H_2O(liq)$	-546.96	-562.94
$C(graphite) + O_2(g) \rightarrow CO_2(g)$	-94.05	-94.26
$2H_2(g) + O_2(g) \rightarrow 2H_2O(liq)$	-136.64	-113.38

	$C(graphite)$	H_2	O_2	CO_2	$H_2O(liq)$	$(CH_2OH)_2(liq)$
$\bar{C}_P°$, cal °K^{-1} mole^{-1}	2.04	6.84	6.98	8.76	17.98	35.45

Assume that all gases are ideal and that each $\bar{C}_P°$ is constant between 280 and 370°K. For the reaction

$$2C\,(graphite) + 3H_2 + O_2 \rightarrow (CH_2OH)_2(liq),$$

find

(a) $\Delta H°$ at 300°K.
(b) $\Delta G°$ at 300°K.
(c) $\Delta E°$ at 300°K.
(d) $\Delta A°$ at 300°K.
(e) $\Delta H°$ as a function of temperature. For what range of temperature is your expression valid?
(f) $\Delta H°$ at 350°K.
(g) K_p (or log K_p) at 300°K.
(h) Explain the significance of the superscript ° (as in $\Delta H°$, not as in 300°). Indicate and explain in which of the above cases the omission of this superscript would be a serious error.

8-II-25. For a certain element the heat capacity of the solid is

$$\bar{C}_P(s) = a + bT \qquad \text{cal °K}^{-1} \text{mole}^{-1}$$

and the heat capacity of the liquid is

$$\bar{C}_P(liq) = e + fT \qquad \text{cal °K}^{-1} \text{mole}^{-1}$$

where a, b, e, and f are all constants. The standard enthalpy of fusion at temperature T_1 is $\Delta H_1°$ cal mole^{-1}, and the standard free energy of fusion at this temperature is $\Delta G_1°$. Derive an equation for $\Delta G°$ as a function of temperature.

8-II-26. Given the following standard enthalpies of formation, standard third-law entropies, and standard molar heat capacities at 25°C:

	$\bar{H}_f^\circ$ kcal mole^{-1}	$\bar{S}_f^\circ$ cal °K^{-1} mole^{-1}	$\bar{C}_P^\circ$ cal °K^{-1} mole^{-1}
$H_2(g)$	0	53.29	6.84
$HCl(g)$	-22.06	44.62	7.07
$Na(s)$	0	12.2	6.79
$NaCl(s)$	-98.23	17.30	12.11

(a) Express the equilibrium constant K_p (or log K_p) for the reaction

$$NaCl(s) + \tfrac{1}{2}H_2(g) \rightarrow Na(s) + HCl(g)$$

as a function of temperature. Your result should contain only T and actual numbers. Point out any approximations that you make in this calculation.

(b) Find K_p at 25°C.

(c) Find the partial pressure of HCl at equilibrium at 25°C in the presence of $Na(s)$, $NaCl(s)$, and $H_2(g,$ 4.00 atm). Assume that the gases are ideal.

8-II-27. For the reaction $2Hg(g) + O_2(g) \rightleftharpoons 2HgO(s)$ at 600°K, $\Delta H^\circ = -71.5$ kcal and $\Delta S^\circ = -91.9$ cal °K^{-1} mole^{-1}. The heat capacities at constant pressure are

$O_2(g)$	$6.31 + 0.0023\ T$	cal °K^{-1} mole^{-1}
$HgO(s)$	$6.24 + 0.016\ T$	cal °K^{-1} mole^{-1}

Assume that the gases are ideal.

(a) What is $\bar{C}_P$ for Hg(g)?

(b) Find the equilibrium constant K_p for this reaction at 600°K.

(c) A closed vessel of fixed volume was kept at 600°K. It contained, initially, O_2 at a pressure of 1.00 atm. A sample of $HgO(s)$ was then introduced into the container without changing the volume available to the gases. At equilibrium some $HgO(s)$ was still present. Find the pressure of Hg(g) at equilibrium.

(d) The vapor pressure of Hg(liq) at 600°K is 400 torr. Find the equilibrium constant K_p' for the reaction

$$2Hg(liq) + O_2(g) \rightleftharpoons 2HgO(s)$$

at 600°K.

(e) Calculate K_p for the reaction

$$2Hg(g) + O_2(g) \rightleftharpoons 2HgO(s)$$

at 300°K.

8-II-28.

cal °K^{-1} mole^{-1} at 27 °C:	$\bar{S}°$	$\bar{C}_P°$
$O_2(g)$	49.0	7.0
$S(s)$	7.6	4.4
$Te(s)$	11.9	6.0
$H_2O(liq)$	16.7	18.0
$H_2S(g)$	48.6	8.3
$SO_2(g)$	69.2	8.6
$TeO_2(s)$	17.2	13.5 (estimated)

$\Delta H°$ for reactions at 27°C in kcal mole^{-1}

$S(s) + O_2(g) \rightarrow SO_2(g)$	-70.96
$Te(s) + O_2(g) \rightarrow TeO_2(s)$	-77.69
$2H_2S(g) + 3O_2(g) \rightarrow 2H_2O(liq) + 2SO_2(g)$	-268.92

Assuming that the gases are ideal, calculate with the aid of the above data:

(a) $\Delta H°$ at 27°C for the reaction

$$2H_2S + TeO_2(s) \rightarrow Te(s) + 2S(s) + 2H_2O(liq)$$

(b) $\Delta H°$ at 77°C for the same reaction.

(c) $\Delta G°$ at 77°C for the same reaction.

(d) The pressure of H_2S that can exist in equilibrium with a mixture of liquid water and the solids S, Te, and TeO_2 at 77°C.

8-II-29. (a) Find the equilibrium constant K_p for the reaction

$$NO(g) + \tfrac{1}{2}O_2(g) \rightleftharpoons NO_2(g)$$

at 500°K using the data given below.

(b) Without using any data other than those needed in (a), estimate the temperature at which $K_p = 1$ for this reaction. (Hint.: What quantity remains roughly constant as the temperature changes and is, therefore, known approximately in advance, even though the desired temperature is unknown?)

	$-(\bar{G}° - \bar{H}_0°)/T$ at 500°K, cal °K^{-1} mole^{-1}	$\bar{H}_0°$ (enthalpy of formation at 0°K), kcal mole^{-1}
$O_2(g)$	45.68	0
$NO(g)$	46.76	21.48
$NO_2(g)$	53.60	8.68

8-II-30. On the basis of the following data, calculate $\Delta H_0°$ for the reaction

$$NaOH \cdot H_2O(s) \rightleftharpoons NaOH(s) + H_2O(g)$$

at 298.15°K [L. E. Murch and E. F. Giauque, *J. Phys. Chem.*, **66**, 2052 (1962)]. The vapor pressure of water over the monohydrate is 0.15 torr.

	$-(\bar{G}° - \bar{H}_0°)/T$, cal °K^{-1} mole^{-1}
$NaOH \cdot H_2O(s)$	11.281
$NaOH(s)$	6.995
$H_2O(g)$	37.17

8-II-31.

	$\dfrac{\bar{G}_{1000}° - \bar{H}_{298}°}{1000}$, cal °K^{-1} mole^{-1}	$\bar{H}_{298}°$, kcal mole
Cu_2O	−31.48	−40.4
O_2	−52.78	0
CuO	−16.09	−37.6

(a) Calculate K_p for the reaction

$$2CuO(s) \rightleftharpoons Cu_2O(s) + \tfrac{1}{2}O_2(g)$$

at 1000°K.

(b) Estimate the temperature at which the pressure of O_2 in equilibrium with CuO and Cu_2O would be 10^{-6} atm.

8-II-32. Vapor pressures of water-ethanol solutions at 20°C:

Weight percent ethanol	0	20	50	80	100
P_{H_2O}, torr	17.5	15.9	14.5	11.3	0
$P_{C_2H_5OH}$, torr	0	12.6	23.5	31.2	43.6

For the reaction

$$C_2H_4(g) + H_2O(liq) \rightleftharpoons C_2H_5OH(liq)$$

$K = 10.0$ at 25°C. Find the pressure of C_2H_4 in equilibrium with a solution containing equal weights of H_2O and C_2H_5OH at 25°C (a) assuming that the solution is ideal, (b) using the best information available to you.

8-II-33.

	HI(g)	Hg₂I₂(s)
$\Delta G°$ of formation at 25°C, kcal mole⁻¹	+0.31	−26.60
$\Delta H°$ of formation at 25°C, kcal mole⁻¹	+6.20	−28.91

Assume that the following heat capacities are constant between 25 and 125°C.

	Hg(liq)	H₂(g)	Hg₂I₂(s)	HI(g)
$\bar{C}_P°$, cal °K⁻¹ mole⁻¹	6.6	6.9	25.0	7.0

Find $\Delta H°$, $\Delta S°$, $\Delta G°$, and K_p at 125°C for the reaction

$$2Hg(liq) + 2HI(g) \rightarrow Hg_2I_2(s) + H_2(g)$$

SECTION 8-III

8-III-1. A pure liquid A and its vapor are in equilibrium. Assume that the vapor is an exactly ideal gas. The two following results can be derived by exact thermodynamic reasoning:

(a) Clapeyron equation:

$$\frac{dP}{dT} = \frac{\bar{H}_g - \bar{H}_{liq}}{T(\bar{V}_g - \bar{V}_{liq})}$$

(b) Van't Hoff equation for the reaction

$$A(liq) \rightleftharpoons A(g)$$

where $K = P$:

$$\frac{d \ln P}{dT} = \frac{d \ln K}{dT} = \frac{\bar{H}_g - \bar{H}_{liq}°}{RT^2}$$

or

$$\frac{dP}{dT} = \frac{P(\bar{H}_g - \bar{H}_{liq}^{\circ})}{RT^2} = \frac{\bar{H}_g - \bar{H}_{liq}^{\circ}}{T\bar{V}_g}$$

How does it come about that the results of (a) and (b), both purportedly exact, are not identical (unless one makes the inexact assumptions that $\bar{V}_{liq} = 0$ and $\bar{H}_{liq} = \bar{H}_{liq}^{\circ}$)?

8-III-2. A person who has a superficial acquaintance with thermodynamics consults you about the following difficulties:

(a) "I was under the impression that the free energy change for a system at equilibrium was supposed to be equal to zero. Yet the equilibrium free energy change for the reaction $N_2 + 3H_2 \rightleftharpoons 2NH_3$ according to our textbook is not equal to zero but -7.88 kcal at $298°K$. If the system is at equilibrium, why isn't the free energy change equal to zero?"

(b) "Ice and salt water are in equilibrium at, say, $-3°C$. The activity of the ice is 1.00. The activity of the water in the solution is less than 1.00. In order for the solid and liquid water to be in equilibrium, is it not necessary that their activities be equal?"

In each case explain what incorrect assumptions have been made, what the corresponding correct statements are, and under what special circumstances, if any, the original assumptions and conclusions would become correct.

8-III-3. An ideal gas A_2 undergoes partial dissociation to the ideal gas A: $A_2 \rightleftharpoons 2A$. The equilibrium constant for this reaction (in terms of partial pressures) is K.

(a) Show that $\alpha = (1 + 4P/K)^{-1/2}$, where α is the fractional degree of dissociation of A_2 and P is the total pressure of A_2 and A.

(b) Write the apparent equation of state for this gas mixture, in terms of P, $\bar{V}$, T, K, and R, assuming (i) that its molecular weight is that of A_2; (ii) that its molecular weight is that of A.

(c) A person who is unaware of the dissociation attempts to determine the fugacity coefficient for this gas by calculation from observed P-V-T data. Show that he will succeed if he makes assumption (ii) but not if he makes assumption (i). Obtain an approximate expression for γ, valid when $P \ll K$, based on assumption (ii). A useful approximation is $(1 + x)^n \approx 1 + nx$, $|x| \ll 1$.

$$\int \frac{dx}{x\sqrt{a + bx}} = \frac{1}{\sqrt{a}} \ln \left(\frac{\sqrt{a + bx} - \sqrt{a}}{\sqrt{a + bx} + \sqrt{a}} \right) + C, \quad a > 0$$

8-III-4. Solutions of A and B are ideal and their vapors are ideal gases. B exists in these solutions as the dimer B_2, but exists in the vapor as the monomer B. The vapor pressures of these solutions are studied by a chemist who does not know about the dimerization and assumes that the apparent deviation of the vapor pressure from Raoult's law is a case of ordinary nonideality.

(a) Express the vapor pressures P'_A and P'_B of A and B, predicted without knowledge of dimerization, in terms of n_A, n_B, P°_A, and P°_B, where n_B is the number of moles of B (not B_2) used in preparing the solution.

(b) Express the actual vapor pressures P_A and P_B of A and B in terms of the same variables. (Observe that the vaporization of B involves a chemical reaction.)

(c) Find the activity coefficients γ_A and γ_B that the chemist would assign on the basis of his measurements and assumptions. (He takes the pure substance as the standard state for each component.) Express γ_A and γ_B in terms of n_A and n_B; for the case of a dilute solution of B ($n_B \ll n_A$), express γ_A and γ_B in terms of the apparent (ignoring dimerization) mole fraction X_B.

8-III-5. The following data refer to the reaction $Br_2(g) \rightleftharpoons 2Br(g)$.

Temperature, °K	1400	1600
K_p(pressures in atm)	0.0303	0.255

(a) Calculate the fraction of Br_2 dissociated into Br atoms at 1600°K and a total pressure of 0.10 atm. Assume that the gases are ideal.

(b) Calculate ΔH° for the reaction given.

(c) ΔH° varies with temperature. Just what does your answer to (b) mean? Is it the value of ΔH° at 1400°K? at 1600°K? or what?

8-III-6.   At 300°K, the compound A is crystalline; the element B and the compound AB_2 are ideal gases. B is crystalline below 100°K and it sublimes (its vapor pressure becomes 1 atm) at this temperature, with the enthalpy of sublimation equal to 2000 cal mole⁻¹. For B(c) below 100°K the heat capacity is given approximately by the equation

$$\bar{C}_P^\circ = 2.50 \times 10^{-4}T^3 - 2.40 \times 10^{-10}T^6 \text{ cal } °K^{-1} \text{ mole}^{-1}$$

Above 100°K, $\bar{C}_P^\circ = 6.00$ cal °K⁻¹ mole⁻¹ for B(g). Enthalpies of formation and third-law entropies for the compounds at 300°K are as follows:

	$\bar{H}_{300}^\circ$	$\bar{S}_{300}^\circ$
A(c)	− 10 kcal mole⁻¹	15 cal °K⁻¹ mole⁻¹
AB₂(g)	−41	55

(a) Find the standard third-law entropy of B(g) at 300°K.

(b) Find $\Delta G°$ and K_p for the reaction

$A(c) + 2B(g) \rightleftharpoons AB_2(g)$.

(c) 1.00 mole each of B and of AB_2 are introduced into a container in which solid A is present. At equilibrium, 1.10 mole of AB_2 is present and solid A is still present. The vapor pressure of A is negligible. What is the total pressure at equilibrium?

8-III-7.   Show how the free energy function $(\bar{G}_T^\circ - H_0^\circ)/T$ is affected if the entropy of the substance at 0°K is taken to have the value σ instead of 0.

CHAPTER 9

The phase rule

SECTION 9-1

9-I-1. For water,

$$\Delta H(freezing) = -80 \text{ cal g}^{-1}$$
$$C_P(liq) = 1.00 \text{ cal } °K^{-1} g^{-1}$$
$$C_P(ice) = 0.49 \text{ cal } °K^{-1} g^{-1}$$

ΔS_{system} for the freezing of 1 g of supercooled liquid water at $-10°C$ is given by which of the following?

(a) $(0.49 - 1.00) \ln \dfrac{263}{273}$

(b) $-\dfrac{80}{273} + (0.49 - 1.00) \ln \dfrac{263}{273}$

(c) 0

(d) $-\dfrac{80}{263} + (0.49 - 1.00) \ln \dfrac{263}{273}$

(e) None of these.

9-I-2. Make a sketch representing schematically each of the following:

(a) A temperature-composition phase diagram for a binary system A-B having a single eutectic, a single peritectic (corresponding to the incongruently melting compound AB), and no solid solutions. Label all areas.

(b) A temperature-composition phase diagram for a binary system A-B having a vapor phase and two partially miscible liquid phases. Assume that there are no solid phases in the system. Label all areas.

(c) A pressure-composition phase diagram at a given temperature for a binary salt hydrate system A-W (where A is the anhydrous salt and W is water) having the compounds A, $A \cdot W$, $A \cdot 2W$, $A \cdot 4W$, and $A \cdot 6W$ present as solids in equilibrium with water vapor. Assume that no liquid phases are formed. Label the lines.

9-I-3. The table below gives vapor pressure data for pure chlorobenzene and pure water.

t, °C	$P^{\circ}_{H_2O}$, torr	$P^{\circ}_{C_6H_5Cl}$, torr
50	93	42
60	149	66
70	234	98
80	355	145
90	526	208
100	760	293
110	1075	403

(a) Assuming that chlorobenzene and water are completely immiscible with each other in the liquid state, estimate the temperature at which chlorobenzene would steam distill at a total pressure of 1 atm.

(b) What would be the proportion (in weight percent) of chlorobenzene in the distillate?

9-I-4. The system carbon tetrachloride (C)-dioxane (D) has two eutectics, one at 5.2 mole percent D and -24.7°C, and the other at 49.5 mole percent D and -20.2°C. There is one binary compound, C_2D, with a congruent melting point at -18.2°C. The melting point of pure C is -22.7°C; that of pure D is 11.8°C. Make a sketch of the temperature-composition phase diagram for this system, assuming that there are no solid solutions. [Kennard and McCusker, *J. Am. Chem. Soc.*, **70**, 3375 (1948)].

9-I-5. The pressure-temperature phase diagram of carbon [Bundy, *Science*, **137**, 1057 (1962)] is shown. 1 bar = 0.987 atm.

(a) What pressure would be required to convert graphite into diamond at 2000°K?

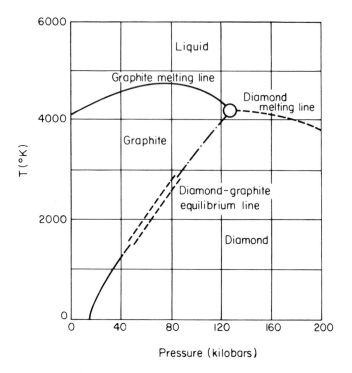

Pressure (kilobars)

(b) At any given temperature and pressure, which phase is denser, graphite or diamond?

(c) If this diagram is correct, at what temperature and pressure do graphite and molten carbon have the same density?

9-I-6.   (a) Label the areas in the figure in a logical manner.

(b) Draw cooling curves for the compositions x_1, x_2, and x_3, from temperature t_i to temperature t_f.

(c) What would be the maximum weight of pure D (uncontaminated with other solids) obtainable by crystallization from 150 g of a melt having the initial composition of 90 weight percent D?

9-I-7.   The temperature-composition phase diagram for the binary system A-B is given.

(a) Label all areas in a meaningful manner.

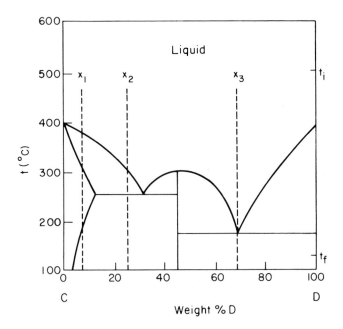

Fig. 9-I-6.

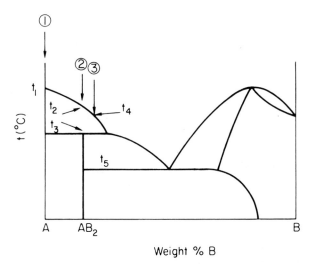

Fig. 9-I-7.

(b) Sketch representative cooling curves for the system compositions indicated by the broken lines numbered (1), (2), (3).

9-I-8. Using the data given below, plot the phase diagram of the system sodium chloride (S)-water (W). Assume that no solid solutions are formed. Label all areas.

Freezing point, °C	Saturated solution composition, weight percent NaCl	Solid phase
0	0	W
−0.4	0.69	W
−0.8	1.35	W
−2.86	4.7	W
−3.42	5.53	W
−6.6	9.90	W
−9.25	13.0	W
−12.7	16.7	W
−16.66	20.0	W
−21.12 (eutectic)	23.1	W + S · 2W
−14	24.6	S · 2W
+0.1 (peritectic)	26.3	S · 2W + S
10.0	26.34	S
15.0	26.34	S
20.0	26.40	S
30.0	26.52	S
40.0	26.67	S
60.0	27.07	S
80.0	27.55	S
100.0	28.15	S

9-I-9. The following data were obtained for the freezing points (beginning of freezing) of ethylene glycol (K)-water (W) mixtures [Ewert, *Bull. Soc. Chim. Belg.*, **46**, 90 (1937)].

Freezing point, °C	Solution composition, mole percent K	Solid phase
0	0	W
−14.1	10.5	W
−20.9	14.1	W
−28.3	18.1	W
−41.8	24.9	W
−51.2	28	W + K · 2W
−49.6	31.8	K · 2W
−49.6	34.1	K · 2W

Freezing point, °C	Solution composition, mole percent K	Solid phase
−58.6	44.0	K · 2W
−63.3	47.5	K · 2W + 3K · 2W
−54.6	50.2	3K · 2W
−40.7	60.9	3K · 2W
−49.4	66.0	3K · 2W + K
−45.3	67.8	K
−36.4	75.3	K
−22.4	90.1	K
−12.8	100	K

(a) Plot the temperature-composition phase diagram, assuming that no solid solutions are formed. Label all areas.

(b) If you wished to prepare an antifreeze mixture consisting of K and W and freezing at −10°C, what composition would you recommend?

(c) What is the composition of the lowest-freezing mixture of K and W that it is possible to prepare?

9-I-10. Referring to the figure,

(a) What phase(s) are in equilibrium in the region *abc*?

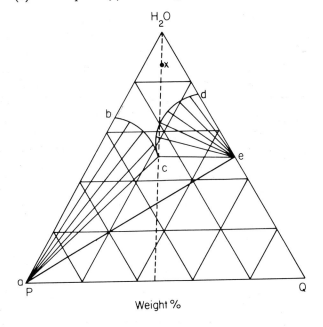

Weight %

(b) Give the empirical chemical formula of any binary or ternary compound(s) occurring in the system. Formula weights: H_2O, 18; P, 25; Q, 36.

(c) For the evaporation of water from a mixture having the initial composition x, sketch a schematic curve showing the weight percent of H_2O in the liquid phase as a function of the weight of water evaporated.

9-I-11. The three-component system F_2-O_3-O_2 has been investigated because of the possible use of such mixtures as oxidizers in rocket engines [Stokes and Streng, *J. Chem. Phys.*, **37**, 920 (1962)]. The liquids O_3 and O_2 are only partially miscible at 77.4°K; the two saturated solutions have the compositions 7 and 84 mole percent O_3. However, F_2 is completely miscible with both O_3 and O_2.

(a) Sketch the triangular phase diagram as far as you can with this information.

(b) Draw a few tie lines on your diagram, based on the assumption that F_2 distributes itself between O_3 and O_2 so that its concentration is greater in the O_2-rich phase. (It is not known whether this assumption is correct.)

9-I-12. The following data for the system benzene-acetic acid-water at 25°C were obtained by Waddell [*J. Phys. Chem.*, **2**, 233 (1898)]. In this system there are two immiscible liquids (L_1 and L_2) existing in equilibrium with each other. (a) Plot the data on triangular graph paper and draw in the tie lines; (b) estimate the composition at the consolute point; and

	Concentrations, weight percent			
	L_1		L_2	
Tie-line no.	CH_3COOH	C_6H_6	CH_3COOH	C_6H_6
1	0.46	99.52	9.4	0.18
2	3.1	96.75	28.2	0.53
3	7.0	92.66	43.9	1.5
4	8.9	90.67	49.5	1.93
5	16.3	82.91	61.4	6.1
6	22.8	76.10	65.0	10.0
7	32.8	64.76	65.0	17.8
8	52.8	39.6	52.8	39.6

(c) determine the compositions and weights of the phases resulting when 30 g of CH_3COOH, 60 g of C_6H_6, and 10 g of H_2O are mixed and allowed to come to equilibrium at this temperature.

9-I-13. Point out any errors or inconsistencies that appear in the following phase diagrams. Any given diagram may contain 0 or 1 mistake. In each case indicate the principle or convention that is violated and if sufficient information is given, indicate what the correct diagram should look like.

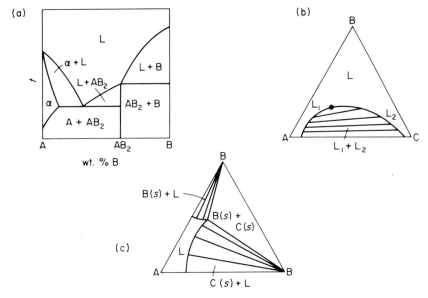

SECTION 9-II

9-II-1. Indicate precisely the conditions under which the formula $P + F = C + 2$ is valid, where P = the number of phases, F = the number of degrees of freedom, and C = the number of components in a system.

9-II-2. Why would it be incorrect to apply the formula

$$\ln \frac{P_2}{P_1} = \frac{\Delta H}{R} \left(\frac{1}{T_2} - \frac{1}{T_1} \right)$$

to the diamond-graphite phase transition?

9-II-3. Prove that the liquid-vapor (L-V) equilibrium line in a one-component system must always have a positive slope on a pressure-temperature diagram.

9-II-4. For the system shown in the figure, prove that at equilibrium

$$\frac{W_1}{W_2} = \frac{x_2 - x_T}{x_T - x_1}$$

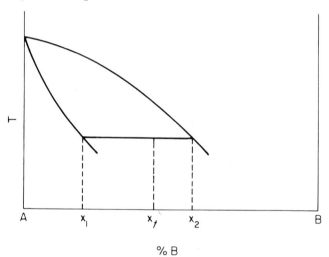

% B

where W_1 = the weight of phase 1, W_2 = the weight of phase 2, x_1 = the weight percent of B in phase 1, x_2 = the weight percent of B in phase 2, and x_T = the weight percent of B in the total system.

9-II-5. Referring to the figure indicate the relative magnitudes of the specific entropies, s, and specific volumes, v, of the phases in the neighborhood of the 1-2-3 triple point.

9-II-6. A certain substance exists in two solid forms, Q and R, as well as liquid and vapor. The following triple points are observed; all equilibria are stable.

Temperature, °C	Pressure, atm	Phases
10	1.0	Q, R, vapor
80	10	R, liquid, vapor
50	1000	Q, R, liquid

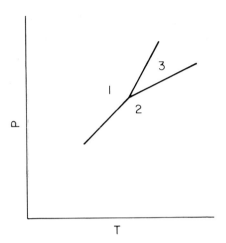

Fig. 9-II-5.

(a) Sketch the pressure-temperature phase diagram for this substance. Indicate the phase or phases present in each region.

(b) In each pair select the form with greater density in the vicinity of 50°C and 100 atm if you have enough information to decide: Q and R; R and liquid; Q and liquid. If you cannot decide, explain why not.

9-II-7.   Element X exists in three solid allotropic modifications, known, respectively, as 1, 2, and 3. In the vicinity of the 1-2-3 triple point,

$$s_2 > s_3 > s_1$$

and

$$v_3 > v_1 > v_2$$

where s is the specific entropy and v is the specific volume. Sketch an arrangement of the three two-phase equilibrium lines around the 1-2-3 triple point on a pressure-temperature diagram consistent with the given information and correct in all other aspects as well. Label all lines and areas.

9-II-8.   Under the range of conditions involved in this problem, element Y exists in the form of a vapor, V, a liquid, L, and three solid allotropic modifications known as 1, 2, and 3. Complete the phase diagram shown in a logical manner and label all lines and areas. The only triple points existing in the system are as follows: 1-2-V, 2-3-V, 3-L-V. These are shown on the diagram in their respective positions.

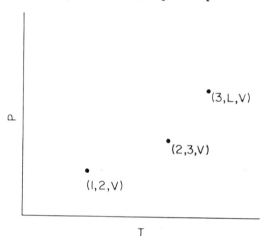

9-II-9. A certain substance exists in two solid modifications, α and β, as well as liquid and vapor. Under a pressure of one atmosphere, α is stable at lower temperatures than β, which melts at a still higher temperature to form the liquid. α is denser than the liquid, but β is less dense than the liquid. No metastable equilibria are observed. Sketch the pressure-temperature phase diagram indicating the significance of each point, line, and region. Include in your diagram every triple point that can be observed.

9-II-10. In studying water at pressures up to 3000 atm the following triple points have been observed:

Temperature, °C	Pressure, atm	Phases
+0.008	6.1×10^{-3}	vapor, liquid, ice I
−22.0	2450	ice I, ice III, liquid
−34.7	2100	ice I, ice II, ice III

Under a pressure of 1660 atm, ice I and ice II are in equilibrium at −60°C. Ice II is denser than ice III, which is denser than the liquid.

(a) Sketch, roughly to scale, the pressure-temperature phase diagram for water, covering the region -60 to $0°C$ and 0 to 3000 atm. Label each region. Show clearly the direction of slope of each curve. Omit curves that are invisible on the scale of your diagram.

(b) In each pair which has the greater molar enthalpy: ice I or ice II ? ice I or ice III ? ice II or ice III ?

9-II-11. A certain substance, X, has its normal freezing point at $300°K$. At $300°K$ the heat of fusion $(\overline{\Delta H})$ of X is 3000 cal mole^{-1}. The heat capacities of solid and liquid X are $\overline{C}_P(s) = 20.0$ cal$°K^{-1}$ mole^{-1}; $\overline{C}_P(liq) = 25.0$ cal$°K^{-1}$ mole^{-1}.

(a) Is $\overline{\Delta G}$ for the fusion of solid X positive, negative, or zero at $290°K$? Explain.

(b) Calculate $\overline{\Delta H}$ at $290°K$.

(c) Calculate $\overline{\Delta S}$ for the fusion of 1 mole of solid X at $300°K$.

(d) Calculate $\overline{\Delta S}$ for the fusion of 1 mole of solid X at $290°K$.

(e) Calculate $\overline{\Delta G}$ for the fusion of 1 mole of solid X at $290°K$. Compare the result with your prediction in (a).

9-II-12. The vapor pressure P_{liq} of a certain pure liquid is given by

$$\ln P_{liq} = A_{liq} + B_{liq} \ln T + C_{liq}/T$$

The vapor pressure of the corresponding solid is given by

$$\ln P_s = A_s + B_s \ln T + \frac{C_s}{T}$$

(a) Express the molar heat of vaporization of the liquid, $\overline{\Delta H}_{liq}$, and of the solid, $\overline{\Delta H}_s$, in terms of any or all of A_{liq}, B_{liq}, C_{liq}, A_s, B_s, C_s, and T.

(b) Express the molar heat of fusion in terms of the same quantities.

(c) Express similarly the difference in molar heat capacities between liquid and solid $(\overline{C}_{P,liq} - \overline{C}_{P,s})$.

(d) Write one equation that could be solved for the melting point of the substance if A_{liq}, A_s, B_{liq}, etc., were known.

9-II-13. At a given temperature the vapor pressures of pure C and pure D are 550 and 250 torr, respectively. By a simple graphical construction, estimate (a) the total vapor pressure above a solution that is 25 mole percent D; (b) the partial pressure of D in that mixture; (c) the composition of a solution with a vapor pressure of 500 torr. Assume ideal solution behavior.

9-II-14. The following table gives the vapor pressures of water and acetone in equilibrium with their solutions of the compositions given, at 25°C.

Mole fraction of acetone in liquid	Partial vapor pressures, torr	
	Acetone	Water
0	0	24
0.0333	38	23
0.117	105	23
0.236	146	22
0.420	164	22
0.737	192	17
1.00	229	0

(a) Plot a phase diagram showing the total vapor pressure of water-acetone solutions as functions of the mole fractions of acetone in the liquid and in the vapor. Label each region in your diagram to show the phases present when the pressure and gross composition of the system are represented by a point in that region.

(b) Calculate (as nearly as you can from the data given) the Henry's law constant for acetone in the solvent water.

(c) Find the activity coefficient of acetone in the solution in which its mole fraction is 0.420 (i) taking pure acetone as the standard state; (ii) treating acetone as the solute, so that the activity coefficient of acetone becomes 1.00 in the limit of pure water. Use the mole fraction as the measure of composition in both cases.

9-II-15. The phase diagram of the system composed of the two partially miscible liquids, A and B, is given. 30 g of pure A is mixed with 70 g of pure B.

(a) What will be the boiling point of this mixture at 1 atm?

(b) What will be the composition of the vapor in equilibrium with the liquid when the mixture just begins to boil at 1 atm?

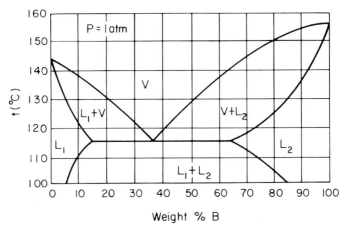

Fig. 9-II-15

(c) What is the maximum amount of pure B recoverable by fractional distillation only?

9-II-16. Referring to the figure,

(a) At what temperature would a liquid mixture consisting initially of 50 g of A and 150 g of B begin to boil?

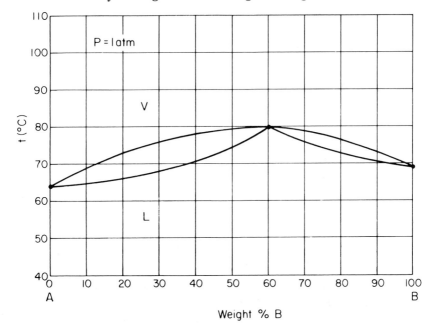

(b) What would be the composition of the vapor in equilibrium with the liquid at the initial boiling point?

(c) If the original mixture were distilled until the boiling point changed 5 degrees (i) what would be the composition of the residue left in the still? (ii) What would be the composition and weight of the distillate collected over the 5 degree interval (estimate)?

9-II-17. The temperature-composition phase diagram for the 2-component system A-B at $P = 1$ atm is given. 200 g of a mixture of A and B boiling initially at 65°C is distilled until the boiling point of the residue remaining in the still reaches 75°C.

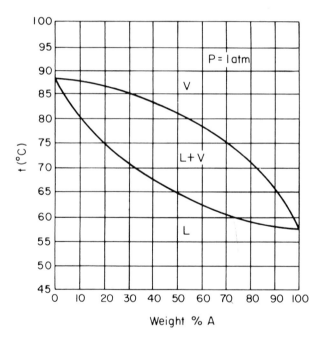

(a) What is the composition of the residue?

(b) What is the composition of the total distillate?

(c) What is the weight of the total distillate?

9-II-18. The temperature-composition phase diagram of the system A-B is shown.

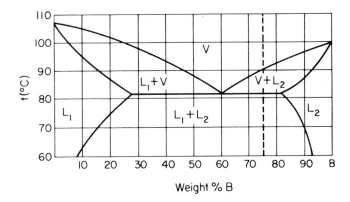

Weight % B

(a) At what temperature would a mixture consisting of 25 weight percent A–75 weight percent B begin to boil?

(b) If the mixture described in (a) is distilled until the boiling point of the residue has risen 10 degrees, what is the composition of the residue?

(c) If all of the distillate produced over this 10-degree range has been collected in a single fraction, what is its overall composition?

(d) If the distillate mentioned above is redistilled, what is the initial boiling point and what is the composition of the first drop of the new distillate?

9-II-19. The figure gives the boiling points of A-B mixtures at one atm. A liquid mixture consisting of 60 weight percent A and 40 weight percent B is placed in a closed container of variable volume. The pressure is kept constant at 1 atm, while the

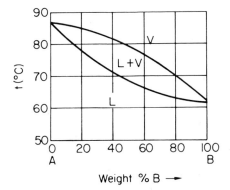

Weight % B →

temperature and volume are so adjusted that one half the mixture (by weight) vaporizes. Estimate the temperature and the composition of each phase.

9-II-20. A certain compound is found to exist in two solid modifications, known, respectively, as α and β. The α-V, β-V, and L-V equilibrium lines are shown, An α-β-L triple point is also shown. Complete the diagram as far as possible and label all lines and areas.

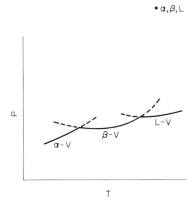

9-II-21.

	Au	Pb
Melting point, °C:	1063	327
	Au_2Pb	$AuPb_2$
Incongruent melting point, °C:	418	254
Atom percent Pb in liquid:	44	71

Eutectic point: $AuPb_2$ + Pb, 215 °C, 84 atom percent Pb

No solid solutions are observed in this system. Sketch the temperature-atom percent phase diagram for the Au-Pb system. Label each region to show the phase(s) present when the system is represented by a point in that region.

9-II-22. At 30°C and 1 atm, lithium and ammonium sulfates form a double salt, $LiNH_4SO_4$. Lithium sulfate forms a hydrate, $Li_2SO_4 \cdot H_2O$. Ammonium sulfate does not form a hydrate. Aqueous solutions in equilibrium with the solid phases have the following compositions:

Solid(s)	Mole percent in solution	
	Li_2SO_4	$(NH_4)_2SO_4$
$Li_2SO_4 \cdot H_2O$	5.2	0
$Li_2SO_4 \cdot H_2O + LiNH_4SO_4$	5.3	4.8
$LiNH_4SO_4 + (NH_4)_2SO_4$	1.9	9.1
$(NH_4)_2SO_4$	0	9.6

[Schreinemakers, *Z. Physik. Chem.*, **59**, 641 (1907)].

(a) Sketch the triangular phase diagram. Label each area to indicate what phases are present when the system has a gross composition corresponding to a point in that region.

(b) Describe the changes that occur as $(NH_4)_2SO_4$ is added in small increments to $Li_2SO_4 \cdot H_2O$ at 30°C.

9-II-23. Sulfuric acid forms three hydrates. All have congruent melting points. There are no solid solutions.

Compound	Melting point, °C
H_2SO_4 (anhydrous)	10.5
$H_2SO_4 \cdot H_2O$	8.6
$H_2SO_4 \cdot 2H_2O$	−38.9
$H_2SO_4 \cdot 4H_2O$	−24.5

(a) Sketch the temperature-mole fraction phase diagram. Label each area to indicate what phases are present when the system has a temperature and gross composition corresponding to a point in that region.

(b) Describe all the changes that occur when sulfuric acid is added in small increments to a sample of ice, the temperature being maintained constant at −30°C. If the information given leaves room for doubt as to the sequence of events, give all possible answers and indicate what additional data you would need to choose among them.

9-II-24. A and B form two solid compounds. A_2B melts at 800°C to a liquid having the composition A_2B. AB_2 decomposes at 700°C to solid B and a liquid phase. The melting point of A is 500°C; of B, 1000°C. No solid solutions are formed.

(a) Sketch the temperature-mole fraction phase diagram for the system A-B. Label each region to show the phase(s) present when the system is represented by a point in that region.

(b) A liquid solution containing 70 mole percent B is cooled slowly from 1100 to 400°C. Sketch a graph showing temperature as a function of time in this cooling process. Show how each major feature of the cooling curve is related to the phase diagram.

9-II-25. Gold and antimony form a compound, $AuSb_2$. These three substances are completely miscible as liquids, but do not form solid solutions with each other. The melting points are as follows:

Au	Sb	$AuSb_2$
1064°	631°	460°C

The following eutectic points are observed:

$Au + AuSb_2 + L$	$AuSb_2 + Sb + L$
360°C, 35 atom percent Sb	456°C

[Vogel, *Z. Anorg. Chem.*, **50**, 145 (1906)].

(a) Sketch the temperature-atom percent phase diagram for this system. Label each region to show the phases present when the system is represented by a point in that region.

(b) A liquid solution containing 20 atom percent Sb and 80 atom percent Au is cooled slowly from 1100 to 200°C. Sketch a curve showing the dependence of temperature on time in this cooling process. Explain each noteworthy feature of the curve in terms of the phase diagram.

(c) You are given the two pure substances Au (X) and $AuSb_2$ (Y), without being told that one of them is a compound containing the other. You proceed to determine the phase diagram for the X-Y system by thermal analysis. How could you then decide by inspection of the phase diagram that Y is a compound containing X and X is not a compound containing Y? Explain.

9-II-26. CaF_2 and $CaCl_2$ are completely miscible as liquids. The following data were obtained on cooling various liquid solutions of CaF_2 and $CaCl_2$:

Mole percent CaCl$_2$	Start of freezing, °C	Completion of freezing, °C
0	1300	1300
30	1050	737
40	950	737
50	820	737
58	737	644
60	735	644
70	700	644
80	644	644
90	710	644
100	774	774

(a) Sketch the temperature-mole percent phase diagram for this system. Label each region to show the phase or phases present when the system is represented by a point in that region.

(b) Describe with the aid of a curve the variation of temperature with time when a mixture of 55 mole percent CaCl$_2$ and 45 mole percent CaF$_2$ is cooled from 1000 to 600°C. Explain each noteworthy feature of the curve in terms of the phase diagram.

9-II-27. A number of liquid solutions of magnesium and copper were prepared. Each solution was allowed to cool slowly and its temperature was plotted as a function of time. Each cooling curve showed one or more breaks or halts as listed in the following table:

Weight percent Cu	Break(s), °C	Halt, °C
0		648
8.57	619	485
16.53	580	485
24.78	531	485
30.10	489	485
34.40	500	485
43.29	540	485
51.60	564.5	485
56.61	567.5	485
56.79	567.5	552
61.70	563	552
65.41		552
73.63	692	552
80.08	793	552

Weight percent Cu	Break(s), °C	Halt, °C
84.43	816	552
84.54	808	722
88.77	753.5	722
90.36		722
96.00	958	722
97.38	1005	722
97.75	1010, 804	
98.50	1042, 874	
100		1083

[Jones, *J. Inst. Metals*, **46**, 395 (1931). The data have been smoothed in places.]

(a) Sketch the temperature-weight percent phase diagram for the Mg-Cu sytem. Label each region to show the phases present when the system is represented by a point in that region.

(b) If any compounds are formed, find their formulas.

9-II-28. The following data were obtained by Keavney and Smith [*J. Phys. Chem.*, **64**, 737 (1960)] for the vapor pressures of liquid and solid $SnBr_4$ at various temperatures:

	Solid		Liquid	
t, °C	9.8	21.0	30.7	41.4
P, torr	0.116	0.321	0.764	1.493

Calculate (a) the triple point, (b) the molar enthalpy of sublimation, and (c) the molar enthalpy of fusion, of $SnBr_4$. Solve (b) and (c) both by an algebraic method and by a graphical method.

9-II-29. Hudson [*Z. Physik. Chem.*, **47**, 113 (1904)] made a phase rule study of the liquid region of the system nicotine-water and discovered an unusual phenomenon. Over a certain range of system composition, as an initially homogeneous solution of nicotine and water is heated it reaches a certain temperature at which the originally homogeneous solution suddenly separates into two different liquid phases coexisting in equilibrium with one another. As the temperature of the system is further increased, the proportions of the two liquid phases gradually change until a temperature is reached at which one of the two phases disappears entirely and the system is completely homogeneous again. Outside this concentration range the system remains homogeneous over the entire temperature interval. Thus on heating solutions of nicotine and water Hudson obtained the following data:

Weight percent nicotine in the total system	Temperature, °C, at which second phase appears	Temperature, °C, at which the system becomes homogeneous again
6.8	94	95
7.8	89	155
10	75	
14.8	65	200
32.2	61	210
49.0	64	205
66.8	72	190
80.2	87	170
82.0	129	130

Draw the temperature-composition phase diagram of this system. Label all areas and indicate the composition(s) of all phase(s) in equilibrium with one another under the following conditions:

	Weight percent nicotine in total system	Temperature, °C
(a)	20	45
(b)	20	120
(c)	20	220
(d)	90	120

9-II-30. Beard and Lyerly [*Anal. Chem.*, **33**, 1781 (1961)] report that arsenic (III) can be separated quantitatively from bismuth (III) and antimony (III) in 8N aqueous HCl by extraction with benzene, the distribution ratio for the arsenic being $c_{H_2O}/c_{benzene} = 0.05$. The bismuth and antimony are virtually insoluble in benzene under these conditions. Determine the number of times it would be necessary to treat a 50-ml portion of an aqueous 8N HCl solution containing originally 0.1000 g of arsenic (III) with fresh 50-ml portions of benzene in order to remove all but 0.1 mg of the arsenic from the aqueous layer.

9-II-31. The phase diagram for the ternary system A-B-H₂O at 25°C is shown.

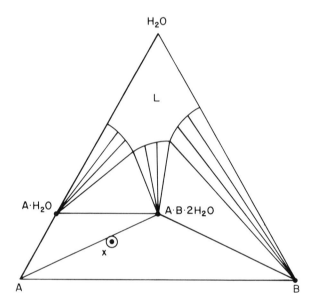

(a) Would it be possible to obtain solid A · B · 2H₂O at this temperature by adding B to A · H₂O ? Explain.

(b) What total system composition is indicated by point x on the diagram ?

9-II-32. The following wet residues data were obtained for the three-component system A-B-C (See figure):

Tie-line No.	Saturated solution composition	Wet residue composition
1	L_1	R_1
2	L_2	R_2
3	L_3	R_3

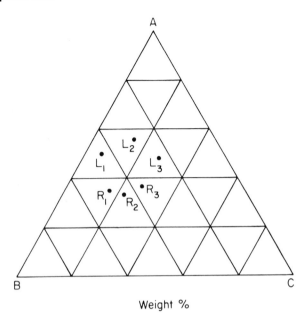

Weight %

(a) Construct the tie lines in the usual manner and indicate the composition of the pure, dry solid phase that is in equilibrium with the saturated solution.

(b) State the system composition indicated by point L_1.

9-II-33. The following data were obtained in a wet residues investigation of the ternary system A-B-C at 25°C:

	Weight percent B	Weight percent C
Tie line No. 1		
Saturated solution	16.0	47.0
Wet residue	32.0	37.0
Tie line No. 2		
Saturated solution	17.0	55.0
Wet residue	30.0	42.0

On triangular graph paper plot all of the data given above, draw in the tie lines, and indicate the composition of the solid phase in weight percent.

9-II-34. In an investigation of phase equilibria in the system NH_4F-KF-H_2O at 25°C, Haendler and Jache [*J. Am. Chem. Soc.*, **72**, 4137 (1950)] obtained the following results:

Saturated Solutions		Wet Residues	
Weight percent NH_4F	Weight percent KF	Weight percent NH_4F	Weight percent KF
0.00	48.96		
1.70	48.76	0.27	63.08
6.53	48.15	1.41	59.32
8.75	48.44	1.60	62.93
10.08	47.88	2.99	58.65
10.94	47.04	43.46	29.58
11.98	44.88	67.94	16.57
12.92	42.93	61.14	19.50
13.93	40.82	70.00	14.96
14.85	38.63	60.34	18.01
17.07	35.01	60.53	16.4
20.37	29.92	70.48	10.99
26.44	23.76	41.23	18.83
31.59	16.85	76.99	5.43
41.27	4.57	80.74	1.64
44.85	0.00		

Plot these data on triangular graph paper, draw in the tie lines, and give the formulas of all solid phases present in the system.

9-II-35. The salts A and B have a common ion. In the system A-B-H_2O at a certain temperature the following saturated solutions are observed to be in equilibrium with the solid phases given:

	Solution	
Solid(s)	Mole percent A	Mole percent B
$A \cdot H_2O$	25	0
$B \cdot 2H_2O$	0	12
$A \cdot H_2O + B \cdot 2H_2O$	20	10

(a) Sketch the triangular phase diagram as far as you can with the data given. Label each region to show the phases present when the system is represented by a point in that region.

(b) Describe what additional information you would need in order to fill in all of the qualitative features of the diagram.

SECTION 9-III

9-III-1. An infinitesimal change in surface tension, γ, is given by

$$d\gamma = \frac{k\,dt}{M^{2/3}v^{2/3}} - \frac{2k(t_c - t - 6)\,dv}{3M^{2/3}v^{5/3}},$$

where M is the molecular weight, v is the specific volume, k is a constant, t is temperature in °C, and t_c is the critical temperature in °C. Instead of using the usual coordinates, such as P, V, T, x, etc., it is desired to plot a phase diagram using surface tension and temperature as the coordinates. Prove that it is valid to do this.

9-III-2. Show that on the basis of slope sign there are 8 and only 8 possible unique configurations of the 2-phase lines around a triple point in a 1-component pressure-temperature diagram. Sketch them.

9-III-3. Explain why the system $KCl\text{-}NaCl\text{-}H_2O$ should be regarded as a 3-component system, whereas $KCl\text{-}NaBr\text{-}H_2O$ should be regarded as a 4-component system.

9-III-4. For each of the following systems determine the number of components.

(a) $NH_4Cl(c)$, $NH_4^+(aq)$, $Cl^-(aq)$, $H_2O(liq)$, $H_3O^+(aq)$, $H_2O(g)$, $NH_3(g)$, $OH^-(aq)$, $NH_4OH(aq)$.

(b) $NH_4Cl(c)$, $NH_3(g)$, $HCl(g)$, where the partial pressure of NH_3 is always equal to the partial pressure of HCl as in the case where all the gas is formed by the sublimation of $NH_4Cl(c)$.

(c) $NH_4Cl(c)$, $NH_3(g)$, $HCl(g)$, where the partial pressure of NH_3 is not necessarily equal to the partial pressure of HCl.

(d) $CH_3COONH_4(c)$, $CH_3COO^-(aq)$, $NH_4^+(aq)$, $H_3O^+(aq)$, $NH_3(aq)$, $OH^-(aq)$, $CH_3COOH(aq)$, $H_2O(liq)$, $H_2O(g)$, taking hydrolysis into account.

(e) $NaCl(c)$, $KBr(c)$, $K^+(aq)$, $Na^+(aq)$, $Cl^-(aq)$, $Br^-(aq)$, $H_2O(liq)$, $H_2O(g)$.

(f) $NaCl(c)$, $KCl(c)$, $Na^+(aq)$, $Cl^-(aq)$, $H_2O(liq)$, $H_2O(g)$.

(g) $CaCl_2 \cdot 6H_2O(c)$, $Ca^{2+}(aq)$, $Cl^-(aq)$, $H_2O(liq)$, $H_2O(g)$.

(h) $CaCO_3(c)$, $CaO(c)$, $CO_2(g)$, where all the CaO and CO_2 in the system are formed by the decomposition of $CaCO_3(c)$.

9-III-5. The salts MX and MY form hydrates $MX \cdot 2H_2O$ and $MY \cdot H_2O$. At 25°C a solution consisting of 20 mole percent MX and 80 mole percent H_2O is saturated with $MX \cdot 2H_2O$; a solution consisting of 30 mole percent MY and 70 mole percent H_2O is saturated with $MY \cdot H_2O$. A solution saturated with both hydrates contains 15 mole percent MX and 20 mole percent MY. The pressures of water vapor in equilibrium with certain mixtures are as follows:

Mixture	Vapor pressure, torr
$MX + MX \cdot 2H_2O$	13
$MX \cdot 2H_2O$ + saturated solution (MY absent)	19
$MY + MY \cdot H_2O$	10
$MY \cdot H_2O$ + saturated solution (MX absent)	17
$MX \cdot 2H_2O + MY \cdot H_2O$ + doubly saturated solution	14

(a) Sketch the triangular phase diagram, in terms of mole fractions, for the system MX-MY-H_2O at 25°C and 1 atm. Label each region.

(b) Describe the changes that will occur in the condensed phases as water vapor is gradually pumped off at 25°C from a solution consisting, initially, of 10 mole percent MX, 10 mole percent MY, and 80 mole percent H_2O until all water has been removed. Indicate, as far as you can with the information given, the pressure of water vapor at each stage of the pumping process.

CHAPTER 10

Electrochemistry

SECTION 10-I

Table 10.1

*Standard Reduction Potentials
in Aqueous Solution at 25°C*

	$E°$, volts
$Ag^+ + e^- \rightarrow Ag(s)$	+0.7996
$Ag(NH_3)_2^+ + e^- \rightarrow Ag(s) + 2NH_3(aq)$	+0.373
$Cl_2(g) + 2e^- \rightarrow 2Cl^-$	+1.358
$Cu^{2+} + 2e^- \rightarrow Cu(s)$	+0.337
$Cu^+ + e^- \rightarrow Cu(s)$	+0.522
$Fe^{2+} + 2e^- \rightarrow Fe(s)$	−0.440
$Fe^{3+} + e^- \rightarrow Fe^{2+}$	+0.771
$2H^+ + 2e^- \rightarrow H_2(g)$	0
$Hg_2^{2+} + 2e^- \rightarrow 2Hg(liq)$	+0.7986
$Hg^{2+} + 2e^- \rightarrow Hg(liq)$	+0.854
$Hg_2Cl_2(s) + 2e^- \rightarrow 2Hg(liq) + 2Cl^-$	+0.2676
$Na^+ + e^- \rightarrow Na(s)$	−2.7132
$O_2(g) + 4H^+ + 4e^- \rightarrow 2H_2O$	+0.1129
$Pb^{2+} + 2e^- \rightarrow Pb(s)$	−0.126
$Tl^+ + e^- \rightarrow Tl(s)$	−0.3363
$Tl^{3+} + 2e^- \rightarrow Tl^+$	+0.125
$Zn^{2+} + 2e^- \rightarrow Zn(s)$	−0.7628

10-I-1. The following data were obtained by Brönsted and King [*J. Am. Chem. Soc.*, **49**, 193 (1927)] for the equivalent conductance of nitramide solutions in water at 15°C:

c, M	0.03	0.015	0.0075	0.00375	0.001875
Λ, ohm^{-1} cm^2 equiv^{-1}	1.017	1.446	2.052	2.89	4.053

$\lambda^{\circ}_{H^+} = 298$, $\lambda^{\circ}_{Na^+} = 39.9$, and $\Lambda^{\circ}_{NaHN_2O_2} = 93$ ohm^{-1} cm^2 equiv^{-1}. Evaluate the equilibrium constant for the dissociation of nitramide in accordance with the equation

$$H_2N_2O_2 \rightleftharpoons H^+ + HN_2O_2^-$$

10-I-2. For the balanced Wheatstone bridge circuit shown prove that

$$\frac{R_1}{R_2} = \frac{R_3}{R_4}$$

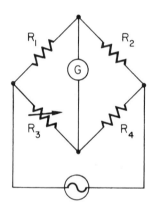

10-I-3. At 25°C the limiting equivalent conductance of potassium picrate is 103.97 ohm^{-1} cm^2 equiv^{-1}, and that of the potassium ion is 73.58 ohm^{-1} cm^2 equiv^{-1} [McDowell and Kraus, *J. Am. Chem. Soc.*, **73**, 2170 (1951)]. Calculate the limiting equivalent conductance of the picrate ion and its transference number at infinite dilution.

10-I-4. The conductance of potassium iodate (KIO$_3$) at 25°C was measured by Monk [*J. Am. Chem. Soc.*, **70**, 3281 (1948)]. The data are presented below. c is the concentration of potassium iodate in gram equivalents per liter, and Λ is the equivalent conductance of the solution corrected for that of the water. Evaluate Λ_0, the limiting equivalent conductance of KIO$_3$.

c	Λ
0.00018265	113.07
0.00035295	112.61
0.00070430	111.91
0.00099845	111.45
0.0017117	110.55
0.0025362	109.78
0.0032859	109.19
0.0039118	108.78

10-I-5. Basiński, Szymański, and Betto [*Roczniki Chem.*, **33**, 289 (1959)] determined the solubility of the sparingly soluble salt cobaltous ferrocyanide, $Co_2Fe(CN)_6$, by measuring the specific conductance of its saturated solution. They found that at 25°C the saturated solution had a specific conductance of 2.06×10^{-6} ohm^{-1} cm^{-1}, while the specific conductance of the water used was 4.1×10^{-7} ohm^{-1} cm^{-1}. The equivalent conductance of the Co^{2+} ion is 43 ohm^{-1} cm^2 equiv^{-1}, and that of the $Fe(CN)_6^{4+}$ ion is 111 ohm^{-1} cm^2 equiv^{-1}. Calculate the solubility of $Co_2Fe(CN)_6$ in water at 25°C.

10-I-6. The equivalent conductance (Λ) of silver chlorate at a series of concentrations c (g equiv liter^{-1}) are reported below [Jones, *J. Am. Chem. Soc.*, **69**, 2066 (1957)]:

c	Λ
0.0010256	123.43
0.0013694	122.94
0.0029782	121.14
0.0032500	120.95

Find Λ_0 for this compound.

10-I-7. A 0.1000 molar aqueous solution of LiX has specific conductance 0.009000 ohm^{-1} cm^{-1} at 25°C. The ionic conductance of Li^+ is 39.5 ohm^{-1} cm^2 equiv^{-1}.

(a) Find the equivalent conductance of the solution.

(b) Find the ionic conductance of X^- as accurately as you can with the information available to you.

10-I-8. A solution of the strong electrolyte AB was electrolyzed in a Hittorf apparatus with a current of 0.100 amp for 9650 sec.

The electrode reactions were $A \rightarrow A^+ + e^-$, $A^+ + e^- \rightarrow A$. The solution was initially 0.100 molal in AB (0.100 mole AB per kg H_2O). After completion of the electrolysis, it was found that the solution in the anode compartment consisted of 100 g H_2O and 0.0165 mole AB. Find the transference (transport) number of A^+ in this solution.

10-I-9. Longsworth [*J. Am. Chem. Soc.*, **54**, 2741 (1932)] determined the transference number of the sodium ion in 0.0200 M NaCl at 25°C by the moving boundary method and obtained the following data:

l, cm (distance traveled by moving boundary)	0	1.00	6.00	10.00
t, sec	0	344	2070	3453

The cathode was Ag | AgCl and the anode was Cd. The cross-sectional area of the tube was 0.1115 cm². The current was 0.0016001 amp. Calculate the transference number of the sodium ion under these conditions.

10-I-10. A moving boundary experiment was performed at 25°C with 0.100 M KCl on the bottom and (initially) 0.0700 M NaCl on top. The transport numbers of K^+ and Na^+ in these solutions are 0.490 and 0.388, respectively. The boundary moved downward. The cross-sectional area of the tube was 0.100 cm². The charge passed through was 96.5 coulombs.

(a) How far did the boundary move?

(b) While the current was flowing, what was the concentration of NaCl just above the boundary?

10-I-11. The following solubility data for the sparingly soluble tritrivalent salt $[Co(NH_3)_6]^{III} [Fe(CN)_6]^{III}$ in the presence of KNO_3 were obtained by La Mer, King, and Mason [*J. Am. Chem. Soc.*, **49**, 363 (1927)]:

Concentration of added KNO_3, M	S, Solubility $\times$ 10^5, M at 25°C
0.0000	2.900
0.0005	3.308
0.0010	3.586
0.0020	4.080

Show that the data are in agreement with the Debye-Hückel theory and calculate the mean activity coefficient of the $[Co(NH_3)_6]^{3+}$ and $[Fe(CN)_6]^{3-}$ ions at each concentration.

10-I-12. The ionization constant of lactic acid at 25°C is 1.4×10^{-4}. A buffer solution is prepared by adding 1.00 mole of lactic acid and 0.80 mole of sodium lactate to 1 kg of water. Assume that water is at unit activity and that the activity coefficient of each univalent ion is 0.65 throughout this problem.

(a) Find the pH (in the activity sense) of this solution at 25°C.

(b) Find the change in the pH of the solution resulting from the addition of 0.50 mole of sodium hydroxide to the quantity of solution containing 1 kg of water.

(c) Find the change in pH resulting from the addition of 0.50 mole of sodium hydroxide to 1 kg of pure water at 25°C.

10-I-13. The solubility product of CuCl at 25°C is 2.29×10^{-7}. From this information and standard reduction potentials given in Table 10.1 calculate (a) $E°$ for the half cell $Cl^- \mid CuCl(s) \mid Cu(s)$, and (b) the standard free energy of formation (in cal mole^{-1}) of CuCl(s).

SECTION 10-II

10-II-1. From the values given below for the equivalent conductance of cadmium perchlorate in dilute aqueous solutions at 25°C [Matheson, *J. Phys. Chem.*, **66**, 439 (1962)] what conclusions

Concentration, g equiv liter^{-1}	Λ, cm^2 ohm^{-1} equiv^{-1} at 25°C
0.1	92.64
0.08	94.21
0.06	96.22
0.04	98.93
0.02	103.30
0.01	107.15
0.005	110.45
0.001	115.74

can be drawn about the completeness of dissociation of the dissolved salt under these conditions? The tabulated values have been corrected for hydrolysis. Suggestion: plot Λ vs $c^{1/2}$.

10-II-2. Outline the steps involved in going from the expression $K = ka/l$ to the expression $\Lambda = 1000\,k/c$, where K is conductance, c is concentration, k is specific conductance, a is area, l is length, and Λ is equivalent conductance.

10-II-3. A solution containing, initially, 0.0250 mole Na_2SO_4 per 100 g H_2O was electrolyzed at 25°C in a Hittorf apparatus between inert electrodes. The anode reaction was

$$2H_2O \rightarrow 4H^+ + O_2 + 4e^-.$$

At the conclusion of the experiment the anode compartment contained 100 g H_2O and titration showed that 0.0100 mole H^+ was also present. The transport number of Na^+ in this solution is 0.390. Find the number of moles of Na^+ and of SO_4^{2-} in the anode compartment at the end of the experiment.

10-II-4. A Hittorf apparatus contained an aqueous solution of AgX with 1.500 g AgX per 101.50 g solution. Direct current was passed through the solution until 1.0787 g Ag had been deposited at the cathode. After the current was shut off, the solution in the cathode section was removed; it weighed 100.50 g and contained 0.500 g AgX. The molecular weight of AgX is 150.0 g mole^{-1}. Find the transference number of Ag^+ in the AgX solution.

10-II-5. A solution of $CuSO_4$ was electrolyzed in a Hittorf apparatus with Pt (inert) electrodes. The electrode processes were

$$2H_2O \rightarrow 4H^+ + O_2(g) + 4e^-$$
$$Cu^{2+} + 2e^- \rightarrow Cu$$

The solution was initially 0.1000 molal. At the end of the electrolysis the anode compartment contained 100.0 g H_2O, 0.00500 mole H_2SO_4, and 0.00800 mole $CuSO_4$. Assume that the only ions present initially, and outside the anode compartment at all times, were Cu^{2+} and SO_4^{2-}.

(a) How many faradays passed through the circuit?

(b) Calculate the transport number of Cu^{2+} in $CuSO_4$.

(c) At the end of the electrolysis the cathode compartment contained 100.0 g H_2O. How many moles of $CuSO_4$ did it contain?

(d) The equivalent conductance of $CuSO_4$ at infinite dilution is 133.6 ohm^{-1} cm^2 equiv^{-1}. Calculate the equivalent ionic conductance of Cu^{2+} at infinite dilution. What approximation(s) are you making in this calculation?

10-II-6. An aqueous solution of $K_4Fe(CN)_6$, initially 1.000 m (molal), was electrolyzed at 25°C in a Hittorf apparatus with Pt electrodes until 0.010 faraday had passed through. The only anode reaction was $Fe(CN)_6^{4-} \rightarrow Fe(CN)_6^{3-} + e^-$. The solution in the anode compartment, after electrolysis, contained 100.0 g H_2O and was 1.015 m with respect to total Fe.

(a) How many equivalents are there in a mole of $Fe(CN)_6^{4-}$ (i) from the point of view of conductance? (ii) from the point of view of the reaction at the electrode?

(b) How many moles of $Fe(CN)_6^{4-}$ reacted at the anode?

(c) How many moles of $Fe(CN)_6^{4-}$ entered or left (state which) the anode compartment?

(d) Calculate the transport number of $Fe(CN)_6^{4-}$ in $K_4Fe(CN)_6$.

(e) Calculate the ionic conductance of $Fe(CN)_6^{4-}$ at infinite dilution at 25°C given that the corresponding quantity for K^+ is 73.52 ohm^{-1} cm^2 equiv^{-1}. Point out any approximations that you make in this calculation.

10-II-7. The apparent transference numbers t_+ of the Zn^{2+} ion in ZnI_2 solutions were measured by Stokes and Levien [*J. Am. Chem. Soc.*, **68**, 1852 (1946)] using concentration cells with and without transference. The transference number was found to vary with m (molality of ZnI_2) as follows (selected values):

m	0.05	0.1	1.0	2.5	4.0	5.0	10.0
t_+	0.382	0.363	0.291	0.115	−0.050	−0.190	−0.550

How do you account for this strange trend in t_+? How can t_+ be negative?

10-II-8. The formula $t_{\pm} = E_t/E$ (where E_t is the potential of a cell with transference and E is the potential of the corresponding cell without transference) for calculating transference numbers from emf data is valid only if the transference numbers can be considered independent of concentration. If the transference numbers vary with concentration, as in the case of LiCl solutions, t_+ can be calculated from the formula

$$dE_t = \pm 2t_\pm \frac{RT}{\mathscr{F}} d \ln a_\pm$$

where $a_\pm$ is the geometrical mean of the activities of the ions in one of the solutions. t_+ appears if the electrodes are reversible with respect to the negative ion, and conversely. The following empirical equation was obtained for an emf equivalent to that of the cell Ag | AgCl | LiCl(c_1) ¦ LiCl(c_2) | AgCl | Ag with transference, by MacInnes and Beattie [*J. Am. Chem. Soc.*, **42**, 1117 (1920)].

$$E_t = -43.865 + 45.363(\log A) - 1.4902(\log A)^2$$

where A is 10^4 times the mean ionic activity of LiCl at concentration c_1; E_t is in millivolts; $a_\pm$ at concentration c_2 is 10^{-3} (this choice merely fixes the constant term in E_t). The activity coefficient of a 0.010 M solution of LiCl is 0.905. Evaluate t_+ for a 0.010 M solution of LiCl.

10-II-9. The mean ionic activity coefficient of an electrolyte in a dilute solution is given approximately by

$$\ln \gamma_\pm = -A\sqrt{m}$$

where m is the molality and A is a constant. Using the Gibbs–Duhem equation find the activity coefficient γ_1 of the solvent in this dilute solution in terms of A, m, and constants characteristic of the solvent and solute. Observe that

$$\ln X_1 = \ln \left(\frac{n_1}{n_1 + m\nu}\right) = \ln \left(\frac{1}{1 + m\nu/n_1}\right) \approx -\frac{m\nu}{n_1}$$

where ν is the number of ions in the formula (for example $\nu = 2$ for NaCl) and n_1 is the number of moles of solvent in 1000 g of solvent. All quantities except γ_1, the unknown, can thus be expressed in terms of the variable m.

10-II-10. The solubility product constant of AgCl is 1.71×10^{-10} at 25°C.

(a) What is the mean ionic activity on the molality scale of AgCl in a saturated aqueous solution at 25°C?

(b) What is the mean ionic activity on the mole fraction scale, referred to the infinitely dilute solution, of AgCl in a saturated aqueous solution at 25°C?

10-II-11. An improvement on the Debye-Hückel limiting law gives the following equation for the activity coefficient of a single ion M with charge z_M:

$$\log \gamma_M = \frac{-A z_M^2 \sqrt{I}}{1 + \sqrt{I}} + \sum_i B_{MX_i} m_{X_i}$$

where A is the usual Debye-Hückel constant, I is the ionic strength, the summation is over all ions present with charge *opposite* to M, B_{MX_i} is a parameter characteristic of the MX_i pair, and m_{X_i} is the molality of X_i. Show that for the electrolyte $M_{\nu_+} X_{\nu_-}$ the mean ionic activity coefficient is given by

$$\log \gamma_\pm = \frac{-A |z_M z_X| \sqrt{I}}{1 + \sqrt{I}} + \frac{\nu_+}{\nu_+ + \nu_-} \sum_i B_{MX_i} m_{X_i} + \frac{\nu_-}{\nu_+ + \nu_-} \sum_i B_{MX_i} m_{M_i}$$

where the first summation is over all negative ions and the second is over all positive ions.

10-II-12. The thermodynamic ionization constant of α-chloropropionic acid at 25°C is 1.47×10^{-3}. Calculate the degree of ionization of this acid in 0.010 m aqueous solution at 25°C. Use the Debye-Hückel limiting law to estimate activity coefficients.

10-II-13. The ionization constant of 2-thiophenecarboxylic acid (C_4H_3SCOOH or HA) is $K_a = 3.3 \times 10^{-4}$ at 25°C.

(a) Find the standard electrode potential E^0 for the half reaction

$$HA(aq) + e^- \rightarrow A^-(aq) + \tfrac{1}{2} H_2(g)$$

(b) Calculate the fraction of HA ionized in a 0.200 m aqueous solution of HA that is also 1.00 m with respect to $MgCl_2$. Make reasonable approximations in calculating activity coefficients but do not assume that they are equal to one.

For problems 10-II-14 to 19, note that the ionization constant of water at 25°C is 1.00×10^{-14}.

10-II-14. The ionization constants of H_2CO_3 at 25°C are

$K_1 = 4.30 \times 10^{-7}$,

$K_2 = 5.61 \times 10^{-11}$.

For a 0.10 m aqueous solution of $NaHCO_3$ at 25°C (a) Write all the equations necessary for calculation of the molalities of all species present; (b) Making appropriate simplifying assumptions, find the molalities of H^+ and of CO_3^{2-} in this solution. Assume that activities are equal to molalities.

10-II-15. The acidic ionization constant of HF is 3.5×10^{-4}. The basic ionization constant of novocaine is 7×10^{-6}. A solution was prepared by dissolving 0.100 mole HF and 0.200 mole novocaine in 1000 g H_2O.

(a) Write six equations in which the unknowns are the molalities of HF, novocaine (B), F^-, novocainium ion (BH^+), H^+, and OH^-. Assume that activities are equal to molalities.

(b) By making suitable approximations (state what they are) solve these equations for the molalities of HF and H^+.

10-II-16. At 25°C the ionization constant of nicotinic acid is 1.4×10^{-5}; the basic ionization constant of quinoline is 8.7×10^{-6}. A solution was prepared by adding 0.100 mole of quinolinium chloride and 0.050 mole of potassium nicotinate to 1000 g of water at 25°C.

(a) Write all the equations that, when solved, will yield the molality of every chemical species in this solution except water. Assume that water is at unit activity and that the activity coefficient of each univalent ion is 0.70.

(b) Making simplifying assumptions when necessary find the molalities of H_3O^+ and of nicotinic acid in this solution.

10-II-17. Quinine $(C_{20}H_{24}N_2O_2)$ is a base that can accept two protons. Its first and second basic ionization constants are $K_1 = 2.0 \times 10^{-6}$ and $K_2 = 1.35 \times 10^{-10}$. A solution was prepared by adding 0.10 mole of quinine and 0.10 mole of HCl to 1.00 kg of water at 25°C.

(a) Estimate the ionic strength of the solution. Use this estimate and the Debye-Hückel equation to find the approximate activity coefficient of each ion in the solution.

(b) Write all the equations that, when solved, will yield the molality of every chemical species except water in this solution. Assume that water is at unit activity.

(c) Making simplifying approximations when necessary find the molalities of OH^- and of quinine in this solution.

10-II-18. At 25°C in aqueous solution the ionization constant of mandelic acid is 4.29×10^{-4}; the basic ionization constant of p-anisidine is 5.13×10^{-6}. A solution was prepared by dissolving 0.040 mole mandelic acid and 0.060 mole p-anisidine in 1000 g H_2O at 25°C. Only one phase is present at equilibrium.

(a) Estimate the ionic strength of this solution. Use this estimate and the Debye-Hückel equation to find the activity coefficient of each ionic species in the solution.

(b) Write a set of equations that, when solved, will yield the molality of every chemical species except water in this solution. Assume that the activity and the mole fraction of water are unity.

(c) Making appropriate simplifying assumptions find the molalities of mandelic acid and of H^+ in this solution.

10-II-19. The acidic ionization constants at 25°C of glycinium ion

$$H_2C \text{------} C-OH$$
$$| \quad\quad ||$$
$$NH_3^+ \quad O$$

are $K_1 = 4.47 \times 10^{-3}$, $K_2 = 1.66 \times 10^{-10}$. A solution was prepared by dissolving 0.100 mole of glycine and 0.040 mole NaOH in 1000 g H_2O at 25°C.

(a) Estimate the ionic strength of this solution. Use your estimate and the Debye-Hückel equation to find the activity coefficient of each ion present in the solution.

(b) Write the equations that could be solved to give the molalities of all species present in this solution except water.

(c) With the aid of appropriate simplyfying assumptions

obtain one equation in which the unknown is the molality of the glycinium ion.

(d) Solve the equation of (c) making further approximations if needed.

10-II-20. (a) Devise a galvanic cell in which the process is

$Pb(s) + CuBr_2(aq, 0.0100 \; m, \text{strong electrolyte}) \rightarrow PbBr_2(s) + Cu(s)$

Describe the cell in the conventional notation.

(b) For the cell in (a) at 25°C, $E = +0.442$ volt. Assume that the mean ionic activity coefficient of $CuBr_2$ is $\gamma_\pm = 0.707 = 10^{-0.150}$. Find $E°$ for the cell.

(c) Find the solubility product of $PbBr_2$ at 25°C.

10-II-21. $Na(s) \mid NaI$ in $C_2H_5NH_2(liq) \mid Na(0.206 \text{ percent in Hg})$
$$E = 0.8453 \text{ volt}$$
$Na(0.206\% \text{ in Hg}) \mid NaCl(aq, 0.1005 \; m) \mid Hg_2Cl_2(s) \mid Hg(liq)$
$$E = 2.2676 \text{ volt}$$
For 0.1005 m NaCl, $\log \gamma_\pm = -0.1019$.
Calculate the standard potential $E°$ for the hypothetical half cell $Na(s) \mid Na^+(aq)$. Compare your result with the tabulated value.

10-II-22. The following data refer to the cell $Zn(s) \mid ZnSO_4(aq)$, molality $= m \mid PbSO_4(s) \mid Pb$ at 25°C:

m	$\sqrt{m}$	$\dfrac{RT}{\mathscr{F}} \ln m$ (volts)	E (volts)
0.001000	0.03162	−0.17745	0.59714
0.005000	0.07071	−0.13611	0.56598

(a) Write the chemical equation for the cell process.
(b) Write the Nernst equation for this cell, in terms of m and the mean ionic activity coefficient $\gamma_\pm$ of $ZnSO_4$. Assume that $PbSO_4$ is completely insoluble.
(c) By a process of linear extrapolation, either graphical or numerical, find $E°$ for the cell.
(d) Find $\gamma_\pm$ in the 0.005 m solution from the emf data.

10-II-23. (a) For the reaction

$$2Ag(s) + PbSO_4(s) \rightarrow Pb(s) + 2Ag^+(aq) + SO_4^{2-}(aq)$$

$$\Delta H^{\circ}_{298} = 53.22 \text{ kcal}, \quad \Delta G^{\circ}_{298} = 53.41 \text{ kcal},$$

and $\Delta C^{\circ}_{P,298} = -8.7 \text{ cal } {}^{\circ}K^{-1}$.

Find the equilibrium constant K as a function of temperature. Your expression should contain only T and actual numbers. Make any reasonable and necessary approximations.

(b) Devise a galvanic cell, or combination of cells, that can be used to determine K for the reaction of (a) at one temperature. Show what measurements would have to be made and how they would be used to calculate K. Illustrate with roughly drawn graphs when appropriate. Assume that $PbSO_4$ is completely insoluble in water and that Ag_2SO_4 is sufficiently soluble.

(c) Show how K would be changed if the activities of the ions were expressed on the "rational" (mole fraction) scale instead of the "practical" (molality) scale.

10-II-24. For the galvanic cell Pt | H_2(1 atm) | HBr (aq, c mole liter^{-1}) | AgBr(s) | Ag at 25°C, the following reversible emf's were observed:

	(1)	(2)	(3)
$10^4 c$	4.042	8.444	37.19
E (volts)	0.47381	0.43636	0.36173

(a) Write the equation for the cell process.

(b) From the data on each of the solutions (1) and (2), considered separately, calculate E° for the cell as predicted by the Debye-Hückel limiting law. Assume that molarity and molality are equal.

(c) With the aid of a graph of the results of (b), estimate the actual value of E°.

(d) Find the mean ionic activity coefficient of HBr in solution (3) from (i) the experimental data; (ii) the Debye-Hückel limiting law.

10-II-25. The following potentials of the cell Pt | H$_2$(g, 1 atm) | HBr(m) | AgBr | Ag at 25°C were obtained by Hetzer, Robinson, and Bates [*J. Phys. Chem.*, **66**, 1423 (1962)]:

m	E
0.005125	0.34594
0.010021	0.31265
0.015158	0.29225
0.02533	0.26718
0.03006	0.25901

Evaluate $E°$ for this cell at 25°C.

10-II-26. On the basis of the following information [Danner, *J. Am. Chem. Soc.*, **44**, 2832 (1922)] calculate the dissociation constant of ethyl alcohol at 25°C; that is, K for the reaction

$C_2H_5OH \rightarrow C_2H_5O^- + H^+$.

	$E°$ at 25°C (volts)
(a) H$_2$	HCl(in alcohol)| Hg$_2$Cl$_2$	Hg	−0.0216
(b) Hg	Hg$_2$Cl$_2$	NaCl(in alcohol)| Na(2-phase amalgam)	−1.8562
(c) Na(2-phase amalgam)| NaOC$_2$H$_5$(in C$_2$H$_5$OH)| H$_2$	0.7458

10-II-27. (a) Write the equation for the overall reaction in the cell

Pt | H$_2$(1 atm)| HA, NaA, NaCl, H$_2$O | AgCl | Ag

where HA represents a *weak* acid.

(b) Express $E - E°$ for this cell in terms of T, universal constants, and the molalities and activity coefficients (mean ionic when appropriate) of HA, NaA, and NaCl. Describe how E^0 for this cell could be determined experimentally.

(c) Answer (a) and (b) for a cell like that of (a) except that HA has been replaced by HCl and NaA has been eliminated. Use primes to label quantities referring to the new cell.

(d) Show how the cells of (a) and (c) could be combined so that the overall reaction for the combined cells is HA + H$_2$O $\rightleftharpoons$ H$_3$O$^+$ + A$^-$.

(e) Express the equilibrium constant K (or ln K) for the reaction of (d) in terms of $E°$ and $E°'$. Show how measurements on the combination of cells can be used to obtain K.

10-II-28. (a) Find the mean ionic activity coefficient of $ZnCl_2$ in a 0.00500 m aqueous solution of $ZnCl_2$ at 25°C by using the Debye-Hückel equation.

(b) The emf of the cell

$Zn(s)|\ ZnCl_2(aq, 0.00500\ m)|\ Hg_2Cl_2(s)|\ Hg(liq)$

is $+1.2272$ volt at 25°C. Find $E°$ for this cell assuming that the Debye-Hückel equation is valid.

(c) Calculate $E°$ for the cell from Table 10.1. Compare with the results of (b).

10-II-29. In the cell

$Cd(X_1)$ in $Hg\ |\ CdSO_4$ solution $|\ Cd(X_2)$ in Hg

the electrodes are solutions (amalgams) of cadmium in mercury with the mole fractions of cadmium equal to X_1 and X_2, respectively. Mercury may be considered inert.

(a) For $X_1 = 1.75 \times 10^{-2}$, $X_2 = 1.75 \times 10^{-4}$ calculate the reversible emf (with sign) of the cell at 25°C, assuming that Cd and Hg form ideal solutions.

(b) The observed emf is 0.05926 volts. Find the ratio of the activity coefficients of cadmium (on the mole fraction scale) in the two amalgams.

10-II-30. Using emf's in Table 10.1, calculate the emf of the half reaction $2Hg^{2+} + 2e^- \rightarrow Hg_2^{2+}$.

10-II-31. Evaluate $E°$ for the half reaction $Fe \rightarrow Fe^{3+} + 3e^-$ from the data in Table 10.1.

10-II-32. Ewing and Eldridge [*J. Am. Chem. Soc.*, **44**, 1484 (1922)] titrated 10 ml of a uranium (III) solution with 0.09064 $N\ K_2Cr_2O_7$ potentiometrically and obtained the following data. Plot E vs V and $\Delta E/\Delta V$ vs $\bar{V}$ (the average between consecutive V's) and determine the total volume of $K_2Cr_2O_7$ added at the U(IV) and the U(VI) end points.

V, ml $K_2Cr_2O_7$ added	E, mV	V, ml $K_2Cr_2O_7$ added	E, mV
0.0	−570	4.4	110
0.05	−565	6.5	120
0.15	−560	8.7	130
0.2	−530	10.3	140
0.25	−490	10.4	150
0.3	−440	10.5	170
0.35	−70	10.6	350
0.4	50	10.8	370
0.5	65	10.9	390
2.5	90	11.1	420
		11.55	440

10-II-33. State the conditions under which each of the following formulas is valid:

(a) $E = 0$ (b) $E^\circ = 0$

(c) $\Lambda = \Lambda_0 - \text{constant} \times c^{1/2}$ (d) $\log \gamma_\pm = -0.509 \sqrt{I}$

(e) $t_+ = \dfrac{u_+}{u_+ + u_-}$ (f) $a_\pm^3 = 4m^3\gamma_\pm^3$

(g) $c = 1000 \dfrac{k}{\Lambda_0}$ (h) $\Delta H = -n\mathscr{F}\left[E - T\left(\dfrac{\partial E}{\partial T}\right)_P\right]$

(i) $t_- = \dfrac{E_t}{E}$

10-II-34. A certain gaseous compound, X, has molecular weight 100.0 g mole^{-1}. Its density is kept constant at 1.000×10^{-3} g cm^{-3}. Its dielectric constant is 1.001212 at 200°K and 1.0007575 at 400°K. Find the permanent dipole moment μ and the polarizability α of the X molecule. Show how the units of your answer are arrived at.

SECTION 10-III

10-III-1. A solution of $FeCl_3$ was initially 2.0000 molal. It was electrolyzed between Pt (inert) electrodes in a Hittorf experiment at

25°C. The only cathode reaction was $Fe^{3+} + e^- \rightarrow Fe^{2+}$. After electrolysis the solution in the cathode compartment contained 50.00 g H_2O and was 1.5750 m in $FeCl_3$ and 0.5000 m in $FeCl_2$.

(a) How many faradays passed through the circuit?

(b) Find the transference number of Cl^- in this solution.

(c) The equivalent ionic conductance of Cl^- at infinite dilution at 25°C is 76.35 ohm^{-1} cm^2 eq^{-1}. Find the equivalent conductance of Fe^{3+} at infinite dilution at 25°C. What approximations, if any, do you make in this calculation?

10-III-2. An aqueous solution containing NaBr and Br_2 was used in a Hittorf experiment. The only electrode reactions were $2Br^- \rightarrow Br_2 + 2e^-$, $Br_2 + 2e^- \rightarrow 2Br^-$. After electrolysis the anode compartment contained 100.0 g H_2O, 0.1100 mole Br_2, and 0.0920 mole NaBr; the cathode compartment contained 100.0 g H_2O, 0.0900 mole Br_2, and 0.1080 mole NaBr. No Br_2 was allowed to escape from the solution. Find the transport numbers of Na^+ and Br^- in this solution.

(Hint: How much Br_2 was initially present in each compartment?)

10-III-3. (a) Suppose that the mean ionic activity coefficient of a certain electrolyte is given by $\ln \gamma_\pm = -B\sqrt{m} + Cm$, where m is the molality of the electrolyte and B and C are constants. Obtain an exact expression for the activity coefficient γ_1 of the solvent in terms of B, C, m, and quantities characteristic of solvent and solute.

(b) Use your formula to find γ_1 in a 0.0010 m aqueous solution of Na_2SO_4 at 25°C, assuming that $C = 0$, that B is given by the Debye-Hückel limiting law, and that molarity and molality may be considered equal.

(c) Find the osmotic pressure of a 0.0010 m aqueous solution of Na_2SO_4 at 25°C.

10-III-4. In the Debye-Hückel theory we assume that the solution as a whole is electrically neutral: $\sigma_0 = 0$, where $\sigma_0 = \sum_i C_i Q_i$, C_i is the concentration of ions of species i in ions cm^{-3}, and Q_i is the corresponding ionic charge in esu ion^{-1}. Let us obtain a more general theory by abandoning this assumption. Then

$$\frac{1}{r^2}\frac{d}{dr}\left(r^2\frac{dU}{dr}\right) = b^2 U - \frac{4\pi\sigma_0}{\epsilon}$$

where U is the electrostatic potential at the distance r from a certain ion,

$$b = \left(\frac{4\pi e^2}{\epsilon k T}\sum_i C_i z_i^2\right)^{1/2}$$

e is the electronic charge, ϵ is the dielectric constant of the medium, $z_i = Q_i/e$, and k and T have the usual meaning. The general solution of this differential equation is

$$U = \frac{A\exp(-br) + B\exp(br)}{r} + \frac{4\pi\sigma_0}{b^2\epsilon}$$

where A and B are constants of integration. For an ion of charge z obtain an expression for the activity coefficient (or its logarithm) based on this more general theory, in terms of b, σ_0, z, ϵ, T, and universal constants. Assume that the limit at infinite dilution of $\sigma_0/b^2 = 0$.

10-III-5. What is the pH of a $10^{-8}\ M$ solution of HCl at 25°C?

10-III-6. A person who has a superficial acquaintance with thermodynamics consults you about the following difficulty: "The emf of the cell Pt | H$_2$(g)| HCl(aq)| AgCl | Ag is given by

$$E = E° - \frac{RT}{\mathscr{F}}\ln\frac{a_{H^+}a_{Cl^-}}{f_{H_2}^{1/2}}$$

But $a_{H^+}a_{Cl^-}/f_{H_2}^{1/2}$ is the equilibrium constant of the reaction $\frac{1}{2}H_2 + AgCl \rightarrow Ag + H^+ + Cl^-$, and I can look up this constant at any given temperature in a table. I can also look up $E°$. Should we conclude that E depends only on temperature?" Explain what incorrect assumptions have been made, what the corresponding correct statements are, and under what special conditions, if any, the assumptions and conclusions would be correct.

10-III-7. (a) Devise a galvanic cell, or combination of cells, that can be used to determine $\Delta G°$ for the process

$$Ag(s) + \tfrac{1}{2}Br_2(liq) \rightarrow AgBr(s)$$

at one temperature. Show how $\Delta G°$ can be calculated from the data obtained with your cell(s).

(b) The value of $\Delta G°$ obtained by such measurements is -96 kilojoules at 25°C. What meaning, if any, should be attached to an equilibrium constant calculated from this figure? Explain.

10-III-8. (a) Find the equilibrium constant for the reaction

$$Ag(NH_3)_2{}^+ \rightleftharpoons Ag^+ + 2NH_3(aq)$$

at 25°C.

(b) Describe a cell, or combination of cells, *not involving liquid junctions* in which the reaction of (a), or its reverse, will occur. (Hint: Ag_2SO_4 is moderately soluble in H_2O, but $PbSO_4$, like AgCl, is nearly insoluble.)

(c) Write the Nernst equation (E as a function of activities) for your invention (b) and show that E actually depends on mean ionic activities rather than on single-ion activities.

10-III-9. A solution initially $0.10\ M$ in Tl^+ and $1.0\ M$ in HCl is exposed to the atmosphere, where the ambient temperature is 25°C and the total pressure is 1.0 atm, until as much Tl^+ as possible has been oxidized to the Tl^{3+} state. What mole percent of the Tl^+ originally present will remain unoxidized?

10-III-10. Calculate the value of n in the formula $Co(NH_3)_n^{2+}$ from the following emf data obtained by Lamb and Larson [*J. Am. Chem. Soc.*, **42**, 2024 (1920)] at 25°C:

$$Co \mid 0.050\ M\ CoCl_2 + xM\ NH_3 \mid 1.00\ M\ NaOH \mid HgO \mid Hg$$

Concentration of NH_3, M	Emf of the cell, V	Vapor pressure of NH_3, torr
6	0.715	107.7
4	0.693	63.4
3	0.659	44.7
2	0.620	27.8

The concentration of NH_3 is varied but the total cobalt concentration is kept constant. You may assume that $[Co^{2+}]$ is very small in comparison with $[Co(NH_3)_n^{2+}]$ and that the total $[Co(NH_3)_n^{2+}]$ is therefore essentially constant. You may also assume that the concentration of free NH_3 in the solution is proportional to the vapor pressure of NH_3 above the solution.

10-III-11. In general we cannot add intensive properties of parts of a system to obtain the corresponding properties of the entire system. Thus, for example, the specific volume (milliliters per gram) of a system is not the sum of the specific volumes of its parts. To calculate the specific volume v of a system consisting of two parts we would first multiply the specific volume of each part by the mass of that part to obtain the total volumes of the parts (extensive properties); then we would add these volumes and divide by the total mass,

$$v = \frac{m_1 v_1 + m_2 v_2}{m_1 + m_2}$$

Electric potential is an intensive property (joules per coulomb). However, we simply add the potentials of two half cells to obtain the potential of the entire cell without taking account of the sizes of the half cells or the quantity of reaction taking place in them. How do you resolve this paradox?

10-III-12. Suppose that the effective field acting on a molecule is given by

$$\mathbf{F} = \mathbf{E} + \frac{4\pi}{n} \mathbf{P}$$

where n is a constant. (This equation is a generalization of the familiar equation in which $n = 3$.) Obtain an equation (analogous to the Clausius-Mosotti equation) for the polarizability α in terms of n, the dielectric constant ϵ, the molecular weight, the density, and universal constants.

CHAPTER 11

Kinetics

SECTION 11-I

11-I-1. The decomposition of benzoyl peroxide in diethyl ether, a first-order reaction, is 75.2 percent complete in 10 min at 60°C [Bartlett and Nozaki, *J. Am. Chem. Soc.*, **69**, 2299 (1947)]. Calculate the rate constant for the reaction.

11-I-2. In a study of the reaction between Br^- and ClO^-

$$ClO^- + Br^- \rightarrow BrO^- + Cl^-$$

Farkas, Lewin, and Bloch [*J. Am. Chem. Soc.*, **71**, 1988 (1949)] mixed 100 ml of 0.1 N NaClO, 48 ml of 0.5 N NaOH, and 21 ml of distilled water and immersed this mixture in a thermostat at 25°C. To this mixture 81 ml of a 1 percent KBr solution, also at 25°C, was added. At certain intervals, t, samples were withdrawn for the determination of BrO^-. The results of the analyses are given below:

t, min	x, conc of BrO^- in moles liter^{-1} $\times$ 10^2
0.0	0.0
3.65	0.0560
7.65	0.0953
15.05	0.1420
26.00	0.1800
47.60	0.2117
90.60	0.2367

The concentration of NaClO in the reaction mixture at $t = 0$ was 0.003230 M, and that of KBr was 0.002508 M.

The pH was 11.28. Determine the reaction order and the value of the reaction rate constant.

11-I-3. To investigate the decomposition of oxalic acid in concentrated H_2SO_4 at 50°C, Lichty [*J. Phys. Chem.*, 11, 225 (1907)] prepared a $1/40$ M solution of oxalic acid in 99.5 percent H_2SO_4, then removed aliquots at various reaction times t, and then determined the volumes v of a potassium permanganate solution required to react with a 10 ml portion. The results are given below:

t, min	v, ml
0	11.45
120	9.63
240	8.11
420	6.22
600	4.79
900	2.97
1440	1.44

Determine the reaction order with respect to oxalic acid and evaluate the specific rate constant.

11-I-4. The kinetics of the reaction between sodium thiosulfate and n-propyl bromide

$$S_2O_3^{2-} + RBr \rightarrow RSSO_3^- + Br^-$$

was investigated at 37.50°C by Crowell and Hammett [*J. Am. Chem. Soc.*, 70, 3444 (1948)]. The concentration of $S_2O_3^{2-}$, initially 0.100 M, was determined at various intervals t by titration with v ml of 0.02572 N iodine solution per 10.02 ml sample of reaction mixture. Thiosulfate was present in excess. The results are given below:

t, sec	v, ml
0	37.63
1110	35.20
2010	33.63
3192	31.90
5052	29.86
7380	28.04
11232	26.01
78840	22.24

Evaluate the second-order rate constant k.

11-I-5. The rate of the reaction

$$(C_2H_5)_3N + \overset{}{C}H_3I \rightarrow [(C_2H_5)_3\overset{+}{N}(CH_3)] \, I^-$$

in nitrobenzene at 25°C was investigated by Brown and Eldred [*J. Am. Chem. Soc.*, **71**, 445 (1949)] who found that:

t, sec	x, moles liter^{-1}
1200	0.00876
1800	0.01066
2400	0.01208
3600	0.01392
4500	0.01476
5400	0.01538

where t is the reaction time in seconds and x is the moles liter^{-1} of $(C_2H_5)_3N$ or CH_3I reacted at time t. The initial concentrations of amine and alkyl iodide were each 0.0198 moles liter^{-1}. The reaction is second order. Find the rate constant.

11-I-6. Calculate the order of the rate-controlling step in the pyrolysis of diborane (B_2H_6, g) at 100°C from the following data on the rate of pressure increase in the system as a function of B_2H_6 concentration [Bragg, McCarty, and Norton, *J. Am. Chem. Soc.*, **73**, 2134 (1951)]:

Concentration of B_2H_6, moles liter^{-1} $\times$ 10^2	Rate of pressure increase, moles liter^{-1} hr^{-1} $\times$ 10^4
2.153	7.4
0.433	0.73

11-I-7. The kinetics of the catalytic decomposition of NH_3 into the elements on a hot tungsten filament at 1100°C was investigated by Kunsman [*J. Am. Chem. Soc.*, **50**, 2100 (1928)] who found that the times $t_{1/2}$ required for half of the NH_3 to decompose with no N_2 or H_2 present at the start depended on the initial NH_3 pressures as follows:

p, torr	$t_{1/2}$, min
265	7.6
130	3.7
58	1.7

Determine (a) the order of the reaction, and (b) the rate constant.

11-I-8. The kinetics of the reaction of methanol with 3,3'-dicarbazylphenylmethyl ion (a green dye) in alkaline water-acetone solution was investigated spectrophotometrically at 25°C by Branch and Tolbert [*J. Am. Chem. Soc.*, **69**, 523 (1947)]. They found that for a solution initially 0.25 M in methanol, the difference $A - A_\infty$ between the absorbance of the solution at time t (A) and the absorbance of the solution when the reaction has reached equilibrium (A_∞) at 730 nm varied with time t as follows, when the NaOH concentration is maintained at 2.03 × 10⁻² M (selected data):

t, min	$A - A_\infty$
2.7	0.562
8.7	0.243
14.7	0.111
21.7	0.045
33.7	0.010

Show that the reaction is first order with respect to the 3,3'-dicarbazylphenylmethyl ion and evaluate the rate constant. For light passed through a sample, let P be transmitted power and P_0 be incident power. Then absorbance, A, is given by

$$A = \log \frac{P_0}{P}$$

Absorbance is directly proportional to the concentration of the absorbing species.

11-I-9. The rate of inversion of sucrose in the presence of HCl was studied by Fales and Morrell [*J. Am. Chem. Soc.*, **44**, 2071 (1922)] who obtained the following data:

t, time elapsed, sec	α, observed angle of rotation, deg
0	11.20
1035.00	10.35
3113	8.87
4857	7.64
9231	5.19
12834	3.61
18520	1.60
26320	−0.16
32640	−1.10
76969	−3.26
∞	−3.37

Determine the order of the reaction and evaluate the specific rate constant.

11-I-10. In order to study the kinetics of the reaction

$$
\begin{array}{ccc}
CH_2 & & CH_2-OH \\
\diagdown & & | \\
& O + H_2O \xrightarrow{H^+} & \\
\diagup & & | \\
CH_2 & & CH_2-OH
\end{array}
$$

a solution initially $0.12\,M$ in ethylene oxide and $0.007574\,M$ in perchloric acid was prepared and the progress of the reaction was followed dilatometrically (that is, by measuring the volume of the solution as a function of time). The following data were obtained at $20°C$:

t, min	Dilatometer reading
0	18.48
30	18.05
60	17.62
135	16.71
300	15.22
∞	12.29

Determine the order of the reaction with respect to ethylene oxide and evaluate the specific rate constant.

11-I-11. Show that the third-order dependence of the reaction

$$2NO + O_2 \rightarrow 2NO_2$$

can be accounted for by either of the mechanisms

(a) $NO + O_2 \overset{K}{\rightleftharpoons} NO_3$

   $NO_3 + NO \xrightarrow{k} 2\,NO_2$

(b) $2\,NO \overset{K'}{\rightleftharpoons} N_2O_2$

   $N_2O_2 + O_2 \xrightarrow{k'} 2\,NO_2$

no step of which is termolecular.

11-I-12. Show that for a

(a) first-order reaction, $A \rightarrow$ products, $t_{1/2} = 0.693/k$

(b) second-order reaction, $2A \rightarrow$ products, $t_{1/2} = 1/ka$

(c) third-order reaction, $3A \rightarrow$ products, $t_{1/2} = 3/2ka^2$
where a is the initial concentration of A and $t_{1/2}$ is the half-life.

11-I-13. Lalor and Lang [*J. Chem. Soc.*, **1963**, 5620] studied the kinetics of the reaction

$$Co(NH_3)_5NO_2^{2+} + OH^- \rightarrow Co(NH_3)_5OH^{2+} + NO_2^-$$

and found the following dependence of the rate constant k on ionic strength I:

I	$5 + \log k$
2.34	1.7640
5.61	1.7130
8.10	1.6800
11.22	1.6467
11.73	1.6418
16.90	1.5990

Evaluate k_0, the rate constant at zero ionic strength.

11-I-14. It is often said that the rate of a typical chemical reaction doubles with every 10-degree rise in temperature. What must be the activation energy of a reaction for which this statement is true in the vicinity of $300°K$?

11-I-15. The rate of the gas reaction

$$N + O_2 \rightarrow NO + O$$

has been studied [Wilson, *J. Chem. Phys.*, **46**, 2017 (1967)] by generating N atoms in a flow system by a microwave discharge and monitoring their concentration by electron-spin resonance. The following rate constants were found:

T, °K	k, cm^3 $mole^{-1}$ sec^{-1}
586	$(1.63 \pm 0.05) \times 10^{10}$
910	$(1.77 \pm 0.08) \times 10^{11}$

Calculate the activation energy of this reaction. Obtain two values corresponding to the upper and lower limits permitted by the given uncertainties in the data.

SECTION 11-II

11-II-1. In an investigation of the kinetics of the reaction

$$MnO_4^- + Cr^{3+} \rightarrow CrO_4^{2-} + Mn^{4+} \text{ at } 25.1°C$$

Fales and Roller [*J. Am. Chem. Soc.*, **51**, 345 (1929)] measured the times required to carry the reaction to various degrees of completion, first as a function of CrO_4^{2-} concentration and then as a function of MnO_4^- concentration. In a set of three experiments, the results were as follows:

Experiment No.	I	II	III
Relative MnO_4^- conc.	1	2	1
Relative CrO_4^{2-} conc.	1	1	0.5
$Cr_2O_7^{2-}$, ml (0.1 N)			
0.1	23 min	11 min	40 min
0.2	36	18	70
0.4	58	32	113
0.6	77	44	148

In each case after definite intervals of time 25 ml aliquots of the reaction mixtures were removed and added rapidly to a solution consisting of 60 ml of 1.2 M H_2SO_4 and 25 ml of 0.5 M KBr. Free bromine was instantly liberated by the reaction

$$2MnO_4^- + 10Br^- + 16H^+ \rightarrow 2Mn^{2+} + 5Br_2 + 8H_2O$$

and was extracted by CS_2. The $Cr_2O_7^{2-}$ that had been formed by the reaction

$$2CrO_4^{2-} + 2H^+ \rightarrow Cr_2O_7^{2-} + H_2O$$

was titrated with 0.01 N FeSO$_4$ in accordance with the reaction

$$Cr_2O_7^{2-} + 6Fe^{2+} + 16H^+ + 2SO_4^{2-} \rightarrow 2Cr^{3+} + 6Fe^{3+} + 2HSO_4^-$$
$$+ 7H_2O$$

The number of milliliters of 0.01 N $Cr_2O_7^{2-}$ present in the mixture at the indicated reaction time is given in the table. This volume may be thought of simply as a number that is proportional to the concentration of CrO_4^{2-} in the reaction mixture at the indicated time. What is the reaction order (a) with respect to Cr^{3+}, (b) with respect to MnO_4^-?

11-II-2. The kinetics of the hydrolysis of *t*-butyl chloride (net reaction:

$$(CH_3)_3CCl + H_2O \rightarrow (CH_3)_3COH + H^+ + Cl^-)$$

at 25°C was investigated by Swain and Ross [*J. Am. Chem. Soc.*, **68**, 658 (1946)] by means of a concentration cell of the type Ag | AgCl | A ‖ B | AgCl | Ag. At zero time both half cells contained a 95 percent water—5 percent acetone solution which was 0.144 M in sodium perchlorate; but, in addition, A contained 0.001 M *t*-butyl chloride. The rate measurements were then carried out by running small measured additions of 0.0499 M HCl into cell B every few seconds and the time was recorded at each moment when a galvanometer placed between the two electrodes registered zero for each addition. The following data were obtained for one such series of runs:

t, sec	ml HCl in B
30	0.90
44	1.10
62	1.30
83	1.40
111	1.50
∞	1.61

Show that the hydrolysis reaction is first order, and evaluate the rate constant.

11-II-3. In an investigation of the kinetics of the alkaline hydrolysis of of ethyl acetate, Potts and Amis [*J. Am. Chem. Soc.*, **71**, 2112 (1949)] carried out the following experiment. 300 ml of water at 0°C was pipetted into a 600-ml flask and 100.00 ml of 0.0500 M ethyl acetate was added at the same temperature. The flask was stoppered and allowed to reach thermal equilibrium in a thermostat. The hydrolysis reaction was then initiated by adding 100.00 ml of 0.1000 M NaOH, also at 0°C, and shaking vigorously. If we assume that the volumes of the starting solutions are strictly additive on mixing, the resulting solution was initially 0.0100 M in ethyl acetate and

0.0200 M in NaOH. At various intervals, t, 50.00-ml samples of the reaction mixture were withdrawn, drained into a measured excess of 0.0200 M HCl at 0°C (v_{HCl}), and titrated at 0°C with 0.0200 M NaOH, v_{NaOH} ml being required. The concentration of NaOH in the reaction mixture at equilibrium time ($t = \infty$) was determined on samples permitted to stand at the reaction temperature until no further change in the composition of the mixture as a function of time could be detected. The results were as follows:

t, min	v_{HCl}, ml	v_{NaOH}, ml
0	60.0	11.50
15	50.0	7.35
30	50.0	11.20
45	50.0	13.95
60	50.0	15.95
75	50.0	17.55
∞	50.0	24.00

Determine the order of this reaction and the rate constant k.

11-II-4. The reaction rate of the photochemical decomposition of $K_2S_2O_8$

$$K_2S_2O_8 + H_2O \xrightarrow{h\nu} 2KHSO_4 + \tfrac{1}{2}O_2$$

in the presence of 0.1 M K_2SO_4 and 0.28 M KOH was investigated by Morgan and Crist [*J. Am. Chem. Soc.*, **49**, 16 (1927)] who titrated aliquots of the reaction mixture removed at the times indicated and obtained the following data:

time, min	ml FeSO$_4$ consumed
0	9.25
150	8.75
360	8.24
540	7.86
720	7.51
940	7.07
1160	6.64
1340	6.27

0.0500 M FeSO$_4$ was the reagent and the titration reaction was

$$K_2S_2O_8 + FeSO_4 \rightarrow Fe_2(SO_4)_3 + K_2SO$$

The initial concentration of $K_2S_2O_8$ was 0.100 M. Find the order of the reaction with respect to $K_2S_2O_8$.

11-II-5. In the presence of sodium methoxide in methanol solution, chloroform reacts first in accordance with the equation

$$CHCl_3 + OMe^- \leftrightharpoons CCl_3^- + MeOH \ (fast, \ K \gg 1)$$

and then

$$CCl_3^- \to CCl_2 + Cl^- \ (slow)$$

followed by $CCl_2 \to$ products (fast). The slow middle step is believed to be the rate-controlling one. In an experiment to determine the order of the slow step with respect to CCl_3^-, the amount of Cl^- produced in time t at 59.7°C was determined by titration with 0.0100 N $AgNO_3$, v ml being required [O'Ferrall and Ridd, *J. Chem. Soc.*, **1963**, 5035]. The results were as follows:

t, min	v, ml
0	1.71
4	3.03
9	4.49
15	5.97
22	7.39
30	8.87
41	10.48
50	11.7
∞	15.98

The initial $[CHCl_3]$ was $9.95 \times 10^{-3} \, M$ and the mean $[NaOMe]$ during the reaction was $1.10 \pm 0.01 \, M$ (a large excess, practically constant during the run). Show that the reaction is first order with respect to CCl_3^- and evaluate the rate constant.

11-II-6. The kinetics of the oxidation of oxalic acid by ceric sulfate was investigated by Ross and Swain [*J. Am. Chem. Soc.*, **69**, 1325 (1947)] by means of a concentration cell of the type Pt | S$_1$ ‖ S$_2$ | Pt. Initially S$_1$ and S$_2$ contained equal amounts of sulfuric acid, ammonium bisulfate (added to maintain the mixture at a constant ionic strength of 2.0 M), and ceric sulfate. At zero time a standard solution of oxalic acid was added to S$_1$ and an equal volume of water to S$_2$. The rate measurements were then carried out by adding measured excesses of ferrous sulfate to solution S_2 and noting the times at which a galvanometer placed between the two Pt electrodes registered zero for each addition. The following data were obtained for one series of runs using 0.00253 M Ce(SO$_4$)$_2$, 0.00125 M H$_2$C$_2$O$_4$, and 2.0 M H$_2$SO$_4$:

t, min	ml FeSO$_4$ (*cumulative*)
0.31	7.00
0.51	9.00
0.65	10.00
0.86	11.00
1.01	11.50
1.15	12.00
1.36	12.50
1.58	13.00
2.19	13.80
∞	16.50

Show that the reaction between oxalic acid and ceric sulfate is second order, and evaluate the rate constant.

11-II-7. The thermal decomposition of arsine on glass,

$$2AsH_3(g) \rightarrow 2As(s) + 3H_2(g)$$

was investigated by K. Tamaru [*J. Phys. Chem.*, **59**, 777 (1955)] who found that the total pressure of the system varied with time as indicated below at 350°C:

Time, hr	Total pressure, cm
0	39.2
4.33	40.3
16	43.65
25.5	45.35
37.66	48.05
44.75	48.85

(a) Determine the order of the reaction with respect to arsine and (b) evaluate the specific rate constant.

11-II-8. In an investigation of the hydrolysis of methyl tosylate (methyl p-toluenesulfonate), Swain and Morgan [*J. Org. Chem.*, **29**, 2097 (1964)] obtained the following spectrophotometric data at 261 nm and 25°C on a solution in water initially $1.22 \times 10^{-3} M$ with respect to methyl tosylate.

Time, hr	Absorbance (see p. 146)
0.0	0.791
5.0	0.746
9.0	0.709
18.0	0.645
24.0	0.611
32.0	0.570
44.0	0.526
55.0	0.498
67.0	0.471
290.0	0.420

Assuming that methyl tosylate is the only absorbing species at this wavelength, show that the reaction is first order with respect to methyl tosylate and evaluate the rate constant in sec^{-1}.

11-II-9. A gas that undergoes a unimolecular reaction is mixed with an inert gas. Using the Lindemann theory, find the rate of the reaction in terms of the concentrations of the reacting gas and the inert gas and of the rate constants of the elementary reactions involved.

11-II-10. The following mechanism for the thermal decomposition of ozone has been proposed:

$$O_3 \xrightarrow{k_1} O_2 + O$$
$$O + O_2 \xrightarrow{k_{-1}} O_3$$
$$O + O_3 \xrightarrow{k_2} 2 O_2$$

(a) By the method of the stationary state obtain an expression for the rate of decomposition in terms of the rate constants of these three reactions and the concentrations of O_2 and O_3.

(b) The reaction is found experimentally to be of the second order with respect to O_3, and of the -1 order with respect to O_2. State the relations of magnitude that must exist among the concentrations and rate constants in order that your expression may agree with these facts.

11-II-11. The following mechanism (i) for the reaction

$$H_2(g) + I_2(g) \rightarrow 2HI(g)$$

was generally accepted until 1967:

$H_2 + I_2 \rightarrow 2HI$ Rate constant : k

In that year it was shown (Sullivan, *J. Chem. Phys.*, **46**, 73) that the reaction probably proceeds by the mechanism (ii):

		Rate constant
$I_2 \rightarrow 2I$	(1)	k_1
$2I \rightarrow I_2$	(2)	k_2
$2I + H_2 \rightarrow 2\,HI$	(3)	k_3

(a) Obtain the rate law for $d[HI]/dt$ predicted by each of the mechanisms (i) and (ii). Use the steady state method where appropriate.

(b) Obtain the rate law predicted by mechanism (ii) under the assumption that reactions (1) and (2) comprise an equilibrium, with K being the equilibrium constant for the reaction $I_2 \rightleftharpoons 2I$. Under what conditions do the results of (a) and (b) for mechanism (ii) agree ?

(c) By producing I atoms photochemically in known concentration it is possible to measure k_3 ,

$T\,(^\circ K)$	417.9	520.1
k_3 (liter^2 mole^{-2} sec^{-1})	1.12×10^5	4.0×10^5

(k_3 is defined with reference to $-d[H_2]/dt$.) Calculate the activation energy for reaction (3).

11-II-12. The following mechanism has been proposed by Anderson and Freeman [*J. Phys. Chem.*, **65**, 1648 (1961)] for the reaction between sodium nitrite and oxygen:

$$NO_2^- + O_2 \xrightarrow{k_1} NO_3^- + O$$

$$O \quad + NO_2^- \xrightarrow{k_2} NO_3^-$$

$$O \quad + O \xrightarrow{k_3} O_2$$

(a) Show that

$$\frac{d[NO_3^-]}{dt} = k_1[NO_2^-][O_2] \left(1 + \frac{k_2[NO_2^-]}{k_3[O] + k_2[NO_2^-]}\right)$$

(b) Show that the expression given in (a) reduces to

$$\frac{d[NO_3^-]}{dt} = 2k_1[NO_2^-][O_2]$$

if we assume that reaction (3) is much slower than reaction (2).

11-II-13. The decomposition of nitramide in aqueous solution,

$$O_2NNH_2 \rightarrow N_2O + H_2O$$

is first order with respect to nitramide. It is believed that the reaction proceeds in three steps,

$$
\begin{align}
O_2NNH_2 + B &\rightarrow BH^+ + O_2NNH^- \tag{1}\\
O_2NNH^- &\rightarrow N_2O + OH^- \tag{2}\\
OH^- + BH^+ &\rightarrow B + H_2O \tag{3}
\end{align}
$$

B is some base, for example, acetate ion.
Two hypotheses have been proposed.
(a) Reaction (1) is fast in both directions with equilibrium constant K; (2) is slow and rate determining with rate constant k_2.
(b) Reaction (1) is rate determining with rate constant k_1 and (2) is much faster.
Ascertain whether either, or both, of these hypotheses predicts the first-order rate law correctly. (Assume that activities are equal to concentrations.) If both are consistent with the facts, suggest a further experiment that might serve to exclude one or the other.

11-II-14. The following mechanism has been proposed for the radiation-induced decomposition of several inorganic nitrates at room temperature [Chen and Johnson, *J. Phys. Chem.*, **66**, 2249 (1962)].

$$NO_3^- \xrightarrow{k_1\phi} NO_2^- + O \tag{1}$$

$$O + NO_2^- \xrightarrow{k_2} NO_3^- \tag{2}$$

$$O + NO_3^- \xrightarrow{k_3} NO_2^- + O_2 \tag{3}$$

The symbol ϕ represents the incident dose of the radiation and indicates that ionizing radiation (instead of light) was used.
(a) Making the steady state assumption about O, derive the rate expression for the formation of NO_2^-.

(b) Integrate the rate expression obtained in (a) assuming that the concentration of NO_3^- remains constant.

11-II-15. The following mechanism for the homogeneous pyrolysis of methane has been proposed:

$$CH_4 \xrightarrow{k_1} CH_3 + H$$

$$CH_3 + CH_4 \xrightarrow{k_2} C_2H_6 + H$$

$$H + CH_4 \xrightarrow{k_3} CH_3 + H_2$$

$$H + CH_3 + M \xrightarrow{k_4} CH_4 + M$$

M is any molecule (perhaps CH_4 or C_2H_6) that can carry away the energy of recombination of H and CH_3.
Deduce the rate law for the formation of C_2H_6 predicted by this mechanism. The concentrations of CH_3 and H, which are present in very small, steady concentrations, should not appear in the result. [Cagle, *J. Chem. Phys.*, **25**, 1300 (1956)].

11-II-16. The hypothetical reaction A → B is of the −1 order; that is, $-dc/dt = kc^{-1}$, where $c = [A]$.
(a) Obtain an equation for c as a function of t, k, and the initial concentration c_0.
(b) Find the time required for the concentration to fall to 10 percent of its initial value, in terms of k and c_0.
(c) Does this reaction ever reach completion?
Does a first-order reaction ever reach completion? Explain any difference between the two cases.

SECTION 11-III

11-III-1. The following mechanism has been proposed for the reaction $NO_2Cl → NO_2 + \frac{1}{2}Cl_2$:

$$NO_2Cl \xrightarrow{k_1} NO_2 + Cl$$

$$NO_2Cl + Cl \xrightarrow{k_2} NO_2 + Cl_2$$

(a) Find the rate law predicted by this mechanism. Assume that Cl is present in a small, steady concentration.

(b) At NO_2Cl concentrations below 10^{-4} mole liter^{-1} the reaction becomes second order in NO_2Cl. Write a modified version of the above mechanism that is consistent with this rate law and explain why the modification is necessary only at low concentration.

11-III-2. H. Johnson, L. Foering, and R. J. Thompson [*J. Phys. Chem.*, **57**, 390 (1953)] propose that nitric acid decomposes by the following mechanism:

$$HNO_3 \xrightarrow{k_a} HO + NO_2$$

$$HO + NO_2 \xrightarrow{k_b} HNO_3$$

$$HO + HNO_3 \xrightarrow{k_c} H_2O + NO_3$$

(a) Making the steady state assumption about HO, show that the rate expression for the decomposition of HNO_3 is given by

$$\frac{d[HNO_3]}{dt} = -2k_a[HNO_3] \cdot \frac{1}{1 + (k_b[NO_2])/(k_c[HNO_3])}$$

(b) If NO_2 is consumed by the fast reaction

$$NO_3 + NO_2 \xrightarrow{k_d} NO_2 + O_2 + NO$$

what form does the above rate expression reduce to?

11-III-3. Making the steady state assumption about HO_2, show that the following mechanism for the reduction of neptunium (VI) by hydrogen peroxide leads to the rate expression

$$\frac{d[NpO_2^+]}{dt} = \frac{2Kk_1[NpO_2^{2+}][H_2O_2]}{[H^+]\{1 + (k_3[NpO_2^+])/(k_2[NpO_2^{2+}])\}}$$

[Zielen, Sullivan, Cohen, and Hindman, *J. Am. Chem. Soc.*, **80**, 5632 (1958).]

$$H_2O_2 \xrightleftharpoons{K} H^+ + HO_2^-$$

$$HO_2^- + NpO_2^{2+} \xrightarrow{k_1} NpO_2^+ + HO_2$$

$$HO_2 + NpO_2^{2+} \xrightarrow{k_2} NpO_2^+ + O_2 + H^+$$

$$HO_2 + NpO_2^+ \xrightarrow{k_3} NpO_2^{2+} + HO_2^-$$

11-III-4. Assume that the thermal decomposition of gaseous N_2O_5 proceeds by the following mechanism:

$$N_2O_5 \xrightarrow{k_1} NO_2 \quad + \quad NO_3$$

$$NO_2 + NO_3 \xrightarrow{k_{-1}} N_2O_5$$

$$NO_2 + NO_3 \xrightarrow{k_2} NO_2 + O_2 + NO$$

$$NO + N_2O_5 \xrightarrow{k_3} 3NO_2$$

(a) By the method of the steady state applied to NO_3 and NO find the rate law that this mechanism predicts.

(b) It is believed that the activation energy of reaction (-1) is close to 0 but that the activation energy of reaction (2) is about 5 kcal. Making reasonable simplifying assumptions, estimate roughly the ratio k_2/k_{-1} at $320°K$. Explain why your assumptions are reasonable.

(c) Show how essentially the same rate law obtained in (a) can be deduced by treating reactions (1) and (-1) as an equilibrium. Under what conditions is this approach justified?

11-III-5. The following mechanism for the formation of phosgene, $COCl_2$, has been proposed:

$$Cl_2 \xrightarrow{k_1^*} 2Cl$$

$$2Cl \xrightarrow{k_2^*} Cl_2$$

$$Cl + CO \xrightarrow{k_3} COCl$$

$$COCl \xrightarrow{k_4} Cl + CO$$

$$COCl + Cl_2 \xrightarrow{k_5} COCl_2 + Cl$$

* for $d[Cl_2]/dt$

(a) Use the steady state approximation to find the rate equation implied by this mechanism for the formation of $COCl_2$. Assume that Cl and COCl are present in small, steady concentrations. The rate equation may contain any or all of the constants $k_1, ..., k_5$ and the concentrations of all species other than Cl or COCl.

(b) Assume that reactions (1)–(4) are much faster than reaction (5). Show how the rate equation can be simplified in this case.

(c) Show that the result of (b) can also be obtained by treating reactions (1)–(2) and reactions (3)–(4) as equilibria. Explain why the assumptions of (b) and (c) lead to the same result.

11-III-6. If two first-order reactions are operating in succession, viz.

$$A \xrightarrow{k_1} B \xrightarrow{k_2} C$$

(starting with A but no B or C), prove that the concentration of the intermediate B reaches a maximum and then declines, evaluate the time at which the maximum concentration of B occurs, and evaluate the maximum concentration of B. (Note: This problem requires a little knowledge of linear differential equations beyond the usual introductory course in calculus. Remember that $e^{a \ln b} = b^a$. The case $k_1 = k_2$ requires separate consideration.)

CHAPTER 12

Photochemistry

and Spectrophotometry

SECTION 12-I

12-I-1. On the basis of the following data, selected from the work of Discher, Smith, Lippman, and Turse [*J. Phys. Chem.*, **67**, 2501 (1963)], evaluate the quantum efficiency of the uranyl oxalate system at each wavelength.

Wavelength, nm	Fraction of oxalate decomposed	Molecules decomposed $\times 10^{-18}$	Photons absorbed $\times 10^{-18}$
365.5	0.0592	5.18	10.58
365.5	0.0498	4.32	8.93
435.8	0.0242	2.10	3.64
435.8	0.0208	1.79	3.10

SECTION 12-II

12-II-1. In an experiment to determine the concentrations of the two substances A and B in a certain solution simultaneously by spectrophotometry the following data were obtained:

	[A], mole liter^{-1}	[B], mole liter^{-1}	Percent transmitted at $\lambda = 400$ nm	Percent transmitted at $\lambda = 500$ nm
Solution 1	0.001	0	10	60
Solution 2	0	0.005	80	20
Solution 3	unknown	unknown	40	50

Determine the concentrations of A and B in solution 3.

12-II-2. In order to determine the dissociation constant K of the indicator *m*-nitrophenol (HIn), Robinson and Peiperl [*J. Phys. Chem.*, **67**, 2860 (1963)] prepared a $6.36 \times 10^{-4}\ M$ solution of it and carried out the following spectrophotometric measurements on the solution at 25°C and 390 nm. In one experiment the solution was made strongly acidic and the absorbance A_1 was found to be 0.142. Under these conditions essentially all of the indicator is in the HIn form. In another experiment the solution was made strongly basic and the absorbance A_2 was found to be 0.943. Under these conditions essentially all of the indicator is in the In$^-$ form. Then in a series of additional experiments the pH of the indicator solution was adjusted with a buffer mixture of ionic strength I and the absorbances A were measured. (Absorbance is defined on p. 146.) The results were as follows:

I	pH	A
0.10	8.321	0.527
0.08	8.302	0.518
0.06	8.280	0.505
0.04	8.251	0.493
0.02	8.207	0.470

Evaluate the apparent pK (in terms of concentrations) of the indicator at each of the ionic strengths listed.

12-II-3. The percent transmittance (percent T) of a series of solutions of the acid-base indicator bromophenol blue were determined at 590 nm, and the results are as follows (Labowitz, unpublished data):

Relative concentration	Buffered at pH 4.39, percent T	Strongly basic, percent T
0.8	20.0	5.4
0.6	29.0	11.0
0.4	44.2	22.7
0.2	66.8	46.4

At the indicated wavelength, the base form absorbs strongly, but the absorbance of the acid form is negligible. Calculate the pK_a of this indicator.

12-II-4. The following mechanism [Buxton and Walker, *J. Phys. Chem.*, **67**, 2835 (1963)] is proposed for the photochemical decomposition of hydrogen peroxide in the presence of carbon monoxide. Making the steady state assumption about OH, CO_2H, and HO_2, obtain the rate law for $d[H_2O_2]/dt$. Let ϕ represent the primary quantum efficiency for H_2O_2 photolysis and I_a represent einsteins absorbed per liter per second.

$$H_2O_2 + h\nu \longrightarrow 2OH$$

$$OH + CO \xrightarrow{k_1} CO_2H$$

$$CO_2H + H_2O_2 \xrightarrow{k_2} CO_2 + H_2O + OH$$

$$H_2O_2 + OH \xrightarrow{k_3} H_2O + HO_2$$

$$2HO_2 \xrightarrow{k_4} O_2 + H_2O$$

12-II-5. The following alternative mechanism is proposed for the photolytic decomposition of hydrogen peroxide in the presence of carbon monoxide [Buxton and Walker, *J. Phys. Chem.*, **67**, 2835 (1963)]. Making the steady state assumption about OH and CO_2H, evaluate $d[H_2O_2]/dt$ as in the preceding problem.

$$H_2O_2 + h\nu \longrightarrow 2OH$$

$$OH + CO \xrightarrow{k_1} CO_2H$$

$$CO_2H + H_2O_2 \xrightarrow{k_2} CO_2 + H_2O + OH$$

$$2CO_2H \xrightarrow{k_5} products$$

SECTION 12-III

12-III-1. In a spectrophotometric analysis, at what value of T (fractional transmittance) will the relative error in concentration ($\Delta c/c$) be minimal for a given error in the measurement of T?

12-III-2. (a) In the photochemical gas reaction $2HI \rightarrow H_2 + I_2$ the quantum yield is approximately 2. Find the number of grams of HI decomposed per calorie of radiant energy absorbed when HI is irradiated with monochromatic radiation with wavelength 2070 Å.

(b) Is the following mechanism in agreement with the observed quantum yield? Explain.

(1) $HI + h\nu \rightarrow H + I$
(2) $H + HI \rightarrow H_2 + I$
(3) $2I \rightarrow I_2$ (on wall or third body)

(c) In the reaction $H_2 + Cl_2 \rightarrow 2HCl$, which has a mechanism similar in some ways, quantum yields of 10^4 to 10^6 are obtained. Explain the great difference between the quantum yields in the two reactions, with reference to relevant energies of activation, bond energies, or other data. The energy of the H—I bond is 71 kcal mole^{-1}. That of I—I is 36 kcal mole^{-1}. Energies of activation are

$Cl + H_2 \rightarrow HCl + H$ 8 kcal
$H + Cl_2 \rightarrow HCl + Cl$ 2 kcal
$H + HI \rightarrow H_2 + I$ 1.5 kcal

12-III-3. The photolysis of O_3 in liquid Ar solution at 87°K has been studied [De Mare and Raper, *J. Chem. Phys.*, **44**, 1780 (1966)]. Radiation of wavelengths 2537 Å and 3130 Å was used. The primary quantum yield, ϕ, is so defined that the rate of decomposition of O_3 by the reaction

$$O_3 + h\nu \rightarrow O_2 + O^* \tag{1}$$

is ϕI_a mole liter^{-1} sec^{-1}, where I_a is einsteins absorbed per liter per second and O^* is an O atom in an excited electronic state (^1D). The reactions following reaction (1) were assumed to be

$$O^* + O_3 \rightarrow 2O_2 \tag{2}$$
$$O^* \rightarrow O \tag{3}$$
$$O + O_2 + M \rightarrow O_3 + M \tag{4}$$

where M is any molecule that can carry away the energy liberated in reaction (4). The overall quantum yield Φ is so defined that the net rate of O_3 disappearance is $-d[O_3]/dt = \Phi I_a$.

(a) On the basis of the mechanism given obtain an expression for Φ in terms of ϕ, rate constants, and concentrations of stable species (O_2, O_3).

(b) The experimental results for Φ at 2537 Å fit an equation of the form $\Phi^{-1} = 0.538 + 0.81[O_3]^{-1}$. Find ϕ and any available information about the rate constants.

12-III-4. The kinetics and mechanism of the vapor phase photochlorination of trifluoroethylene

$$CF_2=CFH + Cl_2 \xrightarrow{h\nu} CF_2Cl=CFHCl \text{ (or TfCl}_2)$$

were investigated at room temperature by Bunbury, Lacher, and Park [*J. Am. Chem. Soc.*, 80, 5104 (1958)], who observed that

I. There is practically no dark reaction.

II. In the range 25 to 400 torr the reaction rate is independent of the olefin pressure.

III. When the chlorine pressure is 90 torr, the reaction rate $(-dP_{Cl_2}/dt)$ varies with the light intensity I_0 in the manner indicated below.

I_0, arbitrary units	$(-dP_{Cl_2}/dt) \times 10^3$, torr sec^{-1}
0.0144	2.2
0.122	6.1
0.421	9.5
1.88	17.2
1.90	18.0
1.90	18.4
1.90	18.4
1.93	19.6

IV. When the light intensity is constant, the reaction rate changes with Cl_2 pressure in the manner indicated below.

P_{Cl_2}, torr	$(-dP_{Cl_2}/dt) \times 10^3$, torr sec^{-1}
9.1	1.5
22.2	6.98
35	11.66
45	17.3
94	47.5
137.2	77.5
180.7	101

V. The reaction is completely stopped when traces of NO are added to the system.

(a) Referring to the data in III above it is seen that when the Cl_2 pressure is constant, the reaction rate is proportional to I_0^n. Evaluate n.

(b) Referring to the data in IV above it is seen that when the light intensity is constant, the reaction rate is proportional to $P_{Cl_2}^m$. Evaluate m.

(c) On the basis of your findings in (a) and (b) write the empirical rate equation for the overall reaction.

(d) The following mechanism (where Tf stands for $CF_2{=}CFH$) was proposed by the investigators. Apply the steady state approximation method and show that the proposed mechanism is consistent with the empirical rate law. Simplify the results as much as possible.

$$Cl_2 + h\nu(\text{incident light}) \rightarrow 2Cl \tag{1}$$
$$Cl + Tf \rightarrow TfCl \tag{2}$$
$$TfCl + Cl_2 \rightarrow TfCl_2 + Cl \tag{3}$$
$$TfCl + TfCl \rightarrow \text{products} \tag{4}$$

(e) In equation (4) the products were not identified. Under what conditions is it legitimate to disregard the identity of products?

(f) If you wished to show experimentally that reaction (3) is not reversible, how would you proceed?

(g) What is the significance of observation V?

CHAPTER 13

Radiochemistry

SECTION 13-1

13-I-1. C^{14} has a half-life of 5760 years. How many years would it take for the activity of a sample of C^{14} to fall to 90 percent of its initial value?

13-I-2. A certain isotope X decays at the rate of 1.00×10^5 atoms $sec^{-1} g^{-1}$. Radium decays at the rate of 3.71×10^{10} atoms $sec^{-1} g^{-1}$. What is the activity of X in millicuries per gram?

13-I-3. The half-life of Na^{24} is 14.9 hr and the atomic mass is 24.0. Calculate the activity of 1.000 μg of Na^{24} in Curies (Ci).

13-I-4. A sample of Na^{24} ($t_{1/2} = 14.9$ hr, atomic mass 24.0) with an activity of 1.00 μCi is administered to a patient. What will be the activity of the sample when it is voided in 5.00 hr?

13-I-5. What mass of Na^{24} ($t_{1/2} = 14.9$ hr, atomic mass 24.0) would give the same activity as 1.000 mg of Mg^{27} ($t_{1/2} = 10.2$ min, atomic mass 27.0)?

13-I-6. Calculate the mass of Rn^{222} ($t_{1/2} = 3.82$ days) in secular equilibrium with 1.00 g of Ra^{226} ($t_{1/2} = 1.62 \times 10^3$ years).

13-I-7. Assuming that Ra^{226} ($t_{1/2} = 1.6 \times 10^3$ yr) is in secular equilibrium with U^{238} ($t_{1/2} = 4.5 \times 10^9$ yr) in a certain mineral, how many grams of Ra^{238} would be present per gram of U^{238} in this mineral?

13-I-8. A hospital has a 0.100-g sample of Ra^{226} ($t_{1/2} = 1.62 \times 10^3$ yr). Every 24 hr, the $Rn^{222}(g)$ produced by the disintegration of this radium sample is pumped off. Estimate the activity of this Rn^{222} at the time it is pumped off. λ for Rn^{222} is 0.182 day^{-1}. The law describing the simultaneous decay of a pair of isotopes A and B in successive nuclear disintegrations

$$A \xrightarrow{\lambda_A} B \xrightarrow{\lambda_B} C$$

is

$$N_B = \frac{\lambda_A N_A^0}{\lambda_B - \lambda_A}(e^{-\lambda_A t} - e^{-\lambda_B t})$$

where λ is the decay constant (first-order rate constant).

13-I-9. In radiochemical dating the age of a specimen can be estimated by measuring the ratio of the amount of daughter isotope D to the amount of the parent isotope remaining, P. Show that the age of a specimen t is related to the daughter/parent ratio D/P by the equation

$$t = \frac{1}{\lambda} \ln\left(1 + \frac{D}{P}\right)$$

where the daughter is nonradioactive and λ is the decay constant for the parent.

13-I-10. The analysis of a 30-g sample of a certain mineral specimen gave 450 mg Rb and 0.90 mg Sr. The Rb is 27 mass percent Rb^{87} ($\lambda = 1.47 \times 10^{-11}$ yr^{-1}) and the Sr is 80 mass percent Sr^{87}. Rb^{87} decays to Sr^{87}. Calculate the age of the specimen.

13-I-11. Complete the following:
  (a) $_1D^2 + \gamma \rightarrow ? + _0n^1$
  (b) $_4Be^9 + _2He^4 \rightarrow _0n^1 + ?$

13-I-12. Complete the following:
  (a) $Au^{197}(n, \gamma)$?
  (b) $Ca^{40}(n, \alpha)$?
  (c) $Mg^{24}(d, \alpha)$?
  (d) $H^3(\alpha, n)$?

13-I-13. Calculate the mass defect and the binding energy for $_8O^{16}$. The isotopic atomic mass of $_8O^{16}$ is 15.99448 atomic mass units (amu). The masses of the proton and neutron are 1.007277 and 1.008657 amu, respectively, and the mass of the electron is 0.000549 amu.

13-I-14. The rest mass of a β particle is 0.000549 amu. What would be the effective relativistic mass if the β particle is moving at a velocity 0.99 that of light?

13-I-15. When a beam of neutrons of flux density ϕ passes through an absorbing medium, the fractional change in flux density $d\phi/\phi$ at any given point within the medium is directly proportional to the path length dx: $d\phi/\phi = N\sigma\,dx$. N is the number of target atoms per cubic centimeter of medium and σ is the microscopic cross section. Show that σ can be evaluated from a plot of $\ln \phi$ vs x.

SECTION 13-II

13-II-1. At 4:00 P.M. on August 22 a pharmacist wishes to prepare a medication containing Au^{198} ($t_{1/2} = 2.70$ days) that will have an activity of 0.50 μCi per g at 8:00 A.M. the following morning. At the time that the material was shipped by the manufacturer, 12:00 noon on August 21, it had an activity of 3.00 μCi per g. How much nonradioactive diluent should the pharmacist add per gram of the Au^{198} as supplied by the manufacturer?

SECTION 13-III

13-III-1. Show that the age of a radioactive specimen that decays with branching into two nonradioactive daughters is given by

$$t = \frac{1}{\lambda} \ln \left[1 + \frac{D_1}{P}\left(\frac{R+1}{R}\right)\right]$$

where P is the amount of parent, D_1 is the amount of daughter number 1, and D_2 is the amount of daughter number 2, at time t. λ is the decay constant of the parent, and $R = D_1/D_2$.

13-III-2. A parent isotope (1) and its radioactive daughter (2) are in secular equilibrium with one another, the daughter decomposing into a stable isotope, (3), viz.,

$$(1) \xrightarrow{\lambda_1} (2) \xrightarrow{\lambda_2} (3)$$

Let $N_1^0 =$ the number of atoms of (1) at $t = 0$.
Derive the expression

$$N_2 = \frac{N_1^0 \lambda_1}{\lambda_2 - \lambda_1} (e^{-\lambda_1 t} - e^{-\lambda_2 t})$$

for N_2, the number of atoms of (2) present at any given time, t. Assume that $\lambda_1 \neq \lambda_2$ (the case $\lambda_1 = \lambda_2$ requires special treatment) and that $N_2^0 = N_3^0 = 0$. (Note: The solution of this problem requires knowledge of linear differential equations slightly beyond the usual introductory course in calculus.) This problem is similar to 11-III-6.

13-III-3. Show that the mean lifetime (not half-life) of an isotope is given by the formula

$$t_{\text{mean}} = \frac{1}{\lambda}$$

You will need the integral

$$\int x e^{ax} \, dx = \frac{e^{ax}}{a^2} (ax - 1) + C$$

13-III-4. Assume that radiation is emitted equally in all directions from a point source. Thus points of equal intensity describe a spherical surface with its center at the point source. Only part of the total radiation emitted from such a source is captured by a Geiger counter. The fraction of the radiation that *is* captured by the counter is called the *geometry factor*, G. G is the ratio of the section of the spherical surface inter-

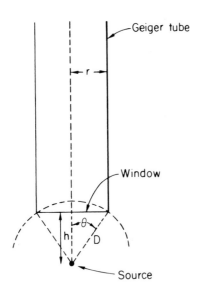

cepted by the flat circular counter window to the area of the entire sphere. Referring to the figure, show that

$$G = \frac{1 - \cos \theta}{2} = \frac{1}{2}\left(1 - \frac{h}{\sqrt{h^2 + r^2}}\right)$$

and show that for large distances between the point source and the counter window this reduces to the inverse square law,

$$G \approx \frac{r^2}{4h^2}$$

CHAPTER 14

Surface Chemistry
and Colloids

SECTION 14-1

14-I-1. A suspension of 1.00 g of hemoglobin in 1.00 liter of water has an osmotic pressure of 3.6×10^{-4} atm at 25°C. Estimate the particle weight of the hemoglobin.

14-I-2. Oncley, Scatchard, and Brown [*J. Phys. Chem.*, **51**, 184 (1947)] measured the osmotic pressure of solutions of γ globulin in 0.15 M NaCl at 37°C and obtained the following results:

c, concentration of γ globulin, g per 100 ml	P, osmotic pressure, mm H_2O
19.27	453
12.35	253
5.81	112

Calculate the molecular weight of the γ globulin.

14-I-3. According to Fox and Flory [*J. Phys. Chem.*, **53**, 197 (1949)], the relationship between intrinsic viscosity and molecular weight for solutions of polyisobutylene at 20°C is given by the formula $[\eta] = 3.60 \times 10^{-4} M^{0.64}$. What is the molecular weight of a polyisobutylene fraction that gives a solution with intrinsic viscosity 1.80 deciliter g^{-1}? Intrinsic viscosity is defined by the equation

$$[\eta] = \lim_{c \to 0} \left(\frac{\eta - \eta_0}{\eta_0 c} \right)$$

where η_0 is the viscosity of the solvent and c is the concentration in grams per deciliter.

14-I-4. Fox and Flory [*J. Phys. Chem.*, **53**, 197 (1949)] obtained the following data for the intrinsic viscosity of polyisobutylene in CCl_4 solutions at 30°C as a function of molecular weight. Show that the data fit the relationship $[\eta] = KM^a$ and evaluate the constants K and a. Intrinsic viscosity is defined in the preceding problem.

M	$[\eta]$, deciliter g^{-1}
1,260,000	4.30
463,000	2.06
110,000	0.78
92,700	0.73
48,000	0.43
10,000	0.15
9,550	0.138
7,080	0.115

14-I-5. By a graphical method evaluate a and K in the formula $[\eta] = KM^a$ for Buna N (a synthetic rubber) in toluene solution from the following data [Scott, Carter, and Magat, *J. Am. Chem. Soc.*, **71**, 220 (1949)]:

M	$[\eta]$
25,000	0.30
31,800	0.35
39,500	0.40
57,000	0.48
100,000	0.71
224,000	1.16
380,000	1.76

$[\eta]$ is intrinsic viscosity defined in Problem 14-I-3. M is the number average molecular weight.

14-I-6. (a) What is the surface area of a cube having an edge length of 1 cm?

(b) What would be the total surface area of this same material if it were subdivided into colloidal-size cubes, each having an edge length of 10^{-7} cm? Express the result in acres. $(1 \text{ m}^2 = 2.47 \times 10^{-4} \text{ acres.})$

14-I-7. The adsorption of oxygen on smooth iron at $-183°C$ was investigated by Armbruster and Austin [*J. Am. Chem. Soc.*, **68**, 1347 (1946)]. On the basis of the following data selected from their work show that the adsorption rate follows first-order kinetics and evaluate the specific rate constant. V is the volume adsorbed on a particular specimen of iron up to time t. The volume adsorbed at equilibrium (V_e) was found to be 0.451 cm³.

t, sec	V, cm³
1380	0.167
3000	0.272
4260	0.330
7320	0.408
10020	0.432

14-I-8. Explain qualitatively the reason for the difference in shape of the two following adsorption curves:

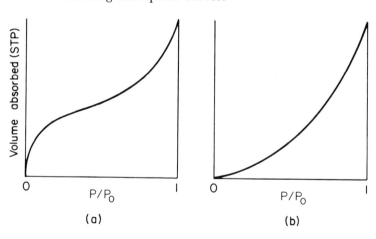

(a) N_2 on Fe at $-195°C$.

(b) Br_2 on SiO_2 at $79°C$.

$P_0 =$ vapor pressure of adsorbate.

SECTION 14-II

14-II-1. According to Szyszkowski [*Z. Physik. Chem.*, **64**, 385 (1908)] the surface tension γ of an aqueous solution of butyric acid is related at 18°C to the bulk concentration c by the empirical equation $\gamma_0 - \gamma = 29.8 \log(1 + 19.64c)$, where γ_0 is the surface tension of pure water. Apply the Gibbs adsorption equation,

$$S = \frac{-c}{RT} \frac{d\gamma}{dc}$$

and calculate the value of S, the excess concentration of solute per square centimeter of surface when $c = 0.01 \ M$. If c could increase indefinitely, what would be the limiting value of S as c becomes infinite?

14-II-2. McBain and Britton [*J. Am. Chem. Soc.*, **52**, 2198 (1930)] investigated the adsorption of nitrogen on charcoal at $-77°C$ and found that a 0.0946-g sample of charcoal adsorbed the following weights of nitrogen at the pressures indicated:

P, atm	x, weight N_2, g
3.5	0.0119
10.0	0.0161
16.7	0.0181
25.7	0.0192
33.5	0.0195
39.2	0.0196
48.6	0.0199

Plot these data in such a manner as to obtain a straight line in accordance with each of the following relationships and evaluate the constants in each. Do not necessarily plot the equations in their given form. First convert them, if necessary, into a form that will yield a straight-line graph. m = mass of charcoal in grams.

(a) $\dfrac{P}{(x/m)} = \dfrac{1 + k_2 P}{k_1}$

(b) $\dfrac{x}{m} = kP^{1/n}$

(c) $\log\left(\dfrac{x/m}{P}\right) = k\left(\dfrac{x}{m}\right)$

14-II-3. The following data for the adsorption of aqueous acetic acid on charcoal were obtained by Labowitz (unpublished data):

c_0, molarity of acetic acid in solution before addition to charcoal	c_e, molarity of acetic acid remaining in solution at equilibrium	m, grams of charcoal
0.503	0.434	3.96
0.252	0.202	3.94
0.126	0.0899	4.00
0.0628	0.0347	4.12
0.0314	0.0113	4.04
0.0157	0.00333	4.00

In all cases the volume of the solution in contact with the charcoal was 200 ml. Show that these data fit the Freundlich adsorption isotherm,

$$\frac{x}{m} = kc_e^{1/n}$$

where x is the number of grams of acetic acid adsorbed. Evaluate the constants k and n.

CHAPTER 15

Quantum Chemistry
and Spectroscopy

15-1. (a) Calculate the amount of work required to separate two hydrogen atoms, each of mass 1.7×10^{-24} g, from their equilibrium distance, 0.74 Å, to infinity, assuming that gravitational attraction between the two hydrogen atoms is the only force to be taken into account. The universal gravitational constant $G = 6.670 \times 10^{-8}$ dyne cm^2 g^{-2}.

(b) The experimental value for the H—H bond strength indicates that the actual amount of energy required to separate the two atoms in H_2 is 6.7×10^{-12} ergs. What is the significance of the discrepancy between this figure and the figure calculated in (a)?

15-2. Calculate the electrostatic charge in esu on an oil drop of density 0.920 g cm^{-3} and radius 1.24×10^{-4} cm that is suspended motionless at sea level when an electric field of strength 1 V cm^{-1} is imposed upon it. 1 V $= 3.34 \times 10^{-3}$ statV. Assume that the density of air is negligible.

15-3. A dark-adapted human eye can perceive yellow light when the rate of incidence of photons on the retina is about 500 per sec. Calculate the power in watts corresponding to this rate of incidence, assuming a wavelength of 5000 Å.

15-4. A certain system has four energy levels E_n, labeled by a quantum number n, with the following energies:

$E_0 = 0$

$E_1 = 1.000 \times 10^{-11}$ erg
$E_2 = 3.000 \times 10^{-11}$ erg
$E_3 = 3.500 \times 10^{-11}$ erg

The selection rule for radiative transitions in this system is $\Delta n = \pm 1$ or ± 3. List the energy differences, frequencies, and wave numbers (cm^{-1}) corresponding to all the lines that might be observed in the absorption spectrum of this system.

15-5. Starting with the Planck radiation law,

$$\rho_\lambda = \frac{8\pi hc}{\lambda^5 (e^{hc/\lambda kT} - 1)}$$

derive the Stefan-Boltzmann law, $\rho = \sigma T^4$. ρ in the latter case means the total radiation energy from $\lambda = 0$ to $\lambda = \infty$; that is,

$$\rho = \int_0^\infty \rho_\lambda \, d\lambda = \sigma T^4.$$

(Hint: Let $x = hc/\lambda kT$.) You will need the integral

$$\int_0^\infty \frac{x^3 \, dx}{(e^x - 1)} = \frac{\pi^4}{15}$$

15-6. Starting with the Planck radiation law, derive the Wien displacement law, $\lambda_{max} = \text{constant}/T$, where λ_{max} is the wavelength where ρ is a maximum for the given temperature.

15-7. Starting with the Planck radiation law, derive the Rayleigh-Jeans equation, $\rho_\lambda = 8\pi kT/\lambda^4$, which is applicable only at long wavelengths.

15-8. Starting with the Planck radiation law, derive the Wien equation, $\rho_\lambda = C_1 e^{-C_2/\lambda T}/\lambda^5$, which is applicable only at short wavelengths.

15-9. Imagine that radiation is in equilibrium with the walls (ends) of a one-dimensional cavity of length l at temperature T. An equivalent way to visualize this situation is to imagine that in a three-dimensional cavity in the shape of a right cylinder or prism, the only possible electromagnetic waves are those that propagate along the axis of the cavity.

(a) Find the number of distinct electromagnetic standing waves in this one-dimensional cavity with frequencies between v and $v + dv$.

(b) Find the amount of electromagnetic energy corresponding to the frequency interval between v and $v + dv$, according to Planck's theory, in this cavity.

15-10. (a) Assume that the possible energies of a mode of electromagnetic radiation of frequency v are nbv^2, where $n = 0$, 1, 2,..., and b is a constant. Using this assumption (in place of Planck's assumption that the possible energies are nhv), obtain an expression for the energy density of radiation of frequency between v and $v + dv$ in equilibrium with the walls of a cavity at temperature T.

(b) From the result of (a) find how the total energy density, at all frequencies, in the cavity depends on T.

15-11. When applying the Ritz combination principle,

$$\bar{v} = Z^2 R \left(\frac{1}{n_1^{\,2}} - \frac{1}{n_2^{\,2}} \right)$$

in each of the following circumstances what values would you substitute for n_1 and n_2?

(a) The calculation of $\bar{v}$ for the absorption line produced by the complete ionization of a hydrogen atom from the ground state.

(b) The calculation of $\bar{v}$ for the absorption line in the Paschen series produced by the transfer of an electron in a hydrogen atom from the lowest possible level for this series ($n_1 = 3$) to the third from the lowest possible level in the same series.

15-12. Calculate the frequency in cm^{-1} of the third line in the Pfund series ($n_1 = 5$) in the spectrum of atomic hydrogen. The Rydberg constant for atomic hydrogen is 109,677.76 cm^{-1}.

15-13. On the basis of the Pauli exclusion principle show that the maximum possible number of electrons in the M shell ($n = 3$) of any individual atom is 18.

15-14. Two trains of traveling waves may be specified by the functions

$$\psi_1 = \sin(ax + bt) \quad \text{and} \quad \psi_2 = \sin(ax - bt)$$

(a) For each of these trains find the speed and direction of propagation and the wavelength. (Hint: Locate the nodes (where $\psi = 0$) for each train and see how they move.)

(b) Show that

$$\psi_+ = \psi_1 + \psi_2 \quad \text{and} \quad \psi_- = \psi_1 - \psi_2$$

represent standing waves. Locate the nodes in each wave.

15-15. A postulate of quantum mechanics is that the operator corresponding to energy is $-(h/2\pi i)(\partial/\partial t)$, where t is time.

(a) What must be the time dependence of an eigenfunction of energy? (In other words, what kind of function is a solution of the equation $-(h/2\pi i)(\partial\psi/\partial t) = E\psi$?)

(b) When ψ is an eigenfunction of energy, how does the probability density $|\psi|^2$ depend on time? How does this result help to explain why eigenfunctions of energy are so important, especially in chemistry?

15-16. In classical mechanics the energy of a particle is given by $E = (p^2/2m) + V(x)$, where p is momentum and V is potential energy. In quantum mechanics an operator (H) corresponding to energy can be obtained by replacing p by the operator (in one dimension) $(h/2\pi i)(\partial/\partial x)$.

(a) By performing this substitution obtain the form of the operator H. (Observe that squaring an operator means operating twice.)

(b) It is postulated (Problem 15-15) that energy also corresponds to the operator $-(h/2\pi i)(\partial/\partial t)$. Combine the result of (a) with this postulate to obtain a partial differential equation that involves the dependence of a wave function ψ on both x and t.

(c) Substitute in this differential equation the function obtained in Problem 15-15(a) to obtain a differential equation not involving t. (Assume that ψ does not depend on y and z.)

15-17. The time-independent one-dimensional Schrödinger equation is

$$\left(\frac{-h^2}{8\pi^2 m}\right)\left(\frac{\partial^2 \psi}{\partial x^2}\right) + V(x)\,\psi = E\psi$$

where V is the potential energy. It is well known that only differences in V are physically significant; nothing is essentially changed if a constant is added to V. Show how the Schrödinger equation is affected by such a change in V and why the effect is inessential.

15-18. A particle of mass m, moving in one dimension, is confined to that part of the x axis between $x = 0$ and $x = a$. The potential function is

$$V(x) = \begin{cases} 0, 0 \leqslant x \leqslant a \\ \infty, x < 0 \text{ or } x > a. \end{cases}$$

(a) Obtain a set of wave functions ψ for this particle that are finite and continuous everywhere, including $x = 0$ and $x = a$, and that satisfy the Schrödinger equation

$$-\left(\frac{h^2}{8\pi^2 m}\right)\left(\frac{d^2\psi}{dx^2}\right) + V(x)\,\psi = E\psi$$

Give the value of E corresponding to each function.

(b) Ascertain whether your functions are eigenfunctions of the momentum operator $(h/2\pi i)(d/dx)$. If they are, find the eigenvalues; if they are not, explain in physical terms why more than one momentum corresponds to a given function.

15-19. A particle of mass m is confined to a one-dimensional box with the origin at the center of the box. The box extends from $-a/2$ to $+a/2$. The potential energy is

$$V(x) = \begin{cases} 0, -\dfrac{a}{2} \leqslant x \leqslant \dfrac{a}{2} \\[2mm] \infty, |x| > \dfrac{a}{2} \end{cases}$$

(a) Write the Schrödinger equation for this problem showing separate equations for the inside and the outside of the box.

(b) Assume a solution (inside the box) of the form

$$\psi(x) = A\sin(cx) + B\cos(cx).$$

Give a rule that determines all the possible values of c, and for each possible c give the conditions on A and B that make ψ a satisfactory solution.

(c) Express the energy in terms of c.

15-20. Each of the following particles is confined to a one-dimensional box as described in Problem 15-18. For each case calculate (a) the energy (in ergs) corresponding to the lowest energy level ($n = 1$); (b) the separation ($E_2 - E_1$) between the lowest and next-to-lowest energy levels; (c) the number of levels with energy less than the mean thermal energy $\frac{1}{2}kT$ at $T = 300°K$.

	Particle	Mass (m)	Length (a)
(i)	Electron	9.11×10^{-28} g	1 Å
(ii)	H_2 molecule	3.35×10^{-24} g	1 cm
(iii)	Ball	100 g	1 m

15-21. (a) Discover a function that is an eigenfunction of the momentum operator, $(h/2\pi i)(d/dx)$, with eigenvalue p.

(b) Show how a linear combination of such functions with eigenvalues $\sqrt{2mE}$ and $-\sqrt{2mE}$ is equivalent to any one of the energy eigenfunctions found in Problem 15-18(a). Discuss the relation of this result to Problem 15-18(b).

15-22. According to the de Broglie relation, $p = h/\lambda$, where p is momentum and λ is wavelength. For the eigenfunctions of momentum in Problem 15-21 (a) verify that the wavelength obtained from the de Broglie relation is indeed the wavelength of the wave that ψ represents.

15-23. Take the difference between the two possible momenta in Problem 15-21(b) as a measure of the uncertainty in the momentum of the particle, $\Delta p = 2\sqrt{2mE}$. Take the permitted interval a as a measure of the uncertainty in position, $\Delta x = a$. Calculate $\Delta p \, \Delta x$ and compare the result with the Heisenberg uncertainty principle.

15-24. Consider a wave function ψ for a one-dimensional problem. In order that $|\psi|^2 \, dx$ should represent the actual probability of finding a particle between x and $x + dx$, $\int_{-\infty}^{\infty} |\psi|^2 \, dx$

should be equal to 1 since this integral represents the probability of finding the particle somewhere. This condition can usually be satisfied by multiplying the wave function by a suitable constant, called a *normalization constant*; the resulting wave function is said to be *normalized*. Convert the wave functions obtained in Problem 15-18(a) to normalized functions.

15-25. A particle of mass m in one-dimensional space is confined to the positive x axis by a potential such that

$$V(x) = 0, x > 0 \qquad V(x) = \infty, x < 0$$

(a) Find a set of wave functions for this particle that are eigenfunctions of energy. What restrictions, if any, must be imposed on the energy in order to obtain an acceptable set of functions?

(b) Ascertain whether they are also eigenfunctions of momentum. Interpret your result in physical terms.

15-26. The potential energy of a particle is given by

$$V = 0, \qquad -a \leqslant x \leqslant a$$
$$V = V_1 > 0, \qquad -b \leqslant x < -a \text{ or } a < x \leqslant b \quad (b = 2a)$$
$$V = V_2 = 2V_1, \qquad x < -b \text{ or } x > b$$

Sketch roughly the distribution of the energy levels available to the particle. Show clearly any distinctions between wider and narrower spacing of levels. Explain your conclusions.

15-27. A particle of mass m moves on the x axis in the following potential:

Region		
1	$x < 0$	$V = \infty$
2	$0 \leqslant x \leqslant a$	$V = 0$
3	$x > a$	$V = V_0$

For a bound state of the particle ($E < V_0$) find wave functions that satisfy the Schrödinger equation, the conditions of finiteness and continuity everywhere, and the requirement that the first derivative be continuous except where V is infinite. The functions will contain parameters that must satisfy certain equations. Exhibit these equations, especially the equation(s) that determine(s) the possible values of E. (It is not necessary to solve explicitly for these values.)

15-28. For a rigid rotator constrained to rotate in a plane about a fixed point but subject to no other forces, the energy is $L^2/2I$, where L is the angular momentum and I is the moment of inertia. The operator corresponding to L is $(h/2\pi i)(\partial/\partial\phi)$. ϕ is the angle between the rotator and the x axis.

(a) Find the operator corresponding to the energy of the rotator.

(b) Find the allowed energy levels and energy eigenfunctions of this rotator. (Remember that ψ must be single valued.)

15-29. A simple harmonic oscillator is described in quantum mechanics by the differential equation

$$\left(\frac{-h^2}{8\pi^2 m}\right)\left(\frac{d^2\psi}{dx^2}\right) + \frac{1}{2}kx^2\psi = E\psi \tag{1}$$

where h is Planck's constant, m is the mass of the oscillating particle, k is the restoring force constant, x is the displacement of the particle from its equilibrium position, ψ is the wave function, and E is the energy of the oscillator. Show by direct substitution that each of the following functions is a solution of Equation (1), provided that the constant a (or b) is given a certain value. (A function ψ is a *solution* of (1) if the entire left side reduces to a constant E times ψ.) For each function express a (or b) and E in terms of k, m, and h, and then express E in terms of the classical frequency ν, where $\nu = (1/2\pi)\sqrt{k/m}$.

(a) $\psi_1 = e^{-ax^2}$
(b) $\psi_2 = xe^{-bx^2}$

15-30. According to the harmonic oscillator wave function ψ_1 of Problem 15-29 the particle can be anywhere from $x = -\infty$ to $x = \infty$, but it is most likely to be near $x = 0$.

(a) Find the length Δx such that when $x = \pm\frac{1}{2}\Delta x$, ψ_1 has fallen to 10 percent of its value at $x = 0$. Express the result in terms of the energy E and other necessary parameters.

(b) According to classical mechanics the momentum of the oscillating particle varies from $\sqrt{2mE}$ to $-\sqrt{2mE}$. (Prove this statement.) In quantum mechanics for momentum as for position there are no sharp limits, but it is still correct to take $\Delta p = 2\sqrt{2mE}$ as a measure of the range within which the momentum of the particle is probably found. Calculate the product $\Delta p \, \Delta x$. Compare the result with the Heisenberg uncertainty principle.

15-31. Make a set of sketches representing all the possible modes of vibration of the carbon dioxide molecule (which is linear) and indicate which of these modes would be active in the infrared.

15-32. The vibrational frequency of H^1Cl^{35} (in wave numbers) is 2989 cm^{-1}. The isotopic atomic weights are $H^1 = 1.008$, $Cl^{35} = 34.97$ amu (atomic mass units). $(6.023 \times 10^{23}$ amu $= 1$ g$)$

(a) Convert this frequency to sec^{-1}.

(b) Calculate the reduced mass of the two atoms in HCl, in amu and in grams. (See Problem 15-33(c).)

(c) Calculate the force constant for stretching in HCl in dynes/Å.

15-33. The vibrational potential energy of a diatomic molecule can be represented approximately by the *Morse function*,

$$V = A(1 - e^{-B(r-r_0)})^2$$

where r is the internuclear distance, r_0 is the equilibrium value of r, and A, B are positive constants characteristic of the molecule.

(a) Show that V has a minimum when $r = r_0$.

(b) Calculate the dissociation energy D of the molecule in terms of A, B, and r_0. (The dissociation energy is the difference between the energy at $r = r_0$ and at $r = \infty$ with no kinetic energy in either case.)

(c) Express similarly the vibrational frequency ν. (Note that if this were a harmonic oscillator, we would have $V = \frac{1}{2}k(r - r_0)^2$, and $\nu = (1/2\pi)(k/\mu)^{1/2}$, where μ is the reduced mass of the two atoms: $\mu = (m_1 m_2)/(m_1 + m_2)$. To obtain k, and thus ν, we must approximate the Morse function by a harmonic oscillator function near $r = r_0$.)

(d) Correct the dissociation energy calculated in (b) by recognizing that the minimum energy of the molecule is not that corresponding to $r = r_0$ but is higher by $\frac{1}{2}h\nu$ (the zero-point energy).

15-34. For a molecule with the symmetry of BF_3 (planar, equilateral triangle) calculate the moment of inertia about each of two mutually perpendicular axes in the plane of the molecule and passing through the center of mass, in terms of the masses m_B and m_F and the bond length r. Show that the two moments are equal.

15-35. When an atom (or ion) is surrounded by six identical negative charges in an octahedral array along the coordinate axes, the atomic d orbitals are split into two sets: $3z^2 - r^2$ and $x^2 - y^2$ with higher energy; xy, yz, and zx with lower energy. Suppose that instead of six negative charges, there are four, arranged (a) in a square on the x and y axes; (b) tetrahedrally at alternate corners of a cube whose faces are perpendicular to the three axes. Describe qualitatively the energy levels of the d orbitals to be expected in each of these cases.

15-36. (a) The $2s$ and $2p_z$ orbitals for a hydrogen atom are

$$\psi_{2s} = \frac{1}{4\sqrt{2\pi}} a_0^{-3/2} \left(2 - \frac{r}{a_0}\right) e^{-r/2a_0}$$

$$\psi_{2p_z} = \frac{1}{4\sqrt{2\pi}} a_0^{-3/2} \frac{r}{a_0} e^{-r/2a_0} \cos\theta$$

($a_0 = $ Bohr radius $= 0.529$ Å)

Using these orbitals write explicit expressions for the two digonal (sp) hybrid orbitals along the z axis given by

$$D_{1,2} = (1/\sqrt{2})(\psi_{2s} \pm \psi_{2p_z}).$$

(b) For either (not both) of your hybrid functions, calculate the probability density $|\psi|^2$ on the z axis at $z = 3a_0$ and $z = -3a_0$, in terms of a_0 and other universal constants.

(c) Make the same calculation separately for the $2s$ function and for the $2p_z$ function.

(d) How are your results related to the relative strengths of bonds formed from the s, p, and sp orbitals?

15-37. The electron in a certain hydrogen atom is in the $2p_z$ orbital (see Problem 15-36). Evaluate the probability that this electron is inside a sphere of radius a_0 centered at the nucleus.

15-38. Sketch the proton magnetic resonance spectrum to be expected for the hypothetical molecule $H_2C—OH_2$ (a) containing a trace of acid or base; (b) rigorously purified. Assume that the acidic properties of the protons attached to O are the same as in CH_3OH. Label each feature of your spectra. (c) Explain any difference between the spectra in (a) and (b).

CHAPTER 16

Statistical
thermodynamics

SECTION 16-I

16-I-1. Evaluate the limiting high-temperature heat capacity C_V in cal mole^{-1} deg^{-1} for the nonlinear gas molecule PH_3 (phosphine).

16-I-2. (a) For each of the following gases, assumed ideal—(i) He; (ii) CF_4 (nonlinear); (iii) C_2F_2 (linear)—find the molar heat capacity at constant volume that is predicted by the application of classical mechanics to all motions of the nuclei.

(b) Would you expect the actual heat capacity of each gas at ordinary temperatures to be greater than, equal to, or less than that calculated in (a)? Explain.

16-I-3. Why is the heat capacity of a solid or liquid usually greater than that of the same substance as a gas at the same temperature?

16-I-4. The energy change at 0°K in the reaction

$$NaCl(g) \rightleftharpoons Na^+(g) + Cl^-(g)$$

is $\Delta\epsilon_0 = 8.63 \times 10^{-12}$ erg molecule^{-1}. Calculate the ratio of the equilibrium constant for the reaction

$$NaCl(aq) \rightleftharpoons Na^+(aq) + Cl^-(aq)$$

to K_c for the gas reaction at 300°K. Assume that the only difference between the gas and solution reactions is that $\Delta\epsilon_0$ is divided by the dielectric constant of water, about 80.

SECTION 16-II

16-II-1. In three dimensions the number of modes of vibration of a nonlinear n-atomic molecule is $3n - 6$. Consider an imaginary nonlinear n-atomic molecule existing only in a hypothetical two-dimensional space (for example, the plane of this paper). What is the number of modes of vibration for such a molecule? Would the result be different if the molecule were linear?

16-II-2. A large number of particles confined to a plane are attracted to the origin with a force such that the potential energy of each particle is $u(r) = ar^2$, where r is the distance from the origin. The temperature is T.

(a) Give an expression (containing an unknown proportionality constant) for the number of particles per unit area at the distance r.

(b) Give a similar expression for the total number of particles between the distance r and the distance $r + dr$.

(c) Evaluate $\overline{u(r)}$, the potential energy averaged over the collection of particles, in terms of given quantities and universal constants.

16-II-3. Consider a set of molecules, each of mass m, that are confined to two dimensions but that behave like ideal gas molecules. The distribution law for each *component* of velocity is

$$\frac{dN_{v_x}}{N_{\text{total}}} = Ae^{-mv_x^2/2kT}\,dv_x$$

(a) Obtain the distribution law with respect to *speed v*, that is,

$$\frac{dN_v}{N_{\text{total}}} = F(v)\,dv$$

No unknown constant, such as A, should appear in the result.

(c) Find the average speed $\bar{v}$ of the molecules, in terms of m, T, and universal constants.

16-II-4. For a certain hypothetical molecule the partition function is $q = 2 + \beta\epsilon$, where $\beta = 1/kT$ and ϵ is a constant characteristic of the molecule. Calculate in terms of β, ϵ, and universal constants (a) the average energy $\bar{E}$, (b) the average entropy $\bar{S}$, (c) the heat capacity, $(\partial\bar{E}/\partial T)_\epsilon$.

16-II-5. A certain molecule can exist in either a singlet (paired electron spins) or triplet (unpaired spins) level. The degeneracies of the singlet and triplet levels are 1 and 3, respectively. The energy of the singlet state exceeds by ϵ the energy of the triplet.

(a) Write the electronic factor in the partition function of this molecule. Indicate any approximations that you make.

(b) For $\epsilon = 1.38 \times 10^{-14}$ erg and $T = 100°K$ find the ratio of the population of the singlet level to the population of the triplet level. What assumptions are you making about the energy levels corresponding to rotational and vibrational motion of the molecule? What more general expression would be needed if these assumptions could not be made?

16-II-6. Let us divide the possible states of a molecule into two classes, A and B. Let N_A and N_B be the equilibrium numbers of molecules in states of the two classes, let $N = N_A + N_B$, and let $\bar{\epsilon}_A$ and $\bar{\epsilon}_B$ be the average energies of molecules in the two classes. We assume that the molecules form an ideal gas and that they can undergo transitions between class A and class B. The energies are measured from the same zero level for the two classes.

(a) Express the populations N_A and N_B and the energies $\bar{\epsilon}_A$ and $\bar{\epsilon}_B$ in terms of partial partition functions q_A and q_B confined to levels belonging to one class. (T, N, and universal constants may also appear here and in later answers.)

(b) Express the total energy of the system in terms of N_A, N_B, $\bar{\epsilon}_A$, and $\bar{\epsilon}_B$.

(c) Express the heat capacity C_V of the system in a way derivable directly from the result of (b). How would your answer be changed if transitions between the two classes were impossible?

(d) Use the results of (a)–(c) to show that

$$C_V = N_A \bar{C}_{VA} + N_B \bar{C}_{VB} + \frac{N_A N_B (\bar{\epsilon}_A - \bar{\epsilon}_B)^2}{NkT^2}$$

16-II-7. (a) For each of the following gases, assumed ideal—(i) He; (ii) CF_4 (nonlinear); (iii) C_2F_2 (linear)—find the molar heat capacity at constant volume that is predicted by the application of classical mechanics to all motions of the nuclei.

(b) Would you expect the actual heat capacity of each gas at ordinary temperatures to be greater than, equal to, or less than that calculated in (a)? Explain.

(c) The second lowest electronic energy level of the helium atom is 3.13×10^{-11} erg above the lowest level. Estimate roughly the highest temperature at which the heat capacity of helium would agree with your answer to (a). Explain.

16-II-8. The SO_2 molecule is nonlinear.

(a) Find the molar heat capacity $\bar{C}_V$ of gaseous SO_2, as predicted by applying classical mechanics to all motions of the nuclei.

(b) The vibrational frequencies of SO_2 are 1.57×10^{13}, 3.45×10^{13}, and 4.08×10^{13} sec^{-1}. What is the lowest temperature (roughly) at which you would expect $\bar{C}_V$ for gaseous SO_2 to agree with the result of (a)? Explain.

16-II-9. A molecule A_2B is nonlinear. Its vibration frequencies are 1.00×10^{13}, 9.00×10^{13}, and 1.00×10^{14} sec^{-1}.

(a) Estimate the molar heat capacity $\bar{C}_V$ of gaseous A_2B at $100°K$ and $1000°K$. Explain.

(b) Find $\bar{C}_V$ at very high temperatures, assuming that the molecules do not dissociate and that the electrons remain in their state of lowest energy.

(c) Estimate roughly the temperature above which $\bar{C}_V$ would have the value found in (b). Explain.

16-II-10. The vibrational frequencies of a certain nonlinear molecule AB_2 are 4.0×10^{12}, 5.0×10^{12}, and 7.0×10^{13} sec^{-1}. Estimate the molar heat capacity $\bar{C}_V$ of gaseous AB_2 at (a) $500°K$; (b) $5000°K$ (assuming no dissociation). Explain.

16-II-11. The acetylene molecule, HCCH, is linear. Its modes of vibration include three stretchings and four bendings. Its observed heat capacity $\bar{C}_V$ is 8.0 cal°K^{-1} mole^{-1}.

(a) Find the value of $\bar{C}_V$ for acetylene that is predicted by the application of classical mechanics to all motions of the nuclei.

(b) Estimate $\bar{C}_V$ by assuming that the stretchings have very high frequency ($\nu \gg kT/h$) and that the bendings have very low frequency ($\nu \ll kT/h$).

(c) Estimate $\bar{C}_V$ by assuming that all the vibrations have very high frequency ($\nu \gg kT/h$).

(d) Explain the relation between these estimates and the experimental value of $\bar{C}_V$.

16-II-12. Explain, in terms of the assumptions made by the respective theories, why

(a) The Einstein and Debye theories of the heat capacity of solids both predict that $\lim_{T\to 0} C_V = 0$, whereas C_V is independent of the temperature in the classical theory.

(b) The Einstein theory predicts that C_V approaches zero more rapidly than the Debye theory predicts.

SECTION 16-III

16-III-1. A number, N, of particles, each of mass m, are confined to a square planar region of edge L, but are otherwise subject to no forces.

(a) Find the force per unit length exerted by these particles on the boundary of the square, in terms of N, m, L, the average kinetic energy $\bar{\epsilon}$ of the particles, and universal constants.

(b) These particles are in equilibrium with an environment at temperature T. What is the relation between $\bar{\epsilon}$ and T? Explain.

(c) Find the average speed $\bar{v}$ of the particles, in terms of T, $\bar{\epsilon}$, m, and universal constants.

16-III-2. A dilute monomolecular film on the surface of a liquid contains N identical molecules per unit area. The molecules move independently of each other and of the solvent molecules. The mass of each molecule is m. The answers to the following questions should be expressed in terms of m, N, T, and universal constants.

(a) Determine the two-dimensional speed distribution function $f(v)$ for these molecules, normalized so that

$$\int_0^\infty f(v)\, dv = 1$$

(b) Calculate the averages $\bar{v}$, $\overline{v^2}$, and $\overline{v^3}$.

(c) Find the number of collisions, per unit length per unit time, with a line segment on the edge of the surface layer.

(d) Find the surface pressure (that is, depression of surface tension) exerted by this surface film on a partition separating the film from a region devoid of film.

(e) Find the average kinetic energy of those molecules that escape through a small gap in the partition.

16-III-3. Molecules, each of mass m, are confined to one dimension in which they move to and fro randomly with a distribution of speeds determined by the temperature T. The molecules are not impenetrable but can pass through each other.

(a) What is the average velocity $\bar{v}$ of these molecules?

(b) Calculate the average speed $\overline{|v|}$, in terms of m, T, and universal constants.

(c) Calculate the average relative speed $\overline{|v_{21}|}$ and the ratio $\overline{|v_{21}|}/\overline{|v|}$.

16-III-4. A certain hypothetical "molecule" can exist in any one of only three states, with energies 0, ϵ, and ϵ. (Two states have the same energy.)

(a) Find the partition function Q and the molar heat capacity $\bar{C}_V$ for 1 mole of these "molecules," in terms of ϵ, T, and universal constants.

(b) Sketch the behavior of $\bar{C}_V$ as a function of T for these "molecules."

(c) Sketch the behavior of $\bar{C}_V$ as a function of T for ordinary molecules. Use the Debye crystal as a typical example of a collection of ordinary molecules.

(d) Explain the physical reasons for any noteworthy differences between the graphs in (b) and (c).

16-III-5. A certain oscillator has available to it an infinite number of equally spaced energy levels with spacing b between levels,

$$\epsilon_0 = 0, \epsilon_1 = b, \epsilon_2 = 2b,..., \epsilon_n = nb$$

The number of different states (the degeneracy or multiplicity) corresponding to the nth energy level is 3^n,

$$g_0 = 1, g_1 = 3, g_2 = 9,..., g_n = 3^n,... .$$

If several of these oscillators are present, they do not interact.

(a) Find the partition function for 1 mole (Avogadro's number) of these oscillators as an infinite series and then as a finite function of b, T, and universal constants.

(b) Find $\bar{E}$, $\bar{S}$, and $\bar{C}_V$ for a substance composed of these oscillators. Ignore any nonvibrational contributions.

(c) Is it likely that anyone will ever discover actual oscillators having these energy levels and degeneracies (i) for all energies from zero to infinity? (ii) for low energies with the spacings and degeneracies becoming different at higher energies? Explain with special reference to the behavior of a collection of these oscillators at various temperatures.

16-III-6. Physical systems are usually of Type I: the possible energy levels range from a finite value, ϵ_0, to $+\infty$. Some degrees of freedom are of Type II: there is a finite number of energy levels between finite limits, say ϵ_0 and ϵ_m. We shall now consider also two hypothetical types: Type III, $-\infty < \epsilon < \epsilon_0$; Type IV, $-\infty < \epsilon < +\infty$.

(a) For each of the four types discuss the question of what values of the reciprocal temperature $\beta = 1/kT$ are possible (positive, negative, real, imaginary, between certain limits, etc.). Include all three types of statistics in your discussion.

(b) Describe what would happen if a system of Type III were placed in thermal contact with a system of Type I or II.

16-III-7. The free energy (and therefore the chemical potential μ) contains an arbitary linear function of temperature, $a + bT$, and therefore depends on the two arbitrary constants a and b. If the equation $\alpha = -\mu/RT$ is correct, two corresponding arbitrary constants must appear in α, where α is the parameter in the Boltzmann distribution law, $N_i = g_i e^{-\alpha} e^{-\epsilon_i/kT}$. $e^\alpha = Q/N$, where Q is the partition function and N is the number of particles.

(a) By what convention(s) are a and b fixed in phenomenological thermodynamics?

(b) Discuss the effect of changes in these arbitrary constants on the equations of statistical mechanics and describe the conventions (perhaps tacit) by which these constants are usually fixed. Confine yourself to Boltzmann statistics.

16-III-8. The phrase "absolute entropy" has a natural meaning in quantum statistical mechanics, but it can be given a meaning in classical mechanics or in phenomenological (that is, empirical, nonstatistical) thermodynamics only by adopting an arbitrary convention. Explain.

16-III-9. Imagine a universe in which Planck's constant is replaced by a function of temperature of the form $h = aT^n$, where a and n are constants. Obtain an expression for the entropy $\bar{S}$ of 1 mole of identical (but distinguishable) harmonic oscillators in such a universe. Ascertain for what values of n we would have $\lim_{T \to 0} \bar{S} = 0$, for what values $\lim_{T \to 0} \bar{S}$ would be infinite, and for what values it would be finite but not zero. Use the bottom of the potential energy curve, not the lowest energy level, as the zero of energy. (Note that $\lim_{T \to 0} T^0 = 1$, even though 0^0 is not defined.)

16-III-10. (a) The distribution laws for material particles (with nonzero rest mass) allow for an arbitrary choice of the zero level of energy. Show how the three distribution laws are affected by a shift $\Delta\epsilon$ in the energy of each level and show that the laws are not essentially changed by this shift.

(b) The distribution law for photons requires that the energy of a photon have a definite absolute value. Show how the law imposes such a requirement and explain the requirement in physical terms.

16-III-11. A Hohlraum (cavity) of volume V at temperature T contains phonyons (phony photons) in equilibrium with the walls. The phonyons resemble photons in that they are bosons, each with energy $h\nu$, and their total energy is conserved but they are subject to an additional constraint: the sum of the squares of their frequencies is conserved. Obtain an equation, analogous to Planck's distribution law, for the number of phonyons with frequency between ν and $\nu + d\nu$.

16-III-12. A new kind of particle (the *ficton*) has the property of not being conserved; in an isolated collection of these particles the only restriction is that the total energy is conserved. Fictons thus resemble photons, which can be created or destroyed at the walls of the container, but differ from them in being distinguishable.

(a) Obtain a distribution law giving, in terms of $\beta = 1/kT$, the number of fictons in the ith state, in which each particle has energy ϵ.

(b) Express the total energy and the total number of particles in terms of β and the ϵ_i's.

(c) Point out any peculiar or paradoxical features of this distribution law.

16-III-13. A new kind of particle will be known as the *novon*. These particles are distinguishable in the sense that interchanging two particles results in a new state but they resemble fermions in that there can be no more than one novon in each state.

(a) Obtain an expression for the number of states corresponding to a given distribution of novons in terms of the degeneracies g_i and occupation numbers N_i.

(b) Derive the distribution law for these particles.

(c) Point out and discuss any peculiar or paradoxical features of this law.

16-III-14. Consider the possibility that molecules can undergo "spontaneous absorption" from the state n to the higher state m with transition probability A_{nm}. (This would be possible if the radiation field could have less energy than a vacuum.)

(a) Use Planck's distribution law to show that $A_{nm} = 0$.

(b) How would Planck's distribution law be modified if $A_{nm} \neq 0$?

16-III-15. For a diatomic molecule with identical atoms the possible rotational energies are

$$\epsilon_J = \frac{h^2 J(J+1)}{4\pi^2 mr^2}$$

where h is Planck's constant, m is the mass of each atom, r is the internuclear distance, and $J = 0, 1, 2, 3,\ldots$. Some internuclear distances are:

H_2	O_2	Cl_2
7.4×10^{-9}	1.21×10^{-8}	1.99×10^{-8} cm

(a) Calculate $(\epsilon_1 - \epsilon_0)/kT$ at 100°C for each of these gases.

(b) Discuss how the results of (a) help to explain some of the data in the following table:

Molar heat capacity at constant volume, cal °K^{-1} mole^{-1}

	0°C	100°C	200°C
H_2	4.87	4.93	5.05
O_2	4.99	5.05	5.15
Cl_2	5.95	6.3	6.7

16-III-16. Apply the Debye theory to a one-dimensional crystal (a chain) of N atoms in which each atom is able to vibrate only longitudinally. Obtain an expression for the heat capacity of the chain. Reduce the results to approximate forms applicable near 0°K and at high temperatures.

16-III-17. At low temperatures ($\gtrsim 70°K$) the only vibrations of graphite that are not frozen out are the vibrations perpendicular to the benzenoid planes. We can treat graphite as a two-dimensional crystal in which each atom has one degree of freedom. Use the Debye approach to obtain an equation for the low-temperature heat capacity $\bar{C}_V$ of graphite.

>
>
>
>
>

Solutions
to Problems >

CHAPTER 1

Gases

SECTION 1-I

1-I-1.

$$\frac{P_1 V_1}{T_1} = \frac{P_2 V_2}{T_2}; \quad V = \frac{4}{3}\pi\left(\frac{d}{2}\right)^3;$$

$$\frac{3 \times (4\pi/3)(1/2)^3}{278} = \frac{1 \times (4\pi/3)(d/2)^3}{298};$$

$$\frac{3}{278} = \frac{d^3}{298}; \quad d^3 = 3.22; \quad d = 1.48 \text{ cm}$$

1-I-2. Weight of ozone $= W = 6.7624 - 6.5998 = 0.1626$ g

$$M = \frac{WRT}{PV} = \frac{0.1626 \times 82.06 \times 301.4}{(274.4/760.0) \times 235.67} = 47.3 \text{ g mole}^{-1}$$

1-I-3.

$$M = \frac{WRT}{PV} = \frac{0.1023 \times 82.06 \times 305.7}{(743.95/760) \times 35.33} = 74.19 \text{ g mole}^{-1}$$

Making a correction for relative humidity, Mac Innes and Kreiling found 75.72. The value calculated from atomic weights is 74.12.

1-I-4.

P	0.400	0.8000	1.0000	atm
d/P	3.780	3.860	3.900	g liter^{-1} atm^{-1}

For an ideal gas, $PM = dRT$, or $M = dRT/P$. For a real gas, $M = RT \lim_{P\to 0}(d/P)$. We plot d/P as a function of P and extrapolate to $P = 0$. From the graph we see that $\lim_{P \to 0}(d/P) = 3.700$ g liter^{-1} atm^{-1}.

$M = 0.08206$ liter atm °K^{-1} mole$^{-1} \times 300.0$°K $\times 3.700$ g liter^{-1} atm^{-1}
$= 91.09$ g mole^{-1}

1-I-5. Plot (d/P) vs P and extrapolate to $P = 0$.

P, atm	0.2	0.5	0.8
d/P, g liter^{-1} atm^{-1}	1.398	1.416	1.4344

$\text{Lim}_{P \to 0}(d/P) = 1.3857$ (from graph)

$M = \left(\dfrac{d}{P}\right)_0 RT = 1.3857 \times 0.08206 \times 273.15 = 31.07$

(Theoretical for $CH_3NH_2 = 31.06$)

1-I-6. $\text{Fraction} = \dfrac{\int_{\epsilon_0}^{\infty} e^{-\epsilon/kT} \sqrt{\epsilon}\, d\epsilon}{\int_0^{\infty} e^{-\epsilon/kT} \sqrt{\epsilon}\, d\epsilon} = \dfrac{2}{\pi^{1/2}(kT)^{3/2}} \int_{\epsilon_0}^{\infty} e^{-\epsilon/kT} \sqrt{\epsilon}\, d\epsilon$

1-I-7. $\dfrac{RT}{N} \ln \dfrac{n_1}{n_2} = \dfrac{4}{3} \pi r^3 g(h_2 - h_1)(d - d')$

$\dfrac{8.31 \times 10^7 \times 288.2 \times 2.303}{N} \log \dfrac{100}{47}$

$= \dfrac{4}{3} \pi (2.12 \times 10^{-5})^3 \times 981 \times (35 - 5) \times 10^{-4} \times (1.206 - 0.999)$

$N = 7.44 \times 10^{23}$

(Note: Use R in ergs °K^{-1} mole^{-1}.)

1-I-8. The maximum will occur at the most probable velocity,

$v_p = \left(\dfrac{2RT}{M}\right)^{1/2} = \left(\dfrac{2 \times 8.314 \times 10^7 \times 273.2}{2.016}\right)^{1/2}$
$= 1.50 \times 10^5$ cm sec^{-1}

At this velocity

$f(v) = 4\pi v^2 \left(\dfrac{M}{2\pi RT}\right)^{3/2} \cdot e^{-Mv^2/2RT}$

$= 4\pi(1.50 \times 10^5)^2 \left(\dfrac{2.016}{2\pi \times 8.314 \times 10^7 \times 273.2}\right)^{3/2}$

$\times \exp\left(-\dfrac{2.016(1.51 \times 10^5)^2}{2 \times 8.314 \times 10^7 \times 273.2}\right)$

$f(v) = 5.54 \times 10^{-6}$

The values of $f(v)$ at various v's, calculated in a similar manner, are given below:

$v \times 10^{-5}$	0.50	1.00	1.50	2.00	3.00	4.00	cm sec^{-1}
$f(v) \times 10^6$	1.49	4.28	5.54	4.53	1.11	0.89	

The graph is shown.

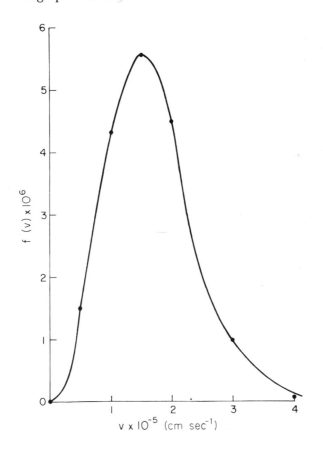

$v \times 10^{-5}$ (cm sec^{-1})

1-I-9.

$$C = \frac{PN}{RT} = \frac{(1/760) \times 1.013 \times 10^6 \times 6.023 \times 10^{23}}{8.314 \times 10^7 \times 298.2}$$
$$= 3.24 \times 10^{16} \text{ molecules cm}^{-3}$$
$$l = \frac{1}{\sqrt{2}\,\pi\sigma^2 C} = \frac{1}{\sqrt{2}\,\pi(2.86 \times 10^{-8})^2 \times 3.24 \times 10^{16}}$$
$$= 8.49 \times 10^{-3} \text{ cm}$$

1-I-10.

$$C = \frac{PN \times 10^{-3}}{RT} = \frac{(1/760) \times 1.013 \times 10^6 \times 6.023 \times 10^{23} \times 10^{-3}}{8.314 \times 10^7 \times 298.2}$$

$$= 3.24 \times 10^{13} \text{ molecules cm}^{-3}$$

$$\bar{v} = \left(\frac{8RT}{\pi M}\right)^{1/2} = \left(\frac{8 \times 8.314 \times 10^7 \times 298.2}{\pi \times 28.02}\right)^{1/2}$$

$$= 4.75 \times 10^4 \text{ cm sec}^{-1}$$

$$Z = \frac{\sqrt{2}}{2} \pi \sigma^2 \bar{v} C^2$$

$$= \frac{\sqrt{2}}{2} \pi (3.16 \times 10^{-8})^2 \times (4.75 \times 10^4) \times (3.24 \times 10^{13})^2$$

$$= 1.11 \times 10^{17} \text{ collisions cm}^{-3} \text{ sec}^{-1}$$

1-I-11. The effusion rate of $H_2 = dn_{H_2}/dT = n_{H_2} \bar{v}_{H_2} A$ and the effusion rate of $D_2 = dn_{D_2}/dT = n_{D_2} \bar{v}_{D_2} A$, or

$$\frac{dn_{H_2}/dt}{dn_{D_2}/dt} = \frac{n_{H_2} \bar{v}_{H_2} A}{n_{D_2} \bar{v}_{D_2} A} = \frac{n_{H_2}}{n_{D_2}} \cdot \frac{\bar{v}_{H_2}}{\bar{v}_{D_2}} = \frac{90}{10} \cdot \frac{\bar{v}_{H_2}}{\bar{v}_{D_2}}.$$

Graham's law contains the root-mean-square velocities but since these are proportional to the arithmetical mean velocities and the proportionality constant cancels out, we may write

$$\frac{dn_{H_2}/dt}{dn_{D_2}/dt} = \frac{90}{10} \sqrt{\frac{M_{D_2}}{M_{H_2}}} = \frac{90}{10} \sqrt{\frac{4.028}{2.016}} = 9\sqrt{2.00} = 12.7.$$

Thus the relative effusion rate is 12.7 molecules H_2 per molecule D_2. Therefore the percent composition of the initial gas passing through will be

$$\text{mole percent } D_2 = \frac{1 \times 100}{12.7 + 1} = 7.30$$

$$\text{mole percent } H_2 = 100 - 7.30 = 92.7$$

The temperature, pressure, and area data are extraneous.

1-I-12.

(a) $P = \dfrac{nRT}{V} = \dfrac{2 \times 0.08206 \times 298.2}{10.0} = 4.90 \text{ atm}$

(b) $P = \dfrac{nRT}{V - nb} - \dfrac{n^2 a}{V^2}$

$$= \frac{2 \times 0.08206 \times 298.2}{10.0 - 2(0.1453)} - \frac{2^2 \times 25.43}{10.0^2}$$

$$= 4.02 \text{ atm}$$

1-I-13. (a) $V = \dfrac{nRT}{P} = \dfrac{0.1 \times 0.08206 \times 273.2}{100} = 22.4 \times 10^{-3}$ liter

(b) $V = \dfrac{ZnRT}{P} = \dfrac{0.2007 \times 0.1 \times 0.08206 \times 273.2}{100}$

$= 4.50 \times 10^{-3}$ liter

1-I-14. $V_2 = \dfrac{P_1 V_1}{P_2} \cdot \dfrac{Z_2 T_2}{Z_1 T_1} = \dfrac{800 \times 1.00 \times 1.10 \times 373.2}{200 \times 1.95 \times 223.2} = 3.77$ liters

1-I-15. $Z_c = \dfrac{P_c \bar{V}_c}{RT_c} = \dfrac{a}{27b^2} \cdot \dfrac{3b}{R} \cdot \dfrac{27bR}{8} = \dfrac{3}{8} = 0.375$

1-I-16. It is approximately true for many substances that the normal boiling point in °K is two-thirds of the critical temperature in °K. Thus

$\tfrac{2}{3} T_c = T_b = (68.9 + 273.2) = 342.1$

$T_c = 513°\text{K (accepted, 507.9°K)}$ or $240°\text{C}$

SECTION 1-II

1-II-1. Plot α vs P; α at $P = 0$ is 3660.9×10^{-6} (from graph). Gay-Lussac's law: $V_t = V_0(1 + \alpha t)$, where $\alpha = (1/V_0)(\partial V/\partial t)_P$. When $P \to 0$, the behavior of the gas approaches ideality and Gay-Lussac's law is obeyed. Therefore use α at $P = 0$. When $t = t_0$, V_t should be zero, and under these conditions

$1 + \alpha t_0 = 0, \qquad t_0 = -\dfrac{1}{\alpha} = -\dfrac{1}{3660.9 \times 10^{-6}} = -273.16$

1-II-2. $M = RT \lim\limits_{P \to 0} \left(\dfrac{\rho}{P} \right)$

$\dfrac{\rho}{P} = (2.000 + 0.0200\,P)$ g (liter atm)$^{-1}$

$$M = RT(2.000)$$
$$= 0.082056 \text{ liter atm deg}^{-1} \text{ mole}^{-1} \times 300.00° \times 2.000 \text{ g (liter atm)}^{-1}$$
$$= 49.23 \text{ g mole}^{-1}$$

1-II-3. Applying the ideal gas law we find that at $0°$ C and 760 mm Hg (pressure not yet corrected) the weight of 1.000 liter of HCl is, for example,

$$\frac{1000}{465.856} \times \frac{760}{756.76} \times 0.76097 = 1.64053 \text{ g}$$

The average for all four sets of data is 1.64016 g liter^{-1}. Since the pressure was measured in London where the force of gravity is 1.000588 times that at $45°$ latitude, the true pressures were $P_{\text{observed}} \times 1.000588$ and the corrected average weight per liter is

$$\frac{1.64016}{1.000588} = 1.63919 \text{ g liter}^{-1}$$

Then plotting PV vs P we find that at $P = 0$, the PV product is $P_0 V_0 = 55213$; and at $P = 760$ torr, $PV = P_1 V_1 = 54803$. Let y be the density of the HCl at 760 torr and $0°$C. Then

$$\frac{P_0 V_0}{P_1 V_1} = \frac{55213}{54803} = \frac{1.63919}{y}$$

and

$$y = 1.62702 \text{ g liter}^{-1}$$

Now let x be the formula weight of HCl. Then

$$\frac{1.62702}{1.42762} = \frac{x}{31.9988} \quad \text{and} \quad x = 36.467$$

Then the atomic weight of Cl is

$$36.467 - 1.008 = 35.459$$

This is based on the 1961 atomic weight scale. The accepted atomic weight of Cl on this scale is 35.453. Gray and Burt, using an older atomic weight scale, obtain a slightly different answer.

1-II-4.

$$t_{\text{Hg}} = \frac{(V_{50} - V_0)_{\text{Hg}}}{(V_{100} - V_0)_{\text{Hg}}} \times 100$$

$$V_{50} - V_0 = \int_0^{50} \alpha V_0 \, dt$$
$$= (1.817 \times 10^{-4}t + 2.95 \times 10^{-9}t^2 + 1.15 \times 10^{-10}t^3]_0^{50} \, V_0$$
$$= 0.009107 \, V_0$$
$$V_{100} - V_0 = \int_0^{100} \alpha V_0 \, dt$$
$$= (1.817 \times 10^{-4}t + 2.95 \times 10^{-9}t^2 + 1.15 \times 10^{-10}t^3]_0^{100} \, V_0$$
$$= 0.01831 \, V_0$$
$$t_{Hg} = \frac{0.009107 V_0}{0.01831 V_0} \times 100 = 49.8°.$$

1-II-5. (a) This definition is based on the special properties of Hg; a Hg thermometer that is calibrated to agree with an ideal gas thermometer at two points will not agree at other points. The international scale, being based on the properties of any ideal gas (more precisely, any real gas in the limit of zero pressure), is more satisfactory than a scale that singles out a preferred thermometric medium. Also this scale has as fixed points the freezing and boiling points of water (as the international scale had before 1954); temperatures near $0°K$ can be specified more reproducibly if absolute zero is taken as one of the fixed points.

(b) This definition makes T proportional to the volume of O_2, a nonideal gas, at a fixed pressure. The international scale defines T by $T = 1/nR \lim_{P \to 0}(PV)$ for any gas, and thus avoids any dependence on the peculiarities of a specific gas. The ideal gas scale, thus defined, has the decisive advantage of being identical with the thermodynamic scale.

1-II-6. Let

W_{Ar} = the weight of argon in grams
W_{He} = the weight of helium in grams

Then

$W_{Ar} + W_{He} = 5.00$

Let

P = the total pressure = 1.00 atm
P_{Ar} = the partial pressure of argon
P_{He} = the partial pressure of helium

Then

$$P = P_{Ar} + P_{He}$$

$$= n_{Ar}\frac{RT}{V} + n_{He}\frac{RT}{V} = \frac{W_{Ar}RT}{M_{Ar}V} + \frac{W_{He}RT}{M_{He}V}$$

$$= \left(\frac{W_{He}}{4.00} + \frac{5.00 - W_{He}}{39.9}\right) \times \frac{0.0821 \times 298}{10.0}$$

$$= 1.00$$

$$W_{He} = 1.26 \text{ g}$$

Weight percent He $= 100 \times \dfrac{1.26}{5.00} = 25.2$

Weight percent Ar $= 100 - 25.2 = 74.8$

1-II-7. n_{H_2O} in RT liters saturated air $= PV/RT = 0.0312$ mole. $R\hat{T} = 24.47$ liter atm per mole. The total number of moles of $N_2 + O_2 + Ar$ remaining in 24.47 liters saturated air $= 1 - 0.0312 = 0.9688$. Therefore the total weight of all gases plus water vapor in 24.47 liters saturated air $= 2 \times 14.0067 \times 0.781 \times 0.9688 + 2 \times 15.9994 \times 0.210 \times 0.9688 + 39.948 \times 0.009 \times 0.9688 + 0.0312 \times 18.02 = 21.18 + 6.51 + 0.35 + 0.56 = 28.60$ g per 24.47 liters. The density of water-saturated air at 25°C and 1 atm total pressure is therefore

$$\frac{28.60}{24.47} = 1.169 \text{ g liter}^{-1}$$

1-II-8. (a)

$$\ln\frac{P_0}{P} = \frac{Mg(h - h_0)}{RT}$$

$$\log\frac{1}{P} = \frac{29 \times 980.6(1248 \times 12 \times 2.54 - 0)}{2.303 \times 8.314 \times 10^7 \times 298.2} = 0.0190$$

$$\log P = -0.0190 = 9.9810 - 10$$

$$P = 0.957 \text{ atm}$$

(b) Plot $\log P$ vs h. The plot must pass through the point $\log P = \log 1 = 0$ (if P is in atm), $h = 0$, with a slope of $Mg/2.303RT$.

1-II-9.

$$-dP = \rho g \, dz \quad \text{(where } \rho = \text{density)}$$
$$= \frac{PMg}{RT} \, dz$$
$$\frac{dP}{P} = \frac{-Mg \, dz}{RT}$$
$$\ln\left(\frac{P}{P_0}\right) = \frac{-Mgz}{RT}$$
$$P = P_0 \, e^{-Mgz/RT}$$

1-II-10.

$$\frac{dP}{P} = \frac{-Mg \, dz}{RT} \; ; \qquad g = \frac{Gm_E}{r^2}$$
$$\frac{dP}{P} = \frac{-MgGm_E \, dz}{RTr^2} \; ; \qquad z = r - r_E$$

where r_E is the radius of the earth.

$$\frac{dP}{P} = \frac{-MgGm_E \, dz}{RT(z + r_E)^2}$$
$$\ln\left(\frac{P}{P_0}\right) = \frac{MgGm_E}{RT}\left(\frac{1}{z + r_E} - \frac{1}{r_E}\right)$$

1-II-11.

$$\frac{dP}{P} = \frac{-Mg \, dz}{RT} \; ; \qquad \frac{dP}{P} = \frac{-Mg \, dz}{R(T_0 - az)}$$

Let $(T_0 - az) = x$. Then $dx = -a \, dz$, and $dz = -dx/a$.

$$\int_{x_0}^{x} -\frac{dx}{ax} = -\frac{1}{a}\ln\frac{x}{x_0} = +\frac{1}{a}\ln\left(\frac{T_0}{T_0 - az}\right)$$
$$\ln\left(\frac{P}{P_0}\right) = \frac{Mg}{Ra}\ln\left(\frac{T_0 - az}{T_0}\right)$$

1-II-12.

(a) The number of molecules having speeds between v and $v + dv$ is $Ce^{-mv^2/2kT}v^2 \, dv$, where C is some constant; this is proportional to the Boltzmann factor and to the volume $4\pi v^2 \, dv$ of the region in velocity space between two concentric spheres of radii v and $v + dv$. The number of molecules having speeds greater than v_0 is $C\int_{v_0}^{\infty} e^{-mv^2/2kT}v^2 \, dv$. The total number of molecules is

$$C\int_0^{\infty} e^{-mv^2/2kT}v^2 \, dv = C\frac{\sqrt{\pi}}{4}\left(\frac{2kT}{m}\right)^{3/2}$$

The fraction having $v > v_0$ is

$$\frac{\int_{v_0}^{\infty} e^{-mv^2/2kT} v^2 dv}{\int_0^{\infty} e^{-mv^2/2kT} v^2 \, dv} = \frac{4}{\sqrt{\pi}} \left(\frac{m}{2kT}\right)^{3/2} \int_{v_0}^{\infty} e^{-mv^2/2kT} v^2 \, dv$$

This integral cannot be expressed as a finite combination of elementary functions.

(b) In two dimensions the number of molecules having speeds between v and $v + dv$ is $Ce^{-mv^2/2kT} v \, dv$; we are now considering the region between circles of radii v and $v + dv$ and the area of this region is $2\pi v \, dv$. The fraction having $v > v_0$ is

$$\frac{\int_{v_0}^{\infty} e^{-mv^2/2kT} v \, dv}{\int_0^{\infty} e^{-mv^2/2kT} v \, dv} = e^{-mv_0^2/2kT}$$

1-II-13.

$$\overline{|v_x|} = \frac{\int_0^{\infty} v_x e^{-mv_x^2/2kT} \, dv_x}{\int_0^{\infty} e^{-mv_x^2/2kT} \, dv_x} = \sqrt{\frac{2kT}{\pi m}} = \sqrt{\frac{2RT}{\pi M}}$$

Z coll cm^{-2} sec$^{-1} = \frac{1}{2}N$ molecules cm$^{-3} \times \sqrt{2RT/\pi M}$ cm sec^{-1}, where $\frac{1}{2}$ is the fraction of molecules moving *toward* the surface, and $2RT/M$ is the volume of the cylinder, 1 cm^2 in cross section, the molecules in which will strike the surface in 1 sec (if they are moving in the proper sense, that is, toward the surface),

$$Z = \frac{\frac{1}{2} \times 1 \text{ atm} \times 6.023 \times 10^{23} \text{ molecules mole}^{-1}}{82.06 \text{ cm}^3 \text{ atm deg}^{-1} \text{ mole}^{-1} \times 298 \text{ deg}}$$

$$\times \sqrt{\frac{2 \times 8.314 \times 10^7 \times 298}{\pi}} \left(\frac{0.2}{\sqrt{32}} + \frac{0.8}{\sqrt{28}}\right)$$

$$= 2.885 \times 10^{23} \text{ collisions cm}^{-2} \text{ sec}^{-1}$$

$$A = 2.0 \times 10^4 \text{ cm}^2$$

$$ZA = 2.885 \times 10^{23} \times 2 \times 10^4$$

$$= 5.77 \times 10^{27} \text{ collisions sec}^{-1}$$

1-II-14.   The area of the orifice $= A = \pi r^2 = 3.14 \times (0.2965/2)^2 = 0.0692$ cm^2.

$$\mu = \frac{\Delta m}{A \, \Delta t} = \frac{9.57 \times 10^{-3}}{0.0692 \times 110.5 \times 60} = 2.085 \times 10^{-5} \text{ g cm}^{-2} \text{ sec}^{-1}$$

$$P = \mu\sqrt{\frac{2\pi RT}{M}} = 2.09 \times 10^{-5} \sqrt{\frac{2 \times 3.14 \times 8.31 \times 10^7 \times 1555.4}{44.96}}$$

$$= 2.80 \text{ dynes cm}^{-2}$$

$$P = 2.80 \times 9.87 \times 10^{-7} = 2.77 \times 10^{-6} \text{ atm}$$

1-II-15.

(a) $\dfrac{T_A}{T_B}$ (b) $\left(\dfrac{T_A M_B}{T_B M_A}\right)^{1/2}$

(c) $\dfrac{\sigma_B^2 c_B}{\sigma_A^2 c_A}$ (d) $\left(\dfrac{T_A M_B}{T_B M_A}\right)^{1/2} \dfrac{\sigma_A^2 c_A}{\sigma_B^2 c_B}$

1-II-16. (a) Gas viscosity results from the lateral transport of momentum between layers moving at different speeds. The higher the temperature, the faster the molecules move and the more momentum they transport, per unit time.

(b) The larger the molecule, the more frequently it collides with other molecules, the shorter is its mean free path, and the less is the average momentum difference between the layers of gas between which the molecule travels in each free path. Therefore viscosity decreases as molecular diameter increases.

(c) As the pressure decreases, the number of momentum-transporting molecules decreases proportionately. However, the mean free path varies inversely with the pressure and thus as the pressure decreases, the effectiveness of each molecule in transporting momentum between layers moving at different speeds increases. These two effects just compensate. At very low pressure, however, the mean free path becomes comparable to the dimensions of the container. It can increase no further and the viscosity approaches zero as the pressure (and thus the number of molecules) approaches zero.

1-II-17.

(a) $\lambda = \dfrac{1}{\sqrt{2}\,\pi C \sigma^2}$

$$= \frac{1}{\sqrt{2}\,\pi (10^{-5} \text{ atom cm}^{-3})(4 \times 10^{-16} \text{ cm}^2)} \times \frac{1 \text{ light-yr}}{9.464 \times 10^{17} \text{ cm}}$$

$$= 59 \text{ light-yr}$$

(b) $\bar{v} = \sqrt{\dfrac{8RT}{\pi \bar{M}}}$

$= \sqrt{\dfrac{8 \times 8.314 \times 10^7 \times 7.8 \times 10^5 \text{ erg (g atom)}^{-1}}{\pi \times 1.008 \text{ g (g atom)}^{-1}}}$

$= \sqrt{1.64 \times 10^{14} \text{ erg g}^{-1}} = 1.28 \times 10^7 \text{ cm sec}^{-1}$

$t = \dfrac{\lambda}{\bar{v}} = \dfrac{59 \text{ light-yr} \times 9.464 \times 10^{17} \text{ cm (light-yr)}^{-1}}{1.28 \times 10^7 \text{ cm sec}^{-1}}$

$\times \dfrac{1 \text{ yr}}{3.156 \times 10^7 \text{ sec}}$

$= 1.38 \times 10^5 \text{ yr}$

(Only approximate because the average of the ratio is not the ratio of the averages.)

1-II-18. (a) The Boyle temperature of a gas according to one definition is the temperature at which the so-called "second virial coefficient," $B(T)$ or $b(T)$, is zero. By examination of equation (a) we see that this condition is fulfilled when the quantity $[b - (A/RT^{3/2})] = 0$. This will happen when $T = T_B = (A/bR)^{2/3}$.

(b) For equation (b) it can be seen that the equation will reduce to $P\bar{V}^2/RT = 1$ (and thus Boyle's law will be obeyed) when the quantity $[1 - 6(T_c/T)^2] = 0$. This will happen when $T = T_B = T_c\sqrt{6}$.

1-II-19.
$$P = \frac{nRT}{V - nb} - \frac{n^2a}{V^2}$$

$$PV = nRT\left(\frac{V}{V - nb}\right) - \frac{n^2a}{V}$$

$$\left(\frac{\partial[PV]}{\partial P}\right)_T = \left[\frac{nRT}{V - nb} - \frac{nRTV}{(V - nb)^2} + \frac{n^2a}{V^2}\right]\left(\frac{\partial V}{\partial P}\right)_T$$

$(\partial V/\partial P)_T < 0$ under all conditions

If $(\partial[PV]/\partial P)_T = 0$, as it should at $P = 0$, $T = T_B$, then the expression in square brackets equals 0, and hence

$$\frac{nRT}{V - nb} - \frac{nRTV}{(V - nb)^2} + \frac{n^2a}{V^2} = 0$$

$$nRTV^2(V - nb) - nRTV^3 + n^2a(V - nb)^2 = 0$$
$$-nRT[V^2(V - nb) - V^3] = n^2a(V - nb)^2$$
$$-RT(V^3 - nbV^2 - V^3) = na(V - nb)^2$$
$$RT = \frac{a}{b}\left[\frac{(V - nb)}{V}\right]^2 = \frac{a}{b}\left(1 - \frac{nb}{V}\right)^2$$

At the Boyle point $T = T_B$, $P = 0$, and $V = \infty$, so

$$RT_B = \frac{a}{b} \quad \text{and} \quad T_B = \frac{a}{Rb}$$

An alternate method is to let $c = n/V$ and proceed as follows:

$$P = \frac{nRT}{V - nb} - \frac{n^2a}{V^2}$$
$$PV = nRT\left(\frac{V}{V - nb}\right) - \frac{n^2a}{V}$$

Since $c = n/V$, then

$$P = \frac{cRT}{1 - bc} - ac^2$$

and

$$PV = n\frac{RT}{1 - bc} - ac$$
$$\left(\frac{\partial[PV]}{\partial P}\right)_T = \left(\frac{\partial[PV]}{\partial c}\right)_T\left(\frac{\partial c}{\partial P}\right)_T = n\left[\frac{bRT}{(1 - bc)^2} - a\right]\left(\frac{\partial c}{\partial P}\right)_T$$
$$\left(\frac{\partial c}{\partial P}\right)_T = \frac{1}{(\partial P/\partial c)_T}$$
$$= \left[\frac{bcRT}{(1 - bc)^2} + \frac{RT}{1 - bc} - ac^2\right]^{-1} \xrightarrow[\{c \to 0}^{\{P \to 0}]{} \frac{1}{RT} \neq 0$$

Therefore at the Boyle temperature the factor

$bRT/(1 - bc)^2 - a$,

evaluated at $c = 0$, must vanish.

$$bRT_B - a = 0, \qquad T_B = \frac{a}{bR}$$

1-II-20. Expanding the Dieterici equation by means of the infinite series for e^x, we obtain

$$P = \frac{RT}{(\bar{V} - b)} - \frac{a}{\bar{V}(\bar{V} - b)} + \frac{a^2}{2RT\,\bar{V}^2(\bar{V} - b)} - \cdots$$

At low densities it is reasonable to assume that the third and subsequent terms are negligible and that $\bar{V}(\bar{V} - b) \approx \bar{V}^2$. Thus we obtain

$$P = \frac{RT}{(\bar{V} - b)} - \frac{a}{\bar{V}^2}$$

which is identical to the van der Waals equation.

1-II-21.
$$P = \frac{RT}{\bar{V} - bT} - \frac{a}{\bar{V}^3}$$

$$\left.\begin{array}{l} \left(\dfrac{\partial P}{\partial \bar{V}}\right)_T = \dfrac{-RT}{(\bar{V} - bT)^2} + \dfrac{3a}{\bar{V}^4} = 0 \\[4mm] \left(\dfrac{\partial^2 P}{\partial \bar{V}^2}\right)_T = \dfrac{2RT}{(\bar{V} - bT)^3} - \dfrac{12a}{\bar{V}^5} = 0 \end{array}\right\} \text{at critical point}$$

$$\frac{RT_c}{(\bar{V}_c - bT_c)^2} = \frac{3a}{\bar{V}_c^4}$$

$$\frac{2RT_c}{(\bar{V} - bT_c)^3} = \frac{12a}{\bar{V}_c^5}$$

Dividing

$$\frac{2}{\bar{V}_c - bT_c} = \frac{4}{\bar{V}_c}$$

$$b = \frac{\bar{V}_c}{2T_c}, \qquad a = \frac{RT_c\bar{V}_c^4}{3(\bar{V}_c - bT_c)^2} = \frac{4RT_c\bar{V}_c^2}{3}$$

1-II-22. $P\bar{V} = RT + APT - BP$

$$P = \frac{RT}{\bar{V} - AT + B}$$

(a) $P\bar{V} = \dfrac{RT}{1 + [(B - AT)/\bar{V}]}$

$$\approx RT\left[1 - \frac{B - AT}{\bar{V}}\right] \quad \text{if } \left|\frac{B - AT}{\bar{V}}\right| \ll 1$$

At the Boyle temperature T_B

$$\lim_{\bar{V} \to \infty} \left[\frac{\partial(P\bar{V})}{\partial(1/\bar{V})}\right]_T = 0$$

$$B - AT_B = 0$$

$$T_B = \frac{B}{A}$$

(b) $\left(\dfrac{\partial P}{\partial \overline{V}}\right)_T = \dfrac{-RT}{(\overline{V} - AT + B)^2}$

$\left(\dfrac{\partial^2 P}{\partial \overline{V}^2}\right)_T = \dfrac{2RT}{(\overline{V} - AT + B)^3}$

At the critical point $(\partial P/\partial \overline{V})_T = 0$ and $(\partial^2 P/\partial \overline{V}^2)_T = 0$. For this gas these derivatives can be 0 only when $T = 0$ or $\overline{V} - AT + B$ is infinite. Neither case corresponds to a real critical point.

1-II-23. At the critical point, $(\partial P/\partial \overline{V})_T = 0$ and $(\partial^2 P/\partial \overline{V}^2)_T = 0$.

$\left(\dfrac{\partial P}{\partial \overline{V}}\right)_T = \dfrac{-RT}{(\overline{V} - b)^2} + \dfrac{a}{\overline{V}^2} = 0$

or

$\dfrac{RT}{(\overline{V} - b)^2} = \dfrac{a}{\overline{V}^2}$

$\left(\dfrac{\partial^2 P}{\partial \overline{V}^2}\right)_T = \dfrac{2RT}{(\overline{V} - b)^3} - \dfrac{2a}{\overline{V}^3} = 0$

or

$\dfrac{2RT}{(\overline{V} - b)^3} = \dfrac{2a}{\overline{V}^3}$

Divide the second equation by the first: $2/(\overline{V} - b) = 2/\overline{V}$, from which $b = 0$. Therefore the two derivatives can never vanish simultaneously unless $b = 0$, contrary to the stipulation that a and b are distinct from zero, and the gas has no critical point.

1-II-24. $P = \dfrac{RT}{\phi \overline{V}_c - b} e^{-a/(R\phi V_c T_c)}$

$\pi \dfrac{a}{4e^2 b^2} = \dfrac{R\theta(a/4Rb)}{\phi(2b) - b} \exp\left(\dfrac{-a}{R\phi 2b\theta a/4Rb}\right)$

$\pi = \dfrac{\theta}{2\phi - 1} e^{2-2/\phi\theta}$

SECTION 1-III

1-III-1. Choose as the volume unit a volume equal to 1 mm times the cross-sectional area of this barometer tube. In these units the volume is numerically equal to the tube length in millimeters. The pressure will be in torr. The correction ΔP to be applied to the reading is equal to the pressure exerted by the entrapped air: $\Delta P = KT/V$, where $V = 780 - P_{\text{apparent}}$, and K is a constant as yet unknown. To determine K, we apply this equation to the conditions given:

$$K = \frac{V\,\Delta P}{T} = \frac{(780 - 717) \times 3.0}{293.2} = 0.64$$

Then

$$\Delta P = \frac{0.64T}{780 - P_{\text{apparent}}}$$

1-III-2. Let $P_2 =$ the final pressure of the entrapped air, in cm Hg
$\quad\quad\quad h =$ the final height of the Hg in the cylinder, in cm

Then

$$P_2 = 76 \times \frac{100}{100 - h}$$

Also

$$P_2 = 100 - h + 76$$

$$\frac{76 \times 100}{100 - h} = 176 - h$$

$$h^2 - 276h + 10{,}000 = 0$$

(a) $h = 42.9$ cm, 233 cm (the 233 root is extraneous)

(b) $P_2 = 176 - 42.9 = 133$ cm Hg

1-III-3. Let $P_2 =$ the final pressure of the entrapped air, in cm Hg
$\quad\quad\quad h =$ the final height of the Hg in the long arm, in cm

Then

$$P_2 = P_1 \frac{V_1}{V_2}$$

$$P_2 = 76 \times \frac{100}{100 - h}$$

$$P_2 = 50 - h + 76$$

$$\frac{76 \times 100}{100 - h} = 50 - h + 76$$

$$h^2 - 226h + 5000 = 0$$

$$h = 25.4 \text{ cm}, 201 \text{ cm} \text{ (201 is extraneous)}.$$

(b) $\quad P_2 = 76 \times \dfrac{100}{100 - 25.4} = 102 \text{ cm Hg}$

1-III-4. The total number of moles of N_2 in the whole system is 2.00. Let $n =$ the final number of moles of N_2 in the 100°C sphere (Sphere 1). Then $2 - n =$ the final number of moles of N_2 in the 0°C sphere (Sphere 2).

$$V_1 = V_2 = 22.4 \text{ liters}$$

$$T_1 = 373°\text{K}$$

$$T_2 = 273°\text{K}$$

$$P_1 = P_2$$

$$\frac{nRT_1}{V_1} = \frac{(2 - n)RT_2}{V_2}$$

$$(2 - n)273 = 373n$$

$$n = 0.846 \text{ moles} = \text{number of moles in sphere 1}$$

$$P_1 = P_2 = \frac{0.846 \times 0.08206 \times 373.2}{22.4} = 1.16 \text{ atm}$$

$$2 - n = 2 - 0.846 = 1.154 \text{ moles}$$

$$= \text{number of moles in sphere 2}$$

1-III-5. The error is in step 5, where equations 3 and 4 are combined. Equation 3 assumes constant temperature but not constant volume or constant pressure. Equation 4 assumes constant pressure but not constant volume or constant temperature. Equations 3 and 4 should be (3') $V = [k_1(T)]/P$ and (4') $V = k_2(P) T$, where k_1 and k_2 are unspecified functions of T and P, respectively. Now when the equations are combined, we obtain (5')

$$\frac{k_1(T)}{P} = k_2(P)T \quad \text{or} \quad \frac{k_1(T)}{T} = k_2(P)P$$

The left side does not depend on P and the right side does not depend on T. But the two sides are equal for all T and P; therefore neither side depends on T or P—both are constants:

$$\frac{k_1(T)}{T} = K_1, \quad k_1(T) = K_1 T$$

$$k_2(P)P = K_2, \quad k_2(P) = \frac{K_2}{P}$$

We have now ascertained the forms of the functions k_1 and k_2. When these are substituted into (5'), we obtain $K_1 = K_2$. Then from (3') or (4') we obtain $V = (K_1 T)/P$.

1-III-6. (a) Plot density of mixture in g liter^{-1} vs composition of mixture in mole percent. This will be a linear plot with slope $= [P(M_1 - M_2)]/100 \, RT$; the intercept on the density axis when $n_1 = 0$ will be PM_2/RT, and the intercept on the density axis when $n_2 = 0$ will be PM_1/RT. The reasoning is as follows:

Let

$$M = \text{the apparent molecular weight of the mixture}$$
$$M_1 = \text{the molecular weight of oxygen}$$
$$M_2 = \text{the molecular weight of helium}$$
$$n_1 = \text{the mole percent of oxygen in the mixture}$$
$$n_2 = \text{the mole percent of helium in the mixture}$$
$$W = \text{the weight of the mixture}$$
$$d = \text{the density of the mixture}$$

Then

$$PV = nRT = \frac{WRT}{M}$$

$$d = \frac{W}{V} = \frac{PM}{RT}$$

$$M = \frac{M_1 n_1}{100} + \frac{M_2 n_2}{100}$$

$$n_2 = 100 - n_1$$

$$M = \frac{M_1 n_1 + M_2(100 - n_1)}{100} = \frac{n_1(M_1 - M_2) + 100 M_2}{100}$$

$$d = \frac{P}{RT} \frac{n_1(M_1 - M_2) + 100 M_2}{100} = \frac{P(M_1 - M_2)n_1}{100 RT} + \frac{PM_2}{RT}$$

The last equation is the algebraic representation of the desired plot. It can be seen by inspection that this equation gives the slope and $n_1 = 0$ intercept specified above. If we had elimina-ted n_1 instead of n_2, we would have an analogous equation showing that the density intercept at $n_2 = 0$ is PM_1/RT, as specified above.

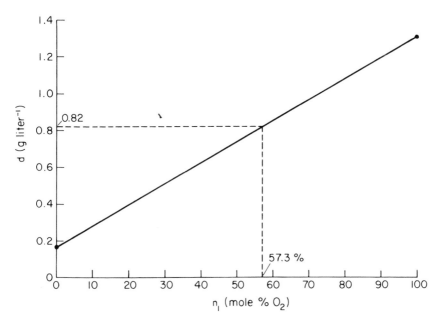

(b) See the figure. At $n_1 = 100$

$$d = \frac{PM_2}{RT} = \frac{1 \times 32.0}{0.0821 \times 298} = 1.31 \text{ g liter}^{-1}$$

At $n_1 = 0$

$$d = \frac{PM_1}{RT} = \frac{1 \times 4.00}{0.0821 \times 298} = 0.163 \text{ g liter}^{-1}$$

We draw a straight line between these two points and read off a composition of 57.3 mole percent O_2 corresponding to a density of 0.820 g liter^{-1}.

1-III-7.

(a) $\overline{v_x^4} = \dfrac{\int_{-\infty}^{\infty} v_x^4 \exp(-\frac{1}{2}mv_x^2/kT)\, dv_x}{\int_{-\infty}^{\infty} \exp(-\frac{1}{2}mv_x^2/kT)\, dv_x}$

(b) $\overline{v^4} = \dfrac{\int_0^{\infty} v^4 e^{-mv^2/2kT} v^2 \, dv}{\int_0^{\infty} e^{-mv^2/2kT} v^2 \, dv}$

(c) The change in limits of integration is inessential; if the limits in (a) were 0 to ∞, the result would be the same. The important difference is the presence of an additional factor v^2 in the integrand of (b). This factor appears because the molecules with speeds between v and $v + dv$ include all those with representative points (in velocity space) in a spherical shell of volume $4\pi v^2\, dv$. Equivalently the integrals in (b) are evaluated in spherical coordinates, in which the volume element is $v^2 \sin \theta\, dv\, d\theta\, d\phi$; the angular integrals are the same in numerator and denominator.

1-III-8. $P\bar{V} = RT + bP$; slope $= [\partial(P\bar{V})/\partial P]_T = b$ (see figure). Significance of slope: slope = the constant b in the equation of state.

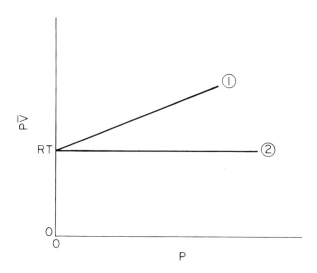

Significance of intercept: at $P = 0$, $P\bar{V} = RT$ (ideal gas behavior at zero pressure). For a real gas if $b > 0$, the gas would have to be above its Boyle temperature if this equation of state were to apply at low pressures inasmuch as the slope is positive near $P = 0$.

1-III-9.

$$dV = \left(\frac{\partial V}{\partial P}\right)_T dP + \left(\frac{\partial V}{\partial T}\right)_P dT$$

From α,

$$\left(\frac{\partial V}{\partial T}\right)_P = \frac{k_1 V C_P T^{(C_P/C_V)-1}}{C_V}$$

and from β,

$$\left(\frac{\partial V}{\partial P}\right)_T = \frac{-k_2 V}{P}$$

$$\frac{dV}{V} = -k_2 \frac{dP}{P} + k_1 \frac{C_P}{C_V} T^{(C_P/C_V)-1} dT$$

$$\ln V = -k_2 \ln P + k_1 \frac{C_P}{C_V} \cdot \frac{C_V}{C_P} T^{C_P/C_V} + \text{constant}$$

$$= -k_2 \ln P + k_1 T^{C_P/C_V} + \text{constant}$$

Therefore the desired equation of state is

$$P^{k_2} V = k \exp(k_1 T^{C_P/C_V})$$

1-III-10. We shall present two different methods for doing this problem. The first method depends on the expansion of the van der Waals equation into cubic form at the critical point and comparing coefficients of V with the equation $(V - V_c)^3 = 0$. The details are as follows:

(1) The van der Waals equation

$$\left(P + \frac{n^2 a}{V^2}\right)(V - nb) = nRT$$

(2) Expanding (1)

$$PV + \frac{n^2 a}{V} - Pnb - \frac{n^3 ab}{V^2} = nRT$$

(3) Multiplying (2) by V^2

$$PV^3 + n^2 aV - PnbV^2 - n^3 ab = nRTV^2$$

(4) Dividing (3) by P

$$V^3 + \frac{n^2 aV}{P} - nbV^2 - \frac{n^3 ab}{P} = \frac{nRTV^2}{P}$$

(5) Rearranging (4) in descending powers of V,

$$V^3 - \left(\frac{nRT}{P} + nb\right) V^2 + \frac{n^2 aV}{P} - \frac{n^3 ab}{P} = 0$$

(6) Now at the critical point all three V roots are equal; hence

$$V_1 = V_2 = V_3 = V_c, \quad \text{as for the 3 roots of} \quad (V - V_c)^3 = 0$$

(7) Expanding (6)

$$(V - V_c)^3 = V^3 - 3V_c V^2 + 3V_c^2 V - V_c^3 = 0$$

(8) At the critical point

$$V^3 - \left(\frac{nRT_c}{P} + nb\right) V^2 + \frac{n^2 a V}{P_c} - \frac{n^3 ab}{P_c} = 0$$

Now, comparing coefficients of V^3, V^2, V^1 and V^0 in (7) and (8), we obtain

(9) $V^3 : 1 = 1$

(10) $V^2 : 3V_c = nRT_c/P_c + nb$

(11) $V^1 : 3V_c^2 = n^2 a/P_c$

(12) $V^0 : V_c^3 = n^3 ab/P_c$

(13) Equating P_c's in (11) and (12) we obtain $n^2 a/3V_c^2 = n^3 ab/V_c^3$, which readily reduces to $V_c = 3nb$.

(14) Substituting (13) into (11)

$$P_c = \frac{n^2 a}{3V_c^2} = \frac{n^2 a}{27 n^2 b^2} = \frac{a}{27 b^2}$$

Alternatively we could have substituted (13) into (12) to get the same final result.

(15) By substituting (13) and (14) into (10)

$$3V_c = \frac{nRT_c}{P_c} + nb$$

$$T_c = \frac{P_c(3V_c - nb)}{nR} = \frac{a(9nb - nb)}{27 b^2 nR} = \frac{8a}{27 Rb}$$

The second method depends upon the generation of two new equations by means of partial differentiation.

(1′) First, we start with the van der Waals equation in the form

$$P = \frac{nRT}{(V - nb)} - \frac{n^2 a}{V^2}$$

(2') Then we take the first derivative to obtain

$$\left(\frac{\partial P}{\partial V}\right)_T = \frac{-nRT}{(V - nb)^2} + \frac{2n^2a}{V^3}$$

(3') And we differentiate (2') to obtain the second derivative

$$\left(\frac{\partial^2 P}{\partial V^2}\right)_T = \frac{2nRT}{(V - nb)^3} - \frac{6n^2a}{V^4}$$

At the critical point the isothermal curve that represents P as a function of V has a horizontal point of inflection. Because the curve is horizontal, $(\partial P/\partial V)_T = 0$; and because it has a point of inflection, $(\partial^2 P/\partial V^2)_T = 0$. Then

(4') $$\frac{RT}{(V - nb)^2} = \frac{2na}{V^3}$$

(5') $$\frac{2RT}{(V - nb)^3} = \frac{6na}{V^4}$$

Dividing the left side of equation (4') by the right side of (5'), and similarly for the right sides, we have

(6') $$\frac{(V - nb)}{2} = \frac{V}{3} \quad \text{and} \quad V_c = 3nb$$

Substituting this result into (4'), we obtain

(7') $$\frac{RT}{(2nb)^2} = \frac{2na}{(3b)^3} \quad \text{and} \quad T_c = \frac{8a}{27Rb}$$

(8') And, finally, from (1')

$$P_c = \frac{8a}{27(b)(2b)} - \frac{a}{(3b)^2} = \frac{a}{27b^2}$$

The advantage of the first method is that it does not require the use of the calculus. The advantage of the second method is that it is simpler, requires less mathematical intuition, and is more generally applicable to other problems of a similar nature.

1-III-11. At the critical point (if any) $(\partial P/\partial V)_T = 0$ and $(\partial^2 P/\partial V^2)_T = 0$. The equation can be solved (as a quadratic equation) for P but it is simpler to obtain the first derivative by the formula

$$\left(\frac{\partial P}{\partial V}\right)_T = -\frac{(\partial T/\partial V)_P}{(\partial T/\partial P)_V} = \frac{-(P + aP^2)}{(V - b)(1 + 2aP)}$$

Before we go to the trouble of evaluating $(\partial^2 P/\partial V^2)_T$, we should consider whether, or in what cases, the first derivative vanishes. $(\partial P/\partial V)_T = 0$ if, and only if, $P + aP^2 = 0$. But $P + aP^2 = 0$ only when $T = 0$, and the gas does not have a critical point.

1-III-12. (1) $P = \dfrac{RT}{\overline{V} - b} - \dfrac{a}{T\overline{V}^2}$

(2) $\left(\dfrac{\partial P}{\partial \overline{V}}\right)_T = \dfrac{-RT}{(\overline{V} - b)^2} + \dfrac{2a}{T\overline{V}^3} = 0$ ⎫

(3) $\left(\dfrac{\partial^2 P}{\partial \overline{V}^2}\right)_T = \dfrac{2RT}{(\overline{V} - b)^3} - \dfrac{6a}{T\overline{V}^4} = 0$ ⎬ at the critical point
                                                                             ⎭

From (2) and (3)

$$\dfrac{2}{\overline{V}_c - b} = \dfrac{3}{\overline{V}_c} \quad \text{and} \quad b = \overline{V}_c/3$$

From (2) we get

(4) $a = \dfrac{RT_c^2 \overline{V}_c^3}{2(\overline{V}_c - b)^2} = \dfrac{9RT_c^2 \overline{V}_c}{8}$

Substituting a and b into (1) and simplifying

$$P_c = \dfrac{3RT_c}{8\overline{V}_c} \; ; \quad R = \dfrac{8P_c\overline{V}_c}{3T_c}$$

Substituting R into (4)

$$a = 3P_c\overline{V}_c^2 T_c$$

Then (1) becomes, in terms of reduced variables (π, θ, ϕ) and critical constants,

$$\pi P_c = \dfrac{(8P_c\overline{V}_c/3T_c)(\theta T_c)}{\phi\overline{V}_c - \tfrac{1}{3}\overline{V}_c} - \dfrac{3P_c\overline{V}_c^2 T_c}{\theta T_c \phi^2 \overline{V}_c^2}$$

$$\pi = \dfrac{8\theta}{3\phi - 1} - \dfrac{3}{\theta\phi^2}$$

1-III-13. We shall proceed as in Problem 1-III-10, method 2, by taking first and second derivatives to generate two new equations.

(1) $P = \dfrac{RT}{(\overline{V} - b)} e^{-A/RT^{3/2}\overline{V}}$

(2) $\left(\dfrac{\partial P}{\partial \overline{V}}\right)_T = \dfrac{RT}{(\overline{V}-b)} e^{-A/RT^{3/2}\overline{V}} \left(\dfrac{A}{RT^{3/2}\overline{V}^2} - \dfrac{1}{(\overline{V}-b)}\right)$

(3) $\left(\dfrac{\partial^2 P}{\partial \overline{V}^2}\right)_T = \left\{\left[\dfrac{A}{RT^{3/2}\overline{V}^2} - \dfrac{1}{(\overline{V}-b)}\right]\left[\dfrac{-1}{(\overline{V}-b)^2} + \dfrac{A}{RT^{3/2}\overline{V}^2}\right]\right.$

$\left. + \left(\dfrac{1}{(\overline{V}-b)}\right)\left[\dfrac{-2A}{RT^{3/2}\overline{V}^3} + \dfrac{1}{(\overline{V}-b)^2}\right]\right\}$

$\times RT\, e^{-A/RT^{3/2}\overline{V}}$

At the critical point, $(\partial P/\partial V)_T = 0$ and $(\partial^2 P/\partial \overline{V}^2)_T = 0$. In (2) there is only one factor that can vanish

(4) $\dfrac{A}{RT_c^{3/2}\overline{V}_c^{\,2}} - \dfrac{1}{\overline{V}_c - b} = 0$

The first term in (3) is then 0 also. For the second term to vanish we must have

(5) $\dfrac{-2A}{RT_c^{3/2}\overline{V}_c^{\,3}} + \dfrac{1}{(\overline{V}_c - b)^2} = 0$

From (4) and (5) $2/\overline{V}_c = 1/(\overline{V}_c - b)$, $\overline{V}_c = 2b$. Substituting into (4), $T_c^{3/2} = A/4bR$, or $T_c = (A/4bR)^{2/3}$. Finally, substituting $\overline{V}_c$ and T_c into (1),

$P_c = \dfrac{R}{b}\left(\dfrac{A}{4bR}\right)^{2/3} e^{-2}$

1-III-14. (a) $\dfrac{P\overline{V}}{RT} = \dfrac{1}{1 - B/\overline{V}} - \dfrac{A\overline{V}^{m+1}}{RT}$

(b) $\overline{V}^{m+1}$ must approach 0 as $\overline{V}$ becomes infinite. This requires that $m + 1 < 0$, or $m < -1$.

(c) (1) $P = \dfrac{RT}{\overline{V} - B} - A\overline{V}^m$

    (2) $\left(\dfrac{\partial P}{\partial \overline{V}}\right)_T = \dfrac{-RT}{(\overline{V} - B)^2} - mA\overline{V}^{m-1}$

    (3) $\left(\dfrac{\partial^2 P}{\partial \overline{V}^2}\right)_T = \dfrac{2RT}{(\overline{V} - B)^3} - m(m-1)A\overline{V}^{m-2}$

(d) At the critical point $(\partial P/\partial \bar{V})_T = 0$ and $(\partial^2 P/\partial \bar{V}^2)_T = 0$. We write (2) and (3), then, as

(2′) $\dfrac{-RT}{(\bar{V} - B)^2} = mA\bar{V}^{m-1}$

(3′) $\dfrac{2RT}{(\bar{V} - B)^3} = m(m - 1) A\bar{V}^{m-}$

and divide (3′) by (2′)

$\dfrac{-2}{(\bar{V} - B)} = \dfrac{m - 1}{\bar{V}}$

(4) $\bar{V}_c = \left(\dfrac{m - 1}{m + 1}\right) B$

(e) If we already know that $m < -1$, then we also know that $m - 1$ and $m + 1$ are both negative, and $\bar{V}_c$ has the same sign as B. In order for $\bar{V}_c$ to be positive, B must be positive. (If we do not take account of the result of (b), all we can say is that $(m - 1)/(m + 1)$ and B must have the same sign. If $m < -1$ or $m > +1$, $B > 0$; if $-1 < m < +1$, $B < 0$. If $m = -1$, $\bar{V}_c$ is infinite; if $m = +1$, $\bar{V}_c = 0$, regardless of B.)

(f) From (2′)

$T_c = \dfrac{-(\bar{V}_c - B)^2 \, mA\bar{V}_c^{m-1}}{R}$

From (4)

$\bar{V}_c - B = \dfrac{-2}{m + 1} B$

Then

$T_c = \dfrac{-4B^2 mA\bar{V}_c^{m-1}}{(m + 1)^2 R} = \dfrac{-4B^{m+1} m(m - 1)^{m-1} A}{(m + 1)^{m+1} R}$

(g) Since $m < 0$ and $B > 0$, T_c will be > 0 if, and only if, $A > 0$. This is more easily seen in the first form of the result than in the second.

(h) B is related to the volume occupied by the molecules. The requirement $B > 0$ means merely that the molecules must have a positive volume. The term containing A and m is intended to correct for intermolecular forces. If $A < 0$, then

P is increased by these forces, which must in this case be repulsive. A gas in which the molecules repel would never condense and there would be no critical point; accordingly we find a real critical point only when $A > 0$ corresponding to attraction and a diminution in pressure by the term $A\overline{V}^m$. In order for the gas to behave ideally at low pressure the attractive forces must decrease, and decrease rapidly enough, as the distance between molecules increases, and thus as $\overline{V}$ increases. The condition $m < -1$ results from this requirement.

CHAPTER 2

The first law

of thermodynamics
and thermochemistry

SECTION 2-1

2-1-1.

$$\Delta E + (P_2 V_2 - P_1 V_1) = \Delta E + (nRT_2 - nRT_1)$$
$$= \Delta E + nR(T_2 - T_1)$$
$$= n\bar{C}_V(T_2 - T_1) + nR(T_2 - T_1)$$
$$= (n\bar{C}_V + nR)(T_2 - T_1)$$
$$= n(\bar{C}_V + R)(T_2 - T_1)$$
$$= n\bar{C}_P(T_2 - T_1)$$

2-1-2.

$$P\bar{V} = RT$$

$$P\,d\bar{V} + \bar{V}\,dP = R\,dT$$

$$\left(\frac{\partial P}{\partial T}\right)_V = \frac{R}{\bar{V}}$$

$$\left(\frac{\partial E}{\partial V}\right)_T = T\frac{R}{\bar{V}} - P = \frac{P\bar{V}}{\bar{V}} - P = 0$$

2-1-3.

$$PV = nRT - \frac{n^2 a}{V}$$

$$P = \frac{nRT}{V} - \frac{n^2 a}{V^2}$$

$$P \, dV = \frac{nRT \, dV}{V} - \frac{n^2 a \, dV}{V^2}$$

$$w = \int_{V_i}^{V_f} P \, dV = \int_{V_i}^{V_f} \frac{nRT \, dV}{V} - \int_{V_i}^{V_f} \frac{n^2 a \, dV}{V^2}$$

$$= nRT \ln \frac{V_f}{V_i} - n^2 a \left(\frac{1}{V_f} - \frac{1}{V_i} \right)$$

2-I-4.

$$P\bar{V} = RT + APT - BP$$
$$P(\bar{V} - AT + B) = RT$$
$$P = \frac{RT}{\bar{V} - AT + B}$$
$$w = P \, dV = RT \int_{\bar{V}_1}^{\bar{V}_2} \frac{dV}{\bar{V} - AT + B}$$
$$= RT \ln \left(\frac{\bar{V}_2 - AT + B}{\bar{V}_1 - AT + B} \right)$$

2-I-5. Under normal conditions the heat transfer from the room to the cylinder would not be rapid enough to maintain iso-thermality, but assuming that the temperature of the expanding gas does remain at 25°C we proceed as follows. Remembering that the resisting pressure is constant at 1 atm, $w = P_2(V_2 - V_1)$, where P_2 is the resisting pressure. $V_1 = 10$ liters.

$$nRT_1 = P_1 V_1 = 25 \text{ atm} \times 10 \text{ liters} = 250 \text{ liter atm}$$
$$V_2 = \frac{nRT_2}{P_2} = \frac{nRT_1}{P_1} = \frac{250 \text{ liter atm}}{1.00 \text{ atm}} = 250 \text{ liters}$$
$$w = 1 \times (250 - 10) = 240 \text{ liter atm}$$

2-I-6.

Stage	1	2	3	
P, atm	1	2	2	
Step	q, cal	w, cal	ΔE, cal	ΔH, cal
$1 \rightarrow 2$	889	0	889	1480
$2 \rightarrow 3$	−1480	−591	−889	−1480
$3 \rightarrow 1$	411	411	0	0
Total cycle	−180	−180	0	0

The details of the calculations are as follows:

Step $1 \rightarrow 2$

$$w = \int_{V_1}^{V_2} P \, dV = 0$$

$$\Delta E = \int_{T_1}^{T_2} n\bar{C}_V \, dT = 1 \times \tfrac{3}{2}R(596 - 298) = 889 \text{ cal}$$

$$\Delta H = \int_{T_1}^{T_2} n\bar{C}_P \, dT = 1 \times \tfrac{5}{2}R(596 - 298) = 1480 \text{ cal}$$

$$q = \Delta E + w = 889 + 0 = 889 \text{ cal}$$

Step $2 \rightarrow 3$

$$w = \int_{V_1}^{V_2} P \, dV = P(V_2 - V_1) = 2(12.2 - 24.4)$$

$$= -24.4 \text{ liter atm}$$

$$w = -24.4 \text{ liter atm} \times 24.22 \text{ cal (liter atm)}^{-1} = -591 \text{ cal}$$

$$\Delta E = \int_{T_1}^{T_2} n\bar{C}_V \, dT = 1 \times \tfrac{3}{2}R(T_2 - T_1) = 1 \times \tfrac{3}{2}R(298 - 596)$$

$$= -889 \text{ cal}$$

$$\Delta H = \int_{T_1}^{T_2} n\bar{C}_P \, dT = 1 \times \tfrac{5}{2}R(T_2 - T_1) = 1 \times \tfrac{5}{2}(298 - 596)$$

$$= -1480 \text{ cal}$$

$$q = \Delta E + w = 889 + (-591) = -1480 \text{ cal}$$

Step $3 \rightarrow 1$

$$w = \int_{V_1}^{V_2} P \, dV = nRT \ln \frac{V_2}{V_1}$$

$$= 1 \times 1.987 \times 298 \times 2.303 \times \log \frac{24.4}{12.2} = 411 \text{ cal}$$

$\Delta E = 0$ (isothermal expansion of an ideal gas)
$\Delta H = 0$ (isothermal expansion of an ideal gas)
$$q = \Delta E + w = 0 + 411 = 411 \text{ cal}$$

2-I-7.

Stage	1	2	3
T, °K	300	600	300

Step	q, cal	w, cal	ΔE, cal	ΔH, cal
$1 \to 2$	1485	591	894	1490
$2 \to 3$	−894	0	−894	−1490
$3 \to 1$	−413	−413	0	0
Total cycle	178	178	0	0

The details of the calculations are as follows:

Step $1 \to 2$

$$w = \int_{V_1}^{V_2} P\,dV = P(V_2 - V_1) = 1 \times (48.8 - 24.4)$$

$$= 24.4 \text{ liter atm}$$

$$w = 24.4 \times 24.22 \text{ cal} = 591 \text{ cal}$$

$$\Delta E = \int_{T_1}^{T_2} n\bar{C}_V\,dT = \tfrac{3}{2}R(600 - 300) = 894 \text{ cal}$$

$$\Delta H = \int_{T_1}^{T_2} n\bar{C}_P\,dT = \tfrac{5}{2}R(600 - 300) = 1490 \text{ cal}$$

$$q = \Delta E + w = 894 + 591 = 1485 \text{ cal}$$

Step $2 \to 3$

$$w = \int_{V_1}^{V_2} P\,dV = 0$$

$$\Delta E = \int_{T_1}^{T_2} n\bar{C}_V\,dT = \tfrac{3}{2}R(300 - 600) = -894 \text{ cal}$$

$$\Delta H = \int_{T_1}^{T_2} n\bar{C}_P\,dT = \tfrac{5}{2}R(300 - 600) = -1490 \text{ cal}$$

$$q = \Delta E + w = -894 \text{ cal}$$

Step $3 \to 1$

$$w = \int_{V_1}^{V_2} P \, dV = nRT \ln \frac{V_2}{V_1}$$

$$= 1 \times 1.987 \times 300 \times 2.303 \log \frac{24.4}{48.8} = -413 \text{ cal}$$

$\Delta E = 0 \qquad \Delta H = 0$ (isothermal expansion of an ideal gas)

$q = \Delta E + w = -413 \text{ cal}$

2-I-8.

Stage V, liters		1 24.4	2 48.8	3 24.4
Step	q, cal	w, cal	ΔE, cal	ΔH, cal
$1 \to 2$	1480	591	889	1480
$2 \to 3$	-822	-822	0	0
$3 \to 1$	-889	0	-889	-1480
Total cycle	231	-231	0	0

The details of the calculations are as follows:

Step $1 \to 2$

$$w = \int_{V_1}^{V_2} P \, dV = P(V_2 - V_1) = 1 \times (48.8 - 24.4)$$

$$= 24.4 \text{ liter atm}$$

$$w = 24.4 \times 24.22 \text{ cal} = 591 \text{ cal}$$

$$\Delta E = \int_{T_1}^{T_2} n\bar{C}_V \, dT = \tfrac{3}{2}R(596 - 298) = 889 \text{ cal}$$

$$\Delta H = \int_{T_1}^{T_2} n\bar{C}_P \, dT = \tfrac{5}{2}R(596 - 298) = 1480 \text{ cal}$$

$$q = \Delta E + w = 1480 \text{ cal}$$

Step $2 \to 3$

$$w = P \, dV = nRT \ln \frac{V_2}{V_1}$$

$$= 1 \times 1.987 \times 596 \times 2.303 \log \frac{24.4}{48.8} = -822 \text{ cal}$$

$\Delta E = 0 \qquad \Delta H = 0$ (isothermal compression of an ideal gas

$q = \Delta E + w = -822 \text{ cal}$

Step $3 \rightarrow 1$

$$w = \int_{V_1}^{V_2} P\, dV = 0 \qquad (V_1 = V_2)$$

$$\Delta E = \int_{T_1}^{T_2} n\bar{C}_V\, dT = \tfrac{3}{2}R(298 - 596) = -889 \text{ cal}$$

$$\Delta H = \int_{T_1}^{T_2} n\bar{C}_P\, dT = \tfrac{5}{2}R(298 - 596) = -1480 \text{ cal}$$

$$q = \Delta E + w = -889 \text{ cal}$$

2-I-9. $\bar{C}_V = \tfrac{3}{2}R$ (ideal monatomic gas)

$$\frac{3}{2} R \ln \frac{T_2}{T_1} = -R \ln \frac{V_2}{V_1}$$

$$\log T_2 = -\frac{2}{3} \log \frac{V_2}{V_1} + \log T_1$$

$$= -\frac{2}{3} \log \frac{50}{10} + \log 298.2$$

$$= -0.466 + 2.475 = 2.009$$

$$T_2 = 102°\text{K}$$

2-I-10.   (a) $w_{\max} = nRT \ln \dfrac{V_2}{V_1}$

$$= 2 \times 1.987 \times 298.2 \times 2.303 \log \frac{20}{10} = 822 \text{ cal}$$

(b) $-C_V \ln \dfrac{T_2}{T_1} = R \ln \dfrac{V_2}{V_1}$

$$-\frac{5}{2} \ln \frac{T_2}{T_1} = \ln \frac{V_2}{V_1}$$

$$\log T_2 = -\frac{2}{5} \log \frac{V_2}{V_1} + \log T_1$$

$$= -\frac{2}{5} \log \frac{20}{10} + \log 298.2 = 2.354$$

$$T_2 = 226°\text{K}$$

$$w = -\Delta E$$

$$= -n\bar{C}_V(T_2 - T_1) = 2 \times \tfrac{5}{2} \times 1.987(298.2 - 226)$$

$$= 717 \text{ cal}$$

2-I-11. $H = E + PV$

$$\mu_{JT} = -\frac{1}{C_P}\left[\left(\frac{\partial E}{\partial P}\right)_T + \left(\frac{\partial(PV)}{\partial P}\right)_T\right]$$

$$= -\frac{1}{C_P}\left[\left(\frac{\partial E}{\partial V}\right)_T\left(\frac{\partial V}{\partial P}\right)_T + \left(\frac{\partial(PV)}{\partial P}\right)_T\right]$$

2-I-12. $\mu_{JT} = \left(\frac{\partial T}{\partial P}\right)_H = +0.366$

$dT = 0.366\, dP$

$T_2 - T_1 = 0.366(1 - 20) = -6.96$

Since $\mu_{JT} > 0$, the expanded gas is colder than it was initially and the final temperature is $-6.96°C$.

2-I-13. $\Delta E = \dfrac{-2660.0 \times 4.0630 \times 128.11}{1.1226} = -1231.6 \text{ kcal mole}^{-1}$

$\Delta H = \Delta E + (\Delta n_{gas})RT$

$C_{10}H_8(s) + 12O_2 \rightarrow 10CO_2 + 4H_2O(l)$

$\Delta n_{gas} = -2$

$\Delta H = -1231.6 - 2 \times 1.987 \times 291.2 \times 10^{-3}$

$\quad = -1232.8 \text{ kcal mole}^{-1}$

2-I-14. $\Delta H° = \Delta E° + (\Delta n_{gas})RT$

$\quad = 10,000 + (20 - 27) \times 3.00 \times 10^{-3} \times 1.987 \times 310.2$

$\quad = 10,000 - 12.9 = 9987 \text{ cal}$

2-I-15. $\Delta H_{T_2} = \Delta H_{T_1} + \displaystyle\int_{T_1}^{T_2} \Delta C_P \, dT = 1435 + (18 - 9)(T_2 - T_1)$

$\quad = 1435 + 9(263 - 273) = 1435 - 90 = 1345 \text{ cal mole}^{-1}$

2-I-16. $\Delta H_{298} = 3\Delta H_5 + \Delta H_6 - \Delta H_1 = -60,003 \text{ cal}$

2-I-17. $\Delta H = \Delta E + (\Delta n_{gas})RT = 15,000 + (2 - 5) \times 1.99 \times 298$

$\quad = 15,000 - 1778 = 13,222 \text{ cal}$

2-I-18. The equation for the combustion reaction is

$$C_{10}H_8(c) + 12O_2(g) \rightarrow 10CO_2(g) + 4H_2O(l)$$

$$\quad x \qquad\quad 0 \qquad\quad -94.0518 \quad -68.3174 \text{ kcal mole}^{-1}$$

The standard molar enthalpy of formation of each substance has been written below its formula. For this reaction

$$\Delta H° = 10(-94.0518) + 4(-68.3174) - x$$
$$= -1231.6 \text{ kcal} \qquad x = +17.8 \text{ kcal mole}^{-1}$$

2-I-19. (a) The combustion reaction is

$$C_6H_5COOH(c) + \frac{15}{2} O_2(g) \rightarrow 7CO_2(g) + 3H_2O(l), \Delta H° = -771.72 \text{ kcal}$$

$$\quad x \qquad\qquad\qquad 0 \quad (-94.0518) \quad (-68.3174)$$

$\Delta H°$ of formation (from Table 2.1) has been written under each formula. Then for the reaction

$$\Delta H° = 7(-94.0518) + 3(-68.3174) - x - \frac{15}{2}(0)$$
$$= -771.72 \text{ kcal}$$
$$x = -91.59 \text{ kcal} = \Delta H° \text{ of formation for } C_6H_5COOH(c)$$

The formation reaction is

$$7C\,(graphite) + 3H_2(g) + O_2(g) \rightarrow C_6H_5COOH(c)$$

In this reaction the number of moles of gas decreases by **4.**

$$\Delta E° = \Delta H° - RT(-4) \text{ kcal} = -93.96 \text{ kcal}$$

(b) For the formation reaction

$$\Delta C_P° = 35.1 - 7(2.0) - 3(4.9) - 5.0 = 1.4 \text{ cal°K}^{-1}$$
$$\Delta H_{373}° = \Delta H_{298}° + \Delta C_P°(373 - 298)$$
$$= -91.59 + 75 \times 0.0014 = -91.49 \text{ kcal}$$

2-I-20.
$$m\text{-CP}(l) + OH^-(aq) \rightarrow m\text{-CP}^-(aq) + H_2O(l)$$
$$m\text{-CP}(aq) \rightarrow m\text{-CP}(l)$$
$$H_2O(l) \rightarrow H^+(aq) + OH^-(aq)$$

$$\overline{\qquad\qquad m\text{-CP}(aq) \rightarrow m\text{-CP}^-(aq) + H^+(aq)\qquad\qquad}$$
$$\Delta H° = \Delta H_2° - \Delta H_1° + \Delta H_3° = -7540 - 674 + 13{,}500$$

$$= 5286 \text{ cal per mole } m\text{-CP}(aq)$$

2-I-21.

$$9CO_2(g) + 8H_2O(l) \rightarrow cis\text{-}C_9H_{16}(l) + 13O_2(g) \qquad (1)$$
$$9C(graphite) + 9O_2(g) \rightarrow 9CO_2(g) \qquad (2)$$
$$\underline{8H_2(g) + 4O_2(g) \rightarrow 8H_2O(l) \qquad (3)}$$
$$9C(graphite) + 8H_2(g) \rightarrow cis\text{-}C_9H_{16}(l) \qquad (4)$$
$$\Delta H_4^\circ = \Delta H_1^\circ + \Delta H_2^\circ + \Delta H_3^\circ$$
$$= -1 \times (-1351.60) + 9 \times (-94.0518) + 8 \times (-68.3174)$$
$$= 1351.60 - 846.4662 - 546.5392 = -41.41 \text{ kcal mole}^{-1}$$

Usually graphite is taken to be the standard state of carbon but if diamond were chosen instead, the new standard enthalpy of formation of $CO_2(g)$ would be

$C(graphite) + O_2 \rightarrow CO_2$	-94.05 kcal
$C(diamond) \rightarrow C(graphite)$	-0.45 kcal
$C(diamond) + O_2 \rightarrow CO_2$	-94.50 kcal

-94.50 kcal mole^{-1}, and ΔH_{298}° for the formation of cis-hexahydroindan would be -45.46 kcal mole^{-1}.

2-I-22. $\Delta H_{f_{298}}^\circ = -94.052 - 200.16 + 285.80 = -8.41$ kcal for the reaction $W(s) + C(graphite) \rightarrow WC(s)$.

2-I-23. From (a), $\Delta H^\circ = -3 \times 28.59 = -85.77$ kcal mole^{-1}. Difference $= 85.77 - 49.80 = 35.97$ kcal mole^{-1} = resonance energy of benzene. The calculated ΔH did not take into account the delocalization of the "double bonds" in benzene.

2-I-24. $\Delta H_f^\circ = \frac{1}{2}(-399.09) + \frac{3}{2}(-303) + 6(-68.3174) - (-989.1) + 7.2 = -199.55 - 454.5 - 409.9044 + 989.1 + 7.2 = -67.7$ kcal mole^{-1}. The paper says -72.1 kcal mole^{-1}.

2-I-25.

$Mg(s) + N_2(g) + 3O_2(g) \rightarrow Mg(NO_3)_2(s)$	$-188,770$
$Mg(NO_3)_2(s) + aq \rightarrow Mg^{2+}(aq) + 2NO_3^-(aq)$	$-21,530$
$2NO_3^-(aq) \rightarrow N_2(g) + 3O_2(g) + 2e^-$	$-2(-49,320)$
$Mg(s) \rightarrow Mg^{2+}(aq) + 2e^- \quad \Delta H_f^\circ =$	$-111,660$
	cal (g ion)$^{-1}$

2-I-26.
$$\Delta H°$$

$$C_5H_5N(l) + \frac{25}{4} O_2(g) \rightarrow 5CO_2(g)$$

$$+ \frac{5}{2} H_2O(l) + \frac{1}{2} \cdot _2(g) \qquad\qquad -664.95$$

$$5CO_2(g) \rightarrow 5C(graphite) + 5O_2(g) \qquad -5 \times (-94.0518)$$

$$\frac{5}{2} H_2O(l) \rightarrow \frac{5}{2} H_2(g) + \frac{5}{4} O_2(g) \qquad -\frac{5}{2} \times (-68.3174)$$

$$C_5H_5N(l) \rightarrow 5C(graphite)$$

$$+ \frac{5}{2} H_2(g) + \frac{1}{2} N_2(g) \qquad\qquad -23.90$$

$$5C(graphite) + \frac{5}{2} H_2(g) + \frac{1}{2} N_2(g) \rightarrow C_5H_5N(l) \qquad +23.90 \text{ kcal mole}^{-1}$$

2-I-27. (a) $\Delta H°_{298} = 6(-68.3174) - 4(-11.04) = -365.74$ kcal

$$\Delta E°_{298} = \Delta H°_{298} - RT(-5) = -365.74 + 2.96$$

$$= -362.78 \text{ kcal}$$

(b) $\Delta C°_P = 6(18.02) + 2(6.94) - 4(8.89) - 3(6.97)$

$$= 65.53 \text{ cal°K}^{-1} = 0.06553 \text{ kcal°K}^{-1}$$

$$\Delta H°_{323} = \Delta H°_{298} + \Delta C°_P(323 - 298) = -365.74 + 1.64$$

$$= -364.10 \text{ kcal}$$

2-I-28. (a) $\Delta H°_{300} = -80.00 - 0 - 2(-50.00) = 20.00$ kcal

$$\Delta C°_P = 8.00 - (5.00 + 0.0020\ T) - 2(7.00)$$

$$= -11.00 - 0.0020\ T \text{ cal°K}^{-1}$$

$$\Delta H°_T = \Delta H°_{300} + \int_{300}^{T} \Delta C°_P\ dT$$

$$= 20,000 + \int_{300}^{T} (-11.00 - 0.0020T)\ dT$$

$$= 20,000 - 11.00(T - 300) - 0.0010(T^2 - 300^2) \text{ cal}$$

$$= 23,390 - 11.00T - 0.0010T^2 \text{ cal}$$

(b) $\Delta H°_{1000} = 23,390 - 11.00 \times 1000 - 0.0010 \times 1000^2$

$$= 11,390 \text{ cal or } 11.39 \text{ kcal}$$

2-I-29. (a) $\Delta H^\circ_{291} = -21.0 - (-19.5) + 2(-17.5) - 44.0 = -80.5$ kcal

for the reaction

$Fe(s) + Cl_2(g) \rightarrow FeCl_2(s)$

(b) $\Delta E^\circ_{291} = \Delta H^\circ_{291} - RT(-1) = -79.9$ kcal

(c) $\Delta C^\circ_P = 18.5 - 8.2 - 6.0 = 4.3$ cal°K⁻¹

$\Delta H^\circ_{391} = \Delta H^\circ_{291} + \Delta C_P(391 - 291) = -80.1$ kcal

2-I-30.

Bonds broken:		Bonds formed:	
O—H 1 × (+111) =	+111	C—O 1 × (−84) =	−84
C—C 1 × (+ 83) =	+ 83	C—H 1 × (−99) =	−99
Total	+194	Total	−183

$\Delta H = +194 - 183 = 11$ kcal

2-I-31. (a)

dU	dW
$\dfrac{\partial(xy^2)}{\partial y} = 2xy$	$\dfrac{\partial(\sin y)}{\partial y} = \cos y$
$\dfrac{\partial(x^2 y)}{\partial x} = 2xy$	$\dfrac{\partial(\sin x)}{\partial x} = \cos x \neq \cos y$

The differential is exact.   The differential is inexact.

(b)

$$\int_{0,0}^{x,y} dU = \int_{(i)} xy^2\, dx + \int_{(ii)} x^2 y\, dy$$

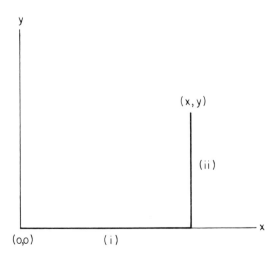

On segment (i), $y = 0$. The first integral is 0. On segment (ii), x is constant and y varies from 0 to y. Therefore

$$\int dU = x^2 \int_0^y y \, dy = \tfrac{1}{2} x^2 y^2$$

$$U = \tfrac{1}{2} x^2 y^2 + \text{constant}$$

SECTION 2-11

2-II-1. The special circumstances are that $(\partial E/\partial V)_T = 0$ or $dV = 0$ (constant volume). In general,

$$dE = \left(\frac{\partial E}{\partial T}\right)_V dT + \left(\frac{\partial E}{\partial V}\right)_T dV$$

and $dE = C_V \, dT$ only under the special circumstances mentioned. Likewise $dH = C_P \, dT$ only when $(\partial H/\partial P)_T = 0$ or $dP = 0$.

2-II-2. For an adiabatic process, $dq = 0$ and hence $dE = -P \, dV$. Therefore $C_V \, dT = -dw$ and $w = -C_V(T_2 - T_1)$. For the adiabatic reversible expansion of an ideal gas

$$\frac{T_2}{T_1} = \left(\frac{P_2}{P_1}\right)^{R/C_P}$$

Therefore,

$$w = -C_V \left[T_1 \left(\frac{P_2}{P_1}\right)^{R/C_P} - T_1\right] = C_V T_1 \left[1 - \left(\frac{P_2}{P_1}\right)^{R/C_P}\right]$$

2-II-3.

$$d\bar{E} = -dw$$

$$\bar{C}_V \, dT + (kT - P) \, d\bar{V} = -P \, d\bar{V}$$

$$\bar{C}_V \, dT + kT \, d\bar{V} = 0$$

$$\frac{\bar{C}_V \, dT}{T} = -R \, a\bar{V}$$

$$\bar{C}_V \ln \frac{T_2}{T_1} = -k(\bar{V}_2 - \bar{V}_1)$$

2-II-4.   (a) $dq = 0$, $dE = -dw$, $C_V dT = -P dV$. From the equation of state, $P = (n^2 KT)/V^2$. Then $C_V dT = (-n^2 KT\, dV)/V^2$. $C_V = n\bar{C}_V$.

$$n\bar{C}_V \ln\left(\frac{T_2}{T_1}\right) = n^2 K\left(\frac{1}{V_2} - \frac{1}{V_1}\right)$$

(b) $\bar{C}_P - \bar{C}_V = \left(\frac{\partial \bar{E}}{\partial \bar{V}}\right)_T + P\left(\frac{\partial \bar{V}}{\partial T}\right)_P$

$$\bar{V} = \left(\frac{KT}{P}\right)^{1/2}$$

$$\left(\frac{\partial \bar{V}}{\partial T}\right)_P = \frac{1}{2}\left(\frac{K}{PT}\right)^{1/2}$$

$$\bar{C}_P - \bar{C}_V = P\left(\frac{\partial \bar{V}}{\partial T}\right)_P = \frac{1}{2}\left(\frac{KP}{T}\right)^{1/2}$$

2-II-5.

$$q = 0 \qquad dw = -dE \qquad P\, dV = -C_V dT - \left(\frac{\partial E}{\partial V}\right)_T dV$$

$$\left(\frac{RT}{\bar{V}-b} - \frac{a}{\bar{V}^2}\right) d\bar{V} = -(A + BT)\, dT - \frac{a}{\bar{V}^2}\, d\bar{V}$$

$$\frac{R}{\bar{V}-b}\, d\bar{V} = -\left(\frac{A}{T} + B\right) dT$$

$$R \ln\left[\frac{\bar{V}_2 - b}{\bar{V}_1 - b}\right] = -A \ln\left(\frac{T_2}{T_1}\right) - B(T_2 - T_1)$$

2-II-6.   By definition $\mu_{JT} = (\partial T/\partial P)_H$. Making use of the general formula

$$\left(\frac{dy}{dx}\right)_z = -\frac{(\partial z/\partial x)_y}{(\partial z/\partial y)_x}$$

we find that

$$\mu_{JT} = -\frac{(\partial H/\partial P)_T}{(\partial H/\partial T)_P} = -\frac{1}{C_P}\left(\frac{\partial H}{\partial P}\right)_T$$

2-II-7.

$$V = \frac{nRT}{P} - \frac{na}{R^2 T^2}$$

$$\left(\frac{\partial V}{\partial T}\right)_P = \frac{nR}{P} + \frac{2na}{R^2 T^3}$$

$$T\left(\frac{\partial V}{\partial T}\right)_P = \frac{nRT}{P} + \frac{2na}{R^2 T^2}$$

$$T\left(\frac{\partial V}{\partial T}\right)_P - V = \frac{nRT}{P} + \frac{2na}{R^2T^2} - \frac{nRT}{P} + \frac{na}{R^2T^2}$$

$$= \frac{3na}{R^2T^2}$$

$$\mu_{\mathrm{JT}} = \frac{3na}{C_P R^2 T^2}$$

At the inversion temperature $\mu_{\mathrm{JT}} = 0$. This could happen only if $C_P = \infty$, $T = \infty$, or $a = 0$. Thus this gas does not have an inversion temperature.

2-II-8.   At the inversion temperature T_i, $\mu_{\mathrm{JT}} = 0$; hence

$$\frac{2a}{RT_i} - b - \frac{3abP}{R^2T_i^2} = 0$$

Thus, $bR^2T_i^2 - 2aRT_i + 3abP = 0$. This is a quadratic equation. Solving for T_i, we obtain

$$T_i = \frac{2aR \pm \sqrt{4a^2R^2 - 12ab^2R^2P}}{2bR^2} = \frac{a \pm \sqrt{a^2 - 3ab^2P}}{bR}$$

Since we are dealing with a quadratic equation, we have two values for the inversion temperature corresponding to any given pressure. Real gases do in fact have two inversion temperatures at any given pressure.

2-II-9.

$$\left(\frac{\partial C_P}{\partial P}\right)_T = \left[\frac{\partial}{\partial P}\left(\frac{\partial H}{\partial T}\right)_P\right]_T = \frac{\partial^2 H}{\partial P \, \partial T} = \left[\frac{\partial}{\partial T}\left(\frac{\partial H}{\partial P}\right)_T\right]_P$$

$$dH = \left(\frac{\partial H}{\partial T}\right)_P dT + \left(\frac{\partial H}{\partial P}\right)_T dP$$

$$0 = \left(\frac{\partial H}{\partial T}\right)_P + \left(\frac{\partial H}{\partial P}\right)_T\left(\frac{\partial P}{\partial T}\right)_H$$

$$\left(\frac{\partial H}{\partial P}\right)_T = -\left(\frac{\partial H}{\partial T}\right)_P\left(\frac{\partial T}{\partial P}\right)_H = -C_P\mu_{\mathrm{JT}}$$

$$\left(\frac{\partial C_P}{\partial P}\right)_T = \frac{\partial}{\partial T}(-C_P\mu_{\mathrm{JT}}) = -\mu_{\mathrm{JT}}\left(\frac{\partial C_P}{\partial T}\right)_P - C_P\left(\frac{\partial \mu_{\mathrm{JT}}}{\partial T}\right)_P$$

2-II-10.

$$C_P - C_V = \left(\frac{\partial H}{\partial T}\right)_P - \left(\frac{\partial E}{\partial T}\right)_V = \left[\frac{\partial(E + PV)}{\partial T}\right]_P - \left(\frac{\partial E}{\partial T}\right)_V$$

$$= \left(\frac{\partial E}{\partial T}\right)_P + P\left(\frac{\partial V}{\partial T}\right)_P - \left(\frac{\partial E}{\partial T}\right)_V$$

$$dE = \left(\frac{\partial E}{\partial T}\right)_V dT + \left(\frac{\partial E}{\partial V}\right)_T dV$$

$$\left(\frac{\partial E}{\partial T}\right)_P = \left(\frac{\partial E}{\partial T}\right)_V + \left(\frac{\partial E}{\partial V}\right)_T \left(\frac{\partial V}{\partial T}\right)_P$$

$$C_P - C_V = \left(\frac{\partial E}{\partial T}\right)_V + \left(\frac{\partial E}{\partial V}\right)_T \left(\frac{\partial V}{\partial T}\right)_P + P\left(\frac{\partial V}{\partial T}\right)_P - \left(\frac{\partial E}{\partial T}\right)_V$$

$$= \left[P + \left(\frac{\partial E}{\partial V}\right)_T\right]\left(\frac{\partial V}{\partial T}\right)_P$$

2-II-11. (a) $\quad \bar{C}_P - \bar{C}_V = \left[P + \left(\frac{\partial E}{\partial V}\right)_T\right]\left(\frac{\partial \bar{V}}{\partial T}\right)_P$

but for an ideal gas,

$$\left(\frac{\partial E}{\partial V}\right)_T = 0$$

thus

$$\bar{C}_P - \bar{C}_V = P\left(\frac{\partial \bar{V}}{\partial T}\right)_P$$

Since $\bar{V} = RT/P$,

$$P\left(\frac{\partial V}{\partial T}\right)_P = \frac{PR}{P} = R$$

and therefore $\bar{C}_P - \bar{C}_V = R$.

(b) $\qquad \bar{V} = \frac{RT}{P}$

$$\left(\frac{\partial \bar{V}}{\partial P}\right)_T = \frac{-RT}{P^2}$$

$$\left(\frac{\partial \bar{V}}{\partial T}\right)_P = \frac{R}{P}$$

Substituting into the formula given in the problem statement, we find that $\bar{C}_P - \bar{C}_V = R$.

(c) Using $(\partial \bar{V}/\partial T)_P$ and $(\partial \bar{V}/\partial P)_T$ as evaluated in (b)

$$\alpha = \frac{1}{\bar{V}} \frac{R}{P} = \frac{1}{T} \quad \text{and} \quad \beta = \left(-\frac{1}{\bar{V}}\right)\left(-\frac{\bar{V}}{P}\right) = \frac{1}{P}$$

and

$$\bar{C}_P - \bar{C}_V = T\bar{V}\left(\frac{1}{T}\right)^2 P = R$$

2-II-12.

(a) $\Delta H = \dfrac{C_P \Delta T}{\text{moles } H_2O \text{ formed}} + \text{correction}$

$$= \frac{-223.9 \times 10^{-3} \times 0.2064}{3.4075 \times 10^{-3}} + 0.155$$

$$= -13.562 + 0.155 = -13.41 \text{ kcal mole}^{-1}$$

(b) HCl and $HClO_4$ are strong acids and completely dissociated. Acetic acid is a weak acid and is only partially dissociated. The difference between the observed enthalpies is
equal to the enthalpy of dissociation of acetic acid.

2-II-13. $\Delta H^\circ_{298} = 41.220 \text{ kcal}$

$$\Delta C^\circ_P = -1.02 - 1.28 \times 10^{-3}T + 3.88 \times 10^5 T^{-2} \text{ cal}^\circ K^{-1}$$

$$\Delta H^\circ_T = 41.220 - 1.02 \times 10^{-3}(T - 298)$$

$$- 6.4 \times 10^{-7}(T^2 - 298^2)$$

$$- 3.88 \times 10^2 \left(\frac{1}{T} - \frac{1}{298}\right) \text{ kcal}$$

The expression is valid in the range $298 - 2000^\circ K$.

2-II-14.   (a) $\Delta H^\circ_{298} = -57.7979 - 70.96 - (-4.815) - 0 = -123.94 \text{ kcal}$

$$\Delta E^\circ_{298} = \Delta H^\circ_{298} - RT(\Delta n)_{gas}$$

$$= -123.94 - 1.987 \times 10^{-3} \times 298 \times \left(-\tfrac{1}{2}\right)$$

$$= -123.64 \text{ kcal}$$

(b) $\Delta C_P^\circ = -2.162 + 5.634 \times 10^{-3}T$
$\qquad\qquad - 6.100 \times 10^{-7}T^2 + 2.057 \times 10^{-9}T^3$ cal

$$\Delta H^\circ_{1000} = \Delta H^\circ_{298} + \int_{298}^{1000} \Delta C_P^\circ \, dT$$

$\qquad = -123.94 - 2.162 \times 10^{-3}(1000 - 298)$
$\qquad\quad + 2.817 \times 10^{-6}(1000^2 - 298^2)$
$\qquad\quad - 2.033 \times 10^{-10}(1000^3 - 298^3)$
$\qquad\quad + 5.14 \times 10^{-13}(1000^4 - 298^4)$ kcal
$\qquad = -122.58$ kcal

(c) The given data apply only to the range 298 to 1500°K. They tell us nothing about the behavior of the heat capacities above 1500°K. Therefore we cannot find ΔH° at 2000°K.

2-II-15. $\Delta C_P = 6.00 + 5.00 \times 10^{-3}T + 4.00 \times 10^5 \dfrac{1}{T^2}$

$$\Delta H^\circ_{T_2} = \Delta H^\circ_{300} + \int_{300}^{T_2} 6.00 \, dT + \int_{300}^{T_2} 5.00 \times 10^{-3}T \, dT$$

$$\qquad\qquad + \int_{300}^{T_2} \frac{4.00 \times 10^5}{T^2} \, dT$$

$\Delta H^\circ_{T_2} = -35,000 + 6.00(T_2 - 300)$

$\qquad\quad + \tfrac{1}{2} \times 5.00 \times 10^{-3}(T_2{}^2 - 300^2)$

$\qquad\quad - 4.00 \times 10^5 \left(\dfrac{1}{T_2} - \dfrac{1}{300} \right)$

$\qquad = -35,692 + 6.00T_2 + 2.50 \times 10^{-3}T_2{}^2 - 4.00 \times 10^5 \dfrac{1}{T_2}$

$\Delta H^\circ = -35,692 + 6.00T + 2.50 \times 10^{-3}T^2$

$\qquad\quad - \dfrac{4.00 \times 10^5}{T}$ cal°K^{-1} mole^{-1}

2-II-16. $\Delta C_P^\circ = 2 \times 4.968 - 6.148 - 3.102 \times 10^{-3}T$
$\qquad\qquad + 9.23 \times 10^{-7}T^2$ cal°K^{-1}

For the given reaction

$$\Delta H^\circ_{1000} = \Delta H^\circ_{298} + \int_{298}^{1000} \Delta C_P \, dT$$

$\qquad = 117,040 + 3.787(1000 - 298)$
$\qquad\quad - \tfrac{1}{2} \times 3.102 \times 10^{-3}(1000^2 - 298^2)$
$\qquad\quad + \tfrac{1}{3} \times 9.23 \times 10^{-7}(1000^3 - 298^3)$ cal

$\qquad = 118.58$ kcal

2-II-17.

$$\Delta C_P = \bar{C}_P(AB_4) - \bar{C}_P(A) - 2\bar{C}_P(B_2) = -10.00 - 6.00 \times 10^{-3}T$$

$$\Delta H_T = \Delta H_{300} + \int_{300}^{T} \Delta C_P \, dT$$

$$= 500,000 + \int_{300}^{T} (-10.00) \, dT + \int_{300}^{T} (-6.00 \times 10^{-3}) \, T \, dT$$

$$= 500,000 - 10.00(T - 300) - \frac{6.00 \times 10^{-3}}{2}(T^2 - 300^2)$$

$$= 503,270 - 10.00T - 3.00 \times 10^{-3}T^2$$

2-II-18.

$$\Delta H_{T_2} - \Delta H_{T_1} = \int_{T_1}^{T_2} \Delta C_P \, dT$$

$$0 - (-5000) = \int_{298}^{T} (1.00 + 2.00 \times 10^{-3}T) \, dT$$

$$= 1.00(T - 298) + 1.00 \times 10^{-3}(T^2 - 298^2)$$

$$5000 = -298 + 1.00T - 89 + 1.00 \times 10^{-3}T^2$$

$$0 = 1.00 \times 10^{-3}T^2 + 1.00T - 5387$$

Solving for T and disregarding the negative root, we obtain $T = 1880°K$.

2-II-19. The reaction is

$$2H_2 + O_2 + 4N_2 \to 2H_2O(g) + 4N_2$$

$$\Delta H_{298}° = 2 \times (-57,800) = -115,600 \text{ cal}$$

Thus, $+115,600$ cal go into heating up 2 moles of $H_2O(g)$ and 4 moles of $N_2(g)$ from $298.2°K$ to the final temperature, T_2.

$$2\bar{C}_P H_2O(g) + 4\bar{C}_P N_2(g) = 40.234 + 10.400 \times 10^{-3}T$$

$$115,600 = \int_{298.2}^{T_2} 40.234 \, dT + \int_{298.2}^{T_2} 10.400 \times 10^{-3} \, T \, dT$$

$$= 40.234(T_2 - 298.2) + \tfrac{1}{2} \times 10.400 \times 10^{-3}(T_2^2 - 298.2^2)$$

$$115,600 = 40.234T_2 - 11,996 + 5.200 \times 10^{-3}T_2^2 - 462$$

$$0 = 5.200 \times 10^{-3}T_2^2 + 40.234T_2 - 128,058$$

Applying the quadratic formula we obtain, disregarding the negative root, $T_2 = 2425°K$. The result is valid only if the given expressions for $\bar{C}_P$ are correct over the range 298 to

2425°K. If they fail at the higher temperatures within this range, the result is erroneous.

2-II-20. $\Delta H_c = -6c + 3a + 3b - 3e + 2g + h = -978.5 \text{ kcal mole}^{-1}$

Experimental value: $-970.8 \text{ kcal mole}^{-1}$

2-II-21. $\dfrac{\partial(xy)}{\partial y} = x \qquad \dfrac{\partial(\frac{1}{2}x^2)}{\partial x} = x$

Exact differential.

$$\int dz = \int_{x_1}^{x_2} xy\,dx + \int_{y_1}^{y_2} \tfrac{1}{2}x^2\,dy$$
$$(y = y_1) \qquad (x = x_2)$$
$$= y_1(\tfrac{1}{2}x_2^2 - \tfrac{1}{2}x_1^2) + \tfrac{1}{2}x_2^2(y_2 - y_1)$$
$$= \tfrac{1}{2}x_2^2 y_2 - \tfrac{1}{2}x_1^2 y_1$$
$$z = \tfrac{1}{2}x^2 y + \text{constant}$$

2-II-22. (a) $\dfrac{\partial(xy)}{\partial x} = y \qquad \dfrac{\partial(xy)}{\partial y} = x \neq y \qquad$ inexact differential

(b) See figure.

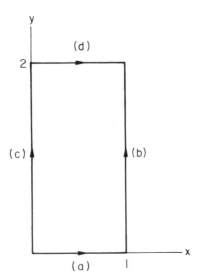

Path (a, b)

$$\int dz = \underbrace{0 \cdot \int_0^1 x\, dx + 0 \cdot \int_1^0 x\, dy}_{(a)} + \underbrace{1 \cdot \int_1^1 y\, dx + 1 \cdot \int_0^2 y\, dy}_{(b)}$$

$$= \int_0^2 y\, dy = \tfrac{1}{2} y^2 \big|_0^2 = 2$$

Path (c, d)

$$\int dz = \underbrace{0 \cdot \int_0^0 y\, dx + 0 \cdot \int_0^2 y\, dy}_{(c)} + \underbrace{2 \int_0^1 x\, dx + 2 \int_2^2 x\, dy}_{(d)}$$

$$= 2 \int_0^1 x\, dx = 2(\tfrac{1}{2} x^2)\big|_0^1 = 1$$

SECTION 2-III

2-III-1.

(a) $\quad \left(\dfrac{\partial T}{\partial \overline{V}} \right)_{\overline{E}} = \dfrac{-(\partial \overline{E}/\partial \overline{V})_T}{(\partial \overline{E}/\partial T)_{\overline{V}}} = -\dfrac{a}{C_V \overline{V}^2} = -\dfrac{2a}{3R\overline{V}^2}$

(b) $\quad \varDelta T = \displaystyle\int_{\overline{V}_1}^{\overline{V}_2} \left(\dfrac{\partial T}{\partial \overline{V}} \right)_{\overline{E}} = -\dfrac{2a}{3R} \int_{1.0}^{2.0} \dfrac{d\overline{V}}{\overline{V}^2}$

$\qquad = \dfrac{-2a}{3R} \left(\dfrac{1}{1.0} - \dfrac{1}{2.0} \right)$

$\qquad = \dfrac{-a}{3R} (1.0 \text{ mole liter}^{-1})$

$\qquad = \dfrac{-4.19 \text{ liter}^2 \text{ atm mole}^{-2} \times 1.0 \text{ mole liter}^{-1}}{3 \times 0.0821 \text{ liter atm mole}^{-1} \text{ deg}^{-1}}$

$\qquad = -17.0°$

2-III-2. The error consists of applying an equation that is valid only at constant pressure to a process that is being carried out at constant volume. In general $H = E + PV$ and $\varDelta H = \varDelta E + \varDelta(PV)$. At constant pressure since $\varDelta P = 0$, it follows that $\varDelta H = \varDelta E + P\varDelta V$ and at constant volume (such as in the bomb calorimetry process) $\Delta V = 0$, and $\Delta H = \Delta E + V \, \Delta P$.

2-III-3.

$$dH = dE + P \, dV + V \, dP = 0$$

$$dq = dE + P \, dV = -V \, dP$$

$$C_H = \frac{dq}{dT} = -V \left(\frac{\partial P}{\partial T} \right)_H = V \frac{(\partial H / \partial T)_P}{(\partial H / \partial P)_T} = \frac{V C_P}{V - T(\partial V / \partial T)_P}$$

2-III-4.

$$dE = \left(\frac{\partial E}{\partial P} \right)_V dP + \left(\frac{\partial E}{\partial V} \right)_P dV$$

$$\left(\frac{\partial E}{\partial P} \right)_T = \left(\frac{\partial E}{\partial P} \right)_V + \left(\frac{\partial E}{\partial V} \right)_P \left(\frac{\partial V}{\partial P} \right)_T$$

$$\left(\frac{\partial E}{\partial V} \right)_T = \left(\frac{\partial E}{\partial V} \right)_P + \left(\frac{\partial E}{\partial P} \right)_V \left(\frac{\partial P}{\partial V} \right)_T$$

If $(\partial E / \partial V)_T = 0$, then

$$\left(\frac{\partial E}{\partial V} \right)_P = - \left(\frac{\partial E}{\partial P} \right)_V \left(\frac{\partial P}{\partial V} \right)_T \text{ or } \left(\frac{\partial E}{\partial V} \right)_P \left(\frac{\partial V}{\partial P} \right)_T = - \left(\frac{\partial E}{\partial P} \right)_V$$

Therefore

$$\left(\frac{\partial E}{\partial P} \right)_T = \left(\frac{\partial E}{\partial P} \right)_V - \left(\frac{\partial E}{\partial P} \right)_V = 0$$

2-III-5.　$dH = dE + d(PV)$

$$\left(\frac{\partial H}{\partial V} \right)_T = \left(\frac{\partial E}{\partial V} \right)_T + \left(\frac{\partial (PV)}{\partial V} \right)_T$$

If $(\partial E / \partial V)_T = 0$, then

$$\left(\frac{\partial H}{\partial V} \right)_T = \left(\frac{\partial (PV)}{\partial V} \right)_T \text{ and } \left(\frac{\partial (PV)}{\partial V} \right)_T = 0$$

only if $(PV)_T = $ constant (Boyle's law). This is why *both* Boyle's law *and* $(\partial E / \partial V)_T = 0$ are necessary for the complete thermodynamic definition of an ideal gas (a gas whose energy and enthalpy are functions of temperature alone).

2-III-6.

$$\pi = \frac{8\theta}{3\phi - 1} - \frac{3}{\phi^2}$$

$$d\pi = \frac{(3\phi - 1) \cdot 8d\theta - 8\theta \cdot 3d\phi}{(3\phi - 1)^2} + \frac{6}{\phi^3} \, d\phi = 0$$

$$\left(\frac{\partial \phi}{\partial \theta}\right)_\pi = -\frac{(\partial \pi/\partial \theta)_\phi}{(\partial \pi/\partial \phi)_\theta}$$

$$\left(\frac{\partial \pi}{\partial \phi}\right)_\theta = \frac{-24\theta}{(3\phi - 1)^2} + \frac{6}{\phi^3}$$

$$\left(\frac{\partial \phi}{\partial \theta}\right)_\pi = \frac{8}{(3\phi - 1)} \Big/ \left[\frac{24\theta}{(3\phi - 1)^2} - \frac{6}{\phi^3}\right]$$

$$\theta_i = \phi \Big/ \left(\frac{\partial \phi}{\partial \theta}\right)_\pi$$

$$= \phi \cdot \frac{3\phi - 1}{8} \left[\frac{24\theta_i}{(3\phi - 1)} - \frac{6}{\phi^3}\right]$$

$$\theta_i \left[1 - \frac{\phi(3\phi - 1)}{8} \cdot \frac{24}{(3\phi - 1)^2}\right] = -\frac{3(3\phi - 1)}{4\phi^2}$$

$$\theta_i = \frac{3(3\phi - 1)}{4\phi^2[1 - 3\phi/(3\phi - 1)]} = -\frac{3(3\phi - 1)^2}{4\phi^2[3\phi - 1 - 3\phi]}$$

$$= \frac{3(3\phi - 1)^2}{4\phi^2}$$

$$\pi_i = \frac{8\theta_i}{3\phi - 1} - \frac{3}{\phi^2} = \frac{6(3\phi - 1)}{\phi^2} - \frac{3}{\phi^2}$$

$$= \frac{18\phi - 9}{\phi^2} = \frac{9(2\phi - 1)}{\phi^2}$$

2-III-7.

(a) $\quad V = \frac{nRT}{P} + n';\quad \left(\frac{\partial V}{\partial T}\right)_P = \frac{nR}{P};\quad \alpha = \frac{nR}{PV}$

We cannot substitute nRT for PV in the last equation to get $\alpha = 1/T$ here because this gas is not ideal.

(b) $\quad P = \frac{nRT}{(V - nb)};\quad P \, dV = \frac{nRT \, dV}{(V - nb)}$

$$w = \int_{V_i}^{V_f} P \, dV = \int_{V_i}^{V_f} \frac{nRT \, dV}{(V - nb)}$$

Integrating with the assumption that T is constant

$$w = nRT \ln \left[\frac{V_f - nb}{V_i - nb} \right]$$

(c) $q = 0$ (adiabatic), so $\Delta E = q - w = 0 - w = -w$.

Since $\Delta E = -w$, then $n\bar{C}_V \, dT = -P \, dV$, since $(\partial E/\partial V)_T = 0$

$$n\bar{C}_V \, dT = - \frac{nRT \, dV}{(V - nb)}$$

$$n\bar{C}_V \frac{dT}{T} = - \frac{nR \, dV}{(V - nb)}$$

On integration

$$\bar{C}_V \ln \left(\frac{T_2}{T_1} \right) = - R \ln \left[\frac{(V_2 - nb)}{(V_1 - nb)} \right]$$

or

$$\left(\frac{T_2}{T_1} \right)^{\bar{C}_V} = \left[\frac{(V_2 - nb)}{(V_1 - nb)} \right]^{-R}$$

or

$$\frac{T_1}{T_2} = \left[\frac{(V_2 - nb)}{(V_1 - nb)} \right]^{-R/\bar{C}_V}$$

We cannot substitute $(\bar{C}_P - \bar{C}_V)$ for R in the exponent $R/\bar{C}_V$ because this gas is not ideal and $\bar{C}_P - \bar{C}_V = R$ only for an ideal gas.

(d) $\left(\dfrac{\partial \bar{V}}{\partial T} \right)_P = \dfrac{R}{P}$

$$\mu_{JT} = \frac{1}{\bar{C}_P} \left[\frac{RT}{P} - \bar{V} \right] = \frac{1}{\bar{C}_P} \left[\frac{(\bar{V} - b)P}{P} - \bar{V} \right]$$

$$= - \frac{b}{\bar{C}_P}$$

CHAPTER 3

The second law
of thermodynamics

SECTION 3-1

3-I-1. (e)

3-I-2. (d)

3-I-3.

$$\Delta S = \int_{300}^{1000} \frac{\bar{C}_P \, dT}{T} = \int_{300}^{1000} 6.4492 \frac{dT}{T} + \int_{300}^{1000} 1.4125 \times 10^{-3} \, dT$$

$$- \int_{300}^{1000} 0.807 \times 10^{-7} T \, dT$$

$$= 6.4492 \times 2.303 \log \frac{1000}{300} + 1.4125 \times 10^{-3}(1000 - 300)$$

$$- \frac{0.807}{2} \times 10^{-7}(1000^2 - 300^2)$$

$$= 7.77 + 0.99 - 0.04$$

$$= 8.72 \text{ cal} °\text{K}^{-1} \text{ mole}^{-1}$$

3-I-4. (a) Let t_f = the final temperature

$$\frac{100}{18.0} \times 18.0 \times (t_f - 25) = \frac{200}{118.7} \times 6.1(100 - t_f)$$

$$t_f = 31.9°\text{C}$$

(b) $\quad \Delta S_{water} = \int_{298.2}^{330.1} \dfrac{n\bar{C}_P \, dT}{T}$

$\qquad = \dfrac{100}{18.0} \times 18.0 \times 2.303 \log \dfrac{330.1}{298.2}$

$\qquad = 10.21 \text{ cal deg}^{-1}$

$\Delta S_{tin} = \int_{373.2}^{330.1} \dfrac{n\bar{C}_P \, dT}{T}$

$\qquad = \dfrac{200}{118.7} \times 6.1 \times 2.303 \log \dfrac{330.1}{373.2}$

$\qquad = -1.26 \text{ cal deg}^{-1}$

$\Delta S_{universe} = \Delta S_{water} + \Delta S_{tin} = 10.21 - 1.26$

$\qquad\qquad = 8.95 \text{ cal deg}^{-1}$

3-I-5. $\quad \dfrac{w}{q_2} = \dfrac{T_2 - T_1}{T_2} = \dfrac{373 - 298}{373} = \dfrac{75}{373} = 0.201 \quad \text{or} \quad 20.1 \text{ percent}$

3-I-6. (a) $\quad \omega_{max} = \dfrac{T_1}{T_2 - T_1} = \dfrac{268.2}{298.2 - 268.2} = 8.94$

(b) $\quad -w_{min} = \dfrac{T_2 - T_1}{T_1} q_1 = \dfrac{298.2 - 268.2}{268.2} \times 1 \text{ cal}$

$\qquad\qquad = \dfrac{30.0}{268.2} = 0.112 \text{ cal}$

3-I-7. $\quad \omega = -\dfrac{q_1}{w} = \dfrac{T_1}{T_2 - T_1} = 7.0$

$\qquad w = q_1 + q_2$

$\qquad q_1 = w - q_2$

$\qquad \dfrac{q_2 - w}{w} = 7.0$

$\qquad \dfrac{q_2}{w} = 8.0$

Thus this heat pump would produce 8 times as much heat as a 100 percent efficient resistor per calorie of energy input.

3-I-8. The process is represented in the figure.

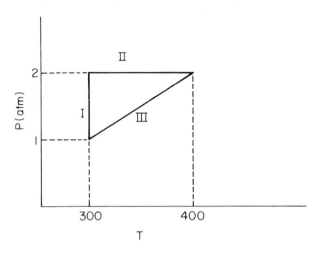

$$\Delta E_{\mathrm{I}} = \int_{300}^{300} n\bar{C}_V \, dT = 0$$

$$\Delta E_{\mathrm{II}} = \int_{300}^{400} n\bar{C}_V \, dT = 2 \times \tfrac{3}{2} \times 1.99(400 - 300) = 597 \text{ cal}$$

$$\Delta E_{\mathrm{III}} = \int_{400}^{300} n\bar{C}_V \, dT = 2 \times \tfrac{3}{2} \times 1.99(300 - 400) = -597 \text{ cal}$$

$$dS_{\mathrm{I}} = \frac{dw + dE}{T} = P\frac{dV}{T} + \frac{n\bar{C}_V \, dT}{T} = \frac{nRT \, dV}{TV} + \frac{n\bar{C}_V \, dT}{T}$$

$$\Delta S_{\mathrm{I}} = nR \ln \frac{V_2}{V_1} + n\bar{C}_V \ln \frac{T_2}{T_1} = 2 \times 1.99 \times 2.303 \log \frac{1}{2} + 0$$

$$= -2 \times 1.99 \times 2.303 \times 0.3010 = -2.76 \text{ cal}^\circ\text{K}^{-1}$$

$$\Delta S_{\mathrm{II}} = nR \ln \frac{V_2}{V_1} + n\bar{C}_V \ln \frac{T_2}{T_1} = 2 \times 1.99 \times 2.303 \log \frac{400}{300}$$

$$+ 2 \times \frac{3}{2} \times 1.99 \times 2.303 \log \frac{400}{300} = 2.86 \text{ cal}^\circ\text{K}^{-1}$$

$$\Delta S_{\mathrm{I}} + \Delta S_{\mathrm{II}} + \Delta S_{\mathrm{III}} = 0$$

$$\Delta S_{\mathrm{III}} = -\Delta S_{\mathrm{I}} - \Delta S_{\mathrm{II}} = 2.76 - 2.86 = -0.10 \text{ cal}^\circ\text{K}^{-1}$$

3-I-9.

$$\Delta \bar{S} = -R(X_1 \ln X_1 + X_2 \ln X_2)$$

where $X_1 =$ mole fraction of nitrogen and $X_2 =$ mole fraction of oxygen

$$\Delta \bar{S} = -1.987 \times 2.303(0.250 \log 0.250 + 0.750 \log 0.750)$$
$$= -4.58(-0.2442)$$
$$= 1.12 \text{ cal}^\circ K^{-1}$$

3-I-10.   (a) and (b)

3-I-11.   For this gas

$$\bar{V} = \frac{RT}{P} + b$$

$$\alpha = \bar{V} - \frac{RT}{P} = b$$

$$d \ln \gamma = d \ln \left(\frac{f}{P} \right) = \frac{\alpha}{RT} dP = \frac{b \, dP}{RT}$$

$$\ln \gamma = \int_{\gamma=1}^{\gamma} d \ln \gamma = \frac{1}{RT} \int_0^P \alpha \, dP = \frac{bP}{RT}$$

3-I-12.   Trouton's rule: $\Delta \bar{H}_v / T_b \approx 21$ cal deg^{-1} mole^{-1}

$\Delta \bar{H}_v \approx T_b \times 21 = 353 \times 21 = 7400$ cal mole^{-1}

The experimental value is 7220 cal mole^{-1}.

SECTION 3-II

3-II-1.   (a) No. The product would be steam at a much higher temperature and pressure.

(b) Yes. $\Delta G < 0$ and the process is possible. These are the conditions which one usually has in mind when he says that a process is or is not "spontaneous."

(c) No. If V and T are kept constant, the pressure will fall because of the loss of gas.

3-II-2.

$$\psi = A + RT = E - TS + RT$$

$$d\psi = dE - T\,dS - S\,dT + R\,dT$$

$$= dq - dw - T\,dS - S\,dT + R\,dT$$

$$= dq - P\,dV - T\,dS - S\,dT + R\,dT$$

$$d\psi_{T,V} = dq - T\,dS$$

If the process is reversible,

$$dq = T\,dS, \quad d\psi_{T,V} = 0, \quad \varDelta\psi_{T,V} = 0$$

If the process is spontaneous,

$$dq < T\,dS, \quad d\psi_{T,V} < 0, \quad \varDelta\psi_{T,V} < 0$$

3-II-3. (a) $dS = \dfrac{dq_{\text{rev}}}{T} = \dfrac{dE - dw}{T}; \quad dE = 0$

$$\varDelta S = \int_{V_1}^{V_2} \frac{P\,dV}{T} = \int_{V_1}^{V_2} \frac{nRT\,dV}{VT} = nR\ln\frac{V_2}{V_1}$$

(b) $\varDelta S = \dfrac{\varDelta H_{\text{transition}}}{T}$

(c) $\varDelta S = 0$

(d) $dS = \dfrac{dE - dw}{T}; \quad dE = 0; \quad \varDelta S = \int_{V_1}^{V_2} \dfrac{P\,dV}{T}$

$$= \int_{V_1}^{V_2} \frac{nRT\,dV}{VT} = nR\ln\frac{V_2}{V_1}$$

3-II-4. $dS = \dfrac{dq_{\text{rev}}}{T} = \dfrac{dE + dw}{T} = \dfrac{n\bar{C}_V\,dT}{T} + \dfrac{P\,dV}{T}$

Let us evaluate $(n\bar{C}_V\,dT)/T$ and $(P\,dV)/T$ separately.

$$\int_{T_i}^{T_f} \frac{\bar{C}_V\,dT}{T} = \int_{T_i}^{T_f} \frac{a\,dT}{T} + \int_{T_i}^{T_f} b\,dT + \int_{T_i}^{T_f} cT\,dT$$

$$= a\ln\frac{T_f}{T_i} + b(T_f - T_i) + \frac{c}{2}(T_f^2 - T_i^2)$$

$$P = \frac{RT}{V - b}$$

$$\frac{P\,dV}{T} = \frac{R}{V-b}\,dV$$

$$\int_{V_i}^{V_f} \frac{P\,dV}{T} = R \ln \left(\frac{V_f - b}{V_i - b} \right)$$

$$\Delta S_{\text{gas}} = a \ln \frac{T_f}{T_i} + b(T_f - T_i) + \frac{c}{2}(T_f^2 - T_i^2)$$
$$+ R \ln \left(\frac{V_f - b}{V_i - b} \right)$$

3-II-5.   Resolve the process into the following steps:

(i) Heat from 20° to 100°C:

$$\Delta H = \bar{C}_P(T_2 - T_1) = 18.0(80) = 1440 \text{ cal mole}^{-1}$$

$$\Delta S = \bar{C}_P \ln \frac{T_2}{T_1} = 18.0 \ln \frac{373.15}{293.15} = 4.35 \text{ cal}°K^{-1} \text{ mole}^{-1}$$

(ii) Vaporize at 100°C:

$$\Delta H = 9720 \text{ cal mole}^{-1}$$

$$\Delta S = \frac{\Delta H - \Delta G}{T} = \frac{9720 - 0}{373.15} = 26.02 \text{ cal}°K^{-1} \text{ mole}^{-1}$$

(iii) Heat from 100° to 250°C:

$$\Delta H = \bar{C}_P(T_2 - T_1) = 8.6(150) = 1290 \text{ cal mole}^{-1}$$

$$\Delta S = \bar{C}_P \ln \frac{T_2}{T_1} = 8.6 \ln \frac{523.15}{373.15} = 2.9\text{i cal}°K^{-1} \text{ mole}^{-1}$$

(a) $\Delta S = 4.35 + 26.02 + 2.91 = 33.28 \text{ cal}°K^{-1} \text{ mole}^{-1}$
(b) $\Delta H = 1440 + 9720 + 1290 = 12,450 \text{ cal mole}^{-1}$
(c) $\Delta E = \Delta H - \Delta(PV) = \Delta H - P\,\Delta V$
$$\Delta V = \bar{V}_{g,523} - \bar{V}_{liq,293} \approx \bar{V}_{g,523}$$

if we make the approximation that the volume of the liquid is negligible in comparison to the volume of the gas.

$$P\,\Delta V = P\bar{V}_{g,523} = RT = 1.987 \frac{\text{cal}}{\text{deg mole}} \times 523.15°$$
$$= 1040 \text{ cal mole}^{-1}$$

if we assume that the gas is ideal.

$$\Delta E = 12,450 - 1,040 = 11,410 \text{ cal mole}^{-1}$$

3-II-6.

(a) $\Delta H^\circ_{1000} = \Delta H^\circ_{298} + \int_{298}^{1000} \Delta C^\circ_P \, dT$

$= 124{,}100 - 1.585(1000 - 298) - \dfrac{3.82}{2}$

$\times 10^{-3}(1000^2 - 298^2) - \dfrac{0.34 \times 10^5(1000 - 298)}{1000 \times 298} \text{ cal}$

$= 121.2 \text{ kcal}$

(b) For any isothermal process

$$\Delta S^\circ = \frac{\Delta H^\circ - \Delta G^\circ}{T}$$

and $\Delta S^\circ = \Delta H^\circ / T$ only when $\Delta G^\circ = 0$.

(i) No; we know by experience that $\Delta G^\circ \gg 0$ for this highly nonspontaneous process.

(ii) No; for this process, also, $\Delta G^\circ \gg 0$. The superscript $^\circ$ implies that the fugacity of NaCl(g) is 1 atm and we know that the fugacity of saturated NaCl vapor is much less than 1 atm at 25°C.

(iii) Yes; the fugacity (and the vapor pressure, since we assume ideality) of NaCl at its boiling point is 1 atm and when the process is carried out reversibly and isothermally at this constant pressure, the work done, excluding pressure-volume work, is 0. Thus $\Delta G^\circ = 0$.

3-II-7. $\Delta \bar{C}_P = \bar{C}_{P_{liq}} - \bar{C}_{P_s} = 9.1 \text{ cal deg}^{-1} \text{ mole}^{-1}$

(a) $\Delta \bar{H}_{263} = \Delta \bar{H}_{273} + \int_{273}^{263} \Delta \bar{C}_P \, dT$

$= 1436 + 9.1(-10)$

$= 1345 \text{ cal mole}^{-1}$

(b) $\Delta \bar{S}_{263} = \Delta \bar{S}_{273} + \int_{273}^{263} \frac{\Delta \bar{C}_P}{T} \, dT$

$= \dfrac{1436}{273} + 9.1 \ln \dfrac{263}{273}$

$= 5.25 - 0.34$

$= 4.91 \text{ cal } °\text{K}^{-1} \text{ mole}^{-1}$

(Note that $\Delta\bar{G}_{273} = 0$; therefore, $\Delta\bar{S}_{273} = \Delta\bar{H}_{273}/273$. As (c) will illustrate $\Delta\bar{S}$ and $\Delta\bar{H}$ are not related in this way at other temperatures).

(c) Method I:
$$\Delta\bar{G} = \Delta\bar{H} - T\,\Delta\bar{S}$$
$$= 1345 - 263 \times 4.91$$
$$= 53\,\text{cal mole}^{-1}$$

Method II:
$$\Delta\bar{G}_{263} = \Delta\bar{G}_{273} - \int_{273}^{263} \Delta\bar{S}\,dT$$
$$= 0 - \Delta\bar{S}_{\text{mean}}(-10)$$
$$\Delta\bar{S}_{\text{mean}} \approx \tfrac{1}{2}(5.25 + 4.91) = 5.08 \text{ cal } °\text{K}^{-1} \text{ mole}^{-1}$$
$$\Delta\bar{G}_{263} = 51 \text{ cal mole}^{-1}$$

Method III:
$$\frac{\Delta\bar{G}_{263}}{263} = \frac{\Delta\bar{G}_{273}}{273} - \int_{273}^{263} \frac{\Delta\bar{H}}{T^2}\,dT$$
$$= 0 - \Delta\bar{H}_{\text{mean}}\left(\frac{1}{273} - \frac{1}{263}\right)$$
$$\Delta\bar{H}_{\text{mean}} \approx \tfrac{1}{2}(1436 + 1345) = 1390 \text{ cal mole}^{-1}$$
$$\Delta\bar{G}_{263} = \frac{263 \times 1390 \times 10}{273 \times 263}$$
$$= 51 \text{ cal mole}^{-1}$$

3-II-8.
$$\left[\frac{\partial(\Delta G°/T)}{\partial T}\right]_P = -\frac{\Delta H°}{T^2} = -\frac{D}{T^2} - \frac{a}{T} - b - cT$$

$$\int_{(\Delta G°/T_1)}^{(\Delta G°/T_2)} d(\Delta G°/T) = -\int_{298}^{T} \frac{D\,dT}{T^2} - \int_{298}^{T} \frac{a\,dT}{T}$$

$$-\int_{298}^{T} b\,dT - \int_{298}^{T} cT\,dT$$

$$\frac{\Delta G}{T} = \frac{\Delta G_{298}}{298} + D\left(\frac{1}{T} - \frac{1}{298}\right) - a \ln\left(\frac{T}{298}\right)$$

$$-b(T - 298) - \frac{c}{2}(T^2 - 298^2)$$

$$\Delta G° = T\left[\frac{B}{298} - \frac{D}{298} + 2.303a \log 298 + 298b + \frac{c}{2}(298)^2\right]$$

$$+ D - 2.303aT \log T - bT^2 - \frac{cT^3}{2}$$

3-II-9.   See figure. The steps in the cycle are labeled A, B, C.

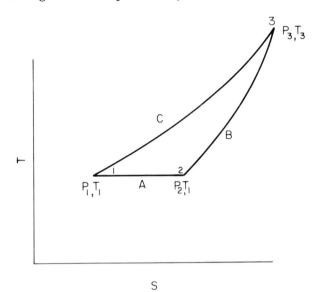

Step A.   Straight line, parallel to the S axis.

Step B. $dS_V = \dfrac{dE}{T} = \dfrac{(C_V\,dT)}{T}$

$$\left(\frac{\partial S}{\partial T}\right)_V = \frac{C_V}{T}$$

$$\left(\frac{\partial T}{\partial S}\right)_V = \frac{T}{C_V}$$

$(\partial T/\partial S)_V$ gives the slope of the curve.

Step C. $dS_P = \dfrac{dH}{T} = \dfrac{(C_P\,dT)}{T}$

$$\left(\frac{\partial S}{\partial T}\right)_P = \frac{C_P}{T}$$

$$\left(\frac{\partial T}{\partial S}\right)_P = \frac{T}{C_P}$$

$(\partial T/\partial S)_P$ gives the slope of the curve.

3-II-10.

$\quad$ I. $\quad dS = 0; \quad dq = 0 \text{ (rev)}; \quad \text{or} \quad q_\mathrm{I} = 0$

$\qquad w_\mathrm{I} = -\Delta E_\mathrm{I} = -C_V(T_2 - T_1)$

II. $dV = 0$; $w_{II} = 0$; $q_{II} = \Delta E_{II} = C_V(T_3 - T_1)$ (heat in)

III. $dS = 0$; $q = 0$ (rev); $w_{III} = -\Delta E_{III} = -C_V(T_4 - T_3)$

IV. $dV = 0$; $w = 0$; $q_{IV} = \Delta E_{IV} = -C_V(T_1 - T_4)$

$$\eta = \frac{w_{\text{net}}}{q_{\text{in}}} = \frac{-C_V(T_2 - T_1) - C_V(T_4 - T_3)}{C_V(T_3 - T_2)}$$

$$= \frac{-T_2 + T_1 - T_4 + T_3}{T_3 - T_2}$$

$$= \frac{(T_3 - T_2) + (T_1 - T_4)}{T_3 - T_2}$$

$$= 1 + \frac{T_1 - T_4}{T_3 - T_2}$$

Since $dS_I = 0$, $S_1 = S_2$; since $dS_{III} = 0$, $S_3 = S_4$.
Therefore

$$S_3 - S_2 = S_4 - S_1.$$

Therefore

$$\int_{T_2}^{T_3} \frac{C_V\, dT}{T} = \int_{T_1}^{T_4} \frac{C_V\, dT}{T}$$

$$C_V \ln \frac{T_3}{T_2} = C_V \ln \frac{T_4}{T_1}$$

$$\frac{T_3}{T_2} = \frac{T_4}{T_1}; \quad \text{or} \quad T_4 = \frac{T_1 T_3}{T_2}$$

$$\frac{T_1 - T_4}{T_3 - T_2} = \frac{-(T_1 T_3 / T_2) + T_1}{T_3 - T_2}$$

$$= \frac{T_1(-T_3/T_2 + 1)}{T_3 - T_2}$$

$$= \frac{T_1(T_2 - T_3)/T_2}{T_3 - T_2} = -\frac{T_1}{T_2}$$

$$\eta = 1 - \frac{T_1}{T_2}$$

For a reversible isentropic process $dq = 0$ and $dE = -dw$.

$$C_V\, dT = -P\, dV; \quad C_V\, dT = -RT \frac{dV}{V}; \quad \frac{C_V\, dT}{T} = -\frac{R\, dV}{V}$$

$$\frac{C_V}{R} \ln \frac{T_2}{T_1} = -\ln \frac{V_2}{V_1} \; ; \quad \frac{T_1}{T_2} = \left(\frac{V_2}{V_1}\right)^{R/C_V}$$

$$\frac{R}{C_V} = \frac{C_P - C_V}{C_V} = \frac{C_P}{C_V} - 1 = \gamma - 1$$

$$\eta = 1 - \left(\frac{V_2}{V_1}\right)^{\gamma-1} = 1 - \left(\frac{1}{r}\right)^{\gamma-1}$$

$$\eta = 1 - r^{1-\gamma}$$

Since $C_P > C_V$, $\gamma > 1$ and $(1 - \gamma) < 0$; as r increases, η increases.

3-II-11. (a) Process A:

$$q_A = w_A = 0$$

Process B:

$$q_B = w_B = RT \ln V_2/V_1 = 1.987 \times 300 \ln 2 = 413 \text{ cal}$$

Either process:

$$\Delta E = \Delta H = 0$$

$$\Delta A = \Delta G = -RT \ln 2 = -413 \text{ cal}$$

(b) The gas can be compressed isothermally and reversibly from 20 liters to 10 liters. The work done *on* the gas in this process is 413 cal. In process B this amount of work was done by the gas and stored in the surroundings from which it can now be withdrawn, thus restoring the surroundings as well as the gas to the initial state. In process A, however, the gas did no work and the 413 cal needed must be obtained by, for example, letting a weight fall, thus leaving the surroundings in a state different from the initial state. If the reverse process is carried out irreversibly, more than 413 cal of work must be done on the gas and the restoration of the surroundings to their initial state is even more clearly impossible.

3-II-12. (a) $\quad \bar{C}_V = \frac{3}{2} R, \quad \bar{C}_P = \frac{5}{2} R$

$$\left(\frac{P_2}{P_1}\right) = \left(\frac{T_2}{T_1}\right)^{\bar{C}_P/R} = \left(\frac{T_2}{T_1}\right)^{\frac{5}{2}}$$

	q	w	ΔE	ΔS
(b) (i)	0	$-\dfrac{3}{2}(T_2 - T_1)$	$\dfrac{3}{2}R(T_2 - T_1)$	0
(ii)	$RT_2 \ln \dfrac{P_2}{P_1}$	$RT_2 \ln \dfrac{P_2}{P_1}$	0	$R \ln \dfrac{P_2}{P_1}$
	$= \dfrac{5}{2}RT_2 \ln \dfrac{T_2}{T_1}$	$= \dfrac{5}{2}RT_2 \ln \dfrac{T_2}{T_1}$		$= \dfrac{5}{2}R \ln \dfrac{T_2}{T_1}$
(iii)	$\dfrac{5}{2}R(T_1 - T_2)$	$R(T_1 - T_2)$	$\dfrac{3}{2}R(T_1 - T_2)$	$\dfrac{5}{2}R \ln \dfrac{T_1}{T_2}$
Total	$\dfrac{5}{2}R\left[(T_1 - T_2) + T_2 \ln \dfrac{T_2}{T_1}\right]$	$\dfrac{5}{2}R\left[(T_1 - T_2) + T_2 \ln \dfrac{T_2}{T_1}\right]$	0	0
(c) (ii)	0	0	0	$\dfrac{5}{2}R \ln \dfrac{T_2}{T_1}$
Total	$\dfrac{5}{2}R(T_1 - T_2)$	$\dfrac{5}{2}R(T_1 - T_2)$	0	0

3-II-13. (a) Constant total volume:

$w = 0$

$q = \Delta E = \Delta H - \Delta(PV) = \Delta H - RT(\Delta n_{\text{gas}})$

$\quad = 540 - 1.987 \times 373 \times \dfrac{1}{18.02} = 499$ cal

For ΔS construct a two-step process in which the initial and final states of the water are the same as in the given process: Vaporization to gas at 1 atm:

$\Delta S = \dfrac{\Delta H}{T} = \dfrac{540 \text{ cal/g}}{373°} = 1.448 \text{ cal deg}^{-1}\text{ g}^{-1}$

Expansion from 1 atm to 0.10 atm:

$\Delta S = nRT \ln \dfrac{P_1}{P_2} = \dfrac{1}{18.02} \times 1.987 \ln 10 = 0.254 \text{ cal deg}^{-1}\text{ g}^{-1}$

Total:

$\Delta S_w = 1.702 \text{ cal deg}^{-1}$

(b) $q_r = -q_w = -499$ cal,

$\quad \Delta S_r = \dfrac{-499 \text{ cal}}{373°} = -1.337 \text{ cal deg}^{-1}$

(For the reservoir, $w = 0$ and $\Delta E = q$. The change in the state of the reservoir, determined only by its energy, is the same whether a given amount of heat is withdrawn reversibly or irreversibly. Therefore $\Delta S = q/T$, even though the process described is irreversible.)

(c) $\quad q_u = 0, \quad \Delta S_u = 1.702 - 1.337 = 0.365$ cal deg^{-1}

(d) (i) The water is allowed to evaporate reversibly against a constant opposing pressure of 1 atm.

(ii) The water is allowed to evaporate reversibly against an opposing pressure equal to its own pressure. Both steps are isothermal at 100°C.

In the reversible process the evaporating and expanding water does work in, for example, lifting a weight, and this work is stored in the surroundings available for use in the reverse process if desired. In the irreversible process the water did no work and the possibility of obtaining work from it has been lost. Correspondingly less heat was withdrawn from the reservoir in the irreversible process.

3-II-14. (a) $\qquad dH = T\,dS + V\,dP.$ Since dH is an exact differential,

$$\left(\frac{\partial V}{\partial S}\right)_P = \left(\frac{\partial T}{\partial P}\right)_S$$

(b) $\left(\dfrac{\partial V}{\partial S}\right)_P = \left(\dfrac{\partial T}{\partial P}\right)_S = -\dfrac{(\partial \bar{S}/\partial P)_T}{(\partial \bar{S}/\partial T)_P} = \dfrac{T}{\bar{C}_P}\left(\dfrac{\partial \bar{V}}{\partial T}\right)_P = \dfrac{RT}{P\bar{C}_P}$

3-II-15. $dE = dq - dw$ (first law)

$dw = P\,dV$ (definition of P-V work)

$dE = dq - P\,dV$

$dS = \dfrac{dq_{\text{rev}}}{T}$ (second law)

(Since the final equation is to apply only to systems at equilibrium, we can use this relationship.)

$\qquad dE = T\,dS - P\,dV$ (combined first and second laws)

$\left(\dfrac{\partial E}{\partial V}\right)_T = T\left(\dfrac{\partial S}{\partial V}\right)_T - P$

$\qquad A = E - TS$ (definition of A)

$\qquad dA = dE - T\,dS - S\,dT$

$\qquad\quad = T\,dS - P\,dV - T\,dS - S\,dT = -P\,dV - S\,dT$

Applying Euler's relation to dA we obtain

$$\left(\frac{\partial P}{\partial T}\right)_V = \left(\frac{\partial S}{\partial V}\right)_T$$

Therefore

$$dE = T\left(\frac{\partial P}{\partial T}\right)_V - P$$

3-II-16.

$$H = E + PV$$

$$dH = dE + d(PV) = dq - dw + P\,dV + V\,dP$$

$$= T\,dS + V\,dP$$

$$\left(\frac{\partial H}{\partial P}\right)_T = T\left(\frac{\partial S}{\partial P}\right)_T + V$$

$$G = H - TS = E + PV - TS$$

$$dG = dE + P\,dV + V\,dP - T\,dS - S\,dT$$

$$= dq - dw + P\,dV + V\,dP - T\,dS - S\,dT$$

$$= V\,dP - S\,dT$$

By the Euler reciprocity relation since dG is a perfect differential, $-(\partial V/\partial T)_P = (\partial S/\partial P)_T$. Therefore

$$\left(\frac{\partial H}{\partial P}\right)_T = V - T\left(\frac{\partial V}{\partial T}\right)_P$$

3-II-17. $dq = dE + dw;\quad dE = 0;\quad dq = dw = P\,dV$

$$\varDelta S = \int_{V_1}^{V_2} \frac{P\,dV}{T} = \int_{V_1}^{V_2} \frac{(RT + A)\,dV}{TV}$$

$$\varDelta S = \left(R + \frac{A}{T}\right)\ln\frac{V_2}{V_1}$$

3-II-18. $dG = V\,dP - S\,dT$

Since dG is a perfect (exact) differential, we can apply the Euler reciprocity relation to this equation obtaining

$(\partial S/\partial P)_T = -(\partial V/\partial T)_P$. Now we must evaluate $(\partial V/\partial T)_P$ for the equation of state.

$$P\,dV + V\,dP = nRT\,dT + \frac{2n^2a}{V^2}\,dV$$

$$\left(\frac{\partial V}{\partial T}\right)_P = \frac{nR}{(P - 2n^2a/V^2)}$$

$$\left(\frac{\partial S}{\partial P}\right)_T = -\left(\frac{\partial V}{\partial T}\right)_P = \frac{nR}{[(2n^2a/V^2) - P]} = \frac{nRV^2}{2n^2a - PV^2}$$

3-II-19.

$$P\bar{V} = RT + \frac{RTB}{\bar{V}}$$

$$dG = \bar{V}\,dP - S\,dT$$

$$dG_T = \bar{V}\,dP$$

$$P\,d\bar{V} + \bar{V}\,dP = -\frac{RTB}{\bar{V}^2}\,d\bar{V}$$

$$\bar{V}\,dP = -P\,d\bar{V} - \frac{RTB}{\bar{V}^2}\,d\bar{V}$$

$$P = \frac{RT}{\bar{V}} + \frac{RTB}{\bar{V}^2}$$

$$\bar{V}\,dP = -\left(\frac{RT}{\bar{V}} + \frac{2RTB}{\bar{V}^2}\right)d\bar{V}$$

$$\Delta G_T = -\int_{\bar{V}_1}^{\bar{V}_2} RT\,\frac{d\bar{V}}{\bar{V}} - \int_{\bar{V}_1}^{\bar{V}_2} 2RTB\,\frac{d\bar{V}}{\bar{V}^2}$$

$$= -RT\ln\left(\frac{\bar{V}_2}{\bar{V}_1}\right) + 2RTB\left(\frac{1}{\bar{V}_2} - \frac{1}{\bar{V}_1}\right)$$

$$\left(\frac{\partial A}{\partial \bar{V}}\right)_T = -P$$

$$\Delta A_T = -\int_{\bar{V}_1}^{\bar{V}_2} P\,d\bar{V} = -RT\int_{\bar{V}_1}^{\bar{V}_2}\left(\frac{1}{\bar{V}} + \frac{B}{\bar{V}^2}\right)d\bar{V}$$

$$= -RT\left[\ln\frac{\bar{V}_2}{\bar{V}_1} - B\left(\frac{1}{\bar{V}_2} - \frac{1}{\bar{V}_1}\right)\right]$$

We can also evaluate ΔG by

$$\Delta G = \Delta A + \Delta(PV) = -RT\ln\left(\frac{\bar{V}_2}{\bar{V}_1}\right) + RTB\left(\frac{1}{\bar{V}_2} - \frac{1}{\bar{V}_1}\right)$$

$$+ RTB\left(\frac{1}{\bar{V}_2} - \frac{1}{\bar{V}_1}\right)$$

$$= -RT\ln\left(\frac{\bar{V}_2}{\bar{V}_1}\right) + 2RTB\left(\frac{1}{\bar{V}_2} - \frac{1}{\bar{V}_1}\right)$$

3-II-20.

$$\left(\frac{\partial T}{\partial \bar{V}}\right)_E = -\frac{(\partial \bar{E}/\partial \bar{V})_T}{(\partial \bar{E}/\partial T)_{\bar{V}}}$$

$$\left(\frac{\partial \bar{E}}{\partial \bar{V}}\right)_T = T\left(\frac{\partial P}{\partial T}\right)_V - P$$

$$P = \frac{RT}{\bar{V} - b} - \frac{a}{\bar{V}^2}$$

$$\left(\frac{\partial \bar{E}}{\partial \bar{V}}\right)_T = \frac{a}{\bar{V}^2}$$

$$\left(\frac{\partial T}{\partial \bar{V}}\right)_E = -\frac{a}{\bar{C}_V \bar{V}^2}$$

3-II-21. (a) $\left(\frac{\partial \bar{V}}{\partial T}\right)_S = -\frac{(\partial \bar{S}/\partial T)_V}{(\partial \bar{S}/\partial \bar{V})_T} = -\frac{\bar{C}_V}{T(\partial P/\partial T)_V}$

$$P = \frac{RT}{\bar{V} - b} - \frac{a}{\bar{V}^2}$$

$$\left(\frac{\partial P}{\partial T}\right)_V = \frac{R}{\bar{V} - b}$$

$$\left(\frac{\partial \bar{V}}{\partial T}\right)_S = -\frac{\bar{C}_V(\bar{V} - b)}{RT}$$

(b) S is constant in this process. Then

$$d\bar{V} = \left(\frac{\partial \bar{V}}{\partial T}\right)_S dT$$

$$\frac{d\bar{V}}{\bar{V} - b} = -\frac{\bar{C}_V \, dT}{RT}$$

$$\ln\left(\frac{\bar{V}_2 - b}{\bar{V}_1 - b}\right) = -\frac{\bar{C}_V}{R}\ln\left(\frac{T_2}{T_1}\right)$$

3-II-22. $\left(\frac{\partial E}{\partial V}\right)_T = T\left(\frac{\partial P}{\partial T}\right)_V - P$

$$\left(\frac{\partial P}{\partial T}\right)_V = \exp(-a/RT\bar{V})\left[\frac{R}{\bar{V} - b} + \left(\frac{RT}{\bar{V} - b}\right)\left(\frac{a}{RT^2\bar{V}}\right)\right]$$

$$= \frac{R\exp(-a/RT\bar{V})}{\bar{V} - b}\left(1 + \frac{a}{RT\bar{V}}\right)$$

$$\left(\frac{\partial E}{\partial V}\right)_T = \frac{a\exp(-a/RT\bar{V})}{(\bar{V} - b)\bar{V}}$$

3-II-23.

$$\Delta G = \int_{P_1}^{P_2} \bar{V}\, dP = \int_{P_1}^{P_2} \frac{RT\, dP}{P} + \int_{P_1}^{P_2} \frac{9R}{128}\left(\frac{T_c}{P_c}\right)\left[1 - 6\left(\frac{T_c}{T}\right)^2\right] dP$$

$$= RT \ln\left(\frac{P_2}{P_1}\right) + \frac{9R}{128}\left(\frac{T_c}{P_c}\right)\left[1 - 6\left(\frac{T_c}{T}\right)^2\right](P_2 - P_1)$$

3-II-24. (a) $\left(\dfrac{\partial S}{\partial V}\right)_T = \left(\dfrac{\partial P}{\partial T}\right)_V = \dfrac{R}{\bar{V} - b} + \dfrac{a}{T^2\bar{V}^2}$

(b) $\left(\dfrac{\partial E}{\partial V}\right)_T = T\left(\dfrac{\partial P}{\partial T}\right)_V - P$

$$= \frac{RT}{\bar{V} - b} + \frac{a}{T\bar{V}^2} - \frac{RT}{\bar{V} - b} + \frac{a}{T\bar{V}^2} = \frac{2a}{T\bar{V}^2}$$

(c) $\left(\dfrac{\partial C_V}{\partial V}\right)_T = \dfrac{\partial^2 E}{\partial T\, \partial V} = -\dfrac{2a}{T^2\bar{V}^2}$

(d) $\left(\dfrac{\partial \bar{V}}{\partial T}\right)_S = -\dfrac{(\partial \bar{S}/\partial T)_V}{(\partial \bar{S}/\partial \bar{V})_T} = -\dfrac{\bar{C}_V}{T}\left[\dfrac{R}{\bar{V} - b} + \dfrac{a}{T^2\bar{V}^2}\right]^{-1}$

(e) $\left(\dfrac{\partial \bar{V}}{\partial T}\right)_P = -\dfrac{(\partial P/\partial T)_V}{(\partial P/\partial \bar{V})_T} = \dfrac{-R/(\bar{V} - b) - a/T^2\bar{V}^2}{-RT/(\bar{V} - b)^2 + 2a/T\bar{V}^3}$

(f) $\bar{C}_P - \bar{C}_V = T\left(\dfrac{\partial P}{\partial T}\right)_V\left(\dfrac{\partial \bar{V}}{\partial T}\right)_P$

$$= \frac{-T[R/(\bar{V} - b) + a/T^2\bar{V}^2]^2}{-RT/(\bar{V} - b)^2 + 2a/T\bar{V}^3}$$

(g) In a reversible adiabatic process S is constant.

$$\frac{d\bar{V}}{dT} = \left(\frac{\partial \bar{V}}{\partial T}\right)_S = -\frac{\bar{C}_V}{T}\left[\frac{R}{\bar{V} - b} + \frac{a}{T^2\bar{V}^2}\right]^{-1}$$

Here $a = 0$ and $\bar{C}_V$ is constant.

$$\frac{d\bar{V}}{dT} = \frac{-\bar{C}_V(\bar{V} - b)}{RT}$$

$$\frac{R\, d\bar{V}}{\bar{V} - b} = -\frac{\bar{C}_V\, dT}{T}$$

$$R \ln\frac{\bar{V}_2 - b}{\bar{V}_1 - b} = -\bar{C}_V \ln\frac{T_2}{T_1}$$

3-II-25.

(a) $\quad \varDelta G = \int_{P_1}^{P_2} \bar{V}\, dP = RT \ln \dfrac{P_2}{P_1} = 1.987 \times 273.2 \times 2.303 \log \dfrac{60}{3}$

$\qquad = 1628$ cal

(b) $\quad \varDelta G = RT \ln \dfrac{f_2}{f_1} = 1.987 \times 2.303 \times 273.2 \log \left(\dfrac{60 \times 0.6961}{3 \times 0.9847} \right)$

$\qquad = 1440$ cal

3-II-26.

$$d \ln \gamma = \frac{\alpha}{RT}\, dP; \quad \alpha = \bar{V} - \frac{RT}{P};$$

$$\bar{V} = \frac{RT}{P} + aP^{-1/2} + b + cP^{1/2}$$

$$\alpha = \frac{RT}{P} + aP^{-1/2} + b + cP^{1/2} - \frac{RT}{P}$$

$$\ln \gamma = \int_{0}^{\ln\gamma} d \ln \gamma = \frac{1}{RT} \int_{0}^{P} (aP^{-1/2} + b + cP^{1/2})\, dP$$

$$\ln \gamma = \frac{1}{RT} \left(2\, aP^{1/2} + bP + \frac{2}{3} cP^{3/2} \right)$$

3-II-27.

$$\bar{V} = \frac{RT}{P}(1 + AP + BP^2)$$

$$\frac{\bar{V}}{RT} = \frac{1}{P} + A + BP$$

$$\ln \gamma = \int_{0}^{P} \left(\frac{\bar{V}}{RT} - \frac{1}{P} \right) dP = \int_{0}^{P} (A + BP)\, dP = AP + \frac{1}{2} BP^2$$

$$\gamma = \exp \left(AP + \frac{1}{2} BP^2 \right)$$

3-II-28.

$$\bar{V}_{\text{ideal}} = \frac{RT}{P} = \frac{0.0821 \times 258}{10.31} = 0.2056$$

$$\alpha = \bar{V}_{\text{observed}} - \bar{V}_{\text{ideal}} = 1.857 - 2.056 = -0.199 \text{ liter}$$

$$\ln \gamma = \frac{1}{RT} \int_{0}^{P} \alpha\, dP$$

If we assume that α is independent of pressure between 0 and 10.3 atm,

$$\log \gamma = \frac{1}{2.303 \times 0.0821 \times 258} \times (-0.199)(10.3084 - 0)$$

$$= -0.0420$$

$$\gamma = 0.908$$

3-II-29.

(a) $\qquad V = RT\left[\frac{n_x + n_y}{P} + \beta(n_x + n_y) + \alpha(n_x n_y)^{1/2}\right]$

$$\bar{V}_x = \left(\frac{\partial V}{\partial n_x}\right)_{n_y, P, T} = RT\left[\frac{1}{P} + \beta + \frac{1}{2}\alpha\left(\frac{n_y}{n_x}\right)^{1/2}\right]$$

(b) $\quad \Delta\bar{G}_x = \int_{P_1}^{P_2} \bar{V}_x \, dP$

$$= RT\left[\ln\frac{P_2}{P_1} + \left(\beta + \frac{1}{2}\alpha\left(\frac{n_y}{n_x}\right)^{1/2}\right)(P_2 - P_1)\right]$$

3-II-30.

$$\left(\frac{\partial E}{\partial V}\right)_T = T\left(\frac{\partial P}{\partial T}\right)_V - P = -T\frac{(\partial V/\partial T)_P}{(\partial V/\partial P)_T} - P$$

$$\left(\frac{\partial V}{\partial T}\right)_P = V_0(-6.427 \times 10^{-5} + 2 \times 8.5053 \times 10^{-6}t$$

$$- 3 \times 6.79 \times 10^{-8}t^2) = -4.746 \times 10^{-5}V_0$$

$$\left(\frac{\partial V}{\partial P}\right)_T = -5.25 \times 10^{-5}V_0$$

$$\left(\frac{\partial E}{\partial V}\right)_T = \frac{-274(-4.746 \times 10^{-5}V_0)}{-5.25 \times 10^{-5}V_0} - 1.00 \text{ atm}$$

$$= -249 \text{ atm}$$

Usually $(\partial E/\partial V)_T$ for a liquid or solid is large and positive, signifying that the energy decreases on compression. Here, however, the energy increases on compression because a decrease in volume can occur only at the expense of some of the hydrogen bonds, which impose a rather open structure on water.

SECTION 3-III

3-III-1.   No. The motion is not perpetual, but the retarding forces are so small in comparison with the momentum of the earth that it would take eons before any appreciable slowing down would occur. (The rate of slowing is 1.6×10^{-10} parts per yr.) If the retarding forces were zero, the motion would be perpetual, but there is nothing wrong with perpetual motion as long as the system is not called on to do any work.

3-III-2.   No. There is nothing wrong with perpetual motion of the first kind as long as the moving object is not called on to do any work (against friction, for example). The moving molecules often lose energy by collision but they gain just as much by other collisions. Friction does not destroy energy but merely randomizes it. In the gas the motion is already as random as it can be. As for perpetual motion of the second kind (violating the second law), it would occur only if the random motion of the molecules (heat) were to be converted into orderly motion (work) with no other process occurring.

3-III-3.   (a) The process is irreversible. Restoration by the same path would mean that the gas would have to flow through the porous plug from the lower to the higher pressure—a manifest impossibility. The gas can be restored to its initial state but only by a different process involving different amounts of work and heat.

(b) $dH = T \, dS + V \, dP = 0$

$$\left(\frac{\partial S}{\partial P} \right)_H = -\frac{V}{T}$$

3-III-4.   The process is irreversible because (a) the process cannot be reversed along the same path—heat will not flow along the wire from a cold to a hot body, or (b) ΔS for the universe is positive for the process described, no less so because of its slowness. A reversible process is infinitely slow, but an infinitely slow process is not necessarily reversible.

3-III-5.   No. The entropy of an *isolated* system must increase in every process. If H_2 and O_2 react in an isolated system, the product will be steam at a very high temperature; its entropy will be greater than that of the starting materials. ΔS calculated from the tables of third-law entropies refers to a process in which the product is restored to the initial temperature of the reactants. This process is indeed impossible in an isolated system.

3-III-6. The incorrect assumption is that the entropy of the *system* (that is, the water) must increase for a spontaneous change. The correct criterion for spontaneity is that the entropy of the *universe* (system plus surroundings) must increase for the process. To consider the surroundings let us imagine that the freezing of the supercooled water takes place in an oil bath so large that the temperature of the bath is not significantly affected by the process. Then the entropy change for the bath (that is, the surroundings) would be $\Delta S = q_{\text{rev}}/T$. ΔH at $-5°C$ can be calculated by the Kirchhoff law to be 1376 cal mole^{-1}, so that $\Delta S_{\text{bath}} = 1376/268 = 5.14$ cal $°K^{-1}$ mole^{-1}. Therefore the entropy change for the universe is $-5.04 + 5.14 = +0.10$ cal $°K^{-1}$ mole^{-1}, and we see that the process is indeed accompanied by an increase in entropy.

3-III-7. (a) The statement $dG = -S\,dT + V\,dP$ is true for a closed system with a single pressure throughout when no work is done other than pressure-volume work. In general

$$dG = -S\,dT + \underset{\substack{i \\ \text{(regions)}}}{\sum} V_i\,dP_i + \underset{\substack{j \\ \text{(components)}}}{\sum} \mu_j\,dn_j + \underset{\substack{k \\ \text{(degrees of freedom)}}}{\sum} F_k\,dx_k$$

The second term on the right provides for the possibility of different pressures in different regions. It is based on the generalized definition $G = A + \sum_i P_i V_i$. The third term accounts for the addition and removal of components (an open system). In the fourth term x_k is a generalized coordinate and F_k is the corresponding generalized force. Examples:

x	F
electric charge	potential
surface area	surface tension

(b) In general for an isothermal process $\Delta S = (\Delta H - \Delta G)/T$. If the freezing occurs at the melting point, $\Delta G = 0$ and $\Delta S = \Delta H/T$. When a supercooled liquid freezes, $\Delta G < 0$, and $\Delta S > \Delta H/T$.

(c) In general

$$\mu_{i\alpha} = \mu_{i\beta} \quad \text{at equilibrium}$$
$$\mu_{i\alpha}^{\circ} + RT \ln a_{i\alpha} = \mu_{i\beta}^{\circ} + RT \ln a_{i\beta}$$

If $\mu_{i\alpha}^{\circ} = \mu_{i\beta}^{\circ}$, then $a_{i\alpha} = a_{i\beta}$. Usually, however, $\mu_{i\alpha}^{\circ} \neq \mu_{i\beta}^{\circ}$. For example, if i is H_2O, α is ice, and β is an aqueous solution of NaCl, then $\mu_{i\alpha} = \mu_{i\alpha}^{\circ}$ and $a_i = 1$, while $\mu_{i\beta} < \mu_{i\beta}^{\circ}$ ($\mu_{i\beta}^{\circ}$ is the chemical potential of pure *liquid* H_2O at the same temperature) and $a_{i\beta} < 1$. However, if the two phases are aqueous solutions (as in an osmotic pressure experiment), then $\mu_{i\alpha}^{\circ} = \mu_{i\beta}^{\circ}$ and $a_{i\alpha} = a_{i\beta}$ at equilibrium.

3-III-8. It is not true, in general, that $\Delta S = q/T$. This is true only for a reversible, isothermal process. In general $\Delta S = \int dq_{rev}/T$. If the gas is expanded reversibly to the same final state, $\Delta S = \int dq_{rev}/T > 0$. This reversible expansion cannot be adiabatic; if it were, the final state would not be the same as in the irreversible adiabatic expansion. The gas would finish by being too cold because it would have done more work than in the irreversible expansion.

3-III-9. For any isothermal process $\Delta S = q_{rev}/T$, where q_{rev} is the heat absorbed when the system is taken from the initial state to the final state by a reversible path. We must ask then whether $q = q_{rev}$ for the process described here. Certainly $\Delta E = \Delta E_{rev}$, and $q = \Delta E + w$. The question thus becomes does $w = w_{rev}$? In the present case we are justified in assuming that $w = w_{rev}$; for a melting process there is practically no work in any case and $w_{rev} - w$ would be even more negligible than w. The only difference would result from expansion (or contraction) so rapid that the atmosphere could not keep up with it—a thoroughly insignificant effect.

3-III-10. Place the system in an insulated thermostat at the temperature T and constant pressure. The system, s, and thermostat, t, together comprise an isolated system; therefore,

$$\Delta S_s + \Delta S_t = \Delta S_{universe} > 0.$$

Now the only interaction of the thermostat with its surroundings (the system) is the absorption and emission of heat. The thermostat reaches the same final state whether a given amount of heat is absorbed reversibly or not and, at constant pressure, $q_t = \Delta H_t$. Therefore

$$\Delta S_t = \frac{q_{t,\text{rev}}}{T} = \frac{q_t}{T} = \frac{\Delta H_t}{T}.$$

But $q_s = -q_t$ and $\Delta H_s = q_s = -\Delta H_t$. Then

$$\Delta S_s + \Delta S_t = \Delta S_s + \frac{\Delta H_t}{T} = \Delta S_s - \frac{\Delta H_s}{T}$$

$$= \frac{-\Delta G_s}{T} > 0, \quad \text{or} \quad \Delta G_s < 0$$

The function G is defined precisely for the purpose of making it unnecessary to consider the surroundings explicitly for this special type of process at constant T and P.

3-III-11. Both dq and $T dS$ are inexact differentials (though dS is exact); the dX thus defined would also be inexact. (It is possible for the sum or difference of two inexact differentials to be an exact differential but this is exceptional: $dE = dq - dw$ is an example.) In other words we would not have defined a function X determined by the state of the system. The change in X would depend on the path by which the new state was reached from the old state. On the other hand the general definitions of A and G are such that their differentials are exact:

$$A = E - TS$$
$$dA = dE - T dS - S dT$$
$$\quad = dq - dw - T dS - S dT$$

If V is constant and there is no work other than pressure-volume work, $dw = 0$; if T is constant, $S dT = 0$. Then $dA_{V,T} = dq - T dS$ and this difference of inexact differentials is exact when the paths are thus restricted. Similarly

$$dG = dA + P dV + V dP$$
$$\quad = dq - (dw - P dV) + V dP - T dS - S dT$$
$$dG_{P,T} = dq - T dS$$

when P and T are constant and $dw = P dV$.

3-III-12. (a) $\Delta S = q/T$ (1) if (i) the process is reversible. $\Delta H = q$ (2) if (ii) pressure is constant and (iii) the only work done is pressure-volume work : $w = \int_{V_1}^{V_2} P \, dV$. (No electrical work).

There is nothing wrong with (3). Therefore the conclusion (4) follows if conditions (i) — (iii) are all satisfied. The only common process that satisfies these conditions is a phase transition (freezing, vaporization, etc.) under equilibrium conditions: freezing at the freezing point, for example, not freezing of a supercooled liquid.

(b) Let q' be the heat absorbed when the process occurs in such a way that $w = P \Delta V$ (P constant, no electrical work). Then $q' = \Delta H$. Let q'' be the heat absorbed when the process occurs reversibly. Then $q'' = T \Delta S$.

$$\Delta G = \Delta H - T \Delta S = q' - q''$$

3-III-13.
$$dE = T \, dS - P \, dV$$

$$\left(\frac{\partial E}{\partial S}\right)_P = T - P \left(\frac{\partial V}{\partial S}\right)_P$$

$$dH = dE + V \, dP + P \, dV = T \, dS + V \, dP$$

Therefore $(\partial V/\partial S)_P = (\partial T/\partial P)_S$ (Euler's relation). Then

$$\left(\frac{\partial E}{\partial S}\right)_P = T - P \left(\frac{\partial T}{\partial P}\right)_S$$

3-III-14. Let

$$X = T \left(\frac{\partial S}{\partial E}\right)_H, \qquad Y = T \left(\frac{\partial S}{\partial H}\right)_E$$

Then

$$T \, dS = X \, dE + Y \, dH \tag{1}$$
$$= dE + P \, dV \tag{2}$$

Now

$$dE = \left(\frac{\partial E}{\partial P}\right)_T dP + \left(\frac{\partial E}{\partial T}\right)_P dT$$

$$dH = \left(\frac{\partial H}{\partial P}\right)_T dP + C_P \, dT$$

$$dV = \left(\frac{\partial V}{\partial P}\right)_T dP + \left(\frac{\partial V}{\partial T}\right)_P dT = V(-\beta \, dP + \alpha \, dT)$$

Thus

$$
T\,dS = X\left(\frac{\partial E}{\partial P}\right)_T dP + X\left(\frac{\partial E}{\partial T}\right)_P dT
$$

$$
+ Y\left(\frac{\partial H}{\partial P}\right)_T dP + YC_P\,dT \tag{1'}
$$

$$
= \left(\frac{\partial E}{\partial P}\right)_T dP + \left(\frac{\partial E}{\partial T}\right)_P dT - PV\beta\,dP + PV\alpha\,dT \tag{2'}
$$

Equating coefficients of dP and dT

$$
X\left(\frac{\partial E}{\partial P}\right)_T + Y\left(\frac{\partial H}{\partial P}\right)_T = \left(\frac{\partial E}{\partial P}\right)_T - PV\beta
$$

$$
X\left(\frac{\partial E}{\partial T}\right)_P + YC_P = \left(\frac{\partial E}{\partial T}\right)_P + PV\alpha
$$

Solving,

$$
X = \frac{\left[\left(\frac{\partial E}{\partial P}\right)_T - PV\beta\right] C_P - \left[\left(\frac{\partial E}{\partial T}\right)_P + PV\alpha\right]\left(\frac{\partial H}{\partial P}\right)_T}{\left(\frac{\partial E}{\partial P}\right)_T C_P - \left(\frac{\partial H}{\partial P}\right)_P \left(\frac{\partial E}{\partial T}\right)_P}
$$

Now,

$$
\left(\frac{\partial H}{\partial P}\right)_T = V - T\left(\frac{\partial V}{\partial T}\right)_P = V(1 - T\alpha)
$$

$$
\left(\frac{\partial E}{\partial P}\right)_T = \left(\frac{\partial H}{\partial P}\right)_T - P\left(\frac{\partial V}{\partial P}\right)_T - V = V(1 - T\alpha) + PV\beta - V
$$
$$
= V(P\beta - T\alpha)
$$

$$
\left(\frac{\partial E}{\partial T}\right)_P = C_P - P\left(\frac{\partial V}{\partial T}\right)_P = C_P - PV\alpha
$$

Thus

$$
X = \frac{\{[V(P\beta - T\alpha) - PV\beta] C_P - (C_P - PV\alpha + PV\alpha) V(1 - T\alpha)\}}{V(P\beta - T\alpha) C_P - V(1 - T\alpha)(C_P - PV\alpha)}
$$

$$
= \frac{-C_P}{C_P(P\beta - 1) + PV\alpha(1 - T\alpha)}
$$

$$
\left(\frac{\partial S}{\partial E}\right)_H = \frac{-C_P}{T[C_P(P\beta - 1) + PV\alpha(1 - T\alpha)]}
$$

3-III-15. (a) $\qquad dH = T\,dS + V\,dP$

$$
\left(\frac{\partial S}{\partial P}\right)_H = -\frac{V}{T}
$$

(b) Method (i)

$$dS = \left(\frac{\partial S}{\partial P}\right)_T dP + \left(\frac{\partial S}{\partial T}\right)_P dT$$

$$\left(\frac{\partial S}{\partial V}\right)_P = \left(\frac{\partial S}{\partial T}\right)_P \left(\frac{\partial T}{\partial V}\right)_P = \frac{C_P}{T} \cdot \frac{1}{V\alpha}$$

$$C_P = C_V + \frac{TV\alpha^2}{\beta} \text{ (a known equation)}$$

$$\left(\frac{\partial S}{\partial V}\right)_P = \frac{C_V}{TV\alpha} + \frac{\alpha}{\beta}$$

Method (ii)

$$dS = \left(\frac{\partial S}{\partial V}\right)_T dV + \left(\frac{\partial S}{\partial T}\right)_V dT$$

$$\left(\frac{\partial S}{\partial V}\right)_P = \left(\frac{\partial S}{\partial V}\right)_T + \left(\frac{\partial S}{\partial T}\right)_V \left(\frac{\partial T}{\partial V}\right)_P$$

$$= \left(\frac{\partial P}{\partial T}\right)_V + \frac{C_V}{T} \cdot \frac{1}{V\alpha}$$

$$\left(\frac{\partial P}{\partial T}\right)_V = -\frac{(\partial V/\partial T)_P}{(\partial V/\partial P)_T} = \frac{\alpha}{\beta}$$

$$\left(\frac{\partial S}{\partial V}\right)_P = \frac{\alpha}{\beta} + \frac{C_V}{TV\alpha}$$

3-III-16. (a) $\qquad dV = \left(\frac{\partial V}{\partial P}\right)_T dP + \left(\frac{\partial V}{\partial T}\right)_P dT$

$$\left(\frac{\partial V}{\partial S}\right)_P = \left(\frac{\partial V}{\partial T}\right)_P \left(\frac{\partial T}{\partial S}\right)_P = \frac{T}{C_P}\left(\frac{\partial V}{\partial T}\right)_P$$

(b) $\left(\frac{\partial V}{\partial H}\right)_P = \left(\frac{\partial V}{\partial T}\right)_P \left(\frac{\partial T}{\partial H}\right)_P = \frac{1}{C_P}\left(\frac{\partial V}{\partial T}\right)_P$

$$\left(\frac{\partial T}{\partial P}\right)_H = -\frac{(\partial H/\partial P)_T}{(\partial H/\partial T)_P} = -\frac{1}{C_P}\left[V - T\left(\frac{\partial V}{\partial T}\right)_P\right]$$

$$= -\frac{V}{C_P} + \frac{T}{C_P}\left(\frac{\partial V}{\partial T}\right)_P$$

$$= -V\left(\frac{\partial T}{\partial H}\right)_P + T\left(\frac{\partial V}{\partial H}\right)_P$$

3-III-17. $\bar{C}_P - \bar{C}_V = T\left(\frac{\partial P}{\partial T}\right)_{\bar{V}}\left(\frac{\partial \bar{V}}{\partial T}\right)_P$

$$P = \frac{RT}{\bar{V} - AT + B}$$

$$\left(\frac{\partial P}{\partial T}\right)_{\bar{V}} = \frac{R}{\bar{V} - AT + B} + \frac{ART}{(\bar{V} - AT + B)^2}$$

$$= \frac{R\bar{V} - ART + RB + ART}{(\bar{V} - AT + B)^2} = \frac{R(\bar{V} + B)}{(\bar{V} - AT + B)^2}$$

$$\bar{V} = \frac{RT}{P} + AT - B$$

$$\left(\frac{\partial \bar{V}}{\partial T}\right)_P = \frac{R}{P} + A$$

$$\bar{C}_P - \bar{C}_V = \frac{RT(\bar{V} + B)(R/P + A)}{(\bar{V} - AT + B)^2}$$

$$= \frac{RT^2(R/P + A)^2}{(RT/P)^2} = \frac{P^2}{R}\left(\frac{R}{P} + A\right)^2$$

$$= R\left(1 + \frac{AP}{R}\right)^2$$

3-III-18. (a) The heat gained by 1 is equal to the heat lost by 2:

$$\bar{C}_V(T_3 - T_1) = \bar{C}_V(T_2 - T_3), \qquad T_3 = \tfrac{1}{2}(T_1 + T_2)$$

(b) The following process is one of several possibilities: Let gas 1 be compressed and gas 2 expanded, adiabatically and reversibly, so that each has the final temperature T_3. To find their volumes (V_1 and V_2) we use the equation $PV^\gamma =$ constant $= RTV^{\gamma-1}$, where $\gamma = \bar{C}_P/\bar{C}_V = (\bar{C}_V + R)/\bar{C}_V$.

For gas 1

$$T_1V^{\gamma-1} = T_3V_1^{\gamma-1}, \qquad \frac{V_1}{V} = \left(\frac{T_1}{T_3}\right)^{1/(\gamma-1)}$$

For gas 2

$$T_2V^{\gamma-1} = T_3V_2^{\gamma-1}, \qquad \frac{V_2}{V} = \left(\frac{T_2}{T_3}\right)^{1/(\gamma-1)}$$

We now expand gas 1 from V_1 to V and compress gas 2 from V_2 to V, isothermally and reversibly, keeping them in contact with a heat reservoir at the temperature T_3.

(c) In the adiabatic steps there are no entropy changes. In the isothermal steps we have

$$\Delta S_{\text{gas1}} = R \ln \frac{V}{V_1} = \frac{R}{\gamma - 1} \ln \frac{T_3}{T_1} = \bar{C}_V \ln \frac{T_3}{T_1}$$

$$\Delta S_{\text{gas2}} = R \ln \frac{V}{V_2} = \bar{C}_V \ln \frac{T_3}{T_2}$$

The heat emitted (or absorbed) by each gas is absorbed (or emitted) by the reservoir at the same temperature T_3:

$$\Delta S_{\text{surroundings}} = -(\Delta S_{\text{gas1}} + \Delta S_{\text{gas2}}) = \bar{C}_V \ln \frac{T_1 T_2}{T_3^2}$$

$$= \bar{C}_V \ln \frac{4 T_1 T_2}{(T_1 + T_2)^2}$$

$$\Delta S_{\text{universe}} = 0$$

(d) In process A there is no change in the state of the surroundings: $\Delta S_{\text{surroundings}} = 0$. For the gases the entropy changes are the same as in process B, since the initial and final states are the same. Then

$$\Delta S_{\text{universe}} = \Delta S_{\text{gas1}} + \Delta S_{\text{gas2}} = \bar{C}_V \ln \left[\frac{(T_1 + T_2)^2}{4 T_1 T_2} \right]$$

It is an interesting mathematical exercise to show that this quantity is always positive when $T_1 \neq T_2$.

3-III-19. (a)
$$P = \frac{nRT}{V} - \frac{n^2 \beta R}{V^2}$$

$$PV = nRT - \frac{n^2 \beta R}{V}$$

$$\left(\frac{\partial S}{\partial V} \right)_T = \left(\frac{\partial P}{\partial T} \right)_V = \frac{nR}{V} = \frac{R}{V} \quad \text{(for } n = 1 \text{ mole)}$$

$$\left(\frac{\partial E}{\partial V} \right)_T = T \left(\frac{\partial P}{\partial T} \right)_V - P = \frac{\beta R}{V^2}$$

$$\left(\frac{\partial H}{\partial V} \right)_T = \left(\frac{\partial E}{\partial V} \right)_T + \left(\frac{\partial (PV)}{\partial V} \right)_T = \frac{2 \beta R}{V^2}$$

(b) The gas is placed in a cylinder of volume V with a frictionless, leakproof piston; the cylinder is placed in the same thermostat as in process A; and the gas is expanded infinitely slowly from volume V to volume $2V$.

(c) $\Delta E = \int_V^{2V} \left(\frac{\partial E}{\partial V} \right)_T dV = \int_V^{2V} \frac{\beta R}{V^2} dV$

$$= \beta R \left(\frac{1}{V} - \frac{1}{2V} \right) = \frac{\beta R}{2V}$$

$$\Delta S = \int_V^{2V} \left(\frac{\partial S}{\partial V} \right)_T dV = \int_V^{2V} \frac{R}{V} dV = R \ln 2$$

Process A				
	q	w	ΔE	ΔS
(i) Gas	$\dfrac{\beta R}{2V}$	0	$\dfrac{\beta R}{2V}$	$R \ln 2$
(ii) Surroundings	$-\dfrac{\beta R}{2V}$	0	$-\dfrac{\beta R}{2V}$	$-\dfrac{\beta R}{2VT}$
(iii) Universe	0	0	0	$R\left(\ln 2 - \dfrac{\beta}{2VT}\right)$

Process B				
	q	w	ΔE	ΔS
(i) Gas	$RT \ln 2$	$RT \ln 2 - \dfrac{\beta R}{2V}$	$\dfrac{\beta R}{2V}$	$R \ln 2$
(ii) Surroundings	$-RT \ln 2$	$-RT \ln 2 + \dfrac{\beta R}{2V}$	$-\dfrac{\beta R}{2V}$	$-R \ln 2$
(iii) Universe	0	0	0	0

3-III-20.

$$\bar{V} = \frac{RT}{P + aP^2} + b = RT\left(\frac{1}{P} - \frac{a}{1 + aP}\right) + b$$

$$d\bar{G} = \bar{V}\,dP$$

$$\bar{G} = \int \bar{V}\,dP = RT \int \left(\frac{1}{P} - \frac{a}{1 + aP}\right) dP + b \int dP$$
$$= RT[\ln P - \ln(1 + aP)] + bP + C$$

$$\bar{G}^\circ = \lim_{P \to 0} (\bar{G} - RT \ln P) = \lim_{P \to 0} [-RT \ln(1 + aP) + bP + C]$$
$$= C \text{ (constant of integration)}$$
$$\bar{G} - \bar{G}^\circ = \bar{G} - C = RT[\ln P - \ln(1 + aP)] + bP$$
$$\bar{S} - \bar{S}^\circ = -\left(\frac{\partial(\bar{G} - \bar{G}^\circ)}{\partial T}\right)_P = -R[\ln P - \ln(1 + aP)]$$
$$\bar{H} - \bar{H}^\circ = \bar{G} - \bar{G}^\circ + T(\bar{S} - \bar{S}^\circ) = bP$$

3-III-21. van der Waals' equation may be written in the three forms

$$\left(P + \frac{n^2 a}{V^2}\right)(V - nb) = nRT \tag{1}$$

$$P = \frac{nRT}{V - nb} - \frac{n^2a}{V^2} \tag{2}$$

$$PV = \frac{nRT}{(1 - nb/V)} - \frac{n^2a}{V}$$

(a) $\left(\dfrac{\partial S}{\partial V}\right)_T = \left(\dfrac{\partial P}{\partial T}\right)_V = \dfrac{nR}{V - nb}$

$\left(\dfrac{\partial S}{\partial P}\right)_T = -\left(\dfrac{\partial V}{\partial T}\right)_P$

Differentiating (1) implicitly,

$$\left(P + \frac{n^2a}{V^2}\right)\left(\frac{\partial V}{\partial T}\right)_P - \frac{2n^2a}{V^3}\left(\frac{\partial V}{\partial T}\right)_P (V - nb) = nR$$

$$\left(\frac{\partial S}{\partial P}\right)_T = -\left(\frac{\partial V}{\partial T}\right)_P = \frac{nR}{(2n^2a/V^3)(V - nb) - (P + n^2a/V^2)}$$

$$= \frac{nR}{(2n^2a/V^3)(V - nb) - nRT/(V - nb)}$$

$$= \frac{V - nb}{(2na/RV^3)(V - nb)^2 - T}$$

$$\left(\frac{\partial E}{\partial V}\right)_T = T\left(\frac{\partial S}{\partial V}\right)_T - P = \frac{n^2a}{V^2}$$

$$\left(\frac{\partial H}{\partial P}\right)_T = T\left(\frac{\partial S}{\partial P}\right)_T + V = \frac{V - nb}{(2na/RTV^3)(V - nb)^2 - 1} + V$$

$$\left(\frac{\partial E}{\partial P}\right)_T = \left(\frac{\partial H}{\partial P}\right)_T - V - P\left(\frac{\partial V}{\partial P}\right)_T$$

Differentiating (1) implicitly

$$\left(1 - \frac{2n^2a}{V^3}\left(\frac{\partial V}{\partial P}\right)_T\right)(V - nb) + \left(P + \frac{n^2a}{V^2}\right)\left(\frac{\partial V}{\partial P}\right)_T = 0$$

$$\left(\frac{\partial V}{\partial P}\right)_T = \frac{V - nb}{(2n^2a/V^3)(V - nb) - nRT/(V - nb)}$$

$$= \frac{(V - nb)^2}{nRT[(2na/RTV^3)(V - nb)^2 - 1]}$$

$$P\left(\frac{\partial V}{\partial P}\right)_T = \frac{V - nb}{(2na/RTV^3)(V - nb)^2 - 1}$$

$$- \frac{na(V - nb)^2}{V^2RT[(2na/RTV^3)(V - nb)^2 - 1]}$$

Therefore

$$\left(\frac{\partial E}{\partial P}\right)_T = \frac{(V - nb)^2}{(2/V)(V - nb)^2 - V^2 RT/na}$$

(b) $\quad \Delta E = \int_{V_1}^{V_2} \frac{n^2 a}{V^2} \, dV = -n^2 a \left(\frac{1}{V_2} - \frac{1}{V_1}\right)$

$$\Delta H = \Delta E + \Delta(PV)$$

$$\Delta(PV) = nRT \left(\frac{1}{1 - nb/V_2} - \frac{1}{1 - nb/V_1}\right) - n^2 a \left(\frac{1}{V_2} - \frac{1}{V_1}\right)$$

$$\Delta H = 2n^2 a \left(\frac{1}{V_1} - \frac{1}{V_2}\right) + nRT \left(\frac{1}{1 - nb/V_2} - \frac{1}{1 - nb/V_1}\right)$$

$$\Delta A = -\int_{V_1}^{V_2} P \, dV = -nRT \ln \left(\frac{V_2 - nb}{V_1 - nb}\right)$$

$$- n^2 a \left(\frac{1}{V_2} - \frac{1}{V_1}\right)$$

$$\Delta G = \Delta A + \Delta(PV) = -nRT \ln \left(\frac{V_2 - nb}{V_1 - nb}\right)$$

$$- 2n^2 a \left(\frac{1}{V_2} - \frac{1}{V_1}\right)$$

$$+ nRT \left(\frac{1}{1 - nb/V_2} - \frac{1}{1 - nb/V_1}\right)$$

$$\Delta S = \int_{V_1}^{V_2} \left(\frac{\partial S}{\partial V}\right)_T dV = nR \ln \frac{V_2 - nb}{V_1 - nb}$$

(c) We may write the free energy per mole as

$$\bar{G} = \frac{G}{n} = -RT \ln \left(\frac{V}{n} - b\right) - \frac{2na}{V} + \frac{RT}{(1 - nb/V)} + K$$

where K is an unknown constant. In order that only intensive quantities shall appear, we have rewritten $(V_2 - nb)/(V_1 - nb)$ as

$$\frac{V_2/n - b}{V_1/n - b}$$

The standard free energy per mole is defined as

$$\bar{G}^\circ = \lim_{V/n \to \infty} \left(\frac{G}{n} - RT \ln P\right)$$

$$= \lim_{V/n \to \infty} \left(\frac{G}{n} - RT \ln \frac{nRT}{V}\right)$$

$$= \lim_{V/n \to \infty} \left(\frac{G}{n} + RT \ln \frac{V}{n}\right) - RT \ln RT$$

since $P = nRT/V$ in the limit of low pressures. But

$$\frac{G}{n} + RT \ln \frac{V}{n} = -RT \ln \left[\frac{V/n - b}{V/n} \right] - \frac{2na}{V} + \frac{RT}{1 - nb/V} + K$$

and

$$\lim_{V/n \to \infty} \left(\frac{G}{n} + RT \ln \frac{V}{n} \right) = RT + K = \bar{G}^\circ + RT \ln RT$$

Then $K = \bar{G}^\circ + RT(\ln RT - 1)$ and we have found K in terms of the more conventional constant of integration $\bar{G}^\circ$. Thus

$$\frac{G}{n} = \bar{G}^\circ - RT \ln \left(\frac{V}{n} - b \right) - \frac{2na}{V} + \frac{RT}{1 - nb/V} - RT(1 - \ln RT)$$

The fugacity f is defined by $\bar{G} = G/n = \bar{G}^\circ + RT \ln f$, or $f = \exp(\bar{G} - \bar{G}^\circ)/RT$, or

$$f = \frac{RT}{V/n - b} \exp \left(\frac{1}{1 - nb/V} - 1 - \frac{2na}{VRT} \right)$$

$$\gamma = \frac{f}{P} = \frac{[nRT/(V - nb)] \exp[1/(1 - nb/V) - 1 - 2na/VRT]}{nRT/(V - nb) - n^2a/V^2}$$

$$= \frac{\exp[1/(1 - nb/V) - 1 - 2na/VRT]}{1 - [na(V - nb)]/V^2RT}$$

Observe that $\lim_{V/n \to \infty} \gamma = 1$ as it must be. V and T are more convenient variables than P and T in working with van der Waals' equation because P can easily be expressed in terms of T and V, but not V in terms of P and T.

3-III-22. $q = 0, \qquad w = 0, \qquad \Delta E = 0$

$$P = \frac{nRT}{V - nb} - \frac{n^2a}{V^2}$$

$$\left(\frac{\partial S}{\partial V} \right)_T = \frac{nR}{V - nb}$$

$$\left(\frac{\partial E}{\partial V} \right)_T = \frac{n^2a}{V^2}$$

$$C_V = -\frac{3}{2} nR$$

$$\left(\frac{\partial T}{\partial V} \right)_E = -\frac{(\partial E/\partial V)_T}{(\partial E/\partial T)_V} = -\frac{n^2a}{(V^2 \cdot (3/2) nR)} = -\frac{2na}{3RV^2}$$

$$\Delta T = \int_V^{2V} \left(\frac{\partial T}{\partial V} \right)_E dV = -\frac{2na}{3R} \int_V^{2V} \frac{dV}{V^2} = -\frac{na}{3RV}$$

For ΔS we replace the expansion by two steps leading to the same final state:

Isothermal expansion:

$$\Delta S_1 = \int_V^{2V} \left(\frac{\partial S}{\partial V}\right)_T dV = nR \ln \frac{2V - nb}{V - nb}$$

Isochoric cooling:

$$\Delta S_2 = \int_{T_0}^{T_0 + \Delta T} \frac{C_V \, dT}{T} = \frac{3}{2} nR \int_{T_0}^{T_0 + \Delta T} \frac{dT}{T} = \frac{3}{2} nR \ln \left(1 + \frac{\Delta T}{T_0}\right)$$

$$= \frac{3}{2} nR \ln \left(1 - \frac{na}{3RVT_0}\right)$$

$$\Delta S = \Delta S_1 + \Delta S_2 = nR \left[\ln \frac{2V - nb}{V - nb} + \frac{3}{2} \ln \left(1 - \frac{na}{3RVT_0}\right)\right]$$

3-III-23. We first note that

$$\left(\frac{\partial \bar{E}}{\partial \bar{V}}\right)_T = T\left(\frac{\partial P}{\partial T}\right)_V - P = \frac{a}{\bar{V}^2}$$

(a) $\left(\frac{\partial \bar{C}_V}{\partial \bar{V}}\right)_T = \frac{\partial^2 E}{\partial \bar{V} \, \partial T} = \left(\frac{\partial}{\partial T} \frac{a}{\bar{V}^2}\right)_V = 0$

(b) $\left(\frac{\partial T}{\partial \bar{V}}\right)_E = -\frac{(\partial E/\partial V)_T}{(\partial E/\partial T)_V} = -\frac{a}{\bar{C}_V \bar{V}^2}$

(c) $\left(\frac{\partial T}{\partial \bar{V}}\right)_S = -\frac{(\partial \bar{S}/\partial \bar{V})_T}{(\partial \bar{S}/\partial T)_V} = -\frac{(\partial P/\partial T)_V}{\bar{C}_V/T} = -\frac{RT}{\bar{C}_V(\bar{V} - b)}$

Because this gas is monatomic, $\bar{C}_V = (3/2) R$ in the ideal limit of infinite volume; because of (a) we know that $\bar{C}_V$ is independent of volume. Therefore $\bar{C}_V = (3/2)R$ at all volumes.

(d) $w = 0$, $q = 0$; therefore, $\Delta E = 0$.

$$T_2 = T_1 + \int_{V_1}^{V_2} \left(\frac{\partial T}{\partial \bar{V}}\right)_E d\bar{V} = T_1 - \frac{a}{\bar{C}_V} \int_{V_1}^{V_2} \frac{d\bar{V}}{\bar{V}^2}$$

$$= T_1 + \frac{2a}{3R} \left(\frac{1}{V_2} - \frac{1}{V_1}\right)$$

(e) In an adiabatic reversible process $\Delta S = 0$.

$$dT = \left(\frac{\partial T}{\partial \bar{V}}\right)_S d\bar{V} = -\frac{RT}{\bar{C}_V(\bar{V} - b)} d\bar{V}$$

$$\frac{dT}{T} = -\frac{R}{\bar{C}_V} \frac{d\bar{V}}{\bar{V} - b}$$

$$\ln \frac{T_2}{T_1} = \frac{R}{\bar{C}_V} \ln \frac{V_1 - b}{V_2 - b} = \frac{2}{3} \ln \frac{V_1 - b}{V_2 - b}$$

or

$$T_2 = T_1 \left(\frac{V_1 - b}{V_2 - b}\right)^{2/3}$$

(f) (d) $T_2 = 300 + \dfrac{2 \times 10}{3 \times 0.08206} \left(\dfrac{1}{100} - \dfrac{1}{1.00}\right) = 219.5°\text{K}$

(e) $T_2 = 300 \left(\dfrac{1}{100}\right)^{2/3} = 3 \times 100^{1/3} = 13.9°\text{K}$

3-III-24.

(a) $\left(\dfrac{\partial H}{\partial P}\right)_T = V - T\left(\dfrac{\partial V}{\partial T}\right)_P = 0$

$\dfrac{T}{V}\left(\dfrac{\partial V}{\partial T}\right)_P = 1$

$\left(\dfrac{\partial \ln V}{\partial \ln T}\right)_P = 1$

$\ln V = \ln T + \ln f(P)$, where $f(P)$ is an arbitrary function of P.

$$V = Tf(P) \tag{1}$$

$\left(\dfrac{\partial E}{\partial V}\right)_T = T\left(\dfrac{\partial P}{\partial T}\right)_V - P = 0$

$\dfrac{T}{P}\left(\dfrac{\partial P}{\partial T}\right)_V = 0$

$\left(\dfrac{\partial \ln P}{\partial \ln T}\right)_V = 0$

$\ln P = \ln T + \ln g(V)$

$$P = Tg(V) \tag{2}$$

Comparing (1) and (2), we see that

$$T = \frac{V}{f(P)} = \frac{P}{g(V)}, \quad \text{or} \quad Pf(P) = Vg(V)$$

The left side depends only on P and the right side only on V; therefore both sides must be constant:

$$Pf(P) = Vg(V) = k; \quad f(P) = \frac{k}{P}, \quad g(V) = \frac{k}{V}$$

Thus

$$T = \frac{PV}{k} \quad \text{or} \quad PV = kT$$

(b) Equation (1) alone requires only that V be proportional to T; it leaves unspecified the dependence of V on P. Similarly equation (2) alone makes P proportional to T but fails to fix the dependence of P on V. Thus neither equation alone implies that the substance is an ideal gas. For example,

$$P = \frac{nRT}{V - nb}$$

is an instance of equation (2) but describes a nonideal gas.

3-III-25.

(a) $\left(\frac{\partial \bar{G}}{\partial P}\right)_T = \bar{V}$ $\bar{G} = \bar{G}^\circ - \frac{rT}{P}$

where $\bar{G}^\circ$ is a constant of integration.

(b) $\bar{G} = \int \bar{V}\, dP = \int \left(\bar{V} - \frac{rT}{P^2}\right) dP - \frac{rT}{P}$

$$= \int_0^P \left(\bar{V} - \frac{rT}{P^2}\right) dP + C - \frac{rT}{P}$$

where C is a constant of integration. The limits 0 and P are chosen to maintain the analogy with real gases.
Let

$$\bar{G}^\circ = \lim_{P \to 0} \left(\bar{G} + \frac{rT}{P}\right) = \lim_{P \to 0} \left[\int_0^P \left(\bar{V} - \frac{rT}{P^2}\right) dP + C\right] = C$$

Therefore

$$\bar{G} = \bar{G}^\circ - \frac{rT}{P} + \int_0^P \left(\bar{V} - \frac{rT}{P^2}\right) dP$$

The last term is a correction for "nonideality." Define f so that $\bar{G} = \bar{G}^\circ - rT/f$. Then

$$\frac{rT}{f} = \bar{G}^\circ - \bar{G} = \frac{rT}{P} - \int_0^P \left(\bar{V} - \frac{rT}{P^2}\right) dP$$

$$f = \frac{1}{1/P - \int_0^P (\bar{V}/rT - 1/P^2)\, dP}$$

$$\gamma = \frac{f}{P} = \frac{1}{1 - P \int_0^P (\bar{V}/rT - 1/P^2)\, dP}$$

$\lim_{P \to 0} \gamma = 1$ as required.

3-III-26.

$$\bar{I} = \frac{\bar{C}_1 \mathscr{H}}{T^2}$$

$$\left(\frac{\partial \bar{I}}{\partial T}\right)_{\mathscr{H},P} = -\frac{2\bar{C}_1 \mathscr{H}}{T^3}$$

$$\left(\frac{\partial^2 \bar{I}}{\partial T^2}\right)_{\mathscr{H},P} = \frac{6\bar{C}_1 \mathscr{H}}{T^4}$$

$$\bar{C}_{\mathscr{H}} = \bar{C}_0 + \int_0^{\mathscr{H}} T \left(\frac{\partial^2 \bar{I}}{\partial T^2}\right)_{\mathscr{H},P}$$

$$d\mathscr{H} = \bar{C}_0 + \frac{3\bar{C}_1 \mathscr{H}^2}{T^3}$$

$$d\bar{G} = -\bar{S}\,dT + \bar{V}\,dP - \bar{I}\,d\mathscr{H}$$

$$\left(\frac{\partial \bar{S}}{\partial \mathscr{H}}\right)_{T,P} = \left(\frac{\partial \bar{I}}{\partial T}\right)_{\mathscr{H},P}$$

by Euler's relation. Also

$$\left(\frac{\partial \bar{S}}{\partial T}\right)_{\mathscr{H},P} = \frac{\bar{C}_{\mathscr{H}}}{T}$$

Then

$$\left(\frac{\partial T}{\partial \mathscr{H}}\right)_{S,P} = \frac{-(\partial \bar{S}/\partial \mathscr{H})_{T,P}}{(\partial \bar{S}/\partial T)_{\mathscr{H},P}} = -\frac{T}{\bar{C}_{\mathscr{H}}}\left(\frac{\partial \bar{I}}{\partial T}\right)_{\mathscr{H},P}$$

$$= \frac{2\bar{C}_1 \mathscr{H}}{T^2(\bar{C}_0 + 3\bar{C}_1 \mathscr{H}^2/T^3)}$$

3-III-27. (a) $A = E - TS$ $G = A - fl$

(b) $\underbrace{-dw = dE - dq}_{\text{first law}} \geqslant dE - T\,dS = dA$ (at constant T)

$$w_u = w_{useful} = w + \int f\,dl = w + f\,\varDelta l$$

(Work done by or against the constant force is excluded from w_u.)

$$-dw_u = -dw - f\,dl \geqslant dA - f\,dl = dG \quad \text{(at constant } f\text{)}$$

(c) $dE = T\,dS + f\,dl$ if there is no work other than $f\,dl$ and this work is done reversibly (that is, $f =$ equilibrium force).

$$dA = -S\,dT + f\,dl$$

$$-\left(\frac{\partial S}{\partial l}\right)_T = \left(\frac{\partial f}{\partial T}\right)_l$$

$$\left(\frac{\partial E}{\partial l}\right)_T = T\left(\frac{\partial S}{\partial l}\right)_T + f = -T\left(\frac{\partial f}{\partial T}\right)_l + f$$

(d) $-T\left(\dfrac{\partial f}{\partial T}\right)_l + f = 0$

$$\left(\frac{\partial \ln f}{\partial \ln T}\right)_l = 1$$

$\ln f = \ln T + \ln C(l)$ where $C(l) =$ arbitrary function of l.
$f = TC(l)$
f must be directly proportional to T at constant l.

CHAPTER 4

The third law

of thermodynamics

SECTION 4-I

4-I-1. $\bar{C}_P \approx \bar{C}_V = aT^3$

$$a = \frac{\bar{C}_V}{T^3} = \frac{0.727}{(20)^3} = 9.09 \times 10^{-5}$$

$$\bar{C}_V = 9.09 \times 10^{-5}T^3$$

$$\Delta S = \int_{T_1}^{T_2} \frac{\bar{C}_V \, dT}{T} = \int_0^{20} 9.09 \times 10^{-5}T^2 \, dT$$

$$= \tfrac{1}{3} \times 9.09 \times 10^{-5}(20^3 - 0^3) = 0.242 \text{ cal } °\text{K}^{-1} \text{ mole}^{-1}$$

4-I-2. In the solid state NO is capable of existing in two orientations, which have practically equal chances of existence. These are NO NO and NO ON. The zero-point entropy is therefore

$$k \ln 2^N = Nk \ln 2 = R \ln 2 = 1.99 \times 2.30 \times 0.301$$

$$= 1.38 \text{ cal } °\text{K}^{-1} \text{ mole}^{-1}$$

where $k = $ Boltzmann's constant and $N = $ Avogadro's number.

SECTION 4-II

4-II-1. (a) $S = k \ln W$, where W is the number of detailed (molecular) states corresponding to the given gross (macroscopic) state. Usually at $0°K$, $W = 1$ for each reactant and product; therefore $S = 0$ for each reactant and product and $\Delta S = 0$ at $0°K$.

(b) For C and O_2, $W = 1$ and $S = 0$ as usual. For CO, however, the dipole moment is so small that the orientation of the molecules (CO or OC) in the crystal is nearly random, even at $0°K$. Thus $W > 1$ and $S > 0$ for CO and $\Delta S > 0$ for the reaction.

4-II-2.

(a)
$$\int_0^{50} \frac{\bar{C}_P}{T} dT = \int_0^{50} 4.0 \times 10^{-5} T^2 dT$$
$$= \frac{4.0 \times 10^{-5} \times 50^3}{3} = 1.67 \text{ cal } °K^{-1} \text{ mole}^{-1}$$

$$\int_{50}^{150} \frac{\bar{C}_P}{T} dT = 5.00 \ln \left(\frac{150}{50}\right)$$
$$= 5.00 \times 1.09861 = 5.49 \text{ cal } °K^{-1} \text{ mole}^{-1}$$

$$\Delta S_{\text{fusion}} = \frac{300 \text{ cal mole}^{-1}}{150°K} = 2.00 \text{ cal } °K^{-1} \text{ mole}^{-1}$$

$$\int_{150}^{300} \frac{\bar{C}_P}{T} dT = 6.00 \ln \left(\frac{300}{150}\right)$$
$$= 6.00 \times 0.69315 = 4.16 \text{ cal } °K^{-1} \text{ mole}^{-1}$$

$$\bar{S} = 1.67 + 5.49 + 2.00 + 4.16$$
$$= 13.32 \text{ cal } °K^{-1} \text{ mole}^{-1}$$

(b) $\Delta \bar{H}_{100} = \Delta \bar{H}_{150} + \int_{150}^{100} \Delta \bar{C}_P \, dT = 300 + 1.00(100 - 150)$
$$= 250 \text{ cal mole}^{-1}$$

$$\Delta \bar{S}_{100} = \Delta \bar{S}_{150} + \int_{150}^{100} \frac{\Delta \bar{C}_P}{T} dT = 2.00 + 1.00 \ln \left(\frac{100}{150}\right)$$

$$= 2.00 + 1.00(0.69315 - 1.09861)$$
$$= 1.59 \text{ cal } °K^{-1} \text{ mole}^{-1}$$

$$\Delta \bar{G}_{100} = \Delta \bar{H} - 100 \Delta \bar{S}_{100} = 250 - 159 = 91 \text{ cal mole}^{-1} > 0$$

Fusion is not spontaneous below the melting point ($150°K$). Therefore it is reasonable that $\Delta \bar{G}$ is positive.

4-II-3.

0 to 15°K (Debye extrapolation)	0.20 cal °K^{-1} mole^{-1}
15 to 160.65°K (graphical)	16.55
Fusion, 1236.4/160.65	7.70
160.65 to 283.60°K (graphical)	11.25
Vaporization, 6101/283.66	21.51
Entropy of actual gas at the boiling point	57.21

In the work by Giauque and Gordon a small correction is applied, bringing the value to 57.38 for the corresponding ideal gas. The graphical integrations can be carried out by plotting either $\bar{C}_P$ vs log T or $\bar{C}_P/T$ vs T.

4-II-4. Method I

$$S_T = \frac{\bar{H}_T - \bar{G}_T}{T} = \frac{\bar{H}_T - \bar{H}_{298}}{T} - \frac{\bar{G}_T - \bar{H}_{298}}{T}$$

$$\frac{\bar{G}^\circ_{1000} - \bar{H}^\circ_{298}}{1000} = -49.17 \text{ cal °K}^{-1} \text{ mole}^{-1}$$

$$\bar{C}_P = \bar{C}_V + R = \frac{5}{2}R \text{ for an ideal monatomic gas}$$

$$\bar{H}^\circ_T - \bar{H}^\circ_{298} = \frac{5}{2}R(T - 298) = \frac{5}{2}R \times 702$$
$$= 3488 \text{ cal mole}^{-1} \quad \text{for } T = 1000°K$$

$$\bar{S}^\circ_{1000} = \frac{\bar{H}^\circ_{1000} - \bar{H}^\circ_{298}}{1000} - \frac{\bar{G}^\circ_{1000} - \bar{H}^\circ_{298}}{1000}$$
$$= 3.49 + 49.17 = 52.66 \text{ cal °K}^{-1} \text{ mole}^{-1}$$

Method II

$$\bar{S}^\circ_{298} = -\frac{\bar{G}^\circ_{298} - \bar{H}^\circ_{298}}{298} = 45.96$$

$$\bar{S}^\circ_{1000} = \bar{S}^\circ_{298} + \int_{298}^{1000} \frac{\bar{C}_P \, dT}{T}$$

$$= 45.96 + \frac{5}{2}R \ln\left(\frac{1000}{298}\right)$$

$$= 45.96 + 6.01 = 51.97 \text{ cal °K}^{-1} \text{ mole}^{-1}$$

The discrepancy is probably attributable to electronic excitation at high temperature.

4-II-5.   The calculation of ΔG_f° from the measurement of the equilibrium constant was not based on the assumption of the validity of the third law, whereas the calculation of ΔG_f° from the heat capacities was. The agreement between the two results is therefore evidence that it was valid to apply the third law in the latter case.

CHAPTER 5

Liquids
and the liquefaction
of gases

SECTION 5-1

5-I-1.   Plot log P vs $100/T$. (See figure.) Draw a straight line through the two data points. From the graph, log P at $500°K = 3.05$ and $P = 1120$ torr.

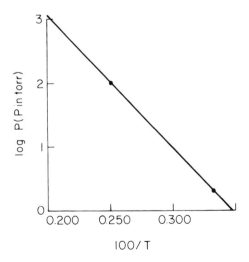

P, torr	log P	T, °K	1/T
2	0.30	300	0.00333
100	2.00	400	0.00250
		500	0.00200

5-I-2. Trouton's rule: $\Delta \bar{H}_v / T \approx 21$ cal °K^{-1} mole^{-1}

$\Delta \bar{H}_v = 21T = 21 \times 309 = 6500$ cal mole^{-1}

The experimentally observed value is 6160 cal mole^{-1}.

5-I-3. $P = \dfrac{n_x RT}{V} = \dfrac{n_x RT}{(n_x + n_{N_2})\, RT/P_{N_2}} = \dfrac{n_x P_{N_2}}{n_x + n_{N_2}} = \dfrac{1}{100} \times \dfrac{1.00}{0.501}$

$= 0.0200$ atm $= 3.80$ torr

5-I-4. $\eta_{OF_2} = \dfrac{\rho_{OF_2} t_{OF_2} \eta_{H_2O}}{\rho_{H_2O} t_{H_2O}} = \dfrac{1.523 \times 67.6 \times 1.00}{0.9982 \times 363.4}$

$= 0.2852$ cP (centipoise)

5-I-5. $\eta = \dfrac{2 \times 980.7 \times 0.100^2 \times (7.87 - 1.26)}{9 \times 10.0}$

$= 1.44$ P $= 144$ cP

5-I-6. The area of a circle is $a = \pi r^2$. For one capillary

$a_1 = \pi r_1^2, \quad r_1 = \sqrt{a_1/\pi}$

for the other capillary

$a_2 = 2a_1 = \pi r_2^2, \quad r_2 = \sqrt{2a_1/\pi}$

$\gamma = \frac{1}{2} ghr; \ h = 2\gamma/gr$
where $h =$ the height risen

$\dfrac{h_2}{h_1} = \dfrac{r_1}{r_2} = \dfrac{1}{\sqrt{2}} = 0.707$

The height of rise in the wider tube would be 0.707 that in the narrower tube.

5-I-7.

(a) $\quad r = \dfrac{2\gamma}{h\rho g} = \dfrac{2 \times 28.8}{2.71 \times 0.878 \times 981} = 0.0247$ cm

(b) $\quad \gamma = \tfrac{1}{2}hr\rho g = \tfrac{1}{2} \times 2.18 \times 0.0247 \times 981 = 23.8$ dynes cm^{-1}

In (a) it is assumed that the contact angle is zero. In (b) it is assumed that the contact angle of benzene is the same as that of ethyl acetate (not necessarily zero).

5-I-8.

$$k = \frac{\mathit{\Delta}[\gamma(M/\rho)^{2/3}]}{\mathit{\Delta}(-t - 6)} = \frac{344 - 407}{26 - 81} = 1.15$$

$$407 = 1.15(t_c - 20 - 6) = 1.15(t_c - 26)$$

$$t_c = 380°C$$

(Experimental value, 322°C)

5-I-9. Mean density at $100°C = \tfrac{1}{2}(0.74 + 0.01) = 0.375$. Mean density at $200°C = \tfrac{1}{2}(0.53 + 0.10) = 0.315$. Plot the mean densities vs t. (See figure.) Draw a straight line through the

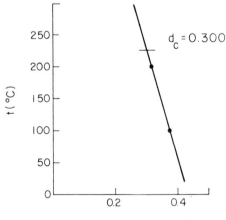

Mean density (g cm^{-3})

two points that were plotted. The density at which the extrapolation of this line intersects $t = 225°C$ is the critical density, 0.300 g cm^{-3}.

5-I-10. The orthobaric densities, $\frac{1}{2}(\rho_v + \rho_{liq})$, are 0.68, 0.65, 0.62, 0.59, 0.56, 0.53, 0.52 g cm^{-3}, respectively. Plot both the actual densities and the orthobaric densities vs t. (See figure.)

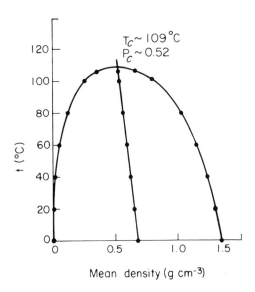

Mean density (g cm^{-3})

Draw a curve through the density points and a straight line through the orthobaric densities.

(a) From the maximum of the curve drawn through the actual densities, $t_c = 109°C$.

(b) From the point of intersection between the curve and the straight line, the critical density is 0.51 g cm^{-3}.

(c) The critical volume, in liter mole^{-1}, is

$$100/(0.51 \times 10^3) = 0.196 \text{ liter mole}^{-1}.$$

SECTION 5-II

5-II-1.

(a) $\overline{V}_v - \overline{V}_{liq} \approx \overline{V}_v$ if $\overline{V}_{liq} \ll \overline{V}_v$

$\bar{V}_v \approx RT/P$ if the pressure is low enough so that the ideal gas law can be applied to the vapor.

$$\frac{dP}{dT} = \frac{\Delta \bar{H}_v}{T(\bar{V}_v - \bar{V}_{liq})} \approx \frac{P \, \Delta \bar{H}_v}{RT^2} \quad \text{or} \quad \frac{1}{P}\frac{dP}{dT} \approx \frac{\Delta \bar{H}_v}{RT^2}$$

(b) $\dfrac{1}{P}\dfrac{dP}{dT} = \dfrac{d \ln P}{dT}$

$$\ln \left(\frac{P_2}{P_1}\right) = \int_{T_1}^{T_2} \frac{d \ln P}{dT} \, dT = \int_{T_1}^{T_2} \frac{\Delta \bar{H}_v}{RT^2} \, dT$$

$$= \frac{\Delta \bar{H}_v}{R}\left(\frac{1}{T_1} - \frac{1}{T_2}\right)$$

if ΔH is independent of temperature.

$$P_2 = P_1 \exp\left[\frac{\Delta \bar{H}_v}{R}\left(\frac{1}{T_1} - \frac{1}{T_2}\right)\right]$$

5-II-2. $\dfrac{dP}{dT} = \dfrac{\Delta \bar{H}_v}{T(\bar{V}_v - \bar{V}_{liq})} \approx \dfrac{\Delta \bar{H}_v}{T\bar{V}_v} = \dfrac{\Delta \bar{H}_v \cdot P}{T(RT + K)}$

$$\frac{dP}{P} = \frac{\Delta \bar{H}_v \, dT}{T(RT + K)}$$

$$\frac{1}{T(RT + K)} = \frac{1}{KT} - \frac{R}{K(RT + K)}$$

$$\frac{dP}{P} = \frac{\Delta \bar{H}_v \, dT}{KT} - \frac{R \, \Delta \bar{H}_v \, dT}{K(RT + K)}$$

$$\ln \frac{P_2}{P_1} = \frac{\Delta \bar{H}_v}{K} \ln \frac{T_2}{T_1} - \frac{\Delta \bar{H}_v}{K} \ln \frac{RT_2 + K}{RT_1 + K}$$

$$\ln \frac{P_2}{P_1} = \frac{\Delta \bar{H}_v}{K} \ln \frac{T_2(RT_1 + K)}{T_1(RT_2 + K)}$$

5-II-3. $\ln P = -\dfrac{\Delta \bar{H}_v}{RT} + \text{constant}$

$$P = e^{-\Delta \bar{H}_v/RT + \text{constant}} = e^{-\Delta \bar{H}_v/RT} \times e^{\text{constant}} = ke^{-\Delta \bar{H}_v/RT}$$

$$e^x = 1 + x + \frac{x^2}{2!} + \frac{x^3}{3!} + \cdots$$

Here, $x = -\Delta H_v / RT$.

$$P = k\left[1 - \left(\frac{\Delta \bar{H}_v}{RT}\right) + \frac{1}{2}\left(\frac{\Delta \bar{H}_v}{RT}\right)^2 - \frac{1}{6}\left(\frac{\Delta \bar{H}_v}{RT}\right)^3 + \cdots\right]$$

5-II-4.   Boiling point $= 197°C$ (vapor pressure at $197°C = 760$ torr)

$\Delta \bar{H}_v = 191 \times 62.1$ cal mole^{-1}

$197°C = 470°K$

$$\log \frac{P_2}{P_1} = -\frac{\Delta \bar{H}_v}{2.303R}\left(\frac{1}{T_2} - \frac{1}{T_1}\right)$$

$$\log \frac{760}{30} = -\frac{191 \times 62.1}{2.303 \times 1.987}\left(\frac{1}{470} - \frac{1}{T_1}\right)$$

$$\log 25.3 = -2590\left(\frac{1}{470} - \frac{1}{T_1}\right)$$

$$T_1 = 375°K = 102°C$$

5-II-5.   The fraction of the molecules that have more than a given amount of kinetic energy increases rapidly as temperature increases. Viscous flow in a liquid involves motion of molecules to new positions, passing through regions of high potential energy (where a molecule is "pushing its way" past others). The higher the temperature, the larger is the fraction of the molecules that have enough energy to pass through potential barriers and the more rapid is the flow.

5-II-6. $\gamma = \frac{1}{2}\rho g h r$

$$h = \frac{2\gamma}{\rho g r}$$

$$h_1 - h_2 = \Delta h = \frac{2\gamma}{\rho g r_1} - \frac{2\gamma}{\rho g r_2} = \frac{2\gamma}{\rho g}\left(\frac{1}{r_1} - \frac{1}{r_2}\right) = \frac{2\gamma}{\rho g}\left(\frac{r_2 - r_1}{r_1 r_2}\right)$$

$$\gamma = \frac{1}{2}\Delta h\left(\frac{r_1 r_2}{r_2 - r_1}\right)\rho g$$

5-II-7. $\log \gamma = \log k + n \log(t_c - t)$

Plot log $(t_c - t)$ as abscissa vs log γ as ordinate. (See figure.)

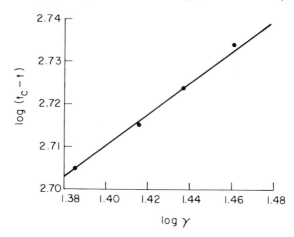

t, °C	log γ	log$(t_c - t)$
20.0	1.4606	2.7337
32.5	1.4362	2.7235
41.5	1.4163	2.7161
54.8	1.3853	2.7048

Slope $= 2.60 = n$

$1.3853 = \log k + 2.60(2.7048)$

$\quad k = 2.2 \times 10^{-6}$

$\quad \gamma = 2.2 \times 10^{-6}(561.5 - t)^{2.60}$

5-II-8.   Plot $\gamma(M/\rho)^{2/3}$ vs t. (See figure.)

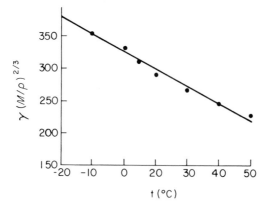

t, °C	$\gamma(M/\rho)^{2/3}$	t, °C	$\gamma(M/\rho)^{2/3}$
−20.3	378	20	294
−10	354	30	270
0.2	332	40	250
9.9	313	50	228

Slope $= 2.27 = k$ (Stowe gets 2.134, but the data are badly scattered and some judgment is required in drawing the curve).

$t_c = 152.2$ (Stowe gets 157.5) from the equation

$$378 = 2.27(t_c - 6 + 20.3)$$

5-II-9. (a) The equation $n^2 = \epsilon$ is correct if ϵ and n are measured at the same frequency. But ϵ and thus n vary with frequency; we cannot expect that ϵ measured at 10^4 or 10^6 sec^{-1} will be the same as n^2 measured at 5.10×10^{14} sec^{-1}. The most important reason for the dependence of ϵ on frequency is that polar molecules can align themselves with the applied field at low frequencies $(< \sim 10^{10}$ sec$^{-1})$, while this orientation effect is lost at high frequencies. The large drop in ϵ for o-$C_6H_4Cl_2$ in going from 10^6 to 10^{14} sec^{-1} can be attributed to this loss of the orientation contribution. For p-$C_2H_2Cl_2$, which is nonpolar and thus has no orientation effect anyway, the change is much less drastic.

(b) The dipole moment of m-$C_6H_4Cl_2$ is intermediate between those of the *ortho* and *para* isomers. The ratio ϵ/n^2 should similarly be intermediate between 1.24 and 3.10. (Experimentally $\epsilon = 5.04$ in the limit of zero frequency and $n = 1.5457$; then $\epsilon/n^2 = 2.11$.)

5-II-10. $n \approx \sqrt{\epsilon} = \sqrt{2.647} = 1.63$ (this agrees with experiment). From its symmetry we can see that CS_2 has dipole moment zero. Therefore orientation polarization, which is manifested only at relatively low frequencies $(< 10^{10}$ sec^{-1}, roughly), is absent and the only polarization arises from distortion of the molecules. This effect is more or less independent of frequency up to the visible range so that the dielectric constant at visible or infrared frequencies is about the same as at 9×10^5 sec^{-1} and we can apply the Maxwell relation $n^2 = \epsilon$.

5-II-11. (a) Polar molecules tend to align themselves so that their dipole moments are parallel to the electric field. The degree of alignment decreases as the temperature rises because the thermal agitation tends to randomize their orientations. Alignment of the molecules contributes to the polarizability of the substance. The molar polarization (actually polarizability) therefore decreases as the temperature rises.

(b) The molar refraction is actually the molar polarization measured at the frequency of visible light. At such a high frequency the molecules cannot reorient themselves as the field alternates in direction and the orientation effect therefore does not contribute to the polarizability. The molar polarization, however, is measured at low frequency (usually $\leqslant 10^6$ sec^{-1}) and the molecules can easily reorient to keep up with this frequency of alternation. The orientation effect thus is present in the molar polarization but absent in the molar refraction.

CHAPTER 6

Solids

SECTION 6-1

6-I-1. The unit cell contains 8 ● atoms, each shared with 8 other unit cells, so the net number of ● atoms that can be assigned to a unit cell is $8 \times \frac{1}{8} = 1$. The unit cell contains 2 ○ atoms, each one shared between two unit cells, so the net number of ○ atoms that can be assigned to a unit cell is $2 \times \frac{1}{2} = 1$.

6-I-2. To determine the Miller indices we take the reciprocals of the Weiss indices, giving 2/1, 3/2, 0, and then multiply the latter by the denominator 2 to eliminate the fractions, giving 4, 3, 0.

6-I-3. The Weiss indices are the coordinates of the intercepts of the plane, 2, 1, 3. To obtain the Miller indices, take the reciprocals of the Weiss indices, giving 1/2, 1/1, 1/3, and then multiply through by 6 to eliminate the fractions, giving 3, 6, 2.

6-I-4. (a) See figure. ○ = K, ● = Si. For clarity the 100, 010, and 001 faces are not shown in the drawing. The K atoms are at the corners and face centers. The Si atoms are at the body center and at the edge centers.

(b) Nearest K—Si neighbors are 7.15/2 = 3.57 Å apart.

(c) Volume of unit cell = $(7.15 \times 10^{-8})^3 = 365 \times 10^{-24}$ cm³. Number of unit cells per gram formula weight KSiH$_3$ = $\frac{1}{4} \times 6.023 \times 10^{23}$. Volume occupied by 1 g formula weight KSiH$_3$ = $\frac{1}{4} \times 6.023 \times 10^{23} \times 365 \times 10^{-24} = 54.9$ cm³. Density = 70.18/54.9 = 1.28 g cm⁻³.

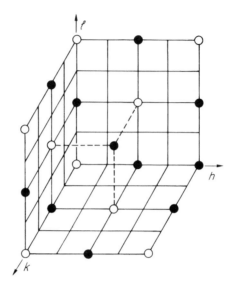

Fig. 6-1-4.

6-I-5.   (a) See figure.

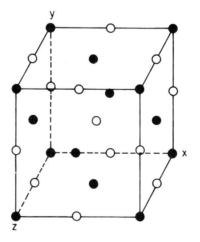

(b) Formula weight of $NaBH_4 = 37.8$
Na atoms at corners $= 8 \times \frac{1}{8} = 1$
Na atoms at face centers $= 6 \times \frac{1}{2} = 3$
Total: 4Na atoms per unit cell
B atoms at edge centers $= 12 \times \frac{1}{4} = 3$

B atom at body center $= 1 \times 1 = 1$
Total: 4B atoms per unit cell
Volume of unit cell $= (6.15 \times 10^{-8})^3 \, cm^3 = 233 \times 10^{-24} \, cm^3$
Volume of 1 g formula weight of unit cells $=$
$\frac{1}{4} \times 6.023 \times 10^{23} \times (6.15 \times 10^{-8})^3 \, cm^3 = 35.1 \, cm^3$
Density $= 37.8 \, g/35.1 \, cm^3 = 1.08 \, g \, cm^{-3}$

6-I-6.   (a) The unit cell contains $1 Cs^+$ and $1 Br^-$.

$$\frac{212.81 \text{ g mole}^{-1}}{4.44 \text{ g cm}^{-3} \times 6.023 \times 10^{23} \text{ unit cells mole}^{-1}}$$

$$= 7.97 \times 10^{-23} \, cm^3 \, (\text{unit cell})^{-1} = e^3$$

$e = \sqrt[3]{79.7 \times 10^{-24}} \, cm = 4.30 \times 10^{-8} \, cm = 4.30 \, Å$

(b) $d_{200} = \frac{1}{2} \times d_{100} = \frac{1}{2} \times 4.30 \, Å = 2.15 \, Å$.

6-I-7.   (a) If I^- ions are in contact along the edge,

$e = 2 \times 2.16 \, Å = 4.32 \, Å$

If Cs^+ and I^- ions are in contact along the body diagonal,

$e \sqrt{3} = 2(1.69 + 2.16) = 7.70 \, Å; \qquad e = 4.44 \, Å$

The latter (larger) figure must be the correct one (experimental value: $e = 4.562 Å$ at $25°C$).

$e^3 = 4.44^3 \, Å^3 = 87.5 \, Å^3 = 8.75 \times 10^{-23} \, cm^3$

(b) $\dfrac{259.8 \text{ g mole}^{-1}}{6.023 \times 10^{23} \text{ unit cells mole}^{-1} \times 8.75 \times 10^{-23} \, cm^3 \, (\text{unit cell})^{-1}}$
$\qquad = 4.93 \, g \, cm^{-3}$

(experimental density : $4.510 \, g \, cm^{-3}$).

6-I-8. $d_{100}^3 =$ volume per unit cell;   formula weight: 65.11

$d_{100}^3 = \dfrac{(65.11/1.52) \, cm^3 \, mole^{-1}}{6.023 \times 10^{23} \times \frac{1}{4} \, \text{unit cells mole}^{-1}}$

$\qquad = 284 \times 10^{-24} \, cm^3 \, mole^{-1}$

$d_{100} = \sqrt[3]{284 \times 10^{-24}} = 6.57 \times 10^{-8} \, cm = 6.57 \, Å$

6-I-9. The unit cell contains 4Ag atoms ($\frac{1}{8} \times 8 + \frac{1}{2} \times 6 = 4$).
The nearest neighbors are indicated in the figure. From this
diagram it can be seen that 2.87 Å $= \frac{1}{2} \cdot \sqrt{2} \times d_{100}$. Therefore $d_{100} = 2.87/0.707 = 4.06$ Å.

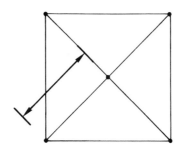

$$V = \tfrac{1}{4} \times 6.023 \times 10^{23} \times (4.06 \times 10^{-8})^3$$
$$= 10.08 \text{ cm}^3 \text{ (g-atom)}^{-1}$$

$$\text{Density} = \frac{107.87}{10.08} \frac{\text{g(g-atom)}^{-1}}{\text{cm}^3 \text{ (g-atom)}^{-1}} = 10.7 \text{ g cm}^3$$

6-I-10. Volume occupied by 1 mole of complex is

$$V = 7.96 \times 8.34 \times 11.7 \times (10^{-8})^3 \times \frac{6.023}{4} \times 10^{23} \text{ cm}^3 = 117 \text{ cm}^3$$

Mass of 1 mole of complex is $M = 285$ g; density $= M/V = $
2.44 g cm^{-3}; experimental value, 2.4.

6-I-11. Volume occupied by 1 mole of LiBH$_4$ $= V$
$$= \tfrac{1}{4} \times 6.81 \times 4.43 \times 7.17 \times (10^{-8})^3 \times 6.023 \times 10^{23} \text{ cm}^3$$
$$= 32.6 \text{ cm}^3$$

Mass of 1 mole $= M = 21.76$ g;   density $= M/V = 0.668$ g cm^{-3}

6-I-12. Volume per molecule $= 12.05 \times 15.05 \times 2.69$
$$= 488 \text{ Å}^3 \text{ (unit cell)}^{-1}$$
$$= 244 \text{ Å}^3 \text{ molecule}^{-1}$$
$$= 2.44 \times 10^{-22} \text{ cm}^3 \text{ molecule}^{-1}$$

Molecular weight $= 1.419$ g cm$^{-3} \times 2.44 \times 10^{-22}$ cm^3 molecule^{-1}
$$\times 6.023 \times 10^{23} \text{ molecule mole}^{-1}$$
$$= 209 \text{ g mole}^{-1}$$

SECTION 6-II

6-II-1. n (the "order" of the x-rays) is the number of wavelengths of the x-rays between the given atomic planes.

6-II-2.

θ	$\sin^2 \theta$	$\sin^2 \theta / \sin^2 (4°40')$	$h^2 + k^2 + l^2$	hkl
5°23′	0.00881	1.33 = 4/3	4	200
10°51′	0.03545	5.35 = 16/3	16	400
4°47′	0.00696	1.05 = 3/3	3	111
4°40′	0.00662	1 = 3/3	3	111

The calculated hkl values are all odd or all even. Therefore the structure is face-centered cubic. Actually it is the NaCl structure—two interpenetrating face-centered cubic lattices. In general,

simple cubic h, k, l may have any values
face-centered cubic h, k, l are all odd or all even, including zero
body-centered cubic $h + k + l$ must be even

6-II-3. Rb^+ and Br^- have the same number of electrons (36). Thus they are practically equivalent for the purpose of reflecting x-rays. A RbBr crystal appears to be simple cubic if the two kinds of ion are treated as identical. In the other three crystals the two kinds of ions have different numbers of electrons. Each kind of ion occupies a face-centered cubic lattice. The x-rays "see" each of these two lattices (which have identical dimensions) and the result is a diffraction pattern characteristic of a face-centered lattice with variations of intensity resulting from interference between the reflections from the two lattices. (For RbBr the effect of these interferences is to give a pattern identical with that of a simple cubic lattice.)

6-II-4.   Any axis of symmetry must have a plane of lattice points perpendicular to it. The overall lattice plane formed by all the adjacent sets of corresponding lattice points must consist of regular polygons that fit together exactly. This is possible only when the symmetry axis is 3-, 4-, or 6-fold.

6-II-5.   One 3-fold axis (a to center of face bcd). Three reflection planes (through ab and midpoint of cd, etc.).

6-II-6.   One $\bar{4}$ axis (4-fold improper axis, or 4-fold axis of rotary inversion) from midpoint of *ab* to midpoint of *gh*.
One 2 axis (twofold proper axis) from midpoint of *ab* to midpoint of *gh*.
One plane of symmetry containing line *ab* and the midpoint of line *gh*.
One plane of symmetry containing line *gh* and the midpoint of line *ab*.

6-II-7.   There are three. Referring to the figure (p. 62) suitable answers are line *ab*, line *cd*, line *ef*. The diagonal drawn through the beveled corners is not acceptable.

6-II-8.   As can be seen in the figure the 2-fold rotation of ① to ② followed by inversion of ② through the point shown on the

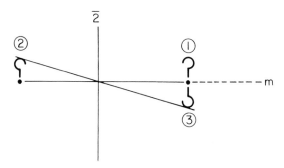

$\bar{2}$ axis gives ③ · ③ is a mirror image of ② reflected in the plane m perpendicular to the plane of the paper.

6-II-9.   (a) See figure. *ABCD* is a suitable unit cell.
(b) Let *r* be the radius of a circle. The unit cell shown in the figure is composed of two equilateral triangles, *ABC* and

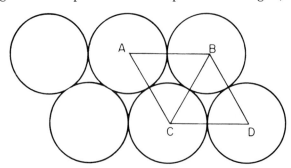

BCD, each with side $2r$ and $s = 3r$; the area of the unit cell is $2(3r \cdot r^3)^{1/2} = 2r^2 \sqrt{3}$. The unit cell contains $\frac{1}{6} + \frac{1}{3} + \frac{1}{6} + \frac{1}{3} = 1$ circle of area πr^2. The fractional void area is

$$\frac{2r^2 \sqrt{3} - \pi r^2}{2r^2 \sqrt{3}} = 0.093$$

6-II-10.

(a)

	AX	AY	AZ
$\dfrac{r_<}{r_>} = R$	1	0.5	0.33

AX has $R > \sqrt{3} - 1 = 0.732$ and therefore will probably have the CsCl structure. AY has $0.732 > R > 0.414 = \sqrt{2} - 1$, and should have the NaCl structure. AZ, with $R < 0.414$, might have a structure with still lower coordination number to permit contact between unlike ions but if the choice is only between CsCl and NaCl structures, we should expect the latter. A similar situation is observed in LiCl, LiBr, and LiI, all of which have the NaCl structure with negative ions in contact.

(b) Let l be the edge of the unit cell.

AX. Body diagonal $= l \sqrt{3} = 2r_+ + 2r_- = 4$. $l = 2.31$.
$$V = l^3 = 12.3$$

AY. $l = 2r_+ + 2r_- = 2 + 4 = 6$. $V = 216$

AZ. Here negative ions are in contact along the face diagonal.
Face diagonal $= l \sqrt{2} = 4r_- = 12$. $l = 8.48$. $V = 609.8$.

SECTION 6-III

6-III-1. (a) CsCl. Consider the Cl^- ions to be at the corners of the unit cell and the Cs^+ ion at the body center. The unit cell contains $1Cs^+ + 8/8 \, Cl^-$. If the Cl^- ions are in contact along the edge, the edge length is $1.81 + 1.81 = 3.62$ Å. If the Cs^+ and Cl^- ions are in contact along the body diagonal, this diagonal is $1.81 + 2 \times 1.69 + 1.81 = 7.00$ Å and the edge is $7.00/\sqrt{3} = 4.04$ Å. The larger of these figures must be correct: $e = 4.04$ Å. The volume of the unit cell is $e^3 = 65.9$ Å^3. The volume of the ions is $\frac{4}{3}\pi(1.81^3 + 1.69^3) = 45.1$ Å^3. The fractional void volume is $(65.9 - 45.1)/65.9 = 0.316$.

(b) NaCl. Unit cell contains $4Na^+ + 4Cl^-$. If Na^+ and Cl^- are in contact along an edge, the edge is $2(0.95 + 1.81) = 5.52$ Å. If Cl^- ions are in contact along a face diagonal, this diagonal is $4 \times 1.81 = 7.24$ Å and the edge is $7.24/\sqrt{2} = 5.12$ Å. If Na^+ and Cl^- are in contact along the body diagonal, this diagonal is $2(0.95 + 1.81) = 5.52$ Å, and the edge is $5.52/\sqrt{3} = 3.19$ Å. The largest of these figures must be the correct one: $e = 5.52$ Å, $e^3 = 168$ Å^3. The volume of the ions is $4 \times \frac{4}{3}\pi(0.95^3 + 1.81^3) = 114$ Å^3. $(168 - 114)/168 = 0.32$.

(c) LiCl. Edge contact: $e = 2(0.60 + 1.81) = 4.82$ Å. Face diagonal contact: $e = 4 \times 1.81/\sqrt{2} = 5.12$ Å. Body diagonal contact: $e = 4.82/\sqrt{3} = 2.78$ Å. Correct value: $e = 5.12$ Å. $e^3 = 134$ Å^3. Volume of ions $= 4 \times \frac{4}{3}\pi(0.60^3 + 1.81^3) = 103$ Å^3. $(134 - 103)/134 = 0.23$.

CHAPTER 7

Solutions

SECTION 7-I

7-I-1. In a very dilute solution a solvent molecule usually has only other solvent molecules as neighbors. The energy that it needs to escape from the surface is practically the same as for the same molecule in pure solvent. The vapor pressure of the solvent over the solution is less than over the pure solvent, not because each molecule is held more firmly in the solution but merely because there are fewer solvent molecules present. The number of solvent molecules is less in the ratio X_A (the mole fraction of the solvent), and the vapor pressure is less in the same ratio: $P_A/P_A^\circ = X_A$, which is Raoult's law.

7-I-2. $$M_2 = K_f \frac{1000 w_2}{\Delta T w_1} = 40.27 \times \frac{1000 \times 0.0113}{27.0 \times 0.0961} = 177$$

The paper by Rozenberg and Ushakova says $M_2 = 173$. The value calculated from atomic weights is 178.

7-I-3. $$m = \frac{\Delta T}{K_f} = \frac{0.01573}{5.085} = 0.00309 = \text{apparent molality}$$

$$\text{Association number} = \frac{\text{molality based on formula weight}}{\text{observed molality}}$$

$$= \frac{0.07734}{0.00309} = 25.0$$

7-I-4.   If 1.4020 g anthracene were dissolved in 100 g CS_2, the boiling-point elevation would be $0.220 \times (86.52)/100 = 0.190°C$. Let x be the number of moles of anthracene in 100 g CS_2. Then

$$\frac{23.7°}{1 \text{ mole}} = \frac{0.190°}{x \text{ moles}} \quad \text{and} \quad x = 0.00802 \text{ moles}$$

Since 1.4020 g anthracene = 0.00802 moles anthracene, 1 mole of anthracene = 1.4020/0.00802 = 175 g. Thus the molecular weight of anthracene is 175 g mole^{-1}. The value calculated from atomic weights is 178.

7-I-5.   We assume that $\overline{V}_1$ is the same as the molar volume of the pure solvent A.

$$\overline{V}_1 = \frac{100 \text{ g mole}^{-1}}{1.00 \text{ g ml}^{-1}} = 100 \text{ ml mole}^{-1}$$

$$\text{Then } X_2 = \frac{\pi \overline{V}_1}{RT} = \frac{0.50 \text{ atm} \times 100 \text{ ml mole}^{-1}}{82.06 \text{ ml atm } °K^{-1} \times 300°K} = 2.03 \times 10^{-3}$$

Let M_2 be the molecular weight of B. Then

$$X_2 = \frac{10/M_2}{10/M_2 + 1000/100} = \frac{1}{1 + M_2}$$

$$M_2 = \frac{1}{X_2} - 1 = 492 \text{ g mole}^{-1}$$

7-I-6. $\gamma = \dfrac{10.27}{0.0250 \times 213} = 1.93$

7-I-7.   Moles O_2 dissolved per liter water $= \dfrac{0.03097}{22.4} \times 0.21 = 0.000290$

7-I-8. $\alpha = \dfrac{273.2}{303.2} \times \dfrac{2.265}{244.0} = 0.00836$

7-I-9.
$$\log \frac{\alpha_2}{\alpha_1} = \frac{\Delta H}{2.303R} \left(\frac{T_2 - T_1}{T_1 T_2} \right)$$

$$\log \frac{0.04889}{0.03802} = \frac{\Delta H}{2.303 \times 1.987} \left(\frac{283.2 - 273.2}{283.2 \times 273.2} \right)$$

$$\Delta H = 3870 \text{ cal (mole } O_2)^{-1}$$

7-I-10.

(a) $a_1 = \dfrac{P_1}{P_1^\circ} = 0.920$

(b) $\gamma_1 = \dfrac{a_1}{X_1}$

$$= 0.920 \Big/ \frac{(25.23/200.61)}{(25.23/200.61) + (1.046/112.41)} = 0.989$$

SECTION 7-II

7-II-1. $P_A^\circ - P_A = X_B P_A^\circ$

$100.00 - 95.00 = X_B(100.00)$

$X_B = 0.0500$

$$X_B = \frac{w_B/M_B}{w_A/M_A + w_B/M_B} = \frac{1}{(M_B w_A/M_A w_B) + 1}$$

$$\frac{M_B w_A}{M_A w_B} = \frac{1}{X_B} - 1 = 19.0$$

$$\frac{M_B}{M_A} = 19.0 \times \frac{w_B}{w_A} = 1.90$$

7-II-2. $\dfrac{\Delta P}{P^\circ} \Big/ \left(\dfrac{n_{Na}}{n_{Na} + n_{NH_3}}\right) = 0.48, 0.52, 0.54, 0.53, 0.55,$ respectively

Assuming that the dissolved compound does not dissociate, the number of moles of compound formed per mole of Na used is equal to (the relative vapor pressure depression)/(the mole fraction of Na) $\approx \frac{1}{2}$. In other words there are two Na atoms per molecule of compound, so the correct formula is Na_2Te_x, not $NaTe_x$.

7-II-3. $$\frac{dP}{P} = \frac{\Delta H \, dT}{RT^2} = -\frac{6997 \, dT}{RT^2} + \frac{63.68 \, dT}{RT} - \frac{0.1586 \, dT}{R}$$

$$\ln \frac{P}{P^\circ} = \frac{6997}{R}\left(\frac{1}{T} - \frac{1}{T_0}\right) + \frac{63.68}{R}\ln\left(\frac{T}{T_0}\right)$$
$$- \frac{0.1586}{R}(T - T_0)$$

$$\ln(1 - X_2) = 3521\left(\frac{T_0 - T}{T_0 T}\right) + 73.8\log\left(\frac{T}{T_0}\right) - 0.0798(T - T_0)$$

$$X_2 \approx 3521\left(\frac{T - T_0}{T_0 T}\right) - 73.8\log\left(\frac{T}{T_0}\right) + 0.0798(T - T_0)$$

7-II-4.

$$\bar{V}_2 = a + bm$$
$$d\bar{V}_2 = b\, dm$$
$$n_1\, d\bar{V}_1 + n_2\, d\bar{V}_2 = 0$$
$$n_1 = \frac{1000}{M_1} \qquad (M_1 = \text{molecular weight of solvent})$$
$$n_2 = m$$
$$d\bar{V}_1 = -\frac{n_2}{n_1}\, d\bar{V}_2 = -\frac{mM_1 b\, dm}{1000}$$
$$\bar{V}_1 = -\frac{M_1 bm^2}{2000} + C \qquad (C = \text{integration constant})$$

When $m = 0$,

$$\bar{V}_1 = V_1^\circ = C \qquad (V_1^\circ = \text{molar volume of pure solvent})$$
$$\bar{V}_1 = V_1^\circ - \frac{M_1 bm^2}{2000}$$

7-II-5. Molecular weights: $C_2H_5OH = 46.07$, $H_2O = 18.02$. Mole fractions in 40 percent solution:

$$X_{C_2H_5OH} = \frac{40.0/46.07}{40.0/46.07 + 60.0/18.02} = 0.207$$

$$X_{H_2O} = \frac{60.0/18.02}{60.0/18.02 + 40.0/46.07} = 0.793$$

Activities:

$$a_{C_2H_5OH} = \frac{P_{C_2H_5OH}}{P_{C_2H_5OH}^\circ} = \frac{20.7}{43.6} = 0.475$$

$$a_{H_2O} = \frac{P_{H_2O}}{P_{H_2O}^\circ} = \frac{14.7}{17.5} = 0.840$$

Activity coefficients:

$$\gamma_{C_2H_5OH} = \frac{a_{C_2H_5OH}}{X_{C_2H_5OH}} = \frac{0.475}{0.207} = 2.30$$

$$\gamma_{H_2O} = \frac{a_{H_2O}}{X_{H_2O}} = \frac{0.840}{0.793} = 1.06$$

7-II-6. Let the alcohol be component 2. Its mole fraction in solution B is

$$X_2{}^B = \frac{83.2/74.12}{83.2/74.12 + 16.8/18.02} = 0.546$$

If we assume that the fugacity of the alcohol in this solution is given by Raoult's law (a crude approximation for a solution consisting of nearly half the other component in terms of mole fraction), then the activity is $a_2{}^B = X_2{}^B = 0.546$. For the two solutions in equilibrium $a_2{}^A = a_2{}^B = 0.546$, provided that such activities are defined in terms of the same standard state (pure alcohol, in this case).

7-II-7. (a) $\mu_A^\circ = \lim_{y_A \to 1} (\mu_A - RT \ln y_A) = \mu_A^*$

(b) $\mu_A = \mu_A^\circ + RT \ln b_A = \mu_A^* + RT \ln a_A$

$b_A = a_A$

(c) $\dfrac{\gamma_A^{(y)}}{\gamma_A^{(x)}} = \dfrac{b_A}{y_A} \cdot \dfrac{X_A}{a_A} = \dfrac{X_A}{y_A} = \dfrac{y_A/M_A}{y_A(y_A/M_A + y_B/M_B)}$

$= \dfrac{1}{y_A + y_B M_A/M_B}$

(d) $\gamma_A^{(x)} = 1$ for an ideal solution.

$\gamma_A^{(y)} = \dfrac{1}{0.50 + 0.50 M_A/M_B} = \dfrac{2.0}{1 + M_A/M_B}$

7-II-8. Define the standard chemical potentials

$$\lambda_2^\circ = \lim_{x_1 \to 1} (\mu_2 - RT \ln X_2)$$

$$\mu_2^\circ = \lim_{y_1 \to 1} (\mu_2 - RT \ln y_2)$$

When $X_1 \to 1$, $y_1 \to 1$; the limits therefore correspond to the same state of infinite dilution.

$$\mu_2 = \lambda_2^{\circ} + RT \ln a_2 = \mu_2^{\circ} + RT \ln b_2$$

$$RT \ln \left(\frac{b_2}{a_2}\right) = \lambda_2^{\circ} - \mu_2^{\circ}$$

$$= \lim_{X_1 \to 1} \left(\mu_2 - RT \ln X_2 - \mu_2 + RT \ln y_2\right)$$

$$= \lim_{X_1 \to 1} \left(RT \ln \frac{y_2}{X_2}\right)$$

$$= RT \ln \left(\lim_{X_1 \to 1} \frac{y_2}{X_2}\right)$$

In terms of molecular weights, M and numbers of moles, n,

$$X_2 = \frac{n_2}{n_1 + n_2}, \qquad y_2 = \frac{n_2 M_2}{n_1 M_1 + n_2 M_2}$$

$$\frac{y_2}{X_2} = \frac{n_2 M_2 (n_1 + n_2)}{n_2 (n_1 M_1 + n_2 M_2)} = \frac{M_2 (1 + n_2/n_1)}{M_1 + (n_2/n_1) M_2}$$

$$\lim_{X_1 \to 1} \frac{y_2}{X_2} = \frac{M_2}{M_1}$$

7-II-9. Let n = number of moles, M = molecular weight, c = molarity, and V = volume in liters.

$$c_2 = \frac{n_2}{V} \qquad V = \frac{n_1 M_1 + n_2 M_2}{1000\rho} \frac{g}{\text{g/liter}}$$

$$= \frac{1000 \rho n_2}{n_1 M_1 + n_2 M_2} \text{ liters}$$

$$m_2 = \frac{1000 n_2}{n_1 M_1} \qquad \frac{c_2}{m_2} = \frac{\rho n_1 M_1}{n_1 M_1 + n_2 M_2} = \frac{\rho}{1 + n_2 M_2/n_1 M_1}$$

$$\frac{a_2}{a_2'} = \lim_{n_2 \to 0} \left(\frac{c_2}{m_2}\right) = \rho_0 \qquad \frac{\gamma_2}{\gamma_2'} = \frac{a_2 m_2}{c_2 a_2'} = \frac{\rho_0}{\rho} \left(1 + \frac{n_2 M_2}{n_1 M_1}\right)$$

Choose n_1 so that $n_1 M_1 = 1000$ g. Then $n_2 = m_2$.

$$\frac{\gamma_2}{\gamma_2'} = \frac{\rho_0}{\rho} \left(1 + \frac{m_2 M_2}{1000}\right)$$

7-II-10.

$$\ln \gamma_2 = AX_2^2$$

$$d \ln \gamma_2 = 2AX_2 \, dX_2 = -2A(1 - X_1) \, dX_1$$

$$d \ln \gamma_1 = -\frac{X_2}{X_1} d \ln \gamma_2$$
$$= -\frac{(1 - X_1)}{X_1}[-2A(1 - X_1) dX_1]$$
$$= 2A\left(\frac{1}{X_1} - 2 + X_1\right) dX_1$$
$$\ln \gamma_1 = 2A \int_1^{X_1} \left(\frac{1}{X_1} - 2 + X_1\right) dX_1$$
$$= 2A[\ln X_1 - 2X_1 + \tfrac{1}{2}X_1^2]_1^{X_1}$$
$$= 2A[\ln X_1 - 2(X_1 - 1) + \tfrac{1}{2}(X_1^2 - 1)]$$
$$X_1^2 - 1 = (X_1 + 1)(X_1 - 1) = (2 - X_2)(-X_2) = -2X_2 + X_2^2$$
$$\ln \gamma_1 = 2A[\ln(1 - X_2) + X_2 + \tfrac{1}{2}X_2^2]$$

7-II-11.

$$\text{Pressure at } 100 \text{ ft} = \frac{100 \text{ ft} \times 62.5 \text{ lb ft}^{-3}}{14.7 \text{ lb in}^{-2} \text{ atm}^{-1} \times 144 \text{ in}^2 \text{ ft}^{-2}}$$
$$= 2.95 \text{ atm}$$

He goes from 2.95 atm to 1.00 atm, so the pressure differential is $2.95 - 1.00 = 1.95$ atm.

$$\Delta V = 5(\alpha_{He} \Delta P_{He} + \alpha_{O_2} \Delta P_{O_2})$$
$$= 5(0.00861 \times 0.80 \times 1.95 + 0.02831 \times 0.20 \times 1.95)$$
$$= 0.122 \text{ liter} = 122 \text{ ml at } 0°C$$
$$122 \times \frac{298}{273} = 133 \text{ ml at } 25°C$$

7-II-12.

t, °C	30	40	50	100
α	0.665	0.530	0.436	
$\log \alpha$	−0.177	−0.276	−0.361	
T, °K	303.2	313.2	323.2	373.2
$1/T$, °K^{-1}	0.00330	0.00319	0.00309	0.00268

Plot $\log \alpha$ vs $1/T$. (See figure.)
At 100°C, $\log \alpha = -0.700$ (from graph); $\alpha = 0.200$

$$\text{Moles } CO_2 = 0.03 \times \frac{0.200}{22.4} = 0.00027 \text{ mole per liter } H_2O$$

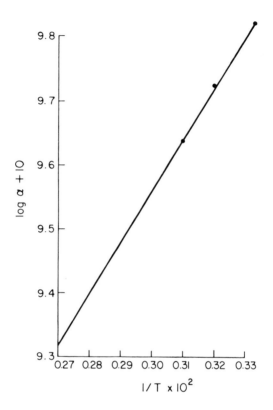

Fig. 7-II-12.

7-II-13. (See figure in problem.)

$$\Delta H = \overline{\Delta H}_1 \cdot n_1 + \overline{\Delta H}_2 \cdot n_2 = -15,300$$

$$= -192 \times 10 + \overline{\Delta H}_2 \times 1$$

$$\overline{\Delta H}_2 = -13,380 \text{ cal}$$

7-II-14. $n_1 = 9; \qquad n_2 = 1$

$$\Delta H = 2.00(9)^{1/2} + 3.00(9)^{3/2} + 4.00(9)^{5/2} = 1059 \text{ cal}$$

$$\overline{\Delta H}_1 = \left(\frac{\partial H}{\partial n_1}\right)_{P,T,n_2}$$

$$= \frac{1}{2} \times 2.00 n_1^{-1/2} + \frac{3}{2} \times 3.00 n_1^{1/2} + \frac{5}{2} \times 4.00 n_1^{3/2}$$

$$= 1.00(9)^{-1/2} + 4.50 \times (9)^{1/2} + 10.00(9)^{3/2}$$

$$= 284 \text{ cal mole}^{-1}$$

$$n_2 \overline{\Delta H_2} = \Delta H - n_1 \overline{\Delta H_1}$$

$$1 \cdot \overline{\Delta H_2} = 1059 - 9(284) = -1497$$

$$\overline{\Delta H_2} = -1497 \text{ cal mole}^{-1}$$

7-II-15. Moles H_2O/mole NaCl = 889, 280, 139, 73.9, 55.2, 28.5, 17.9,

13.9, 11.1, 9.25

Plot ΔH vs moles H_2O/mole NaCl. (See figure.) Draw a smooth curve through data points.

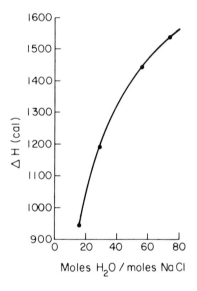

Moles H_2O / moles Na Cl

The initial concentration of the solution = $(90/18.0)/(10/58.5)$ = 29.2 moles H_2O/mole NaCl. At this concentration $\Delta H = 1195$ cal mole^{-1} (from graph). The final concentration of the solution = $(216/18.0)/(10/58.5)$ = 70.3 moles H_2O/mole NaCl. At this concentration $\Delta H = 1518$ cal mole^{-1} (from graph).

$$\Delta(\Delta H) = \frac{10}{58.5} (1518 - 1195) = 55.2 \text{ cal}$$

7-II-16. (a) The initial composition of the solution = 6 moles H_2O per mole H_2SO_4 and the final composition = 10 moles H_2O per mole H_2SO_4 .

$$\Delta H = -16{,}240 - (-14{,}740) = -1500 \text{ cal}$$

(b) (3 moles H_2O)/(6 moles H_2SO_4)

$$= 0.5 \text{ mole } H_2O \text{ per mole } H_2SO_4$$

$$\overline{\Delta H_1} = -6740 \text{ cal mole}^{-1}$$

and

$$\overline{\Delta H_2} = -438 \text{ cal mole}^{-1}$$

$$\Delta H = \overline{\Delta H_1} \cdot n_1 + \overline{\Delta H_2} \cdot n_2 = (-6{,}740 \times 3) + (-438 \times 6)$$
$$= -22{,}848 \text{ cal}$$

7-II-17. (a) $\log \dfrac{s_2}{s_1} = \dfrac{-\Delta H^\circ}{2.303R} \left(\dfrac{1}{T_2} - \dfrac{1}{T_1} \right)$

where s = solubility. Using the third and fifth values of s and T we find that $\Delta H = +9990$ cal mole^{-1}. We can also plot $\log s$ vs $1/T$ and obtain ΔH from the slope.

(b) The "$\circ$" means that the reactants and the products are in their respective standard states. For the solvent the standard state is the pure substance. For the solute the standard state is a hypothetical state of infinite dilution. (More precisely, for the solute $H^\circ = \lim H$, the limit being that of zero concentration.)

7-II-18. $X_{H_2O} = \dfrac{23.8}{760} = 0.031$

$$X_{H_2} = 1 - X_{H_2O} = 0.969$$

$$0.969 n_{\text{total}} = n_{H_2} = 1.500$$

$$n_{\text{total}} = 1.548$$

$$n_{H_2O} = X_{H_2O} n_{\text{total}} = 0.031 \times 1.548 = 0.048$$

$$\Delta H = 0.048 \times 582.2 \text{ cal} \times 18.01 = 0.50 \text{ kcal}$$

The paper by Argue, Mercer, and Cobble says $\Delta H = 0.4$ kcal.

SECTION 7-III

7-III-1.

(a) $\quad P_A = \left(\dfrac{n_A}{n_A + n_B} \right) P_A^\circ \qquad P_B = \left(\dfrac{n_B}{n_A + n_B} \right) P_B^\circ$

(b) $\quad \Delta H_I = n_A \overline{\Delta H_A} + n_B \overline{\Delta H_B}$

$\Delta H_{II} = \Delta H_{III} = 0$

$\Delta H_{IV} = -(n_A \overline{\Delta H_A} + n_B \overline{\Delta H_B})$

$\Delta H_{total} = 0$

$\Delta G_I = \Delta G_{III} = \Delta G_{IV} = 0$

$\Delta G_{total} = \Delta G_{II} = RT \left(n_A \ln \dfrac{P_A}{P_A^\circ} + n_B \ln \dfrac{P_B}{P_B^\circ} \right)$

$\qquad\qquad = RT \left(n_A \ln \dfrac{n_A}{n_A + n_B} + n_B \ln \dfrac{n_B}{n_A + n_B} \right)$

(c) $\quad \Delta S = \dfrac{\Delta H_{total} - \Delta G_{total}}{T}$

$\qquad = -R \left(n_A \ln \dfrac{n_A}{n_A + n_B} + n_B \ln \dfrac{n_B}{n_A + n_B} \right)$

ΔS is the same for the mixing process whether it is carried out by the usual irreversible path (simple mixing) or by the reversible path described in (b).

(d) The result would be the same because the initial and final states would be the same: two pure liquids and an ideal solution. ΔS_{total} would not be changed if the process in (b) passed through nonideal instead of ideal vapors, though, of course, ΔS for each of the steps would be changed.

7-III-2. (a) $\quad V = \dfrac{1 + w_2}{\rho}, \qquad v_1^\circ = \dfrac{1}{\rho_1^\circ}$

$\phi_2 = \dfrac{V - v_1^\circ}{w_2} = \dfrac{1}{\rho} \left(\dfrac{1}{w_2} + 1 \right) - \dfrac{1}{\rho_1^\circ w_2}$

$\qquad = \dfrac{1}{w_2} \left(\dfrac{1}{\rho} - \dfrac{1}{\rho_1^\circ} \right) + \dfrac{1}{\rho}$

$\dfrac{\partial \phi_2}{\partial w_2} = \left(\dfrac{1}{\rho} - \dfrac{1}{\rho_1^\circ} \right) - \left(\dfrac{1}{w_2{}^2} \right) - \dfrac{1}{\rho^2} \dfrac{\partial \rho}{\partial w_2} \left(\dfrac{1}{w_2} + 1 \right)$

(b) $V = w_2\phi_2 + v_1^\circ$

$$\bar{v}_2 = \frac{\partial V}{\partial w_2} = \phi_2 + w_2 \frac{\partial \phi_2}{\partial w_2}$$

Here

$$\rho = 1.1263 \text{ g ml}^{-1}, \quad \rho_1^\circ = 0.9982 \text{ g ml}^{-1}, \quad w_2 = 1$$

$$\frac{\partial \rho}{\partial w_2} \approx \frac{\Delta \rho}{\Delta w_2} = \frac{1.1263 - 1.1236}{1 - (49/51)} = 0.069 \text{ g ml}^{-1}$$

Then

$$\phi_2 = 0.774 \text{ ml g}^{-1}$$

$$\frac{\partial \phi_2}{\partial w_2} = 0.0099 \text{ ml g}^{-1}$$

$$\bar{v}_2 = 0.774 + 0.0099 = 0.784 \text{ ml g}^{-1}$$

7-III-3. (a) $V = \dfrac{M_1 n_1 + M_2 n_2}{\rho}$

$$\bar{V}_2 = \left(\frac{\partial V}{\partial n_2}\right)_{n_1} = \frac{M_2}{\rho} - (M_1 n_1 + M_2 n_2)\frac{1}{\rho^2}\left(\frac{\partial \rho}{\partial n_2}\right)_{n_1}$$

(b) $X_2 = \dfrac{n_2}{n_1 + n_2}$

$$\left(\frac{\partial X_2}{\partial n_2}\right)_{n_1} = \frac{n_1}{(n_1 + n_2)^2}$$

$$\left(\frac{\partial \rho}{\partial n_2}\right)_{n_1} = \frac{d\rho}{dX_2}\left(\frac{\partial X_2}{\partial n_2}\right)_{n_1} = \frac{n_1}{(n_1 + n_2)^2}\frac{d\rho}{dX_2}$$

$$\bar{V}_2 = \frac{M_2}{\rho} - (M_1 n_1 + M_2 n_2)\frac{n_1}{\rho^2(n_1 + n_2)^2}\frac{d\rho}{dX_2}$$

$$= \frac{M_2}{\rho} - (M_1 X_1 + M_2 X_2)\frac{X_1}{\rho^2}\frac{d\rho}{dX_2}$$

(c) Differentiating the given equation for ρ

$$\frac{d\rho}{dX_2} = -0.28930 + 0.59814 X_2 - 1.82628 X_2^2 + 2.37752 X_2^3$$
$$- 1.02905 X_2^4$$

When $X_2 = 0.100$, $\rho = 0.97061$ g ml^{-1} and $\partial\rho/\partial X_2 = -0.24547$ g ml^{-1}.

Substituting these values and $M_1 = 18.016$ g mole^{-1}, $M_2 = 32.043$ g mole^{-1}, $X_1 = 0.900$ into the result of (b),

$$\bar{V}_2 = 37.56 \text{ ml mole}^{-1}$$

7-III-4. (a) $\gamma_C = \dfrac{P_C}{X_C P_C^\circ} = \dfrac{117.8}{0.5143 \times 293.1} = 0.782$

$\gamma_A = \dfrac{P_A}{X_A P_A^\circ} = \dfrac{135.0}{0.4857 \times 344.5} = 0.802$

(b) $k_C = \dfrac{P_C}{X_C} = \dfrac{9.2 \text{ torr}}{0.0588} = 156 \text{ torr}$

We use P_C and X_C for the most dilute solution for which data are given.

$k_A = \dfrac{P_A}{X_A} = \dfrac{13.0 \text{ torr}}{0.0825} = 158 \text{ torr}$

(c) $\gamma_C' = \dfrac{P_C}{k_C X_C} = \dfrac{117.8}{156 \times 0.5143} = 1.468$

(d) $\dfrac{\gamma_C'}{\gamma_C} = \dfrac{P_C}{k_C X_C} \cdot \dfrac{P_C^\circ X_C}{P_C} = \dfrac{P_C^\circ}{k_C} = \dfrac{293.1}{156} = 1.88$

$\dfrac{\gamma_A'}{\gamma_A} = \dfrac{P_A^\circ}{k_A} = \dfrac{344.5}{158} = 2.18$

These ratios are independent of the composition of the solution.

(e) $\Delta G = 0.5143\mu_C + 0.4857\mu_A - (0.5143\mu_C^\circ + 0.4857\mu_A^\circ)$

$= 0.5143(\mu_C - \mu_C^\circ) + 0.4857(\mu_A - \mu_A^\circ)$

$= 0.5143RT \ln a_C + 0.4857RT \ln a_A$

$= RT[0.5143 \ln(\gamma_C X_C) + 0.4857 \ln(\gamma_A X_A)]$

$= 2.303RT[0.5143 \log(0.782 \times 0.5143)$

$\qquad + 0.4857 \log(0.802 \times 0.4857)]$

$= 2.303 \times 1.987 \times 308.32 \times (-0.4026) \text{ cal}$

$= -568 \text{ cal}$

7-III-5. $G = n_A \mu_A^\circ + n_B \mu_B^\circ + RT(n_A \ln X_A + n_B \ln X_B) + \dfrac{C n_A n_B}{n_A + n_B}$

(a) $\mu_A = \left(\dfrac{\partial G}{\partial n_A}\right)_{n_B, T, P} = \mu_A^\circ + RT \ln X_A$

$\qquad + RT \left[n_A \left(\dfrac{\partial \ln X_A}{\partial n_A}\right)_{n_B} + n_B \left(\dfrac{\partial \ln X_B}{\partial n_A}\right)_{n_B} \right]$

$\qquad + C \left[\dfrac{(n_A + n_B) n_B - n_A n_B}{(n_A + n_B)^2} \right]$

$\quad = \mu_A^\circ + RT \ln X_A + RT \underbrace{\left(1 - \dfrac{n_A}{n_A + n_B} - \dfrac{n_B}{n_A + n_B} \right)}_{0}$

$\qquad + \dfrac{C n_B^2}{(n_A + n_B)^2}$

$\quad = \mu_A^\circ + RT \ln X_A + C X_B^2$

(b) $\mu_A = \mu_A^\circ + RT \ln a_A = \mu_A^\circ + RT \ln X_A + RT \ln \gamma_A$

By comparison, $RT \ln \gamma_A = C X_B^2$

$\gamma_A = e^{C X_B^2 / RT} = 1$

when $X_B = 0$ (pure A). Alternatively we may require that $\gamma_A' \to 1$ as $X_B \to 1$ (infinitely dilute solution of A in B). Then

$\mu_A^{\circ\prime} = \lim\limits_{X_A \to 0} (\mu_A - RT \ln X_A)$

$\qquad = \lim\limits_{X_B \to 1} (\mu_A^\circ + C X_B^2)$

$\qquad = \mu_A^\circ + C$

$\mu_A = \mu_A^{\circ\prime} + RT \ln X_A + C(X_B^2 - 1)$

$\qquad = \mu_A^\circ + RT \ln X_A + RT \ln \gamma_A'$

$\ln \gamma_A' = \dfrac{C(X_B^2 - 1)}{RT} = 0 \qquad$ when $\quad X_B = 1$

7-III-6. (a) Let the solute activity be referred to molality ($\gamma_2 = a_2/m$). Define

$n_1 = 1\,000/M_1$

$n_1 d \ln a_1 = -m d \ln a_2$

$\qquad = -m d \ln(\gamma_2 m)$

$\qquad = -m \left(-\dfrac{3}{2} k m^{1/2} + \dfrac{1}{m} \right) dm$

$\qquad = \left(\dfrac{3}{2} k m^{3/2} - 1 \right) dm$

$$\ln X_1 = -\ln \left(1 + \frac{m}{n_1}\right)$$

$$n_1 \, d \ln X_1 = \frac{-n_1 \, dm}{n_1 + m}$$

$$a_1 = \gamma_1 X_1$$

$$n_1 \, d \ln \gamma_1 = n_1 \, d \ln(\gamma_1 X_1) - n_1 \, d \ln X_1$$

$$= \left(\frac{3}{2} km^{3/2} - 1\right) dm + \frac{n_1 \, dm}{n_1 + m}$$

$$= \left(-\frac{m}{n_1 + m} + \frac{3}{2} km^{3/2}\right) dm$$

Integrating from $m = 0 \ (\gamma_1 = 1)$ to $m = m$

$$n_1 \ln \gamma_1 = -m + n_1 \ln \frac{n_1 + m}{n_1} + \frac{3}{5} km^{5/2}$$

$$\ln \gamma_1 = -\frac{mM_1}{1000} + \ln \left(1 + \frac{mM_1}{1000}\right) + \frac{3M_1 km^{5/2}}{5000}$$

(b) Expand $\ln(1 + mM_1/1000)$ in a series and retain the first two terms,

$$\ln \gamma_1 \approx \underbrace{-\frac{mM_1}{1000} + \frac{mM_1}{1000}}_{0} - \frac{1}{2}\left(\frac{mM_1}{1000}\right)^2 + \cdots + \frac{3M_1 km^{5/2}}{5000}$$

$$\lim \left(\frac{\ln \gamma_1}{m^2}\right) = -\frac{M_1^2}{2 \times 10^6}; \quad n = 2$$

For $n \neq 2$, the limit is 0 or $-\infty$.

7-III-7. (a) $\gamma_2 = 1 - 3.92 X_2$; $\quad d \ln \gamma_2 = \frac{d\gamma_2}{\gamma_2} = \frac{-3.92 \, dX_2}{1 - 3.92 X_2}$

$X_1 \, d \ln \gamma_1 + X_2 \, d \ln \gamma_2 = 0$ for activity coefficients on the mole fraction scale.

$$\ln \gamma_1 = -\int_{X_2=0}^{X_0 = X_2} \frac{X_2}{X_1} \, d \ln \gamma_2$$

$$= 3.92 \int_0^{X_2} \frac{X_2 \, dX_2}{(1 - X_2)(1 - 3.92 X_2)}$$

$$= \frac{3.92}{2.92} \int_0^{X_2} \left(\frac{-X_2}{1 - X_2} + \frac{3.92 X_2}{1 - 3.92 X_2}\right) dX_2$$

$$= \frac{3.92}{2.92} \left\{ -1 + X_2 + \ln(1 - X_2) \right.$$

$$+ \frac{1}{3.92} \left[1 - 3.92X_2 - \ln(1 - 3.92X_2) \right] \right\} \Big|_0^{X_2}$$

$$= \frac{1}{2.92} \left[3.92 \ln(1 - X_2) - \ln(1 - 3.92X_2) \right]$$

(b) $\ln \gamma_1 = \ln[1 - (1 - \gamma_1)] \approx -(1 - \gamma_1)$ if $|1 - \gamma_1| \ll 1$,

that is, in a sufficiently dilute solution.

$$\begin{matrix} \ln(1 - X_2) \approx -X_2 - \tfrac{1}{2}X_2^2 \\ \ln(1 - 3.92X_2) \approx -3.92X_2 - \tfrac{1}{2}(3.92X_2)^2 \end{matrix} \right\} \text{ if } X_2 \ll 1$$

$$1 - \gamma_1 \approx -\ln \gamma_1 \approx -\frac{1}{2.92} \left[-3.92X_2 - \tfrac{1}{2}(3.92) X_2^2 \right.$$

$$\left. + 3.92X_2 + \tfrac{1}{2}(3.92X_2)^2 \right]$$

$$\approx -\frac{3.92}{2 \times 2.92} (-1 + 3.92) X_2^2 = -\frac{3.92}{2} X_2^2$$

7-III-8. (a) $n_1 \, d \ln a_1 + n_2 \, d \ln a_2 = 0$

$\ln \gamma_2 = Am^p$

$n_1 \, d \ln \gamma_1 + n_1 \, d \ln X_1 + m \, d \ln \gamma_2 + m \, d \ln m = 0$

$d \ln \gamma_2 = Apm^{p-1} \, dm$

$\ln X_1 = \ln n_1 - \ln(n_1 + m)$

$d \ln X_1 = -\dfrac{dm}{n_1 + m}$

$m \, d \ln m = dm$

Therefore,

$$n_1 \, d \ln \gamma_1 - \frac{n_1 \, dm}{n_1 + m} + Apm^p \, dm + dm = 0$$

$$d \ln \gamma_1 = \left[\frac{1}{n_1 + m} - \frac{Apm^p + 1}{n_1} \right] dm$$

$$\ln \gamma_1 = \int_{m=0}^m d \ln \gamma_1$$

$$= \ln \frac{n_1 + m}{n_1} - \frac{1}{n_1} \left(\frac{Apm^{p+1}}{p + 1} + m \right)$$

if $\int_0^m m^p \, dm$ exists and is equal to $m^{p+1}/(p + 1)$.

(b) The integral $\int_0^m m^p \, dm$ exists only if $p > -1$. The expression for $\ln \gamma_1$ was evaluated using this assumption.

7-III-9.   (a) $\mu_{B}^{\circ} = \lim\limits_{X_{B} \to 1} (\mu_{B} - RT \ln X_{B}^{2}) = \mu_{B}^{*}$

Since the solution is ideal,

$\mu_{B} = \mu_{B}^{*} + RT \ln X_{B}$

$\quad\ = \mu_{B}^{\circ} + RT \ln X_{B}$

Activity is defined by $\mu_{B} = \mu_{B}^{\circ} + RT \ln a_{B}$. Therefore $a_{B} = X_{B}$.

$$\gamma_{B} = \frac{a_{B}}{X_{B}^{2}} = \frac{X_{B}}{X_{B}^{2}} = \frac{1}{X_{B}}$$

$\lim\limits_{X_{B} \to 1} \gamma_{B} = 1$

as required. However, we have the awkward situation that γ_{B} becomes infinite in the limit of pure A.

(b) $\mu_{B}^{\circ} = \lim\limits_{X_{B} \to 0} (\mu_{B} - RT \ln X_{B}^{2}) = \lim\limits_{X_{B} \to 0} (\mu_{B} - 2RT \ln X_{B})$

$\quad \mu_{B} = \mu_{B}^{*} + RT \ln X_{B}$

$\quad \mu_{B}^{\circ} = \lim\limits_{X_{B} \to 0} (\mu_{B}^{*} - RT \ln X_{B}) = \infty$

The limit does not exist and this activity scale cannot be used. An attempt to use it would lead to

$\quad\quad \mu_{B} = \mu_{B}^{\circ} + RT \ln a_{B}$

$RT \ln a_{B} = \mu_{B} - \mu_{B}^{\circ} = -\infty$

$\quad\quad\ a_{B} = 0$

$\quad\quad\ \gamma_{B} = \frac{a_{B}}{X_{B}^{2}} = 0$

except when $X_{B} = 0$. This activity scale would be appropriate if B dissociated into $2B_{1/2}$ at infinite dilution (as with electrolytes). In that case, of course, the solution would not be ideal in terms of X_{B} .

CHAPTER 8

Free energy
and chemical equilibrium

SECTION 8-I

8-I-1.

$$\Delta G^\circ = -RT \ln K$$

$$\ln K = \frac{-\Delta G^\circ}{RT} = -\frac{1}{R}\left(\frac{\Delta G^\circ}{T}\right)$$

$$d \ln K = -\frac{1}{R} d\left(\frac{\Delta G^\circ}{T}\right)$$

$$d\left(\frac{\Delta G^\circ}{T}\right) = \frac{-\Delta H^\circ \, dT}{T^2}$$

$$d \ln K = -\frac{1}{R}\left(\frac{-\Delta H^\circ \, dT}{T^2}\right) = \frac{\Delta H^\circ \, dT}{RT^2}$$

$$\int d \ln K = \int \frac{\Delta H^\circ \, dT}{RT^2}$$

$$\ln K = -\frac{\Delta H^\circ}{RT} + C$$

8-I-2. (i) The vapor is an ideal gas.

(ii) ΔH_v is independent of temperature.

(iii) The volume of the liquid is negligible in comparison with the volume of the vapor.

(iv) The system is at equilibrium.

8-I-3. (a) $\Delta G < 0$. Therefore the reaction is spontaneous.

(b) No.

(c) "Spontaneous," in thermodynamics, means "not impossible." There is no *thermodynamic* reason why C_2H_4 cannot decompose at 25°C. For some extrathermodynamic reason (for example, high activation energy), the rate of the reaction is essentially zero.

8-I-4.

$$\text{Moles Na}(g) = \frac{71.30}{22.990} = 3.103$$

$$\text{Moles Na}_2(g) = \frac{28.70}{45.980} = 0.624$$

Total number of moles $= 3.103 + 0.624 = 3.727$

$$\text{Mole fraction of Na}(g) = \frac{3.103}{3.727} = 0.832$$

$$\text{Mole fraction of Na}_2(g) = \frac{0.624}{3.727} = 0.167$$

$$K_p = \frac{P_{Na_2}}{P_{Na}^2} = \frac{0.832 \times 10}{(0.167 \times 10)^2} = 2.98$$

8-I-5. (a) Since $K_p = P_{BiI}/P_{BiI_3}^{1/3} =$ constant at constant temperature, then $\log K_p = \log(P_{BiI}) - \frac{1}{3}\log(P_{BiI_3}) =$ constant. This second equation is the equation of a straight line.

(b) $0 = d(\text{constant}) = d(\log P_{BiI}) - \frac{1}{3}d(\log P_{BiI_3})$

$$\text{Slope} = \frac{dy}{dx} = \frac{1}{1/3} = 3$$

Physical significance of the slope: ratio of coefficients in the chemical equation.

8-I-6.

$\Delta G°$

$Mg + Cl_2 + 6H_2 + 3O_2$	
$\quad \rightarrow MgCl_2 \cdot 6H_2O$	$-505,410$
$6H_2O \rightarrow 6H_2 + 3O_2$	$-6(-56,693) = +340,158$
$2Cl^-(aq) \rightarrow Cl_2 + 2e^-$	$-2(-31,340) = +62,680$
$MgCl_2 \cdot 6H_2O + aq \rightarrow Mg^{2+}(aq)$	
$\quad + 2Cl^-(aq) + 6H_2O$	-6180

$Mg \rightarrow Mg^{2+}(aq) + 2e^-$	$-108,752$ cal per g-ion

The original article gives $\Delta G = -108,760$

8-I-7. $\Delta G° = 29{,}760 - 3(50{,}000) = -120{,}240$ cal

$$\log K = \frac{-\Delta G°}{2.303\ RT} = \frac{-(-120{,}240)}{2.303 \times 1.987 \times 298.2} = 88.2$$

$$K = 2 \times 10^{88}$$

Since the equilibrium constant is so large this might be a practical method.

8-I-8. $N_2O_4 \rightleftharpoons 2NO_2$

$(1 - \alpha)$ 2α moles at equilibrium

Total number of moles at equilibrium $= 1 + \alpha$

$$K = \frac{[2\alpha/(1 + \alpha)]^2 \cdot 1^2}{[(1 - \alpha)/(1 + \alpha)] \cdot 1} = 0.174$$

$$\frac{4\alpha^2}{1 - \alpha^2} = 0.174$$

$$\alpha = 0.204$$

Mole fraction $N_2O_4 = X_{N_2O_4} = \dfrac{1 - \alpha}{1 + \alpha} = 0.661$

Mole fraction $NO_2 = X_{NO_2} = \dfrac{2\alpha}{1 + \alpha} = 0.339$

Apparent molecular weight $= (M_{N_2O_4})(X_{N_2O_4}) + (M_{NO_2})(X_{NO_2})$

$$= (92.0)(0.661) + (46.0)(0.339)$$

$$= 76.5$$

8-I-9. $Fe_3O_4 + CO \rightleftharpoons 3FeO + CO_2$

$(1 - y)$ $(2 - y)$ $(0.5 + 3y)$ $(0.3 + y)$ moles at equilibrium

Total number of moles of gas $= 2.3$

$$P_{CO} = \frac{(2 - y)}{2.3} \times 5.00 \text{ atm}$$

$$P_{CO_2} = \frac{(0.3 + y)}{2.3} \times 5.00 \text{ atm}$$

$$K_p = \frac{P_{CO_2}}{P_{CO}} = \frac{(0.3 + y)/2.3}{(2 - y)/2.3} = 1.15$$

$$y = 0.93$$

Number of moles of CO_2 at equilibrium $= 0.3 + y = 1.23$

Number of moles of CO at equilibrium $= 2 - y = 1.07$

Number of moles of Fe_3O_4 at equilibrium $= 1 - y = 0.07$

Number of moles of FeO at equilibrium $= 0.5 + 3y = 3.29$

8-I-10. (a) $\Delta G^{\circ}_{298} = 46.5$ kcal

$$\log K_p = \frac{-\Delta G^{\circ}}{2.303RT} = \frac{-46.5}{2.303 \times 1.987 \times 10^{-3} \times 298.15} = -34.1$$

$$K_p = 8 \times 10^{-35}$$

(b) $\Delta H^{\circ}_{298} = 55.5$ kcal

$$\log K_{T_2} = \log K_{T_1} + \frac{1}{2.303R} \int_{T_1}^{T_2} \frac{\Delta H^{\circ}}{T^2} \, dT$$

$$\approx \log K_{T_1} + \frac{\Delta H^{\circ}(T_2 - T_1)}{2.303RT_1T_2}$$

$$\log K_{398} = -34.1 + \frac{55.5 \times 100}{2.303 \times 1.987 \times 10^{-3} \times 298.15 \times 398.15}$$

$$= -34.1 + 10.2 = -23.9$$

$$K_{398} = 1.3 \times 10^{-24}$$

(c) The assumption was made that ΔH° is independent of temperature in the range 25 to 125°C and could therefore be taken outside the integral sign and set equal to its value at 25°C. Equivalently it was assumed that $\Delta C_P^{\circ} \approx 0$, or, more precisely, that

$$\int_{298}^{398} \Delta C_P^{\circ} \, dT \ll \Delta H^{\circ}$$

8-I-11. (a) $\dfrac{\Delta G^{\circ}_{398}}{398} = \dfrac{\Delta G^{\circ}_{298}}{298} - \displaystyle\int_{298}^{398} \dfrac{\Delta H^{\circ}}{T^2} \, dT$

$$= \frac{-44.72}{298} + 44.14 \left(\frac{1}{298} - \frac{1}{398} \right) = -0.113 \text{ kcal } {}^{\circ}\text{K}^{-1}$$

$$\Delta G^{\circ}_{398} = -45.0 \text{ kcal}$$

(b) $\ln K_p = -\dfrac{\Delta G^{\circ}}{RT}$

$$\log K_p = \frac{0.113}{2.303 \times 1.987 \times 10^{-3}} = 24.7$$

$$K_p = 5 \times 10^{24}$$

8-I-12. $\log \left(\dfrac{K_{p_2}}{K_{p_1}} \right) = \dfrac{-\Delta H^{\circ}}{2.303R} \left(\dfrac{1}{T_2} - \dfrac{1}{T_1} \right)$

$$\log \left(\frac{0.54}{1.46} \right) = \frac{-\Delta H^\circ}{2.303 R} \left(\frac{1}{413.2} - \frac{1}{373.2} \right)$$

$$\Delta H^\circ = 7630 \text{ cal} = -7.63 \text{ kcal}$$

The original article gives -7.56 kcal.

8-I-13. Plot $\log P$ vs $1/T$ (see figure). Slope $= -\Delta H_s/2.303R$.

$$\text{Slope} = \frac{\Delta(\log P)}{\Delta(1/T)} = \frac{(1.800 - 0.400)}{(6.90 - 7.72) \times 10^{-4}} = -1.95 \times 10^4 \text{ }^\circ\text{K}$$

$$\overline{\Delta H_s^\circ} = -2.303R \times \text{Slope}$$
$$= 2.303 \times 1.987 \times 1.95 \times 10^4$$
$$= 89,200 \text{ cal mole}^{-1} \text{ or } 89.2 \text{ kcal mole}^{-1}$$

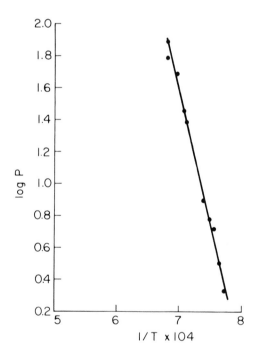

8-I-14. $\overline{\Delta H_s}:$ $\log \dfrac{P_2}{P_1} = \dfrac{\overline{\Delta H_s}(T_2 - T_1)}{2.303 R T_1 T_2}$

$$\overline{\Delta H_s} = \frac{\log(75/25) \times 2.303R \times (250 \times 200)}{50}$$
$$= 2190 \text{ cal mole}^{-1}$$

$$\overline{\Delta H_v} : \quad \log \frac{P_2}{P_1} = \frac{\overline{\Delta H_v}(T_2 - T_1)}{2.303 R T_1 T_2}$$

$$\overline{\Delta H_v} = \frac{\log(300/150) \times 2.303 R \times (400 \times 300)}{100}$$

$$= 1654 \text{ cal mole}^{-1}$$

$$\overline{\Delta H_f} : \quad \overline{\Delta H_s} = \overline{\Delta H_f} + \overline{\Delta H_v}$$

$$\overline{\Delta H_f} = \overline{\Delta H_s} - \overline{\Delta H_v} = 2190 - 1654 = 536 \text{ cal mole}^{-1}$$

8-I-15. (a) Plot $\log P$ vs $1/T$. (See figure.) Slope $= -\overline{\Delta H_v}/2.303 R$

$$\text{Slope} = \frac{\Delta(\log P)}{\Delta(1/T)} = \frac{2.068 - 1.114}{0.004228 - 0.004921} = -1378$$

$$\overline{\Delta H_v} = 2.303 \times 1.987 \times 1378 = 6300 \text{ cal mole}^{-1}$$

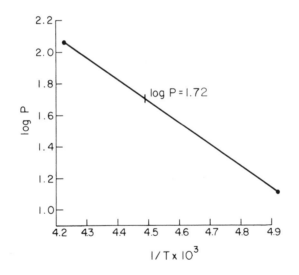

(b) At $-50°C$, $T = 223.2°K$, $1/T = 0.00448°K^{-1}$. From graph, $\log P = 1.72$ at $1/T = 0.00448$. $P = 52$ torr.

8-I-16. $\Delta\left(\dfrac{\bar{G}° - \bar{H}_0°}{T}\right) = 26.74 \text{ cal °K}^{-1}$

$$\Delta H_0° = -26.138 \text{ kcal}$$

$$\Delta(\bar{G}° - \bar{H}_0°) = 298.15 \times 26.74 = 7972 \text{ cal}$$

$$\Delta G° = \Delta(\bar{G}° - \bar{H}_0°) + \Delta H_0° = 7972 - 26{,}138$$

$$= -18{,}166 \text{ cal}$$

$$\log K_p = \frac{-\Delta G°}{2.303RT} = \frac{18{,}166}{4.576 \times 298.15} = 13.3$$

$$K_p = 2 \times 10^{13}$$

8-I-17. $$\frac{\Delta G°}{T} = \Delta\left(\frac{\bar{G}° - \bar{H}_0°}{T}\right) + \frac{\Delta H_0°}{T}$$

$$= -61.11 + 57.29 + 32.74 + \frac{-16{,}520 - 14{,}520}{1000}$$

$$= -2.12 \text{ cal °K}^{-1}$$

$$\log K_p = \frac{-\Delta G°}{2.303RT} = \frac{2.12}{4.576} = 0.463$$

$$K_p = 2.90$$

8-I-18. $$\Delta\left[-\left(\frac{\bar{G}° - \bar{H}_0°}{T}\right)\right] = 2(27.0) - 1(48.0) = 6.0$$

$$-(\Delta G° - \Delta H_0°) = 6.0 \times T = 6.0 \times 600 = 3600 \text{ cal}$$

$$\Delta H_0° = 2(-27{,}000) - 1(-94{,}000) = 40{,}000 \text{ cal}$$

$$-\Delta G° = 3600 - \Delta H_0° = 3600 - 40{,}000 = -36{,}400 \text{ cal}$$

$$\Delta G° = 36{,}400 \text{ cal}$$

$$\log K_p = \frac{-36{,}400}{2.303 \times 1.987 \times 600} = -13.26$$

$$K_p = 5.50 \times 10^{-14}$$

SECTION 8-II

8-II-1. $$dA = -P \, dV - S \, dT$$

$$\left(\frac{\partial A}{\partial T}\right)_V = -S; \quad \left(\frac{\partial A_2}{\partial T}\right)_V = -S_2$$

and

$$\left(\frac{\partial A_1}{\partial T}\right)_V = -S_1$$

$$\left(\frac{\partial \Delta A}{\partial T}\right)_V = -\Delta S$$

$$\left(\frac{\partial(\Delta A/T)}{\partial T}\right) = \frac{T\left(\frac{\partial \Delta A}{\partial T}\right) - \Delta A}{T^2} = \frac{-T\,\Delta S - \Delta A}{T^2} = \frac{-\Delta E}{T^2}$$

8-II-2.

$$\frac{dP}{dT} = \frac{\Delta H}{T\,\Delta V} = \frac{80}{(273.2[(0.92 - 1.00)/(1.00 \times 0.92)])}$$

$$= -3.4 \text{ cal cm}^{-3}\,{}^\circ K^{-1}$$

$$\Delta P = -3.4\,\Delta T = -3.4(-1) = +3.4\,\frac{\text{cal}}{\text{cm}^3} \times \frac{41.3 \text{ cm}^3 \text{ atm}}{\text{cal}}$$

$$= 1.4 \times 10^2 \text{ atm}$$

8-II-3. Rhombic is stable.

$$d(\Delta G) = \Delta V\,dP$$

$$\Delta G_2 - \Delta G_1 = \Delta V(P_2 - P_1)$$

$$0 - 18 \text{ cal mole}^{-1} = \left(\frac{1}{2.07} - \frac{1}{1.96}\right) \text{cm}^3 \text{ g}^{-1} \times 32.0 \text{ g mole}^{-1}$$

$$\times (P_2 - 1) \text{ atm} \times \frac{1 \text{ cal}}{41.3 \text{ cm}^3 \text{ atm}}$$

$$P_2 = 858 \text{ atm}$$

8-II-4. Since the equilibrium conditions have the same form, $K = P_{CO_2}/P_{CO}$, there is only one temperature at which both reactions could be in equilibrium simultaneously—the temperature at which $K_1 = K_2$. Plot $\log K_1$ vs $1/T$ and $\log K_2$ vs $1/T$ on the same graph. (See figure.) The point of intersection gives $1/T = 11.9 \times 10^{-4}$, $T = 840°K$ (567°C) and $\log K_1 = \log K_2 = -0.01$, $K = 0.98$. (The original paper gives $\log K = -0.1$ but apparently this is in error.)

8-II-5. The standard state for a solid, or a liquid that appears pure or as a solvent, is the pure substance. $\mu = \mu° + RT \ln a$. When the substance is pure, $\mu = \mu°$ and $a = 1$. Thus we replace each activity of a pure substance by 1 in the equilibrium condition, which is equivalent to omitting it. If the substance is not quite pure, a first approximation to the activity is the mole fraction (according to Raoult's law), not the concentration.

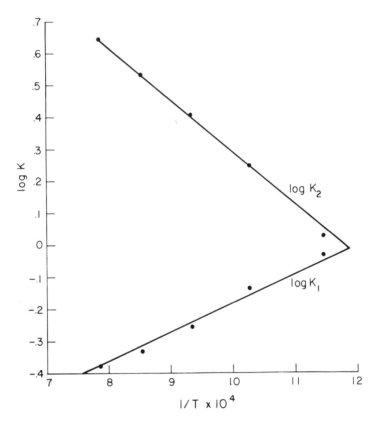

Fig. 8-II-4.

8-II-6. (a) $M = \dfrac{\rho\, RT}{P} = 0.344 \text{ g liter}^{-1} \times \dfrac{0.08206 \text{ liter atm } {}^{\circ}\text{K}^{-1} \text{ mole}^{-1}}{1.00 \text{ atm}}$

$\times\ 1300\ {}^{\circ}\text{K}$

$= 36.7 \text{ g mole}^{-1}$

(b) $\text{ZnO} + \quad \text{CO} \quad \leftrightharpoons \text{Zn} + \text{CO}_2$

$\qquad\qquad n_0(1-\alpha) \quad n_0\alpha \quad n_0\alpha \quad$ moles present at equilibrium

$n_{\text{total}} = n_0(1 + \alpha)$

The total weight of the gases is

$w = n_0[(1-\alpha) \times 28.01 + \alpha \times 65.37 + \alpha \times 44.01]$

(The numbers are the molecular weights of the gases.)

$$w = n_0(28.01 + 81.37\alpha)$$

$$M = \frac{w}{n_{\text{total}}} = \frac{28.01 + 81.37\alpha}{1 + \alpha} = 36.7$$

$$\alpha = 0.194$$

(c) $P_{CO_2} = P_{Zn} = \dfrac{n_0\alpha}{n_0(1 + \alpha)} P = 0.162$ atm

$$P_{CO} = \frac{n_0(1 - \alpha)}{n_0(1 + \alpha)} P = 0.675 \text{ atm}$$

$$K_p = \frac{P_{CO_2}P_{Zn}}{P_{CO}} = 3.89 \times 10^{-2} \text{ atm}$$

8-II-7. $\quad XY_2 \leftrightharpoons X + 2Y$

$(0.40 - z) \quad z \quad 2z \quad$ moles present at equilibrium

$$n_{\text{total}} = 0.40 + 2z$$

$$n = \frac{PV}{RT} = \frac{1.20 \text{ atm} \times 10.0 \text{ liters}}{0.08206 \text{ liter atm } °K^{-1} \text{ mole}^{-1} \times 300°K} = 0.487$$

$0.40 + 2z = 0.487, \quad z = 0.044$

$$K_p = \frac{P_X P_Y^2}{P_{XY_2}} = \frac{z(2z)^2 (1.20)^2}{(0.40 - z)(0.40 + 2z)^2} = 5.8 \times 10^{-3}$$

8-II-8. (a) $\quad 2SO_2 + O_2 \leftrightharpoons 2SO_3$

$(0.100 + 2y) \quad y \quad (0.100 - 2y) \quad$ moles present at equilibrium

$$n_{\text{total}} = 0.200 + y$$

$$\frac{V}{RT} = \frac{2.00 \text{ liters}}{0.08206 \text{ liter atm } °K^{-1} \text{ mole}^{-1} \times 300°K}$$

$$= 0.0812 \text{ mole atm}^{-1}$$

$$n_{\text{total}} = \frac{PV}{RT} = 2.78 \text{ atm} \times 0.0812 \text{ mole atm}^{-1} = 0.226 \text{ mole}$$

$$y = 0.026 \text{ mole}$$

$$X_{O_2} = \frac{y}{n_{\text{total}}} = \frac{0.026}{0.226} = 0.115$$

(b) $K_p = \dfrac{P_{SO_3}^2}{P_{SO_2}^2 P_{O_2}} = \dfrac{n_{SO_3}^2}{n_{SO_2}^2 n_{O_2}} \cdot \dfrac{V}{RT}$

$\qquad = \dfrac{0.048^2 \times 0.0812}{0.152^2 \times 0.026} = 0.32$

(c) $2SO_2 + O_2 \leftrightharpoons 2SO_3$

$\qquad 2y \qquad y \qquad (0.100 - 2y)$ moles present at equilibrium

$\dfrac{n_{SO_3}^2}{n_{SO_2}^2 n_{O_2}} = \dfrac{K_p RT}{V} = \dfrac{0.32}{0.0812} = 3.94$

$\dfrac{(0.100 - 2y)^2}{(2y)^2 y} = 3.94$

$\dfrac{(0.100 - 2y)^2}{y^3} = 15.76$

This equation is best solved by trial and error. A possible procedure is the following. It is obvious that y must be between 0 and 0.050. We first try the midpoint of this interval:

y	$(0.100 - 2y)^2/y^3$	
0.025	160	y is too small
0.040	6.3	y is too large
0.036	16.79	
0.0365	14.99	interpolate
0.0363	15.70	

$\dfrac{2y}{0.100} = 0.73$ or 73 percent = fraction of SO_3 dissociated

8-II-9. Moles HOAc (assuming 100 percent monomer)

$\qquad = 13.80 \times 10^{-3} \times 0.0568$

$\qquad = 7.84 \times 10^{-4}$

Moles $(HOAc)_2$ (assuming 100 percent dimer)

$\qquad = \frac{1}{2} \times 7.84 \times 10^{-4}$

$\qquad = 3.92 \times 10^{-4}$

Assuming 100 percent dimer, the pressure of the ideal gas would be

$P_i = \dfrac{nRT}{V} = \dfrac{3.92 \times 10^{-4} \times 82.06 \times 324.4}{359.8}$

$P_i = 0.0290$ atm $= 22.0$ torr

$(HOAc)_2 (g) \rightleftharpoons 2HOAc (g)$

$(1 - \alpha)$ 2α moles present at equilibrium

Total number of moles $= 1 + \alpha$

$P_i(1 + \alpha) = P_{\text{observed}} = 22.0(1 + \alpha) = 25.98$ torr

$\alpha = 0.181;$

$$K = \frac{P_{HOAc}^2}{P_{(HOAc)_2}} = \frac{(2\alpha)^2 P}{(1 - \alpha)(1 + \alpha)} = 3.52 \text{ (for pressures in torr)}$$

8-II-10.   Aqueous: $[HBz] + [K \cdot HBz] = 20.40 \times 10^{-3}$ moles liter^{-1}

Skellysolve: $[HBz] = 28.43 \times 10^{-3}$ moles liter^{-1}

Aqueous: $[K] + [K \cdot HBz] = 26.91 \times 10^{-3}$ moles liter^{-1}

$$(HBz)_2 (Sk) \rightleftharpoons 2HBz(aq)$$

$$\frac{[HBz]_{aq}^2}{[(HBz)_2]_{Sk}} = 5.02 \times 10^{-3}$$

$$[HBz]_{aq}^2 = \frac{28.43 \times 10^{-3}}{2} \times 5.02 \times 10^{-3} = 71.4 \times 10^{-6}$$

$$[HBz]_{aq} = 8.45 \times 10^{-3} \text{ moles liter}^{-1}$$

$$[K \cdot HBz]_{aq} = 20.40 \times 10^{-3} - [HBz]_{aq}$$
$$= 20.40 \times 10^{-3} - 8.45 \times 10^{-3} = 11.95 \times 10^{-3}$$

$$[K]_{aq} = 26.91 \times 10^{-3} - 11.95 \times 10^{-3}$$
$$= 14.96 \times 10^{-3} \text{ moles liter}^{-1}$$

$$K_c = \frac{[HBz]_{aq} [K]_{aq}}{[K \cdot HBz]_{aq}} = \frac{[8.45 \times 10^{-3}][14.96 \times 10^{-3}]}{[11.95 \times 10^{-3}]}$$
$$= 1.06 \times 10^{-2}$$

8-II-11.   (a) $CO(g) + H_2O(g) \rightleftharpoons CO_2(g) + H_2(g)$ (1)

$\Delta G_1^\circ = -6.818$ kcal

$$\log K_{p_1} = \frac{6818}{2.303 \times 1.987 \times 298.15} = 5.00$$

$$K_{p_1} = 1.00 \times 10^5$$

(b) $H_2O(liq) \rightleftharpoons H_2O(g)$ (2)

$\Delta G_2^\circ = 2.055$ kcal

$$\log K_{p_2} = \frac{-2055}{2.303 \times 1.987 \times 298.15} = -1.506$$

$P_{H_2O} = K_{p_2} = 3.12 \times 10^{-2}$ atm

(c) $\quad CO(g) + H_2O(liq) \rightleftharpoons CO_2(g) + H_2(g)$ (3)

$\quad (1.00 - x) \qquad\qquad\qquad (1.00 + x) \quad (1.00 + x)$

atm at equilibrium

$$\frac{P_{CO_2} P_{H_2}}{P_{CO}} = K_{p_3} = K_{p_1} K_{p_2}$$

$$\frac{(1.00 + x)^2}{(1.00 - x)} = 3.12 \times 10^3$$

Let $y = 1 - x$. Then $1 + x = 2 - y$.

$$\frac{(2 - y)^2}{y} = 3.12 \times 10^3$$

Assume $y \ll 2$,

$$\frac{4}{y} = 3.12 \times 10^3$$

$y = 1.28 \times 10^{-3}$ atm $= P_{CO}$

$P_{CO_2} = P_{H_2} = 2.00 - y = 2.00$ atm

$P_{H_2O} = 3.12 \times 10^{-2}$ atm

8-II-12.

(a) $\qquad\qquad\qquad A(g) + 2B(g) = C(s) + 2D(g)$

Moles present
initially $\qquad\qquad\qquad n_0 \qquad\qquad n_0 \qquad\qquad 0 \qquad 0$

Moles present
at equilibrium $\quad n_0(1 - \alpha) \quad n_0(1 - 2\alpha) \quad [n_0\alpha] \quad n_0(2\alpha)$

Total moles of gas at equilibrium $= n_0(2 - \alpha)$. We are told that $1 - \alpha = 0.750$; then

$\alpha = 0.250.$ $\qquad P = 2.00$ atm

$$P_A = \frac{n_0(1 - \alpha)}{n_0(2 - \alpha)} P = \frac{6}{7} \text{ atm}$$

$$P_B = \frac{n_0(1 - 2\alpha)}{n_0(2 - \alpha)} P = \frac{4}{7} \text{ atm}$$

$$P_D = \frac{n_0(2\alpha)}{n_0(2-\alpha)} \, P = \frac{4}{7} \, \text{atm}$$

$$K_p = \frac{P_D^2}{P_A P_B^2} = \frac{7}{6}$$

(b) $A(g) \quad + \quad 2B(g) \leftrightarrows C(s) + 2D(g)$

Partial pressure

at equilibrium, atm $1.00 - \frac{1}{2}x$ $1.00 - x$ x

$$K_p = \frac{x^2}{(1 - \frac{1}{2}x)(1 - x)^2} = \frac{7}{6}$$

(c) In (a) the total pressure is always 2 atm; in (b) the pressure at equilibrium is less, because when the reaction proceeds from left to right, 3 moles of gas become 2 moles of gas and, the volume being constant, the pressure must diminish. The forward reaction is favored by increased pressure and we therefore expect a larger yield of D in (a).

(d) This cubic equation is most easily solved by trial and error. We look for a solution between 0 and $4/7 = 0.57$. The result is $x = 0.48$ atm $= P_D$.

8-II-13. (a) $2IBr(g) \rightleftharpoons I_2(s) + Br_2(g)$

$0.50 - 2x = 0.16$ atm $x = 0.17$ atm (at equilibrium)

$$K_p = \frac{P_{Br_2}}{P_{IBr}^2} = \frac{0.17}{(0.16)^2} = 6.64$$

(b) $2IBr(g) \rightleftharpoons I_2(s) + Br_2(g)$

$n_0(1 - 2\alpha)$ $n_0\alpha$ (moles at equilibrium)

$n_{total} = n_0(1 - \alpha)$

$P_{Br_2} + P_{IBr} = 0.50 - 4 \times 10^{-4}$ atm $= 0.50$ atm

$$P_{Br_2} = \frac{n_0\alpha}{n_0(1-\alpha)} \, 0.50 = \frac{\alpha}{2(1-\alpha)}$$

$$P_{IBr} = \frac{n_0(1-2\alpha)}{n_0(1-\alpha)} \, 0.50 = \frac{1-2\alpha}{2(1-\alpha)}$$

$$\frac{P_{Br_2}}{P_{IBr}^2} = K_p$$

$$\frac{2\alpha(1-\alpha)}{(1-2\alpha)^2} = 6.64$$

$$14.28\alpha^2 - 14.28\alpha + 3.32 = 0$$

$$\alpha = \frac{1}{2}\left(1 \pm \sqrt{\frac{1}{14.28}}\right)$$

Since $\alpha < \frac{1}{2}$, the minus sign must be chosen.

$\alpha = 0.368$

$$P_{Br_2} = \frac{\alpha}{2(1-\alpha)} = \frac{0.368}{2 \times 0.632} = 0.29 \text{ atm}$$

8-II-14. $2BrCl(g) \rightleftharpoons Br_2(liq) + Cl_2(g)$

$$K_p = \frac{1}{2.032} = 0.4921$$

$$P_{BrCl} + P_{Cl_2} = 1.000 - 0.281 = 0.719 \text{ atm}$$

Let n_0 = the number of moles of BrCl initially present. At equilibrium

$$n_{BrCl} = n_0(1-\alpha)$$

$$n_{Cl_2} = n_0 \times \tfrac{1}{2}\alpha \qquad (1 BrCl \rightarrow \tfrac{1}{2}Cl_2)$$

$$n_{BrCl} + n_{Cl_2} = n_0(1 - \tfrac{1}{2}\alpha)$$

$$P_{BrCl} = \frac{n_0(1-\alpha)}{n_0(1-\tfrac{1}{2}\alpha)} \times 0.719 \text{ atm}$$

$$P_{Cl_2} = \frac{n_0 \times \tfrac{1}{2}\alpha}{n_0(1-\tfrac{1}{2}\alpha)} \times 0.719 \text{ atm}$$

$$\frac{P_{Cl_2}}{P_{BrCl}^2} = \frac{\tfrac{1}{2}\alpha(1-\tfrac{1}{2}\alpha)}{(1-\alpha)^2 \times 0.719} = 0.4921$$

$$0.604\alpha^2 - 1.208\alpha + 0.354 = 0$$

$$\alpha = 0.357$$

8-II-15. (a) Equilibrium pressure of $F_2 = 1 - P$ atm

Equilibrium pressure of $PuF_6 = P$ atm

$$K_p = \frac{P_{PuF_6}}{P_{F_2}} = \frac{P}{1-P} = 26.6 \times 10^{-4}$$

$$P = 26.5 \times 10^{-4} \text{ atm}$$

$$P_{total} = P_{PuF_6} + P_{F_2} = 1 - P + P = 1 \text{ atm}$$

$$\text{Mole percent } F_2 = \frac{P_{F_2}}{P_{total}} \times 100 = \frac{(1 - 26.5 \times 10^{-4})}{1} \times 100$$

$$= 99.7 \text{ percent}$$

$$\text{Mole percent } PuF_6 = \frac{P_{PuF_6}}{P_{total}} \times 100 = \frac{26.5 \times 10^{-4} \times 100}{1}$$

$$= 0.265 \text{ percent}$$

(b) Formula weight of $PuF_6 = 353$

$$1 \text{ g of } PuF_6 = \frac{1}{353} \text{ mole} = 0.00283 \text{ mole}$$

Let n_{F_2} = the number of moles of F_2 required.

$0.00265\, n_{F_2} = 0.00283$

$\quad\quad n_{F_2} = 1.07 \text{ moles}$

8-II-16. (a) $\quad\quad HD(g) \quad\quad + \quad H_2O(g) \rightleftharpoons H_2(g) + HDO(g)$

$\quad\quad\quad (0.000298 \times 0.5 - x) \quad (0.5 - x) \quad\quad (0.5 + x) \quad\quad x$

$$K_p = \frac{P_{HDO} \times P_{H_2}}{P_{HD} \times P_{H_2O}} = \frac{(0.5 + x)(x)}{(0.000149 - x)(0.5 - x)} = 2.6$$

Since $0.5 \gg x$, $0.5 + x \approx 0.5 - x \approx 0.5$, and we can write

$$\frac{x}{0.000149 - x} = 2.6$$

$$x = 1.078 \times 10^{-4} \text{ atm}$$

Fraction of HD remaining $= \dfrac{0.000149 - 0.000108}{0.000149}$

$$= 0.275$$

(b) $\quad\quad \dfrac{x'}{0.000041 - x'} = 2.6$

$$x' = 0.0000296$$

Fraction of HD remaining $= \dfrac{0.000041 - 0.000030}{0.000149}$

$$= 0.074$$

8-II-17. (a) $\Delta\dfrac{\bar{G}° - \bar{H}°_0}{T} = -32.74 - 52.01 + 57.29$

$$= -27.46 \text{ cal } °K^{-1} \text{ mole}^{-1}$$

$\Delta H°_0 = 54.33 - 14.52 = 39.81 \text{ kcal mole}^{-1}$

$\dfrac{\Delta H°_0}{T} = 39.81 \text{ cal } °K^{-1} \text{ mole}^{-1}$

$\dfrac{\Delta G°}{T} = \Delta\dfrac{\bar{G}° - \bar{H}°_0}{T} + \dfrac{\Delta H°_0}{T} = 12.35 \text{ cal } °K^{-1} \text{ mole}^{-1}$

$\log K_p = \dfrac{-\Delta G°}{2.303RT} = \dfrac{-12.35}{2.303 \times 1.987} = -2.699$

$K_p = 2.00 \times 10^{-3}$

(b) $C_2H_4 \leftrightharpoons H_2 + C_2H_4$
$\qquad n_0(1-\alpha) \quad n_0\alpha \quad n_0\alpha \quad$ moles at equilibrium

$$n_{total} = n_0(1+\alpha)$$

$$P_{C_2H_4} = \frac{1-\alpha}{1+\alpha} \times 10.0 \text{ atm}$$

$$P_{H_2} = P_{C_2H_2} = \frac{\alpha}{1+\alpha} \times 10.0 \text{ atm}$$

$$\frac{P_{H_2}P_{C_2H_2}}{P_{C_2H_4}} = K_p$$

$$\left(\frac{10.0\alpha}{1+\alpha}\right)^2 \left(\frac{1+\alpha}{10.0(1-\alpha)}\right) = 2.00 \times 10^{-3}$$

$$\frac{\alpha^2}{1-\alpha^2} = 2.00 \times 10^{-4}$$

$$\alpha^2 = \frac{2.00 \times 10^{-4}}{1.0002} = 2.00 \times 10^{-4}$$

$$\alpha = 1.41 \times 10^{-2}$$

$$P_{H_2} = \frac{1.41 \times 10^{-2}}{1.0141} \times 10.0 \text{ atm} = 0.139 \text{ atm}$$

8-II-18. $\quad A \quad + \quad 2B \quad \leftrightharpoons C + D(s)$
$\quad n_0(1-\alpha) \quad n_0(1-2\alpha) \quad n_0\alpha \qquad$ moles present at equilibrium

$$\frac{n_0 RT}{V} = 1.00 \text{ atm}$$

(a) $\quad P_A = n_0(1-\alpha)\dfrac{RT}{V} = 1 - \alpha$

$$P_B = n_0(1-2\alpha)\frac{RT}{V} = 1 - 2\alpha$$

$$P_C = n_0\alpha \frac{RT}{V} = \alpha$$

$$\frac{P_C}{P_A P_B^2} = K_p$$

$$\frac{\alpha}{(1-\alpha)(1-2\alpha)^2} = 1.0 \times 10^{-3}$$

If $2\alpha \ll 1$, $\alpha = 1.0 \times 10^{-3} \text{ atm} = P_C$. For an improved result, $1 - \alpha = 0.999$, $1 - 2\alpha = 0.998$.

$$\alpha = 1.0 \times 10^{-3} \times 0.999 \times 0.9982 = 0.995 \times 10^{-3} \text{ atm} = P_C$$

(b) $n_{\text{total}} = n_0(1 - \alpha + 1 - 2\alpha + \alpha) = n_0(2 - 2\alpha)$

$P = 2.00$ atm

$$P_A = \frac{n_0(1 - \alpha)}{n_0(2 - 2\alpha)} P = 1.00 \text{ atm}$$

$$P_B = \frac{n_0(1 - 2\alpha)}{n_0(2 - 2\alpha)} P = \frac{1 - 2\alpha}{1 - \alpha}$$

$$P_C = \frac{n_0 \alpha}{n_0(2 - 2\alpha)} P = \frac{\alpha}{1 - \alpha}$$

$$\frac{P_C}{P_A P_B^2} = K_p$$

$$\frac{\alpha(1 - \alpha)}{(1 - 2\alpha)^2} = 1.0 \times 10^{-3}$$

If $2\alpha \ll 1$, $\alpha = 1.0 \times 10^{-3}$ atm $\approx P_C$. For an improved result (as in (a))

$$\alpha = \frac{1.0 \times 10^{-3} \times 0.998^2}{0.999} = 0.997 \times 10^{-3}$$

$$P_C = \frac{\alpha}{1 - \alpha} = \frac{0.997 \times 10^{-3}}{0.999} = 0.998 \times 10^{-3}$$

(c) Physically: This reaction is accompanied by a decrease in the number of moles of gas. If the volume is held constant, the final pressure will be less than 2.00 atm. The leftward reaction is thus (by Le Châtelier's principle) more favored than it is when the pressure is held constant at 2.00 atm. We therefore expect a higher yield of C at constant pressure. Mathematically:

(a) $\alpha_a = K_p(1 - \alpha_a)(1 - 2\alpha_a)^2$

(b) $\alpha_b = \dfrac{K_p(1 - 2\alpha_b)^2}{1 - \alpha_b}$

$$\frac{\alpha_a}{\alpha_b} \approx (1 - \alpha)^2 < 1$$

8-II-19. $\Delta H_T^\circ = \Delta H_{298}^\circ + \displaystyle\int_{298}^{T} \Delta C_P^\circ \, dT = -1130.5 + 0.0740(T - 298)$

$= -1152.6 + 0.0740 \; T \text{ kilojoules}$

(It has been assumed that ΔC_P° is independent of T.)

$\Delta E_T^\circ = \Delta H_T^\circ - RT \, \Delta n_{\text{gas}} = \Delta H_T^\circ + 3RT$

$= -1152.6 + 0.0989 T \text{ kilojoules}$

(It has been assumed that the gases are ideal and that $P\bar{V}$ for $H_2O(liq)$ is negligible.)

$$\Delta S_T^\circ = \Delta S_{298}^\circ + \int_{298}^T \frac{\Delta C_P^\circ}{T} \, dT = -388.3 + 74.0 \ln \left(\frac{T}{298}\right)$$

$$= -810.0 + 74.0 \ln T \text{ joules } {}^\circ K^{-1}$$

$$\Delta G_T^\circ = \Delta H_T^\circ - T \Delta S_T^\circ$$

$$= -1152.6 + 0.8840T - 0.0740T \ln T \text{ kilojoules}$$

8-II-20. (a) $\Delta H_{298}^\circ = 0 - 94.05 - (-52.40) - (-26.42) = -15.23 \text{ kcal}$

$$\Delta G_{298}^\circ = 0 - 94.26 - (-45.25) - (-32.81) = -16.20 \text{ kcal}$$

$$\log K_p = \frac{-\Delta G^\circ}{2.303RT} = \frac{16.20}{4.576 \times 10^{-3} \times 298} = 11.88$$

$$K_p = 7.6 \times 10^{11}$$

(b) $\Delta C_P^\circ = 6.34 + 8.76 - 11.07 - 6.95 = -2.92 \text{ cal } {}^\circ K^{-1} \text{ mole}^{-1}$

$$\Delta H_T^\circ = \Delta H_{298}^\circ + \int_{298}^T \Delta C_P^\circ \, dT$$

$$= -15.23 - 2.92 \times 10^{-3} \times (T - 298) \text{ kcal}$$

$$= -14.36 - 2.92 \times 10^{-3}T \text{ kcal}$$

(c) $\log K_{p,400} = \log K_{p,298} + \dfrac{1}{2.303R} \displaystyle\int_{298}^{400} \dfrac{\Delta H_T^\circ}{T^2} \, dT$

$$= 11.88 + \frac{1}{4.576 \times 10^{-3}}$$

$$\times \int_{298}^{400} \left(\frac{-14.36}{T^2} - \frac{2.92 \times 10^{-3}}{T}\right) dT$$

$$= 11.88 + \frac{1}{4.576 \times 10^{-3}} \left[\frac{-14.36(400 - 298)}{400 \times 298}\right.$$

$$\left. - 2.92 \times 10^{-3} \ln \frac{400}{298}\right]$$

$$= 7.32$$

$$K_p = 2.1 \times 10^7$$

8-II-21. $\Delta H_{300}^\circ = 2(-150,000) - 1(-250,000)$

$$= -50,000 \text{ cal}$$

$$\Delta S^\circ_{300} = 2(10.00) - 1(30.00) = -10.00 \text{ cal } {}^\circ\text{K}^{-1}$$

$$\Delta G^\circ_{300} = \Delta H^\circ_{300} - 300\Delta S^\circ_{300} = -50,000 - 300(10.00)$$

$$= -47,000 \text{ cal}$$

$$\Delta C_P = 2(3.00 + 2.00 \times 10^{-2}T) - (4.00 + 5.00 \times 10^{-2}T)$$

$$= 2.00 - 1.00 \times 10^{-2}T$$

$$\Delta H_{T_2} = \Delta H_{T_1} + \int_{T_1}^{T_2} \Delta C_P \, dT$$

$$\Delta H_T = -50,000 + \int_{300}^{T} (2.00 - 1.00 \times 10^{-2}T) \, dT$$

$$= -50,000 + 2.00(T - 300) - \frac{1.00 \times 10^{-2}}{2}(T^2 - 300^2)$$

$$= -50,000 + 2.00T - 600 - 5.00 \times 10^{-3}T + 450$$

$$\Delta H_T = -50,150 + 2.00T - 5.00 \times 10^{-3}T^2 \text{ cal}$$

$$-\frac{\Delta G_2}{T_2} + \frac{\Delta G_1}{T_1} = \int_{T_1}^{T_2} \frac{\Delta H \, dT}{T^2} = -\int_{T_1}^{T_2} \frac{50,150}{T^2} + \int_{T_1}^{T_2} \frac{2.00 \, dT}{T}$$

$$-\int_{T_1}^{T_2} 5.00 \times 10^{-3} \, dT$$

$$= 50,150 \left(\frac{1}{T_2} - \frac{1}{T_1}\right) + 2.00 \ln \frac{T_2}{T_1}$$
$$-5.00 \times 10^{-3}(T_2 - T_1)$$

$$-\frac{\Delta G_2}{T_2} + \frac{-47,000}{300} = 50,150 \left(\frac{1}{T_2} - \frac{1}{300}\right) + 2.00 \ln \frac{T_2}{300}$$
$$- 5.00 \times 10^{-3}(T_2 - 300)$$

$$-\frac{\Delta G_2}{T_2} = -23.408 + \frac{50,150}{T_2} + 4.61 \log T_2 - 5.00 \times 10^{-3} T_2$$

Let

$$\Delta G_2 = \Delta G, \qquad T_2 = T$$

$$\Delta G = -50,150 + 23.408T - 4.61T \log T + 5.00 \times 10^{-3}T^2 \text{ cal}$$

8-II-22. (a) $\Delta H^\circ_{298} = 2(-30.36) - 2(-22.06) = -16.60 \text{ kcal}$

$$\Delta G^\circ_{298} = 2(-26.22) - 2(-22.77) = -6.90 \text{ kcal}$$

$$\log K_p = \frac{-\Delta G^\circ_{298}}{2.303RT} = \frac{6.90}{2.303 \times 1.987 \times 10^{-3} \times 298} = 5.06$$

$$K_p = 1.1 \times 10^5$$

(b) $Ag + 2HCl \rightleftharpoons 2AgCl + H_2$

$\qquad n_0(1 - 2\alpha) \qquad\qquad\qquad n_0\alpha$ moles present at equilibrium

$\qquad n_{total} = n_0(1 - \alpha)$

$$P_{H_2} = \left(\frac{\alpha}{1 - \alpha}\right)(0.50) \text{ atm}$$

$$P_{HCl} = \left(\frac{1 - 2\alpha}{1 - \alpha}\right)(0.50) \text{ atm}$$

$$\frac{P_{H_2}}{P_{HCl}^2} = K_p$$

$$\frac{\alpha(1 - \alpha)}{(1 - 2\alpha)^2 (0.50)} = 1.1 \times 10^5$$

Let

$$\beta = 1 - 2\alpha$$

Then

$$\alpha = \tfrac{1}{2}(1 - \beta), \quad 1 - \alpha = \tfrac{1}{2}(1 + \beta)$$

$$\frac{1 - \beta^2}{\beta^2} = 2.2 \times 10^5$$

$$\beta = 2.1 \times 10^{-3}$$

$$P_{HCl} = \frac{0.50\beta}{\tfrac{1}{2}(1 + \beta)} = 2.19 \times 10^{-3} \text{ atm}$$

$$P_{H_2} = \frac{\tfrac{1}{2}(1 - \beta)(0.50)}{\tfrac{1}{2}(1 + \beta)} = 0.50 \text{ atm}$$

(c) $\Delta C_P^\circ = 2 \times 12.61 + 6.80 - 2 \times 6.01 - 2 \times 7.09$

$\qquad = 5.82 \text{ cal } {}^\circ K^{-1} \text{ mole}^{-1}$

$$\Delta H_T^\circ = \Delta H_{298}^\circ + \int_{298}^{T} \Delta C_P^\circ \, dT$$

$\qquad = -16.60 + 5.82 \times 10^{-3}(T - 298) \text{ kcal}$

$\qquad = -14.86 + 5.82 \times 10^{-3}T \text{ kcal}$

(d) $\log K_{p,T} = \log K_{p,298} + \dfrac{1}{2.303R} \displaystyle\int_{298}^{T} \dfrac{\Delta H_T^\circ}{T^2} \, dT$

$$= 5.06 + \frac{1}{4.576 \times 10^{-3}}$$

$$\times \left[14.86 \left(\frac{1}{T} - \frac{1}{298}\right) + 5.82 \times 10^{-3} \ln \frac{T}{298}\right]$$

$$= -13.07 + \frac{3.25 \times 10^3}{T} + 2.93 \log T$$

(d) $\log K_{p,323} = -13.07 + \dfrac{3.25 \times 10^3}{323} + 2.93 \log 323 = 4.34$

$K_{p,323} = 2.2 \times 10^4$

8-II-23. (a) $I_2(s) + Br_2(g) \rightleftarrows 2IBr(g)$

$\qquad\qquad n_0(1 - \alpha) \quad n_0(2\alpha)$ moles present at equilibrium

$n_{total} = n_0(1 + \alpha)$

$P_{IBr} = \dfrac{n_0(2\alpha)}{n_0(1 + \alpha)} P = \dfrac{2\alpha(0.164)}{1 + \alpha}$

$P_{Br_2} = \dfrac{n_0(1 - \alpha)}{n_0(1 + \alpha)} P = \dfrac{(1 - \alpha)(0.164)}{1 + \alpha}$

$\dfrac{P_{IBr}^2}{P_{Br_2}} = K_p$

$\dfrac{(2\alpha)^2 (0.164)}{(1 + \alpha)(1 - \alpha)} = 0.164$

$\dfrac{4\alpha^2}{1 - \alpha^2} = 1$

$\qquad \alpha = 0.447$

$P_{IBr} = \dfrac{2 \times 0.447 \times 0.164}{1.447} = 0.101$ atm

(b) $\Delta C_P^\circ = 2(8.7) - 13.3 - 8.8 = -4.7$ cal $°K^{-1}$

$\Delta H_{298}^\circ = 2(9.75) - 7.34 = 12.16$ kcal $= 12{,}160$ cal

$\Delta H_T^\circ = \Delta H_{298}^\circ + \displaystyle\int_{298}^{T} \Delta C_P^\circ \, dT = 12{,}160 - 4.7(T - 298)$

$\qquad\qquad = 13{,}560 - 4.7T$ cal

$\dfrac{d \ln K_p}{dT} = \dfrac{\Delta H^\circ}{RT^2} = \dfrac{1}{R}\left(\dfrac{13{,}560}{T^2} - \dfrac{4.7}{T}\right)$

$\ln \dfrac{K_{p,398}}{K_{p,298}} = \dfrac{1}{R}\displaystyle\int_{298}^{398}\left(\dfrac{13{,}560}{T^2} - \dfrac{4.7}{T}\right) dT$

$\log \dfrac{K_{p,398}}{K_{p,298}} = \dfrac{1}{R}\left(\dfrac{13{,}560 \times 100}{398 \times 298 \times 2.303} - 4.7 \log \dfrac{398}{298}\right) = 2.20$

$K_{p,398} = K_{p,298} \times 10^{2.20} = 0.164 \times 1.59 \times 10^2 = 26.0$

(c) ΔH° of formation is taken to be 0 at one temperature for an element *in its standard state*, the stable state at 1 atm and that temperature. For Br_2 the liquid is the standard state and 7.34 kcal is ΔH for the process $Br_2(liq) \rightarrow Br_2(g, 1$ atm$)$.

8-II-24.

	ΔH°_{300}	ΔG°_{300}
$2CO_2(g) + 3H_2O(liq)$		
$\rightarrow (CH_2OH)_2 \, (liq) + \frac{5}{2}O_2(g)$	273.48	281.47
$2C(graphite) + 2O_2(g)$		
$\rightarrow 2CO_2(g)$	-188.10	-188.52
$3H_2(g) + \frac{3}{2}O_2(g)$		
$\rightarrow 3H_2O(liq)$	-204.96	-170.07

(a) -119.58 kcal (b) -77.12 kcal

(c) $\Delta E^\circ = \Delta H^\circ - RT\,\Delta n_{gas}$

$= -119.58 - 1.987 \times 10^{-3} \times 300(-4)$

$= -117.20$ kcal

(d) $\Delta A^\circ = \Delta G^\circ - RT\,\Delta n_{gas} = -74.74$ kcal

(e) $\Delta C^\circ_P = 35.45 - 2(2.04) - 3(6.84) - 6.98$ cal $^\circ K^{-1}$

$= 3.87 \times 10^{-3}$ kcal $^\circ K^{-1}$

$$\Delta H^\circ_T = \Delta H^\circ_{300} + \int_{300}^T \Delta C^\circ_P \, dT$$

$= -119.58 + 3.87 \times 10^{-3}(T - 300)$ kcal,

$$280 \leqslant T \leqslant 370\ ^\circ K$$

(f) $\Delta H^\circ_{350} = -119.58 + 3.87 \times 10^{-3} \times 50 = -119.39$ kcal

(g) $\log K_p = \dfrac{-\Delta G^\circ}{2.303RT} = \dfrac{77.12}{2.303 \times 1.987 \times 10^{-3} \times 300} = 56.2$

(h) The superscript $^\circ$ indicates that an ideal gas is at 1.00 atm and that a solid or liquid is pure and under 1.00 atm pressure. E and H are insensitive to pressure or dilution and there is usually not much difference between E and E°, or between H and H°. However, A and G are very sensitive to pressure in the case of a gas:

$$\left(\frac{\partial G}{\partial P}\right)_T = V, \qquad \left(\frac{\partial A}{\partial P}\right)_T = -P\left(\frac{\partial V}{\partial P}\right)_T$$

Thus, A° or G° (for 1 atm) is very different from A or G at some other pressure. For a liquid or a solid, however, V is small and thus A and G are insensitive to pressure. The serious difference in these cases would be between G° (or A°) for the pure substance and G (or A) for one component in a solution.

8-II-25. $\Delta \bar{C}_P(s \to liq) = (e - a) + (f - b)T$ cal °K^{-1} mole^{-1}

$d \Delta H^\circ = \Delta C_P \, dT$

$$\Delta H^\circ = \int (e - a) \, dT + \int (f - b)T \, dT$$
$$= (e - a)T + \tfrac{1}{2}(f - b)T^2 + I_1$$

To evaluate I_1, let $\Delta H^\circ = \Delta H_1^\circ$ when $T = T_1$. Then

$$\Delta H_1^\circ = (e - a)T_1 + \tfrac{1}{2}(f - b)T_1^2 + I_1$$

and

$$I_1 = \Delta H_1^\circ - (e - a)T_1 - \tfrac{1}{2}(f - b)T_1^2$$

$$d \frac{\Delta G^\circ}{T} = \frac{-\Delta H^\circ \, dT}{T^2}$$
$$= \frac{-(e - a)T \, dT}{T^2} - \frac{\tfrac{1}{2}(f - b)T^2 \, dT}{T^2} - \frac{I_1 \, dT}{T^2}$$

$$\frac{\Delta G^\circ}{T} = -(e - a) \ln T - \tfrac{1}{2}(f - b)T + \frac{I_1}{T} + I_2$$

When $T = T_1$, $\Delta G^\circ = \Delta G_1^\circ$, so

$$I_2 = \frac{\Delta G_1^\circ}{T_1} + (e - a) \ln T_1 + \tfrac{1}{2}(f - b)T_1 - \frac{I_1}{T_1}$$

and

$$\Delta G^\circ = -(e - a)T \ln T - \tfrac{1}{2}(f - b)T^2 + I_1 + I_2 T$$

where I_1 and I_2 can be evaluated as indicated above. If desired, I_1 and I_2 can be eliminated in the last equation by substituting in the values for these quantities, leading to

$$\Delta G^\circ = \frac{T \Delta G_1^\circ}{T_1} + \Delta H_1^\circ \left(1 - \frac{T}{T_1}\right) + (e - a)\left(T \ln \frac{T_1}{T} + T - T_1\right)$$
$$- \tfrac{1}{2}(f - b)(T - T_1)^2$$

8-II-26. (a) $\Delta H_{298}^\circ = 76.17$ kcal

$\Delta S_{298}^\circ = 12.9$ cal °K^{-1}

$\Delta C_P^\circ = -1.67$ cal °K^{-1}

$\Delta H_T^\circ = \Delta H_{298}^\circ + \Delta C_P^\circ(T - 298) = 76,170 - 1.67(T - 298)$

$= 76,670 - 1.67T$ cal

$$\Delta S_T^\circ = \Delta S_{298}^\circ + \Delta C_P^\circ \ln \frac{T}{298} = 12.9 - 1.67 \ln \frac{T}{298}$$
$$= 22.4 - 1.67 \ln T \text{ cal } °\text{K}^{-1}$$

$$\log K_p = -\frac{-\Delta G^\circ}{2.303RT} = \frac{1}{2.303R}\left(\frac{-\Delta H^\circ}{T} + \Delta S^\circ\right)$$
$$= \frac{1}{4.576}\left(\frac{-76,670}{T} + 1.67 + 22.4 - 1.67 \ln T\right)$$
$$= \frac{-16,760}{T} + 5.26 - 0.840 \log T$$

(b) $T = 298°\text{K}$

$$\log K_p = -51.39$$
$$K_p = 4.1 \times 10^{-52}$$

(c) $\text{NaCl}(s) + \frac{1}{2}\text{H}_2(g) \rightleftharpoons \text{Na}(s) + \text{HCl}(g)$

$$\frac{P_{\text{HCl}}}{P_{\text{H}_2}^{1/2}} = K_p$$

$$\frac{P_{\text{HCl}}}{4.00^{1/2}} = 4.1 \times 10^{-52}$$

$$P_{\text{HCl}} = 8.2 \times 10^{-52} \text{ atm}$$

8-II-27. (a) $\bar{C}_P^\circ = 5/2R = 4.97 \text{ cal } °\text{K}^{-1} \text{ mole}^{-1}$ for a monatomic ideal gas.

(b) $\Delta G_{600}^\circ = \Delta H_{600}^\circ - T\,\Delta S_{600}^\circ = -71.5 - 600(-91.9 \times 10^{-3})$
$$= -16.4 \text{ kcal}$$

$$\log K_p = \frac{-\Delta G_{600}^\circ}{2.303RT} = \frac{16.4}{4.576 \times 10^{-3} \times 600} = 5.97$$

$$K_p = 9.3 \times 10^5$$

(c) $2\text{Hg} + \text{O}_2 \rightleftharpoons 2\text{HgO}$
$\quad\quad\; 2x \quad\;\; 1.00 + x \quad\quad\quad\quad$ pressure (atm) at equilibrium

$$\frac{1}{P_{\text{Hg}}^2 P_{\text{O}_2}} = K_p$$

$$(2x)^2\,(1.00 + x) = \frac{1}{K_p} = 1.07 \times 10^{-6}$$

If $x \ll 1.00$ atm, then $(2x)^2 = 1.07 \times 10^{-6}$,

$P_{\text{Hg}} = 2x = 1.03 \times 10^{-3}$ atm

(d) $K_p' = \frac{1}{P_\text{O}} = K_p P_{\text{Hg}}^2 = 9.3 \times 10^5 \left(\frac{400}{760}\right)^2 = 2.6 \times 10^5$

(e) $\Delta C_P^\circ = 2(6.24 + 0.016T) - 2(4.97) - (6.31 + 0.0023T)$

        $= -3.77 + 0.0297 \text{ cal } °K^{-1}$

$$\Delta H_{300}^\circ = \Delta H_{600}^\circ + \int_{600}^{300} \Delta C_P^\circ \, dT$$

        $= -71.5 - 3.77 \times 10^{-3}(300 - 600)$

        $+ \frac{1}{2} \times 2.97 \times 10^{-5}(300^2 - 600^2) \text{ kcal}$

        $= -74.4 \text{ kcal}$

$$\Delta S_{300}^\circ = \Delta S_{600}^\circ + \int_{600}^{300} \frac{\Delta C_P^\circ}{T} \, dT$$

        $= -91.9 + \int_{600}^{300} \left(\frac{-3.77}{T} + 0.0297 \right) dT$

        $= -91.9 - 3.77 \ln \frac{300}{600} + 0.0297(300 - 600)$

        $= -98.2 \text{ cal } °K^{-1}$

$\Delta G_{300}^\circ = \Delta H_{300}^\circ - T \Delta S_{300}^\circ = -74.4 - 300(-98.2 \times 10^{-3})$

        $= -44.9 \text{ kcal}$

$\log K_p = \dfrac{-\Delta G^\circ}{2.303RT} = \dfrac{44.9}{4.576 \times 10^{-3} \times 300} = 32.7$

     $K_p = 5 \times 10^{32}$

8-II-28.   (a) $\Delta H_{300}^\circ \text{ kcal}$

$2SO_2$	$\rightarrow$	$2S + 2O_2$	$+141.92$
TeO_2	$\rightarrow$	$Te + O_2$	$+77.69$
$2H_2S + 3O_2$	$\rightarrow$	$2H_2O + 2SO_2$	-268.92
$2H_2S + TeO_2$	$\rightarrow$	$Te + 2S + 2H_2O$	-49.31 kcal

(b) $\Delta C_P^\circ = 6.0 + 2 \times 4.4 + 2 \times 18.0 - 2 \times 8.3 - 13.5$

        $= 20.7 \text{ cal } °K^{-1}$

$$\Delta H_{350}^\circ = \Delta H_{300}^\circ + \int_{300}^{350} \Delta C_P^\circ \, dT$$

        $= -49.31 + 20.7 \times 10^{-3} \times 50 = -48.27 \text{ kcal}$

(c) $\Delta S_{300}^\circ = 11.9 + 2 \times 7.6 + 2 \times 16.7 - 2 \times 48.6 - 17.2$

        $= -53.9 \text{ cal } °K^{-1}$

$$\Delta S_{350}^\circ = \Delta S_{300}^\circ + \int_{300}^{350} \frac{\Delta C_P^\circ}{T} \, dT$$

        $= -53.9 + 20.7 \ln \frac{350}{300} = -50.7 \text{ cal } °K^{-1}$

$$\Delta G^{\circ}_{350} = \Delta H^{\circ}_{350} - T\,\Delta S^{\circ}_{350} = -48.27 - 350(-50.7 \times 10^{-3})$$

$$= -30.52 \text{ kcal}$$

(d) $\log K_p = \dfrac{-\Delta G^{\circ}}{2.303RT} = \dfrac{+30.52}{2.303 \times 1.987 \times 10^{-3} \times 350} = 19.1$

$$K_p = 1 \times 10^{19} = P_{\text{H}_2\text{S}}^{-2}$$

$$P_{\text{H}_2\text{S}} = K_p^{-1/2} = 3 \times 10^{-10} \text{ atm}$$

8-II-29. (a) $\Delta \left(\dfrac{\bar{G}^{\circ} - \bar{H}_0^{\circ}}{T}\right) = -53.60 + 46.76 + \dfrac{1}{2}(45.68)$

$$= 16.00 \text{ cal } {}^{\circ}\text{K}^{-1} \text{ mole}^{-1}$$

$$\Delta H_0^{\circ} = 8.68 - 21.48 = -12.80 \text{ kcal mole}^{-1}$$

$$\dfrac{\Delta H_0^{\circ}}{T} = \dfrac{-12,800}{500} = -25.60 \text{ cal } {}^{\circ}\text{K}^{-1} \text{ mole}^{-1}$$

$$\dfrac{\Delta G^{\circ}}{T} = \Delta \left(\dfrac{\bar{G}^{\circ} - \bar{H}_0^{\circ}}{T}\right) + \dfrac{\Delta H_0^{\circ}}{T} = -9.60 \text{ cal } {}^{\circ}\text{K}^{-1} \text{ mole}^{-1}$$

$$\log K_p = \dfrac{-\Delta G^{\circ}}{2.303RT} = \dfrac{9.60}{2.303 \times 1.987} = 2.098$$

$$K_p = 125$$

(b) When $K_p = 1$, $\Delta G^{\circ} = 0$. $(\bar{G}^{\circ} - \bar{H}_0^{\circ})/T$ varies slowly with temperature. We assume that $\Delta[(\bar{G}^{\circ} - \bar{H}_0^{\circ})/T]$ is constant at 16.00 cal ${}^{\circ}$K^{-1} mole^{-1}.

$$\dfrac{\Delta G^{\circ}}{T} = 16.00 + \dfrac{\Delta H_0^{\circ}}{T} = 16.00 - \dfrac{12,800}{T} = 0$$

$$T = 800{}^{\circ}\text{K}$$

8-II-30. $\text{NaOH} \cdot \text{H}_2\text{O}(s) \rightleftharpoons \text{NaOH}(s) + \text{H}_2\text{O}(g)$

$$K_p = P_{\text{H}_2\text{O}} = \dfrac{0.15}{760} = 1.97 \times 10^{-4}$$

$$-\Delta \left(\dfrac{G^{\circ} - H_0^{\circ}}{T}\right) = 6.995 + 37.17 - 11.281 = 32.884$$

$$\Delta G^\circ_{298} = -RT \ln K_p$$
$$= -1.987 \times 298.2 \times 2.303 \times \log 1.97 \times 10^{-4} \text{ cal}$$
$$= 5057 \text{ cal}$$
$$\Delta G^\circ_{298} = \Delta H^\circ_0 + T \cdot \Delta \left(\frac{\bar{G}^\circ - \bar{H}^\circ_0}{T} \right)$$
$$5057 = \Delta H^\circ_0 - 298.2 \times 32.884 = \Delta H^\circ_0 - 9806$$
$$\Delta H^\circ_0 = 14{,}863 \text{ cal mole}^{-1}$$

The original article gives 14,890 cal mole^{-1}.

8-II-31. (a)

	$\left(\dfrac{\bar{G}^\circ_{1000} - \bar{H}^\circ_{298}}{1000}\right),$ cal °K^{-1} mole^{-1}	$\bar{H}^\circ_{298},$ kcal mole^{-1}
Cu_2O	−31.48	−40.4
$\frac{1}{2}O_2$	−26.39	0
−2CuO	+32.18	+75.2
	−25.69	+34.8

$$\frac{\Delta G^\circ_{1000}}{1000} = \Delta \left(\frac{\bar{G}^\circ_{1000} - \bar{H}^\circ_{298}}{1000} \right) + \frac{\Delta H^\circ_{298}}{1000}$$
$$= -25.69 + 34.8 = 9.1 \text{ cal °K}^{-1} \text{ mole}^{-1}$$
$$\log K_p = \frac{-\Delta G^\circ}{2.303RT} = \frac{-9.1}{4.576} = -1.99$$
$$K_p = 1.0 \times 10^{-2}$$

(b) $P_{O_2}^{1/2} = K_p$

When $P_{O_2} = 10^{-6}$ atm, $K_p = 10^{-3}$,

$$\Delta G^\circ = -4.576T \log(10^{-3}) = 13.728T$$

The free energy function $(\bar{G}^\circ_T - \bar{H}^\circ_{298})/T$ varies slowly with temperature. We assume that this function is the same at the unknown temperature T as at 1000°K. Then

$$\frac{\Delta G^\circ}{T} = -25.69 + \frac{\Delta H^\circ_{298}}{T}$$
$$13.728 = -25.69 + \frac{34{,}800}{T}$$
$$T = 882°K$$

8-II-32.

$$\frac{a_{C_2H_5OH}}{P_{C_2H_4}a_{H_2O}} = K = 10.0$$

where a represents activity

$$P_{C_2H_4} = \frac{a_{C_2H_5OH}}{10.0 a_{H_2O}}$$

(a) In an ideal solution the activity is equal to the mole fraction

$$a_{C_2H_5OH} = X_{C_2H_5OH} = \frac{1/46.07}{1/46.07 + 1/18.02} = 0.281,$$

where 46.07 and 18.02 are the molecular weights of C_2H_5OH and H_2O, respectively.

$$a_{H_2O} = X_{H_2O} = 0.719$$

$$P_{C_2H_4} = \frac{0.281}{10.0 \times 0.719} = 0.0392 \text{ atm}$$

(b) For each component $a = P/P°$, where P is the vapor pressure of the component in solution and $P°$ is the vapor pressure of the pure component.

$$a_{C_2H_5OH} = \frac{23.5}{43.6} = 0.539$$

$$a_{H_2O} = \frac{14.5}{17.5} = 0.828$$

$$P_{C_2H_4} = \frac{0.539}{10.0 \times 0.828} = 0.0651$$

8-II-33. $\Delta C_P° = 25.0 + 6.9 - 2 \times 6.6 - 2 \times 7.0 = 4.7 \text{ cal } °K^{-1}$

$\Delta H_{298}° = -28.91 - 2 \times 6.20 = -41.31 \text{ kcal}$

$\Delta G_{298}° = -26.60 - 2 \times 0.31 = -27.22 \text{ kcal}$

$$\Delta S_{298}° = \frac{\Delta H_{298}° - \Delta G_{298}°}{T} = \frac{-14,090}{298} = -47.2 \text{ cal } °K^{-1}$$

$$\Delta H_{398}° = \Delta H_{298}° + \int_{298}^{398} \Delta C_P° \, dT = -41.31 + 4.7 \times 10^{-3} \times 100$$
$$= -40.84 \text{ kcal}$$

$$\Delta S^{\circ}_{398} = \Delta S^{\circ}_{298} + \int_{298}^{398} \frac{\Delta C^{\circ}_P}{T} dT = -47.2 + 4.7 \ln \frac{398}{298}$$

$$= -45.8 \text{ cal } ^{\circ}\text{K}^{-1}$$

$$\Delta G^{\circ}_{398} = \Delta H^{\circ}_{398} - T \Delta S^{\circ}_{398} = -40.84 - 398(-45.8 \times 10^{-3})$$

$$= 22.61 \text{ kcal}$$

$$\log K_p = \frac{-\Delta G^{\circ}}{2.303RT} = \frac{22.61}{2.303 \times 1.987 \times 10^{-3} \times 398}$$

$$= 12.42$$

$$K_p = 2.6 \times 10^{12}$$

SECTION 8-III

8-III-1. The Clapeyron equation (a) refers to the pressure at which liquid and gas are in equilibrium when both phases are at the pressure P, the vapor pressure of the liquid. The van't Hoff equation (b) refers, strictly, to equilibrium between the gas at the pressure P and the liquid in its standard state under a fixed pressure, usually 1 atm. The following derivations may be compared:

(a) $d\bar{G}_g = -\bar{S}_g dT + \bar{V}_g dP$

$\quad d\bar{G}_{liq} = -\bar{S}_{liq} + \bar{V}_{liq} dP$

$\quad d(\bar{G}_g - \bar{G}_{liq}) = -(\bar{S}_g - \bar{S}_{liq}) dT + (\bar{V}_g - \bar{V}_{liq}) dP = 0$

$$\frac{dP}{dT} = \frac{\bar{S}_g - \bar{S}_{liq}}{\bar{V}_g - \bar{V}_{liq}} = \frac{H_g - H_{liq}}{T(\bar{V}_g - \bar{V}_{liq})}$$

(b) $d\bar{G}_g = -\bar{S}_g dT + \bar{V}_g dP$

$\quad d\bar{G}^{\circ}_{liq} = -\bar{S}^{\circ}_{liq} dT$

($\bar{G}^{\circ}_{liq}$ is independent of the actual pressure of the system.)

$$d(\bar{G}_g - \bar{G}^{\circ}_{liq}) = -(\bar{S}_g - \bar{S}^{\circ}_{liq}) dT + \bar{V}_g dP = 0$$

$$\frac{dP}{dT} = \frac{\bar{S}_g - \bar{S}^{\circ}_{liq}}{\bar{V}_g} = \frac{\bar{H}_g - \bar{H}^{\circ}_{liq}}{T\bar{V}_g}$$

8-III-2.   (a) The person does not understand the distinction between ΔG and $\Delta G°$. The criterion for equilibrium is that $\Delta G = 0$, not $\Delta G° = 0$. $\Delta G° = 0$ only if the equilibrium constant equals 1.

(b) A necessary condition for equilibrium between the two phases (*liq* and *s*) is that $\mu_{1,liq} = \mu_{1,s}$, where 1 refers to water. This condition may be written

$$\mu_{1,liq}^{\circ} + RT \ln a_{1,liq} = \mu_{1,s}^{\circ} + RT \ln a_{1,s} \qquad (1)$$

If $\mu_{1,liq}^{\circ} = \mu_{1,s}^{\circ}$, then, of course, $a_{1,liq} = a_{1,s}$ at equilibrium. But in the present case $\mu_{1,liq}^{\circ}$ is the chemical potential of pure liquid water, and $\mu_{1,s}^{\circ}$ is the chemical potential of pure ice, both under 1 atm at $-3°C$. These are not equal; rather, $\mu_{1,s}^{\circ} < \mu_{1,liq}^{\circ}$, for ice is the stable form. Then it is obvious from (1) that $a_{1,s} > a_{1,liq}$, as we already know. A case where $\mu°$ is the same in the two phases appears in connection with osmotic pressure; there it is true that the activity of the solvent is the same in the two phases at equilibrium.

8-III-3.   (a) $A_2 \rightleftharpoons 2A$

moles of A_2 at equilibrium $= n_0(1 - \alpha)$
moles of A at equilibrium $= 2n_0\alpha$
total moles at equilibrium $= n_0(1 + \alpha)$

$$P_{A_2} = \frac{n_0(1 - \alpha)}{n_0(1 + \alpha)} P \qquad P_A = \frac{2n_0\alpha}{n_0(1 + \alpha)} P$$

$$\frac{P_A^2}{P_{A_2}} = K$$

$$\frac{4\alpha^2 P}{(1 - \alpha)(1 + \alpha)} = K$$

$$\frac{4\alpha^2 P}{1 - \alpha^2} = K$$

$$\alpha^2 = \frac{K}{K + 4P}$$

$$\alpha = \left(1 + \frac{4P}{K}\right)^{-1/2}$$

(b) $V = \dfrac{nRT}{P} = n_0(1 + \alpha)\dfrac{RT}{P}$

(i) Assume that there are n_0 moles of gas,

$$\bar{V} = \frac{V}{n_0} = (1 + \alpha)\frac{RT}{P}$$

$$\bar{V} = \left[1 + \left(1 + \frac{4P}{K}\right)^{-1/2}\right]\frac{RT}{P}$$

(ii) Assume that there are $2n_0$ moles of gas,

$$\bar{V} = \frac{V}{2n_0} = (1 + \alpha)\frac{RT}{2P}$$

$$\bar{V} = \left[1 + \left(1 + \frac{4P}{K}\right)^{-1/2}\right]\frac{RT}{2P}$$

(c) For $P \ll K$, $\alpha \approx 1 - 2P/K$

$$\bar{V} \approx \left(2 - \frac{2P}{K}\right)\frac{RT}{mP}$$

where $m = 1$ or 2

$$\ln\gamma = \int_0^P \left(\frac{\bar{V}}{RT} - \frac{1}{P}\right)dP = \int_0^P \left[\left(2 - \frac{2P}{K}\right)\frac{1}{mP} - \frac{1}{P}\right]dP$$

$$= \int_0^P \left[-\frac{2}{Km} + \left(\frac{2}{m} - 1\right)\frac{1}{P}\right]dP$$

This integral will diverge unless $2/m - 1 = 0$, $m = 2$ (assumption (ii)). In this case

$$\ln\gamma = \frac{-2P}{Km}$$

8-III-4. (a) $P'_A = P^\circ_A X_A = P^\circ_A \dfrac{n_A}{n_A + n_B}$

$\qquad P'_B = P^\circ_B X_B = P^\circ_B \dfrac{n_B}{n_A + n_B}$

(b) $P_A = P^\circ_A \dfrac{n_A}{n_A + n_{B_2}} = P^\circ_A \dfrac{n_A}{n_A + \frac{1}{2}n_B}$,

where n_{B_2}, the actual number of moles of B_2 in the solution, is one half the number of moles of $B(n_B)$ that the chemist thinks to be present.

$B_2(liq) \rightleftharpoons 2B(g)$

$$\frac{P_B{}^2}{X_{B_2}} = K$$

When $X_{B_2} = 1$, $P_B = P_B^{\circ}$ and $K = P_B^2 = (P_B^{\circ})^2$

$$P_B{}^2 = KX_B = (P_B^{\circ})^2\, X_{B_2}$$

$$P_B = P_B^{\circ} X_B^{1/2} = P_B^{\circ}\left(\frac{n_{B_2}}{n_A + n_{B_2}}\right)^{1/2} = P_B^{\circ}\left(\frac{\frac{1}{2}n_B}{n_A + \frac{1}{2}n_B}\right)^{1/2}$$

(c) $\gamma_A = \dfrac{P_A}{P_A'} = \dfrac{n_A + n_B}{n_A + \frac{1}{2}n_B} = \dfrac{1 + n_B/n_A}{1 + n_B/2n_A}$

$\approx 1 + \dfrac{n_B}{n_A} - \dfrac{n_B}{2n_A} = 1 + \dfrac{n_B}{2n_A} \approx 1 + \dfrac{1}{2}X_B$

$\gamma_B = \dfrac{P_B}{P_B'} = \left(\dfrac{\frac{1}{2}n_B}{n_A + \frac{1}{2}n_B}\right)^{1/2}\dfrac{n_A + n_B}{n_B}$

$= \left(\dfrac{n_A}{2n_B}\right)^{1/2}\left(1 + \dfrac{n_B}{n_A}\right)\left(1 + \dfrac{n_B}{2n_A}\right)^{-1/2}$

$\approx \left(\dfrac{n_A}{2n_B}\right)^{1/2}\left(1 + \dfrac{n_B}{n_A}\right)\left(1 - \dfrac{n_B}{4n_A}\right)$

$\approx \left(\dfrac{n_A}{2n_B}\right)^{1/2}\left(1 + \dfrac{3n_B}{4n_A}\right) \approx \left(\dfrac{1}{2X_B}\right)^{1/2}\left(1 + \dfrac{3}{4}X_B\right)$

8-III-5. (a) $Br_2 \rightleftharpoons 2Br$

$\qquad\qquad 1 - \alpha \quad\quad 2\alpha \quad$ moles

Total number of moles $= 1 + \alpha$.

$P_{Br_2} = \dfrac{1 - \alpha}{1 + \alpha}\, P$

$P_{Br} = \dfrac{2\alpha}{1 + \alpha}\, P$

$P = 0.10$ atm

$\dfrac{P_{Br}^2}{P_{Br_2}} = K_p$

$\dfrac{(2\alpha)^2\, P}{(1 - \alpha)(1 + \alpha)} = 0.255$

$\dfrac{\alpha^2}{1 - \alpha^2} = \dfrac{0.255}{0.40} = 0.64$

$\alpha^2 = 0.39$

$\alpha = 0.62$

(b) $\dfrac{d \ln K}{d(1/T)} = -\dfrac{\varDelta H^\circ}{R}$

$\ln \dfrac{K_{1600}}{K_{1400}} = -\dfrac{\varDelta H^\circ}{R}\left(\dfrac{1}{1600} - \dfrac{1}{1400}\right) = \dfrac{\varDelta H^\circ}{1.12 \times 10^4 R}$

$\varDelta H^\circ = 1.12 \times 10^4 R \ln\left(\dfrac{K_{1600}}{K_{1400}}\right)$

$\qquad = 1.12 \times 10^4 \times 4.576 \log\left(\dfrac{K_{1600}}{K_{1400}}\right)$

$\qquad = 1.12 \times 10^4 \times 4.576 \times 0.925 \text{ cal}$

$\qquad = 4.74 \times 10^4 \text{ cal or } 47.4 \text{ kcal}$

(c) This is an average value of $\varDelta H^\circ$ for the range 1400 to 1600°K. The averaging is with respect to the variable $(1/T)$; that is, the result is

$$\overline{\varDelta H^\circ} = \dfrac{\displaystyle\int_{T=1400}^{T=1600} \varDelta H^\circ\, d(1/T)}{\displaystyle\int_{T=1400}^{T=1600} d(1/T)}$$

If we prefer to think of T as the variable of integration, then we have a weighted average, the weighing factor being $1/T^2$:

$$\overline{\varDelta H^\circ} = \dfrac{\displaystyle\int_{1400}^{1600} \varDelta H/T^2\, dT}{\displaystyle\int_{1400}^{1600} dT/T^2}$$

8-III-6. (a) $\bar{S}^\circ = \displaystyle\int_0^{100} \dfrac{\bar{C}_P^\circ}{T}\, dT + \dfrac{2000}{100} + 6.00 \ln \dfrac{300}{100}$

$\qquad = \tfrac{1}{3} \times 2.50 \times 10^{-4} \times 100^3$

$\qquad\quad - \tfrac{1}{6} \times 2.40 \times 10^{-10} \times 100^6 + 20.0 + 6.00 \times 1.099$

$\qquad = 69.9 \text{ cal } °K^{-1} \text{ mole}^{-1}$

(b)

	A(c) +	2B	$\leftrightharpoons$	AB$_2(g)$
$\bar{H}^\circ_{300}$	-10	0		-41 kcal mole^{-1}
$\bar{S}^\circ_{300}$	15	2(69.9)		55 cal $°K^{-1}$ mole^{-1}

$\varDelta H^\circ_{300} = -31 \text{ kcal mole}^{-1}$

$\varDelta S^\circ_{300} = -99.8 \text{ cal } °K^{-1} \text{ mole}^{-1}$

$$\Delta G^\circ_{300} = \Delta H^\circ_{300} - 300\,\Delta S^\circ_{300} = -1060 \text{ cal mole}^{-1}$$

$$\log K_p = \frac{1060}{2.303 \times 1.987 \times 300} = 0.772, \quad K_p = 5.92$$

(c) $A(c) + 2B \rightleftharpoons AB_2(g)$

$$n_B = 1 - 2x; \quad n_{AB_2} = 1 + x = 1.10 \text{ moles}$$

$$x = 0.10 \text{ mole}, \quad n_B = 0.80 \text{ mole}$$

$$n_{total} = 1.90 \text{ moles}$$

$$P_{AB_2} = \frac{n_{AB_2}}{n_{total}}\, P = \frac{1.10}{1.90}\, P$$

$$P_B = \frac{n_B}{n_{total}}\, P = \frac{0.80}{1.90}\, P$$

$$\frac{P_{AB_2}}{P_B{}^2} = K_p$$

$$\frac{1.10P}{1.90}\left(\frac{1.90}{0.80P}\right)^2 = 5.92$$

$$P = 0.55 \text{ atm}$$

8-III-7.
$$\frac{\bar{G}^\circ_T - \bar{H}^\circ_0}{T} = \frac{\bar{G}^\circ_T - \bar{H}^\circ_T}{T} + \frac{\bar{H}^\circ_T - \bar{H}^\circ_0}{T} = -\bar{S}^\circ_T + \frac{\bar{H}^\circ_T - \bar{H}^\circ_0}{T}$$

For $\bar{S}^\circ_0 = 0$

$$\bar{S}^\circ_T = \int_0^T \frac{\bar{C}^\circ_P}{T}\, dT$$

Let $\bar{S}^{\circ\prime}_T = \sigma$. In this case,

$$\bar{S}^{\circ\prime}_T = \sigma + \int_0^T \frac{\bar{C}^\circ_P}{T}\, dT = \sigma + \bar{S}^\circ_T$$

The modified value of the free energy function is

$$\left(\frac{\bar{G}^\circ_T - \bar{H}^\circ_0}{T}\right)' = -\bar{S}^{\circ\prime}_T + \frac{\bar{H}^\circ_T - \bar{H}^\circ_0}{T} = -\sigma - \bar{S}^\circ_T + \frac{\bar{H}^\circ_T - \bar{H}^\circ_0}{T}$$

$$= -\sigma + \frac{\bar{G}^\circ_T - \bar{H}^\circ_0}{T}$$

Thus the free energy function is decreased by σ when $\bar{S}^\circ_0$ is similarly increased.

CHAPTER 9

The phase rule

SECTION 9-I

9-I-1.   (b)

9-I-2.   See figures.

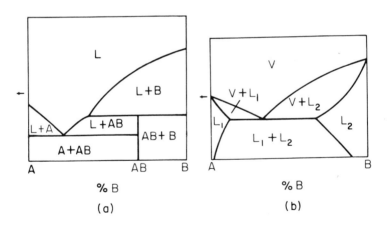

(a)   (b)

9-I-3.   (a) Plot $P^\circ_{\phi Cl}$ vs t (curve 1). $\Big\}$ On same graph (see figure.)
         Plot $P^\circ_{H_2O}$ vs t (curve 2). $\Big\}$

At each of several temperatures add $P^\circ_{\phi Cl}$ and $P^\circ_{H_2O}$, and plot $(P^\circ_{\phi Cl} + P^\circ_{H_2O})$ vs t (curve 3). Curve 3 is the total vapor pressure of the ϕCl-H_2O system as a function of temperature.

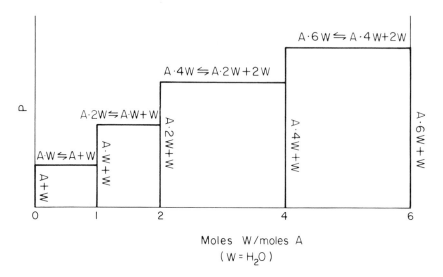

Fig. 9-I-2(c).

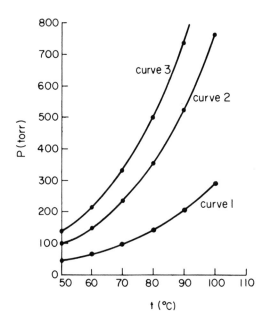

Fig. 9-I-3.

The boiling point of the ϕCl-H_2O system is the temperature at which $P^\circ_{\phi Cl} + P^\circ_{H_2O} = 760$ torr. Reading curve 3 we get $t = 91.2°C$ at $P^\circ_{\phi Cl} + P^\circ_{H_2O} = 760$ torr.

(b)
$$\frac{W_A}{W_B} = \frac{M_A P^\circ_A}{M_B P^\circ_B} \qquad \begin{array}{l} A = C_6H_5Cl \\ B = H_2O \end{array}$$

boiling point $= 91.2°C$

$$P^\circ_A = 216 \text{ torr}$$

$$P^\circ_B = 544 \text{ torr}$$

$$M_A = 113$$

$$M_B = 18.0$$

$$\frac{W_A}{W_B} = \frac{113 \times 216}{18.0 \times 544} = 2.49$$

weight percent B $= \dfrac{1 \times 100}{1 + 2.49} = 28.7$

9-I-4. See figure.

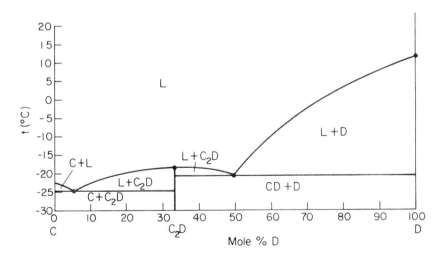

9-I-5. (a) 60 kilobars

(b) Diamond

(c) $\dfrac{dT}{dP} = \dfrac{T(V_{liq} - V_s)}{\Delta H} = 0$ at 70 kilobars and 4700°K

9-I-6.   (a), (b). See figures.

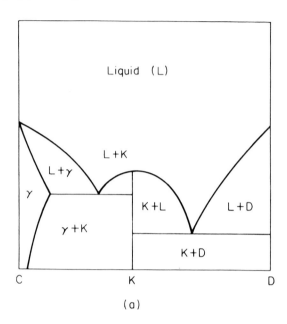

(a)

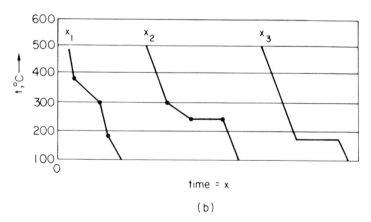

time = x

(b)

(c) The maximum weight of pure D is obtained by cooling to just above the eutectic temperature. The composition of the liquid is then approximately 68% D. By the lever rule, the weight of solid D is

$$150 \text{ g} \times \frac{(90 - 68)}{(100 - 68)} = 103 \text{ g}$$

9-I-7. (a), (b). See figures.

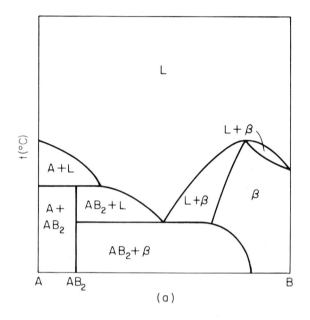

(a)

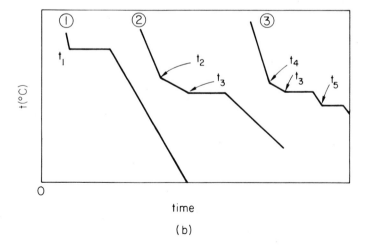

time

(b)

9-I-8.   See figure.

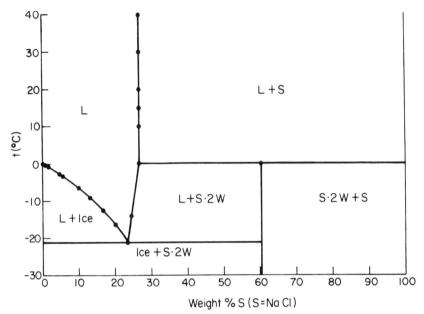

9-I-9.   (a) See figure.

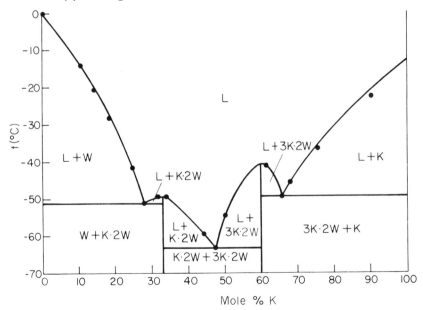

(b) 9 mole percent ethylene glycol, 91 mole percent water.

(c) 47.5 mole percent ethylene glycol, 52.5 mole percent H_2O.

9-I-10. (a) $L + P$

(b) Moles $H_2O = \dfrac{50}{18} = 2.78$

Moles $Q = \dfrac{50}{36} = 1.39$

$\dfrac{\text{Moles } H_2O}{\text{mole } Q} = \dfrac{2.78}{1.39} = 2$

$Q \cdot 2H_2O$

(c) See figure.

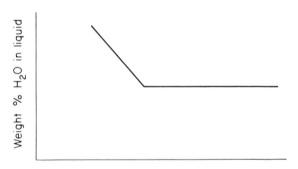

Weight of water evaporated

9-I-11. See figure.

9-I-12. (a) See figure.

(b) Consolute point (the point at which L_1 and L_2 have the same composition): 52.8 percent CH_3COOH, 39.6 percent C_6H_6, 7.6 percent H_2O.

(c) Point b lies on tieline 5.

$L_1 = 16.3$ percent CH_3COOH, 82.9 percent C_6H_6,
0.79 percent H_2O

$L_2 = 61.4$ percent CH_3COOH, 6.1 percent C_6H_6,
32.5 percent H_2O

$\dfrac{L_1}{L_2} = \dfrac{\text{distance } bc}{\text{distance } ab} = \dfrac{52}{23}$

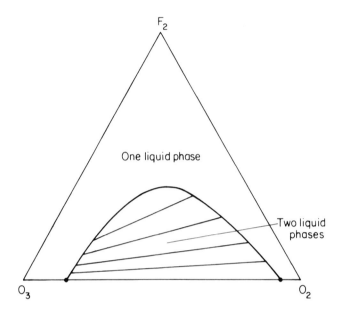

Fig. 9-I-11.

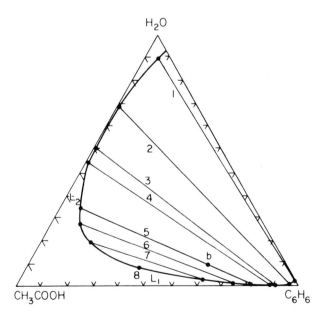

Fig. 9-I-12.

$$L_1 = 100 \times \frac{52}{23 + 52} = 69.4g$$

$$L_2 = 100 \times \frac{23}{23 + 52} = 30.6g$$

9-I-13. (a) 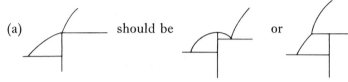 should be or

The original diagram is possible but improbable.

(b) No mistakes.

(c) $B(s) + C(s)$ should read $B(s) + C(s) + L$.

SECTION 9-II

9-II-1. The formula is valid for a system at equilibrium in which phase concentrations plus two other properties of state can be varied.

9-II-2. In the derivation of the given formula it is assumed that one of the phases is an ideal gas and that the molar volume of one of the phases is negligibly small in comparison with the molar volume of the other phase. Neither of these assumptions is valid for the diamond-graphite transition.

9-II-3.

$$\frac{dP}{dT} = \frac{\Delta H}{T(V_v - V_{liq})} = \frac{\Delta S}{(V_v - V_{liq})} = \frac{(S_v - S_{liq})}{(V_v - V_{liq})}$$

$$S_v > S_{liq} \quad \text{and} \quad V_v > V_{liq}$$

Therefore,

$$\frac{dP}{dT} = \frac{+}{+} = +$$

9-II-4. Let W_T = the total weight of the whole system. Then

$$W_T x_T = W_1 x_1 + W_2 x_2$$

$$W_T = W_1 + W_2$$

$$W_1 x_T + W_2 x_T = W_1 x_1 + W_2 x_2$$

$$W_1 x_T - W_1 x_1 = W_2 x_2 - W_2 x_T$$

$$W_1(x_T - x_1) = W_2(x_2 - x_T)$$

$$\frac{W_1}{W_2} = \frac{x_2 - x_T}{x_T - x_1}$$

9-II-5. $s_2 > s_3 > s_1$

$v_2 > v_3 > v_1$

9-II-6. (a) See figure.

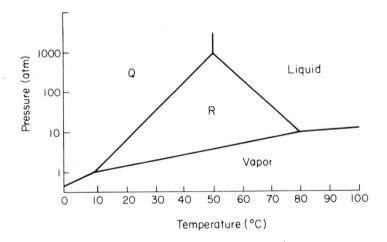

(b) Increasing the pressure at constant temperature favors the denser form: $\rho_Q > \rho_R$; $\rho_{liq} > \rho_R$. We cannot decide about Q and liquid because we do not know whether the Q-liquid equilibrium line has a positive or negative slope.

9-II-7.   See figure.

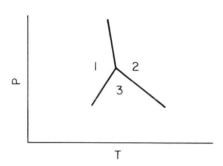

9-II-8.   See figure.

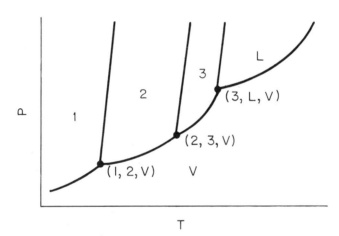

9-II-9.   See figure.

Equilibrium curves: QR, α-vapor; RS, β-vapor; SW, liquid-vapor; RU, α-β; SU, β-liquid; UX, α-liquid.

Triple points: R, α-β-vapor; S, β-liquid-vapor; U, α-β-liquid.

Critical point: W.

The signs of the slopes of RU and SU can be obtained from the Clapeyron equation

$$\frac{dP}{dT} = \frac{H_2 - H_1}{T(V_2 - V_1)}$$

Since higher temperature favors the form with the greater enthalpy, $H_L > H_\beta > H_\alpha$, while from the densities,

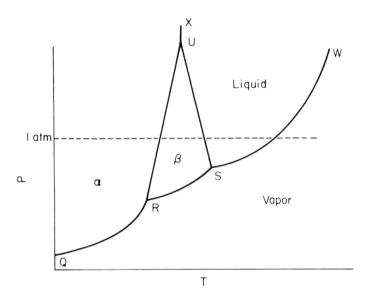

Fig. 9-II-9.

$V_\beta > V_L > V_\alpha$. Thus for the α-β equilibrium, $dP/dT > 0$, but for the β-liquid equilibrium, $dP/dT < 0$, and the curves (if their slopes do not change sign) will intersect at a triple point U.

9-II-10.   (a) See figure.

(b) The form with greater molar enthalpy is that which is favored by an increase of temperature at constant pressure. $\bar{H}_I > \bar{H}_{II}$; $\bar{H}_I > \bar{H}_{III}$; $\bar{H}_{III} > \bar{H}_{II}$.

9-II-11.   (a) $\overline{\Delta G} > 0$; the fusion of X is not spontaneous below 300°K.

(b) $\overline{\Delta C_P} = \bar{C}_{P,liq} - \bar{C}_{P,s} = 25.0 - 20.0 = 5.0 \text{ cal °K}^{-1} \text{ mole}^{-1}$

$\overline{\Delta H}_{290} = \overline{\Delta H}_{300} + \int_{300}^{290} \overline{\Delta C_P}\, dT = 3000 - 5.0 \times 10$

$= 2950 \text{ cal mole}^{-1}$

(c) $\overline{\Delta S}_{300} = \dfrac{\overline{\Delta H}_{300} - \overline{\Delta G}_{300}}{300} = \dfrac{3000 - 0}{300} = 10 \text{ cal °K}^{-1} \text{ mole}^{-1}$

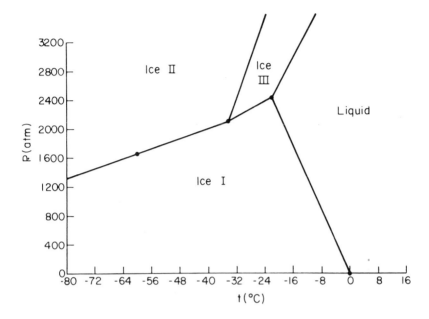

Fig. 9-II-10.

(d) $\overline{\Delta S}_{290} = \overline{\Delta S}_{300} + \displaystyle\int_{300}^{290} \frac{\overline{\Delta C_P}}{T}\, dT = 10 + 5.0 \ln \frac{290}{300}$

$\qquad = 9.83$ cal $°K^{-1}$ mole^{-1}

(e) $\overline{\Delta G}_{290} = \overline{\Delta H}_{290} - 290\, \overline{\Delta S}_{290} = 2950 - 290 \times 9.83$
$\qquad = 99$ cal mole$^{-1} > 0$

as predicted in (a).

9-II-12. (a) $\ln P = A + B \ln T + \dfrac{C}{T}$

$\qquad \overline{\Delta H} = RT^2 \dfrac{d \ln P}{dT} = RT^2 \left(\dfrac{B}{T} - \dfrac{C}{T^2} \right) = R(BT - C)$

$\qquad \overline{\Delta H}_{liq} = R(B_{liq} T - C_{liq})$

$\qquad \overline{\Delta H}_s = R(B_s T - C_s)$

(b) $\overline{\Delta H}_f = \bar{H}_{liq} - \bar{H}_s = \bar{H}_v - \bar{H}_s - (\bar{H}_v - \bar{H}_{liq}) = \overline{\Delta H}_s - \overline{\Delta H}_{liq}$

$\qquad = R[(B_s - B_{liq})T - (C_s - C_{liq})]$

(c) $\bar{C}_{P,liq} - \bar{C}_{P,s} = \dfrac{\partial(\bar{H}_{liq} - \bar{H}_s)}{\partial T} = \dfrac{\partial\,\varDelta\bar{H}_f}{\partial T} = R(B_s - B_{liq})$

(d) $\ln P_{liq} = \ln P_s$

$$A_{liq} + B_{liq}\ln T + \dfrac{C_{liq}}{T} = A_s + B_s\ln T + \dfrac{C_s}{T}$$

9-II-13.

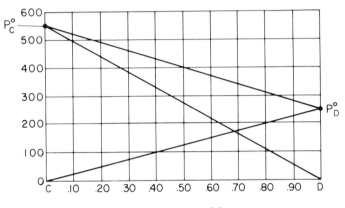

Mole fraction of D

From the graph:

(a) 475 torr

(b) 62.5 torr

(c) 17 percent D

9-II-14. (a) See figure.

(b) $k_A = P_A/X_A$. We take the values given for the most dilute solution:

$$k_A = \frac{38}{0.0333} = 1140 \text{ torr}$$

(c) (i) $\gamma_A = \dfrac{P_A}{X_A P_A^\circ} = \dfrac{164}{0.420 \times 229} = 1.71$

(ii) $\gamma_A = \dfrac{P_A}{X_A k_A} = \dfrac{164}{0.420 \times 1140} = 0.343$

9-II-15. (a) 118°C

(b) 39 percent B

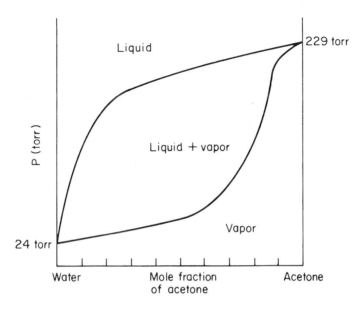

Fig. 9-II-14.

(c) Best distillate = 36 percent B (eutectoid)
best residue = 100 percent B. Let

$$w_D = \text{weight of distillate}$$
$$w_R = \text{weight of residue}$$
$$w_R + w_D = 100 \text{ g}$$

Weight of B in distillate + weight of B in residue = weight of B in original mixture

$$0.39\, w_D + 1.00\, w_R = 70 \text{ g}$$
$$0.39(100 - w_R) + 1.00\, w_R = 70 \text{ g}$$
$$0.61\, w_R = 31$$
$$w_R = 51 \text{ g (pure B)}$$

9-II-16. (a) 74°C

(b) 87 percent B

(c) (i) 62 percent B

(ii) $\frac{1}{2}(87 + 68) = 77.5$ percent B (midway between initial and final compositions of distillate). Let

$$w_R = \text{weight of residue}$$
$$w_D = \text{weight of distillate}$$
$$w_R + w_D = 200$$

Weight of B in residue + weight of B in distillate = 150 g

$$0.62\, w_R + 0.775\, w_D = 150$$
$$0.62(200 - w_D) + 0.775\, w_D = 150$$
$$0.155\, w_D = 26$$
$$w_D = 168 \text{ g}$$

9-II-17. (a) Residue = 20 percent A

(b) Total distillate $\approx \frac{1}{2}(91 + 71) = 81$ percent A (average of initial and final compositions of vapor)

(c) Let

$$w_R = \text{weight of residue}$$
$$w_D = \text{weight of distillate}$$

The initial mixture was **49 percent A.**

$$w_D + w_R = 200 \text{ g}$$
$$0.20\, w_R + 0.81\, w_D = 0.49 \times 200 \text{ g A total}$$
$$0.20(200 - w_D) + 0.81\, w_D = 98$$
$$0.61\, w_D = 58$$
$$w_D = 95 \text{ g}$$

9-II-18. (a) 83°C

(b) 13 percent B (93°C)

(c) $\frac{1}{2}(57 + 41) = 49$ percent B (average of initial and final compositions of distillate)

(d) 82 degrees, 60 percent B (eutectoid)

9-II-19. Let f_{Bl} (or f_{Bv}) be the weight fraction of B in the liquid (or vapor) phase. The total weight of B is

$$w_B = f_{Bl}(\tfrac{1}{2}w) + f_{Bv}(\tfrac{1}{2}w)$$

where w is the total weight of the mixture and $\frac{1}{2}w$ is the weight of each phase. But $w_B/w = 0.40$. Then

$$f_{Bl} + f_{Bv} = 2w_B/w = 0.80$$

Inspection of the figure shows that this condition is satisfied at 77°C, with $f_{Bl} = 0.21$ and $f_{Bv} = 0.59$.

9-II-20. See figure.

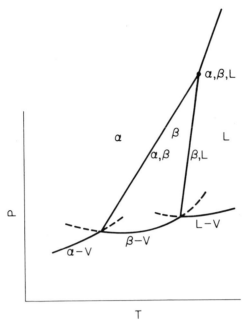

9-II-21. See figure.

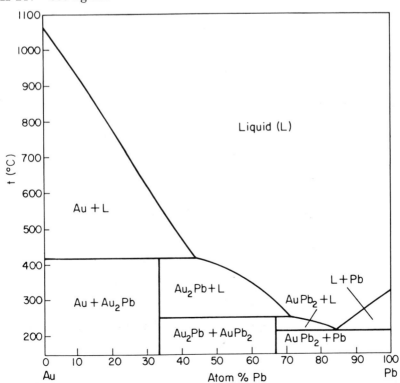

9-II-22. (a) See figure.

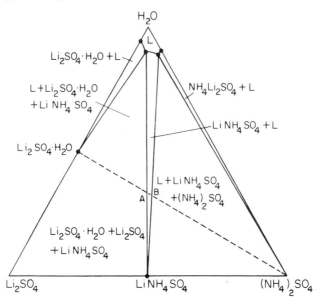

(b) The dashed line represents the addition of $(NH_4)_2SO_4$ to $Li_2SO_4 \cdot H_2O$. Initially a liquid solution and $LiNH_4SO_4$ are formed. [$(NH_4)_2SO_4$ "extracts" Li_2SO_4 from the hydrate to form the double salt leaving behind the water that dissolves both salts to form the solution.] At the composition A all hydrate has been consumed and we have only double salt and solution. This condition persists to B when the solution is saturated with both $LiNH_4SO_4$ and $(NH_4)_2SO_4$. All $(NH_4)_2SO_4$ added thereafter merely remains undissolved.

9-II-23. (a) See figure.

(b) According to the diagram as shown the system at $-30°C$ (dashed line) will pass through the following stages: ice + solution, all solution, $H_2SO_4 \cdot 4H_2O$ + solution, all solid $H_2SO_4 \cdot 4H_2O$, $H_2SO_4 \cdot 4H_2O$ + solution, all solution, $H_2SO_4 \cdot H_2O$ + solution, all solid $H_2SO_4 \cdot H_2O$, $H_2SO_4 \cdot H_2O$ + solution, all solution, solid H_2SO_4 + solution. The diagram shows the actual positions of the eutectic points. Since these were not given, it could have been drawn somewhat differently. If the $H_2O + H_2SO_4 \cdot 4H_2O$ eutectic point were above $-30°C$, the system would remain entirely solid until the mole percent of

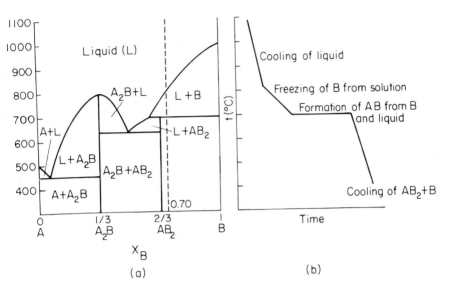

Fig. 9-II-24.

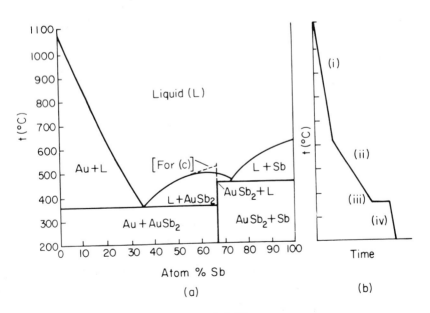

Fig. 9-II-25.

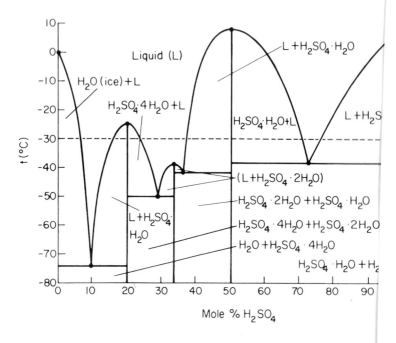

H$_2$SO$_4$ reached some value above 20 percent. The H$_2$SO
would simply combine with the ice to form H$_2$SO$_4$
when this reaction was complete, H$_2$SO$_4$ · 2H$_2$O w
formed (assuming that there is time for these sol
reactions to occur). Similarly if the H$_2$SO$_4$ · H$_2$O +
eutectic were above −30°C, addition of H$_2$SO$_4$
50 mole percent would merely be the addition of o
(H$_2$SO$_4$) to another (H$_2$SO$_4$ · H$_2$O); no liquid would

9-II-24. (a), (b). See figures. Eutectic temperatures and comp
have been guessed.

9-II-25. (a), (b). See figures. The segments of the curve in (b
spond to the following processes:

(i) Cooling of liquid solution.

(ii) Slower cooling because Au is solidifying and its
fusion must be removed.

(iii) Eutectic point. Temperature remains constant until all liquid has frozen to a solid mixture of Au and $AuSb_2$.

(iv) Cooling of solid mixture.

(c) Addition of Y to pure X depresses the freezing point of X in the typical way. However, the initial slope of the freezing point curve of Y is zero (at the maximum). This behavior is characteristic of solid compounds: the freezing point of the pure compound is already depressed below an estimated hypothetical value (shown dotted) by the presence of decomposition products (Au and Sb) in the melt.

9-II-26. (a), (b). See figures. The segments of the curve in (b) correspond to the following processes:

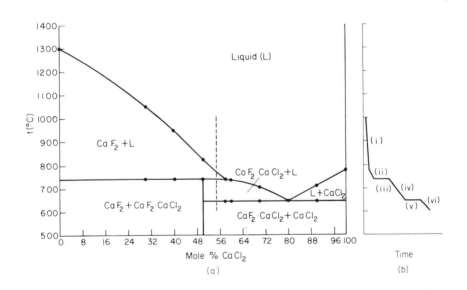

(a)

(b)

(i) Cooling of liquid solution.

(ii) Freezing of CaF_2 from solution.

(iii) Peritectic point. CaF_2, $CaF_2 \cdot CaCl_2$, and liquid are in equilibrium.

(iv) Freezing of $CaF_2 \cdot CaCl_2$ from solution.

(v) Eutectic point. $CaF_2 \cdot CaCl_2$, $CaCl_2$, and liquid are in equilibrium.

(vi) Cooling of solid mixture of $CaF_2 \cdot CaCl_2$ and $CaCl_2$.

9-II-27. (a) See figure. C_1 and C_2 represent compounds.

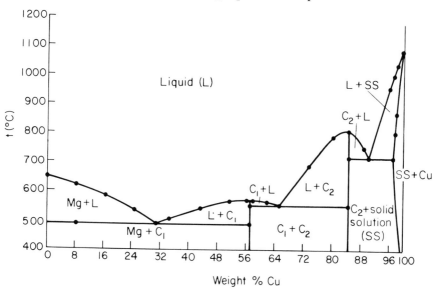

(b) C_1, 56.7 percent Cu

$$\frac{56.7}{63.54} = 0.892 \text{ g-atom Cu}$$

$$\frac{43.3}{24.31} = 1.78 \text{ g-atom Mg}$$

$$\frac{1.78}{0.892} = 2$$

$CuMg_2$

C_2, 84.5 percent Cu

$$\frac{84.5}{63.54} = 1.33 \text{ g-atom Cu}$$

$$\frac{15.5}{24.31} = 0.64 \text{ g-atom Mg}$$

$$\frac{1.33}{0.64} = 2$$

Cu_2Mg

9-II-28. (a) Plot log P vs $1/T$ for the solid and log P vs $1/T$ for the liquid on the same graph. (See figure.) The point of inter-

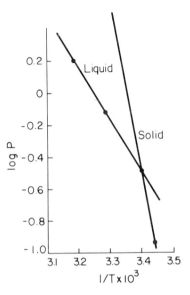

section gives log P and $1/T$ for the triple point. It is not all right to plot P vs T instead of log P vs $1/T$ because log P vs $1/T$ is a straight line function and can be extrapolated whereas the P vs T function is curved, and two data points are not sufficient to plot the function. The intersection is at $T = 308°$K.

	solid		liquid	
t, °C	9.8	21.0	30.7	41.4
T, °K	283.0	294.2	303.9	314.6
$1/T$	0.003534	0.003399	0.003291	0.003179
P, torr	0.116	0.321	0.764	1.493
log P	−0.9355	−0.4935	−0.1169	+0.1741

(b) *Algebraic method*
From the integrated form of the Clausius-Clapeyron equation

$$\log \frac{P_2}{P_1} = \frac{-\Delta H_s}{2.303R}\left(\frac{1}{T_2} - \frac{1}{T_1}\right)$$

$$\log \frac{0.321}{0.116} = \frac{-\Delta H_s}{2.203 \times 1.987 \times 10^{-3}}\left(\frac{1}{294.2} - \frac{1}{283.0}\right)$$

$$\Delta H_s = 15.0 \text{ kcal (literature: } 15.13 \text{ kcal mole}^{-1})$$

Graphical method

From the Clapeyron-Clausius equation in the form of an indefinite integral

$$\log P = \frac{-\Delta H}{R} \frac{1}{T} + \text{constant}$$

This means that a plot of $\log P$ vs $1/T$ should give a straight line with a slope of $-\Delta H/R$. Thus the slope of the sublimation line $= -\Delta H_s/4.58$. The slope can be determined graphically and ΔH_s can then be calculated.

(c) Calculate ΔH_v as well as ΔH_s in the manner outlined in (b). Then

$$\Delta H_f = \Delta H_s - \Delta H_v = 15.0 - 11.9 = 3.1 \text{ kcal mole}^{-1}$$

$$\log \frac{0.764}{1.493} = \frac{-\Delta H_v}{4.576 \times 10^{-3}} \left(\frac{1}{303.9} - \frac{1}{314.6} \right)$$

$$\Delta H_v = 11.9 \text{ kcal mole}^{-1}$$

The calculated values of $1/T$, P, ΔH_s, and ΔH_v differ from those in the original paper because in the original study more data points were used.

9-II-29.   See figure.

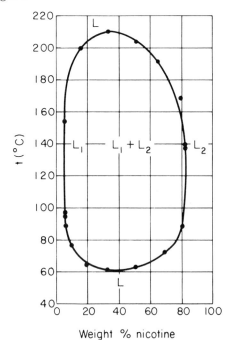

Weight % nicotine

(a) Liquid, 20 percent nicotine.

(b) Liquid I, 7.3 percent nicotine; Liquid II, 82.0 percent nicotine.

(c) Liquid, 20 percent nicotine.

(d) Liquid II, 90 percent nicotine.

9-II-30. $K = \dfrac{w_1/v_1}{(w - w_1)/v_2}$

where

K = distribution constant

w = weight of solute in phase 1 before extraction

w_1 = weight of solute in phase 1 after first extraction

v_1 = volume of liquid 1

v_2 = volume of liquid 2

$Kv_1(w - w_1) = w_1 v_2$

$$w_1 = w \left(\frac{Kv_1}{Kv_1 + v_2} \right)$$

Similarly the weight of solute in phase 1 after n extractions is

$$w_n = w \left(\frac{Kv_1}{Kv_1 + v_2} \right)^n$$

$$\frac{c_w}{c_b} = K = 0.05$$

$$w_n = w \left(\frac{Kv_{H_2O}}{Kv_{H_2O} + v_b} \right)^n$$

$$0.1 = 100.0 \left(\frac{0.05 \times 50}{(0.05 \times 50) + 50} \right) = \left(\frac{2.5}{52.5} \right)^n$$

$$\left(\frac{2.5}{52.5} \right)^n = 10^{-3}$$

$$\left(\frac{52.5}{2.5} \right)^n = 10^3 = (21.0)^n$$

$n \log 21.0 = 3.00$

$n \times 1.32 = 3.00$

$n = 2.3$ times

9-II-31. (a) No. The straight line joining B and A · H₂O does not pass through a region corresponding to the presence of A · B · 2H₂O.

(b) 60 percent A, 30 percent B, 10 percent C.

9-II-32. (a) See figure. Draw in lines $L_1 \rightarrow R_1$, $L_2 \rightarrow R_2$, and $L_3 \rightarrow R_3$ and extrapolate them. The point of intersection of

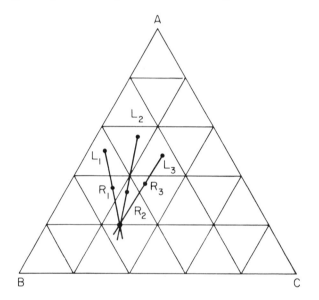

the extrapolations gives the composition of the solid phase (20 percent A, 54 percent B, 26 percent C).

(b) 50 percent A, 44 percent B, 6 percent C.

9-II-33. See figure. Solid phase is 39.7 percent B, 32.2 percent C.

9-II-34. See figure. KF · 2H₂O, NH₄F.

9-II-35. (a) See figure.

(b) If the system A + A · H₂O has a greater vapor pressure than the system B + B · 2H₂O, A · H₂O begins to dehydrate as soon as the last drop of solution disappears (at line I). When all A · H₂O has dehydrated (dashed line II), the pressure falls to the vapor pressure of B + B · 2H₂O and B · 2H₂O then

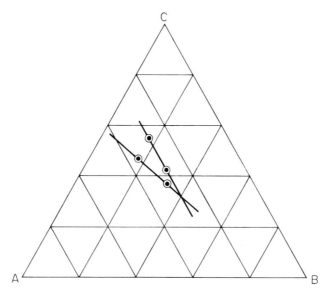

Fig. 9-II-33.

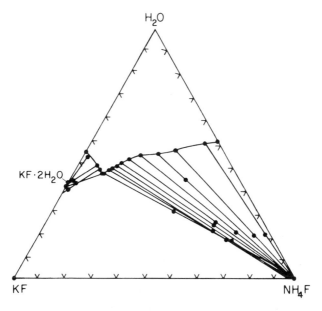

Fig. 9-II-34.

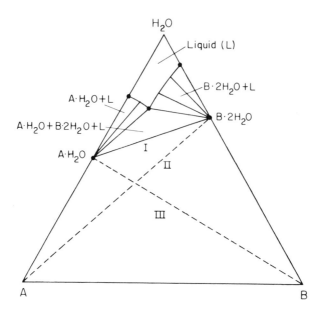

dehydrates. Conversely if $B + B \cdot 2H_2O$ has a greater vapor pressure than $A + A \cdot H_2O$, $B \cdot 2H_2O$ dehydrates first and $A \cdot H_2O$ begins to dehydrate at dashed line III. Either line II or line III, but not both, belongs on the diagram; the decision cannot be made without vapor-pressure data.

SECTION 9-III

9-III-1. To be valid phase diagram coordinates the properties plotted must be functions of state (that is, their differentials must be exact). It is already known that t is a property of state but we must prove this for γ. To do this we apply the Euler reciprocity law to the differential equation $d\gamma = f(t, v) \, dt + g(t, v) \, dv$.

$$\left(\frac{\partial}{\partial v}\right)\left(\frac{k}{M^{2/3}v^{2/3}}\right) = \frac{-2k}{3M^{2/3}v^{5/3}}$$

and

$$\left(\frac{\partial}{\partial t}\right)\left(\frac{-2k(t_c - t - 6)}{3M^{2/3}v^{5/3}}\right) = \frac{-2k}{3M^{2/3}v^{5/3}}$$

Since these two derivatives are equal, γ is a property of state, and γ and t are therefore valid phase diagram coordinates.

9-III-2. The slope of each line must be $+$ or $-$. Labeling the three phases 1, 2, and 3, the possible permutations of these signs are as follows:

1-2 equilibrium line $+$ $+$ $+$ $-$ $+$ $-$ $-$ $-$

2-3 equilibrium line $+$ $+$ $-$ $+$ $-$ $+$ $-$ $-$

1-3 equilibrium line $+$ $-$ $+$ $+$ $-$ $-$ $+$ $-$

These, in all, number 8. The corresponding diagrams are as follows:

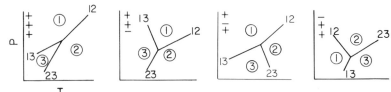

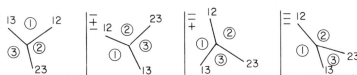

9-III-3. The number of components (C) = the number of possible species (constituents) (N) — the number of independent equations (E) relating their concentrations, mole fractions, etc. Each independent chemical equilibrium involving the constituents counts as one equation. The condition that a solution be electrically neutral also counts as one if ions are considered constituents.

$KCl-NaCl-H_2O$

     $N = 3$ (KCl, NaCl, H_2O)

     $E = 0$

     $C = N - E = 3 - 0 = 3$

$KCl-NaBr-H_2O$

$N = 5$ (KCl, NaBr, NaCl, KBr, H_2O)

$E = 1$ $KCl + NaBr \rightleftharpoons KBr + NaCl$

$C = N - E = 5 - 1 = 4$

9-III-4. (a) $N = 8$ (NH_4Cl, NH_4^+, Cl^-, H_2O, NH_3, NH_4OH, H_3O^+, OH^-)

$E = 5$ electroneutrality

$$NH_4Cl \rightleftharpoons NH_4^+ + Cl^-$$
$$NH_4^+ + H_2O \rightleftharpoons NH_3 + OH^-$$
$$NH_3 + H_2O \rightleftharpoons NH_4OH$$
$$2H_2O \rightleftharpoons H_3O^+ + OH^-$$

(b) $N = 3$ (NH_4Cl, NH_3, HCl)

$E = 2$ $NH_4Cl \rightleftharpoons NH_3 + HCl$

$$P_{NH_3} = P_{HCl}$$

$C = N - E = 3 - 2 = 1$

(c) $N = 3$ (NH_4Cl, NH_3, HCl)

$E = 1$ $NH_4Cl \rightleftharpoons NH_3 + HCl$

$C = N - E = 3 - 1 = 2$

(d) $N = 8$ (CH_3COONH_4, CH_3COO^-, NH_4^+, H_3O^+, NH_3, OH^-, CH_3COOH, H_2O)

$E = 4$ $CH_3COOH + H_2O \rightleftharpoons CH_3COO^- + H_3O^+$

$$CH_3COO^- + H_2O \rightleftharpoons CH_3COOH + OH^-$$
$$NH_4^+ + H_2O \rightleftharpoons NH_3 + H_3O^+$$

electroneutrality

$C = N - E = 8 - 4 = 4$

The equation $2H_2O \rightleftharpoons H_3O^+ + OH^-$ was not counted because it can be derived by the addition of the first two equations.

(e) $N = 9$ (NaCl, KBr, KCl, NaBr, K^+, Na^+, Cl^-, Br^-, H_2O)

$E = 5$ $NaCl \rightleftharpoons Na^+ + Cl^-$

$$KBr \rightleftharpoons K^+ + Br^-$$
$$NaBr \rightleftharpoons Na^+ + Br^-$$
$$NaCl + KBr \rightleftharpoons NaBr + KCl$$

electroneutrality

$C = N - E = 9 - 5 = 4$

(f) $N = 6$ (NaCl, KCl, K$^+$, Na$^+$, Cl$^-$, H$_2$O)

$E = 3$ NaCl $\rightleftharpoons$ Na$^+$ + Cl$^-$

KCl $\rightleftharpoons$ K$^+$ + Cl$^-$

electroneutrality

$C = N - E = 6 - 3 = 3$

(g) $N = 4$ (CaCl$_2 \cdot$ 6H$_2$O, Ca^{2+}, Cl$^-$, H$_2$O)

$E = 2$ CaCl$_2 \cdot$ 6H$_2$O $\rightleftharpoons$ Ca^{2+} + 2Cl$^-$ + 6H$_2$O

electroneutrality

$C = N - E = 4 - 2 = 2$

(h) $N = 3$ (CaCO$_3$, CaO, CO$_2$)

$E = 1$ CaCO$_3$ $\rightleftharpoons$ CaO + CO$_2$

$C = N - E = 3 - 1 = 2$

The restriction that CaO and CO$_2$ are present in stoichio-metrically equal amounts does not count here because it does not affect a phase composition. No matter what the proportions the composition of the gas phase is always 100 percent CO$_2$ and the composition of the CaO phase is always 100 percent CaO.

9-III-5.   (a) See figure.

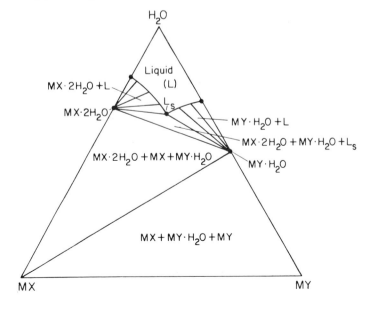

(b) As H_2O is pumped off the composition moves down along the dashed line. This system passes through the following stages:

Region	Phase(s)	Pressure, torr
L	unsaturated solution	>14
$MX \cdot 2H_2O$ + L	saturated solution + $MX \cdot 2H_2O$	$>14, <19$
$MX \cdot 2H_2O$ + $MY \cdot H_2O$ + L_s	two hydrates + doubly saturated solution	14
$MX \cdot 2H_2O$ + MX + $MY \cdot H_2O$	two hydrates + anhydrous MX	13
MX + $MY \cdot H_2O$ + MY	two anhydrous salts + $MY \cdot H_2O$	10

The question that arises in drawing this diagram is whether to draw a line between MX and $MY \cdot H_2O$ or between MY and $MX \cdot 2H_2O$. When the last drop of doubly saturated solution (L_s) disappears, the pressure must drop to the vapor pressure of either (a) $MX + MX \cdot 2H_2O$, 13 torr or (b) $MY + MY \cdot H_2O$, 10 torr. If assumption (a) is correct, $MY \cdot H_2O$ (stable at pressures > 10 torr) can continue to exist until all $MX \cdot 2H_2O$ is dehydrated. If assumption (b) is correct, and the pressure drops immediately to 10 torr, $MX \cdot 2H_2O$ must dehydrate instantaneously for it is unstable below 13 torr. This is impossible; it takes time to remove the H_2O from $MX \cdot 2H_2O$. Assumption (b) is therefore incorrect, and (a) is correct. When L_s has disappeared, $MX \cdot 2H_2O$ dehydrates first at 13 torr; the phase diagram should, accordingly, show a region corresponding to $MX \cdot 2H_2O$, MX, and $MY \cdot H_2O$. When all $MX \cdot 2H_2O$ is gone, $MY \cdot H_2O$ begins to dehydrate at 10 torr.

CHAPTER 10

Electrochemistry

SECTION 10-I

10-I-1. $K = \dfrac{c_{HN_2O_2^-} \times c_{H^+}}{c_{H_2N_2O_2}} = \dfrac{c\alpha^2}{1-\alpha}; \qquad \alpha = \dfrac{\Lambda}{\Lambda^\circ}$

$\Lambda^\circ_{H_2N_2O_2} = 298 + 93 - 39.9 = 351.1$

For $c = 0.03$,

$\alpha = \dfrac{1.017}{351.1} = 0.00290$

$K = 0.03 \dfrac{(2.90 \times 10^{-3})^2}{1 - 0.00290} = 2.53 \times 10^{-7}$

c	0.03	0.015	0.0075	0.00375	0.001875
K	2.53	2.56	2.58	2.56	2.53×10^{-7}

$K_{av} = 2.55 \times 10^{-7}$

10-I-2. $E_1 = I_1R_1; \quad E_2 = I_2R_2; \quad E_3 = I_3R_3; \quad E_4 = I_4R_4$

$I_1R_1 = I_3R_3; \quad I_2R_2 = I_4R_4$

$\dfrac{I_1R_1}{I_2R_2} = \dfrac{I_3R_3}{I_4R_4}$

$I_1 = I_2; \quad I_3 = I_4$

$\dfrac{R_1}{R_2} = \dfrac{R_3}{R_4}$

10-I-3. $\Lambda^\circ = \lambda^\circ_+ + \lambda^\circ_-$

$\lambda^\circ_- = \Lambda^\circ - \lambda^\circ_+ = 103.97 - 73.58 = 30.39$ ohm^{-1} cm^2 equiv^{-1}

$t_- = \dfrac{\lambda^\circ_-}{\Lambda^\circ} = \dfrac{30.39}{103.97} = 0.292$

10-I-4. Plot Λ vs $\sqrt{c}$. $\Lambda = \Lambda^0$ when $\sqrt{c} = 0$; $\Lambda^0 = 114.3$

10-I-5. $\Lambda^\circ = \dfrac{1000k}{c}$; $\Lambda^\circ = 2.06 \times 10^{-6} - 4.1 \times 10^{-7} = 1.65 \times 10^{-6}$

$c = \dfrac{1000k}{\Lambda^\circ} = \dfrac{1000 \times 1.65 \times 10^{-6}}{(111 + 43)} = 1.07 \times 10^{-5}$ eq liter^{-1}

$= 2.7 \times 10^{-6}$ mole liter^{-1}

Basiński, Szymanstli, and Betto, using the Onsager equation, arrive at 1.02×10^{-5}.

10-I-6. Plot Λ vs $c^{1/2}$.

$\Lambda^\circ = 126.62$

10-I-7. (a) $\Lambda = \dfrac{1000k}{c} = \dfrac{9.000}{0.1000} = 90.00$ ohm^{-1} cm^2 eq^{-1}

(b) $\lambda_- = \Lambda - \lambda_+ = 90.00 - 39.5 = 50.5$ ohm^{-1} cm^2 eq^{-1}

10-I-8. $\dfrac{0.100 \text{ amp} \times 9650 \text{ sec}}{9.65 \times 10^4 \text{ coul faraday}^{-1}} = 0.0100$ faraday

$\dfrac{0.100 \text{ mole AB} \times 100 \text{ g H}_2\text{O}}{1000 \text{ g H}_2\text{O}} = 0.0100$ mole AB

In anode compartment :

		moles A$^+$
	Initially	0.0100
	Produced	0.0100
		0.0200
	Present at end	0.0165
	Migrated out	0.0035

$t_+ = \dfrac{0.0035}{0.0100} = 0.35$

10-I-9.

$$t_+ = \frac{cal\mathscr{F}}{Q}$$

where

c = concentration in eq liter^{-1}

a = cross-sectional area of tube

l = distance in cm traveled by boundary

Q = the number of faradays of charge passed

$$t_+ = \frac{0.0200 \times 0.1115 \times 1.00 \times 96{,}500}{344 \times 0.0016001} = 0.391$$

$$t_+ = \frac{0.0200 \times 0.1115 \times 6.00 \times 96{,}500}{2070 \times 0.0016001} = 0.390$$

$$t_+ = \frac{0.0200 \times 0.1115 \times 10.00 \times 96{,}500}{3453 \times 0.0016001} = 0.389$$

mean $t_+ = 0.390$

10-I-10.

(a) Let c = concentration in eq cm^{-3}

$c_{K^+} = 1.00 \times 10^{-4}$ eq cm^{-3}

$t_{K^+} = 0.490$; $\quad t_{Na^+} = 0.388$

$$\frac{Q}{\mathscr{F}} = \frac{96.5 \text{ coul}}{9.65 \times 10^4 \text{ coul faraday}^{-1}} = 1.00 \times 10^{-3} \text{ faraday}$$

Volume swept out by boundary $= \dfrac{t_{K^+}Q/\mathscr{F}}{c_{K^+}} = \dfrac{t_{Na^+}Q/\mathscr{F}}{c_{Na^+}}$

$$= \frac{0.490 \times 1.00 \times 10^{-3} \text{ far}}{1.00 \times 10^{-4} \text{ eq cm}^{-3}}$$

$$= 4.90 \text{ cm}^3$$

Distance traveled $= \dfrac{4.90 \text{ cm}^3}{0.100 \text{ cm}^2} = 49.0$ cm

(b) $\dfrac{t_{Na^+}Q/\mathscr{F}}{c_{Na^+}} = \dfrac{0.388 \times 1.00 \times 10^{-3} \text{ faraday}}{c_{Na^+}} = 4.90 \text{ cm}^3$

$c_{Na^+} = 7.92 \times 10^{-5}$ eq cm^{-3} $= 7.92 \times 10^{-2}$ mole liter^{-1}

10-I-11. Ionic strength $= I = c_{KNO_3} + 9S$

log S/S_0	$\sqrt{I}$	$\sqrt{I} - \sqrt{I_0}$
0	0.01616	0
0.0572	0.02824	0.01208
0.0922	0.03637	0.02021
0.1483	0.04865	0.03249

See graph. Slope of $\log(S/S_0)$ vs $\sqrt{I} - \sqrt{I_0}$ plot $= 4.94$. Data fall on a straight line. Slope predicted by Debye-Hückel theory $= 0.509 \times 3^2 = 4.58$.

$\log \gamma_\pm = -0.509 z_+ z_- \sqrt{I}$	$\gamma_\pm$
-0.0740	0.843
-0.1294	0.742
-0.1667	0.681
-0.2230	0.598

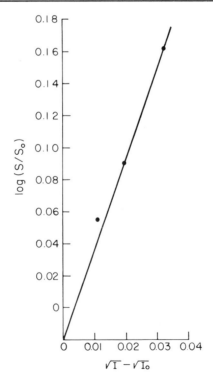

10-I-12. (a) $\quad$ HA $\quad\rightleftharpoons$ H$^+$ $\quad+\quad$ A$^-$
$\qquad\qquad$ $1.0 - x \approx 1.0 \quad x \quad 0.8 + x \approx 0.8$ m at equilibrium

$$\frac{\gamma_{H^+}\gamma_{A^-}m_{H^+}m_{A^-}}{m_{HA}} = K$$

$$\frac{m_{H^+}m_{A^-}}{m_{HA}} = \frac{K}{\gamma_{H^+}\gamma_{A^-}} = \frac{1.4 \times 10^{-4}}{0.65^2} = 3.3 \times 10^{-4}$$

$$\frac{x(0.8)}{1.0} = 3.3 \times 10^{-4}$$

$$x = 4.1 \times 10^{-4} \text{ mole kg}^{-1} = m_{H^+}$$

$$a_{H^+} = \gamma_{H^+}m_{H^+} = 0.65 \times 4.1 \times 10^{-4} = 2.7 \times 10^{-4}$$

$$\text{pH} = -\log a_{H^+} = 3.57$$

(b) $\quad m_{HA} = 1.0 - 0.5 = 0.5 \qquad m_{A^-} = 0.8 + 0.5 = 1.3$

$$\frac{y(1.3)}{0.5} = 3.3 \times 10^{-4}$$

$$y = 1.3 \times 10^{-4} \text{ mole kg}^{-1}$$
$$= m_{H^+}$$

$$a_{H^+} = 0.65 \times 1.3 \times 10^{-4} = 8.3 \times 10^{-5} \qquad \text{pH} = 4.08$$

(c) $\quad m_{OH^-} = 0.5 \text{ mole kg}^{-1} \qquad a_{OH^-} = 0.65 \times 0.5 = 0.33$
$\qquad \text{pOH} = -\log 0.33 = 0.48 \qquad \text{pH} = 14.00 - 0.48 = 13.52$

10-I-13. (a) $\quad E° = \dfrac{RT \ln K}{n(\mathscr{F})} = 0.05915 \log K = 0.05915(-6.64)$

$$= -0.393 \text{ V}$$

	$E°$
CuCl(s) → Cu$^+$ + Cl$^-$	-0.393
Cu$^+$ + e$^-$ → Cu(s)	$+0.522$
CuCl(s) + e$^-$ → Cu(s) + Cl$^-$	$+0.129$ V

(b)

	$E°$
Cu(s) + Cl$^-$ → CuCl(s) + e$^-$	-0.129
$\frac{1}{2}$ Cl$_2$(g) + e$^-$ → Cl$^-$	$+1.358$
Cu(s) + $\frac{1}{2}$ Cl$_2$(g) → CuCl(s)	$+1.229$ V

$$\Delta G° = -n\mathscr{F}E° = -1 \text{ faraday mole}^{-1} \times 9.65$$
$$\times 10^4 \text{ coul faraday}^{-1} \times 1.229 \text{ joule coul}^{-1}$$
$$\times \frac{1}{4.184} \text{ cal joule}^{-1}$$
$$= -2.83 \times 10^4 \text{ cal mole}^{-1}$$

SECTION 10-II

10-II-1. See figure. The definite curvature of the Λ vs $c^{1/2}$ plot at low concentrations shows that dissociation is incomplete.

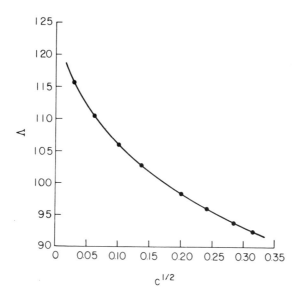

10-II-2. $K = ka/l$. Since equivalent conductance is defined as the conductance of the volume of solution containing one equivalent of electrolyte between electrodes 1 cm apart, then $\Lambda = ka/1$ and a is numerically equal to the volume occupied by one equivalent of solution, or $1000/c$. Therefore $\Lambda = 1000\,k/c$.

10-II-3. Anode reaction: $H_2O \to 2H^+ + \frac{1}{2}O_2 + 2e^-$.

0.0100 mole H^+ formed indicates that 0.0100 faraday passed through the circuit.

0.005 mole $= 0.090$ g H_2O was destroyed; this amount can be neglected relative to 100 g.

$0.0100t_+$ equiv (or mole) Na^+ migrated out of the anode compartment; $0.0100\,t_-$ equiv $= 0.0050\,t_-$ mole SO_4^{2-} migrated in.

$t_+ = 0.39; \quad t_- = 0.61.$

Initially present in 100 g H_2O:

0.0500 mole Na^+ + 0.0250 mole SO_4^{2-}

Finally present:

0.0500 − 0.0100 t_+ = 0.0461 mole Na^+;
0.0250 + 0.00500 t_- = 0.0281 mole SO_4^{2-}

10-II-4. $\dfrac{1.0787 \text{ g Ag}}{107.87 \text{ g Ag faraday}^{-1}} = 0.010000$ faraday

In cathode compartment (associated with 100.00 g H_2O):

Initially   1.500 g AgX
Finally   0.500 g AgX
Change   1.000 g AgX

$\dfrac{1.000 \text{ g AgX}}{150.0 \text{ g mole}^{-1}} = 0.00667$ mole AgX

0.00667 mole X^- migrated out

$t_- = \dfrac{0.00667}{0.010000} = 0.667$

$t_+ = 0.333$

10-II-5. (a) 0.00500 mole H_2SO_4 produced at anode × 2 faradays/ mole = 0.01000 faraday

(b) 0.01000 mole $CuSO_4$ in anode compartment initially (0.1000 mole (kg H_2O)$^{-1}$ × 0.1000 kg H_2O)

0.00800 mole $CuSO_4$ in anode compartment at end

$\overline{0.00200}$ {mole $CuSO_4$ lost from anode compartment mole Cu^{2+} migrated out

0.00400 equivalent Cu^{2+} migrated out

$t_+ = \dfrac{0.00400 \text{ equivalent } Cu^{2+}}{0.01000 \text{ faraday total}} = 0.400$

(A small correction may be made for the fact that 0.00500 mole = 0.0901 g H_2O was consumed in the anode compartment. Therefore the amount of H_2O initially present in this compartment was 100.0 + 0.09 = 100.1 g, which contained 100.1/100.0 × 0.01000 = 0.01001 mole $CuSO_4$.)

(c)   0.01000 mole $CuSO_4$ in cathode compartment initially
$\underline{-0.00500}$ mole Cu^{2+} reduced at cathode
$\underline{+0.00200}$ mole Cu^{2+} migrated in
$\overline{0.00700}$ mole $\begin{Bmatrix} Cu^{2+} \\ CuSO_4 \end{Bmatrix}$ in cathode compartment at end

(d) 133.6 ohm^{-1} cm^2 eq^{-1} × 0.400 = 53.4 ohm^{-1} cm^2 eq^{-1}

We assume that t_+ is the same in the 0.1 m solution as at infinite dilution.

10-II-6.   (a)   (i) 4   (ii) 1

(b)   0.010 mole

(c) $100.0 \text{ g } H_2O \times \dfrac{(1.015 - 1.000) \text{ mole Fe}}{1000 \text{ g } H_2O} = 0.0015 \text{ mole entered}$

(The anode reaction has no effect on total Fe.)

(d) $t_- = \dfrac{4 \text{ eq mole}^{-1} \times 0.0015 \text{ mole}}{0.010 \text{ eq}} = 0.60$

(e) $\lambda_-^\circ = \lambda_+^\circ \left(\dfrac{t_-}{t_+} \right) = 73.52 \times \dfrac{0.60}{0.40} = 110 \text{ ohm}^{-1} \text{ cm}^2 \text{ eq}^{-1}$

We have assumed that the transport numbers and thus the ratio of equivalent conductances are the same at infinite dilution as in the 1 m solution.

10-II-7.   The remaining ZnI_2 is forming a complex with the I^-. The following equilibria are involved:

$Zn^{2+} + I^- \leftrightharpoons ZnI^+$

$ZnI^+ + I^- \leftrightharpoons ZnI_2$

$ZnI_2 + I^- \leftrightharpoons ZnI_3^-$

$ZnI_3^- + I^- \leftrightharpoons ZnI_4^{2-}$

At higher concentrations, ZnI_3^- and ZnI_4^{2-} are favored, so that Zn(II) moves in the direction opposite to that expected for a positive ion.

10-II-8. $dE_t = \dfrac{+2t_+ RT}{\mathscr{F}} d \ln a_{\pm}$

It can be seen by inspection of the cell that increasing c_1 increases E_t (by making the left electrode a better anode); the sign is therefore $+$ when $a_\pm$ refers to the left (c_1) solution.

$$a_\pm = 10^{-4}\, A$$

$$\log a_\pm = -4 + \log A$$

$$\frac{dE_t}{d \log A} = 2 \times 0.05915\, t_+ = 0.11830\, t_+$$

$$E_t = -0.043865 + 0.045363\, (\log A) - 0.0014902\, (\log A)^2$$

$$\frac{dE_t}{d \log A} = 0.045363 - 0.0029804\, (\log A)$$

$$t_+ = \frac{1}{0.11830}\frac{dE_t}{d \log A} = 0.3834 - 0.0252\, (\log A)$$

$$= 0.3834 - 0.0252 \log (0.01 \times 0.905 \times 10^4) = 0.333$$

10-II-9. $\ln \gamma_\pm = -Am^{1/2}$

$d \ln \gamma_\pm = -\tfrac{1}{2}Am^{-1/2}\, dm$

$\ln X_1 = -\dfrac{m\nu}{n_1}$

$d \ln X_1 = -\dfrac{\nu\, dm}{n_1}$

$n_2 = m$

$\ln a_2 = \ln(a_\pm^\nu) = \nu \ln(\gamma_\pm m_\pm)$

$\ln m_\pm = \ln(\text{constant} \times m)$

$d \ln a_2 = \nu d \ln(\gamma_\pm m_\pm) = \nu(d \ln \gamma_\pm + d \ln m)$

Gibbs-Duhem equation:

$n_1 d \ln a_1 + m d \ln a_2 = 0$

$n_1(d \ln \gamma_1 + d \ln X_1) + m\nu(d \ln \gamma_\pm + d \ln m) = 0$

$n_1 d \ln \gamma_1 - \nu\, dm - \tfrac{1}{2}A\nu m^{1/2}\, dm + \nu\, dm = 0$

$d \ln \gamma_1 = \dfrac{A\nu m^{1/2}\, dm}{2n_1}$

$\ln \gamma_1 = \dfrac{A\nu}{2n_1} \displaystyle\int_0^m m^{1/2}\, dm = \dfrac{A\nu}{3n_1} m^{3/2}$

10-II-10. (a) $a_+ a_-/a_{\text{AgCl}} = 1.71 \times 10^{-10}$.

By convention $a_{AgCl} = 1$. Then

$$a_\pm{}^2 = a_+ a_- = 1.71 \times 10^{-10}$$
$$a_\pm = 1.31 \times 10^{-5}$$

(b) $\dfrac{a_\pm{}^{(X)}}{a_\pm{}^{(m)}} = \lim_{m \to 0} \dfrac{X}{m} = \dfrac{M_1}{1000} = 0.018016,$

where X is the mole fraction of either Ag^+ or Cl^- and M_1 is the molecular weight of H_2O.

$$a_\pm{}^{(X)} = 1.31 \times 10^{-5} \times 0.018016 = 2.36 \times 10^{-7}$$

10-II-11. Let

$$U = \frac{-A I^{1/2}}{1 + I^{1/2}}$$

$$\log \gamma_\pm = \frac{\nu_+ \log \gamma_M + \nu_- \log \gamma_X}{\nu_+ + \nu_-}$$

$$= \frac{U(\nu_+ z_M{}^2 + \nu_- z_X{}^2)}{\nu_+ + \nu_-} + \frac{\nu_+}{\nu_+ + \nu_-} \sum_i B_{MX_i} m_{X_i}$$

$$+ \frac{\nu_-}{\nu_+ + \nu_-} \sum_i B_{M_i X} m_M$$

Let

$$z_+ = z_M \quad \text{and} \quad z_- = z_X$$

Introducing in the first term the electroneutrality condition $\nu_+ z_+ + \nu_- z_- = 0$, we have

$$\log \gamma_\pm = U(-z_+ z_-) + \frac{\nu_+}{\nu_+ + \nu_-} \sum_i B_{MX_i} m_{X_i} + \frac{\nu_-}{\nu_+ + \nu_-} \sum_i B_{M_i X} m_{M_i}$$

10-II-12.

$$\begin{array}{ccccccc} & HA & + \ H_2O & \rightleftharpoons & H_3O^+ & + & A^- \\ \text{moles kg}^{-1}: & 0.010(1 - \alpha) & & & 0.010\alpha & & 0.010\alpha \end{array}$$

$$\frac{\gamma_\pm{}^2 m_{H_3O^+} m_{A^-}}{m_{HA}} = K = 1.47 \times 10^{-3}$$

$$\frac{\gamma_\pm{}^2 (0.010\alpha^2)}{1 - \alpha} = K$$

$$\frac{\alpha^2}{1 - \alpha} = \frac{K}{0.010 \gamma_\pm{}^2} = \frac{0.147}{\gamma_\pm{}^2}$$

First approximation:

$I = 0, \quad \gamma_\pm = 1$

$\alpha^2 + 0.147\alpha - 0.147 = 0$

$\alpha = 0.317$

Second approximation:

$$I = 0.01 \times 0.317 = 3.17 \times 10^{-3}$$

$$\sqrt{I} = 5.63 \times 10^{-2}$$

$$\log(\gamma_\pm^2) = 2 \log \gamma_\pm = 2 \times 0.509(1)(-1) \times 5.63 \times 10^{-2}$$
$$= -5.73 \times 10^{-2}$$

$$\gamma_\pm^2 = 0.876$$

$$\frac{\alpha^2}{1 - \alpha} = \frac{0.147}{0.876} = 0.168$$

$$\alpha = 0.334$$

10-II-13. (a) $\quad$ HA $+ e^- \rightarrow A^- + \frac{1}{2}H_2 \quad E_1^\circ = ?$

$\quad\quad\quad \frac{1}{2}H_2 \rightarrow H^+ + e^- \quad\quad\quad\quad E_2^\circ = 0$

$$\overline{\text{HA} \rightleftharpoons H^+ + A^-} \quad\quad\quad E_3^\circ = (RT/\mathscr{F}) \ln K_a$$
$$= E_1^\circ + E_2^\circ = E_1^\circ$$

$$E_1^\circ = 0.05915 \log(3.3 \times 10^{-4}) = -0.206 \text{ V}$$

(b) $\quad I = \frac{1}{2}(1.00 \times 2^2 + 2.00 \times 1^2) = 3.00$

$\quad\quad \sqrt{I} = 1.73$

Let

$$\log \gamma = \log \gamma_{H^+} = \log \gamma_{A^-} \approx \frac{-0.509 \sqrt{I}}{1 + \sqrt{I}}$$

$$= -\frac{0.509 \times 1.73}{2.73} = -0.322$$

$$\gamma = 0.476$$

$$\gamma_{HA} \approx 1$$

$$\frac{a_{H^+}a_{A^-}}{a_{HA}} = K_a$$

$$\frac{\gamma^2 m_{H^+} m_{A^-}}{m_{HA}} = K_a$$

$$\frac{m_{H^+} m_{A^-}}{m_{HA}} = \frac{K_a}{\gamma^2} = \frac{3.3 \times 10^{-4}}{0.476^2} = 1.46 \times 10^{-3}$$

$$\begin{array}{ccc} \text{HA} & \rightleftharpoons \text{H}^+ + & \text{A}^- \\ 0.200(1-\alpha) & 0.200\alpha & 0.200\alpha \end{array}$$

$$\frac{0.200\alpha^2}{1-\alpha} = 1.46 \times 10^{-3}$$

$$\frac{\alpha^2}{1-\alpha} = 7.3 \times 10^{-3}$$

If $\alpha \ll 1$, $\alpha^2 = 7.3 \times 10^{-3}$, $\alpha = 8.5 \times 10^{-2}$

Improved solution:

$$\alpha^2 + 7.3 \times 10^{-3}\alpha - 7.3 \times 10^{-3} = 0$$
$$\alpha = 8.2 \times 10^{-2}$$

10-II-14. (a) Equilibrium:

$$H_2CO_3 \rightleftharpoons H^+ + HCO_3^-$$

$$\frac{m_{H^+} m_{HCO_3^-}}{m_{H_2CO_3}} = K_1 = 4.30 \times 10^{-7} \tag{1}$$

$$HCO_3^- \rightleftharpoons H^+ + CO_3^{2-}$$

$$\frac{m_{H^+} m_{CO_3^{2-}}}{m_{HCO_3^-}} = K_2 = 5.61 \times 10^{-11} \tag{2}$$

$$H_2O \rightleftharpoons H^+ + OH^-$$

$$m_{H^+} m_{OH^-} = K_w = 1.00 \times 10^{-14} \tag{3}$$

Charge balance:

$$m_{Na^+} + m_{H^+} = m_{HCO_3^-} + 2m_{CO_3^{2-}} + m_{OH^-} \tag{4}$$

Material balance:

$$m_{H_2CO_3} + m_{HCO_3^-} + m_{CO_3^{2-}} = 0.10 \tag{5}$$

$$m_{Na^+} = 0.10 \tag{6}$$

(b) Assume

$$m_{H^+}, m_{OH^-} \ll m_{H_2CO_3}, m_{CO_3^{2-}}$$

Then (4) and (5) become, using (6),

$$0.10 = m_{HCO_3^-} + 2m_{CO_3^{2-}} \tag{4'}$$

$$m_{H_2CO_3} + m_{HCO_3^-} + m_{CO_3^{2-}} = 0.10 \tag{5'}$$

From (4') and (5')

$$m_{CO_3^{2-}} = m_{H_2CO_3} = x$$

From (4)

$$m_{HCO_3^-} = 0.10 - 2x$$

Multiply (1) by (2):

$$m_{H^+}^2 = K_1 K_2 = 2.41 \times 10^{-17}$$
$$m_{H^+} = 4.9 \times 10^{-9} \text{ mole kg}^{-1}$$

Divide (1) by (2):

$$\frac{m_{HCO_3^-}^2}{m_{H_2CO_3} m_{CO_3^{2-}}} = \frac{K_1}{K_2}$$

$$\frac{(0.10 - 2x)^2}{x^2} = 7.66 \times 10^3$$

$$\frac{0.10 - 2x}{x} = 87.5$$

$$x = 1.1 \times 10^{-3} \text{ mole kg}^{-1} = m_{CO_3^{2-}}$$

10-II-15. (a) Equilibrium:

$$\frac{m_{H^+} m_{F^-}}{m_{HF}} = 3.5 \times 10^{-4} \tag{1}$$

$$\frac{m_{BH^+} m_{OH^-}}{m_B} = 7 \times 10^{-6} \tag{2}$$

$$m_{H^+} m_{OH^-} = 1.00 \times 10^{-14} \tag{3}$$

Charge balance:

$$m_{H^+} + m_{BH^+} = m_{OH^-} + m_{F^-} \tag{4}$$

Material balance:

$$m_{HF} + m_{F^-} = 0.100 \tag{5}$$

$$m_B + m_{BH^+} = 0.200 \tag{6}$$

(b) Assume

$$m_{H^+}, m_{OH^-} \ll m_{BH^+}, m_{F^-}$$

Then

$$m_{BH^+} = m_{F^-} = x \tag{4'}$$

$$m_{HF} = 0.100 - x \tag{5'}$$

$$m_B = 0.200 - x \tag{6'}$$

Multiply (1) by (2):

$$\frac{m_F - m_{BH^+} K_w}{m_{HF} m_B} = 2.45 \times 10^{-9}$$

$$\frac{m_F - m_{BH^+}}{m_{HF} m_B} = 2.45 \times 10^5$$

or

$$\frac{x^2}{(0.100 - x)(0.200 - x)} = 2.45 \times 10^5$$

Let

$$y = 0.100 - x$$

then

$$x = 0.100 - y, \quad 0.200 - x = 0.100 + y$$

$$\frac{(0.100 - y)^2}{y(0.100 + y)} = 2.45 \times 10^5$$

Assume $y \ll 0.100$; then

$$\frac{0.0100}{0.100y} = 2.45 \times 10^5$$

$$y = 4.1 \times 10^{-7} \text{ mole kg}^{-1} = m_{HF}$$

$$m_{F^-} = 0.100 - y = 0.100 \text{ mole kg}^{-1}$$

$$m_{H^+} = 3.5 \times 10^{-4} \times \frac{m_{HF}}{m_{F^-}} = \frac{3.5 \times 10^{-4} \times 4.1 \times 10^{-7}}{0.100}$$

$$= 1.4 \times 10^{-9} \text{ mole kg}^{-1}$$

10-II-16. (a) Nicotinic acid = HA; quinoline = B

Equilibrium:

$$HA \rightleftharpoons H^+ + A^-$$

$$\frac{0.70^2 m_{H^+} m_{A^-}}{m_{HA}} = 1.4 \times 10^{-5} \tag{1}$$

$$B + H_2O \rightleftharpoons BH^+ + OH^-$$

$$\frac{0.70^2 m_{BH^+} m_{OH^-}}{m_B} = 8.7 \times 10^{-6} \tag{2}$$

$$H_2O \rightleftharpoons H^+ + OH^-$$

$$0.70^2 m_{H^+} m_{OH^-} = 1.00 \times 10^{-14} \tag{3}$$

Charge balance:

$$m_{BH^+} + m_{K^+} + m_{H^+} = m_{A^-} + m_{Cl^-} + m_{OH^-} \tag{4}$$

Material balance:

$$m_{HA} + m_{A^-} = 0.050 \tag{5}$$

$$m_B + m_{BH^+} = 0.100 \tag{6}$$

$$m_{K^+} = 0.050 \tag{7}$$

$$m_{Cl^-} = 0.100 \tag{8}$$

(b) Assume

$$m_{H^+}, m_{OH^-} \ll m_{BH^+}, m_{A^-}$$

Then

$$m_{BH^+} + 0.050 = m_{A^-} + 0.100 \tag{4'}$$

Let

$$x = m_{A^-}$$

Then

$$m_{BH^+} = 0.050 + x$$

$$m_{HA} = 0.050 - x \tag{5'}$$

$$m_B = 0.100 - m_{BH^+} = 0.050 - x \tag{6'}$$

Multiply (1) by (2) and divide by (3):

$$\frac{0.70^4 m_{H^+} m_{A^-} m_{BH^+} m_{OH^-}}{0.70^2 m_{HA} m_B m_{H^+} m_{OH^-}} = \frac{1.4 \times 10^{-5} \times 8.7 \times 10^{-6}}{1.00 \times 10^{-14}}$$

$$\frac{m_{A^-} m_{BH^+}}{m_{HA} m_B} = 2.49 \times 10^4$$

$$\frac{x(0.050 + x)}{(0.050 - x)^2} = 2.49 \times 10^4$$

It appears that $0.050 - x \approx 0$. Let $y = 0.050 - x$. Assume $y \ll 0.050$. Then

$$x = 0.050 - y \approx 0.050, \quad 0.050 + x = 0.100 - y \approx 0.100$$

$$\frac{0.050 \times 0.100}{y^2} = 2.49 \times 10^4$$

$$y = 4.5 \times 10^{-4} \text{ mole kg}^{-1} = m_{HA}$$

(More accurate solution: $y = 4.45 \times 10^{-4}$)

$$m_{A^-} = 0.050 - y = 0.0496 \text{ mole kg}^{-1}$$

From (1)

$$m_{H^+} = \frac{1.4 \times 10^{-5} m_{HA}}{0.70^2 m_{A^-}} = 2.6 \times 10^{-7} \text{ mole kg}^{-1}$$

10-II-17. (a) $Q + H^+ \rightleftharpoons QH^+$

$$m_{QH^+} \approx 0.10$$

$$m_{Cl^-} = 0.10$$

$$I \approx 0.10$$

$$\sqrt{I} \approx 0.32$$

Let

$$\gamma_1 = \gamma_{H^+} = \gamma_{QH^+} = \gamma_{Cl^-} = \gamma_{OH^-}$$

$$\gamma_2 = \gamma_{QH_2^{2+}}$$

$$\log \gamma_1 = -\frac{0.509 \sqrt{I}}{1 + \sqrt{I}} = -0.123, \quad \gamma_1 = 0.753$$

$$\log \gamma_2 = -\frac{0.509 \times 2^2 \sqrt{I}}{1 + \sqrt{I}} = -0.492, \quad \gamma_2 = 0.322$$

(b) Equilibrium:

$$Q + H_2O \rightleftharpoons QH^+ + OH^-, \quad \frac{\gamma_1^2 m_{QH^+} m_{OH^-}}{m_Q} = K_1 = 2.0 \times 10^{-6} \quad (1)$$

$$QH^+ + H_2O \rightleftharpoons QH_2^{2+} + OH^-, \quad \frac{\gamma_2 \gamma_1 m_{QH_2^{2+}} m_{OH^-}}{\gamma_1 m_{QH^+}} = K_2 \quad (2)$$

$$= 1.35 \times 10^{-10}$$

$$H_2O \rightleftharpoons H^+ + OH^-, \quad \gamma_1^2 m_{H^+} m_{OH^-} = K_w = 1.00 \times 10^{-14} \quad (3)$$

Charge balance:

$$m_{QH^+} + 2m_{QH_2^{2+}} + m_{H^+} = m_{Cl^-} + m_{OH} \tag{4}$$

Material balance:

$$m_Q + m_{QH^+} + m_{QH_2^{2+}} = 0.10 \tag{5}$$

$$m_{Cl^-} = 0.10 \tag{6}$$

(c) Assume m_{H^+}, $m_{OH^-} \ll m_Q$, $m_{QH_2^{2+}}$. Then (4) and (5) become, using (6),

$$m_{QH^+} + 2m_{QH_2^{2+}} = 0.10$$

$$\underline{m_Q + m_{QH^+} + m_{QH_2^{2+}} = 0.10}$$

$$m_Q - m_{QH_2^{2+}} = 0$$

Let

$$x = m_Q = m_{QH_2^{2+}}$$

Then

$$m_{QH^+} = 0.10 - 2x$$

Multiply (1) and (2):

$$\frac{\gamma_1^2 \gamma_2 m_{QH^+} m_{OH^-}^2 m_{QH_2^{2+}}}{m_Q m_{QH^+}} = K_1 K_2$$

$$m_{OH^-}^2 = \frac{K_1 K_2}{\gamma_1^2 \gamma_2} = \frac{2.0 \times 10^{-6} \times 1.35 \times 10^{-10}}{0.753^2 \times 0.322} = 1.48 \times 10^{-15}$$

$$m_{OH^-} = 3.8 \times 10^{-8} \text{ mole kg}^{-1}$$

Divide (1) by (2):

$$\frac{\gamma_1^2 m_{QH^+}^2 m_{OH^-}}{\gamma_2 m_Q m_{QH_2^{2+}} m_{OH^-}} = \frac{K_1}{K_2}$$

$$\frac{m_{QH^+}^2}{m_Q m_{QH_2^{2+}}} = \frac{K_1 \gamma_2}{K_2 \gamma_1^2}$$

$$\frac{(0.10 - 2x)^2}{x^2} = 8.41 \times 10^3$$

$$\frac{0.10 - 2x}{x} = 91.7$$

$$x = 1.08 \times 10^{-3} \text{ mole kg}^{-1} = m_Q$$

10-II-18. (a) Mandelic acid = HA; p-anisidine = B.

Assuming complete reaction

$$0.040HA + 0.060B \rightarrow 0.040BH^+ + 0.040A^- + 0.020B$$

$I \approx 0.040 \qquad \sqrt{I} \approx 0.20$

$$\log \gamma \approx \frac{-0.509z^2 \sqrt{I}}{1 + \sqrt{I}} = \frac{-0.509 \times 1^2 \times 0.20}{1.20} = -0.0848$$

$\gamma = 0.823$ for any ion with charge ± 1.

(b) Equilibrium:

$$HA \rightleftharpoons H^+ + A^-$$

$$\frac{\gamma^2 m_{H^+} m_{A^-}}{m_{HA}} = 4.29 \times 10^{-4} \tag{1}$$

$$B + H_2O \rightleftharpoons BH^+ + OH^-$$

$$\frac{\gamma^2 m_{BH^+} m_{OH^-}}{m_B} = 5.13 \times 10^{-6} \tag{2}$$

$$H_2O \rightleftharpoons H^+ + OH^-$$

$$\gamma^2 m_{H^+} m_{OH^-} = 1.00 \times 10^{-14} \tag{3}$$

Charge balance:

$$m_{BH^+} + m_{H^+} = m_{A^-} - m_{OH^-} \tag{4}$$

Material balance:

$$m_{HA} + m_{A^-} = 0.040 \tag{5}$$

$$m_B + m_{BH^+} = 0.060 \tag{6}$$

(c) Assume

$$m_{H^+}, m_{OH^-} \ll m_{BH^+}, m_{A^-}$$

Then

$$m_{BH^+} = m_{A^-} = x \tag{4'}$$

$$m_{HA} = 0.40 - x \tag{5'}$$

$$m_B = 0.60 - x \tag{6'}$$

Multiply (1) by (2) and divide by (3):

$$\frac{\gamma^4 m_{H^+} m_A - m_{BH^+} m_{OH^-}}{\gamma^2 m_{HA} m_B m_{H^+} m_{OH^-}} = \frac{4.29 \times 10^{-4} \times 5.13 \times 10^{-6}}{1.00 \times 10^{-14}}$$

$$\frac{m_A - m_{BH^+}}{m_{HA} m_B} = 3.25 \times 10^5$$

$$\frac{x^2}{(0.040 - x)(0.060 - x)} = 3.25 \times 10^5$$

It appears that $0.040 - x \approx 0$. Let $y = 0.040 - x$. Then

$$x = 0.040 - y, \quad 0.060 - x = 0.020 + y$$

$$\frac{(0.040 - y)^2}{y(0.020 + y)} = 3.25 \times 10^5$$

Assume $y \ll 0.040$.

$$\frac{0.040^2}{0.020y} = 3.25 \times 10^5$$

$$y = 2.46 \times 10^{-7} \text{ mole kg}^{-1} = m_{HA}$$

$y \ll 0.040$ as assumed.

$$m_{A^-} = 0.040 - y = 0.040 \text{ mole kg}^{-1}$$

From (1)

$$m_{H^+} = \frac{4.29 \times 10^{-4} m_{HA}}{\gamma^2 m_{A^-}} = 3.90 \times 10^{-9} \text{ mole kg}^{-1}$$

10-II-19. (a) Glycine = HA; glycinium ion = H_2A^+

For complete reaction

$0.100HA + 0.040Na^+ + 0.040OH^- \rightarrow 0.040Na^+ + 0.040A^-$
$+ 0.040H_2O + 0.060HA$

$$I \approx 0.040 \qquad \sqrt{I} = 0.20$$

$$\log \gamma = \frac{-0.509 \times 1^2 \sqrt{I}}{1 + \sqrt{I}} = -0.0848$$

$\gamma = 0.823$ for any ion with charge ± 1.

(b) Equilibrium:

$$H_2A^+ \rightleftharpoons H^+ + HA \qquad \frac{m_{H^+}m_{HA}}{m_{H_2A^+}} = K_1 = 4.47 \times 10^{-3} \tag{1}$$

$$HA \rightleftharpoons H^+ + A^- \qquad \frac{\gamma^2 m_{H^+}m_{A^-}}{m_{HA}} = K_2 = 1.66 \times 10^{-10} \tag{2}$$

$$H_2O \rightleftharpoons H^+ + OH^- \qquad \gamma^2 m_{H^+}m_{OH^-} = 1.00 \times 10^{-14} \tag{3}$$

Charge balance:

$$m_{Na^+} + m_{H_2A^+} + m_{H^+} = m_{A^-} + m_{OH^-} \tag{4}$$

Material balance:

$$m_{H_2A^+} + m_{HA} + m_{A^-} = 0.100 \tag{5}$$

$$m_{Na^+} = 0.040 \tag{6}$$

(c) Assume

$$m_{H^+}, m_{OH^-} \ll m_{H_2A^+}, m_{A^-}$$

Let

$$x = m_{H_2A^+}.$$

Then

$$m_{A^-} = 0.040 + x \tag{4'}$$

$$m_{HA} = 0.100 - x - (0.040 + x) = 0.060 - 2x \tag{5'}$$

Divide (1) by (2):

$$\frac{m_{H^+}m_{HA}^2}{\gamma^2 m_{H_2A^+}m_{H^+}m_{A^-}} = \frac{K_1}{K_2} = 2.69 \times 10^7$$

$$\frac{m_{HA}^2}{m_{H_2A^+}m_{A^-}} = 1.82 \times 10^7$$

$$\frac{(0.060 - 2x)^2}{x(0.040 + x)} = 1.82 \times 10^7$$

(d) Assume $x \ll 0.030$

$$\frac{0.060^2}{0.040x} = 1.82 \times 10^7$$

$$x = 4.95 \times 10^{-9} \text{ mole kg}^{-1} = m_{H_2A^+}$$

10-II-20. (a) $Pb \mid PbBr_2(s) \mid CuBr_2(aq, 0.0100m) \mid Cu$

(b) $m_\pm = (0.0100 \times 0.0200^2)^{1/3} = 0.0100 \sqrt[3]{4}$

$\log m_\pm = -2 + \frac{1}{3}\log 4 = -1.799$

$$E = E° - \frac{RT}{2\mathscr{F}} \ln\left(\frac{1}{a_{Cu^{2+}}a_{Br-}^2}\right)$$

$$= E° + \frac{3RT}{2\mathscr{F}} \ln a_\pm = E° + \frac{3RT}{2\mathscr{F}}(\ln \gamma_\pm + \ln m_\pm)$$

$$= E° + \tfrac{3}{2} \times 0.05915\,(\log \gamma_\pm + \log m_\pm)$$

$$= E° + \tfrac{3}{2} \times 0.05915(-0.150 - 1.799)$$

$$= E° - 0.173$$

$$E° = E + 0.173 = 0.442 + 0.173 = 0.615 \text{ V}$$

(c)

	$E°$, V
$Pb \rightarrow Pb^{2+} + 2e^-$	$+0.126$ (from table)
$PbBr_2 + Cu \rightarrow Pb + Cu^{2+} + 2Br^-$	-0.615 (from b)
$Cu^{2+} + 2e^- \rightarrow Cu$	$+0.337$ (from table)
$PbBr_2 \rightarrow Pb^{2+} + 2Br^-$	-0.152 V

$$\log K = \frac{2E°}{0.05915} = -5.14$$

$$K = 7.2 \times 10^{-6}$$

10-II-21.

	E, V
$Na(s) \rightarrow Na^+ \text{ (in } C_2H_5NH_2) + e^-$ $\Big\}$ $Na^+ \text{ (in } C_2H_5NH_2) + e^- \rightarrow Na \text{ (in Hg)}$	$+0.8453$
$Na \text{ (in Hg)} \rightarrow Na^+ (aq) + e^-$ $\Big\}$ $\frac{1}{2}Hg_2Cl_2(s) + e^- \rightarrow Hg(liq) + Cl^-(aq)$	$+2.2676$
$Na(s) + \frac{1}{2}Hg_2Cl_2(s) \rightarrow Na^+(aq) + Cl^-(aq) + Hg(liq)$	$+3.1129$

$$E° = E + \frac{RT}{\mathscr{F}} \ln (\gamma_\pm m_\pm)_{NaCl}^2$$

$$= 3.1129 + 2 \times 0.05915[-0.1091 + \log(0.1005)]$$

$$= 2.9820 \text{ V}$$

	$E°$, V
$Na(s) \rightarrow Na^+(aq) + e^-$	$-x$
$\frac{1}{2}Hg_2Cl_2(s) + e^- \rightarrow Hg(liq) + Cl^-(aq)$	$+0.2676$
	2.9820

$$x = -2.9820 + 0.2676 = -2.7144 \text{ V (Table: } -2.7132 \text{ V)}$$

10-II-22. (a) $Zn \rightarrow Zn^{2+} + 2e^-$

$$\frac{PbSO_4 + 2e^- \rightarrow Pb + SO_4^{2-}}{Zn + PbSO_4 \rightarrow Pb + Zn^{2+} + SO_4^{2-}}$$

(b) $a_{Zn^{2+}}a_{SO_4^{2-}} = (\gamma_+ m)(\gamma_- m) = \gamma_\pm^2 m^2$

$$E = E^\circ - \frac{RT}{2\mathscr{F}} \ln(\gamma_\pm^2 m^2) = E^\circ - \frac{RT}{\mathscr{F}} \ln(\gamma_\pm m)$$

(c)   Let

$$E' = E + \frac{RT}{\mathscr{F}} \ln m = E^\circ - \frac{RT}{\mathscr{F}} \ln \gamma_\pm$$

$$E^\circ = \lim_{m \to 0} E'$$

m	$\sqrt{m}$	E'
0.001000	0.03162	0.41969
0.005000	0.07071	0.42987

According to the Debye-Hückel limiting law $\ln \gamma_\pm$ should be proportional to $\sqrt{m}$. Thus E' should be a linear function of $\sqrt{m}$: $E' = E^\circ + k\sqrt{m}$

$$\frac{\begin{array}{l} 0.41969 = E^\circ + k(0.03162) \\ 0.42987 = E^\circ + k(0.07071) \end{array}}{0.01018 = \qquad k(0.03909)}$$

$k = 0.2604;$ $E^\circ = 0.41146$ V

Equivalently, plot E' vs $\sqrt{m}$ and extrapolate to $\sqrt{m} = 0$. (Accepted value, 0.41089 V; Cowperthwaite and La Mer, *J. Am. Chem. Soc.* **53**, 4333 (1931). A correction for the finite solubility of $PbSO_4$ is needed.)

(d) $\dfrac{RT}{\mathscr{F}} \ln \gamma_\pm = E^\circ - E' = 0.41146 - 0.42987 = -0.01841$

$$\log \gamma_\pm = -\frac{0.01841}{0.05915} = -0.3113; \gamma_\pm = 0.488$$

10-II-23. (a) $\ln K_{298} = -\Delta G_{298}^\circ / RT$

$$= \frac{-53.41}{1.987 \times 10^{-3} \times 298} = -90.2$$

$$\Delta H_T^\circ = \Delta H_{298}^\circ + \int_{298}^{T} \Delta C_P^\circ \, dT$$

$$= 53.22 - 8.7 \times 10^{-3} (T - 298)$$

$$= 55.8 - 8.7 \times 10^{-3} \, T \text{ kcal}$$

(It has been assumed that ΔC_P° is independent of T.)

$$\ln K_T = \ln K_{298} + \frac{1}{R} \int_{298}^{T} \frac{\Delta H_T^\circ}{T^2} \, dT$$

$$= -90.2 + \frac{1}{1.987 \times 10^{-3}} \int_{298}^{T} \left(\frac{55.8}{T^2} - \frac{8.7 \times 10^{-3}}{T} \right) dT$$

$$= -90.2 + 2.81 \times 10^4 \left(\frac{1}{298} - \frac{1}{T} \right) - 4.4 \ln \left(\frac{T}{298} \right)$$

$$= +28.8 - \frac{2.81 \times 10^4}{T} - 4.4 \ln T$$

(b) The cell $Ag(s)|\ Ag_2SO_4(aq)|\ PbSO_4(s)|\ Pb(s)$ is suitable. In this cell the process is

$$2Ag(s) + PbSO_4(s) \rightarrow Pb(s) + 2Ag^+(aq) + SO_4^{2-}\ (aq)$$

actually the reverse, since $E < 0$ near room temperature for any reasonable concentration of Ag_2SO_4 . The emf is

$$E = E^\circ - \frac{RT}{2\mathscr{F}} \ln(a_{Ag^+}^2 a_{SO_4^{2-}})$$

$$= E^\circ - \frac{3RT}{2\mathscr{F}} \ln a_\pm$$

Now

$$a_\pm = \gamma_\pm\, m_\pm$$

$$= \gamma_\pm\, \sqrt[3]{4}m$$

The Debye-Hückel limiting law gives $\ln \gamma_\pm \approx -B\sqrt{m}$, where B is a known constant for any one temperature, solvent, and salt type. Let

$$E' = E + \frac{RT}{2\mathscr{F}} (3 \ln m + \ln 4 - 3B \sqrt{m})$$

then

$$E' = E^\circ - \frac{3RT}{2\mathscr{F}} (\ln \gamma_\pm + B \sqrt{m})$$

and $\lim_{m \to 0} E' = E^\circ$. We now measure E (and thus E') with a sequence of cells in which the molality m of Ag_2SO_4 becomes smaller, plot E' against m, and extrapolate to $m = 0$. (See figure.) Finally

$$\ln K = \frac{2\mathscr{F}E^\circ}{RT}$$

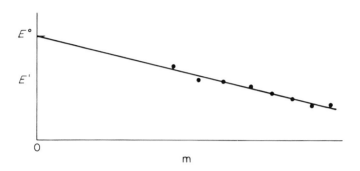

(c) $K_m = a_{Ag^+}^{(m)2} a_{SO_4^{2-}}^{(m)}$ $K_X = a_{Ag^+}^{(X)2} a_{SO_4^{2-}}^{(X)}$

$$\frac{a^{(X)}}{a^{(m)}} = \lim_{\substack{m \\ X}\to 0} \left(\frac{X}{m}\right) = \frac{M_{H_2O}}{1000} = 0.018$$

$$\frac{K_X}{K_m} = (0.018)^3 = 5.83 \times 10^{-6}$$

10-II-24.

(a) $\frac{1}{2}H_2(g) + AgBr(s) \rightarrow H^+ + Br^- + Ag(s)$

(b) $E = E^\circ - \dfrac{RT}{\mathscr{F}} \ln(a_{H^+} a_{Br^-}) = E^\circ + \dfrac{2RT}{\mathscr{F}} \ln a_\pm$

$\qquad = E^\circ - \dfrac{2RT}{\mathscr{F}} \ln (\gamma_\pm c)$

$E^\circ = E + \dfrac{2RT}{\mathscr{F}} \ln (\gamma_\pm c) = E + 0.1183(\log \gamma_\pm + \log c)$

Debye-Hückel limiting law:

$\log \gamma_\pm \approx -0.5091 \sqrt{c}$

Let

$E^{\circ\prime} = E - 0.06023 \sqrt{c} + 0.1183 \log c$

The limiting law predicts $E^{\circ\prime} = E^\circ$.

(c)   (1)   (2)

$\qquad E^{\circ\prime}$, V   0.07110   0.07091 (See figure.)

$E^\circ = 0.0713$ V

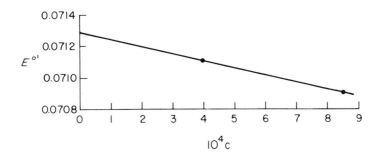

(d)   (i) $\log \gamma_{\pm} = \dfrac{E^\circ - E - 0.1183 \log c}{0.1183} = -0.0248$

   $\gamma_{\pm} = 0.944$

   (ii) $\log \gamma_{\pm} = -0.5091 \sqrt{37.19} \times 10^{-2} = -0.0311$

   $\gamma_{\pm} = 0.931$

10-II-25. $\tfrac{1}{2}H_2(g) + AgBr(s) \rightleftharpoons Ag(s) + H^+ + Br^-$

$$E = E^\circ - \frac{RT}{\mathscr{F}} \ln(a_+ a_-) = E^\circ - \frac{RT}{\mathscr{F}} \ln(\gamma_{\pm} m)^2$$

$$= E^\circ - \frac{2RT}{\mathscr{F}} \ln \gamma_{\pm} - \frac{2RT}{\mathscr{F}} \ln m$$

As

$$m \to 0, \quad \gamma_{\pm} \to 1, \quad \frac{2RT}{\mathscr{F}} \ln \gamma_{\pm} \to 0$$

$$E^\circ = \lim_{\sqrt{m} \to 0} \left[E + \frac{2RT}{\mathscr{F}} \ln m \right]$$

Plot $E + (2RT/\mathscr{F}) \ln m$ vs $\sqrt{m}$, and extrapolate to $\sqrt{m} = 0$. (See figure.)

m	$E + (2RT/\mathscr{F}) \ln m$
0.005125	0.0749
0.010021	0.0762
0.015158	0.0771
0.02533	0.0782
0.03006	0.0790

$E^\circ = 0.0722$ V (Hetzer et al. get 0.07106 V.)

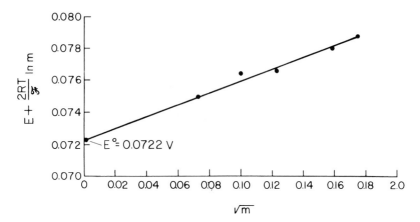

We can also plot

$$E' = E + \frac{2RT}{\mathscr{F}} \ln m + \frac{2RT}{\mathscr{F}} \ln \gamma'_{\pm},$$

where $\gamma'_{\pm}$ is the value predicted by the Debye-Hückel limiting law. This is a better procedure because $E^{\circ} - E' \neq 0$ only because of the deviations from the limiting law. In this method one plots vs m instead of $\sqrt{m}$, since the residual dependence of $\ln \gamma'$ (and thus $E^{\circ} - E'$) on m is approximately linear.

10-II-26. Cell reactions:

		E°, V
(a)	$\frac{1}{2}H_2 + \frac{1}{2}Hg_2Cl_2 \rightarrow H^+ + Hg + Cl^-$	-0.0216
(b)	$Hg + Na^+ + Cl^- \rightarrow \frac{1}{2}Hg_2Cl_2 + Na$	-1.8562
(c)	$Na + C_2H_5OH \rightarrow \frac{1}{2}H_2 + C_2H_5O^- + Na^+$	0.7458
	$C_2H_5OH \rightarrow H^+ + C_2H_5O^-$	-1.1320

$$E^{\circ} = 0.05915 \log K$$

$$\log K = \frac{-1.1320}{0.05915} = -19.138 = 0.862 - 20$$

$$K = 7.28 \times 10^{-20}$$

10-II-27.

(a) $\frac{1}{2}H_2 + A^- + AgCl \rightarrow HA + Cl^- + Ag$

(b) $E - E^{\circ} = -\dfrac{RT}{\mathscr{F}} \ln \left(\dfrac{m_{HA}m_{Cl^-}\gamma_{HA}\gamma_{\pm NaCl}}{m_{A^-}\gamma_{\pm NaA}} \right)$

$\qquad\qquad = -\dfrac{RT}{\mathscr{F}} \ln \left(\dfrac{m_{HA}m_{NaCl}\gamma_{HA}\gamma_{\pm NaCl}}{m_{NaA}\gamma_{\pm NaA}} \right)$

$$E'' = E + \frac{RT}{\mathscr{F}} \ln\left(\frac{m_{HA}m_{NaCl}}{m_{NaA}}\right)$$

$$= E^\circ - \frac{RT}{\mathscr{F}} \ln\left(\frac{\gamma_{HA}\gamma_{\pm NaCl}}{\gamma_{\pm NaA}}\right)$$

E'' can be calculated at once from measurable quantities if HA is weak enough so that m_{HA} and m_{NaA} can be assumed equal to the total molalities introduced. Prepare a series of cells with different molalities of NaCl, NaA, and HA and plot E'' as a function of the ionic strength I (or its square root). The limit of E'' as I approaches zero is E°. Since $\gamma_{HA} \approx 1$ and $\gamma_{\pm NaCl} \approx \gamma_{\pm NaA}$, the approach to E° should be quite rapid in this case.

(c) $\frac{1}{2}H_2 + AgCl \rightarrow H^+ + Cl^- + Ag$

$$E' - E^{\circ\prime} = -\frac{RT}{\mathscr{F}} \ln(m'_{\pm HCl}\gamma'_{\pm HCl})^2$$

where

$$m'_{\pm HCl} = (m'_{H^+}m'_{Cl^-})^{1/2} = [m'_{HCl}(m'_{HCl} + m'_{NaCl})]^{1/2}$$

Let

$$E''' = E' + \frac{2RT}{\mathscr{F}} \ln(m'_{\pm HCl}) = E^{\circ\prime} - \frac{2RT}{\mathscr{F}} \ln \gamma'_{\pm HCl}$$

As in (b) plot E' as a function of I. In this case $\sqrt{I}$ should be used as the abscissa.

$$\lim_{I \to 0} E''' = E^\circ.$$

(d)   Pt| H_2(1 atm)| HCl, NaCl, H_2O| AgCl | Ag| AgCl |
HA, NaA, NaCl, H_2O| H_2(1 atm)| Pt

(e) For the cell of (d) the standard emf is $E^{\circ\prime} - E^\circ$. The measured emf is $E' - E$. Combining the results of (b) and (c),

$$E' - E - E^{\circ\prime} + E^\circ = -\frac{RT}{\mathscr{F}} \ln\left(\frac{m'^2_{\pm HCl}\gamma'^2_{\pm HCl}m_{NaA}\gamma_{\pm NaA}}{m_{HA}m_{NaCl}\gamma_{HA}\gamma_{\pm NaCl}}\right)$$

Let

$$E'''' = E' - E + \frac{RT}{\mathscr{F}} \ln\left(\frac{m'^2_{\pm HCl}m_{NaA}}{m_{HA}m_{NaCl}}\right)$$

$$= E^{\circ\prime} - E^\circ - \frac{RT}{\mathscr{F}} \ln\left(\frac{\gamma'^2_{\pm HCl}\gamma_{\pm NaA}}{\gamma_{HA}\gamma_{\pm NaCl}}\right)$$

Plot E'''' as a function of $\sqrt{I'}$.

$$\lim_{I' \to 0} E'''' = E^{\circ\prime} - E^\circ$$

For the cell of (d) the reaction is $HA \rightleftharpoons H^+ + A^-$ or, in terms of complete electrolytes

$$HA + NaCl \rightleftharpoons HCl + NaA$$

with equilibrium constant K; the relation between K and $E^{\circ\prime} - E^{\circ}$ is

$$\ln K = \frac{\mathscr{F}(E^{\circ\prime} - E^{\circ})}{RT}$$

10-II-28. (a) $\quad I = \frac{1}{2}(0.00500 \times 2^2 + 0.01000 \times 1^2) = 0.01500$

$$\sqrt{I} = 0.1225$$

$$\log \gamma_{\pm} = \frac{-0.509| z_+ z_- | \sqrt{I}}{1 + \sqrt{I}} = -0.1111$$

$$\gamma_{\pm} = 0.774$$

(b) $\quad m_{\pm} = (m_{Zn^{2+}} m_{Cl^-}^2)^{1/3} = \sqrt[3]{4} \times 0.00500$

$$Zn + Hg_2Cl_2 \rightarrow Zn^{2+} + 2Cl^- + 2Hg$$

$$E = E^{\circ} - \frac{RT}{2\mathscr{F}} \ln(a_{Zn^{2+}} a_{Cl^-}^2)$$

$$= E^{\circ} - \frac{3RT}{2\mathscr{F}} \ln a_{\pm} = E^{\circ} - \frac{3RT}{2\mathscr{F}} \ln(\gamma_{\pm} m_{\pm})$$

$$= E^{\circ} - \frac{3}{2} \times 0.05915 \, (-0.1111 + \frac{1}{3} \log 4 + \log 0.00500)$$

$$1.2272 = E^{\circ} + 0.1964$$

$$E^{\circ} = 1.0308 \text{ V}$$

(c) $\quad Zn \rightarrow Zn^{2+} + 2e^- \qquad\qquad\qquad\qquad +0.7628$

$\quad\dfrac{Hg_2Cl_2 + 2e^- \rightarrow 2Hg + 2Cl^-}{Zn + Hg_2Cl_2 \rightarrow Zn^{2+} + 2Cl^- + 2Hg} \qquad\qquad \dfrac{+0.2676}{E^{\circ} = 1.0304 \text{ V}}$

10-II-29. $Cd(X_1) \rightarrow Cd^{2+} + 2e^-$

$\dfrac{Cd^{2+} + 2e^- \rightarrow Cd(X_2)}{Cd(X_1) \rightarrow Cd(X_2)}$

$$E = E^{\circ} - \frac{RT}{2\mathscr{F}} \ln\left(\frac{a_2}{a_1}\right) = 0 - \frac{RT}{2\mathscr{F}}\left(\ln \frac{\gamma_2}{\gamma_1} + \ln \frac{X_2}{X_1}\right)$$

$$= \frac{0.05915}{2}\left(\log \frac{\gamma_1}{\gamma_2} + \log \frac{X_1}{X_2}\right)$$

(a) For ideal solutions

$\gamma_1 = \gamma_2 = 1$

$$E = \frac{0.05915}{2} \log \left(\frac{1.75 \times 10^{-2}}{1.75 \times 10^{-4}} \right) = 0.05915 \text{ V}$$

(b) $\log \dfrac{\gamma_1}{\gamma_2} = \dfrac{2E}{0.05915} - \log \dfrac{X_1}{X_2} = \dfrac{2 \times 0.05926}{0.05915} - 2$

$$= \frac{2(0.05926 - 0.05915)}{0.05915} = 0.0037$$

$$\frac{\gamma_1}{\gamma_2} = 1.0086$$

10-II-30. When the emf of a complete reaction is calculated from the emf's of half reactions, the emf's are merely added. The justification for this procedure, however, is dependent on the equal numbers of electrons in the two half reactions (Problem 10-III-11). Here we must add ΔG°'s or, more simply, $-(\Delta G^{\circ}/\mathscr{F}) = nE^{\circ}$:

	n	E°	nE°
$2\text{Hg} \rightarrow \text{Hg}_2^{2+} + 2e^-$	2	-0.7986	-1.5972
$2\text{Hg}^{2+} + 4e^- \rightarrow 2\text{Hg}$	4	$+0.854$	$+3.416$
$2\text{Hg}^{2+} + 2e^- \rightarrow \text{Hg}_2^{2+}$	2		$+1.819$

$$E^{\circ} = \frac{1.819}{2} = 0.910 \text{ V}$$

10-II-31.

$\text{Fe} \rightarrow \text{Fe}^{2+} + 2e^-$	$+0.440 \times 2 = \quad 0.880$
$\text{Fe}^{2+} \rightarrow \text{Fe}^{3+} + e^-$	$-0.771 \times 1 = -0.771$
$\text{Fe} \rightarrow \text{Fe}^{3+} + 3e^-$	$3E^{\circ} = \quad 0.109$
	$E^{\circ} = \quad 0.036 \text{ V}$

where E° is the standard potential of the new half cell.

10-II-32.

V	$\bar{V}$	ΔV	E	ΔE	$\Delta E/\Delta V$
0.0			-570		
	0.025	0.05		5	100
0.05			-565		
	0.10	0.1		5	50
0.15			-560		
	0.175	0.05		30	600
0.2			-530		
	0.225	0.05		40	800

V	$\bar{V}$	ΔV	E	ΔE	$\Delta E/\Delta V$
0.25			−490		
	0.275	0.05		50	1000
0.3			−440		
	0.325	0.05		370	7400
0.35			−70		
	0.375	0.05		120	2400
0.4			50		
	0.450	0.1		15	150
0.5			65		
	1.500	2.0		25	13
2.5			90		
	3.450	1.9		20	11
4.4			110		
	5.450	2.1		10	5
6.5			120		
	7.600	2.2		10	5
8.7			130		
	9.500	1.6		10	6
10.3			140		
	10.350	0.1		10	100
10.4			150		
	10.450	0.1		20	200
10.5			170		
	10.550	0.1		180	1800
10.6			350		
	10.700	0.2		20	100
10.8			370		
	10.850	0.1		20	200
10.9			390		
	11.000	0.2		30	150
11.1			420		
	11.325	0.45		20	44
11.55			440		

Graphs of E vs V and $\Delta E/\Delta V$ vs $\bar{V}$ (average V) are shown.

10-II-33. (a) Equilibrium.

(b) $K_p = 1$ or $K_c = 1$, depending upon how $E°$ is defined. Another answer would be "concentration cell."

(c) Very dilute solution of strong electrolyte.

(d) Very dilute solution.

(e) No restrictions.

(f) Only for 1 : 2 or 2 : 1 salt.

(g) Very dilute solution.

(h) Reversible reaction in cell.

(i) $E_t = $ emf of cell reversible with respect to cation. $E = $ emf of same cell without transference. Transference number independent of concentration.

10-II-34.

$$\left(\frac{\epsilon - 1}{\epsilon + 2}\right)\frac{3M}{4\pi N\rho} = \alpha + \frac{\beta}{T}$$

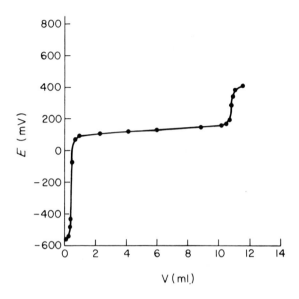

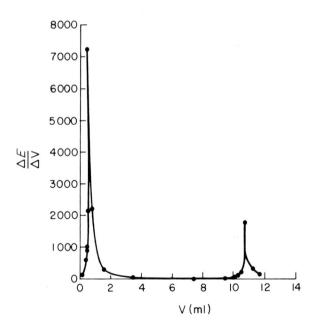

Figs. 10-II-32.

where $\beta = \mu^2/3k$ and N is Avogadro's number.

$$\frac{3M}{4\pi N\rho} = \frac{3 \times 100.0 \text{ g mole}^{-1}}{4\pi \times 6.023 \times 10^{23} \text{ molec mole}^{-1} \times 1.000 \times 10^{-3} \text{ g cm}^{-3}}$$

$$= 3.96 \times 10^{-20} \text{ cm}^3 \text{ molec}^{-1}$$

$$\frac{1.212 \times 10^{-3}}{3.001} \times 3.96 \times 10^{-20} = \alpha + \frac{\beta}{200}$$

$$\frac{7.575 \times 10^{-4}}{3.001} \times 3.96 \times 10^{-20} = \alpha + \frac{\beta}{400}$$

$$1.60 \times 10^{-23} = \alpha + \frac{\beta}{200}$$

$$1.00 \times 10^{-23} = \alpha + \frac{\beta}{400}$$

$$\overline{0.60 \times 10^{-23} = \beta \left(\frac{1}{200} - \frac{1}{400}\right) = \frac{\beta}{400}}$$

$$\beta = 2.40 \times 10^{-21} \text{ deg cm}^3 \text{ molec}^{-1}$$

$$\alpha = 1.00 \times 10^{-23} - \frac{\beta}{400} = 4.0 \times 10^{-24} \text{ cm}^3 \text{ molec}^{-1}$$

$$\mu^2 = 3k\beta = 3 \times 1.38 \times 10^{-16} \text{ erg deg}^{-1} \text{ molec}^{-1}$$
$$\times 2.40 \times 10^{-21} \text{ deg cm}^3 \text{ molec}^{-1}$$
$$= 9.94 \times 10^{-37} \text{ erg cm}^3 \text{ molec}^{-2} \quad \text{or} \quad \text{esu}^2 \text{ cm}^2 \text{ molec}^{-2}$$

$(1 \text{ erg} = 1 \text{ esu}^2 \text{ cm}^{-1})$

$\mu = 1.0 \times 10^{-18} \text{ esu cm}^{-1} \text{ molec}^{-1} \quad \text{or} \quad 1.0 \text{ debye}$

SECTION 10-III

10-III-1. (a) 0.5000 mole kg^{-1} × 0.0500 kg = 0.0250 mole Fe^{2+} produced or 0.0250 faraday passed.

(b) 3 × 1.5750 + 2 × 0.5000 = 5.7250 mole Cl$^-$ kg^{-1} at end

$$3 \times 2.0000 \qquad\qquad\qquad = \underline{6.0000 \text{ mole Cl}^-\text{ kg}^{-1} \text{ at beginning}}$$
$$0.2750 \text{ mole Cl}^-\text{kg}^{-1} \text{ migrated out}$$

0.2750 mole $kg^{-1} \times$ 0.0500 kg = 0.01375 mole or equivalent of Cl^- migrated out.

$$t_- = \frac{0.01375}{0.0250} = 0.550$$

(c) $\lambda_+ = \lambda_- \dfrac{t_+}{t_-} = \dfrac{76.35 \times 0.450}{0.550} = 62.5 \ ohm^{-1} \ cm^2 \ equiv^{-1}$

The assumption is that t_- (and thus t_+) is the same in the $0.5m$ solution as in an infinitely dilute solution. This is a questionable approximation for a tervalent ion like Fe^{3+}, which probably exists in considerable part as $FeCl^{2+}$, etc., in a concentrated solution.

10-III-2. Br_2 produced at anode = Br_2 consumed at cathode
Br_2 initially present in either compartment = $\frac{1}{2} \times$ total Br_2
  present in two compartments = constant = 0.1000 mole
Anode compartment gained 0.0100 mole
Cathode compartment lost 0.0100 mole
Br_2 does not migrate
0.0100 mole $\times$ 2 equiv $mole^{-1}$ = 0.0200 faraday passed.
Br^- initially present in either compartment = $\frac{1}{2} \times$ total Br^-
  present in the two compartments = constant = 0.1000 mole

Moles Br^-	Anode	Cathode
Initial	0.1000	0.1000
Produced	−0.0200	+0.0200
Final in absence of migration	0.0800	0.1200
Final	0.0920	0.1080
Migrated	+0.0120	−0.0120

$$t_- = \frac{0.0120}{0.0200} = 0.600 \qquad\qquad t_+ = 0.400$$

10-III-3.   (a) $n_1 \, d\mu_1 + n_+ \, d\mu_+ + n_- \, d\mu_- = 0$.
When 1 kg of solvent (1) is considered, $n_+ = \nu_+ m$, $n_- = \nu_- m$, $n_1 = 1000/M$, where M_1 is the molecular weight of 1. Introducing activities, we have

$$n_1 d \ln a_1 + m(\nu_+ d \ln a_+ + \nu_- d \ln a_-) = 0$$
$$n_1 d \ln a_1 + \nu m d \ln a_\pm = 0$$

where $\nu = \nu_+ + \nu_-$. Now

$$a_1 = \gamma_1 X_1 , \quad a_\pm = \gamma_\pm (\nu_+^{\nu_+} \nu_-^{\nu_-})^{1/\nu} m$$

thus

$$n_1(d \ln \gamma_1 + d \ln X_1) + \nu m(d \ln \gamma_\pm + d \ln m) = 0$$

It is given that

$$\ln \gamma_\pm = -B \sqrt{m} + Cm$$

Then

$$d \ln \gamma_\pm = (-\tfrac{1}{2}Bm^{-1/2} + C)\, dm.$$

Solving,

$$d \ln \gamma_1 = -d \ln X_1 - \frac{\nu m}{n_1}\left(-\frac{1}{2}Bm^{-1/2} + C + \frac{1}{m}\right) dm$$

$$\ln \gamma_1 = -\int_{X_1=1}^{X_1} d \ln X_1 - \frac{\nu}{n_1}\int_{m=0}^{m}\left(-\frac{1}{2}B\sqrt{m} + Cm + 1\right) dm$$

$$= -\ln X_1 - \frac{\nu}{n_1}\left(-\tfrac{1}{3}Bm^{3/2} + \tfrac{1}{2}Cm^2 + m\right)$$

$$= -\ln\left(\frac{n_1}{n_1 + \nu m}\right) - \frac{\nu}{n_1}\left(-\frac{1}{3}Bm^{3/2} + \frac{1}{2}Cm^2 + m\right)$$

(b) $\nu = 3$

  $n_1 = 55.5$

$$X_1 = \frac{55.5}{55.5 + 0.0030} = \frac{1}{1 + 0.0030/55.5}$$

$$\ln X_1 \approx -\frac{0.0030}{55.5} = -5.41 \times 10^{-5}$$

$$I = \tfrac{1}{2}(2 \times 1^2 + 1 \times 2^2)\, m = 3m$$

$$\ln \gamma_\pm = -0.5091 \times 2.303 \times 1 \times 2\sqrt{3m} = -4.06\sqrt{m}$$

  $B = 4.06$

$$\ln \gamma_1 = 5.41 \times 10^{-5} - \frac{3}{55.5}\left[-\frac{4.06}{3}(0.001)^{3/2} + 0.001\right]$$

$$= 2.31 \times 10^{-6}$$

  $\gamma_1 = 1.00000231$

(c) $\pi = -\dfrac{RT \ln a_1}{V_1} = -\dfrac{RT(\ln X_1 + \ln \gamma_1)}{V_1}$

$$= -\frac{82.06 \times 298.15 \times (-5.41 + 0.23) \times 10^{-5}}{18.016/0.997}$$

$$= 0.070 \text{ atm}$$

10-III-4. $B = 0$ in order that $U(\infty)$ be finite. In the absence of other ions, $b = 0$, $\sigma_0 = 0$, and $\sigma_0/b^2 \to 0$. Then

$$U = \frac{ze}{\epsilon r} = \frac{A \exp(0)}{r} \quad \text{and} \quad A = \frac{ze}{\epsilon}.$$

For any b and σ_0

$$U = \frac{ze \exp(-br)}{\epsilon r} + \frac{4\pi\sigma_0}{b^2\epsilon}$$

$$\approx \frac{ze}{\epsilon r} - \frac{zeb}{\epsilon} + \frac{4\pi\sigma_0}{b^2\epsilon}$$

$$= \frac{ze}{\epsilon r} + U_{xs}$$

$$U_{xs} = -\frac{zeb}{\epsilon} + \frac{4\pi\sigma_0}{b^2\epsilon}$$

For a variable charge Q on the central ion,

$$U_{xs} = -\frac{Qb}{\epsilon} + \frac{4\pi\sigma_0}{b^2\epsilon}$$

$$G_{xs} \text{ (per ion)} = \int_0^{ze} U_{xs}\, dQ = \int_0^{ze} \left(-\frac{Qb}{\epsilon} + \frac{4\pi\sigma_0}{b^2\epsilon}\right) dQ$$

$$= -\frac{bz^2e^2}{2\epsilon} + \frac{4\pi\sigma_0 ze}{b^2\epsilon} = kT \ln \gamma$$

$$\ln \gamma = -\frac{bz^2e^2}{2\epsilon kT} + \frac{4\pi\sigma_0 ze}{b^2\epsilon kT}$$

10-III-5. Let $x = [H^+]$. Then

$$[OH^-] = \frac{K_w}{x} = \frac{10^{-14}}{x}$$

$$[H^+] = [OH^-] + [Cl^-] \text{ for electrical neutrality}$$

$$x = \frac{10^{-14}}{x} + 10^{-8}$$

$$x^2 - 10^{-8}x - 10^{-14} = 0$$

$$x = 1.051 \times 10^{-7}$$

$$pH = 6.978$$

10-III-6. For the cell process

$$\tfrac{1}{2}H_2(g) + AgCl(s) \to Ag(s) + H^+(aq) + Cl^-(aq)$$

the reaction quotient is

$$Q = \frac{a_{H^+} a_{Cl^-}}{f_{H_2}^{1/2}}.$$

Thus

$$E + E^\circ - \frac{RT}{\mathscr{F}} \ln Q$$

We cannot say that $Q = K$ in general; this is true only when the cell process has reached equilibrium. In this case the cell is no longer capable of doing work, so that $E = 0$ and

$$E^\circ = \frac{RT}{\mathscr{F}} \ln Q = \frac{RT}{\mathscr{F}} \ln K$$

When the cell is not entirely discharged, Q is a variable dependent on the concentration of HCl and the pressure of H_2 as well as on the temperature; E depends on these same variables.

10-III-7. (a) $Ag(s) \mid Ag^+, NO_3^-(aq) \mid Br_2(liq) \mid AgBr(s) \mid Pt(s)$

$$Ag(s) \rightarrow Ag^+ + e^-$$

$$\frac{Ag^+ + \frac{1}{2}Br_2(liq) + e^- \rightarrow AgBr(s)}{Ag(s) + \frac{1}{2}Br_2(liq) \rightarrow AgBr(s)}$$

$$E = E^\circ - \frac{RT}{\mathscr{F}} \ln \frac{a_{AgBr}}{a_{Ag} a_{Br_2}^{1/2}} = E^\circ$$

since the activities of the pure solids and liquids are equal to 1.

$$\Delta G^\circ = -\mathscr{F} E^\circ = -\mathscr{F} E$$

(b) Formally $K = e^{-\Delta G^\circ / RT}$. However, the concept of an equilibrium constant is inapplicable to a reaction involving only pure solids and liquids. The reaction above has $\Delta G = \Delta G^\circ < 0$ and will therefore proceed until one reactant or the other is entirely consumed. ΔG does not change as the reaction proceeds. The activity of each substance remains 1, regardless of how far the reaction has progressed, and

$$a_{Ag} a_{Br_2}^{1/2} / a_{AgBr} = 1 \neq K$$

It is possible for the reaction to reach equilibrium only if the activities change as a result of changes in concentrations or partial pressures.

10-III-8.

<table>
<tr><td></td><td></td><td>$E°$ (from table)</td></tr>
<tr><td>(a)</td><td>$Ag(NH_3)_2{}^+ + e^- \rightarrow Ag + 2NH_3$</td><td>0.373</td></tr>
<tr><td></td><td>$Ag \rightarrow Ag^+ + e^-$</td><td>−0.7996</td></tr>
<tr><td></td><td>$Ag(NH_3)^+ \rightarrow Ag^+ + 2NH_3$</td><td>−0.427 V</td></tr>
</table>

$$\log K = \frac{\mathscr{F}E°}{2.303RT} = \frac{E°}{0.05915} = -7.22$$

$$K = 6.0 \times 10^{-8}$$

(b) $Ag|\ Ag^+, SO_4^{2-}\ |\ PbSO_4\ |\ Pb\ \overline{_{(wire)}}\ Pb|\ PbSO_4\ |\ Ag(NH_3)_2{}^+,$

     $SO_4^{2-}, NH_3\ |\ Ag$

$$\left. \begin{array}{l} 2Ag \rightarrow 2Ag^+ + 2e^- \\ PbSO_4 + 2e^- \rightarrow Pb + SO_4^{2-}(a_1) \end{array} \right\} \text{left cell}$$

$$\left. \begin{array}{l} Pb + SO_4^{2-}(a_2) \rightarrow PbSO_4 + 2e^- \\ 2Ag(NH_3)_2{}^+ + 2e^- \rightarrow 2Ag + 2NH_3 \end{array} \right\} \text{right cell}$$

Overall reaction:

$$2Ag(NH_3)_2{}^+ + SO_4^{2-}(a_2) \rightarrow 2Ag^+ + SO_4^{2-}(a_1) + 2NH_3$$

(c) $E = E° - \dfrac{RT}{2\mathscr{F}} \ln \left(\dfrac{a_{Ag^+}^2 \, a_1 a_{NH_3}^2}{a_{Ag(NH_3)_2{}^+}^2 \, a_2} \right)$

$$= E° - \frac{RT}{2\mathscr{F}} \ln \left(\frac{a_{1\pm}^3 a_{NH_3}^2}{a_{2\pm}^3} \right)$$

where $a_{1\pm}$ is the mean ionic activity of Ag_2SO_4 and $a_{2\pm}$ is the mean ionic activity of $[Ag(NH_3)_2]_2 SO_4$.

10-III-9.

<table>
<tr><td></td><td>$E°$ (from table)</td></tr>
<tr><td>$O_2 + 4H^+ + 4e^- \rightarrow 2H_2O$</td><td>0.1129</td></tr>
<tr><td>$2Tl^+ \rightarrow 2Tl^{3+} + 4e^-$</td><td>−0.125</td></tr>
<tr><td>$O_2 + 4H^+ + 2Tl^+ \rightarrow 2Tl^{3+} + 2H_2O$</td><td>−0.012 V</td></tr>
</table>

At equilibrium

$$E° = \frac{0.05915}{4} \log \frac{[Tl^{3+}]^2}{P_{O_2}[H^+]^4[Tl^+]^2}$$

$$P_{O_2} = 0.21 \times 1.0 = 0.21 \text{ atm}$$

Let M = the concentration of Tl^{3+} produced

Let $0.10 - M$ = the concentration of Tl^+ remaining

$$\log \left(\frac{M^2}{[0.21][1.0]^4[0.10 - M]^2} \right) = \frac{-0.012 \times 4}{0.05915} = -0.812$$

$$\frac{M^2}{(0.21)(0.10 - M)^2} = 0.154$$

$$\frac{M^2}{(0.10 - M)^2} = 0.154 \times 0.21 = 3.24 \times 10^{-2}$$

$$\frac{M}{0.10 - M} = 0.18$$

$$M = 0.018 - 0.18M$$

$$M = 0.0153$$

$$0.1 - M = 0.0847$$

$$\text{percent unoxidized} = 100 \times \frac{0.085}{0.1} = 85 \text{ percent}$$

10-III-10. $Co + nNH_3 \rightarrow Co(NH_3)_n^{2+} + 2e^-$

$HgO + H_2O + 2e^- \rightarrow Hg + 2OH^-$

$\overline{Co + nNH_3 + HgO + H_2O \rightarrow Co(NH_3)_n^{2+} + Hg + 2OH^-}$

$$E = E° - \frac{RT}{2\mathscr{F}} \ln \frac{[Co(NH_3)_n^{2+}][OH^-]^2}{[NH_3]^n}$$

$$= \text{const} + \frac{nRT}{2\mathscr{F}} \ln[NH_3]$$

$$= \text{const}' + \frac{nRT}{2\mathscr{F}} \ln P_{NH_3}$$

Plot $\log P_{NH_3}$ as abscissa and E as ordinate.

$$\text{Slope} = \frac{2.303nRT}{2\mathscr{F}} = 0.163$$

$$n = 5.5 \approx 6$$

Answers vary considerably, from 5 to 7, depending upon how the graph is drawn.

10-III-11. The quantity that can clearly be added for the two half cells is ΔG, the change in an extensive property. Now for each half cell $\Delta G = -n\mathscr{F}E$, where n is the number of faradays that pass through the circuit when the half reaction occurs as written. Thus for the entire cell

$$\varDelta G = \varDelta G_1 + \varDelta G_2 = -\mathscr{F}(n_1E_1 + n_2E_2)$$

But to conserve electrons the half reactions must be written so that $n_1 = n_2 = n$. Then

$$\varDelta G = -n\mathscr{F}(E_1 + E_2)$$

For the entire cell n is not $n_1 + n_2$ but is the same n as for each half cell—the electrons gained at one electrode are lost at the other and thus each electron does double duty. Then for the entire cell

$$E = -\frac{\varDelta G}{n\mathscr{F}} = E_1 + E_2$$

The sizes of the half cells are irrelevant; $\varDelta G$ depends on the quantity reacting, not the quantity present.

10-III-12. $\mathbf{P} = \dfrac{(\epsilon - 1)}{4\pi}\,\mathbf{E}$

$$\mathbf{m} = \alpha\mathbf{F} = \alpha\left(\mathbf{E} + \frac{4\pi}{n}\,\mathbf{P}\right)$$

$$\mathbf{P} = \frac{mL\rho}{M} = \alpha\left(\mathbf{E} + \frac{4\pi}{n}\,\mathbf{P}\right)\frac{L\rho}{M}$$

$$= \alpha\left(1 + \frac{\epsilon - 1}{n}\right)\mathbf{E}\,\frac{L\rho}{M}$$

$$\frac{\epsilon - 1}{4\pi}\,\mathbf{E} = \alpha\left(1 + \frac{\epsilon - 1}{n}\right)\mathbf{E}\,\frac{L\rho}{M}$$

$$\frac{\epsilon - 1}{4\pi} = \alpha\left(\frac{n + \epsilon - 1}{n}\right)\frac{L\rho}{M}$$

$$\alpha = \frac{Mn(\epsilon - 1)}{4\pi L\rho(n + \epsilon - 1)}$$

CHAPTER 11

Kinetics

SECTION 11-1

11-I-1. $k = \dfrac{2.303}{t} \log \left(\dfrac{a}{a-x}\right) = \dfrac{2.303}{10} \log \dfrac{100}{24.8} = 0.2303 \log 4.03$

$\qquad = 0.2303 \times 0.606 = 0.140 \text{ min}^{-1}$

11-I-2. Try second order.

$$k = \dfrac{2.303}{t(a-b)} \log \dfrac{b(a-x)}{a(b-x)}$$

$a = [\text{NaClO}]_0 = 0.003230$

$b = [\text{KBr}]_0 = 0.002508$

$a - b = 0.000722$

$$k = \dfrac{2.303}{3.65(7.22 \times 10^{-4})} \log \dfrac{2.508 \times 10^{-3}(0.003230 - 0.000560)}{3.230 \times 10^{-3}(0.002508 - 0.000560)}$$

$\qquad = 23.42 \text{ liters mole}^{-1} \text{ min}^{-1}$

$k = 23.42,\ 23.30,\ 23.52,\ 23.90,\ 23.80,\ 23.80,$ average 23.62 liters mole^{-1} min^{-1}

Second order (as shown by the approximate constancy of k).

11-I-3. Try first order.

$$k = \dfrac{1}{t} \ln \left(\dfrac{c_0}{c}\right)$$

$$k = \frac{2.303}{120} \log \frac{11.45}{9.63} = 0.00144$$

$k = 0.00144, 0.00144, 0.00145, 0.00145, 0.00150, 0.00140$, average 0.00145 min^{-1}

11-I-4. For a second-order reaction

$$k = \frac{2.303}{t(a-b)} \log \frac{b(a-x)}{a(b-x)}$$

where

a = concentration $S_2O_3^{2-}$ at time $t = 0$

$\quad = \dfrac{\text{meq iodine consumed at time } t = 0}{V_{S_2O_3^{2-}}}$

$\quad = \dfrac{37.63 \times 0.02572}{10.02} = 0.0967M$

(At time $t = 0$ for this experiment, some $S_2O_3^{2-}$ had already been consumed, so its concentration was less than the initial $0.100M$.)

b = concentration of n-PrBr at time $t = 0$

$\quad = \dfrac{\text{total meq thiosulfate consumed by } n\text{-PrBr}}{V_{n\text{-PrBr}}}$

$\quad = \dfrac{(37.63 - 22.24) \times 0.02572}{10.02} = 0.0395M$

We assume that at $t = 78{,}840$ sec equilibrium has been attained.

$(b - x)$ = concentration n-PrBr at time t

$(a - x)$ = concentration $S_2O_3^{2-}$ at time t

At $t = 1110$ sec

$(b - x) = \dfrac{\text{meq } S_2O_3^{2-} \text{ consumed at } t = 1110 \text{ sec}}{V_{n\text{-PrBr}}}$

$\quad = \dfrac{(35.20 - 22.24) \times 0.02572}{10.02} = \dfrac{12.96 \times 0.02572}{10.02}$

$(a - x) = \dfrac{\text{meq iodine consumed at } t = 1110 \text{ sec}}{V_{S_2O_3^{2-}}}$

$\quad = \dfrac{35.20 \times 0.02572}{10.02}$

$$\frac{b(a-x)}{a(b-x)} = \frac{0.0395(35.20 \times 0.02572)/(10.02)}{0.0967(12.96 \times 0.02572)/(10.02)}$$

$$= \frac{0.0395(35.20)}{0.0967(12.96)} = 1.110$$

$a - b = 0.0967 - 0.0395 = 0.0572$

$k = 0.0363 \times \log 1.110 = 0.0363 \times 0.0453 = 0.001644$

$k = 0.001644, 0.001644, 0.001649, 0.001636, 0.001618, 0.001618$

Average:

$k = 0.001635$ liter mole^{-1} sec^{-1}

11-I-5. For a second-order reaction in which the two reactants are present in equal concentrations

$$k = \frac{x}{ta(a-x)}$$

$$k = \frac{0.00876}{1200 \times 0.0198(0.01104)} = 0.0334$$

$k = 0.0334, 0.0327, 0.0329, 0.0332, 0.0328, 0.0325$: average 0.0329
liter mole^{-1} min^{-1}

11-I-6. For an nth-order reaction,

$$-\frac{dc}{dt} = kc^n$$

$$\log\left(-\frac{dc}{dt}\right) = \log k + n \log c$$

Thus

$$\frac{\log(-dc/dt)_2 - \log(-dc/dt)_1}{\log c_1 - \log c_2} = n$$

The rate of pressure increase is proportional to $-dc/dt$.

$$n = \frac{\log 7.4 - \log 0.73}{\log 2.153 - \log 0.433} = 1.44 \approx \frac{3}{2}$$

11-I-7. By inspection it can be seen that $t_{1/2}$ is directly proportional to p. Every time p is halved, $t_{1/2}$ is also halved. This suggests a zero-order reaction. For a zero-order reaction $-dx/dt = k$ or, in this case, $-dp/dt = k$, and on integration $k = p_i/2t_{1/2}$, where p_i is the initial pressure. $k = 17.4, 17.6, 17.0$; average 17.3 torr min^{-1}.

11-I-8. A is directly proportional to concentration.
Plot $\log(A - A_\infty)$ vs t. Graph is a straight line with slope $=$
-0.0563; $k = -2.303 \times$ slope $= 0.130 \text{ min}^{-1}$.

11-I-9. $x =$ fraction converted $= \dfrac{\alpha_0 - \alpha_t}{\alpha_0 - \alpha_\infty} = \dfrac{11.20 - 10.35}{11.20 - (-3.37)}$

$= 0.0583$ at $t = 1035$ sec.

Try first order.

$k = \dfrac{2.303}{t} \log\left(\dfrac{1}{1-x}\right) = 5.80 \times 10^{-5}$

$k_{\text{av}} = 5.80 \times 10^{-5} \text{ sec}^{-1}$

First order.

11-I-10. Try first order.

$a = 18.48 - 12.29 = 6.19$

$a - x = 18.05 - 12.29 = 5.76$

$k = \dfrac{2.303}{t} \log\left(\dfrac{a}{a-x}\right) = \dfrac{2.303}{30} \log \dfrac{6.19}{5.76} = 2.40 \times 10^{-3} \text{ min}^{-1}$

$k = 2.40, 2.46, 2.49, 2.49$; average $2.46 \times 10^{-3} \text{ min}^{-1}$.

11-I-11. (a) $K = \dfrac{[\text{NOH}_2]}{[\text{NO}][\text{H}_2]}$

$\dfrac{d[\text{NOH}]}{dt} = 2k[\text{NOH}_2][\text{NO}] = 2kK[\text{NO}]^2[\text{H}_2]$

(b) $K' = \dfrac{[\text{N}_2\text{O}_2]}{[\text{NO}]^2}$

$\dfrac{d[\text{NOH}]}{dt} = 2k'[\text{N}_2\text{O}_2][\text{H}_2] = 2k'K'[\text{NO}]^2[\text{H}_2]$

11-I-12. (a) $t_{1/2} = \dfrac{1}{k} \ln\left(\dfrac{a}{a/2}\right) = \dfrac{1}{k} \ln 2 = \dfrac{0.693}{k}$

(b) $t_{1/2} = \dfrac{1}{k}\left(\dfrac{1}{a/2} - \dfrac{1}{a}\right) = \dfrac{1}{ka}$

(c) $t_{1/2} = \dfrac{1}{2k}\left(\dfrac{1}{(a/2)^2} - \dfrac{1}{a^2}\right) = \dfrac{3}{2ka^2}$

11-I-13.   Plot log k vs $\sqrt{I}$ and extrapolate to $\sqrt{I} = 0$.

$5 + \log k$	$\sqrt{I}$
1.7640	1.53
1.7130	2.37
1.6800	2.85
1.6467	3.35
1.6418	3.42
1.5990	4.11

Extrapolated value:

$$5 + \log k_0 = 1.858, \quad k_0 = 7.21 \times 10^{-4}$$

11-I-14. $$2 = \frac{k_{305}}{k_{295}} = \frac{e^{-E/305R}}{e^{-E/295R}}$$

$$\ln 2 = -\frac{E}{R}\left(\frac{1}{305} - \frac{1}{295}\right) = -\frac{E}{R}\left(\frac{-10}{305 \times 295}\right)$$

$$0.693 = \frac{10E}{1.987 \times 10^{-3} \times 305 \times 295}$$

$$E = 12.4 \text{ kcal mole}^{-1}$$

11-I-15. $k = Ae^{-E/RT}$

$$E = \frac{RT_1 T_2 \ln(k_2/k_1)}{T_2 - T_1}$$

$$\frac{2.303 R T_1 T_2}{T_2 - T_1} = \frac{4.576 \times 910 \times 586}{910 - 586} = 7530 \text{ cal mole}^{-1}$$

$$E_{\max} = 7530 \log\left(\frac{1.85 \times 10^{11}}{1.58 \times 10^{10}}\right)$$

$$= 8046 \text{ cal mole}^{-1} \text{ of activated complex}$$

$$E_{\min} = 7530 \log\left(\frac{1.69 \times 10^{11}}{1.68 \times 10^{10}}\right)$$

$$= 7549 \text{ cal mole}^{-1}$$

(Wilson, using data at temperatures down to 300°K, obtains $E = 7900 \pm 200$ cal mole^{-1}).

SECTION 11-II

11-II-1. It can be seen from inspection of the table that doubling the MnO_4^- concentration doubles the reaction rate, while decreasing the Cr^{3+} concentration by one half decreases the reaction rate by one half. Therefore the reaction is first order with respect to Cr^{3+} and first order with respect to MnO_4^-.

11-II-2.

t	Percent complete $(100\ V_{HCl,t}/V_{HCl,\infty})$
30	55.9
44	68.3
62	80.8
83	87.0
111	93.2
∞	100.0

$$k_1 = \frac{1}{t} \times 2.303 \log\left(\frac{a}{a-x}\right) = \frac{2.303}{30}\log\frac{100}{44.1} = 0.0273\ \text{sec}^{-1}$$

$k_1 = 0.0273, 0.0262, 0.0266, 0.0249, 0.0242$; average $0.0258\ \text{sec}^{-1}$

The approximate constancy of k_1 shows that the reaction is first order.

11-II-3. $EtOAc + NaOH \rightarrow EtOH + NaOAc$

Try second order.

$$k = \frac{2.303}{t(a-b)}\log\left[\frac{b(a-x)}{a(b-x)}\right]$$

$a = 0.0200 = [NaOH]_0$

$b = 0.0100 = [EtOAc]_0$

At $t = 15$ min

$[NaOH] = (50.0 - 7.35) \times 0.0200 \times 10^{-3}\ \text{mole}/0.05000\ \text{liter}$
$= 0.01706N = a - x$

$$x = a - 0.01706 = 0.0200 - 0.01706 = 0.00294$$

$$[EtOAc] = b - x = 0.0100 - 0.00294 = 0.00706$$

$$k = \frac{2.303}{15(0.0100)} \log \left[\frac{0.0100(0.01706)}{0.0200(0.00706)} \right] = 1.260 \text{ liters mole}^{-1} \text{ min}^{-1}$$

$k = 1.260, 1.136, 1.087, 1.053, 1.039,$ average 1.097 liters mole^{-1} min^{-1}

Second order (as shown by the approximate constancy of k).

11-II-4. The data do not fit first, second, or third order. By plotting ml FeSO$_4$ consumed, which is proportional to meq K$_2$S$_2$O$_8$ remaining, it can be seen that the concentration of K$_2$S$_2$O$_8$ varies linearly with time. Thus the reaction rate is independent of K$_2$S$_2$O$_8$ concentration and the reaction is zero order. Alternatively we could calculate meq K$_2$S$_2$O$_8$ and plot that against time, obtaining a straight line. Actually the order of this reaction depends on K$_2$S$_2$O$_8$ concentration and can vary continuously from zero to one. In the concentration range referred to here the order is zero.

11-II-5. The [CHCl$_3$] and [NaOMe] data are not needed to solve the problem.

Method 1. Plot log $(v_\infty - v)$ vs t. If first order, a straight line will be obtained. The value of k can be calculated from the slope of this line.

Method 2. Sample calculation for $t = 4$ min:

$$k = \frac{2.303}{t} \log \frac{v_\infty - v_0}{v_\infty - v}$$

$$= \frac{2.303}{4} \log \frac{14.27}{12.95} = 0.0243 \text{ min}^{-1}$$

$k = 0.0243, 0.0241, 0.0236, 0.0231, 0.0232, 0.0233, 0.0241,$ average 0.0237 min^{-1}

The approximate constancy of k shows that the reaction is first order.

11-II-6.

t (min)	Percent complete $(100\, v_{FeSO_4.t}/v_{FeSO_4.\infty})$
0.31	42.4
0.51	54.6
0.65	60.6
0.86	66.7
1.01	69.7
1.15	72.7
1.36	75.8
1.58	78.8
2.19	83.6
∞	100

$$k = \frac{1}{at}\left(\frac{x}{a-x}\right)$$

where $a = 100$ percent, $x =$ percent complete.

$10^2 k = 2.37, 2.36, 2.36, 2.33, 2.28, 2.32, 2.30, 2.35, 2.33$; average $k = 2.33 \times 10^{-2}$ liter mole^{-1} min^{-1}

11-II-7. (a) $2AsH_3(g) \rightarrow 2As(s) + 3H_2(g)$
$\quad\quad P_0 - 2x \quad\quad\quad\quad 3x$

Let

$P_0 =$ initial pressure (at time t_0) $= 39.2$ cm
$P_0 - 2x =$ partial pressure of AsH_3 at time t

Then $3x =$ partial pressure of H_2 at time t. Therefore

$P_{total} = P_0 - 2x + 3x = P_0 + x$

at time t. At $t = 4.33$ hr,

$P_{total} = 39.2 + x = 40.3, \quad x = 1.1$

Therefore,

$P_{AsH_3} = P_0 - 2x = 39.2 - 2(1.1) = 37.0$ cm

t	0	4.33	16	25.5	37.66	44.75
$\log P_{AsH_3}$	1.593	1.568	1.481	1.430	1.332	1.299

If the reaction is first order with respect to AsH_3, then

$$\frac{dP_{AsH_3}}{dt} = -kP_{AsH_3}$$

Thus

$$\frac{dP_{AsH_3}}{P_{AsH_3}} = -k\,dt$$

and, on integration as an indefinite integral,

$$\ln P_{AsH_3} = -kt + \text{constant}$$

$$2.303 \log P_{AsH_3} = -kt + \text{constant}'$$

$$\log P_{AsH_3} = -\frac{kt}{2.303} + \text{constant}'$$

This is the equation of a straight line with slope $= -k/2.303$. Plot $\log P_{AsH_3}$ vs t. A straight line is obtained. Therefore the reaction is first order.

(b) Slope $= \dfrac{-k}{2.303} = 6.58 \times 10^{-3}$

$k = 1.52 \times 10^{-2}\ \text{hr}^{-1}$

11-II-8. At 5 hr, the fraction of methyl tosylate unchanged $= (0.746 - 0.420)/(0.791 - 0.420) = 0.879$.

$$k = \frac{2.303}{5}\left(\log \frac{1}{0.879}\right) \times \frac{1}{60 \times 60} = 7.17 \times 10^{-6}\ \text{sec}^{-1}$$

$k_{avg} = 7.77 \times 10^{-6}\ \text{sec}^{-1}$

11-II-9. Let A be the reacting gas, B the inert gas, and C and D the products.

$$A + A \underset{k_{-1}}{\overset{k_1}{\rightleftharpoons}} A^* + A$$

$$A + B \underset{k_{-2}}{\overset{k_2}{\rightleftharpoons}} A^* + B$$

$$A^* \overset{k_3}{\rightarrow} C + D$$

$$\frac{d[A^*]}{dt} = k_1[A]^2 - k_1[A^*][A] + k_2[A][B] - k_{-2}[A^*][B] - k_3[A^*] \approx 0$$

$$\frac{d[C]}{dt} = k_3[A^*] = \frac{k_3(k_1[A]^2 + k_2[A][B])}{k_{-1}[A] + k_{-2}[B] + k_3}$$

11-II-10. (a) $\dfrac{d[O]}{dt} = k_1[O_3] - k_{-1}[O][O_2] - k_2[O][O_3] \approx 0$

$$[O] = \frac{k_1[O_3]}{k_{-1}[O_2] + k_2[O_3]}$$

$$\frac{d[O_3]}{dt} = -k_1[O_3] + k_{-1}[O][O_2] - k_2[O][O_3]$$

$$= -k_1[O_3] + \frac{k_{-1}k_1[O_3][O_2] - k_1k_2[O_3]^2}{k_{-1}[O_2] + k_2[O_3]}$$

$$= \frac{-2k_1k_2[O_3]^2}{k_{-1}[O_2] + k_2[O_3]}$$

(b) If

$$k_{-1}[O_2] \gg k_2[O_3]$$

$$\frac{d[O_3]}{dt} \approx \frac{-2k_1k_2[O_3]^2}{k_{-1}[O_2]}$$

11-II-11. (a) Mechanism (i):

$$\frac{d[HI]}{dt} = 2k[H_2][I_2]$$

Mechanism (ii):

$$\frac{d[I]}{dt} = 2k_1[I_2] - 2k_2[I]^2 - 2k_3[I]^2[H_2] \approx 0$$

$$[I]^2 = \frac{k_1[I_2]}{k_2 + k_3[H_2]}$$

$$\frac{d[HI]}{dt} = 2k_3[I]^2[H_2] = \frac{2k_1k_3[H_2][I_2]}{k_2 + k_3[H_2]}$$

(b) $\dfrac{[I]^2}{[I_2]} = K \qquad [I]^2 = K[I_2]$

$$\frac{d[HI]}{dt} = 2k_3K[H_2][I_2]$$

This result agrees with that of (a) if $k_3[H_2] \ll k_2$, that is, if reaction (3) is much slower than reaction (2).

(c) $\ln k_3 = \ln A - \dfrac{E_a}{RT}$

$$\ln\left(\frac{k_{3,T_2}}{k_{3,T_1}}\right) = \frac{E_a}{R}\left(\frac{1}{T_1} - \frac{1}{T_2}\right) = \frac{E_a}{R}\left(\frac{T_2 - T_1}{T_1T_2}\right)$$

$$E_a = \frac{RT_1T_2}{T_2 - T_1} \ln\left(\frac{k_{3,T_2}}{k_{3,T_1}}\right)$$

$$= \frac{2.303 \times 1.987 \times 10^{-3} \times 417.9 \times 520.1}{520.1 - 417.9}$$

$$\times \log\left(\frac{4.0 \times 10^5}{1.12 \times 10^5}\right)$$

$$= 5.38 \text{ kcal mole}^{-1} \text{ of activated complex}$$

11-II-12. (a) $\quad \dfrac{d[NO_3^-]}{dt} = k_1[NO_2^-][O_2] + k_2[O][NO_2^-]$ (1)

$$\frac{d[O]}{dt} = k_1[NO_2^-][O_2] - k_2[O][NO_2^-] - k_3[O]^2 \qquad (2)$$

Assuming steady state for [O], then from equation (2),

$$[O] = \frac{k_1[NO_2^-][O_2]}{k_3[O] + k_2[NO_2^-]} \qquad (3)$$

Substituting (3) into (1)

$$\frac{d[NO_3^-]}{dt} = k_1[NO_2^-][O_2]\left(1 + \frac{k_2[NO_2^-]}{k_3[O] + k_2[NO_2^-]}\right)$$

(b) If reaction (3) is much slower than reaction (1), then $k_3[O] \ll k_2[NO_2^-]$, and

$$\frac{d[NO_3^-]}{dt} = k_1[NO_2^-][O_2]\left(1 + \frac{k_2[NO_2^-]}{k_2[NO_2^-]}\right)$$
$$= 2k_1[NO_2^-][O_2]$$

11-II-13. (a) $\quad \dfrac{[BH^+][O_2NNH^-]}{[O_2NNH_2][B]} = K$

$$\frac{d[O_2NNH_2]}{dt} = -k_2[O_2NNH^-] = \frac{-k_2K[O_2NNH_2][B]}{[BH^+]}$$

(b) $\quad \dfrac{d[O_2NNH_2]}{dt} = -k_1[O_2NNH_2][B]$

Both assumptions are consistent with the first-order rate law. They can be distinguished by performing experiments in which $[BH^+]$ is varied while $[O_2NNH_2]$ and $[B]$ are held constant. If (a) is correct, the rate should be inversely proportional to $[BH^+]$. If (b) is correct, the rate should be constant in these experiments. (It turns out that (b) is correct.)

11-II-14. (a) $\quad \dfrac{d[NO_2^-]}{dt} = k_1\phi[NO_3^-] - k_2[O][NO_2^-] + k_3[O][NO_3^-]$

Since ϕ is the incident (rather than the absorbed) dose rate, the rate of reaction (1) is given by $k_1\phi[NO_3^-]$ (not $k_1\phi$), provided that only a small fraction of the incident radiation is absorbed. Making the steady state assumption about O, we obtain

$$\frac{d[O]}{dt} = k_1[NO_3^-]\phi - k_2[O][NO_2^-] - k_3[O][NO_3^-] = 0$$

$$[O] = \frac{k_1[NO_3^-]\phi}{k_2[NO_2^-] + k_3[NO_3^-]}$$

and therefore

$$\frac{d[NO_2^-]}{dt} = k_1\phi[NO_3^-] + \frac{-k_1k_2[NO_2^-][NO_3^-]\phi + k_1k_3[NO_3^-]^2\phi}{k_2[NO_2^-] + k_3[NO_3^-]}$$

$$= \frac{\left\{\begin{array}{l}k_1k_2\phi[NO_2^-][NO_3^-] + k_1k_3\phi[NO_3^-]^2 \\ - k_1k_2\phi[NO_2^-][NO_3^-] + k_1k_3[NO_3^-]^2\phi\end{array}\right\}}{k_2[NO_2^-] + k_3[NO_3^-]}$$

$$= \frac{2k_1k_3\phi[NO_3^-]^2}{k_2[NO_2^-] + k_3[NO_3^-]}$$

(b) Rearranging the last expression we obtain

$$k_2[NO_2^-]\,d[NO_2^-] + k_3[NO_3^-]\,d[NO_2^-] = 2k_1k_3\phi[NO_3^-]^2\,dt,$$

which, upon integration between limits 0 to $[NO_2^-]$ for $[NO_2^-]$ and between 0 and t for t, gives

$$\tfrac{1}{2}k_2[NO_2^-]^2 + k_3[NO_3^-][NO_2^-] = 2k_1k_3\phi[NO_3^-]^2\,t$$

11-II-15. $\quad \dfrac{d[CH_3]}{dt} = k_1[CH_4] - k_2[CH_3][CH_4] + k_3[H][CH_4]$

$$- k_4[H][CH_3][M] = 0$$

$$\frac{d[H]}{dt} = k_1[CH_4] + k_2[CH_3][CH_4] - k_3[H][CH_4]$$
$$- k_4[H][CH_3][M] = 0$$

Adding

$$k_1[CH_4] - k_4[H][CH_3][M] = 0$$

Subtracting

$$-k_2[CH_3][CH_4] + k_3[H][CH_4] = 0$$

$$[H][CH_3] = \frac{k_1[CH_4]}{k_4[M]}$$

$$\frac{[H]}{[CH_3]} = \frac{k_2}{k_3}$$

Dividing

$$[CH_3]^2 = \frac{k_1 k_3 [CH_4]}{k_2 k_4 [M]}$$

$$\frac{d[C_2H_6]}{dt} = k_2[CH_3][CH_4] = \left(\frac{k_1 k_3 k_2 [CH_4]^3}{k_4[M]}\right)^{1/2}$$

11-II-16. (a) $\quad -\dfrac{dc}{dt} = kc^{-1}$

$$-c\,dc = k\,dt$$
$$\tfrac{1}{2}(c_0^2 - c^2) = kt$$
$$c = (c_0^2 - 2kt)^{1/2}$$

(b) $\quad c = 0.1c_0$

$$c^2 = 0.01c_0^2$$
$$t = \frac{c_0^2 - c^2}{2k} = \frac{0.99c_0^2}{2k}$$

(c) $c = 0$ when $t = c_0^2/2k$. The reaction reaches completion at this time. In a first-order reaction $-dc/dt = kc$. As c decreases the rate of decrease ($-dc/dt$) also decreases, so that the reaction becomes slower and slower without ever attaining completion. In this -1 order reaction, however, the rate of decrease of c *increases* as c decreases, becoming infinite as c approaches zero. The reaction accelerates as it approaches completion and comes to a sudden stop when the last trace of reactant is consumed.

SECTION 11-III

11-III-1. (a)
$$\frac{d[\text{Cl}]}{dt} = k_1[\text{NO}_2\text{Cl}] - k_2[\text{NO}_2\text{Cl}][\text{Cl}] \approx 0$$

$$[\text{Cl}] = \frac{k_1}{k_2}$$

$$\frac{d[\text{NO}_2\text{Cl}]}{dt} = -k_1[\text{NO}_2\text{Cl}] - k_2[\text{NO}_2\text{Cl}][\text{Cl}] = -2k_1[\text{NO}_2\text{Cl}]$$

(b) According to the Lindemann theory of unimolecular reactions, the NO_2Cl molecule must be activated by collision before it can decompose. It can also be deactivated by collision. We treat the activated molecule NO_2Cl^* as a distinct species.

$$2\text{NO}_2\text{Cl} \underset{k_{-3}}{\overset{k_3}{\rightleftharpoons}} \text{NO}_2\text{Cl} + \text{NO}_2\text{Cl}^*$$

$$\text{NO}_2\text{Cl}^* \overset{k_1'}{\rightarrow} \text{NO}_2 + \text{Cl}$$

$$\text{NO}_2\text{Cl} + \text{Cl} \overset{k_2}{\rightarrow} \text{NO}_2 + \text{Cl}_2$$

The steady state approximation can now be applied to both Cl and NO_2Cl^*:

$$\frac{d[\text{Cl}]}{dt} = k_1'[\text{NO}_2\text{Cl}^*] - k_2[\text{NO}_2\text{Cl}][\text{Cl}] \approx 0$$

$$\frac{d[\text{NO}_2\text{Cl}^*]}{dt} = k_3[\text{NO}_2\text{Cl}]^2 - k_{-3}[\text{NO}_2\text{Cl}][\text{NO}_2\text{Cl}^*]$$
$$- k_1'[\text{NO}_2\text{Cl}^*] \approx 0$$

$$[\text{NO}_2\text{Cl}^*] = \frac{k_3[\text{NO}_2\text{Cl}]^2}{k_{-3}[\text{NO}_2\text{Cl}] + k_1'}$$

$$[\text{Cl}] = \frac{k_1'[\text{NO}_2\text{Cl}^*]}{k_2[\text{NO}_2\text{Cl}]} = \frac{k_1'k_3[\text{NO}_2\text{Cl}]}{k_2(k_{-3}[\text{NO}_2\text{Cl}] + k_1')}$$

$$\frac{d[\text{NO}_2\text{Cl}]}{dt} = -k_3[\text{NO}_2\text{Cl}]^2 + k_{-3}[\text{NO}_2\text{Cl}][\text{NO}_2\text{Cl}^*]$$
$$- k_2[\text{NO}_2\text{Cl}][\text{Cl}]$$

$$= -k_1'[\text{NO}_2\text{Cl}^*] - k_2[\text{NO}_2\text{Cl}][\text{Cl}]$$

$$= \frac{-2k_1'k_3[\text{NO}_2\text{Cl}]^2}{k_{-3}[\text{NO}_2\text{Cl}] + k_1'}$$

At high concentration $k_{-3}[NO_2Cl] \gg k_1'$ and

$$\frac{d[NO_2Cl]}{dt} = \frac{-2k_1'k_3[NO_2Cl]}{k_{-3}}$$

This result agrees with (a), provided that $k_1 = k_1'k_3/k_{-3}$. At low concentration $k_{-3}[NO_2Cl] \ll k_1'$ and

$$\frac{d[NO_2Cl]}{dt} = -2k_3[NO_2Cl]^2$$

In the latter case activation by collision is the rate-determining step.

11-III-2. (a) $\dfrac{d[HNO_3]}{dt} = -k_a[HNO_3] + k_b[HO][NO_2] - k_c[HO][HNO_3]$

$$\frac{d[HO]}{dt} = k_a[HNO_3] - k_b[HO][NO_2] - k_c[HO][HNO_3] = 0$$

$$[HO] = \frac{k_a[HNO_3]}{k_b[NO_2] + k_c[HNO_3]}$$

$$\frac{d[HNO_3]}{dt} = -k_a[HNO_3] + \frac{(k_b[NO_2] - k_c[HNO_3])\,k_a[HNO_3]}{k_b[NO_2] + k_c[HNO_3]}$$

$$= \frac{\begin{Bmatrix} -k_a[HNO_3]\,k_b[NO_2] - k_ak_c[HNO_3]^2 \\ + k_a[HNO_3]\,k_b[NO_2] - k_ak_c[HNO_3]^2 \end{Bmatrix}}{k_b[NO_2] + k_c[HNO_3]}$$

$$= \frac{-2k_ak_c[HNO_3]^2}{k_b[NO_2] + k_c[HNO_3]}$$

$$= -2k_a[HNO_3]\,\frac{1}{1 + (k_b[NO_2])/(k_c[HNO_3])}$$

(b) If the consumption of NO_2 is very rapid, then $[NO_2] \approx 0$; therefore

$$\frac{k_b[NO_2]}{k_c[HNO_3]} \ll 1$$

and

$$\frac{d[HNO_3]}{dt} = -2k_a[HNO_3] \cdot \frac{1}{1 + 0} = -2k_a[HNO_3]$$

k_d is not needed.

11-III-3.

$$\frac{d[\text{NpO}_2{}^+]}{dt} = k_1[\text{HO}_2{}^-][\text{NpO}_2^{2+}] + k_2[\text{HO}_2][\text{NpO}_2^{2+}]$$
$$- k_3[\text{HO}_2][\text{NpO}_2{}^+]$$

$$\frac{d[\text{HO}_2]}{dt} = k_1[\text{HO}_2{}^-][\text{NpO}_2^{2+}] - k_2[\text{HO}_2][\text{NpO}_2^{2+}]$$
$$- k_3[\text{HO}_2][\text{NpO}_2{}^+] = 0$$

$$[\text{HO}_2] = \frac{k_1[\text{HO}_2{}^-][\text{NpO}_2^{2+}]}{k_2[\text{NpO}_2^{2+}] + k_3[\text{NpO}_2{}^+]}$$

$$\frac{d[\text{NpO}_2{}^+]}{dt} = k_1[\text{HO}_2{}^-][\text{NpO}_2^{2+}] + \frac{k_1 k_2[\text{NpO}_2^{2+}]^2[\text{HO}_2{}^-]}{k_2[\text{NpO}_2^{2+}] + k_3[\text{NpO}_2{}^+]}$$

$$- \frac{k_1 k_3[\text{HO}_2{}^-][\text{NpO}_2{}^+][\text{NpO}_2^{2+}]}{k_2[\text{NpO}_2^{2+}] + k_3[\text{NpO}_2{}^+]}$$

$$= \frac{\begin{Bmatrix} k_1[\text{HO}_2{}^-](k_2[\text{NpO}_2^{2+}]^2 + k_3[\text{NpO}_2{}^+][\text{NpO}_2^{2+}]) \\ + k_2[\text{NpO}_2^{2+}]^2 - k_3[\text{NpO}_2{}^+][\text{NpO}_2^{2+}]) \end{Bmatrix}}{k_2[\text{NpO}_2^{2+}] + k_3[\text{NpO}_2{}^+]}$$

$$= \frac{k_1[\text{HO}_2{}^-]\, 2k_2[\text{NpO}_2^{2+}]^2}{k_2[\text{NpO}_2^{2+}] + k_3[\text{NpO}_2{}^+]}$$

$$= \frac{2k_1[\text{HO}_2{}^-][\text{NpO}_2^{2+}]}{1 + (k_3[\text{NpO}_2{}^+])/(k_2[\text{NpO}_2^{2+}])}$$

$$K = \frac{[\text{H}^+][\text{HO}_2{}^-]}{[\text{H}_2\text{O}_2]}$$

$$[\text{HO}_2{}^-] = \frac{K[\text{H}_2\text{O}_2]}{[\text{H}^+]}$$

$$\frac{d[\text{NpO}_2{}^+]}{dt} = \frac{2Kk_1[\text{NpO}_2^{2+}][\text{H}_2\text{O}_2]}{[\text{H}^+]\{1 + (k_3[\text{NpO}_2{}^+])/(k_2[\text{NpO}_2^{2+}])\}}$$

11-III-4. (a)

$$\frac{d[\text{NO}_3]}{dt} = k_1[\text{N}_2\text{O}_5] - k_{-1}[\text{NO}_2][\text{NO}_3] - k_2[\text{NO}_2][\text{NO}_3] \approx 0$$

$$[\text{NO}_3] = \frac{k_1[\text{N}_2\text{O}_5]}{(k_{-1} + k_2)[\text{NO}_2]}$$

$$\frac{d[\text{NO}]}{dt} = k_2[\text{NO}_2][\text{NO}_3] - k_3[\text{NO}][\text{N}_2\text{O}_5] \approx 0$$

$$[NO] = \frac{k_2[NO_2][NO_3]}{k_3[N_2O_5]} = \frac{k_1k_2}{k_3(k_{-1} + k_2)}$$

$$\frac{d[N_2O_5]}{dt} = -k_1[N_2O_5] + k_{-1}[NO_2][NO_3] - k_3[NO][N_2O_5]$$

$$= \left\{ -k_1 + \frac{k_1(k_{-1} - k_2)}{k_{-1} + k_2} \right\} [N_2O_5]$$

(b) When NO_2 and NO_3 collide with the N of NO_2 meeting an O of NO_3, the product (if any) will be N_2O_5 (that is, O_2NONO_2). When they collide with O's meeting, the products could be NO (from NO_2) + NO_2 (from NO_3) + O_2 (1 atom from each). Since there are half as many N atoms as O atoms in NO_2, the first kind of collision (needed for reaction (-1)) should be approximately half as probable as the second kind (needed for reaction (2)). Then the frequency factors of reactions (-1) and (2) should be approximately in the ratio $1 : 2$:

$$\frac{k_{-1}}{k_2} = \frac{A_{-1}e^{-E_{-1}/RT}}{A_2e^{-E_2/RT}} = \frac{e^{-0}}{2e^{-5/RT}}$$

$$= \tfrac{1}{2} \times 10^{5/(2.303 \times 1.987 \times 10^{-3} \times 320)}$$

$$= 10^3$$

(c) $N_2O_5 \rightleftharpoons NO_2 + NO_3$

$$\frac{[NO_2][NO_3]}{[N_2O_5]} = K = \frac{k_1}{k_{-1}}$$

$$[NO] = \frac{k_2[NO_2][NO_3]}{k_3[N_2O_5]} = \frac{k_2K}{k_3}$$

$$\frac{d[N_2O_5]}{dt} = [-k_1 + (k_{-1} - k_2)K][N_2O_5]$$

This result is the same as that of (a) if $k_2 \ll k_{-1}$, that is, if most NO_2 + NO_3 reactions result in N_2O_5. In this case reaction (2) can be considered as merely a slow leakage out of the equilibrium system. The calculation in (b) supports this assumption.

11-III-5. (a)
$$\frac{d[Cl]}{dt} = 2k_1[Cl_2] - 2k_2[Cl]^2 - k_3[Cl][CO] + k_4[COCl]$$
$$+ k_5[COCl][Cl_2] = 0 \tag{1}$$

$$\frac{d[COCl]}{dt} = k_3[Cl][CO] - k_4[COCl] - k_5[COCl][Cl_2] = 0 \tag{2}$$

Adding Equations (1) and (2)

$$2k_1[Cl_2] - 2k_2[Cl]^2 = 0$$

$$[Cl] = \left(\frac{k_1[Cl_2]}{k_2}\right)^{1/2}$$

From equation (2)

$$[COCl] = \frac{k_3[Cl][CO]}{k_4 + k_5[Cl_2]}$$

$$= \frac{k_3 k_1^{1/2}[Cl_2]^{1/2}[CO]}{k_2^{1/2}(k_4 + k_5[Cl_2])}$$

Then

$$\frac{d[COCl_2]}{dt} = k_5[COCl][Cl_2] = \frac{k_5 k_3 k_1^{1/2}[Cl_2]^{3/2}[CO]}{k_2^{1/2}(k_4 + k_5[Cl_2])} \tag{3}$$

(b) If $k_4[COCl] \gg k_5[COCl][Cl_2]$, equation (3) becomes

$$\frac{d[COCl_2]}{dt} = \frac{k_5 k_3 k_1^{1/2}[Cl_2]^{3/2}[CO]}{k_2^{1/2}k_4} \tag{4}$$

(c)　　$$\frac{[Cl]^2}{[Cl_2]} = K_1 \qquad [Cl] = K_1^{1/2}[Cl_2]^{1/2}$$

$$\frac{[COCl]}{[Cl][CO]} = K_3 \qquad [COCl] = K_3[Cl][CO]$$
$$= K_3 K_1^{1/2}[Cl_2]^{1/2}[CO]$$

$$\frac{d[COCl_2]}{dt} = k_5[COCl][Cl_2] = k_5 K_3 K_1^{1/2}[Cl_2]^{3/2}[CO] \tag{5}$$

Equation (5) agrees with equation (4) if $K_1 = k_1/k_2$ and $K_3 = k_3/k_4$. This is the familiar relation between an equilibrium constant and the rate constants of the forward and reverse reactions. Treating reactions (1)–(4) as equilibria is equivalent to saying, as in (b), that they are much faster than reaction (5) and their equilibrium is not significantly perturbed by the relatively slow leakage of COCl and Cl_2 out of the equilibrium system.

11-III-6. Let $a = [A]$, $b = [B]$, and $c = [C]$. The initial value of a (at $t = 0$) is a_0, which is assumed to be known. The rate equations are (in the notation $\dot{a} = da/dt$, etc.)

$$\dot{a} = -k_1 a \tag{1}$$

$$\dot{b} = k_1 a - k_2 b \tag{2}$$

$$\dot{c} = k_2 b \tag{3}$$

For conservation $a + b + c = a_0$ or $a = a_0 - b - c$. Then

$$\dot{b} = k_1(a_0 - b - c) - k_2 b$$
$$\ddot{b} = k_1(-\dot{b} - \dot{c}) - k_2 \dot{b} \tag{4}$$

Using (3)

$$\ddot{b} = k_1(-\dot{b} - k_2 b) - k_2 \dot{b}$$

or

$$\ddot{b} + (k_1 + k_2)\,\dot{b} + k_1 k_2 b = 0 \tag{5}$$

We now have one linear homogeneous differential equation in the variable b. The general solution of this equation is

$$b = \alpha e^{+m_1 t} + \beta e^{+m_2 t} \tag{6}$$

where α and β are constants of integration, and m_1, m_2 are the two distinct roots of the equation

$$m^2 + (k_1 + k_2)\,m + k_1 k_2 = 0$$
$$m_1 = -k_1, \quad m_2 = -k_2$$

If $k_1 = k_2$, the roots are not distinct and (6) is not the most general solution. We first consider

Case I. $k_1 \neq k_2$

$$b = \alpha e^{-k_1 t} + \beta e^{-k_2 t}$$

When $t = 0$, $b = 0$; $0 = \alpha + \beta$, $\beta = -\alpha$

$$b = \alpha(e^{-k_1 t} - e^{-k_2 t}) \tag{7}$$

To find α, we start with (4)

$$\dot{b} = k_1(a_0 - b - c) - k_2 b$$

When $t = 0$, $b = c = 0$. Then $\dot{b} = k_1 a_0$. From (7)

$$\dot{b} = \alpha(-k_1 e^{-k_1 t} + k_2 e^{-k_2 t})$$

when $t = 0$, $\dot{b} = \alpha(k_2 - k_1)$

$$\alpha(k_2 - k_1) = k_1 a_0$$

$$\alpha = \frac{k_1 a_0}{k_2 - k_1}$$

When b is a maximum, $\dot{b} = 0$ and $\ddot{b} < 0$.

$$\dot{b} = \alpha(-k_1 e^{-k_1 t} + k_2 e^{-k_2 t}) = 0$$

$$k_1 e^{-k_1 t} = k_2 e^{-k_2 t}$$

$$\ln k_1 - k_1 t = \ln k_2 - k_2 t$$

$$t_{max} = \frac{\ln(k_1/k_2)}{k_1 - k_2}$$

(Can this expression ever be negative?)

$$\ddot{b} = -(k_1 + k_2)\,\dot{b} - k_1 k_2 b \qquad \text{(from 5))}$$

$$= -k_1 k_2 b < 0$$

when $\dot{b} = 0$.

Therefore b has a maximum when $t = t_{max}$, not a minimum or a horizontal point of inflection.

$$b_{max} = \alpha \left\{ \exp\left[\frac{-k_1 \ln(k_1/k_2)}{k_1 - k_2} \right] - \exp\left[\frac{-k_2 \ln(k_1/k_2)}{k_1 - k_2} \right] \right\}$$

$$= \alpha \left[\left(\frac{k_1}{k_2} \right)^{-k_1/(k_1 - k_2)} - \left(\frac{k_1}{k_2} \right)^{-k_2/(k_1 - k_2)} \right]$$

$$= \alpha \left(\frac{k_1}{k_2} \right)^{-k_1(k_1 - k_2)} \left[1 - \left(\frac{k_1}{k_2} \right)^{(-k_2 + k_1)/(k_1 - k_2)} \right]$$

$$= \left(\frac{k_1 a_0}{k_2 - k_1} \right) \left(\frac{k_1}{k_2} \right)^{-k_1/(k_1 - k_2)} \left(1 - \frac{k_1}{k_2} \right)$$

$$= \frac{k_1 a_0}{k_2} \left(\frac{k_1}{k_2} \right)^{-k_1/(k_1 - k_2)}$$

$$= a_0 \left(\frac{k_1}{k_2} \right)^{-k_2/(k_1 - k_2)}$$

Case II. $k_1 = k_2 = k$

The general solution for b is

$$b = \alpha e^{-kt} + \beta t e^{-kt}$$

When $t = 0$, $b = 0$; $0 = \alpha + \beta \cdot 0$, $\alpha = 0$. Then

$$b = \beta t e^{-kt}, \quad \dot{b} = \beta(1 - kt)\,e^{-kt}$$

As in case I

$$\dot{a} = -ka$$

$$-\dot{b} - \dot{c} = -k(a_0 - b - c)$$

$$-\dot{b} - kb = -k(a_0 - b - c)$$

When $t = 0$, $b = c = 0$; $\dot{b} = \beta = ka_0$

When $\dot{b} = 0$, $1 - kt = 0$, and $t_{max} = 1/k$.

$$\ddot{b} = -k_1 k_2 b < 0$$

as before.

$$b_{max} = \beta t_{max} e^{-kt_{max}}$$

$$= ka_0 \cdot \frac{1}{k} e^{-1}$$

$$= \frac{a_0}{e}$$

CHAPTER 12

Photochemistry
and spectrophotometry

SECTION 12-I

12-I-1. At 365.5 mμ

$$\phi = \frac{\text{number of molecules decomposed}}{\text{number of photons absorbed}}$$

$$= \frac{5.18 \times 10^{18}}{10.58 \times 10^{18}} = 0.490$$

The values of ϕ for the four measurements are, respectively, 0.490, 0.483, 0.576, 0.577.

SECTION 12-II

12-II-1. $A = abc$, where A = absorbance, a = the absorptivity of the material, b = thickness of the sample, and c = concentration.

$T = I/I_0 \qquad A = -\log T$

Solution No. 1:

At 400nm, $A = \log \dfrac{1}{0.1} = 1.00$; $a_A = \dfrac{1.00}{0.001} = 1.00 \times 10^3$

At 500nm, $A = \log \dfrac{1}{0.60} = 0.22$; $a_A = \dfrac{0.22}{0.001} = 0.22 \times 10^3$

Solution No. 2:

At 400nm, $A = \log \dfrac{1}{0.80} = 0.097$; $a_B = \dfrac{0.097}{0.005} = 19.4$

At 500nm, $A = \log \dfrac{1}{0.20} = 0.699$; $a_B = \dfrac{0.699}{0.005} = 140$

Solution No. 3:

At 400nm, $1000c_A + 19.4c_B = \log \dfrac{1}{0.40} = 0.398$

At 500nm, $220c_A + 140c_B = \log \dfrac{1}{0.50} = 0.301$

Solving the last two equations simultaneously,

$c_B = 0.00156$ moles liter^{-1}

$c_A = 0.000368$ moles liter^{-1}

12-II-2. $A_{\text{HIn}} = 0.142$; $a_{\text{HIn}} = \dfrac{0.142}{6.36 \times 10^{-4}} = 223$

$A_{\text{In}^-} = 0.943$; $a_{\text{In}^-} = \dfrac{0.943}{6.36 \times 10^{-4}} = 1483$

Let [HIn] = the concentration of HIn in the solution with
$\qquad\qquad I = 0.02$
Let [In$^-$] = the concentration of In$^-$ in the same solution

Then

[HIn] $= 6.36 \times 10^{-4} - $ [In$^-$]

223[HIn] $+ 1483$[In$^-$] $= 0.470$

$223(6.36 \times 10^{-4} - $ [In$^-$]$) + 1483$[In$^-$] $= 0.470$

$0.142 - 223$[In$^-$] $+ 1483$[In$^-$] $= 0.470$

1260[In$^-$] $= 0.328$

$\qquad$ [In$^-$] $= 2.60 \times 10^{-4}$

$\qquad$ [HIn] $= 6.36 \times 10^{-4} - 2.60 \times 10^{-4} = 3.76 \times 10^{-4}$

$\qquad$ pH $= 8.207$; [H$^+$] $= 6.21 \times 10^{-9}$

$\qquad K = \dfrac{[\text{H}^+][\text{In}^-]}{[\text{HIn}]} = \dfrac{6.21 \times 10^{-9} \times 2.60 \times 10^{-4}}{3.76 \times 10^{-4}}$

$\qquad\quad = 4.29 \times 10^{-9}$

$$pK = 8.368 \quad \text{at} \quad I = 0.02$$

I	0.10	0.08	0.06	0.04	0.02
pK	8.36	8.36	8.36	8.36	8.37

12-II-3. $\quad HIn \rightleftharpoons H^+ + In^-$

$$K_a = \frac{[H^+][In^-]}{[HIn]}$$

$$\frac{1}{K_a} = \frac{[HIn]}{[H^+][In^-]} = \frac{[HIn]}{[In^-]} \times \frac{1}{[H^+]}$$

$$pK_a = \log \frac{[HIn]}{[In^-]} + pH$$

$$A = \log \frac{1}{T}$$

where A is absorbance

Relative concentration	pH = 4.39 A	Strongly basic A
0.8	0.699	1.268
0.6	0.538	0.959
0.4	0.355	0.644
0.2	0.175	0.333

Assuming that Beer's law holds, that is, assuming that the concentration of the base form $[In^-]$ is proportional to the absorbance A, we can write, referring to the 0.8 solution, buffered at pH = 4.39,

$$\frac{[HIn]}{[In^-]} = \frac{1.268 - 0.699}{0.699} = 0.814$$

$$pK = \log 0.814 + pH$$
$$= -0.09 + 4.39 = 4.30$$

The corresponding results for the 0.6, 0.4, and 0.2 solutions are, respectively, 4.17, 4.23, 4.34. The average of the four solutions is 4.26.

12-II-4. $\quad \dfrac{d[H_2O_2]}{dt} = -\phi I_a - k_2[H_2O_2][CO_2H] - k_3[H_2O_2][OH]$
$$+ k_4[HO_2]^2 \tag{1}$$

$$\frac{d[OH]}{dt} = 2\phi I_a - k_1[OH][CO] + k_2[H_2O_2][CO_2H]$$
$$-k_3[H_2O_2][OH] = 0 \tag{2}$$

$$\frac{d[CO_2H]}{dt} = k_1[OH][CO] - k_2[H_2O_2][CO_2H] = 0 \tag{3}$$

$$\frac{d[HO_2]}{dt} = k_3[H_2O_2][OH] - k_4[HO_2]^2 = 0 \tag{4}$$

Rearrangement of (4):

$$k_4[HO_2]^2 = k_3[H_2O_2][OH] \tag{5}$$

Substitution of (5) into (1):

$$\frac{d[H_2O_2]}{dt} = -\phi I_a - k_2[H_2O_2][CO_2H] \tag{6}$$

Rearrangement of (3):

$$k_1[OH][CO] = k_2[H_2O_2][CO_2H] \tag{7}$$

Substitution of (7) into (2):

$$2\phi I_a = k_3[H_2O_2][OH] \tag{8}$$

Substitution of (7) into (6):

$$\frac{d[H_2O_2]}{dt} = -\phi I_a - k_1[OH][CO] \tag{9}$$

Rearrangement of (8):

$$[OH] = \frac{2\phi I_a}{k_3[H_2O_2]} \tag{10}$$

Substitution of (10) into (9):

$$\frac{d[H_2O_2]}{dt} = -\phi I_a - \frac{2k_1\phi I_a[CO]}{k_3[H_2O_2]} \tag{11}$$

Rearrangement of (11):

$$\frac{d[H_2O_2]}{dt} = -\phi I_a\left(1 + \frac{2k_1[CO]}{k_3[H_2O_2]}\right) \tag{12}$$

Equation (12) is the form obtained by Buxton and Walker.

12-II-5. $\quad \dfrac{d[H_2O_2]}{dt} = \phi I_a - k_2[H_2O_2][CO_2H] \tag{1}$

$$\frac{d[CO_2H]}{dt} = k_1[OH][CO] - k_2[H_2O][CO_2H] - k_5[CO_2H]^2 = 0 \quad (2)$$

$$\frac{d[OH]}{dt} = 2\phi I_a - k_1[OH][CO] + k_2[H_2O_2][CO_2H] = 0 \quad (3)$$

Sum of (2) and (3):

$$2\phi I_a - k_5[CO_2H]^2 \quad (4)$$

$$[CO_2H] = \sqrt{\frac{2\phi I_a}{k_5}} \quad (5)$$

Substitution of (5) into (1):

$$\frac{d[H_2O_2]}{dt} = -\phi I_a - \frac{k_2[2\phi I_a]^{1/2}[H_2O_2]}{k_5^{1/2}} \quad (6)$$

SECTION 12-III

12-III-1. Absorbance $= abc = A$, where $a =$ absorptivity, $b =$ sample path length, and $c =$ concentration.

$$T = \frac{I}{I_0} = 10^{-abc} = e^{-2.303abc}$$

$$dT = -abe^{-2.303abc} \, dc$$

Let

$$p = \frac{1}{c}\frac{dc}{dT} = \frac{-e^{2.303abc}}{abc}$$

p represents the relative error in c divided by the error in T.

$$\frac{dp}{dc} = \frac{-2.303abe^{2.303abc}}{abc} + \frac{e^{2.303abc}}{abc^2} = 0$$

$$\frac{-2.303}{c} + \frac{1}{abc^2} = 0$$

$$abc = \frac{1}{2.303}$$

$$T = e^{-2.303abc} = e^{-1} = 0.368$$

The error p is a minimum when $T = 36.8$ percent.

12-III-2.

(a) $\dfrac{2 \text{ molecules}}{\text{photon}}$

$\times \dfrac{2.070 \times 10^{-5} \text{ cm}}{6.625 \times 10^{-27} \text{ erg sec/photon} \times 2.998 \times 10^{10} \text{ cm sec}^{-1}}$

$\times 4.184 \times 10^7 \text{ erg cal}^{-1} \times \dfrac{127.9 \text{ g}}{6.023 \times 10^{23} \text{ molecules}}$

$= 1.85 \times 10^{-3} \text{ g cal}^{-1}$

(b) Each photon destroys one HI molecule, producing an H atom that destroys a second HI molecule in agreement with the observed quantum yield of 2.

(c) The high quantum yield of the $H_2 + Cl_2$ reaction is attributed to the self-perpetuating sequence

$$Cl + H_2 \rightarrow HCl + H \tag{1}$$

$$H + Cl_2 \rightarrow HCl + Cl \tag{2}$$

The energies of activation are fairly low: $E_1 = 8$ kcal, $E_2 = 2$ kcal. Thus both reactions are fast and can occur repeatedly before the chain is terminated by recombination of atoms. The HI decomposition would show a similarly high quantum yield if the following chain were possible:

$$H + HI \rightarrow H_2 + I \tag{3}$$

$$I + HI \rightarrow I_2 + H \tag{4}$$

$E_3 = 1.5$ kcal, so that reaction (3) should be fast and it is indeed assumed as one step in the mechanism. E_4 is not given but a lower limit can be obtained from bond energies:

	ΔE, kcal
$HI \rightarrow H + I$	71
$2I \rightarrow I_2$	-36
$I + HI \rightarrow I_2 + H$	$+35$

Thus $E_4 \geqslant 35$ kcal; the energy required to reach the activated state cannot be less than the energy required to reach the final products. We expect reaction (4) with its high activation energy to be slow, so that the chain will not be propagated and I atoms will recombine much more often than they will undergo reaction (4).

12-III-3. (a) $\dfrac{d[O^*]}{dt} = \phi I_a - k_2[O^*][O_3] - k_3[O^*] \approx 0$

$$[O^*] = \frac{\phi I_a}{k_2[O_3] + k_3}$$

$$\frac{d[O]}{dt} = k_3[O^*] - k_4[O][O_2][M] \approx 0$$

$$[O] = \frac{k_3[O^*]}{k_4[O_2][M]}$$

$$-\Phi I_a = \frac{d[O_3]}{dt}$$

$$= -\phi I_a - k_2[O^*][O_3] + k_4[O][O_2][M]$$

$$= -\phi I_a + (k_3 - k_2[O_3])[O^*]$$

$$= \phi I_a \left(-1 + \frac{k_3 - k_2[O_3]}{k_2[O_3] + k_3} \right)$$

$$= \phi I_a \left(\frac{-2k_2[O_3]}{k_2[O_3] + k_3} \right)$$

$$\Phi^{-1} = \phi^{-1} \left(\frac{1}{2} + \frac{k_3}{2k_2[O_3]} \right)$$

(b) $(2\phi)^{-1} = 0.538, \quad \phi = 0.93$

$$\frac{k_3}{2\phi k_2} = 0.81, \quad \frac{k_3}{k_2} = 1.51 \text{ mole liter}^{-1}$$

12-III-4. (a) Rate $= k I_0{}^n$

Log rate $= \log k + n \log I_0$

Plot "log rate" vs "log I_0 "

Slope $= n = \frac{1}{2}$

(b) Rate $= k' P_{Cl_2}^m$

Log rate $= k' + m \log P_{Cl_2}$

Plot "log rate" vs "log P_{Cl_2}"

Slope $= m = 3/2$

(c) Rate $= k'' P_{Cl_2}^{3/2} I_0^{1/2} = $ rate of disappearance of $Cl_2 = $ rate of appearance of $TfCl_2$.

(d) Since $h\nu$ in this case refers to *incident* (rather than *absorbed*) light, the rate of reaction (1) is $k_1 I_0 P_{Cl_2}$, not $k_1 I_0$ (provided $I_a \ll I_0$).

$$\frac{-dP_{Cl_2}}{dt} = k_1 I_0 P_{Cl_2} + k_3 P_{Cl_2} P_{TfCl} \tag{1a}$$

$$\frac{dP_{TfCl_2}}{dt} = k_3 P_{TfCl} P_{Cl_2} \tag{1b}$$

Making the steady state approximation for Cl, we obtain

$$k_2 P_{Cl} P_{Tf} = 2k_1 P_{Cl_2} I_0 + k_3 P_{TfCl} P_{Cl_2} \tag{2}$$

Making the steady state approximation for TfCl, we obtain

$$k_3 P_{TfCl} P_{Cl_2} + k_4 P_{TfCl}^2 = k_2 P_{Cl} P_{Tf} \tag{3}$$

Solving (2) and (3) simultaneously we obtain

$$k_4 P_{TfCl}^2 = 2k_1 P_{Cl_2} I_0 \tag{4}$$

or

$$P_{TfCl} = \left(\frac{2k_1 P_{Cl_2} I_0}{k_4} \right)^{1/2} \tag{5}$$

Substituting this value for P_{TfCl} (5) into (1a), we obtain

$$\frac{-dP_{Cl_2}}{dt} = k_1 I_0 P_{Cl_2} + k_3 P_{Cl_2} \left(\frac{2k_1 P_{Cl_2} I_0}{k_4} \right)^{1/2}$$
$$= k_1 I_0 P_{Cl_2} + k''' P_{Cl_2}^{3/2} I_0^{1/2} \tag{6}$$

If reaction (1) is very much slower than reactions (2), (3), and (4), then the term $k_1 I_0 P_{Cl_2}$ is small and may be neglected with respect to the term $k''' P_{Cl_2}^{3/2} I^{1/2}$ in equation (6), so that (6) reduces to the form

$$\frac{-dP_{Cl_2}}{dt} = k''' P_{Cl_2}^{3/2} I_0^{1/2} \tag{7}$$

Alternatively starting with equation (1b) substituting equation (5) for P_{TfCl}, we obtain

$$\frac{dP_{TfCl_2}}{dt} = k_3 P_{TfCl} P_{Cl_2} = k''' P_{Cl_2}^{3/2} I_0^{1/2} \tag{8}$$

(e) If their concentrations have no effect on the reaction rate.

(f) One would have to work out the new rate law based on the reverse of reaction (3) in addition to the other reactions and compare this law with the experimental results.

(g) Free radicals are involved.

CHAPTER 13

Radiochemistry

SECTION 13-I

13-I-1.
$$\frac{N}{N_0} = 2^{-t/t_{1/2}}$$

$$\log \frac{N_0}{N} = \frac{t}{t_{1/2}} \log 2 = \frac{t}{t_{1/2}} (0.3010)$$

$$t = \frac{t_{1/2} \log(100/90)}{0.3010}$$

$$= \frac{5760 \times 0.0458}{0.3010} = 877 \text{ yr}$$

13-I-2. $\text{Activity} = 1000 \times \dfrac{1.00 \times 10^5}{3.71 \times 10^{10}} = 0.00270 \text{ mCi g}^{-1} \text{ (Ci = curie)}$

13-I-3. $\lambda = \dfrac{0.693}{t_{1/2}} = \dfrac{0.693}{14.9 \times 60 \times 60} = 1.29 \times 10^{-5} \text{ sec}^{-1}$

$$\text{Disintegration rate} = -\frac{dN}{dt} = \lambda N$$

$$= \frac{(1.29 \times 10^{-5})(6.02 \times 10^{23})}{24.0 \times 10^6} = 3.24 \times 10^{11} \text{ sec}^{-1} \mu\text{g}^{-1}$$

$$\text{Activity} = \frac{3.24 \times 10^{11}}{3.71 \times 10^{10}} = 8.74 \text{ Ci}$$

13-I-4. $\ln \dfrac{N}{N_0} = -\lambda t; \quad \ln \dfrac{N_0}{N} = \lambda t$

$$\lambda = \frac{0.693}{t_{1/2}} = \frac{0.693}{14.9} = 4.65 \times 10^{-2} \, \text{hr}^{-1}$$

$$\log N = -\frac{0.2325}{2.303} = -0.1010 = 9.8990 - 10$$

$$N = 0.792 \mu\text{Ci}$$

13-I-5. $\dfrac{dN}{dt} = -\lambda N$

Let $m_{\text{Na}^{24}}$ = the desired mass of Na^{24}.

$$\left(\frac{dN}{dt}\right)_{\text{Na}^{24}} = \frac{-0.693}{14.9 \times 60} \times \frac{6.02 \times 10^{23} \times m_{\text{Na}^{24}}}{24.0}$$

$$= \left(\frac{dN}{dt}\right)_{\text{Mg}^{27}} = \frac{-0.693}{10.2} \times \frac{6.02 \times 10^{23} \times 10^{-3}}{27.0}$$

$$m_{\text{Na}^{24}} = \frac{14.9 \times 60 \times 24.0 \times 10^{-3}}{10.2 \times 27.0} = 0.0780 \, \text{g} = 78.0 \, \text{mg}$$

13-I-6. $N_{\text{Ra}} = \dfrac{6.02 \times 10^{23}}{226} \times 1.00 \, \text{atoms}$

$$\lambda_{\text{Ra}} = \frac{0.693}{t_{1/2}} = \frac{0.693}{1.62 \times 10^3 \times 365} \, \text{day}^{-1}$$

$$N_{\text{Rn}} = \frac{6.02 \times 10^{23}}{222} \, m_{\text{Rn}}$$

$$\lambda_{\text{Rn}} = \frac{0.693}{3.82} \, \text{day}^{-1}$$

$$\lambda_{\text{Ra}} N_{\text{Ra}} = \lambda_{\text{Rn}} N_{\text{Rn}}$$

$$\frac{0.693}{1.62 \times 10^3 \times 365} \times \frac{6.02 \times 10^{23} \times 1.00}{226}$$

$$= \frac{0.693}{3.82} \times \frac{6.02 \times 10^{23}}{222} \, m_{\text{Rn}}$$

$$m_{\text{Rn}} = \frac{3.82 \times 222}{1.62 \times 10^3 \times 365 \times 226} = 6.34 \times 10^{-6} \, \text{g} = 6.34 \, \mu\text{g}$$

13-I-7. $\dfrac{N_{\text{Ra}^{226}}}{N_{\text{U}^{238}}} = \dfrac{1.6 \times 10^3}{4.5 \times 10^9}$

$\dfrac{m_{\text{Ra}^{226}}}{m_{\text{U}^{238}}} = \dfrac{226}{238} \times \dfrac{1.6 \times 10^3}{4.5 \times 10^9} = 3.4 \times 10^{-7}$ g Ra^{226} per g U^{238}

13-I-8. $\lambda_{\text{Ra}} = \dfrac{0.693}{t_{1/2}} = \dfrac{0.693}{1.62 \times 10^3 \times 365} = 1.17 \times 10^{-6}$ day^{-1}

$\lambda_{\text{Rn}} = 0.182$ day^{-1}

$N_{\text{Rn}} = \dfrac{1.17 \times 10^{-6} \times N_{\text{A}}^{\circ}}{0.182 - 1.17 \times 10^{-6}} \left(e^{-1.17 \times 10^{-6}} - e^{-0.182} \right)$

$\quad\quad = \dfrac{1.17 \times 10^{-6} \times N_{\text{A}}^{\circ}}{0.182} (1 - 0.834) = 1.07 \times 10^{-8}\, N_{\text{A}}^{\circ}$

The activity of 0.1 g Ra^{226} is 0.1 Ci; therefore

$N_{\text{Rn}} = 1.07 \times 10^{-8} \times 0.1 = 1.07 \times 10^{-9}$ Ci $= 1.07 \times 10^{-3}\,\mu$Ci

13-I-9. $N = N_0 e^{-\lambda t}$
Let N = parents remaining = P
Let N_0 = parents + daughters = $P + D$

$$P = (P + D)\, e^{-\lambda t}$$

$$\left(\dfrac{P}{P + D} \right) = e^{-\lambda t}$$

$$\ln \left(\dfrac{P + D}{P} \right) = \lambda t$$

$$t = \dfrac{1}{\lambda} \ln \left(1 + \dfrac{D}{P} \right)$$

13-I-10. $t = \dfrac{1}{\lambda} \ln \left(1 + \dfrac{D}{P} \right)$

(for derivation, see preceding problem)

$\quad = \dfrac{2.303}{1.47 \times 10^{-11}} \log \left(1 + \dfrac{(0.90/87) \times 0.80}{(450/87) \times 0.27} \right)$

$\quad = 1.568 \times 10^{11} \times 2.303 \times \log(1 + 0.0059)$

$\quad = 1.568 \times 10^{11} \times 2.303 \times 0.00255 = 3.99 \times 10^8$ years

13-I-11. (a) $_1H^1$ (b) $_6C^{12}$

13-I-12. (a) Au^{198} (b) Ar^{37} (c) Na^{22} (d) Li^6

13-I-13. The mass of 8 electrons must be subtracted from the mass of the O^{16} atom to obtain the mass of the nucleus.

$$\text{Mass defect} = 8(1.007277) + 8(1.008657)$$
$$- [15.99468 - 8(0.000549)]$$
$$= 0.1372 \text{ amu}$$

$$\text{Binding energy} = 931 \text{ MeV amu}^{-1} \times 0.1372 \text{ amu} = 128 \text{ MeV}$$

13-I-14. $m = \dfrac{m_0}{\sqrt{1 - (v/c)^2}} = \dfrac{0.000549}{\sqrt{1 - (0.99/1.00)^2}} = 0.00389 \text{ amu}$

(7.1 times the rest mass)

13-I-15. $\dfrac{d\phi}{\phi} = N\sigma \, dX$

$$\int_{\phi_1}^{\phi_2} \frac{d\phi}{\phi} = \int_{X_1}^{X_2} N\sigma \, dX$$

$$\ln \phi_2 - \ln \phi_1 = N\sigma(X_2 - X_1)$$

$$\sigma = \frac{\ln \phi_2 - \ln \phi_1}{N(X_2 - X_1)}$$

Plot $\ln \phi$ vs X. Slope $= N\sigma$.

SECTION 13-II

13-II-1. $\lambda = \dfrac{0.693}{t_{1/2}} = \dfrac{0.693}{2.70} = 0.257 \text{ day}^{-1}; \quad t = 44 \text{ hr} = \dfrac{44}{24} \text{ days}$

$$\log \frac{N}{N_0} = -\frac{\lambda t}{2.303} = \frac{-0.257 \times 44/24}{2.303} = -0.204 = 9.796 - 10$$

$$\frac{N}{N_0} = 0.625 \text{ at 8 A.M. August 23}$$

The activity of the undiluted material at 8 A.M. on August 22 would be $0.625 \times 3 = 1.875 \, \mu\text{Ci g}^{-1}$. Thus the pharmacist should add 2.75 g diluent per gram of material as supplied by the manufacturer. The time at which the prescription is prepared is irrelevant.

SECTION 13-III

13-III-1.

$$\frac{dN}{dt} = -\lambda N$$

$$\frac{dN}{N} = -\lambda \, dt$$

$$\ln \frac{N}{N_0} = -\lambda t$$

$$N_0 = P + D_1 + D_2$$

$$N = P$$

$$\ln \frac{P}{(P + D_1 + D_2)} = -\lambda t$$

$$\ln \left[\frac{(P + D_1 + D_2)}{P} \right] = \lambda t$$

$$\ln \left[1 + \frac{1}{P} (D_1 + D_2) \right] = \lambda t$$

$$\ln \left[1 + \frac{D_1}{P} \left(1 + \frac{1}{R} \right) \right] = \lambda t$$

$$\ln \left[1 + \frac{D_1}{P} \left(\frac{R + 1}{R} \right) \right] = \lambda t$$

13-III-2.

$$N_1 = N_1^\circ - N_2 - N_3$$

$$\frac{dN_2}{dt} = \lambda_1 N_1 - \lambda_2 N_2 = \lambda_1(N_1^\circ - N_3) - (\lambda_1 + \lambda_2) N_2$$

$$\frac{dN_3}{dt} = \lambda_2 N_2$$

$$\frac{d^2 N_2}{dt^2} = -\lambda_1 \frac{dN_3}{dt} - (\lambda_1 + \lambda_2) \frac{dN_2}{dt}$$

$$= -\lambda_1 \lambda_2 N_2 - (\lambda_1 + \lambda_2) \frac{dN_2}{dt}$$

$$\frac{d^2 N_2}{dt^2} + (\lambda_1 + \lambda_2) \frac{dN_2}{dt} + \lambda_1 \lambda_2 N_2 = 0$$

This is a homogeneous linear differential equation with constant coefficients. The auxiliary equation is

$$m^2 + (\lambda_1 + \lambda_2) m + \lambda_1 \lambda_2 = 0$$

with roots $m = -\lambda_1$ or $-\lambda_2$.

$$N_2 = A e^{-\lambda_1 t} + B e^{-\lambda_2 t}$$

When $t = 0$,

$$N_2 = 0 = A + B$$

$$\frac{dN_2}{dt} = \lambda_1 N_1^\circ = -\lambda_1 A - \lambda_2 B$$

Solving, we obtain

$$A = -B = \frac{\lambda_1 N_1^\circ}{\lambda_2 - \lambda_1}$$

$$N_2 = \frac{\lambda_1 N_1^\circ}{\lambda_2 - \lambda_1} (e^{-\lambda_1 t} - e^{-\lambda_2 t})$$

13-III-3. To obtain the mean lifetime we multiply each possible lifetime t by the number of particles decaying at the end of that time ($-dN = \lambda N\, dt$), "add up" (integrate) the results for all values of t from 0 to ∞, and divide by the number of particles initially present:

$$t_{\text{mean}} = \frac{1}{N_0} \int_0^\infty t\lambda N\, dt = \int_0^\infty t\lambda e^{-\lambda t}\, dt$$

$$= \frac{e^{-\lambda t}}{\lambda} (-\lambda t - 1) \Big|_0^\infty = \frac{1}{\lambda}$$

13-III-4. To find the surface area of the spherical segment intercepted by the flat circular counter window, construct an annulus of length $2\pi R$, where $R = D \sin \theta$, as shown in the figure. The area of this annulus is

$$dA = 2\pi D \sin \theta D \, d\theta = 2\pi D^2 \sin \theta \, d\theta$$

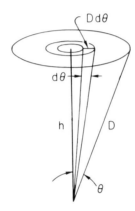

Integrating between 0 and θ

$$A = 2\pi D^2 \int_0^\theta \sin \theta \, d\theta = -2\pi D^2 \cos \theta \Big|_0^\theta$$

$$= 2\pi D^2 (1 - \cos \theta)$$

$G =$ geometry factor

$$= \frac{\text{area enclosed by counter window}}{\text{area of sphere of radius } D}$$

$$= \frac{2\pi D^2 (1 - \cos \theta)}{4\pi D^2} = \frac{1}{2}(1 - \cos \theta)$$

Since

$$\cos \theta = h/D = \frac{h}{\sqrt{h^2 + r^2}}, \quad G = \frac{1}{2}\left(1 - \frac{h}{\sqrt{h^2 + r^2}}\right)$$

For large distances, that is, where $h \gg r$,

$$1 - h(h^2 + r^2)^{-1/2}$$

$$= 1 - \left(1 + \frac{r^2}{h^2}\right)^{-1/2} = 1 - \left(1 - \frac{r^2}{2h^2} + \cdots\right) \approx \frac{r^2}{2h^2}$$

$$G \approx \frac{r^2}{4h^2}$$

CHAPTER 14

Surface chemistry
and colloids

SECTION 14-I

14-I-1. $M = \dfrac{wRT}{PV} = \dfrac{1 \times 0.0821 \times 298}{3.6 \times 10^{-4} \times 1} = 6.8 \times 10^4 \text{ g mole}^{-1}$

14-I-2. $\dfrac{P}{c} = \dfrac{453 \text{ mm H}_2\text{O}}{19.26 \text{ g dl}^{-1}} = 23.5 \text{ mm H}_2\text{O dl g}^{-1}$

For other solutions

$\dfrac{P}{c} = 20.5, \quad 19.3 \text{ mm H}_2\text{O dl g}^{-1}$

Plot P/c vs c.

$$\lim_{c \to 0} \left(\frac{P}{c} \right) = 18.6 \text{ mm H}_2\text{O dl g}^{-1}$$

$$= \frac{18.6 \text{ mm H}_2\text{O dl g}^{-1} \times 0.100 \text{ liter dl}^{-1}}{13.56 \text{ mm H}_2\text{O torr}^{-1} \times 760 \text{ torr atm}^{-1}}$$

$$= 1.804 \times 10^{-4} \text{ liter atm g}^{-1}$$

$$M = RT \lim \left(\frac{P}{c} \right) = \frac{0.08206 \text{ liter atm } °\text{K}^{-1} \text{ mole}^{-1} \times 310°\text{K}}{1.804 \times 10^{-4} \text{ liter atm g}^{-1}}$$

$$= 1.41 \times 10^5 \text{ g mole}^{-1}$$

14-I-3. $1.80 = 3.60 \times 10^{-4} M^{0.64}$

$5.00 \times 10^3 = M^{0.64}$

$\log(5.00 \times 10^3) = 0.64 \log M$

$3.6990 = 0.64 \log M$

$\log M = 5.78$

$M = 6.0 \times 10^5 \text{ g mole}^{-1}$

14-I-4.   Plot $\log[\eta]$ vs $\log M$. Obtain straight line (shows that data fit $[\eta] = K M^a$, or $\log[\eta] = \log K + a \log M$). Intercept on $\log M$ axis is $\log K$. Slope $= a = (d \log[\eta])/(d \log M) = 0.70$. Log $K = -3.58 = 6.42 - 10$. $K = 2.6 \times 10^{-4}$. (Fox and Flory get $a = 0.68$, $K = 2.9 \times 10^{-4}$.)

14-I-5.   Plot $\log[\eta]$ vs $\log M$. Slope $= a$. When $\log M = 0$, $\log[\eta] = \log K$. $K = 4.14 \times 10^{-4}$, $a = 0.65$.

14-I-6.   (a) 6 cm³

(b)   Number of cubes $= \dfrac{1 \text{ cm}^3}{(10^{-7})^3 \text{ cm}^3} = 10^{21}$ cubes

each having a surface area of $6 \times (10^{-7})^2$ cm².

Total surface area $= 10^{21} \times 6 \times (10^{-7})^2 = 6 \times 10^7$ cm² $= 1.48$ acres

14-I-7.   Plot $\log(V_e - V)$ vs t and get a straight line with slope $-k$. $t = 1380$ sec, $V = 0.167$ cm³, $(V_e - V) = 0.284$ cm³, $\log(V_e - V) = -0.547$. The other four cases are treated similarly.

$k = 1.38 \times 10^{-4} \text{ sec}^{-1}$

14-I-8.   Both isotherms represent physical adsorption. In (a) the first layer of molecules is adsorbed more strongly than the other layers; in other words the attraction between N_2 and Fe is greater than the attraction between N_2 and N_2. There is a rapid rise in quantity adsorbed as the pressure is increased from zero, but a temporary leveling off as the first layer is completed. In (b) Br_2 is more attracted to Br_2 than to SiO_2. The quantity adsorbed rises smoothly with pressure and the curve exhibits no special feature corresponding to the completion of a monomolecular layer.

SECTION 14-II

14-II-1. $\gamma_0 - \gamma = 29.8 \log(1 + 19.64c)$

$$\frac{d\gamma}{dc} = -\frac{0.4343 \times 29.8 \times 19.64}{1 + 19.64c} = -\frac{254}{1 + 19.64c}$$

$$S = -\frac{c}{RT} \cdot \frac{d\gamma}{dc} = \frac{254c}{RT(1 + 19.4c)}$$

$$= \frac{254 \times 0.01}{8.31 \times 10^7 \times 291 \times (1 + 19.64 \times 0.01)}$$

$$S = 8.79 \times 10^{-11} \text{ moles cm}^{-2}$$

$$\lim_{c \to \infty} S = \frac{254}{19.64RT} = 5.34 \times 10^{-10}$$

(experimental value, 5.35×10^{-10})

14-II-2. (a) Plot $P/(x/m)$ vs P. Intercept on $P = 0$ axis is $1/k_1$; slope $= k_2/k_1$.

P	3.5	10.0	16.7	25.7	33.5	39.2	48.6
$P/(x/m)$	27.8	58.8	87.9	126.5	162.7	189.3	230.5

$1/k_1 = 12$; $k_1 = 0.083$; $k_2/k_1 = 4.50$; $k_2 = 0.38$

(b) Plot $\log(x/m)$ vs $\log P$. Intercept on $\log P = 0$ axis is $\log k$. Slope $= 1/n$.

P	3.5	10.0	16.7	25.7	33.5	39.2	48.6
$\log(x/m)$	−0.900	−0.770	−0.716	−0.693	−0.686	−0.684	−0.677
$\log P$	0.544	1.000	1.223	1.410	1.526	1.594	1.688

$\log k = -1.048$; $k = 0.0895$; $1/n = 0.271$; $n = 3.69$

(c) Plot $\log[(x/m)/P]$ vs x/m. Slope $= k$

P	3.5	10.0	16.7	25.7	33.5	39.2	48.6
$(x/m)/P$	0.0360	0.0170	0.0114	0.00790	0.00615	0.00528	0.00434
$\log[(x/m)/P]$	−1.444	−1.770	−1.943	−2.102	−2.211	−2.277	−2.362

$k = -7.61$

All three curves show departure from linearity at higher pressures.

14-II-3.   Let x = number of grams of adsorbed CH_3COOH
$$= (c_0 - c_e) \text{ mole liter}^{-1} \times 0.200 \text{ liter} \times 60.0 \text{ g mole}^{-1}$$

$$\frac{x}{m} = kc_e^{1/n}$$

$$\log \frac{x}{m} = \log k + \frac{1}{n} \log c_e$$

Plot $\log(x/m)$ vs $\log c_e$. Get straight line. Intercept for $c_e = 1(\log c_e = 0)$ is $\log k$. Slope $= 1/n$.

c_0	c_e	x	x/m	$\log(x/m)$	$\log c_e$
0.503	0.434	0.828	0.209	-0.680	-0.362

The other five cases are treated similarly. Intercept for $\log c_e = 0$ is $-0.552 = \log k$. $\log k = 9.448 - 10$; $k = 0.28$. Slope $= 0.355 = 1/n$; $n = 2.82$.

CHAPTER 15

Quantum chemistry
and spectroscopy

15-1. (a) $w = \int_{r_1}^{\infty} F \, dr = \int_{r_1}^{\infty} \frac{Gm^2}{r^2} \, dr = -Gm^2 \cdot \frac{1}{r} \Big|_{r_1}^{\infty}$

$$= -Gm^2 \left[\frac{1}{\infty} - \frac{1}{0.74 \times 10^{-8}} \right]$$

$$= -6.670 \times 10^{-8} \times (1.7 \times 10^{-24})^2 \times \frac{-1}{0.74 \times 10^{-8}}$$

$$= 2.6 \times 10^{-47} \text{ erg}$$

(b) The experimentally observed value is much greater than the value calculated on the assumption that gravitational attraction is the only force to be taken into account. Thus it is clear that gravitational attraction is only a negligible part of the total bond strength.

15-2. When the oil drop is suspended motionless in space, the upward electric force, qE, is equal to the downward gravitational force, $(4/3)\,\pi r^3 g(\rho - \rho_0)$. That is,

$$qE = \frac{4}{3} \pi r^3 g(\rho - \rho_0)$$

In order to obtain q in esu, E must be in statvolt cm^{-1}.
$E = 4.50 \times 10^3 \times 3.34 \times 10^{-3} = 15.0$ statV cm^{-1}

$$q = \frac{1}{15.0} \times \frac{4}{3} \pi (1.24 \times 10^{-4})^3 \times 981\,(0.92 - 0)$$

$$= 4.81 \times 10^{-10} \text{ esu}$$

15-3.

$$E = \frac{nhc}{\lambda} = \frac{500 \text{ sec}^{-1} \times 6.625 \times 10^{-27} \text{ erg sec}}{5.000 \times 10^{-5} \text{ cm}}$$

$$\times \frac{2.998 \times 10^{10} \text{ cm sec}^{-1} \times 1 \text{ watt}}{10^7 \text{ erg sec}^{-1}}$$

$$= 2.0 \times 10^{-16} \text{ watt}$$

15-4.

$$\nu = \frac{\Delta E}{h} = \frac{\Delta E \text{ erg}}{6.625 \times 10^{-27} \text{ erg sec}}$$

$$\bar{\nu} = \frac{\nu}{c} = \frac{\nu \text{ sec}^{-1}}{2.998 \times 10^{10} \text{ cm sec}^{-1}}$$

	E, erg	sec^{-1}	cm^{-1}
$0 \rightarrow 1$	1.000×10^{-11}	1.51×10^{15}	5.04×10^4
$0 \rightarrow 3$	3.500×10^{-11}	5.28×10^{15}	1.76×10^5
$1 \rightarrow 2$	2.000×10^{-11}	3.02×10^{15}	1.01×10^5
$2 \rightarrow 3$	5.00×10^{-12}	7.55×10^{14}	2.52×10^4

15-5. Let $x = hc/\lambda kT$. Then $dx = -hcd\lambda/(\lambda^2 kT)$. Also $\lambda = hc/(xkT)$, and $d\lambda = -hcdx/(x^2 kT)$. Therefore

$$\rho_\lambda \, d\lambda = \rho_x \, dx$$

$$= \frac{8\pi hc}{(hc/xkT)^5 (e^x - 1)} \left(\frac{-hc \, dx}{x^2 kT} \right)$$

$$\rho = \int_0^\infty \rho_\lambda \, d\lambda = \int_\infty^0 \rho_x \, dx = \int_\infty^0 \frac{8\pi hc}{(hc/xkT)^5 (e^x - 1)} \cdot \left(\frac{-hc}{x^2 kT} \right) dx$$

$$= -\int_\infty^0 \frac{8\pi x^3 k^4 T^4 \, dx}{(hc)^3 (e^x - 1)}$$

$$= \frac{8\pi k^4 T^4}{(hc)^3} \int_0^\infty \frac{x^3}{(e^x - 1)} \, dx$$

$$= \frac{8\pi k^4 T^4}{(hc)^3} \times \frac{\pi}{15}$$

$$= \frac{8\pi^5 k^4 T^4}{15 (hc)^3} = \sigma T^4$$

where

$$\sigma = \frac{8\pi^5 k^4}{15 (hc)^3}$$

15-6. $d\rho/d\lambda = 0$ when ρ is at ρ_{max}. Find $d\rho/d\lambda$ and then set $d\rho/d\lambda = 0$.

$$\frac{d\rho}{d\lambda} = -\frac{5}{\lambda^6} \cdot \frac{1}{e^{hc/\lambda kT} - 1} + \frac{1}{\lambda^7} \cdot \frac{(hc/kT) \cdot e^{hc/\lambda kT}}{(e^{hc/\lambda kT} - 1)^2} = 0$$

$$\lambda = \frac{hce^{hc/\lambda kT}}{5kT(e^{hc/\lambda kT} - 1)}$$

If the derived relationship is to fit the form of the Wien displacement law, we must assume that $e^{hc/\lambda kT} \gg 1$ and therefore $e^{hc/\lambda kT} - 1 \approx e^{hc/\lambda kT}$. With this assumption

$$\lambda_{max} = \frac{hce^{hc/\lambda kT}}{5kTe^{hc/\lambda kT}} = \frac{hc}{5kT}$$

15-7. $e^x = 1 + x + \frac{1}{2}x^2 + \cdots$

$e^x - 1 \approx x$ if $|x| \ll 1$

$e^{hc/\lambda kT} - 1 \approx \dfrac{hc}{\lambda kT}$ if $\lambda \gg \dfrac{hc}{kT}$

$$\rho_\lambda = \frac{8\pi hc}{\lambda^5(hc/\lambda kT)} = \frac{8\pi kT}{\lambda^4}$$

15-8. $\rho_\lambda = \dfrac{8\pi hc}{\lambda^5(e^{hc/\lambda kT} - 1)}$

As $\lambda \to 0$, then $e^{hc/\lambda kT}$ becomes $\gg 1$ (because $hc/\lambda kT$ becomes very large), and $e^{hc/\lambda kT} - 1 \to e^{hc/\lambda kT}$. Thus

$$\rho_\lambda \approx \frac{8\pi hc}{\lambda^5 e^{hc/\lambda kT}} = \frac{8\pi hce^{-hc/\lambda kT}}{\lambda^5}$$

Let $8\pi hc = c_1$ and $hc/k = c_2$. Then

$$\rho_\lambda = \frac{c_1 e^{-c_2/\lambda T}}{\lambda^5}$$

at short wavelengths.

15-9. (a) The length must be an integral number of half wave lengths: $1 = n\lambda/2$, where n is an integer.

$$\nu = \frac{c}{\lambda} = \frac{cn}{2l} \qquad n = \frac{2l\nu}{c} \qquad dn = \frac{2l\,d\nu}{c}$$

The number of integers between n and $n + dn$ is dn. (We assume that n is so large that an "infinitesimal" increment still includes many integers.) The number of waves, dN, is twice this number of integers because of the two directions of polarization

$$dN = 2dn = \frac{4l\,dv}{c}$$

(b) $dE = \bar{\epsilon}\,dN$

$$\bar{\epsilon} = \frac{hv}{e^{hv/kT} - 1}$$

independently of the number of dimensions.

$$dE = \frac{4lhv\,dv}{c(e^{hv/kT} - 1)}$$

15-10. (a)

$$\epsilon_n = nbv^2$$

The average energy of a mode of radiation of frequency v is

$$\bar{\epsilon}(v) = \frac{\sum_{n=0}^{\infty} \epsilon_n \exp(-nbv^2/kT)}{\sum_{n=0}^{\infty} \exp(-nbv^2/kT)} = \frac{bv^2 \sum_{n=0}^{\infty} ny^n}{\sum_{n=0}^{\infty} y^n}$$

where

$$y = \exp(-bv^2/kT)$$

Let

$$f(y) = \sum_{n=0}^{\infty} y^n = (1 - y)^{-1}$$

Then

$$f'(y) = \sum_{n=0}^{\infty} ny^{n-1} = (1 - y)^{-2}$$

$$yf'(y) = \sum_{n=0}^{\infty} ny^n = y(1 - y)^{-2}$$

$$\bar{\epsilon}(v) = bv^2 y(1 - y)^{-1} = bv^2 \left[\exp(bv^2/kT) - 1\right]^{-1}$$

The number of modes of radiation (standing waves) with frequencies between v and $v + dv$ in a container of volume V is $dn = 8\pi V c^{-3} v^2\,dv$. (This result is derived in many textbooks.) The energy between v and $v + dv$ is $dE = \bar{\varepsilon}(v)\,dn$. The density function is

$$\rho\,dv = \frac{dE}{V} = 8\pi c^{-3}bv^4\,[\exp(bv^2/kT) - 1]^{-1}\,dv$$

(b) $\displaystyle\int_0^\infty \rho\,dv = \frac{8\pi b}{c^3}\int_0^\infty v^4\,[\exp(bv^2/kT) - 1]^{-1}\,dv$

$$= \frac{8\pi b}{c^3}\left(\frac{kT}{b}\right)^{5/2}\int_0^\infty \frac{x^4\,dx}{e^{x^2}-1} = \text{const}\times T^{5/2}$$

with

$$x = v\left(\frac{b}{kT}\right)^{1/2}.$$

15-11. (a) $n_1 = 1$, $n_2 = \infty$
(b) $n_1 = 3$, $n_2 = 5$

15-12. $\bar{\nu} = R_H\left(\dfrac{1}{5^2} - \dfrac{1}{8^2}\right)$

$$= 109{,}677.76\left(\frac{1}{25} - \frac{1}{64}\right)$$

$$= 2673.395\ \text{cm}^{-1}$$

15-13. As we go from any given main shell to the next higher main shell, we add a new subshell and each newly added subshell contains two more orbitals than the preceding subshell. The first (K) main shell contains one subshell, consisting of 1 orbital. The second (L) main shell contains two subshells, consisting of $1 + 3 = 4$ orbitals, and the third (M) main shell contains three subshells, consisting of $1 + 3 + 5 = 9$ orbitals. According to the Pauli exclusion principle no two electrons in the same orbital can have the same spin. Since there are only two possible spins $(+\frac{1}{2}$ and $-\frac{1}{2})$, this means that there can be no more than two electrons in any given orbital; and since the M shell contains 9 orbitals, this means there can be no more than $9 \times 2 = 18$ electrons.

15-14. (a) $\psi_1 = 0$ when $ax + bt = \pi n$, where $n = 0,\ \pm 1,\ \pm 2,\ldots$.

$$x = \frac{\pi n - bt}{a}$$

Each such nodal point moves along the x axis in the negative direction with velocity $dx/dt = -b/a$. Similarly for ψ_2, $dx/dt = +b/a$; this wave propagates along the x axis in the positive direction. The wavelength in each case is twice the distance between adjacent nodes

$$\lambda = 2(x_{n+1} - x_n) = \frac{2\pi}{a}$$

(See figure.)

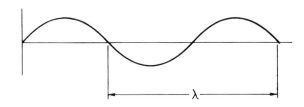

(b) $\psi_+ = \sin(ax + bt) + \sin(ax - bt)$

$\qquad = \sin ax \cos bt + \cos ax \sin bt$

$\qquad\quad + \sin ax \cos bt - \cos ax \sin bt$

$\qquad = 2 \sin ax \cos bt$

This function has a node wherever $x = \pi n/a$. These nodes do not move with time and the function therefore represents a standing wave. Similarly

$$\psi_- = 2 \cos ax \sin bt$$

There is a node wherever

$$x = \frac{\pi(n + \frac{1}{2})}{a}$$

15-15.   (a) $-\dfrac{h}{2\pi i}\dfrac{\partial \psi}{\partial t} = E\psi$

$\qquad -\dfrac{h}{2\pi i}\dfrac{\partial \ln \psi}{\partial t} = E$

$\qquad \ln \psi = \dfrac{-2\pi i E t}{h} + \text{constant}$

$\qquad \psi = \psi_0 e^{-2\pi i E t/h}$

(b) $|\psi|^2 = |\psi_0|^2 \, |\, e^{-2\pi i E t/h}\,|^2 = |\psi_0|^2$

since $| e^{i\phi} | = 1$ for any real ϕ. Thus $| \psi |^2$ does not depend on time. An eigenfunction of energy corresponds to a stable probability distribution. Chemistry is concerned largely with long-lived, stable molecules, in which the electron distribution remains constant in time. (Note that ψ_0, though constant with respect to time, may depend on x, y, and z.)

15-16. (a) $H = \dfrac{1}{2m} \left(\dfrac{h}{2\pi i} \dfrac{\partial}{\partial x} \right)^2 + V(x)$

$$= -\dfrac{h^2}{8\pi^2 m} \dfrac{\partial^2}{\partial x^2} + V(x)$$

(b) $-\dfrac{h^2}{8\pi^2 m} \dfrac{\partial^2 \psi}{\partial x^2} + V(x)\,\psi = -\dfrac{h}{2\pi i} \dfrac{\partial \psi}{\partial t}$

(c) $\psi = \psi_0(x)\, e^{-2\pi i E t / h}$

$$-\dfrac{h^2}{8\pi^2 m} \dfrac{d^2 \psi_0}{dx^2} e^{-2\pi i E t / h} + V(x)\,\psi_0 e^{-2\pi i E t / h}$$

$$= -\dfrac{h}{2\pi i}\,\psi_0 \left(-\dfrac{2\pi i E}{h} \right) e^{-2\pi i E t / h}$$

$$-\dfrac{h^2}{8\pi^2 m} \dfrac{d^2 \psi_0}{dx^2} + V(x)\,\psi_0 = E\psi_0$$

This is the familiar time-independent Schrödinger equation.

15-17. Let $V' = V + C$, or $V = V' - C$.

$$-\dfrac{h^2}{8\pi^2 m} \dfrac{d^2 \psi}{dx^2} + (V' - C)\,\psi = E\psi$$

$$-\dfrac{h^2}{8\pi^2 m} \dfrac{d^2 \psi}{dx^2} + V'\psi = (E + C)\,\psi$$

Thus the equation can equally well be written in terms of V' instead of V but each eigenvalue of energy is then increased by the same constant C. A list of energies is defined relative to a certain choice for the origin of V.

15-18. (a) For $0 \leqslant x \leqslant a$, the Schrödinger equation is

$$-\dfrac{h^2}{8\pi^2 m} \dfrac{d^2 \psi}{dx^2} = E\psi$$

This equation is satisfied by functions of the forms $\sin kx$, $\cos kx$, and e^{ikx}. For $x < 0$ or $> a$

$$-\frac{h^2}{8\pi^2 m}\frac{d^2\psi}{dx^2} + \infty\psi = E\psi$$

and $\psi = 0$ (unless $E = \infty$ or $d^2\psi/dx^2 = \infty$, both unacceptable). For continuity, then, $\psi = 0$ at $x = 0$ and $x = a$. Only $\sin kx$, not $\cos kx$ or e^{ikx}, vanishes at $x = 0$. To have $\psi = 0$ at $x = a$, we require $\psi(a) = \sin ka = 0$; $ka = \pi n$, $n = 0, \pm 1, \pm 2,....$ Then

$$\psi_n(x) = \sin\left(\frac{\pi n x}{a}\right)$$

However, $n = 0$ must be excluded because it makes $\psi = 0$ everywhere. To obtain E_n we substitute ψ_n into the Schrödinger equation:

$$\frac{d^2\psi_n}{dx^2} = -\left(\frac{\pi n}{a}\right)^2 \sin\left(\frac{\pi n x}{a}\right) = -\left(\frac{\pi n}{a}\right)^2 \psi_n$$

$$-\frac{h^2}{8\pi^2 m}\frac{d^2\psi_n}{dx^2} = \frac{1}{8m}\left(\frac{nh}{a}\right)^2 \psi_n = E_n\psi_n$$

$$E_n = \frac{1}{8m}\left(\frac{nh}{a}\right)^2$$

(b) $\dfrac{h}{2\pi i}\dfrac{d\psi_n}{dx} = \dfrac{h}{2\pi i}\dfrac{\pi n}{a}\cos\dfrac{\pi n x}{a} \neq \text{const} \times \psi_n$

ψ_n is not an eigenfunction of momentum. In the interval $0 \leqslant x \leqslant a$ the particle has only kinetic energy, which is related to the momentum p by $E = p^2/2m$, or $p = \pm\sqrt{2mE}$. For a given energy, then, two momenta corresponding to opposite directions of travel of the particle are possible.

15-19. (a) Inside:

$$-\frac{h^2}{8\pi^2 m}\frac{d^2\psi}{dx^2} = E\psi$$

Outside:

$$-\frac{h^2}{8\pi^2 m}\frac{d^2\psi}{dx^2} + \infty\psi = E\psi$$

Then

$$\psi = 0$$

outside.

(b) $\psi = A \sin(cx) + B \cos(cx)$

For continuity of inside and outside functions,

$$\psi\left(-\frac{a}{2}\right) = -A \sin \frac{ca}{2} + B \cos \frac{ca}{2} = 0$$

$$\psi\left(\frac{a}{2}\right) = A \sin \frac{ca}{2} + B \cos \frac{ca}{2} = 0$$

$$2A \sin \frac{ca}{2} = 0$$

Either $A = 0$ or $\sin(ca/2) = 0$

$$\frac{ca}{2} = n\pi, \qquad n = \pm 1, \pm 2, \ldots$$

$$c = \frac{2n\pi}{a}$$

$$\psi = A \sin \frac{2n\pi x}{a}$$

$$2B \cos \frac{ca}{2} = 0$$

Either $B = 0$ or $\cos ca/2 = 0$

$$\frac{ca}{2} = \left(n - \tfrac{1}{2}\right) \pi, \qquad n = 0, \pm 1, \pm 2, \ldots$$

$$c = \frac{(2n - 1) \pi}{a}$$

$$\psi = B \cos \left[\frac{(2n - 1) \pi x}{a}\right]$$

(c) $\dfrac{d^2\psi}{dx^2} = -c^2\psi$

$$\frac{-h^2}{8\pi^2 m} (-c^2\psi) = E\psi$$

$$E = \frac{h^2 c^2}{8\pi^2 m} = \frac{h^2 j^2}{8ma^2}, \qquad \begin{aligned} j &= 2n \text{ or } 2n - 1 \\ &= \pm 1, \pm 2, \ldots \end{aligned}$$

15-20.   (a) $E_1 = \dfrac{h^2}{8ma^2} = \dfrac{5.49 \times 10^{-54}}{ma^2}$

(b) $E_2 - E_1 = \dfrac{3h^2}{8ma^2} = 3E_1$

(c) $E = \frac{1}{2}kT = \frac{1}{2} \times 1.38 \times 10^{-16} \times 300 = 2.07 \times 10^{-14}$ erg

$$E \geqslant E_n = \frac{n^2h^2}{8ma^2} \qquad n \leqslant \frac{2a\sqrt{2mE}}{h}$$

The largest integer that satisfies this inequality is the number of levels below E.

	(a) E_1, erg	(b) $E_2 - E_1$, erg	(c) n
(i)	6.02×10^{-11}	1.81×10^{-10}	0
(ii)	1.64×10^{-30}	4.92×10^{-30}	1.12×10^8
(iii)	5.49×10^{-60}	1.65×10^{-59}	6.15×10^{22}

15-21. (a) $\dfrac{h}{2\pi i}\dfrac{d\psi}{dx} = p\psi$

$$\frac{h}{2\pi i}\frac{d\ln\psi}{dx} = p$$

$$\ln\psi = \frac{2\pi i px}{h} + \text{const}$$

$$\psi = Ce^{2\pi i px/h}, \quad C = \text{any constant}$$

(b) The functions obtained in Problem 15–18(a) are

$$\psi_n = \sin kx = \frac{e^{ikx} - e^{-ikx}}{2i}, \qquad k = \frac{\pi n}{a}$$

These functions are linear combinations of those in (a) if $ikx = \pm 2\pi i px/h$, or $k = \pm 2\pi p/h$, or

$$p = \frac{\pm kh}{2\pi} = \frac{\pm nh}{2a} = \pm\sqrt{2mE_n}$$

Thus ψ_n, which corresponds to a definite energy, is a linear combination of eigenfunctions of the momentum operator, each corresponding to one of the two possible momenta, $\pm\sqrt{2mE_n}$, consistent with the energy E_n. This combination is not an eigenfunction of momentum but corresponds to equal probabilities of observing momenta $\sqrt{2mE_n}$ and $-\sqrt{2mE_n}$, corresponding to opposite directions of travel of the waves.

15-22. $\lambda = \dfrac{h}{p}$

$$\psi(x) = Ce^{2\pi i px/h}$$

$$\psi(x + \lambda) = Ce^{2\pi i px/h} \cdot e^{2\pi i p\lambda/h}$$

$$= Ce^{2\pi i px/h} \cdot e^{2\pi i} = \psi(x)$$

since $e^{2\pi i} = 1$. Thus ψ repeats itself after the interval λ, which must be either the wavelength or an integer times the wavelength. However, there is no integer n (except $n = 1$) such that

$$\psi\left(x + \frac{\lambda}{n}\right) = \psi(x).$$

$$\psi\left(x + \frac{\lambda}{n}\right) = \psi(x)\, e^{2\pi i/n} = \psi(x)$$

only if $n = 1, \frac{1}{2}, \frac{1}{3}, \dots$. Therefore λ is the wavelength.

15-23.
$$\Delta p = 2\sqrt{2mE} = 2\sqrt{\frac{2m}{8m}} \cdot \frac{nh}{a} = \frac{nh}{a}$$

$$\Delta p \cdot \Delta x = \frac{nh}{a}\, a = nh \geqslant h$$

15-24.

$$\psi_n = \begin{cases} C_n \sin\left(\dfrac{\pi n x}{a}\right) & \text{(where } C_n \text{ is the normalization constant),} \\[2mm] & 0 \leqslant x \leqslant a \\[2mm] 0, & x < 0 \quad \text{or } x > a \end{cases}$$

$$\int_{-\infty}^{\infty} |\psi_n|^2\, dx = \int_0^a \left[C_n \sin\left(\frac{\pi n x}{a}\right)\right]^2 dx$$

$$= C_n^2 \left(\frac{a}{\pi n}\right)\left(\frac{1}{2}\pi n\right) = \frac{aC_n^2}{2} = 1$$

$$C_n = \sqrt{\frac{2}{a}} \text{ (the same for all } n \text{ in this special case)}$$

$$\psi_n = \begin{cases} \sqrt{\dfrac{2}{a}} \sin\left(\dfrac{\pi n x}{a}\right), & 0 \leqslant x \leqslant a \\[2mm] 0, & x < 0 \quad \text{or } x > a \end{cases}$$

15-25.   (a) $\psi = 0$ for $x < 0$. For continuity $\psi(0) = 0$. For $x \geqslant 0$ the Schrödinger equation is

$$-\frac{h^2}{8\pi^2 m}\frac{d^2\psi}{dx^2} = E\psi$$

As in Problem 15–18, $\psi = \sin kx$; then $\psi(0) = 0$, as required. Here, however, there is no a such that $\psi(a) = 0$; therefore any real number (except 0) is acceptable for k.

$$-\frac{h^2}{8\pi^2 m} \frac{d^2\psi}{dx^2} = \frac{h^2 k^2}{8\pi^2 m} \psi$$

$$E = \frac{h^2 k^2}{8\pi^2 m}$$

and E can be any positive number.

(b) $\dfrac{h}{2\pi i} \dfrac{d\psi}{dx} = \dfrac{hk}{2\pi i} \cos kx \neq \text{const} \times \psi$.

Therefore ψ is not an eigenfunction of momentum but is, as in Problem 15-18, a linear combination of eigenfunctions of momentum with eigenvalues $\sqrt{2mE}$ and $-\sqrt{2mE}$. A wave train corresponding to definite momentum will necessarily be reflected at the barrier at $x = 0$, giving rise to another wave train moving in the opposite direction.

15-26.   In a square potential well the levels become more widely spaced as the energy increases. The wider the well, the more closely spaced are the levels. Thus, in the present case, the levels will become more widely spaced as one goes up from the bottom, but the spacing will decrease at V_1 because the well widens. The spacing will again increase, but above V_2, where the well becomes infinitely wide, the levels will form a continuum (zero spacing).

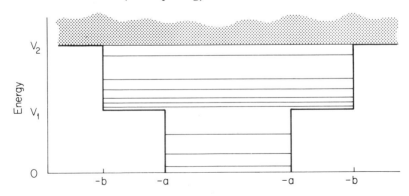

15-27.   Region 1:

$$\psi_1 = 0$$

Region 2:

$$-\frac{\hbar^2}{2m}\frac{d^2\psi_2}{dx^2} = E\psi_2 \qquad (\hbar = h/2\pi)$$

$$\psi_2 = A_2 \sin c_2 x + B_2 \cos c_2 x$$

$$c_2 = \frac{\sqrt{2mE}}{\hbar}$$

Region 3:

$$-\frac{\hbar^2}{2m}\frac{d^2\psi_3}{dx^2} = (E - V_0)\psi_3$$

$$\psi_3 = A_3\, e^{-c_3 x} + B_3 e^{c_3 x}$$

$$c_3 = \frac{\sqrt{2m(V_0 - E)}}{\hbar}$$

$$\psi_1(0) = \psi_2(0) \quad \therefore\ 0 = B_2$$

$$\psi_3(\infty) = 0 \quad \therefore\ B_3 = 0$$

$$\psi_2(a) = \psi_3(a) \quad \therefore\ A_2 \sin c_2 a = A_3\, e^{-c_3 a} \tag{1}$$

$$\psi_2'(a) = \psi_3'(a) \quad \therefore\ A_2 c_2 \cos c_2 a = -A_3 c_3\, e^{-c_3 a} \tag{2}$$

Dividing (2) by (1),

$$c_2 \cot c_2 a = -c_3$$

$$\frac{\sqrt{2mE}}{\hbar} \cot \frac{a\sqrt{2mE}}{\hbar} = -\frac{\sqrt{2m(V_0 - E)}}{\hbar}$$

$$\cot \frac{a\sqrt{2mE}}{\hbar} = -\sqrt{\frac{V_0}{E} - 1}$$

This transcendental equation for E has solutions corresponding to the energy levels. The levels are found to be lower and closer together than in the case $V_0 = \infty$ (Problem 15–18). There is only a finite number of bound states. Equation (1) now gives

$$\frac{A_3}{A_2} = e^{c_3 a} \sin c_2 a = \exp\left(\frac{a\sqrt{2m(V_0 - E)}}{\hbar}\right) \sin \frac{a\sqrt{2mE}}{\hbar}$$

Finally, A_2 or A_3 is determined by normalization:

$$\int_0^a |\psi_2|^2\, dx + \int_a^\infty |\psi_3|^2\, dx = 1$$

$$\int_0^a A_2^2 \sin^2 c_2 x\, dx + \int_a^\infty A_3^2 e^{-2c_3 x}\, dx = 1$$

$$A_2^2 \left(\frac{1}{2} a - \frac{\sin 2c_2 a}{4c_2}\right) + \frac{A_3^2}{2c_3} e^{-2c_3 a} = 1$$

$$A_2^2 \left(\frac{1}{2} a - \frac{\sin 2c_2 a}{4c_2} + \frac{\sin^2 c_2 a}{2c_3}\right) = 1$$

$$A_2 = \left(\frac{1}{2} a - \frac{\sin 2c_2 a}{4c_2} + \frac{\sin^2 c_2 a}{2c_3}\right)^{-1/2}$$

$$= \left\{\frac{a}{2} - \frac{\sin(2a\sqrt{2mE}/\hbar)}{(4\sqrt{2mE})/\hbar} + \frac{\sin^2[a\sqrt{2m(V_0 - E)}/\hbar]}{[2\sqrt{2m(V_0 - E)}]/\hbar}\right\}^{-1/2}$$

15-28. (a) $L \rightarrow \dfrac{h}{2\pi i} \dfrac{\partial}{\partial \phi}$

$$\frac{L^2}{2I} \rightarrow -\frac{h^2}{8\pi^2 I} \frac{\partial^2}{\partial \phi^2} = H$$

(b) $H\psi = E\psi$

$$-\frac{h^2}{8\pi^2 I} \frac{\partial^2 \psi}{\partial \phi^2} = E\psi$$

$$\psi = \sin k\phi \quad \text{or} \cos k\phi \quad \text{or } e^{ik\phi}$$

Substituting any of these functions gives

$$\frac{h^2 k^2}{8\pi^2 I} = E$$

Since the points $\phi = 0$, $\pm 2\pi$, $\pm 4\pi$,... are physically identical, ψ must be periodic with period 2π

$$\sin k\phi = \sin k(\phi + 2\pi) = \sin k\phi \cos 2\pi k + \cos k\phi \sin 2\pi k$$

$\cos 2\pi k = 1$ and $\sin 2\pi k = 0$. This requires that $k = 0$, ± 1, ± 2,... . The same result is obtained on taking $\psi = \cos k\phi$ or $e^{ik\phi}$.

15-29.

(a) $\dfrac{d\psi_1}{dx} = -2axe^{-ax^2}$

$\dfrac{d^2\psi_1}{dx^2} = (4a^2x^2 - 2a)\,e^{-ax^2}$

$\left[-\dfrac{h^2}{8\pi^2 m}(4a^2x^2 - 2a) + \dfrac{1}{2}kx^2\right]e^{-ax^2} = Ee^{-ax^2}$

The terms on the left containing x^2 must add to 0:

$-\dfrac{h^2a^2x^2}{2\pi^2 m} + \dfrac{1}{2}kx^2 = 0$

$a = \dfrac{\pi\sqrt{km}}{h}$

$E = \dfrac{2ah^2}{8\pi^2 m} = \dfrac{h}{4\pi}\sqrt{\dfrac{k}{m}} = \dfrac{1}{2}h\nu$

(b) $\dfrac{d\psi_2}{dx} = (-2bx^2 + 1)\,e^{-bx^2}$

$\dfrac{d^2\psi_2}{dx^2} = (4b^2x^3 - 6bx)\,e^{-bx^2}$

$\left[-\dfrac{h^2}{8\pi^2 m}(4b^2x^3 - 6bx) + \dfrac{1}{2}kx^3\right]e^{-bx^2} = Exe^{-bx^2}$

The terms containing x^3 must add to 0:

$-\dfrac{h^2b^2x^3}{2\pi^2 m} + \dfrac{1}{2}kx^3 = 0$

$b = \dfrac{\pi\sqrt{km}}{h}$ (the same as a)

$E = \dfrac{6bh^2}{8\pi^2 m} = \dfrac{3h}{4\pi}\sqrt{\dfrac{k}{m}} = \dfrac{3}{2}h\nu$

15-30. (a) $\dfrac{\psi_1(\frac{1}{2}\Delta x)}{\psi_1(0)} = \dfrac{e^{-a((1/2)\Delta x)^2}}{1} = e^{-(1/4)a(\Delta x)^2} = 0.10$

$-\frac{1}{4}a(\Delta x)^2 \log e = -1$

$(\Delta x)^2 = \dfrac{4}{a\log e}$

$a = \dfrac{4\pi^2 mE}{h^2}$

$$(\Delta x)^2 = \frac{4h^2}{4\pi^2 mE \log e}$$

$$\Delta x = \frac{h}{\pi \sqrt{mE \log e}}$$

(b) $x = A \sin 2\pi \nu t$

$$p = \frac{m \, dx}{dt} = 2\pi \nu mA \cos 2\pi \nu t$$

$$p_{max} = \pm 2\pi \nu mA$$

(corresponding to $\cos 2\pi \nu t = \pm 1$, $x = 0$)

$$E = \frac{p^2}{2m} + \frac{1}{2} kx^2 = \frac{p_{max}^2}{2m} + 0$$

$$p_{max} = \pm \sqrt{2mE}$$

$$\Delta p \, \Delta x = \frac{2\sqrt{2mE}\, h}{\pi \sqrt{mE \log e}} = \frac{2h}{\pi} \sqrt{\frac{2}{\log e}} = 1.37h$$

The uncertainty principle requires that $\Delta p \, \Delta x \gtrsim h$, the exact value depending on just how "uncertainty" is defined.

15-31.

Any vibrations that are accompanied by changes in the dipole moment of the molecule will be active in the IR, namely: ν_3, ν_{2a}, and ν_{2b}. Note that ν_{2a} and ν_{2b} have the same frequency and are therefore said to be degenerate.

15-32.   (a) $\frac{1}{\lambda} = 2989 \text{ cm}^{-1}$

$$\nu = \frac{c}{\lambda} = 2.998 \times 10^{10} \text{ cm sec}^{-1} \times 2989 \text{ cm}^{-1}$$
$$= 8.96 \times 10^{13} \text{ sec}^{-1}$$

(b) $\mu = \frac{m_1 m_2}{m_1 + m_2} = \frac{1.008 \times 34.97}{35.98} = 0.981 \text{ amu}$

$$0.981 \text{ amu} \times \frac{1 \text{ g}}{6.023 \times 10^{23} \text{ amu}} = 1.63 \times 10^{-24} \text{ g}$$

(c) $\nu = \dfrac{1}{2\pi} \sqrt{\dfrac{k}{\mu}}$

$k = 4\pi^2\nu^2\mu = 4\pi^2 \times (8.96 \times 10^{13})^2 \text{ sec}^{-2}$

$\times 1.63 \times 10^{-24} \text{ g} \times \dfrac{1 \text{ cm}}{10^8 \text{ Å}} \times \dfrac{1 \text{ dyne}}{1 \text{ g cm sec}^-}$

$= 5.17 \times 10^{-3} \text{ dyne/Å}$

15-33.

(a) $\dfrac{dV}{dr} = 2A(1 - e^{-B(r-r_0)}) \, Be^{-B(r-r_0)} = 0$

when $r = r_0$ and when $r = \infty$.

$\dfrac{d^2V}{dr^2} = 2AB[(1 - e^{-B(r-r_0)})(-B) + Be^{-B(r-r_0)}]$

$\times e^{-B(r-r_0)} = 2AB^2 > 0$

when $r = r_0$. Therefore V has a minimum when $r = r_0$. More simply $V(r_0) = 0$ and $V > 0$ when $r \neq r_0$; therefore $V(r_0)$ is a minimum.

(b) $V(r_0) = 0, \quad V(\infty) = A$

$D = V(\infty) - V(r_0) = A$

(c) Near $r = r_0$, $V = \tfrac{1}{2}k(r - r_0)^2$

$e^{-B(r-r_0)} = 1 - B(r - r_0) + \cdots$

$V \approx A[1 - 1 + B(r - r_0) - \tfrac{1}{2}B^2(r - r_0)^2]^2$

$\approx AB^2(r - r_0)^2$

(higher powers of $r - r_0$ neglected)

$k = 2AB^2$

$\nu = \dfrac{1}{2\pi} \left(\dfrac{k}{\mu}\right)^{1/2} = \dfrac{B}{2\pi} \left(\dfrac{2A}{\mu}\right)^{1/2}$

More simply

$k = \left(\dfrac{\partial^2 V}{\partial r^2}\right)_{r=r_0} = 2AB^2$

(d) $D_{\text{corr}} = D - \dfrac{1}{2} h\nu = A - \dfrac{Bh}{4\pi} \left(\dfrac{2A}{\mu}\right)^{1/2}$

15-34.   See figure.

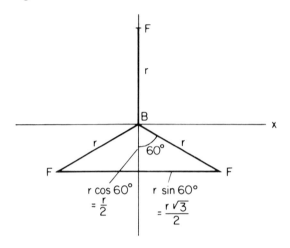

$$I_x = m_F r^2 + 2m_F \left(\frac{r}{2}\right)^2 = \frac{3}{2} m_F r^2$$

$$I_y = 2m_F \left(\frac{r\sqrt{3}}{2}\right)^2 = \frac{3}{2} m_F r^2 = I_x$$

15-35.   (a) The $x^2 - y^2$ orbital is closest to the negative charges and therefore the electrons in this orbital should have the highest energy. The xy orbital is next closest, the yz and zx orbitals somewhat farther, and the $3z^2 - r^2$ orbital the farthest. See figure.

$$\underline{\quad x^2-y^2 \quad}$$

$$\underline{\quad xy \quad}$$

$$\underline{\quad yz \quad} \qquad \underline{\quad zx \quad} \qquad\qquad \underline{\quad xy \quad} \quad \underline{\quad yz \quad} \quad \underline{\quad zx \quad}$$

$$\underline{\quad 3z^2-r^2 \quad} \qquad\qquad\qquad \underline{\quad 3z^2-r^2 \quad} \quad \underline{\quad x^2-y^2 \quad}$$

(a)   (b)

(b) The tetrahedral arrangement treats all axes alike; $3z^2 - r^2$ and $x^2 - y^2$ are therefore equal in energy. (There are three equivalent but linearly dependent orbitals, $x^2 - y^2$, $z^2 - x^2$, and $z^2 - y^2$, any two of which may be combined to obtain a linearly independent set. The usual choice is

$$(z^2 - x^2) + (z^2 - y^2) = 2z^2 - x^2 - y^2 = 3z^2 - r^2.)$$

These two orbitals, which point toward the face centers of the cube, are somewhat farther from the negative -charges than are the other three, which point toward the edge centers of the cube. See figure.

15-36.   (a) $D_{1,2} = \dfrac{1}{\sqrt{2}} (\psi_{2s} \pm \psi_{2p_z})$

$$= \frac{1}{8\sqrt{\pi}} a_0^{-3/2} \left[2 + \frac{r}{a_0} (-1 \pm \cos \theta) \right] e^{-r/2a_0}$$

(b) If $z = \pm 3a_0$, $x = y = 0$, then $r = 3a_0$, $\theta = 0$ or π, $\cos \theta = \pm 1$.

$$D_1 = \frac{1}{8\sqrt{\pi}} a_0^{-3/2} \left[2 + \frac{3a_0}{a_0} (-1 \pm 1) \right] e^{-3a_0/2a_0}$$

$$= \frac{1}{8\sqrt{\pi}} a_0^{-3/2} (-1 \pm 3) e^{-3/2}$$

$$| D_1 |^2 = \frac{a_0^{-3} e^{-3}}{64\pi} (-1 \pm 3)^2$$

$$| D_1(\theta = \pi)|^2 = \frac{a_0^{-3} e^{-3}}{4\pi}$$

$$| D_1(\theta = 0)|^2 = \frac{a_0^{-3} e^{-3}}{16\pi}$$

(c) $\psi_{2s}(r = 3a_0) = \dfrac{-a_0^{-3/2}}{4\sqrt{2\pi}} e^{-3/2}$

$$| \psi_{2s} |^2 = \frac{a_0^{-3} e^{-3}}{32\pi}$$

$$\psi_{2p_z}(r = 3a_0, \ \theta = 0 \text{ or } \pi) = \frac{\pm 3a_0^{-3/2} e^{-3/2}}{4\sqrt{2\pi}}$$

$$| \psi_{2p_z} |^2 = \frac{9a_0^{-3} e^{-3}}{32\pi}$$

(d) For $\theta = \pi$, $|D_1|^2$ is 8 times $|\psi_{2s}|^2$, and about the same as $|\psi_{2p_z}|^2$. D_1 would thus be better suited than ψ_{2s} to forming a covalent bond, with high internuclear electron density, with another atom approaching along the negative z axis. For $\theta = 0$, however, $|D_1|^2$ is much smaller than $|\psi_{2p_z}|^2$ and is generally small along the positive z axis. D_1 would thus be unsuitable for forming a covalent bond with an atom approaching along the positive z axis. The corresponding conclusions, with positive and negative interchanged, apply to D_2. The results, of course, do not apply quantitatively to atoms other than hydrogen but they are qualitatively correct.

15-37. $P = \int_0^{a_0} \int_0^{\pi} \int_0^{2\pi} \left| \psi_{2p_z} \right|^2 r^2 \sin\theta\, dr\, d\theta\, d\phi$

$$= \frac{1}{32\pi}\, a_0^{-5} \int_0^{a_0} (re^{-r/2a_0})^2\, r^2\, dr \int_0^{\pi} \cos^2\theta \sin\theta\, d\theta \cdot 2\pi$$

$$= \frac{1}{16}\, a_0^{-5} \cdot \frac{2}{3}\, e^{-r/a_0}(-a_0 r^4 - 4a_0^2 r^3 - 12a_0^3 r^2 - 24a_0^4 r - 24a_0^5\, |_0^{a_0}$$

$$= \frac{1}{24}\, (-65e^{-1} + 24) = 0.00366$$

15-38.   (a), (b). See figures.

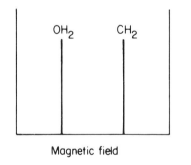

Magnetic field

(a)

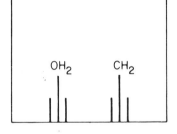

(b)

(c) In (b) a given proton on C may have any one of three different magnetic environments, corresponding to the four possible spin states of the OH_2 protons: ↑↑, ↑↓, ↓↑, ↓↓. (The second and third are equivalent.) A selection rule precludes transitions between states distinguished by the spin of the other proton on C. Thus there are three lines for the CH_2

protons with relative intensities 1 : 2 : 1. Similarly there are three lines for the OH_2 protons as a result of splitting by the CH_2 protons. In (a) rapid exchange of OH_2 protons between different molecules averages out their magnetic environment. In one period of the radio-frequency radiation, each proton has been in many different molecules, and each CH_2 proton has had neighbors on O in all possible spin states. There is only one pair of energy levels for the CH_2 protons and one pair for the OH_2 protons, corresponding to this average state but with alignment parallel or antiparallel to the applied field.

CHAPTER 16

Statistical

thermodynamics

SECTION 16-1

16-I-1.

	Degrees of freedom	Heat capacity contribution
Translation	3	$\frac{3}{2}R$
Rotation	3	$\frac{3}{2}R$
Vibration	$3 \times 4 - 6 = 6$	$6R$
		$9R = 18$ cal mole^{-1} °K^{-1}

16-I-2. (a)

	He	CF_4	C_2F_2
Translation	$\frac{3}{2}R$	$\frac{3}{2}R$	$\frac{3}{2}R$
Rotation	0	$\frac{3}{2}R$	R
Vibration	0	$9R$	$7R$
$\bar{C}_v$	$\frac{3}{2}R$	$12R$	$\frac{19}{2}R$

(b) (i) Equal. Translational energy levels are so close together that translation is classically excited at any temperature at which gases exist.

(ii), (iii) Less. Vibrational energy levels are far enough apart so that each vibrational mode contributes less than R at room temperature. Stretching modes, with high frequency, usually contribute 0; a bending mode contributes between 0 and R.

16-I-3. A gas molecule has 3 translational and 2 or 3 rotational degrees of freedom, each of which contributes $\frac{1}{2}R$ to the molar heat capacity at or above (or even considerably below) room temperature. In a solid these degrees of freedom become lattice vibrations, each of which contributes R to the heat capacity at any temperature such that $kT > h\nu$, where ν is the frequency of the vibration. Since the frequency of the lattice vibrations is low, this condition is well satisfied at or above room temperature. We thus expect the molar heat capacity of a solid to exceed that of a gas by approximately $5/2R$ if the molecules are linear, or $3R$ if they are nonlinear. Similar considerations apply to a liquid. The additional heat capacity may be greater if there are strong intermolecular forces, especially hydrogen bonds, which break with absorption of heat as the temperature increases.

16-I-4. $K_c = \dfrac{q_{Na^+}q_{Cl^-}}{q_{NaCl}} e^{-\Delta\epsilon_0/kT},$

where the q's are partition functions in terms of energies measured from the respective ground states. We are told to assume that these functions are the same for the gas and solution reactions.

$\Delta\epsilon_0(g) = 8.63 \times 10^{-12}$ erg molecule^{-1}

$\Delta\epsilon_0(aq) = \dfrac{8.63 \times 10^{-12}}{80}$ erg molecule^{-1}

$\dfrac{K_c(aq)}{K_c(g)} = \exp\left[\dfrac{-[\Delta\epsilon_0(aq) - \Delta\epsilon_0(g)]}{kT}\right]$

$= \exp\left[\dfrac{8.63 \times 10^{-12}(1 - 1/80)}{1.38 \times 10^{-16} \times 300}\right]$

$= e^{206} = 10^{89}$

SECTION 16-II

16-II-1. The molecule has in all $2n$ degrees of freedom (2 for each atom). There are 2 translational and 1 rotational degrees of freedom and therefore $2n - 3$ vibrational degrees of freedom, each of which corresponds to a mode of vibration.

The argument is unaffected if the molecule is linear. In three dimensions the distinction is important because one rotational degree of freedom becomes vibrational when the molecule becomes linear. In the present case, however, this degree of freedom would correspond to an out-of-plane motion and is therefore absent.

16-II-2. (a) $\dfrac{dN}{dA} = Ce^{-ar^2/kT}$

(b) $dA = 2\pi r\, dr$

$dN = 2\pi C e^{-ar^2/kT} r\, dr$

(c) $\overline{u(r)} = \overline{ar^2} = \dfrac{\int_0^\infty ar^2\, e^{-ar^2/kT} r\, dr}{\int_0^\infty e^{-ar^2/kT} r\, dr} = kT$

16-II-3. (a) The probability of finding a molecule with v_x between v_x and $v_x + dv_x$ and simultaneously with v_y between v_y and $v_y + dv_y$ is the product of the separate probabilities:

$$\dfrac{dN_{v_x v_y}}{N_{\text{total}}} = \left(\dfrac{dN_{v_x}}{N_{\text{total}}}\right)\left(\dfrac{dN_{v_y}}{N_{\text{total}}}\right)$$

$$= A^2 \exp\left[-m\left(\dfrac{v_x^2 + v_y^2}{2kT}\right)\right] dv_x\, dv_y$$

Transforming to polar coordinates in velocity space,

$$\dfrac{dN_{v_x v_y}}{N_{\text{total}}} = A^2 e^{-mv^2/2kT} v\, dv\, d\phi$$

To obtain the number having speeds between v and $v + dv$, we "add up" (integrate) the molecules at all angles ϕ

$$\dfrac{dN_v}{N_{\text{total}}} = \int_0^{2\pi} A^2 e^{-mv^2/2kT} v\, dv\, d\phi$$

$$= 2\pi A^2 e^{-mv^2/2kT} v\, dv$$

This quantity must yield 1 on integration over all speeds:

$$\int_{v=0}^{\infty} \frac{dN_v}{N_{\text{total}}} = 2\pi A^2 \int_0^{\infty} e^{-mv^2/2kT} v \, dv$$

$$= 2\pi A^2 \frac{kT}{m} = 1, \quad A^2 = \frac{m}{2\pi kT}$$

$$\frac{dN_v}{N_{\text{total}}} = \frac{m}{kT} e^{-mv^2/2kT} v \, dv$$

(b) $\quad \bar{v} = \int_{v=0}^{\infty} \frac{v \, dN_v}{N_{\text{total}}} = \frac{m}{kT} \int_0^{\infty} e^{-mv^2/2kT} v^2 \, dv = \left(\frac{\pi kT}{2m}\right)^{1/2}$

16-II-4. (a) $\quad \bar{E} = -\frac{d \ln q}{d\beta} = \frac{-\epsilon}{2 + \beta\epsilon}$

(b) $\quad \bar{S} = k(\ln Q + \beta\bar{E}) = k\left[\ln(2 + \beta\epsilon) - \frac{\beta\epsilon}{2 + \beta\epsilon}\right]$

(c) $\quad \dfrac{\partial \bar{E}}{\partial T} = \dfrac{\partial \bar{E}}{\partial \beta} \dfrac{d\beta}{dT} = -k\beta^2 \dfrac{\partial \bar{E}}{\partial \beta} = k\left(\dfrac{\beta\epsilon}{2 + \beta\epsilon}\right)^2$

16-II-5. (a) $\quad Q_{el} = 3 + e^{-\epsilon/kT}$.

We assume that, for every level i with $\epsilon_i > \epsilon$, $g_i e^{-\epsilon_i/kT} \ll e^{-\epsilon/kT}$

(b) $\quad \dfrac{N_S}{N_T} = \dfrac{e^{-\epsilon/kT}}{3} = \dfrac{1}{3} \exp\left(\dfrac{-1.38 \times 10^{-14}}{1.38 \times 10^{-16} \times 100}\right)$

$$= e^{-1}/3 = 0.123$$

We assume that the same rotational and vibrational levels are available to a molecule whether it is in the singlet or in the triplet state; that is, that its moments of inertia and force constants are the same. If this assumption is not valid, we must write

$$\frac{N_S}{N_T} = \frac{e^{-\epsilon/kT} Q_{rv(T)}}{3 Q_{rv(S)}}$$

where each Q_{rv} is the partition function for rotation and vibration of the molecule in one of the two electronic states. The simplifying assumption above makes $Q_{rv(S)} = Q_{rv(T)}$. Indeed it is only in this case that an electronic factor in the partition function can be written separately as we wrote it in (a).

16-II-6. (a) $q_A = \sum_{i \text{ in } A} g_i e^{-\epsilon_i/kT}$

$$q_B = \sum_{j \text{ in } B} g_j e^{-\epsilon_j/kT}$$

$$\frac{N_A}{N} = \frac{q_A}{q_A + q_B}, \quad \frac{N_B}{N} = \frac{q_B}{q_A + q_B}$$

$$\bar{\epsilon}_A = kT^2 \frac{d \ln q_A}{dT}$$

$$\bar{\epsilon}_B = kT^2 \frac{d \ln q_B}{dT}$$

(b) $E = N_A \bar{\epsilon}_A + N_B \bar{\epsilon}_B$

(c) $C_V = N_A \dfrac{d\bar{\epsilon}_A}{dT} + N_B \dfrac{d\bar{\epsilon}_B}{dT} + \bar{\epsilon}_A \dfrac{dN_A}{dT} + \bar{\epsilon}_B \dfrac{dN_B}{dT}$

If transitions were impossible, the last two terms would be absent.

(d) $\bar{C}_{VA} = \dfrac{d\bar{\epsilon}_A}{dT} \qquad \bar{C}_{VB} = \dfrac{d\bar{\epsilon}_B}{dT}$

(The bar indicates average per molecule.)

$$C_V = N_A \bar{C}_{VA} + N_B \bar{C}_{VB}$$
$$+ \frac{(q_B(dq_A/dT) - q_A(dq_B/dT))\, N(\bar{\epsilon}_A - \bar{\epsilon}_B)}{(q_A + q_B)^2}$$

$$\frac{dq_A}{dT} = \frac{q_A\, d \ln q_A}{dT} = \frac{q_A \bar{\epsilon}_A}{kT^2}$$

$$\frac{dq_B}{dT} = \frac{q_B \bar{\epsilon}_B}{kT^2}$$

$$C_V = N_A \bar{C}_{VA} + N_B \bar{C}_{VB} + \frac{q_A q_B(\bar{\epsilon}_A - \bar{\epsilon}_B)}{(q_A + q_B)^2\, kT^2} \cdot N(\bar{\epsilon}_A - \bar{\epsilon}_B)$$

$$= N_A \bar{C}_{VA} + N_B \bar{C}_{VB} + \frac{N_A N_B(\bar{\epsilon}_A - \bar{\epsilon}_B)^2}{NkT^2}$$

16-II-7. (a)

		Vibra- tional degrees of freedom	Heat capacity contributions			
			Trans- lational	Rota- tional	Vibra- tional	Total
(i)	He	0	$\frac{3}{2}R$	0	0	$\frac{3}{2}R$
(ii)	CF_4	9	$\frac{3}{2}R$	$\frac{3}{2}R$	9R	12R
(iii)	C_2F_2	7	$\frac{3}{2}R$	R	7R	$\frac{19}{2}R$

(b) For He the predicted value should be correct; only translational motion is involved and the translational energy levels are close enough together so that classical mechanics is applicable. The same applies to the translational and rotational motions of the other two gases but not to their vibrations. The vibrational energy levels (at least for stretching motions) are so far apart that at room temperature few molecules are excited to higher levels by a rise in temperature and these vibrations therefore contribute less to the heat capacity than classical mechanics would predict.

(c) The predictions in (a) and (b) assume that the contribution of electronic motions to the heat capacity can be neglected. This is correct as long as the spacing ΔE between the lowest and next-to-lowest electronic levels is large in comparison with kT

$$kT \ll \Delta E$$

$$T \ll \frac{\Delta E}{k} = \frac{3.13 \times 10^{-11} \text{ erg}}{1.38 \times 10^{-16} \text{ erg deg}^{-1}} = 2.27 \times 10^{5}{}^{\circ}\text{K}$$

If this condition is not satisfied, $C_V > \frac{3}{2}R$. Roughly we may say that $C_V = \frac{3}{2}R$ as long as T is below $10^{4}{}^{\circ}\text{K}$.

16-II-8. (a) There are $9 - 6 = 3$ vibrational degrees of freedom.

$$\bar{C}_V = (\tfrac{3}{2} + \tfrac{3}{2} + 3)\, R = 6R$$

(b) The result of (a) is approximately applicable when $h\nu/kT < 1$, or $T > h\nu/k$. If this condition is satisfied for the mode of highest frequency ($\nu = 4.08 \times 10^{13} \text{ sec}^{-1}$), it is necessarily satisfied for the others.

$$\frac{h\nu}{k} = \frac{6.625 \times 10^{-27} \times 4.08 \times 10^{13}}{1.381 \times 10^{-16}}$$

$$= 1.96 \times 10^{3}\ {}^{\circ}\text{K}$$

When $T \gg 2 \times 10^{3}{}^{\circ}\text{K}$, $\bar{C}_V$ is given approximately by (a).

16-II-9. (a) The contribution of each mode of vibration to the heat capacity depends on the ratio of the spacing ($h\nu$) between energy levels to kT:

$$\frac{h\nu}{kT} = 4.80 \times 10^{-11}\, \frac{\nu}{T}$$

with ν in sec^{-1} and T in $^{\circ}\text{K}$.

Mode:		(i)	(ii)	(iii)
T, °K	ν	1.00×10^{13}	9.00×10^{13}	1.00×10^{14} sec^{-1}
100	$\dfrac{h\nu}{kT}$	4.80	43.2	48.0
1000		0.480	4.32	4.80

If $h\nu/kT < 1$, the mode contributes approximately R to $\bar{C}_V$; if $h\nu/kT \gg 1$, the mode contributes practically 0. The second condition is satisfied for all modes at 100°K and at this temperature we expect only translational and rotational contributions: $\bar{C}_V = (\frac{3}{2} + \frac{3}{2}) R = 3R$. At 1000°K modes (ii) and (iii) should still contribute very little but mode (i) has $h\nu/kT < 1$, and $\bar{C}_V \approx (\frac{3}{2} + \frac{3}{2} + 1) = 4R$.

(b) There are three modes of vibration. At high temperatures each contributes R to $\bar{C}_V$:

$$\bar{C}_V = (\tfrac{3}{2} + \tfrac{3}{2} + 3) R = 6R$$

(c) If $h\nu/kT < 1$ for every mode, the result in (b) should be correct. This condition is most difficult to satisfy with the mode (iii) of highest frequency. When $h\nu/kT = 1$ for this mode,

$$T = h\nu/k = 4.80 \times 10^{-11} \times 1.00 \times 10^{14} = 4800°\text{K}$$

16-II-10. A mode of vibration contributes approximately R to the heat capacity if $h\nu/kT < 1$ and approximately 0 if $h\nu/kT \gg 1$.

Mode		i		ii		iii	
T, °K	ν	4.0	$\times 10^{12}$	5.0	$\times 10^{12}$	7.0	$\times 10^{13}$
500	$\dfrac{h\nu}{kT}$	(0.38		0.48		6.7	
5000		(0.038		0.048		0.67	
500	Contri-bution	R		R		0	
5000	to $\bar{C}_V$	R		R		R	

At 500°K, $\bar{C}_V = (\frac{3}{2} + \frac{3}{2} + 2) R = 5R$

At 5000°K, $\bar{C}_V = (\frac{3}{2} + \frac{3}{2} + 3) R = 6R$

16-II-11. (a) There are three translational and two rotational degrees of freedom, each of which contributes $\frac{1}{2}R$ to the heat capacity:

$$\bar{C}_V = \left(\frac{3}{2} + \frac{2}{2} + 7\right) R = \frac{19}{2} R = 18.88 \text{ cal } °\text{K}^{-1} \text{ mole}^{-1}$$

(b) This assumption implies that each bending contributes R to the heat capacity and each stretching contributes 0:

$$\bar{C}_V = \left(\frac{5}{2} + 4\right) R = \frac{13}{2} R = 12.92 \text{ cal } °\text{K}^{-1} \text{ mole}^{-1}$$

(c) In this case the vibrational contribution is 0:

$$\bar{C}_V = \frac{5}{2} R = 4.97 \text{ cal } °\text{K}^{-1} \text{ mole}^{-1}$$

(d) The experimental value is intermediate between the results of (b) and (c). It thus appears that the stretching modes are frozen out and that the bending modes are excited to the extent of contributing $8.0 - 4.97 = 3.0 \text{ cal } °\text{K}^{-1} \text{ mole}^{-1}$ to $\bar{C}_V$.

16-II-12. (a) The classical theory assumes that the spacing between energy levels is 0. In this case the Boltzmann equipartition principle is applicable: the average energy of each oscillator (vibration is the only kind of motion in a solid) is kT, or NkT for N oscillators, and the heat capacity is Nk independent of temperature. The Einstein and Debye theories both take account of the quantization of energy: If the frequency of an oscillator is v, the spacing between energy levels is hv. When $kT \ll hv$, the oscillators are "frozen out": Practically all the oscillators with this frequency are in their ground state, they remain there after a small increase in temperature, and thus they absorb practically no energy and contribute nothing to C_V. In the limit $T = 0$, $C_V = 0$ for all modes.

(b) The Einstein theory assumes that all oscillators have the same frequency v_0. When $kT \ll hv_0$, C_V is practically 0. The Debye theory assumes that there are oscillators with all frequencies from 0 to a maximum v_D. There is no temperature at which $kT \ll hv$ for all frequencies. As the temperature falls fewer and fewer of the oscillators contribute appreciably to C_V but the presence of the low-frequency oscillators results in a heat capacity near $T = 0$ considerably higher than that predicted by the Einstein theory.

SECTION 16-III

16-III-1. (a) For a single particle with velocity (v_x, v_y): Change in momentum per collision with edge parallel to y axis $= \Delta p_x = -2mv_x$. Time between collisions with edge $= \Delta t = 2L/v_x$. Average force exerted by edge on particle $= \Delta p_x/\Delta t = -mv_x^2/L$. Average force exerted by particle on edge $= mv_x^2/L$.

$$v^2 = v_x^2 + v_y^2$$

Averaging over all particles,

$$\overline{v_x^2} = \overline{v_y^2} = \tfrac{1}{2}\,\overline{v^2}$$

$$\bar{\epsilon} = \tfrac{1}{2}\,m\overline{v^2}$$

Force exerted by all N particles on edge $=$

$$\frac{Nm\overline{v_x^2}}{L} = \frac{Nm\overline{v^2}}{2L} = \frac{N\bar{\epsilon}}{L}$$

Force per unit length $= N\bar{\epsilon}/L^2$.

(b) The Boltzmann equipartition principle predicts that the average kinetic energy for each degree of freedom is $\tfrac{1}{2}kT$. Here there are two degrees of freedom and $\bar{\epsilon} = kT$.

(c) $\quad \bar{v} = \dfrac{\int_0^\infty v e^{-(1/2)mv^2/kT} v\,dv}{\int_0^\infty e^{-(1/2)mv^2/kT} v\,dv}$

$\qquad = \dfrac{\sqrt{\pi}}{4(m/2kT)^{3/2}} \cdot \dfrac{m}{kT} = \left(\dfrac{\pi kT}{2m}\right)^{1/2}$

16-III-2. (a) $\qquad f(v) = Ce^{-mv^2/2kT}v$

$$\int_0^\infty f(v)\,dv = C\int_0^\infty e^{-mv^2/2kT}v\,dv = C\,\frac{kT}{m} = 1, \quad C = \frac{m}{kT}$$

$$f(v) = \frac{m}{kT}\,e^{-mv^2/2kT}v\,dv$$

(b) $\quad \bar{v} = \dfrac{m}{kT}\displaystyle\int_0^\infty e^{-mv^2/2kT}v^2\,dv = \dfrac{m}{kT} \cdot \dfrac{\sqrt{\pi}}{4}\left(\dfrac{2kT}{m}\right)^{3/2}$

$\qquad = \left(\dfrac{\pi kT}{2m}\right)^{1/2}$

$$\overline{v^2} = \frac{m}{kT} \int_0^\infty e^{-mv^2/2kT} v^3 \, dv = \frac{m}{kT} \cdot \frac{1}{2} \left(\frac{2kT}{m}\right)^2 = \frac{2kT}{m}$$

$$\overline{v^3} = \frac{m}{kT} \int_0^\infty e^{-mv^2/2kT} v^4 \, dv = \frac{m}{kT} \cdot \frac{3\sqrt{\pi}}{8} \left(\frac{2kT}{m}\right)^{5/2}$$

$$= 3\sqrt{\frac{\pi}{2}} \left(\frac{kT}{m}\right)^{3/2}$$

(c) Consider those molecules with speeds between v and $v + dv$ and with the velocity vector making an angle between θ and $\theta + d\theta$ with the unit line segment AB. (See figure.) These molecules will collide with the segment during the next second if they are now in the parallelogram $ABCD$, where $\overline{AD} = v$. The area of this parallelogram is $(\overline{AB})(\overline{AD}) \sin\theta = v \sin\theta$. The number of molecules in this parallelogram is $Nv \sin\theta$; the number in the given ranges of v and θ is

$$Nv \sin\theta \cdot \frac{m}{kT} e^{-mv^2/2kT} v \, dv \, \frac{d\theta}{2\pi} = \frac{Nm \sin\theta \, d\theta \, e^{-mv^2/2kT} v^2 \, dv}{2\pi kT}$$

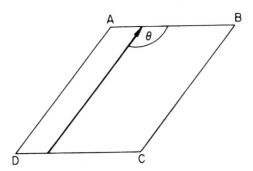

and this gives the number of collisions by molecules in these infinitesimal ranges of v and θ. The total number of collisions is obtained by integrating this expression from $\theta = 0$ to π (molecules with $\theta > \pi$ are going the wrong way) and from $v = 0$ to ∞:

$$Z = \frac{Nm}{2\pi kT} \int_0^\pi \sin\theta \, d\theta \int_0^\infty e^{-mv^2/2kT} v^2 \, dv$$

$$= N \left(\frac{kT}{2\pi m}\right)^{1/2}$$

(d) When a molecule collides with the partition, it suffers a change of momentum equal to $2mv \sin \theta$. The force exerted on the molecules by the partition and on the partition by the molecules is given by the change in momentum per unit time. The calculation is essentially the same as in (c) except that instead of merely counting collisions per unit time, we must "add up" the momentum changes per unit time. This means that we must include a factor $2mv \sin \theta$ before integration. Since the segment is of unit length, we obtain the pressure:

$$P = \frac{Nm}{2\pi kT} \cdot 2m \int_0^\pi \sin^2 \theta \, d\theta \int_0^\infty e^{-mv^2/2kT} v^3 \, dv$$

$$= NkT$$

The resemblance to the ideal gas law is obvious. (Compare 16-III-1(a).)

(e) A particle that "collides" with the gap will escape. We first calculate the total kinetic energy of colliding particles per unit length per unit time. Again the calculation is similar to that of (c) but with a factor $\frac{1}{2}mv^2$,

$$E = \frac{Nm}{2\pi kT} \cdot \tfrac{1}{2}m \int_0^\pi \sin \theta \, d\theta \int_0^\infty e^{-mv^2/2kT} v^4 \, dv$$

$$= \frac{3N}{\sqrt{\pi m}} \left(\frac{kT}{2} \right)^{3/2}$$

We now divide by the number of colliding particles to obtain an average,

$$\bar{\epsilon} = \frac{E}{Z} = \frac{3kT}{2}$$

16-III-3. (a) $\bar{v} = 0$

(b) $\overline{|v|} = \dfrac{\int_0^\infty v e^{-mv^2/2kT} \, dv}{\int_0^\infty e^{-mv^2/2kT} \, dv} = \dfrac{kT/m}{\tfrac{1}{2}\sqrt{(2\pi kT)/m}} = \sqrt{\dfrac{2kT}{\pi m}}$

(c) Let $v_{21} = v_2 - v_1$ and $V_{21} = \frac{1}{2}(v_1 + v_2)$. Then $v_1 = V_{21} - \frac{1}{2}v_{21}$ and $v_2 = V_{21} + \frac{1}{2}v_{21}$

$$v_1^2 + v_2^2 = 2V_{21}^2 + \tfrac{1}{2}v_{21}^2$$

The Jacobian determinant is

$$\frac{\partial(V_{21}, v_{21})}{\partial(v_1, v_2)} = 1$$

Therefore

$$dv_1 \, dv_2 = dV_{21} \, dv_{21}$$

$$| v_{21} | = \frac{\int_{-\infty}^{+\infty} \int_{-\infty}^{+\infty} | v_{21} | \exp[-m(v_1{}^2 + v_2{}^2)/2kT] \, dv_1 \, dv_2}{\int_{-\infty}^{+\infty} \int_{-\infty}^{+\infty} \exp[-m(v_1{}^2 + v_2{}^2)/2kT] \, dv_1 \, dv_2}$$

$$= \frac{\int_{-\infty}^{+\infty} \exp(-mV_{21}^2/kT) \, dV_{21} \int_{-\infty}^{+\infty} | v_{21} | \exp(-mv_{21}^2/4kT) \, dv_{21}}{\int_{-\infty}^{+\infty} \exp(-mV_{21}^2/kT) \, dV_{21} \int_{-\infty}^{+\infty} \exp(-mv_{21}^2/4kT) \, dv_{21}}$$

$$= \frac{\int_0^\infty v e^{-mv^2/4kT} \, dv}{\int_0^\infty e^{-mv^2/4kT} \, dv} = \frac{(2kT/m)}{\frac{1}{2} \sqrt{(4\pi kT)/m}} = 2\sqrt{\frac{kT}{\pi m}}$$

$$\frac{| v_{21} |}{| v |} = \sqrt{2}$$

16-III-4. (a) $\quad q = 1 + 2e^{-\epsilon/kT}$

$$Q = q^N = (1 + 2e^{-\epsilon/kT})^N,$$

where N is Avogadro's number.

$$\frac{d \ln Q}{dT} = \frac{N}{q} \frac{dq}{dT} = \frac{N}{1 + 2e^{-\epsilon/kT}} \frac{2\epsilon}{kT^2} e^{-\epsilon/kT}$$

$$\bar{E} = kT^2 \frac{d \ln Q}{dT} = \frac{2\epsilon N}{e^{\epsilon/kT} + 2}$$

$$\bar{C}_V = \frac{d\bar{E}}{dT} = \frac{2\epsilon N}{(e^{\epsilon/kT} + 2)^2} e^{\epsilon/kT} \frac{\epsilon}{kT^2} = \frac{2Rx^2 e^x}{(e^x + 2)^2}$$

where $x = \epsilon/kT$

(b) See figure.

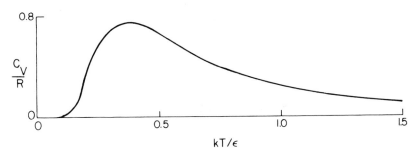

(c) The curve corresponds to the Debye crystal.

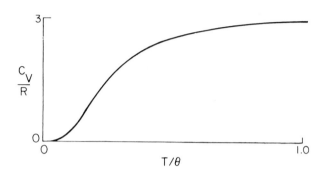

(d) Actual molecules always have available an infinite number of possible states with energies extending to infinitely large values (provided, of course, that we include states corresponding to dissociation). At any temperature there are always energy levels so high that their populations are appreciably less than those of the lower levels; as the temperature rises, additional molecules are promoted to these higher levels. Such promotion represents absorption of heat, so that an actual molecule has a nonzero heat capacity no matter how high the temperature. For our hypothetical molecules, however, the populations of the three states become practically equal at sufficiently high temperatures $(kT \gg \epsilon)$; raising the temperature further can promote only a few more molecules to the higher level and the heat capacity therefore approaches zero at high temperatures. Such behavior is observed for certain degrees of freedom in physical systems, sometimes only if the temperature is not too high.

16-III-5. (a) $\quad q = \sum\limits_{n=0}^{\infty} g_n e^{-\epsilon_n/kT} = \sum\limits_{n=0}^{\infty} 3^n e^{-nb/kT}$

$$= \sum\limits_{n=0}^{\infty} x^n = \frac{1}{1 - x}$$

where $x = 3e^{-b/kT}$.

$Q = q^N = (1 - 3e^{-b/kT})^{-N}$

where N is Avogadro's number.

(b) $\quad \bar{E} = kT^2 \dfrac{d \ln Q}{dT} = RT^2 \dfrac{d \ln q}{dT} = \dfrac{3bN}{e^{b/kT} - 3}$

$\quad \bar{S} = \dfrac{\bar{E}}{T} + k \ln Q = \dfrac{3bN}{T(e^{b/kT} - 3)} - R \ln(1 - 3e^{-b/kT})$

$\quad \bar{C}_V = \dfrac{d\bar{E}}{dT} = \dfrac{3bNe^{b/kT}}{(e^{b/kT} - 3)^2} \cdot \dfrac{b}{kT^2}$

$\qquad\quad = \dfrac{3Ry^2 e^y}{(e^y - 3)^2}$

where $y = b/kT$.

(c) The series for q converges only when $x < 1$ or $T < b/(k \ln 3)$. When $T \geqslant b/(k \ln 3)$, q, $\bar{E}$, $\bar{S}$, and $\bar{C}_V$ are infinite. It is unlikely that anyone will discover a substance in which these properties become infinite at a finite temperature. However, if the higher terms in the series have a different form (case ii), the threatened divergence might never occur—for example, the degeneracies of the higher levels might be less than 3^n. In that case our results would apply only to temperatures such that these higher levels have negligible populations, which they have if $T \ll b/(k \ln 3)$. It would not be too surprising to find oscillators whose lower levels have the energies and degeneracies given, but something would have to change in the higher levels. The degeneracies of the levels of this hypothetical oscillator should be compared with those of a three-dimensional harmonic oscillator for which the partition function is

$(1 - e^{-h\nu/kT})^{-3}$

16-III-6. (a) The distribution laws are

$N_i = \dfrac{1}{e^\alpha e^{\beta \epsilon_i} + \nu}$

where N_i is the population of the i'th state of energy ϵ_i and $\nu = 0$ for Maxwell-Boltzmann statistics, $+1$ for Fermi-Dirac statistics, and -1 for Bose-Einstein statistics.

For a system of Type I if $\beta < 0$, the populations of the states increase as ϵ_i increases. When $\nu = 0$, the population becomes infinite as ϵ_i becomes infinite; when $\nu = -1$, infinite population would occur if there were a state with $\epsilon_i = -\alpha/\beta$ and higher energy states would have negative populations; when $\nu = 1$, the populations would not become infinite but would become equal for states with high energies. In all three types of statistics a negative β would correspond to infinite energy or the absurdity of negative populations. The same calamity occurs, less drastically, when $\beta = 0$: all states have equal populations. We thus conclude that $\beta > 0$ for a system of Type I.

A Type II system can have $\beta < 0$, merely requiring that population increases as energy increases, or $\beta = 0$, with all populations equal. The difficulties at infinite energies do not arise. β can be any real number. A Type III system must have $\beta < 0$. The reasoning is the same as for Type I, but the difficulties would appear at infinitely negative energies if $\beta \geqslant 0$. A Type IV system must have $\beta > 0$, as with Type I, and at the same time $\beta < 0$, as with Type III. Such a system could not have any temperature. One can at least speculate on the possibility of $\beta = 0$, when all states have equal populations and the infinitely positive energies of some might cancel the infinitely negative energies of others.

(b) We first note that the smaller β is (algebraically), the hotter the system is. A negative temperature is hotter than a positive temperature. A Type III system, with $\beta < 0$, would give energy to a Type II system until they had the same negative β. A Type III system would give energy to a Type I system, with both temperatures tending to $\beta = 0$ $(T = \infty)$. Equilibrium would never be reached, for the Type III system would keep falling to lower and lower energy levels, giving an infinite amount of energy to the Type I system. Thus a Type III system would destroy the universe by raising it to an infinite temperature.

16-III-7. (a) $\qquad \mu = \mu' + a + bT$

$$\left(\frac{\partial \mu}{\partial T}\right)_V = \left(\frac{\partial \mu'}{\partial T}\right)_V + b$$

$$-\bar{S} = -\bar{S}' + b$$

Thus b is an arbitrary additive constant in $\bar{S}$, which is usually fixed by taking $\bar{S}_0 = 0$ for each substance at $0°K$. Then $\bar{S}$ is fixed at every other temperature by

$$\bar{S}_T = \int_0^T \frac{\bar{C}_P \, dT}{T} + \sum_{\substack{(\text{phase} \\ \text{transitions})}} \frac{\overline{\Delta H}}{T}$$

The additive constant a is fixed by the convention that $\mu = 0$ for each element in its standard state at some temperature, usually 25°C. Then for a compound at the same temperature $\mu = \Delta G^\circ_{\text{formation}} + RT \ln \text{(activity)}$.

(b) $\alpha = \ln Q - \ln N = -\dfrac{\mu}{RT} = -\dfrac{\mu'}{RT} - \dfrac{a}{RT} - \dfrac{b}{R}$

The arbitrariness of the constant a corresponds to the possibility of shifting the origin of the energy scale. Let $\epsilon_i = \epsilon'_i + \epsilon_0$. Then

$$Q = \sum_i g_i e^{-\epsilon_i/kT} = \sum g_i e^{-\epsilon'_i/kT} e^{-\epsilon_0/kT}$$

$$= Q' e^{-\epsilon_0/kT}$$

$$\ln Q = \ln Q' - \frac{\epsilon_0}{kT}$$

Thus,

$$\frac{\epsilon_0}{k} = \frac{a}{R}$$

A change in b corresponds to multiplying all the degeneracies g_i by a constant:

$$g_i = \gamma g'_i$$

$$Q = \sum_i \gamma g'_i e^{-\epsilon_i/kT} = \gamma Q''$$

$$\ln Q = \ln Q'' + \ln \gamma$$

$$\ln \gamma = -\frac{b}{R}$$

A change in b, unlike a change in a, represents a real physical distinction: it means that there are more, or fewer, states with each energy. A shift in $\bar{S}$ at 0°K has the same significance; we take $\bar{S}_0 = 0$ because there is usually only one state available at this temperature; but if it were later found that there were two (with similar doubling in every level), we could take $\bar{S}'_0 = R \ln 2$. Then $b = -R \ln 2$ and $\gamma = 2$.

16-III-8. The statistical definition of entropy is $S = k \ln W$, where W is the number of detailed (microscopic, molecular) states corresponding to a given gross (macroscopic) state. In classical mechanics W is infinite; each particle in the system can have arbitrary values of position and momentum. At best it is possible to define the ratio W_2/W_1, and thus ΔS, for two states; for example, ΔS in the isothermal compression of an ideal gas containing N molecules is correctly calculated by assuming that $W_2/W_1 = (V_2/V_1)^N$. In quantum mechanics, however, the number of detailed states (linearly independent wave functions) of a confined system corresponding to a given gross state is finite, though it may be enormously large. Therefore $S = k \ln W$ gives meaning to the absolute value of S (not merely to differences) in a natural way.

16-III-9. $q = \dfrac{e^{-h\nu/2kT}}{1 - e^{h\nu/kT}} = \dfrac{e^{-a\nu T^{n-1}/2k}}{1 - e^{-a\nu T^{n-1}/k}}$

Let $c = a\nu/k$

$$q = \frac{e^{-cT^{n-1}/2}}{1 - e^{-cT^{n-1}}}$$

$\ln q = -\tfrac{1}{2}cT^{n-1} - \ln(1 - e^{-cT^{n-1}})$

$\bar{E} = RT^2 \dfrac{d \ln q}{dT}$

$\qquad = RT^2 \left[-\dfrac{1}{2}(n-1)cT^{n-2} - \dfrac{(n-1)cT^{n-2}e^{-cT^{n-1}}}{1 - e^{-cT^{n-1}}} \right]$

$\qquad = R(1-n)cT^n \left(\dfrac{1}{2} + \dfrac{1}{e^{cT^{n-1}} - 1} \right)$

$\bar{S} = R \ln q + \dfrac{E}{T}$

$\qquad = -\dfrac{1}{2}RcT^{n-1} - R\ln(1 - e^{-cT^{n-1}})$

$\qquad\quad + R(1-n)cT^{n-1} \left(\dfrac{1}{2} + \dfrac{1}{e^{cT^{n-1}} - 1} \right)$

$\qquad = \underbrace{-\dfrac{1}{2}RncT^{n-1}}_{X} - \underbrace{R\ln(1 - e^{-cT^{n-1}})}_{Y} + \underbrace{\dfrac{R(1-n)cT^{n-1}}{e^{cT^{n-1}} - 1}}_{Z}$

lim: $T \to 0$	X	Y	Z	$\bar{S}$
$(n-1) < 0, n \neq 0$	$-\infty$	0	0	$-\infty$
$n = 0$	0	0	0	0
$n - 1 = 0$	$-\tfrac{1}{2}Rc$	$-R\ln(1 - e^{-c})$	0	$-R[\tfrac{1}{2}c + \ln(1 - e^{-c})]$
$(n-1) > 0$	0	∞	$R(1-n)$	∞

For the last entry under Z: If $(n - 1) > 0$ and $T \approx 0$,

$$\frac{cT^{n-1}}{e^{cT^{n-1}} - 1} \approx \frac{cT^{n-1}}{1 + cT^{n-1} - 1} = 1$$

Thus $\lim_{T \to 0} \bar{S}$ is finite if $n = 1$, zero if $n = 0$ (our universe), and infinite otherwise. When $n = 0$, $\bar{S}$ is unaffected by inclusion or omission of the zero-point energy. If $n \neq 0$, however, the zero-point energy must be included since it depends on temperature. Omitting it would result in measuring energy from different zero levels for different temperatures.

16-III-10. (a) $\quad n_i = \dfrac{g_i}{e^{\alpha + \epsilon_i / kT} + v}, \quad v = \pm 1 \text{ or } 0$

Let $\mu = -kT\alpha$. Then

$$n_i = \frac{g_i}{e^{(\epsilon_i - \mu)/kT} + v}$$

When ϵ_i is replaced by $\epsilon_i' = \epsilon_i + \Delta\epsilon$, n_i will be unchanged if μ is replaced by $\mu' = \mu + \Delta\epsilon$ or, equivalently, α is replaced by $\alpha' = \alpha - \Delta\epsilon/kT$. In other words a shift in the zero of energy requires an equal shift in the zero level of the chemical potential μ or a temperature-dependent shift in the value of α.
(b) The distribution law for photons is

$$n_i = \frac{g_i}{e^{\epsilon_i / kT} - 1}$$

This equation lacks the parameter α (or μ) because this parameter appears as a result of a conservation condition that is absent in this case. Any change in ϵ_i will necessarily change n_i. This situation can be understood if we recall that the creation or destruction of a photon is associated with the transfer of a definite amount of energy $(h\nu)$ to or from the radiation field. This amount of energy is not subject to choice. On the other hand as long as material particles are conserved, their absolute energies are undefined and any arbitrary constant may be added to all the energies. However, when such particles are not conserved, as in nuclear reactions, we are required to associate a definite amount of energy

$$\frac{mc^2}{\sqrt{1 - (v^2/c^2)}} \approx mc^2 + \frac{1}{2}mv^2$$

with each particle just as in the case of photons.

16-III-11. For a system of bosons

$$\ln W = \sum \left[(N_j + g_j) \ln \left(\frac{g_j}{N_j} + 1 \right) - g_j \ln \frac{g_j}{N_j} \right]$$

where g_j is the number of states with energy ϵ_j, N_j is the number of particles in these states, and W is the number of ways in which this distribution can be realized. We must maximize the function

$$f = \ln W - h\beta \sum_j N_j \nu_j - \gamma \sum_j N_j \nu_j{}^2$$

On differentiation

$$\frac{\partial f}{\partial N_j} = \frac{\partial \ln W}{\partial N_j} - h\beta \nu_j - \gamma \nu_j{}^2$$

$$= \ln \left(\frac{g_j}{N_j} + 1 \right) - h\beta \nu_j - \gamma \nu_j{}^2 = 0$$

$$N_j = \frac{g_j}{\exp(h\beta \nu_j + \gamma \nu_j{}^2) - 1}$$

We now replace g_j and N_j by the numbers of states and particles, respectively, with frequencies between ν and $\nu + d\nu$. The number of modes of radiation per unit volume between ν and $\nu + d\nu$ is

$$g(\nu) \, d\nu = \frac{8\pi \nu^2}{c^3} \, d\nu$$

The number of phonyons in this range is

$$dN = \frac{g(\nu) \, d\nu}{e^{h\beta \nu + \gamma \nu^2} - 1} = \frac{8\pi \nu^2 \, d\nu}{c^3(e^{h\beta \nu + \gamma \nu^2} - 1)}$$

16-III-12. (a) For distinguishable particles

$$W = \frac{N!}{\Pi_i N_i!}$$

$$\ln W = N! - \sum_i \ln N_i! \approx N \ln N - N - \sum_i (N_i \ln N_i - N_i)$$

Let

$$\phi = \ln W - \beta \sum_i N_i \epsilon_i$$

Then

$$\frac{\partial \phi}{\partial N_i} = \frac{\partial \ln W}{\partial N_i} - \beta \epsilon_i = -\ln \frac{N_i}{N} - \beta \epsilon_i = 0$$

$$N_i = N e^{-\beta \epsilon_i}$$

(Note that we cannot treat N as constant in the differentiation. We must recognize that $N = \sum_i N_i$.)

(b) $E = \sum_i N_i \epsilon_i = N \sum_i \epsilon_i e^{-\beta \epsilon_i}$

 $N = \sum_i N_i = N \sum_i e^{-\beta \epsilon_i}$

(c) It is necessary that $\sum_i e^{-\beta \epsilon_i} = 1$. In the case of conserved particles the Lagrange multiplier α can be adjusted to satisfy an analogous condition but no such parameter is present here. The system could have only one reciprocal temperature β.

16-III-13. (a) $W = \prod_i \dfrac{g_i!}{(g_i - N_i)!}$, $N_i \leqslant g_i$

(b) $\ln W = \sum_i [g_i \ln g_i - g_i - (g_i - N_i) \ln(g_i - N_i) + g_i - N_i]$

if g_i , $N_i \gg 1$.

$$\frac{\partial \ln W}{\partial N_i} = \frac{g_i - N_i}{g_i - N_i} + \ln(g_i - N_i) - 1 = \ln(g_i - N_i)$$

In the usual way we introduce the Lagrange multipliers α and β and require that for each i

$$\frac{\partial \ln W}{\partial N_i} - \alpha - \beta \epsilon_i = 0$$

$$\ln(g_i - N_i) - \alpha - \beta \epsilon_i = 0$$

$$N_i = g_i - e^{\alpha + \beta \epsilon_i}$$

(c) All the other distribution laws give expressions for the ratio n_i/g_i in terms of α, β, and ϵ_i only. Thus in these normal cases the number n_i of particles in a group of states of approximately the same energy is proportional to the number g_i of states included in the group. When the levels are very closely spaced, they may be divided arbitrarily into groups of similar energy. With novons, however,

$$\frac{N_i}{g_i} = 1 - \frac{e^{\alpha+\beta\epsilon_i}}{g_i}$$

and a change in the length of an arbitrary interval would change the value of N_i/g_i. For example, if $g'_i = 2g_i$, then

$$\frac{N'_i}{g'_i} = 1 - \frac{e^{\alpha+\beta\epsilon_i}}{2g_i} \neq \frac{N_i}{g_i}$$

This situation is so implausible that we may safely assume the nonexistence of novons.

16-III-14. (a) Let ρ be the energy density at frequency

$$\nu = \frac{\epsilon_m - \epsilon_n}{h}$$

At equilibrium

$$N_m(A_{mn} + \rho B_{mn}) = N_n(A_{nm} + \rho B_{nm})$$

where A_{mn} and A_{nm} are the probabilities of spontaneous transition, B_{mn} and B_{nm} are the probabilities of induced transition, and N_m and N_n are the populations of the two state. The Boltzmann distribution law gives

$$\frac{N_m}{N_n} = e^{-h\nu/kT}$$

By general quantum-mechanical principles $B_{nm} = B_{mn}$.

$$\rho = \frac{N_m A_{mn} - N_n A_{nm}}{N_n B_{nm} - N_m B_{mn}} = \frac{A_{mn} - e^{h\nu/kT} A_{nm}}{B_{mn}(e^{h\nu/kT} - 1)}$$

Planck's law gives

$$\rho = \frac{8\pi h\nu^3}{c^3(e^{h\nu/kT} - 1)}$$

The two expressions agree at all teperatures only if

$$A_{nm} = 0 \quad \text{and} \quad \frac{A_{mn}}{B_{mn}} = \frac{8\pi h\nu^3}{c^3}$$

(b) Planck's law might be of the form

$$\rho = \frac{8\pi h\nu^3(1 - \gamma e^{h\nu/kT})}{c^3(e^{h\nu/kT} - 1)}.$$

Then

$$\frac{A_{nm}}{B_{nm}} = \frac{8\pi h\nu^3\gamma}{c^3}$$

A_{nm} and B_{nm} could not depend on temperature and thus γ must be independent of temperature. Since the equilibrium density of cavity radiation is independent of the nature of the walls, γ could not depend on the identity of the atom or molecule involved. However, γ might depend on frequency.

16-III-15. (a)
$$\epsilon_J = \frac{h^2 J(J+1)}{4\pi^2 mr^2}$$

$$\epsilon_1 - \epsilon_0 = \frac{h^2(2-0)}{4\pi^2 mr^2} = \frac{h^2 N}{2\pi^2 Mr^2}$$

where N is Avogadro's number and M is the atomic weight.

$$\frac{\epsilon_1 - \epsilon_0}{kT} = \frac{h^2 N}{2\pi^2 Mr^2 kT} = \frac{2.60 \times 10^{-17}}{Mr^2}$$

	H_2	O_2	Cl_2
$\dfrac{\epsilon_1 - \epsilon_0}{kT}$	0.47	0.011	0.0019

(b) When translation and rotation are classically excited and vibration is frozen out,

$$\bar{C}_v = \left(\frac{3}{2} + \frac{2}{2}\right) R = \frac{5}{2} R = 4.97 \text{ cal } {}^\circ K^{-1} \text{ mole}^{-1}$$

This result is applicable if (1) the spacing between rotational energy levels is much less than kT and (2) the spacing between vibrational energy levels is much greater than kT. The calculation shows that condition (1) is well satisfied for O_2 and Cl_2 and these gases, accordingly, have $\bar{C}_V \geqslant 4.97$ cal${}^\circ K^{-1}$ mole^{-1}. The fact that $\bar{C}_V$ exceeds 4.97 slightly for O_2 and substantially for Cl_2 indicates that condition (2) is not fully satisfied and that vibration makes some contribution to the heat capacity. For H_2, however, the spacing between the two lowest rotational levels is about $\frac{1}{2}kT$ and condition (1) is not satisfied. H_2 thus has $\bar{C}_V < 4.97$ at 100°C.

16-III-16. The distribution of modes of vibration with respect to frequency depends in detail, but not in its essential features, on the boundary conditions at the ends of the chain. Assume that the end atoms are fixed. Then the m'th mode can be represented by $D_n = A \sin(nm\pi/N)$, where D_n is the displacement of the n'th atom. A is the amplitude with which the mode is excited and $m = 1, 2, 3,\dots$. We make the usual assumption of the Debye theory that all modes have the same phase velocity, that is, $\nu\lambda = v = $ constant, where ν is the frequency, λ is the wavelength, and v is the velocity. Here $\lambda = 2N/m$ atoms, for

$$\sin\left[\frac{(n + 2N/m)\, m\pi}{N}\right] = \sin\left(\frac{nm\pi}{N}\right)$$

Then $\nu = v/\lambda = mv/2N$ or $m = 2N\nu/v$. The number of modes in the frequency interval from ν_1 to ν_2 is proportional to the number of integers between the corresponding m's:

$$m_2 - m_1 = \frac{2N}{v}(\nu_2 - \nu_1)$$

Similarly for an infinitesimal interval $d\nu$ the number of modes between ν and $\nu + d\nu$ is proportional to $d\nu$ and independent of ν. (The usual assumption is made that $d\nu \gg 2N/v$, so that there are many modes in the interval.) The number of modes from 0 to the cutoff frequency ν_D is

$$\int_0^{\nu_D} K\, d\nu = N,$$

where K is a constant.

$$K\nu_D = N, \quad K = \frac{N}{\nu_D}$$

Let $u = h\nu/kT$ and $\theta = h\nu_D/k$. Then

$$K = \frac{Nh}{k\theta}$$

$$C_V = \int_0^{\nu_D} K\,\frac{ku^2 e^u}{(e^u - 1)^2}\, d\nu$$

$$d\nu = \frac{kT}{h}\, du$$

When $v = v_D$,

$$u = \frac{\theta}{T}$$

$$C_V = \frac{Nh}{k\theta} \cdot k \cdot \frac{kT}{h} \int_0^{\theta/T} \frac{u^2 e^u}{(e^u - 1)^2} \, du$$

$$= Nk \left(\frac{T}{\theta}\right) \int_0^{\theta/T} \frac{u^2 e^u}{(e^u - 1)^2} \, du$$

For $T \ll \theta$,

$$C_V \approx Nk \left(\frac{T}{\theta}\right) \int_0^{\infty} \frac{u^2 e^u}{(e^u - 1)^2} \, du = \text{constant} \times T$$

For $T \gg \theta$ only $u \ll 1$ need be considered.

$$\frac{u^2 e^u}{(e^u - 1)^2} \approx \frac{u^2}{(1 + u - 1)^2} = 1$$

$$C_V \approx Nk \left(\frac{T}{\theta}\right) \int_0^{\theta/T} du = Nk$$

16-III-17. In a two-dimensional system the number of modes of vibration n, with frequencies less than v, is proportional to $v^2 : n = Kv^2$. This result can be obtained by the same reasoning commonly used in the three-dimensional case except that we ask how many pairs (instead of triples) of integers there are with sums of squares less than a certain value proportional to v; the answer is the area of a quadrant of an ellipse (instead of the volume of an octant of an ellipsoid) with axes each proportional to v and this area is proportional to v^2 (instead of v^3). Then the number of modes with frequency between v and $v + dv$ is $dn = 2Kv \, dv$. In 1 mole of crystal there are N atoms (Avogadro's number). Each atom has 1 degree of freedom (out-of-plane displacement). Therefore if we integrate dn up to some maximum frequency v_m, we should obtain N:

$$\int_0^{v=v_m} dn = 2K \int_0^{v_m} v \, dv = Kv_m^2 = N$$

$$K = \frac{N}{v_m^2} \qquad dn = \frac{2Nv \, dv}{v_m^2}$$

Let $x = hv/kT$ and $x_m = hv_m/kT$. Then $dn = (2Nx \, dx)/x_m^2$. The contribution of each mode to the heat capacity is given by the Einstein expression, $(kx^2 e^x)/(e^x - 1)^2$. We must multiply this expression by dn for each frequency and integrate from 0 to x_m :

$$\bar{C}_V = \int_0^{x_m} \frac{kx^2 e^x}{(e^x - 1)^2} \cdot \frac{2Nx\,dx}{x_m{}^2} = \frac{2R}{x_m{}^2} \int_0^{x_m} \frac{x^3 e^x\,dx}{(e^x - 1)^2}$$

Let

$$\theta = \frac{h\nu_m}{k} = Tx_m$$

Then

$$\bar{C}_V = 2R \left(\frac{T}{\theta}\right)^2 \int_0^{\theta/T} \frac{x^3 e^x\,dx}{(e^x - 1)^2}$$

If $T \ll \theta$,

$$\bar{C}_V \approx 2R \left(\frac{T}{\theta}\right)^2 \int_0^{\infty} \frac{x^3 e^x\,dx}{(e^x - 1)^2} = \text{constant} \times T^2$$

Appendix

MATHEMATICAL CONSTANTS

$$\pi = 3.141592653589793$$
$$e = 2.718281828459045$$
$$e^{-1} = 0.367879441171442$$
$$\log_e 10 = \ln 10 = 2.302585092994046$$
$$\log_{10} e = 0.434294481903252$$
$$\sqrt{2} = 1.414213562373095$$
$$\sqrt{3} = 1.732050807568877$$

PHYSICAL CONSTANTS

Speed of light in vacuum	$c = 2.997925 \times 10^{10}$ cm sec^{-1}
Electronic charge	$e = 1.6021 \times 10^{-19}$ coulomb
	$= 4.8030 \times 10^{-10} \begin{cases} \text{statcoulomb} \\ \text{cm}^{3/2} \text{ g}^{1/2} \text{ sec}^{-1} \end{cases}$
Avogadro's number	$N = 6.0225 \times 10^{23}$ molecule mole^{-1} (or amu g^{-1})
Faraday's constant	$\mathscr{F} = 9.6487 \times 10^{4}$ coulomb mole^{-1}
Planck's constant	$h = 6.6256 \times 10^{-27}$ erg sec
Bohr radius	$a_0 = 5.29167 \times 10^{-9}$ cm
Gas constant	$R = 8.314$ joule °K^{-1} mole^{-1}
	$= 1.987$ cal °K^{-1} mole^{-1}
	$= 0.08206$ liter atm °K^{-1} mole^{-1}
	$= 62.36$ liter torr °K^{-1} mole^{-1}
	$R \ln 10 = 4.576$ cal °K^{-1} mole^{-1}
Boltzmann constant	$k = 1.3805 \times 10^{-16}$ erg °K^{-1} molecule^{-1}

CONVERSION FACTORS

1 cm $= 10^8$ Å (Ångstrøm)

1 yr $= 3.1557 \times 10^7$ sec

1 joule $= 10^7$ erg

1 cal $= 4.18400 \ldots$ joule

1 liter atm $= 101.325$ joule $= 24.2173$ cal

1 electron volt (eV) $= 1.6021 \times 10^{-12}$ erg

1 atomic mass unit (amu) $= 9.31478 \times 10^8$ eV $= 931.478$ MeV

1 atm $= 760$ torr $= 1.01325$ bar $= 1.01325 \times 10^6$ dyne cm^{-2}

$298.16\ R \ln 10/\mathscr{F} = 0.05915$ volt equiv mole^{-1}

Factor in Debye–Hückel equation $= 0.5091$ for H_2O at 25 °C

>

>

>

>

>

Subject Index

Only the problem statements, not the solutions, are indexed.